D0607232

THIS ITEM HAS BEEN
DISCARDED BY THE
UNIVERSITY OF PUGET SOUND
COLLINS MEMORIAL LIBRARY

SIGGRAPH

Proceedings of InterGraphics '83

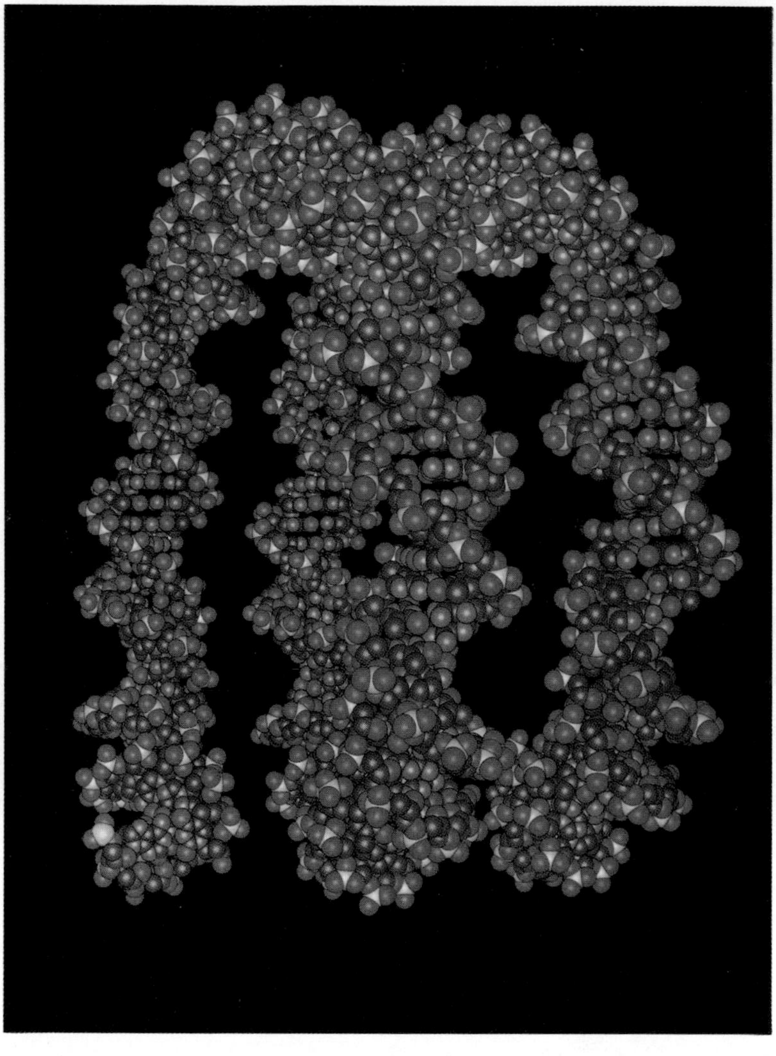

Computer Graphics

Theory and Applications

Intergraphics '83 (1983: Tokyo, Japan)

Edited by Tosiyasu L. Kunii

With 292 Figures, Some in Color

Springer-Verlag
Tokyo Berlin Heidelberg New York
1983

Dr. Tosiyasu L. Kunii
Professor & Director
Kunii Laboratory of Computer Science
Department of Information Science
Faculty of Science
The University of Tokyo

ISBN 4-431-70001-3 Springer-Verlag Tokyo Berlin Heidelberg New York
ISBN 3-540-70001-3 Springer-Verlag Berlin Heidelberg New York Tokyo
ISBN 0-387-70001-3 Springer-Verlag New York Heidelberg Berlin Tokyo

Library of Congress Cataloging in Publication Data
InterGraphics '83 (1983 : Tokyo, Japan) Computer graphics.
Proceedings of InterGraphics '83, held in Tokyo, Apr. 11-14, 1983, and sponsored by the World Computer Graphics Association.
Bibliography: p.
Includes index.
1. Computer graphics—Congresses. I. Kunii, Tosiyasu. II. World Computer Graphics Association. III. Title.
T385.I49 1983 001.64'43 83-26218
ISBN 0-387-70001-3 (U.S.)

All rights reserved. No part of this publication may be reproduced or transmitted in any form or by any means, electronic or mechanical, including photocopy, recording, or any information storage and retrieval system, without permission in writing from the publisher.

© by Springer-Verlag Tokyo 1983

Printed in Japan

Printing and Binding: Sanbi Printing, Tokyo

Preface

This book is an extensive treatise on the most up-to-date advances in computer graphics technology and its applications. Both in business and industrial areas as well as in research and development, you will see in this book an incredible development of new methods and tools for computer graphics. They play essential roles in enhancing the productivity and quality of human work through computer graphics and applications.

Extensive coverage of the diverse world of computer graphics is the privilege of this book, which is the Proceedings of InterGraphics '83. This was a truly international computer graphics conference and exhibit, held in Tokyo, April 11-14, 1983, sponsored by the World Computer Graphics Association (WCGA) and organized by the Japan Management Association (JMA) in cooperation with ACM-SIGGRAPH. InterGraphics has over 15 thousands participants.

This book consists of seven Chapters. The first two chapters are on the basics of computer graphics, and the remaining five chapters are dedicated to typical application areas of computer graphics. Chapter 1 contains four papers on "graphics techniques". Techniques to generate jag free images, to simulate digital logic, to display free surfaces and to interact with 3 dimensional (3D) shaded graphics are presented. Chapter 2 covers "graphics standards and 3D models" in five papers. Two papers discuss the CORE standard and the GKS standard. Three papers describe various 3D models and their evaluations.

Chapter 3 attacks one of the major application areas "CAD/CAM (computer-aided design and manufacturing)" with 11 papers. Four papers cover mechanical CAD/-CAM, two papers CAD/CAM for VLSI, and the remaining five papers report on important topics such as CAD/CAM education, documentation, communication, computer-aided engineering and CAD trends in the 1980s.

In-depth studies of key issues in another important area, "office automation (OA)", are given in Chapter 4 in five papers. It covers management, financial and word processing applications as well as general areas in OA. In Chapter 5 the fascinating area of "computer animation" is presented in four papers emphasizing 3D techniques and dedicated systems design. Diverse "graphic applications" such as automated cartography, graphic design, scientific applications and hard copy are covered in five papers in Chapter 6.

The last chapter, Chapter 7, contains five papers on "image processing", which is the reverse of computer graphics. Computer graphics is a mechanism to generate images from their description, and image processing is the reverse mechanism to generate image description from images.

It is the great pleasure of the editor to acknowledge the following key people who made this InterGraphics '83 possible: Mr. Caby C. Smith, President of WCGA, Mr. Akira Totoki, President of JMA, Mr. Michiya Ishii, Former Secretary General of JCGA, and Prof. Thomas A. DeFanti, Chairman of ACM-SIGGRAPH.

I would like to thank Springer-Verlag Tokyo, especially Mr. M. Tsuchida, Ms. C. Sato and Mr. H. Matthies for their help to publish this beautiful volume.

Dr. Tosiyasu L. Kunii

Chairman, Program Committee,
InterGraphics '83, and
Professor of Computer Science,
The University of Tokyo

List of Contents

List of Contributors

The page numbers given below refer to the page on which contribution begins.

Chapter 1
Graphics Techniques

JAG FREE IMAGES ON A RASTER CRT

Akira Fujimoto*
Kansei Iwata
Graphica Computer Corporation
505 Kaitori, Tama-shi
Tokyo 206, JAPAN

ABSTRACT

This paper presents an algorithm for removing all kinds of jags (staircase-like effects) due to the aliasing phenomenon which is intrinsic in all synthesized wire frame and continuous-tone images displayed on raster CRT's.

This algorithm produces images whose quality is virtually equal to the results obtainable by the use of far more elaborate techniques but nevertheless the implementation and the computational costs of the algorithm are extremely low. This and other important features of the algorithm have been proven by numerous experimental results and succesfull practical implementations.

The actual implementation of the algorithm was carried out for two types of aliasing. First as a smooth vector generator for wire frames and second as an anti-aliasing post processor for continuous-tone image outputs, both being implemented locally as intelligent features on the display sites.

Because of its universality, speed, accuracy and low implementation cost, the algorithm can be inexpensively hardwarized, providing an effective anti-aliasing tool for practical applications.

1. INTRODUCTION

In recent years, sharply decreasing memory costs have resulted in expanding popularity of raster scan displays, making them increasingly competitive with random-scan vector displays. The special properties of the raster-scan display have facilitated greater realism in pictures and posed new challenges for graphic applications. On the other hand the raster-scan display can be and is actually more often used for many of the purposes for which the random-scan display was developed. In raster-scan applications, however, we inevitably face the well known problem which is characteristic to this device: aliasing or rastering. Picture degradation caused by aliasing is often considered as an "Achilles' heel" of the raster display devices. Considerable effort has been expended in attempting to overcome the "jaggy" or "staircase" appearance of lines and edges. All

*former name: Wieslaw Romanowski

solutions are naturally limited to displays with a frame buffer which can handle more than two intensities per pixel. Any algorithm, no matter what sort of approach has been adapted, finally fixes the gray scale intensity level for each pixel. Many different approaches of different levels of complexity have been proposed. Most of the existing solutions, however, in spite of being able to produce high quality anti-aliased images, lack universality or involve a considerable amount of calculation which makes them often prohibitively expensive or just too slow from the view point of practical applications. The decisive factor for succesfull application of any particular anti-aliasing technique is, along with quality, the speed of the anti-aliasing process. In the present paper, the author presents an algorithm which, while producing high quality anti-aliased images, succesfully resolves a problem of speed.

2. SPATIAL FILTERING

As regards the "jaggy line" produced on the raster CRT, one must clearly realize that there exists no medicament which can treat the aliasing problem without side effects. This stems directly from the so called "sampling theorem", which states that a sampled signal cannot reproduce a frequency component higher than half the sampling frequency.

To avoid aliasing, different filtering techniques are applied before actual sampling takes place. The purpose of filtering is to remove spatial frequences of the image which are too high to be representable on the given raster. Obviously, a filtering procedure removes "jag" at the cost of spatial frequencies Images produced on the screen will look more or less blurred, depending on the amount of high frequencies "sacrified" during filtering. In other words, the application of low pass filtering before sampling merely changes the degradation of the image from one from to another. Realizing this fact is especially important when treating vectors on raster CRT's. Preserving the high spatial frequencies for vectors which are relatively thick even without any filtering can be no less important than removing its jags. The filtering procedure involves choosing a filter function which is mathematically tractable. The vector is assumed to have a finite thickness and the actual intensity of each pixel of the vector is obtained by integrating the filter function over the region it covers.

Nishida and Nakamae[2] proposed making the pixel intensity proportional to the area it contributes to the vector. This corresponds to the implied adoption of the Fourier window as the filter function. This function intersects the line in various patterns. The computational effort involved in calculating the area covered by Fourier window makes the proposed algorithm practically unacceptable. On the other hand, S.Gupta and R.F. Sproul[3] adopted a conical filtering function. Because of its circular symmetry, for the given thickness of the line, pixel intensity depends only on the distance from the pixel center to the center line, and it can be precalculated for specific distant values. This requires creating and storing the look up table for each particular gray scale. The table must be referred to in each generation of the particular pixel. Moreover, the algorithm requires separate, time-consuming treatment for the end points of the vector. Also, the problem of intersecting lines is left open. On the other hand, no single experimental result justifying the claimed practical importance of the proposed algorithm was presented.

3. THE ALGORITHM

The solution proposed in the present paper utilizes the special properties of the vector, namely its slope and thickness, which is geometrically equal to zero. The Fourier window is adopted for the spatial filter. The Fourier window is assumed to have a value of 1.0 in the region ± 0.5 of the pixel and is zero everywhere else[4]. In present implementation, however, the filter function is normalized so that the enclosed volume is 1.(see Fig. 1). Furthermore, it is assumed that the size (d) of the window is the function of the slope of the vector, and that its orientation is always ajusted to the slope of the vector as shown in Fig.1. Each pixel intensity is obtained by convoluting the filter function and the line intensity. The integration of the filter function will be performed over the region $2(d/2-dx)d$ (see Fig.1). Integration of the filter function is thus extremely simple. Each pixel intensity is inversely proportional to the vector, i.e., $C'=C\,(d/2-dx)/d$, where C is the overall vector intensity and C' the intensity of the pixel under consideration.

The pixel intensity distribution in the direction perpendicular to the center line of the vector is shown on Fig.2. The intensity of the pixel as it approaches the center line of the vector will converge to the overall vector intensity. If the thickness of the vector is assumed to be finite, then this property is satisfied only when the size of the filter function is equal to or less than the thickness of the vector.

All further discussion will be restricted to the vectors in the first octant (i.e., $0<y<x$); the extention to other regions is obvious.

First, we try to produce a jag free vector which is as thin as possible. The thickness of the displayed vector is limited by the smallest possible size of the Fourier window (see Fig.1). When generating the pixel on the one side of the vector, we must also ensure the existence of its counterpart on the other side of the vector. This obvious requirement sets a limit on the window size for a vector with given slope (see Fig.2). As was noted above, each pixel intensity is a linear function of its distance from the center line of the vector. The principle of superposition can then be applied and the intensity of each pixel can be calculated incrementally without explicit calculation of this distance. The algorithm, in which incremental

d - Fourier window size

dx - distance between pixel and center line of vector

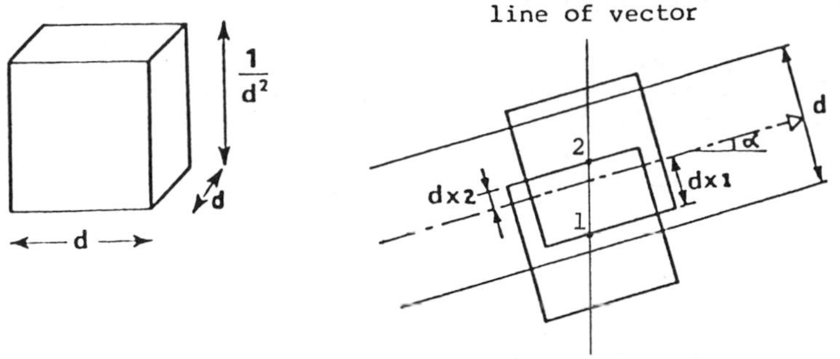

Figure 1: The Fourier window and its orientation along the vector

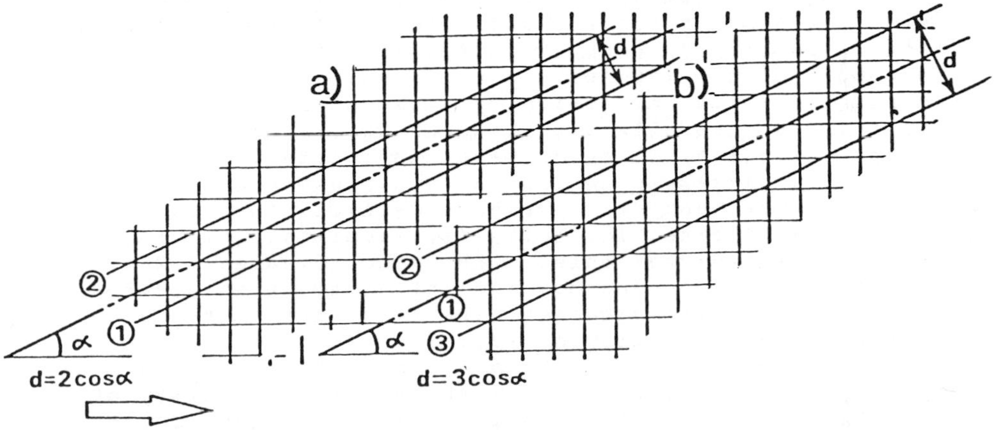

a) smallest possible window involving shading of one pixel on each side.
b) expanded Fourier window in which three pixels are shaded per each column.

Figure 2: Fourier window size for given slope of vector.

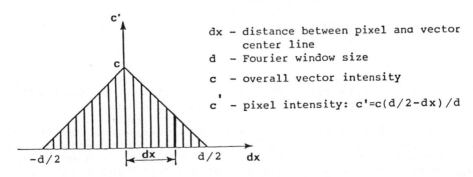

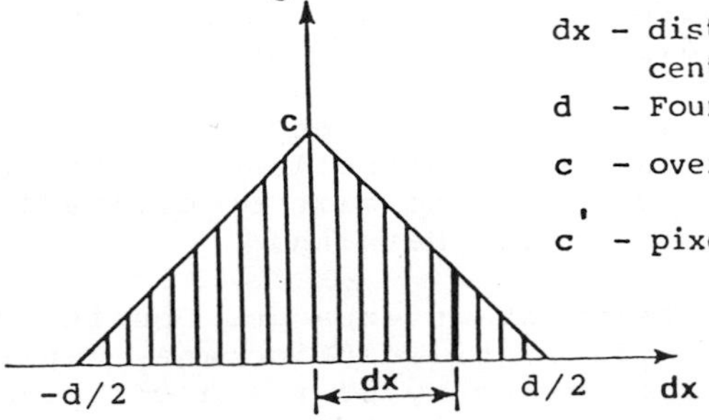

dx - distance between pixel and vector center line

d - Fourier window size

c - overall vector intensity

c' - pixel intensity: $c'=c(d/2-dx)/d$

Figure 3: Intensity distribution of pixels across the vector.

calculation of this pixel intensity was adopted, is shown in Fig.4. The indices 1 and 2 refer to variables relating to pixels lying on the right and left sides, respectively, of the center line of the vector. Such a pair of pixels, however, is placed in the column which is located perpendicular toward the direction of the greatest displacement of the vector. In the first octant, the X axis represents this direction (see Fig.2).

The input data are the coordinates of the initial (XS,YS) and final (XE,YE) points of the vector, together with its intensity C.

The algorithm consists of two parts, i.e., the initialization part and the main part. The initial calculation proceeds as follows. The coordinates of the right pixel (IX1,IY1) are obtained by rounding off the coordinates of the initial points of the vector. Then the slope of the vector (Q) and the value (A) used for checking the y coordinate of the first pixel (IY1) are calculated. After eventual correction of the y coordinate, the increment of the intensity corresponding to one pixel increment (CP) in the direction of greatest displacement is calculated. The initialization process is completed by calculating the value (C2) which corresponds to the initial intensity of the left pixel. In case of a vector where only two pixels are generated per increment, we have C=C1+C2, so the calculation of the right pixel intensity is immediate. The coordinates of the left pixel differ only in the y coordinate: IY2=IY2+1. At this point, the coordinates and intensity of the pair of pixels are sent to frame buffer. The main part of the algorithm then proceeds in the following way. The intensity for the left pixel (C2) is incremented by CP and immediately checked against its maximum possible value, i.e., the overall intensity of the vector (C). If its actual value is still less than (C), the only a move in the direction of the greatest movement is executed, otherwise, an additional increment in the perpendicular direction is made and the actual intensity of the left pixel is corrected by subtracting the overall vector intensity value. The pixel coordinate generation process carried out in the main part of the algorithm happens to resemble Bresenham's one[1]. In the present algorithm, however, it is the pixels' intensity control variable(C2) which directly governs its coordinate generation. This means that the control variable simultanously incorporates two distinct meanings., i.e., physical and geometrical. In Bresenham's algorithm, the controlling error term, which is measured perpendicularly to the axis of greatest displacement, possesses only geometrical meaning.

The variation of the algorithm with an expanded Fourier window size (see Fig.2b) is shown in Fig. 4b. In this case, 3 pixels are shaded in each column. The intensity of the outer pixels will vary between 0 and 2/3 of the overall vector intensity. The intensity of the centrally located pixel oscillates between 2/3 of the overall vector intensity and its maximum value.

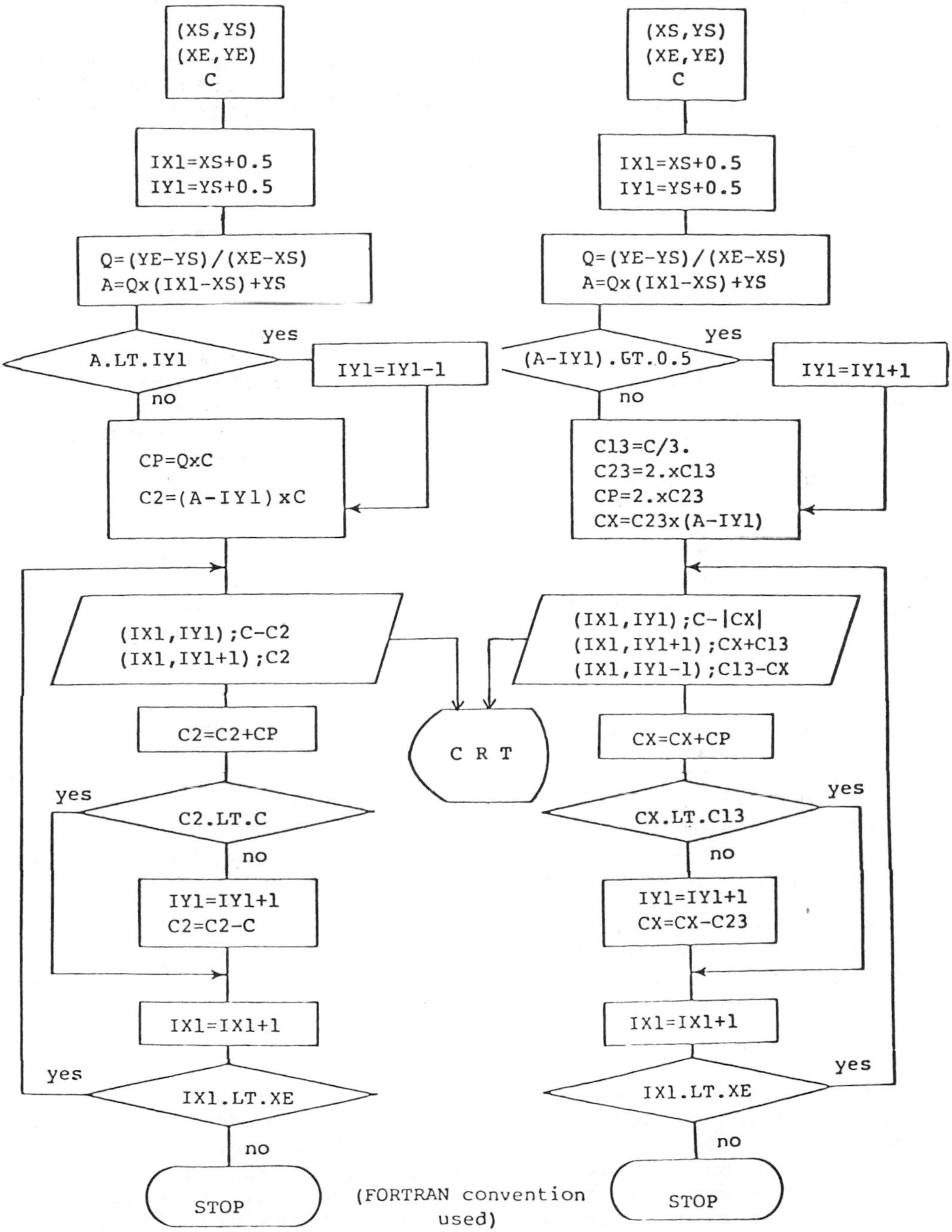

a) smallest possible Fourier window; two pixels shaded in each column

b) expanded Fourier window; three pixels shaded in each column

Figure 4: The flow chart of the algorithm.

4. EXPERIMENTAL RESULTS

A display* with the following characteristics was used for the experiment: 512x512 i.e., rather low range of resolution; 280x 280mm of screen size; 8 bits depth buffer (256 intensities) for each RGB per pixel.

a) Smooth vector generator (straight line)

The results of direct application of the algorithm explained in the previous section are shown in Fig.5.

(1) Variable window size.
Variations in the size of the Fourier window (for vectors having different slopes) does not produce any visual difference in vector thickness, in spite of the fact that the actual change in its size is as large as 30% (a case where only two pixels per column are shaded). This is explained by property of the algorithm, which maintains the sum of the intensities of the pair of two pixels in each column constant.

(2) "Twisted rope" effect.
Lines with slope approaching 0 or infinity still have a somewhat twisted rope-like appearance, even in the case where a generally larger Fourier window was used (upper middle part of Fig.5). This phenomenon is due mainly to the characteristics of the monitor i.e., the light emitted by each pixel is not, in general, distributed uniformly over an idealized square. Actually, however, the twisted rope-like appearance of the smoothed vector cannot be avoided in any anti-aliasing technique unless window size or line thickness is significantly increased[2,3]. The former, however, will result in producing a line which is exessively thick and blurred in comparison with the usual, already thick lines on raster CRT's. The twisted rope effect will obviously diminish significantly or completely disappear in displays with greater resolution.

(3) Bit depth factor.
During the experiments, it became clear that increase of the gray scale above 8 intensities (3 bits per each R,G,B) does not produce visible improvement in the appearance of the vectors.

b) Smooth vector generator (curves)

Any curve can be represented by fitting it with a polygonal line, a standard procedure in graphics. Arcs approximated by using 8,20,30,100,1000 and 10000-sided polygons are shown in Fig.6. In this particular case (radius=320 pixels) no visible change is observed when the number of polygons is increased beyond 30. Experimental results proved that the visually smooth

---

* Graphics and image processing display M508, manufactured by the Graphica Computer Co., Japan.

Upper middle part: 2 pixels shaded in each column.

Bottom left: 3 pixels shaded in each column.

Bottom right: no jag removal performed.

Figure 5: Vectors drawn on a 512 x 512 raster CRT.

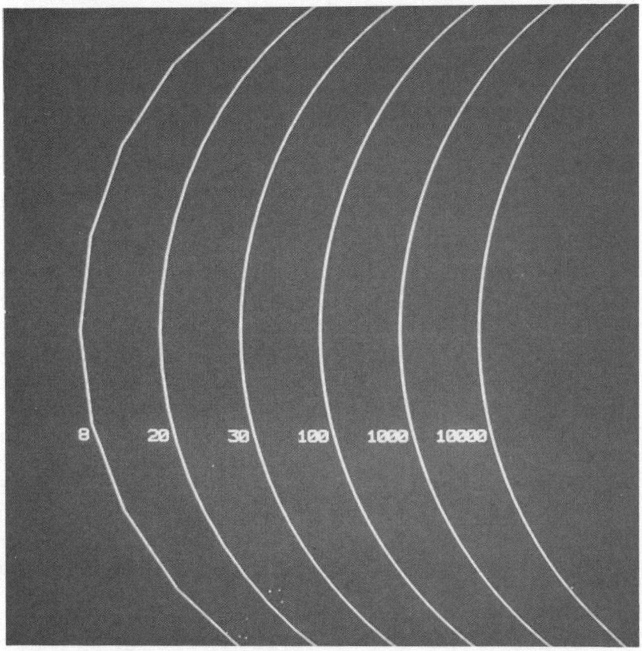

Figure 6: Anti-aliased vectors drawn on a 512 x 512 raster CRT: extention to curve generation.

jag-free arcs can be successfully represented by polygonal lines provided the tolerance (maximum allowed distance between the arc and polygonal line inscribed in it) is kept below 0.2 pixel. This means that the average arc with the radius of, say, a quarter of the screen size (125 pixels) can be represented by relatively low number of 40 sides polygon; the number of sides $n=\pi/(\arccos(1-T/R))$, where T is the tolerance and R the radius of the arc.

The quality of the experimental results shown in Fig.6 confirms another very important feature of the algorithm, that is, no special treatment is necessary for the end points of the vector[3]. It is sometimes argued that nothing is gained by increasing coordinate precision much beyond resolution of the screen because the observer will be unable to detect the difference[1]. The experiments showed, however, that the ability of the algorithm to address the end points of the vector with precision several times higher than the actual resolution, is an essential factor in producing nearly ideal arcs or any other curves. In fact, the sufficient addressability happens to be an important factor for other reasons as well, e.g., it is essential in avoiding jitter when the picture is moved on the screen.

In general, the experiments demonstrated that the proposed algorithm produces highly satisfactory results for both straight lines and curves. Since it became clear that increasing the size of the Fourier window merely produces thicker lines with excessive blurring, the smallest possible window (only two pixels shaded in each column) was chosen for the practical implementation of the algorithm. This choice possibly represents the best compromise between preserving high spatial frequencies and jag free edges. It should be noted that this choice provides lines which actually appears somewhat slimmer than those generated by standard vector generators, e.g., a symmetrical DDA[1].

Practical implementations will be discussed in the next section, however, the results obtained on a display with a resolution of 1024 x 1024 are worthy of comment here (see Fig.7 and 8). First the twisted rope-like effect disappeared completely and the quality of the vectors seemed to be even better than that of the usual vectors displayed on storage tubes and were, in fact, almost comparable with that of those generated by plotters (except, of course, for thickness). The points of intersection of the vectors (see Fig.8) are also worthy of notice, i.e., no special treatment was carried out. Such "negligence" was practically justified because the smallest possible Fourier window was used, which resulted in shading of only one pixel on each side of the vector. Thus, the interaction area around the point of intersection becomes so small that it can be simply ignored without introducing any visible effects.

Some experimental results and practical implementations of

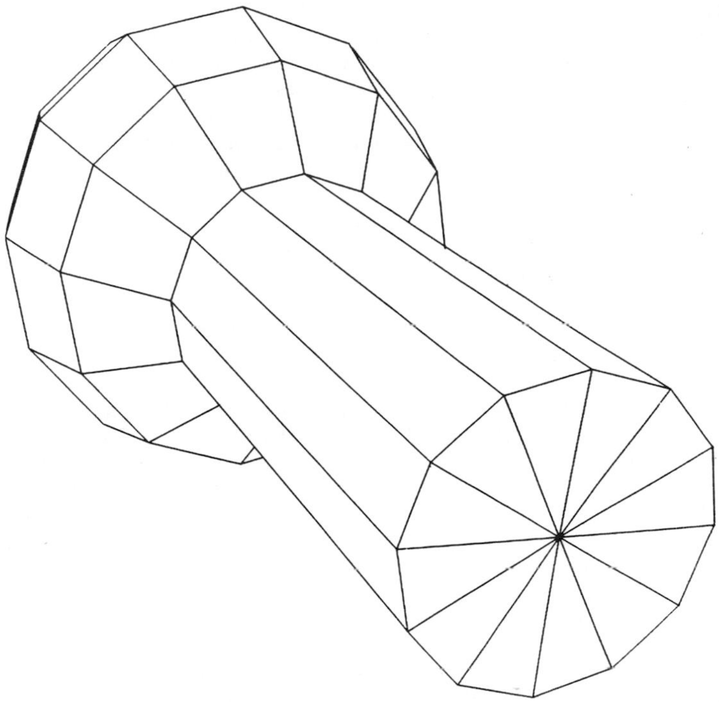

Figure 7: Anti-aliased vectors drawn on a 1024x1024 raster CRT.

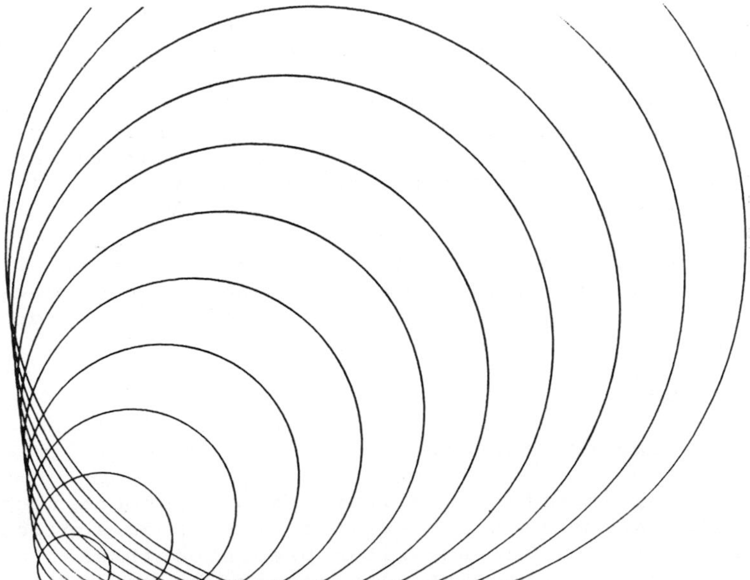

Figure 8: Anti-aliased vectors drawn on a 1024x1024 raster CRT.

anti-aliased vector generators in Japan and the USA are known to the author, but none of the results are actually better than those of Nishida and Nakamae [2]. On the other hand, no visible difference appears between the results of the present experiments and those of Nishida, which were produced on the same display (M508), except that vector produced by the present algorithm actually appears significantly slimmer.

c) Anti-aliasing postprocessor (smooth edge generator)

The smooth vector generator described in a) and b) does not produce acceptable results in the case where the background must be considered. Here, "background" means any kind of image appearing on the screen prior to the actual drawing of the vector. The background is in general nonuniform and essentially unknown, as far as the algorithm is concerned. Taking the background into consideration in the algorithm involves the readout of the intensity values of all subsequently generated pixels. In the case where the background is to be considered, each pixel intensity calculated by the present algorithm must be corrected by adding the term (1-CI/C)x CB, where CI is the pixel intensity before correction, C the overall vector intensity and CB the intensity of the background. This operation requires one division and one multiplication; both operations can be performed with relatively low precision. (The actual number of bits to be considered is just the number of bits of the gray scale.) By introducing slight changes in the algorithm, this division and multiplication can be converted to two multiplications, which can be performed with considerably lower cost when hardwarized. Results obtained considering the background are shown in Fig.6. Background consideration is also essential in smoothing the edges of previously shaded continuous-tone image polygons. Because of the importance of preserving the highest possible frequencies of the anti-aliased image, an algorithm with the smallest possible Fourier window was used as in the case of smooth vector implementation; in any one column, only one pixel from two contiguous polygons is taken into consideration.

The experimental results with smooth edge generator proved to be very satisfactory and are not introduced here because of lack of space. Practical applications with smooth edge generator are presented in the next section.

5. APPLICATIONS

a) Smooth vector generator

Among the many important applications of a smooth vector generator is CAD. We mention one example of such an application (see Figs. 7 and 8). The algorithm presented in section 3 was hardwarized using a display* with resolution of 1024 x 1024.

---

* MB8000-intelligent graphics display for CAD use, made by Graphica Computer Co.

Three bit planes, providing 8 intensities of the gray scale, were implemented. The number of addressable points was, thus increased from 1024 x 1024 to 8192 x 8192. The vector writing speed in this particular implementation is 732 μs for a vector 256 pixels in length, thus, one thousand smooth vectors are drawn within less than one second. Smooth vector quality appears to be better than of the usual vectors displayed on storage tube devices, where a resolution of the order of 4096 x 4096 is commonly used.

b) Smooth edge generator

The smooth edge generator described in the previous section was implemented as an intelligent anti-aliasing postprocessor incorporated in the M508 - graphics display manufactured by Graphica. Numerous graphics packages producing continuous-tone images have been coupled to this postprocessor through the driver which retrieves the list of all visible edges and transmits them to the smooth edge generator. Lack of space limits the author to citing only two examples of practical application. Two different graphics programs were choosen: MOVIE.BYU from Brigham Young University, Utah, USA and LUMINOUS from Graphica Computer Co., Tokyo, Japan (see Figs. 9 and 10 respectively).

The MOVIE.BYU on the VAX PDP 11/750 required 31 seconds to calculate the nonanti-aliased image shown on Fig. 9a. Using an averaging technique (MOVIE.BYU option) requires computation at resolution twice as much as that of the display. Removal of jags, however, is not adequate and only diminishes the aliasing effects. Nevertheless the time required for this partial anti-aliasing is about 55 seconds (basically constant) per frame. This is about 170% of the image calculation time in this particular case. Provided the list of visible edges is buffered somewhere during continuous-tone image calculation, however, the smooth edge generator requires practically no time (less than one second) for post anti-aliasing of the image shown in Fig. 9a. The result is shown in Fig. 9b.

The LUMINOUS on the VAX 11/750 required one and half minutes to output the image shown in Fig. 10a. Using an anti-aliasing feature of LUMINOUS requires computation at resolution three time as much as that of the display. Obtained results are satisfactory but the times required is almost four minutes. To obtain virtually the same results shown in Fig. 10b, again, practically no time is required when the smooth vector generator is put into operation.

6. CONCLUSION

The development and practical implementation of an anti-aliasing algorithm for raster CRT's has been described. The actual application of the algorithm provided smooth vectors and smooth edge generators. Various problems involved in developing anti-aliasing generators, such as the addressability of the vector

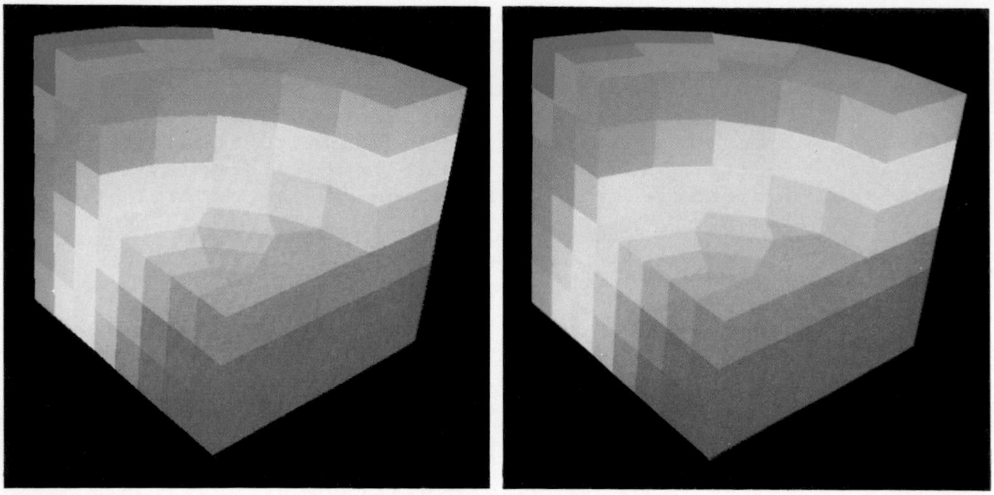

Figure 9: Continuous-tone image output from MOVIE.BYU on a 512 x 512 raster CRT.
a) before anti-aliasing
b) after post anti-aliasing performed locally on the display site.

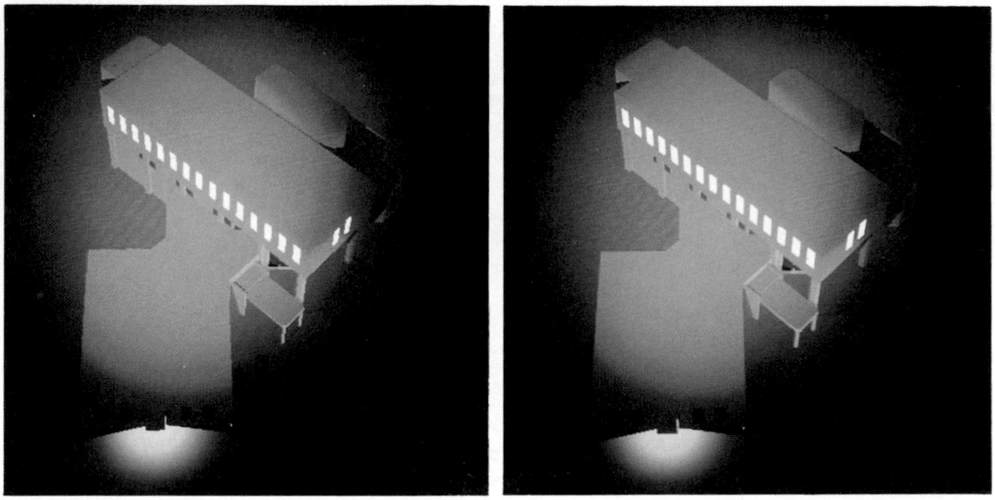

Figure 10: Continuous-tone image output from LUMINOUS on a 512 x 512 raster CRT.
a) before anti-aliasing
b) after post anti-aliasing. The shadow edges are not processed in order to demonstrate that anti-aliasing is performed locally on display site, thus being implemented as an intelligent feature.

end points, background treatment, vector intersection and vector quality have been discussed and the succesful solution of these problems has been demonstrated by experimental results. Both experimental results and numerous examples of applications demonstrated the high capabilities of the proposed algorithm, i.e., high quality anti-aliased images, high processing speed, low implementation and computational costs and universality. These desirable features may result in widespread use of the proposed algorithm.

REFERENCES

(1) William M. Newman, Robert F. Sproul
Principles of Interactive Computer Graphics
McGrow-Hill Kogakusha,Ltd.

(2) T. Nishida, E. Nakamae
Jag Removal Method for Lines on Color Displays (Japanese)
Computer Vision 10-1 (1981.1.22)

(3) Satish Gupta, Robert F. Sproul
Filtering Edges for Gray-Scale Displays
Computer Graphics Vol.15, No.3 August 1981

(4) Blinn, James Frederick
Computer Display of Curved Surfaces
University of Utah, PH.D,1978

AN INTERACTIVE GRAPHIC PROCESSOR FOR DIGITAL LOGIC SIMULATION SYSTEM

Yu-Huei Jea
Tsung-Che Lin*

National Taiwan University
Taipei, Taiwan
Republic of China

ABSTRACT

The growth of computer graphics is remarkable even compared with the growth of the computers. Many computer-aided-design systems have used computer graphics as an important tool. Computer graphics can provide a designer with a visual graphical input and output means, which are usually more convenient and immediately understandable by the user than the conventional method. This paper presents a study in design of a flexible interactive graphic processor for digital logic simulation systems. We design the input means so that it is concise, easy-to-use, error-preventive and menu driven. We provide a powerful graphic editing capability so that the user may create, erase, copy and move symbols, wires, labels and a block of area in the schematic diagram. We apply a relational database support to the graphic processor so that it is suitable for not only one simulation program.

INTRODUCTION

Engineers have long been aware of the computer's enormous capability of analyzing a wide range of engineering problems. Many programs have been developed for engineering purposes. Neverthless, not all the programs have been widely accepted by the engineers. The main obstacles to the acceptance of the computer-aided-design systems are probably due to the design engineers' reluctance to learn sufficiently the input data definitions and to prepare the usually tedious and error-prone data.

Conventional simulation systems usually accept data cards of the design, while drafting a design is a graphical process in its nature. In a typical process, the designer must transcribe the design from a graphical draft into alphanumerical strings of data. However, in transcribing the design draft into data cards, errors are often made. Moreover, since alphanumeric strings can not be so immediately understood as the design draft, errors in the data cards are usually less detectable than in the design draft.

Providing an easy-to-use interactive graphic processor to collect the design data graphically for the simulation systems seems to be a good approach to solve the above-mentioned problems. GTE AE Labs have successfully used graphic processors for circuit design simulation [1].

A graphic processor will let the designer graphically create and edit his design draft. Utility programs should also be provided. After a designer

---

* Lin is with CTCI Corporation, which sponsored his study at NTU.

has completed his design draft, he can use the utility program to extract the required design information for the following simulation system. For example, CASS, a CAD/CAM system for the Norwegian electronic industry, collects the design information graphically, and transmits the collected information to the TEGAS simulation system thru a TEGAS input translation utility program, [2], [3].

Behavioral characteristic of the designer

Human factors are the primary keys concerning whether the designer will accept the interactive system. Certain behavioral characteristics of the human being have been established. The following shows some of the characteristics that have direct relation to an interactive system, [4].

(1) It is difficult to retain in memory a long string of data. The designer may be difficult to remember a long sequence of keystrokes if interruption occurs.
(2) The designer can easily get impatient if he has to wait a long time for a result. Impatience can fatigue the designer and thus reduce the motivation of the designer.
(3) A slow response will arouse uncertainty. Indication or reaction to the designer's actions can free the designer from irritating uncertainty.
(4) Graphic patterns are more acceptable and understandable to the designer than strings of data.
(5) Familiar and consistent terminology are more acceptable to the designer.

Problem definition

Since the main objectives of an interactive graphic processor are to provide an easy means for creating a design draft and to collect required information for the following simulation system, we must solve the following problems to achieve our goal:

(1) Keep in mind the designer's behavioral characteristics and provide an easy-to-learn, easy-to-use graphic input method to allow the designer to create and edit his draft.
(2) Editing functions must be powerful enough to meet the user's needs.
(3) The design draft information must be properly stored so that the user may edit it whenever he wants to, i.e., we must provide the re-run capability.
(4) The stored design draft information can be easily processed to produce input for the simulation system.
(5) We must provide a flexible data structure for the design draft information, if the graphic processor is not limited to only one simulation system.

Design is a process of incorporating a set of known elements together to accomplish a desired function. When a designer is working on his draft, the designer should not be bothered with how to draw an element on the graphic terminal. Therefore, the following problems should also be solved:

(6) The graphical representations and attributes of elements should be properly stored, so that they may be easily retrieved when necessary.
(7) Relations between element occurrences in a draft should be handled properly.

To solve problems (1) and (2), we have to design the graphical input carefully. To solve problems (3) to (7), we apply some relational database management functions to the graphic processor. To increase the flexibility in creating or adding new element types, we provide a graphical capability to add new element types to the graphical database.

SYSTEM OVERVIEW

The system was implemented on a VAX 11/780 computer. A Tektronix Storage/Refresh graphics CRT is used for graphical inputs and outputs. We use FORTRAN IV as the programming language. The overall software structure is shown in Figure 1.

This graphic processor aims at collecting information for not only one digital logic simulation system, therefore the flexibility in data structure is required. We incorporate a Relational Database Support (RDBS) feature in the system to achieve flexibility. The RDBS modules maintain the attributes of digital logic elements, and the schematic diagram in relations, which may be retrieved and used as input to following simulation systems.

The functions of the graphic processor are implemented by the symbol library modules, the schematic drawing modules, and the RDBS interface modules. The symbol library modules are used to create symbols in the symbol library. The schematic drawing modules are used to create schematic diagrams. The RDBS interface modules are used to maintain the Symbol Relation (SYR), the Schematic Relation (SCR), and the Network Relation (NWR).

The symbol library contains the SYR and the Basic Pattern File. The former stores common attributes for each element, and the latter stores the drawing pattern of the basic elements. Before the designer use the graphic processor to draft a design, the information of the required elements should have been already stored in the symbol library. The designer can add new elements to the symbol library thru the symbol library modules.

At completion of a schematic diagram, two relations, i.e., the SCR and the NWR and the Connection File will be created. The SCR stores the attributes of each symbol occurrence, for example, the location, rotation, and scale factor of each symbol occurrence. The NWR stores the fan-in, and fan-out relations of the symbol occurrences. The Connection File stores all the line segments of all the wires in the schematic diagram.

By this graphic processor, the design draft can be shown on the graphic terminal, and the design information can be properly handled by the three relations and two files. Since the purpose of the graphic processor is to collect information for simulation system, an input translation program is needed for each simulation system, as shown in Figure 2. The one we implemented is for the DFSS-1 simulation system [5], a digital simulation system based on three-value precise-delay model.

Graphical command

The interaction between the designer and the graphic processor is thru a sequence of command steps issued by the designer. To provide a better

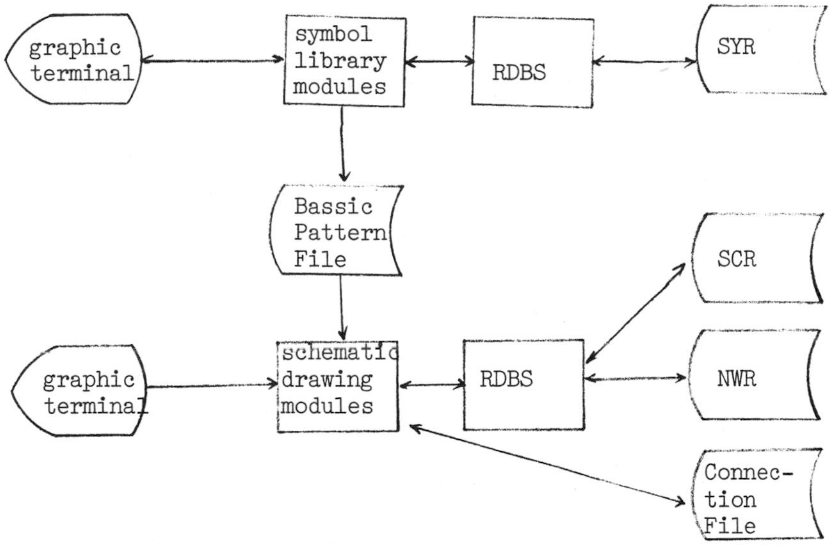

Figure 1 Overall software structure

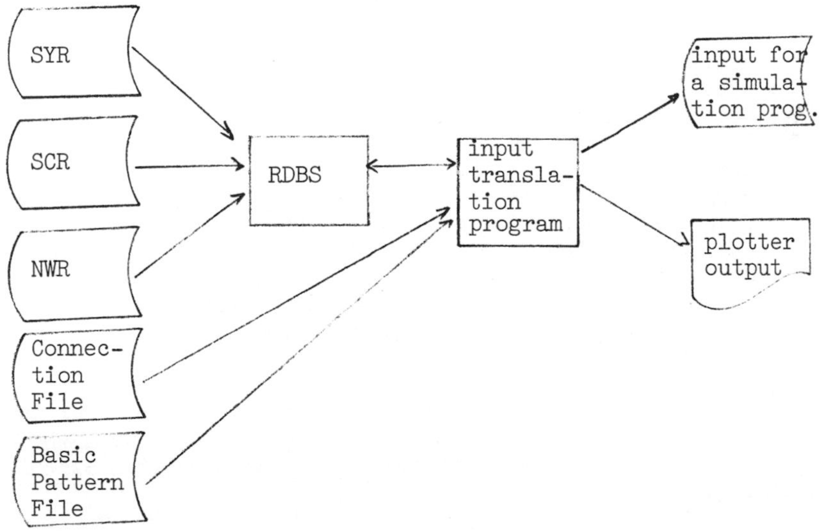

Figure 2 Relationship between the generated relations and files, and the input translation program

interaction with the designer, the command steps should fulfill the following objectives :

(1) Concise
(2) Easy-to-use
(3) Uniform response to user's requests
(4) Consideration for input keystroke assignments
(5) Error-preventive, preventing the user from mis-hitting an undeired 'valid' command
(6) The user can abort any incomplete command at any step of a command sequence

A graphical command is a command to create or manipulate graphical items. Therefore, a graphical command can be divided into the following four parts:

(1) Action
(2) Object of the action
(3) Description of the action
(4) Termination

The action part is given by a hit on the light-button, an area on the screen indicating the action, and is used to initiate the desired command. The object part may be a definition of a symbol, a definition of a wire, an indication of a created symbol, an indication of a created wire, an indication of a created label, or an indication of a block of area on the screen. The description part contains additional information to the action. The termination part is the keystroke ';'. The syntax of the commands is shown as follows:

action object , description ;

Some commands do not need the object and/or description, for example, the WINDOW command.

There are ten commands implemented in the schematic drawing modules, i.e.,

SYMBOL : Create a symbol occurrence
WIRE : Create a wire
LABEL : Give label to a symbol or wire
ERASE : Erase symbol, wire, label, or a block of area
COPY : Copy a block of area
MOVE : Move a block of area to another area
REPLACE: Replace a symbol
WINDOW : Change view window. View window is the part of a schematic diagram that is shown on the screen.
HELP : Show auxiliary information to help the user
RETURN : Return to the calling module

The creation of a design draft is a sequence of commands. In order to minimize to designer's input keystrokes, a sequence of commands with the same action can be activated without hitting the command light-button except at the very beginning.

Information representation of a logic circuit schematic diagram

A schematic diagram is a set of symbols, connection wires, and labels. The symbols and wires may have attributes to indicate their properties. Therefore, we use the following information to represent a schematic diagram:

(1) Symbol occurrences
(2) Attributes of the symbol occurrences
(3) Interconnection information between symbols
(4) Description of each wire

A symbol is the graphical representation of a basic element. Attributes common to a basic element should also be associated with the symbol. The graphical representation of a basic element is a set of lines, circles, curves, and pin location definitions. To draw a symbol we need the drawing information of the symbol. Therefore, the following information will also be needed.

(5) Drawing information of the symbols

(6) Attributes of the basic elements

We provide a symbol library to store the information mentioned in (5) and (6). Each symbol in the library is represented by a row in the SYR and several entries in the Basic Pattern File. The row in SYR will contain the attributes of the symbol. The entries in the Basic Pattern File will contain the line, circle, curve, and pin information of the symbol.

We provide the SCR to store the information mentioned in (1) and (2). Each row of SCR will contain a symbol occurrence and its attributes. The symbol occurrence is a pointer to the symbol library.

We also provide the NWR to store the network relationship between symbols. The Connection File is provided to maintain the routes of the connection wires. Each wire is represented by a row in NWR, which contains information of the pins and symbol identifications at both end points of the wire. Each entry in the Connection File represents a line segment of the wire. The route of a wire is represented by several entries in the Connection File.

CORRELATION

Correlation is the process of identifying a displayed item in the schematic diagram by pointing at the item on the display terminal [6]. During the creation of a schematic diagram, the displayed items are often referred to by the user for editing or assigning attributes. For example, if we want to erase a displayed item or move the item, we must first locate the item, then the desired action can be executed. The correlation mechanism involves the following actions:

(1) The user move the light pen or cursor to the desired item, then the X, Y coordinates are read by the computer.

(2) Tables of the correlatable items are searched for the 'hit' item.

(3) The desired action can be executed if the user hit an item. If no item can be hit, the user will be warned.

Correlatable items

A correlatable item is an item that may be referred to by the user on the display terminal. Information of the correlatable items are stored in tables that may be quickly referenced by the user. In this system, we define symbols, wires, pins of symbols, labels of symbols and wires, and a block of area on the display terminal as correlatable items.

Correlation on these items sometimes is to identify a point, sometimes is to identify the both end points of a wire, and also sometimes is to identify the corners of an area. Therefore, we can classify the correlation into the following three types, i.e., point correlation, wire correlation, and block correlation.

Point correlation

The correlation of symbols, pins, and labels of symbols and wires is a process of point correlation. The reference point of a symbol, stored in the symbol table, is used for the symbol correlation. The location of the pins of each symbol, stored in the pin table, is used for the pin correlation.

During the process of the point correlation, the X, Y coordinates of the cursor is first read and then the corresponding table is searched. Because the cursor can hardly be placed at exactly the reference point, a criterion is set for the possible 'hit' points. If more than one possible hit points exist, then the one that is closest to the cursor position is selected. If no hit point exists, then the user will be warned by a bell ring.

Because the number of pins is much greater than the number of symbols, searching the whole pin table may be time-consuming. A solution for this problem is provided. During the creation of each symbol, the 'maximal span' of the symbol is calculated and stored along with the symbol occurrence table. The maximal span is the maximal distance of the pins to the reference point of the symbol. When we desire a pin correlation, we search the symbol table for the possible symbols of the pin, whose X, Y coordinates lie within the maximal span of the symbol. Then, we search further the pins of the possible symbols for a hit. By doing this, we can reduce the time for searching the hit of a pin.

Wire correlation

The correlation of wires is a process of wire correlation. Correlating a wire will require the user to locate the starting point and ending point of the wire.

A wire can be defined as contiguous line segments starting from an output pin of a symbol and ending at an input pin of a symbol. Therefore, wire correlation require two pin correlations.

A wire may also be defined as contiguous line segments starting from a point on an existing wire and ending at an input pin of a symbol. Wire correlation of this type requires a pin correlation and the correlation of a point on an existing wire.

To find the wire on which a point resides, we have to check all the line segments on the current view window. The 'hit' line segment is that which has the minimal distance with the point and the distance is less than certain criterion. Because the number of line segments on the view window may be many, calculating all the distances between the point and the line segments may be time-consuming. We choose the possible line segments whose 'spanning area' cover the point. The 'spanning area' is a square block easily computed from the coordinates of the two end points of the line segment. Then we compute the distances between the point and the possible line segments. The one that is closest to the point and the distance is smaller than the criterion is chosen.

Block correlation

When we are creating a schematic diagram, it is not unusual that we take actions on a block of area on the view window. For example, we might duplicate group of items to other place, move group of items to other place, or erase group of items. With the block correlation capability, we simply specify the lower left corner and upper right corner of the block, and the desired actions can be executed. The items in the specified block, which can be identified thru the data structures of the system, will be processed with the desired actions. The wires that have something to do with items outside the block are neglected in the duplicate function, and are erased in a move or erase function.

RELATIONAL DATABASE SUPPORT (RDBS)

Different simulation systems usually require different formats of input data, and quite often the data items are different. But from the designer's point of view, he just want to analyze his digital logic circuit, no matter what the simulation is.

Many of the current graphic processors are designed as a part to a certain simulation system. Therefore, a graphic processor is limited to only one simulation system. Our idea about a graphic processor is that it can collect the schematic diagram of a logic circuit and other information, whatever is necessary for the subsequent simulation systems. As different simulation systems may require different data, the data structure of the graphic processor should be flexible enough to absorb the differences.

A database approach seems to be a good idea to tackle this problem. The user may define different databases for different simulation systems or define a database large enough for different simulation systems, and the user still use the same graphic processor. We choose the relational database approach because it is simple and powerful enough to handle the problem.

The RDBS of our graphic processor implements some functions of the general relational database management system which our graphic processor requires. For example, creation of a relation, editing a relation, operation within a relation, etc., are required functions in our graphic processor. The structure of the RDBS closely resembles that of RISS [7].

The RDBS feature in our graphic processor stores the following information in relations : common attributes of basic elements (SYR), attributes of symbols in the schematic diagram (SCR), and network relationship in the schematic diagram (NWR). We provide RDBS interface modules that users can call to extract data from the relations and prepare inputs for different simulation systems. We also provide retrieving modules and editing modules in RDBS. Once the relations are created, the user can querry or revise data in the relations.

For a simulation system, the user may define his own SYR or share the SYR with other simulation systems. In the SAMPLE APPLICATION section, we will provide a sample of SYR for DFSS-1 simualtion system. In this section, we will discuss the SCR and the NWR.

The SCR and the NWR are internal relations to the graphic processor. The attributes of SCR are shown as follows:

SID : Symbol label
SIDX : X coordinate of the label
SIDY : Y coordinate of the label
STYPE : Symbol type (i.e., the SYR entry of the displayed symbol)
SLOCX : X coordinate of the symbol
SLOCY : Y coordinate of the symbol
SCALE : Scale factor of the symbol
ROTATE: Orientation code of the symbol

The attributes of NWR are shown as follows:

WID : Wire label
WIDX : X coordinate of the label
WIDY : Y coordinate of the label
WISYM : The corresponding entry number in SYR, which indicates the symbol whose input pin is connected to the wire.
WIPIN : The input pin number of the above symbol
WOSYM : The corresponding entry number in SYR, which indicates the symbol whose output pin is connected to the wire.
WOPIN : The output pin number of the above symbol
WLF : Pointer to the Connection File, indicating the start of the actual route of the wire
WLT : Pointer to the Connection File, indicating the end of the actual route of the wire

In a schematic diagram for digital logic circuit, the attributes in the SCR and the NWR shown above seem enough. For some applications, if different values on certain attributes for the same type of elements exist in the schematic diagram, it may be necessary to add attributes to the SCR. For example, if resistors are to be used in the schematic diagram, the resistance may be different, therefore we should include the resistance attribute in the SCR. Because we implement the data structures in relations, it is easy to maintain the system if additional attributes are required.

SAMPLE APPLICATION

We take the DFSS-1 as a desired sample simulation system. The following paragraphs will demonstrate the application.

Brief description of DFSS-1 input

The circuit description input for DFSS-1 consists of five decks as follows:

```
*TYPES
 (Type statements)
*GATES
 (Gate statements)
*PULL  (optional)
 (Pull-up statements)
*FAULT
 (Fault statements)
*END
```

The type statements describe the attributes of the symbols. The format is:

Type name Type# Family type# # of input # of output D1 D2 D3 D4 D5 D6 D7 D8

Where D1 thru D8 are the delay values.

The gate statements describe the type and connection of the symbols. The

format is:
Gate name (Type name) IN1 IN2 ... INm, OUT1 OUT2 .. OUTn+
or Gate name (Type name) IN1 IN2 ... INm+
or Gate name (Type name) ,OUT1 OUT2 .. OUTn+
Where INs and OUTs are gate names. '+' is the delimiter.
The pull-up statements are optional and are used to describe gates that have pull-up resistors. The fault statements describe the fault conditions of the circuit. For more detailed information, please see reference 5 .

Basic symbol definition

From the DFSS-1 input description above, we can see the digital elements should have the following attributes:

```
SNAME : A 2 character mnemonic name of the basic symbol
DESC  : A 12 character description of the symbol
TYPEN : A 6 character type name
TYPENO: Type number
FAMNO : Family type number
INP   : Number of inputs
OUT   : Number of outputs
DMIR  : Minimum rise delay
DMAR  : maximun rise delay
DMIF  : Minimum fall delay
DMAF  : Maximum fall delay
D1Z   : From logic 1 to hi-impedance delay
DOz   : From logic 0 to hi-impedance delay
DZ1   : From hi-impedance to logic 1 delay
DZO   : From hi-impedance to logic 0 delay
```

The symbol library modules allow us to create the SYR for this application. The following shows the man-machine interaction to create the relation. The underlined strings are user's inputs.

```
LIBRARAY NAME=?TEST
CREATE NEW LIBRARY? (Y/N)Y
NUMBER OF COLUMN IN RELATION (I2) >15
COLUMN  1 NAME = >SNAME
DATA TYPE 1=1 BYTE CHAR, 2=INTEGER,4=REAL,6=STRING >6
COLUMN  2 NAME = >DESC
DATA TYPE 1=1 BYTE CHAR, 2=INTEGER,4=REAL,6=STRING >6
COLUMN  3 NAME = >TYPEN
DATA TYPE 1=1 BYTE CHAR, 2=INTEGER,4=REAL,6=STRING >6
COLUMN  4 NAME = >TYPENO
DATA TYPE 1=1 BYTE CHAR, 2=INTEGER,4=REAL,6=STRING >2
COLUMN  5 NAME = >FAMNO
DATA TYPE 1=1 BYTE CHAR, 2=INTEGER,4=REAL,6=STRING >2
COLUMN  6 NAME = >INP
DATA TYPE 1=1 BYTE CHAR, 2=INTEGER,4=REAL,6=STRING >2
COLUMN  7 NAME = >OUT
DATA TYPE 1=1 BYTE CHAR, 2=INTEGER,4=REAL,6=STRING >2
COLUMN  8 NAME = >DMIR
DATA TYPE 1=1 BYTE CHAR, 2=INTEGER,4=REAL,6=STRING >4
COLUMN  9 NAME = >DMAR
DATA TYPE 1=1 BYTE CHAR, 2=INTEGER,4=REAL,6=STRING >2
COLUMN 10 NAME = >DMIF
```

```
DATA TYPE 1=1 BYTE CHAR, 2=INTEGER,4=REAL,6=STRING >4
COLUMN 11 NAME = >DMAF
DATA TYPE 1=1 BYTE CHAR, 2=INTEGER,4=REAL,6=STRING >4
COLUMN 12 NAME = >DIZ
DATA TYPE 1=1 BYTE CHAR, 2=INTEGER,4=REAL,6=STRING >4
COLUMN 13 NAME = >DOZ
DATA TYPE 1=1 BYTE CHAR, 2=INTEGER,4=REAL,6=STRING >4
COLUMN 14 NAME = >DZ1
DATA TYPE 1=1 BYTE CHAR, 2=INTEGER,4=REAL,6=STRING >4
COLUMN 15 NAME = >DZO
DATA TYPE 1=1 BYTE CHAR, 2=INTEGER,4=REAL,6=STRING >4
ANY CORRECTION ? Y/N >Y
INPUT COL NO TO BE CORRECTED (I2) >9
COL  9 NAME=DMAR        TO BE CHANGED TO >DMAR
CURRENT DATA TYPE=2 NEW TYPE = > 4
ANY CORRECTION ? Y/N >N
RELATION TEST      HAS BEEN CREATED
```

After we define the SYR, we can define the symbols. The following example shows the definition of a two-input NOR gate. We will define the attributes first, then we define the pattern of the symbol.

```
1=CREATE SYMBOL
2=SHOW SYMBOL
3=REPLACE SYMBOL
4=EXIT
WHICH?1

ASSIGN VALUES
 1. SNAME    >P2
 2. DESC     >2-INPUT NOR
 3. TYPEN    >NOR2
 4. TYPENO   >5
 5. FAMNO    >3
 6. INP      >2
 7. OUT      >1
 8. DMIR     >4.
 9. DMAR     >4.
10. DMIF     >4.
11. DMAF     >4.
12. DIZ      >0
13. DOZ      >0
14. DZ1      >0
15. DZO      >0

P=PRINT,V=VALUE CHANGE,Q=QUIT, WHICH?> Q
```

After the user types Q at the last step described above, light-button and assigned attributes will be shown on the screen. Grid points are also displayed on the screen. Figure 3 shows the hardcopy of the created pattern. In order to describe the operation, points p1 thru p13 are also drawn on this figure.

The steps involved in the creation of this pattern are also shown sequen-

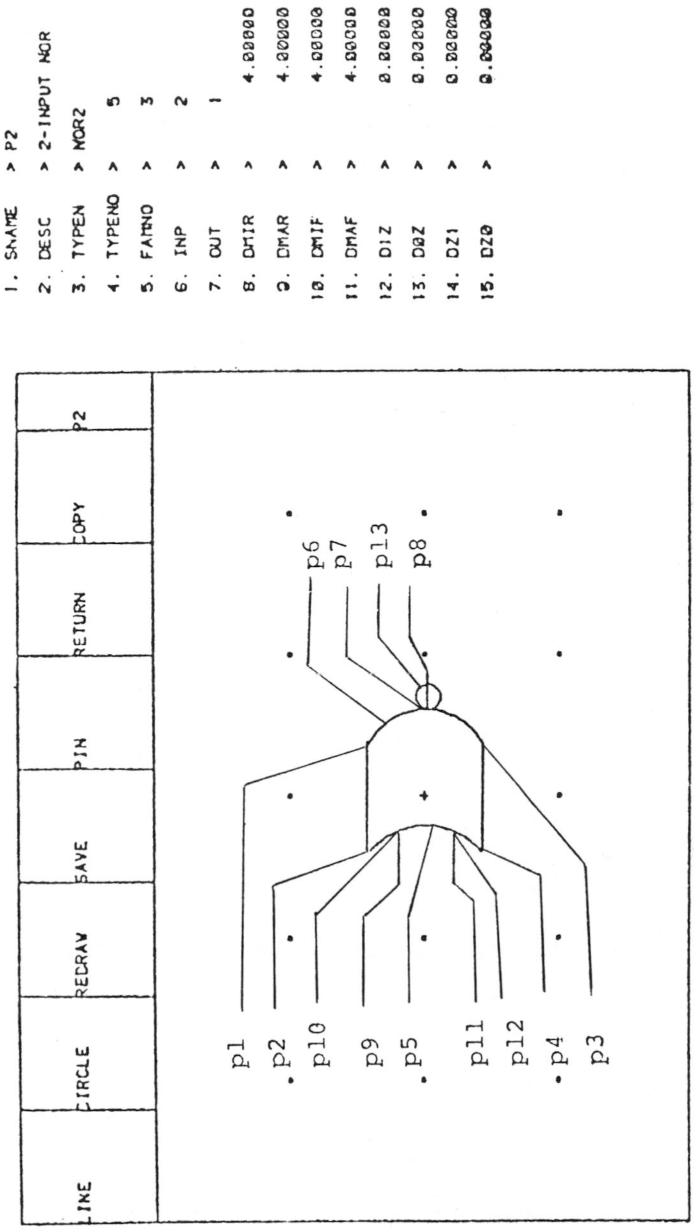

Figure 3 Creation of the basic symbol P2 (NOR2)

tially in the rows of the following table.

Cursor Position	Key-strokes	Result
LINE	space	activate LINE
pl	M	move cursor to pl
p2	D	draw a line from pl to p2
p3	M	
p4	D	draw a line
CIRCLE	space	activate CIRCLE
p4	S	
p2	E	
p5	P	draw a partial circle from p4 to p2 passing p5
p3	S	
pl	E	
p6	p	draw a partial circle
LINE	space	activate LINE
p7	M	
p8	D	draw a line
p9	M	
pl0	D	draw a line
pll	M	
pl2	D	draw a line
CIRCLE	space	activate CIRCLE
pl3	C	
p7	R	draw a circle center pl3 passing p7
PIN	space	activate PIN
p8	O	define output pin at p8
p9	I	define input pin at p9
pll	I	define input pin at pll
SAVE	space	save the pattern and attributes into library
RETURN	space	return to the calling module

Creation of a schematic diagram

The following shows the steps involved in the creation of the schematic diagram in Figure 4.

Cursor position	Key-strokes	Result
SYMBOL	space	activate SYMBOL command
pl	A2;	draw a symbol A2, an AND gate, at pl
p2	*;	draw a symbol same as previous one
p3	B2;	draw a symbol B2, an OR gate
p4	PI;	draw a symbol PI, a primary input
p5	*;	draw a symbol same as previous one
p6	*;	"
p7	*;	"
p8	PO;	draw a symbol PO, a primary output
WIRE	space	activate WIRE command
p9	W	
pl0	W;	draw a wire from p9 to pl0
pll	W	
pl2	W;	draw a wire from pll to pl2

(to be continued)

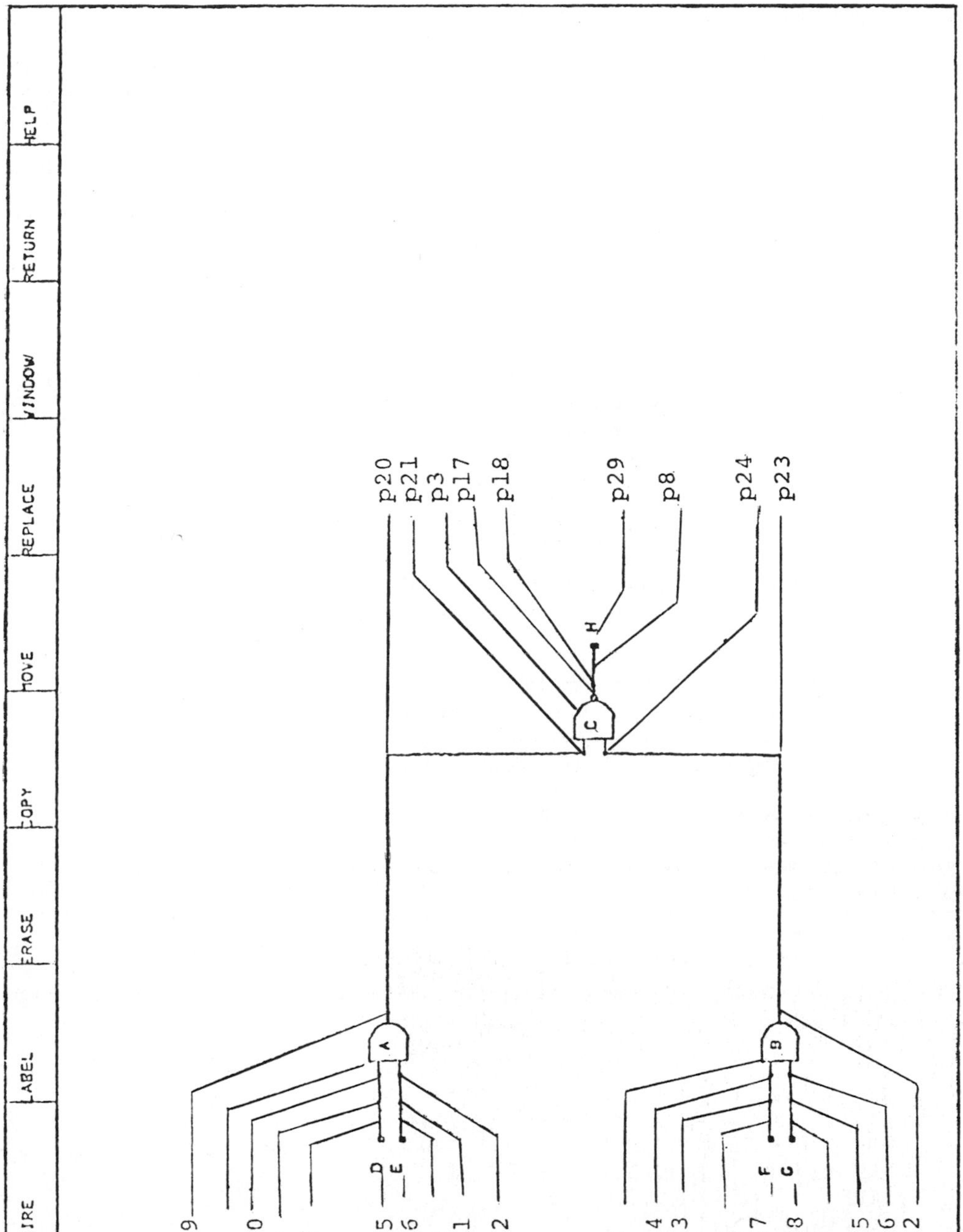

Figure 4 A sample schematic diagram

(continued)

Cursor Position	Key-strokes	Result
p13	W	
p14	W;	draw a wire
p15	W	
p16	W;	draw a wire
p17	W	
p18	W	
p19	W;	draw a wire from p17 passing p18 to p19
p20	W	
p21	W	
p22	W;	draw a wire
p23	W	
p24	W;	draw a wire
LABEL	space	activate LABEL command
p1	S,A;	draw the label 'A' at p1 for the symbol at p1
p2	S,B;	draw the label 'B'
p3	S,C;	draw the label 'C'
p4	S,	
p25	D;	draw the label 'D' at p25 for the symbol at p4
p5	S,	
p26	E;	draw the label 'E' at p26 for the symbol at p5
p6	S,	
p27	F;	draw the label 'F'
p7	S,	
p28	G;	draw the label 'G'
p8	S,	
p29	H;	draw the label 'H'
RETURN	space	return to the calling module

Input for DFSS-1 simulation system

After we create a schematic diagram, we can extract data in the relations, and translate to the input format for the simulation system by a translation program. The user can retrieve the information stored in the relations by calling the RDBS interface modules.

The following shows the translated input of the schematic diagram in Figure 5 for DFSS-1.

```
*TYPES
PO          19 0 1 0 0 0 0 0+
NAND3        4 3 3 1 2 4 2 2+
NAND4        4 3 4 1 2 4 2 2+
PI          18 0 0 1 0 0 0 0+
INV          3 3 1 1 1 3 1 1+
WIRE        17 0 1 1 0 0 0 0+
*GATE
QBAR     (PO       ) F9+
Q        (PO       ) F8+
F8       (NAND3    ) F5 PRESET F9, Q F82 F9+
F9       (NAND3    ) F6 CLEAR F8, QBAR F91 F8+
F5       (NAND3    ) F3 F7 PWR, F8+
F6       (NAND3    ) F4 F7 PWR, F9+
F4       (NAND3    ) F2 CLEAR F3, F6 F3+
```

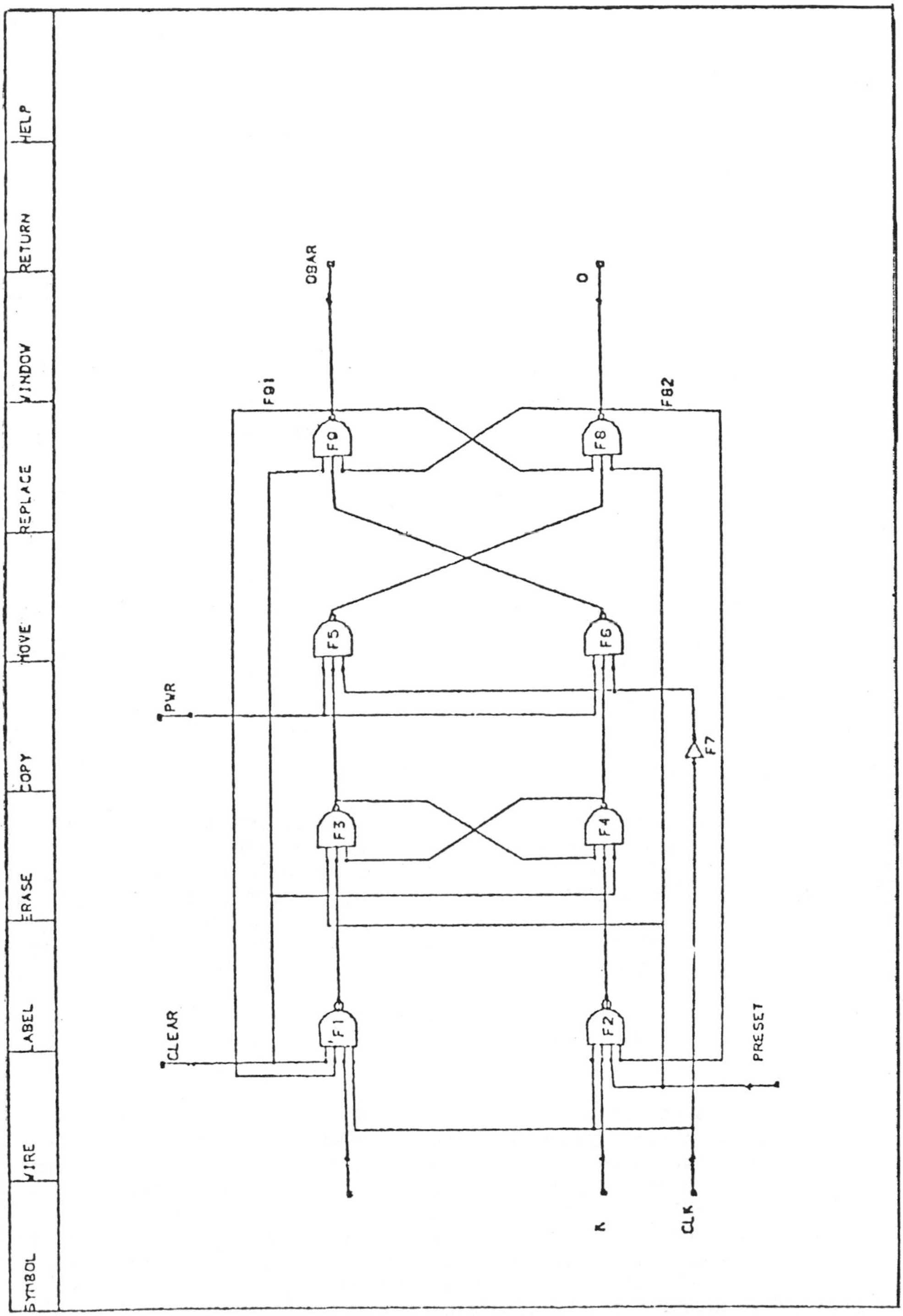

Figure 5 Schematic diagram of a master-slave J-K flip flop

```
F3      (NAND3  ) F1 PRESET F4, F5 F4+
F1      (NAND4  ) J CLK CLEAR F91,F3+
F2      (NAND4  ) K PRESET CLK F82, F4+
K       (PI     ) , F2+
CLK     (PI     ) , F7 F1 F2+
J       (PI     ) , F1+
CLEAR   (PI     ) , F1 F9 F4+
PWR     (PI     ) , F6 F5+
PRESET  (PI     ) , F2 F8 F3+
F7      (INV    ) CLK, F5 F6+
F91     (WIRE   ) F9, F1+
F82     (WIRE   ) F8, F2+
```

CONCLUSION

We have presented the basic concepts and algorithms involved in the design and implementation of an interactive graphic processor for digital logic simulation systems. The significant results that have been obtained in this study are:

(1) Provide powerful editing functions. Editing capabilities are extended to include operations on a group of graphical items.

(2) Incorporate relational database functions into the graphic processor. By this feature, the data structures are more flexible and more suitable for future extension.

(3) Define graphical data structures to store basic symbols and schematic diagrams.

(4) Provide an interactive means to create basic symbols in the symbol library.

(5) Provide an interactive means to create and edit schematic diagrams.

(6) Provide an input translation program for the DFSS-1 simulation system.

The graphic processor described so far has been implemented on a VAX 11/780 computer, with two mega bytes of main memory. Because the VAX 11/780 is a virtual memory computer, the capacity of the elements in a schematic diagram can be very large. The Tektronix 4054 is an intelligent terminal, but we do not use this capability. The reason is that we hope the low cost non-intelligent storage tube terminals may also be used. Another reason is that we hope the system is more portable.

We use FORTRAN IV as the programming language in order to make the system more portable. We also apply the modular programming technique to increase the reliability and maintainability.

Graphic processors can be used in many other applications. GTE AE Labs have developed the AELCAP system for linear circuit analysis [8]. In the application, the attributes of each symbol occurrence besides of the common attributes of each element type should be given. For example, the capacitance values and resistance values should be given for the capacitors and resistors, though the graphical representation and common attributes are the same for each element type. The user can give these values either at the completion of the schematic diagram or at the same time when the user creates the symbol occurrences. A little modification in our graphic processor to let the user define the SCR will make our graphic processor applicable to this type of simulations.

Although our graphic processor is enhanced by the relational database support feature, we are not satisfied with it. We think the system could be enhanced further by incorporating a complete graphical database.

REFERENCES

1. Dyer, J. A., Laha, A. K., Moran, E. J., and Smart, D. W., "The Use of Graphics Processors for Circuit Design Simulation at GTE AE Labs", 17th Design Automation Conference Proc. (1980), pp. 446-550.
2. Bayegan, H. M., "CASS: Computer Aided Schematic System", 14th Design Automation Conference Proc. (1977), pp.396-403.
3. Bayegan, H. M., and Aas, E., "An Integrated System for Interactive Editing of Schematics, Logic Simulation and PCB Layout Design", 15th Design Automation Conference Proc. (1978), pp. 1-8.
4. Spence, R., and Apperley, M., "The Interactive Graphic Man-Computer Dialogue in Computer-Aided Circuit Design", IEEE Trans. Circ. Sys., vol. CAS-24, no. 2 (1977), pp. 49-61.
5. Jea, Y. H., and Shih, H. C., "A Digital Fault Simulation System Based on Three-Value Precision-Delay Model", Proc. of International Computer Symposium, 1980, Taipei, R.O.C., pp. 1158-1170.
6. Weller, D., and Williams, R., "Graphic and Relational Data Base Support for Problem Solving", Tutorial and Selected Readings in interactive Computer Graphics, edited by Herbert Freeman, 1980, pp. 193-199.
7. Meldam, M. J., Mcleod, D. J., Pellicore, R. J., and Squire, M., "RISS: A Relational Data Base Management System for Minicomputers", Van Nostrand Reinhold Company, 1978.
8. Page, W. D., "Interactive Graphics for Linear Circuit Analysis", GTE AE. J., vol. 16, no. 6 (1978), pp. 233-238.

SHIPHULLS, B-SPLINE SURFACES AND CADCAM

David F. Rogers
Steven G. Satterfield
Francisco A. Rodriguez

Computer Aided Design/Interactive Graphics Group
Division of Engineering and Weapons
U.S. Naval Academy
Annapolis, Maryland 21402
U. S. A.

ABSTRACT

A Computer Aided Design/Computer Aided Manufacturing (CADCAM) system for the design of ship hulls and the production of towing tank models is described. The design portion of the system is implemented on and supported by a three dimensional interactive graphics device and a minicomputer.

The hull surface is modeled using B-spline surfaces. Both smooth surfaces and surfaces with internal discontinuities (knuckles and hard chines) may be modeled. The use of a fast incremental algorithm for modifying these surfaces dynamically in real time (rubber sheeting) is described for real ships. The use of color graphics to display the Gaussian curvature of the surface for fairness determination is described for real ships. A simple algorithm for obtaining accurate sections or contours of B-spline surfaces is described. Its use on real ship hulls in a towing tank model production environment is described.

A microprocessor driven, stand alone graphics device simply, directly and inexpensively interfaced to the CNC controller on the shop floor is used to provide support for the manufacturing portion of the system. A program running in the microprocessor based graphics system provides all post-processing, producing a graphical display for the machine operator and drives the machining center. All functions are accomplished on-the-fly in real time.

The integration of these systems into a Computer Integrated Manufacturing system for the production of wooden towing tank models is described.

1. INTRODUCTION

The computer aided design of ships lines and hulls using interactive graphics lines fairing techniques to represent the surface of ship hulls as a net of lines is well known. However, the use of mathematical surfaces is less common. Although the traditional bicubic Coons patch has been used for hull representation [1], recently, a number of authors have investigated the

---

+This work was partially supported by the U.S. Coast Guard.

use of B-spline surfaces for ship hull design [2-6]. Building on this previous work, the present paper describes the integration of an interactive B-spline surface hull description technique into a system for the production of towing tank models.

The task of designing and producing a fair, accurate ship hull using CADCAM techniques can be divided into the following areas:

Development of a preliminary surface description.

Manipulating or modifying this surface.

Determining that the surface is fair and correct.

Interfacing to the production facilities.

Producing the model hull.

Checking the correctness of the hull produced.

Each of these areas is examined in turn.

2. PRELIMINARY SURFACE DESCRIPTION

A preliminary surface description can be generated in one of three ways: ab initio, by modification of an existing surface described hull, or from external data such as a traditional lines plan or set of offsets. For ab initio design in the present system an initially flat B-spline polygon net is interactively modified using the techniques described below. Modification of an existing surface is accomplished in a similar fashion, i.e. by interactively manipulating the existing polygon net and resulting surface until the desired modified surface is obtained.

When the surface is described by external data it is convenient to obtain an initially non-flat B-spline surface approximating the hull for subsequent real time interactive modification. This requires determining the defining polygonal net from an existing network of three dimensional surface data points. Since, in the present context, the algorithm will only be used once to obtain an initial approximate surface some computational inefficiencies are acceptable.

Consider a Cartesian product parametric B-spline surface [7] given by

$$Q(u,w) = \sum_{i=1}^{n} \sum_{j=1}^{m} B_{i,j} N_{i,k}(u) M_{j,\ell}(w) \tag{1}$$

where

$$N_{i,1}(u) = \begin{cases} 1 \text{ if } x_i \leq u < x_{i+1} \\ 0 \text{ otherwise} \end{cases} \tag{2a}$$

$$N_{i,k}(u) = \frac{(u-x_i)N_{i,k-1}(u)}{x_{i+k-1}-x_i} + \frac{(x_{i+k}-u)N_{i+1,k-1}(u)}{x_{i+k}-x_{i+1}}$$

$$M_{j,1}(w) = \begin{cases} 1 \text{ if } y_j \le w < y_{j+1} \\ 0 \text{ otherwise} \end{cases} \tag{2b}$$

$$M_{j,\ell}(w) = \frac{(w-y_j)M_{j,\ell-1}(w)}{y_{j+\ell-1}-y_j} + \frac{(y_{j+\ell}-w)M_{j+1,\ell-1}(w)}{y_{j+\ell}-y_{j+1}}$$

where the x_i, y_j are the elements of a uniform knot vector, k and ℓ are the order of the B-spline surface in the u and w directions, and n and m are the number of polygon net points in the u and w directions respectively. Here the Q(u,w) are the known surface data points. The N and M basis functions can be determined from the knot vector and the parameter values u and w. The $B_{i,j}$ are the unknown required polygon net points. For each known surface data point Eq.1 provides a linear equation in the unknown $B_{i,j}$'s. Writing this out for a single surface data point yields

$$\begin{aligned} Q(u_1,w_1) = N_{1,k}(u_1) & \left[B_{1,1}M_{1,\ell}(w_1) \text{ -- } B_{1,m}M_{m,\ell}(w_1)\right] \\ + N_{2,k}(u_1) & \left[B_{2,1}M_{1,\ell}(w_1) \text{ -- } B_{2,m}M_{m,\ell}(w_1)\right] \\ & \vdots \\ + N_{n,k}(u_1) & \left[B_{n,1}M_{1,\ell}(w_1) \text{ -- } B_{n,m}M_{m,\ell}(w_1)\right] \end{aligned}$$

and similarly for all the surface data points. In matrix notation this can be written as

$$[Q] = [C][B] \tag{3}$$

Since for r x s topologically rectangular surface point data [C] is not normally square, a solution can only be obtained in some mean sense. In particular,

$$[B] = \left[[C]^T [C] \right]^{-1} [C]^T [Q] \tag{4}$$

The u and w parametric values for each surface data point are obtained using a chord length approximation.

As pointed out in [8] for B-spline curves, and in [6] for B-spline surfaces, this technique cannot yield hard points, knuckles or hard chines (discontinues in first and second derivative) in the resulting B-spline curve or surface. To illustrate this consider the bicubic B-spline surface and its defining polygon net shown in Fig. 1. The surface exhibits a hard chine as a result of the three coincident lines in the defining polygon net.

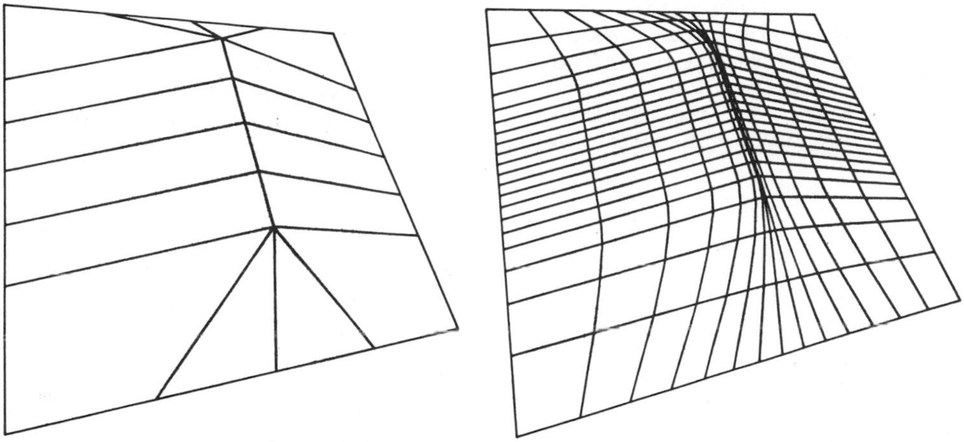

a. Polygon net b. Bicubic B-spline surface

Figure 1. Interactively generated hard chine bicubic B-spline test surface.

Data points from this surface were used to create a new defining polygon net using the mathematical technique described above. The resulting polygon net is shown along with the resulting surface in Fig. 2. Note that the new polygon net does not have any coincident lines and that the resulting surface does not exhibit a hard chine. At present, hard chines or knuckles must be introduced interactively.

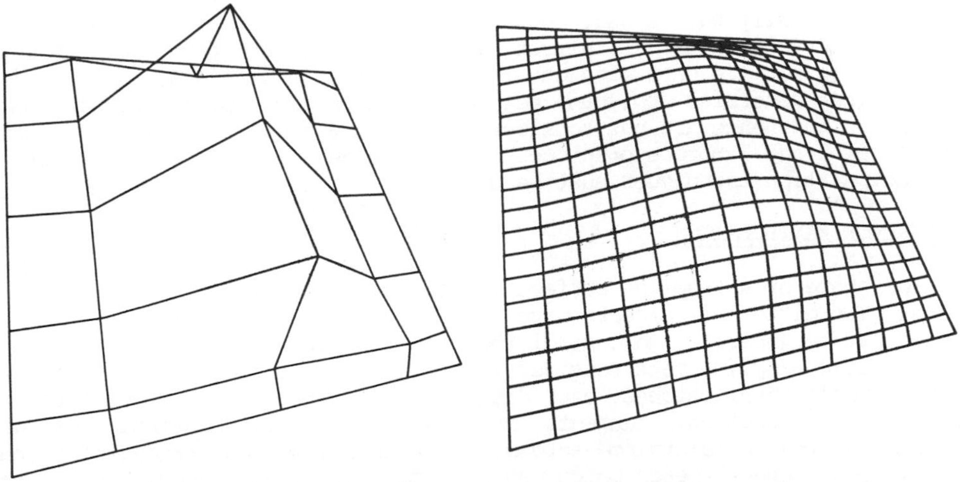

a. Polygon net b. Bicubic B-spline surface

Figure 2. Automatically generated hard chine bicubic B-spline test surface.

Additional difficulties associated with automatically fitting a surface to known three dimensional data points are illustrated in Fig. 3. Figure 3 shows three dimensional digitized data representing the afterbody station lines for a ship. The ship hull is smooth, i.e. does not exhibit any hard chines or knuckles. The resulting automatically generated polygon net and the resulting bicubic B-spline surface is also shown.

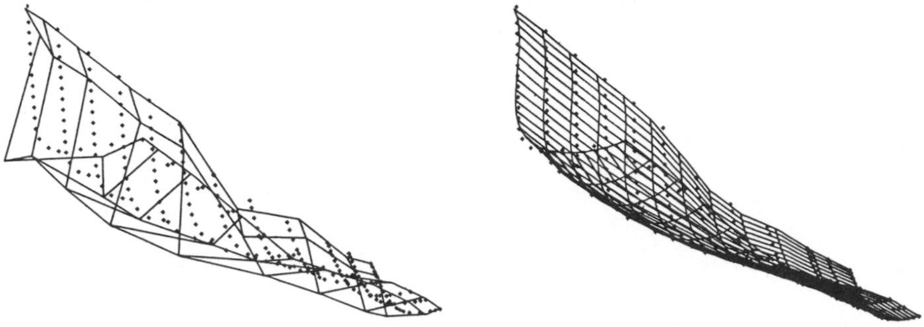

a. Polygon net b. Bicubic B-spline surface

Figure 3. B-spline surface for the afterbody of a ship.

Of particular interest is the digitized data for the midship section and the shape of the polygon net and surface in this region. The midbody of the ship is essentially wall sided. However, since non-analytical sculptured, digitized surface data is almost never fair the data from the deck edge downward does not lie on a straight line but rather exhibits a small oscillation The generated polygon net and resulting surface exhibit the same oscillation and hence are not considered fair (cf. Fig. 3). Thus, either very careful and laborous preprocessing of the data is required or interactive manipulation techniques must be used.

3. SURFACE MANIPULATION

The shape of a B-spline surface is controlled by a polygonal net of points. Two different concepts have been developed with respect to use of a polygon net to generate and control the B-spline surface--local and global. Local bicubic B-spline nets consider that the surface is composed of several (many) quadrilateral patches, each defined by 16 three component vectors at each corner (position, tangent, and twist vectors). Continuity of some arbitrary degree is maintained across the patch boundaries. Except for continuity requirements each patch can be separately manipulated. The global approach assumes that a single large polygonal net controls the entire B-spline surface. Although the resulting surface is constructed of piecewise patches, individual quadrilateral patches, cannot be separately manipulated. The present authors use this latter approach, [5] and [6].

The polygon net defining the B-spline surface, seen as a perspective or an orthographic projection with intensity (gray) scaling on an interactive line drawing refresh graphics display, can be oriented in space by manipulating a set of control dials. The control dials provide rotation about the three coordinate axes, translation along the three coordinate axes and overall scaling. An additional control dial is used to adjust the sensitivity of the other dials. Interactive picking of individual polygon net points is accomplished using a tablet and a cross hair cursor. Once selected, the position of the net point in three space is controlled by three dials. To be useful for interactive design the B-spline surface generated by the polygon net must move dynamically with the net point, i.e. it must be possible to perform rubber sheeting.

To develop a dynamic B-spline surface algorithm, consider the Cartesian product B-spline surface governed by Eq.1. The blending functions in the u,w parametric space are the B-spline basis functions N and M respectively. The basis functions depend upon the number of polygon net points and the character of the knot vector [7]. As shown by the recursion relations given in Eq.1 the B-spline basis function provides only local support for the surface. That is, the extent of the surface influenced by a given net point is limited. A knowledge of the extent of this influence is useful in increasing the speed of calculation for the surface algorithm.

Further, note that if the number of polygon net points in the u and w directions does not change, the knot vector will not change, and that if the parameter values used to calculate lines on the surface do not change, then the basis functions N and M do not change and may be precalculated for any arbitrary location of the polygon net points, i.e. the $B_{i,j}$'s. Examination of Eq.1 then leads to an incremental method for calculating a new or updated surface from a known B-spline surface when a change in a polygon net point occurs [6]. In particular

$$Q_{new}(u,w) = Q_{old}(u,w) + (B_{i,j_{new}} - B_{i,j_{old}}) \left[\sum_{i=1}^{n} \sum_{j=1}^{m} N_{i,k}(u)\, M_{j,\ell}(w) \right]$$

where B is the specific polygon net point that has been changed. A fast algorithm for the dynamic update of the B-spline surface is then

Start:

If surface order or number of polygon net points
or number of required parametric lines for either
u or w has not changed then go to 4

Comment: calculate complete surface

calculate knot vector in the u direction - X
calculate knot vector in the w direction - Y

```
        for u = min to max for increment X max/(number of
                u parametric lines - 1)
        calculate N(u)
        next u

        for w = min to max for increment Y max/(number of
                w parametric lines - 1)
        calculate M(w)
        next w
        Q = Ø

        for I=1 to number of parametric lines in the u
                direction
        if N(I)=Ø then 3
             for J=1 to number of parametric lines in the
                     w direction
             if M(J)=Ø then 2
             Q(I,J) = Q(I,J) + B(I,J)*N(I)*M(J)
           2 next J
    3   next I
        QOLD = Q
        BOLD = B
        Done


Comment:  calculate incremental change in surface

    4   BCHANG = (new polygon net point) - (old polygon
                 net point)

        for I=1 to number of parametric lines in the u
                direction
        if N(I)=Ø then 6
             for J=1 to number of parametric lines in
                     the w direction
             if M(J)=Ø then 5
             Q(I,J) = QOLD(I,J) + BCHANG*N(I)*M(J)
           5 next J
    6   next I
        Done
```

This algorithm, written in FORTRAN and implemented on a PDP-11/45 with floating point processor and a 2K byte Cache memory driving an Evans & Sutherland Picture System I, using the RT-11 operating system, allows real time interactive surface dragging or rubber sheeting at 4-20 updates per second, depending on the complexity of the surface [6]. Examples of surfaces constructed using the dynamic B-spline surface algorithm are shown in Figs. 1, 4 and 5. Figure 4 shows the forebody of the ship shown in Fig. 3 and Fig. 5 shows a modified bulb on the ship of Fig. 4. Modification of the surface required approximately three minutes of user time sitting at the display. The defining polygon is 5 x 8 and the defining surface has 15 x 24 parametric lines. The algorithm allows eight updates per second.

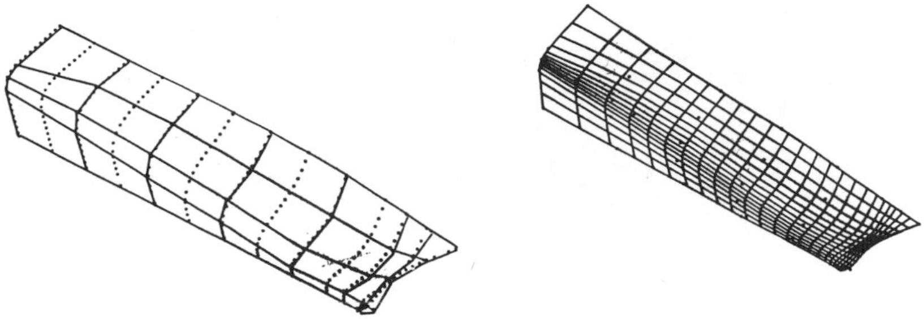

a. Interactively fit B-spline polygon net b. Bicubic B-spline surface

Figure 4. B-spline surfaces for forebody of U.S. Navy Ammunition Ship.

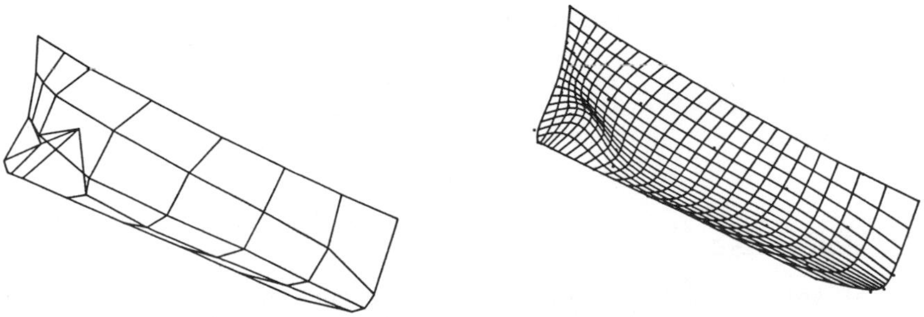

a. Polygon net b. Bicubic B-spline surface

Figure 5. Modified bulb on ammunition ship.

Figure 6 illustrates the technique for creating a surface with a hard chine. Figures 6a and 6b show the initial polygon net and bicubic B-spline surface obtained using the automatic fitting technique discussed above. Notice that the surface does not exhibit a hard chine. Figures 6c and 6d show the defining polygon net and surface after interactively adding the hard chine.+

+A short 16mm film illustrating the dynamic modification of B-spline surfaces accompanied the presentation.

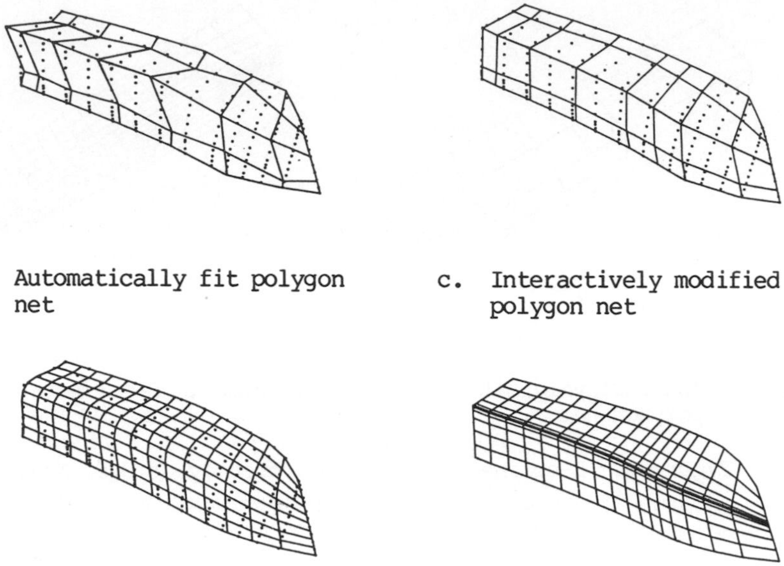

a. Automatically fit polygon net

c. Interactively modified polygon net

b. Automatically fit surface

d. Interactively modified surface

Figure 6. Ship Hull Surface with Hard Chine.

4. SURFACE FAIRNESS

One of the fundamental concerns in Computer Aided Ship Design is to develop appropriate mathematical techniques for determining and/or visualizing the fairness or smoothness of the hull surface. Recently attention has focused on the use of Gaussian curvature as a means for detecting unfairness in surfaces [2, 9-12]. The Gaussian or total curvature at a point on a surface is the product of the maximum and minimum curvatures, and indicates whether the surface is locally elliptic, hyperbolic, or parabolic (Gaussian curvature positive, negative, or zero).

Dill [10] used contours of Gaussian and average curvature combined with color raster graphics to examine surface fairness. He applied this technique to toroidal and catenoidal test surfaces and to automobile hood and fender surfaces. The results clearly show surface curvature discontinuities and hence provide an indication of surface fairness. Dill and Rogers [12] applied the method to a series of B-spline test surfaces and to B-spline ship hull surfaces.

To display the Gaussian curvature of a B-spline surface the surface is first approximated by a quadrilateral polygonal surface. Each polygon is assigned a color encoded according to the curvature value associated with the polygon. The polygon is then shaded using a simple ambient plus Lambertian reflection assuming a single light source. For display purposes, the average of the Gaussian curvature values at the four polygon vertices is assigned to each polygon. To color-encode the curvature the scalar range is divided into a number of intervals with each interval assigned a different color. In general, colors ranging from yellow-green through yellow and red to magenta represent positive values, while colors from yellow-green through turquoise to blue represent negative values.

Figure 7 shows the curvature colored image for the ship shown in Fig. 4. The ship has a sharp bow with a mild underwater bulb flowing back into a parallel midbody and an essentially flat bottom. Figure 8 shows the example of the ship hull with a hard chine previously illustrated in Fig. 6d.

In the curvature images, Figs. 7 and 8, a staircase-like boundary between different colors will be seen. This is not due to the sampling or polygonal approximation (actual polygons are considerably smaller), but to the quantization effects of a limited number of bits per pixel. Since each test surface consists of approximately 2,000 polygons, an image could require up to 2,000 distinct colors, far more than the 256 colors possible with the eight bit color frame buffer.

There is an apparent minor anomaly in Fig. 7. Just aft of the bow will be seen a small patch of relatively high Gaussian curvature (yellow spot) in the middle of a large area of small, negative Gaussian curvature (green). This possible unfairness is not detected in the parametric mesh display, Fig. 4. A similar unfair region in Fig. 6e, the hard chine vessel, is the negative region (green) between two positive regions (red) about halfway along the sheer line.

As the examples of Figs. 7 and 8 illustrate, Gaussian curvature shows the nature of surface curvature. Further, the superimposing of color graphically shows the variation of curvature over a three-dimensional surface and helps to visualize this surface behavior. In sum, color "makes it obvious"; potential problem areas that might otherwise be missed are made immediately apparent.

5. INTERFACING TO THE PRODUCTION FACILITIES

As discussed below the numerical control production technique requires a significant number of waterlines. In general a waterline can be considered as a level contour line for the ship surface. In addition, body or section lines, buttocks and diagonals can also be considered level contour lines. The problem of generating contour lines would seem to be the same as intersecting the B-spline surface with a plane. However, generating true contour lines requires more information than finding a group of planar points. The points must be connected in a logical order that "follows" the desired contour. For an arbitrary surface several disconnected contour lines may exist.

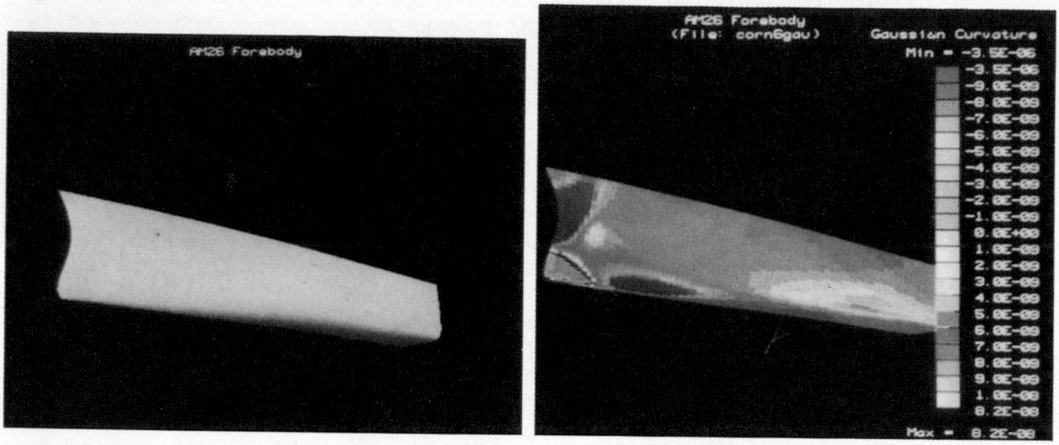

a. Normally colored image

b. Color-encoded gaussian curvature

Figure 7. Forebody of U.S. Navy Ammunition Ship.

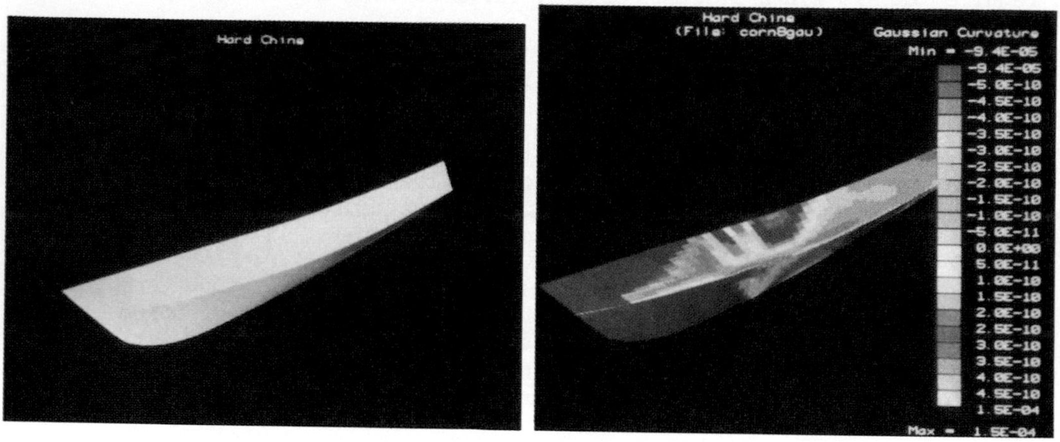

a. Normally colored image

b. Color-encoded gaussian curvature

Figure 8. Ship with Hard Chine.

Satterfield and Rogers [13] present a procedure for obtaining accurate contour lines from a B-spline surface. The procedure is a two step process. The first step uses a modification of a traditional algorithm [14] to obtain the contour on a triangular polygonal approximation to the B-spline surface (ship hull). The second step performs a B-spline surface generation over a limited area to produce an accurate contour.

The Heap algorithm [14] produces contour lines from a triangular surface mesh description. The mesh consists of a set of triangular elements whose vertices are points lying on the surface. For each specified contour plane the algorithm follows the contour element by element. As each triangular element is found the edges of the triangle are intersected by the contour plane. The resultant contour lines consist of straight line segments passing through each triangular element. The accuracy of the resulting contour depends on the density of the triangular mesh. Used directly, a very fine mesh is necessary to meet accuracy requirements. This results in excessive memory and execution requirements.

The Heap algorithm used with a first approximation for the surface is modified to output the triangular surface polygons along a given contour. Each triangular contour line thus specifies a band or limited surface area within which the desired contour line or lines occur. As a result of the algorithm "following" the contours, the correct order for the points of a contour is produced and the existence of multiple disconnected contours within a single contour plane is identified. Figure 9 shows an arbitrary B-spline surface with one triangular contour line.

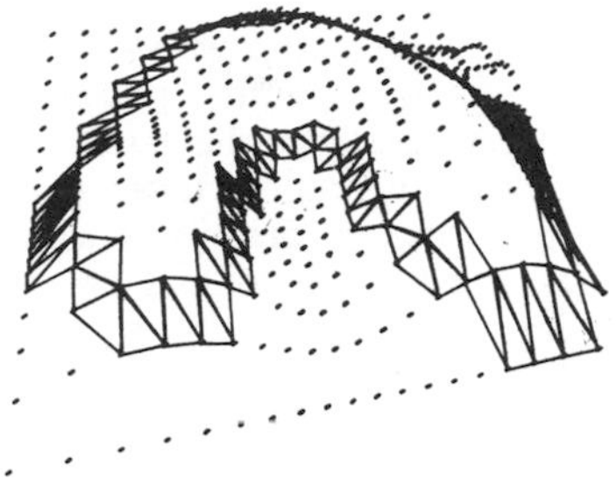

Figure 9. Arbitrary B-spline Surface with One Triangular Contour.

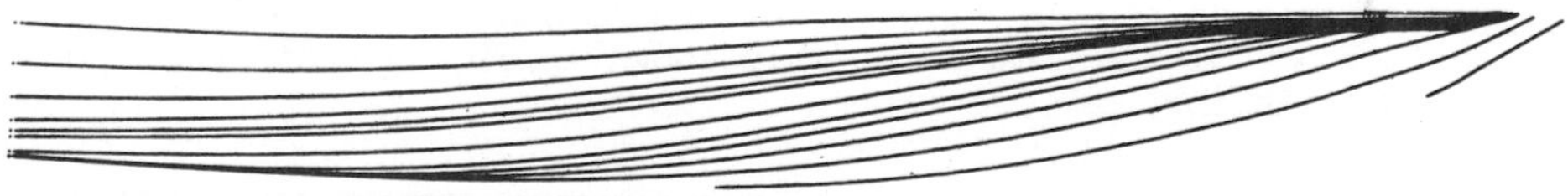

Figure 10. Contoured Waterlines for the Ammunition Ship of Figure 4.

In the second step, the triangular contours produced by the modified Heap algorithm are used as the basis for a piecewise B-spline calculation of the surface. Since the B-spline calculation is controlled by parametric values, any sub-region of the full surface may be calculated from the corresponding known parametric values. Thus, each triangular element is used to accurately identify a small region of the surface that intersects the desired contour plane. Using the B-spline algorithm, points on the surface intersecting the contour plane are found by generating pairs of surface points located within a desired tolerance of each other. When a pair spans the contour plane, the contour point is found by linear interpolation. Waterlines for the forebody of the ammunition ship of Fig. 4 are shown in Fig. 10.

6. PRODUCING THE MODEL HULL

Once the hull surface design is finalized a numerical control (N/C) milling file consisting of waterlines created with the contouring algorithm described above sorted from the keel to the deck is created and stored on disc [15]. Any number of waterlines and any number of points on each waterline can be generated. The actual N/C mill file can be plotted for proofing purposes. Once the milling file is considered satisfactory, it is transferred from the disc file to the magnetic tape unit in a Tektronix 4050 series graphics system. It is this data stored on the tape as waterline data points which represents the direct interface between the design facility and the manufacturing facility. No separate part programming occurs.

The N/C milling program is written in BASIC and runs on the Tektronix 4050 series system. The program provides the N/C machine operator with assistance in setting up the mill. Quantities such as spindle speed, rotation direction, cutter diameter, etc., are interactively supplied by the operator. The program provides all the required post processing of the mill file. The program accesses each waterline sequentially, calculates the necessary cutter path locations, and directs the CNC control of the milling machine. The ship is cut upside down from keel to deck. The N/C program provides the capability to graphically preview the milling file. During the cutting operation the N/C program provides, on the shop floor, a graphical display of the shape of the waterline to be cut, the location of the cutter and all cutter motions.

The hardware interface between the CNC controller for the machining center and the 4050 series computer is accomplished by simulating the normal paper tape input to the CNC controller. Using this technique requires no modification of the standard N/C machine software and no modification to the CNC controller hardware. Figure 11 shows the machining center and the graphics computer system. Figure 12 shows a typical graphical cutter path display available on the shop floor. Figure 13 shows the B-spline surface for the forebody of the ammunition ship shown in Figure 4 after milling but before hand finishing.

Figure 11. N/C machining center.

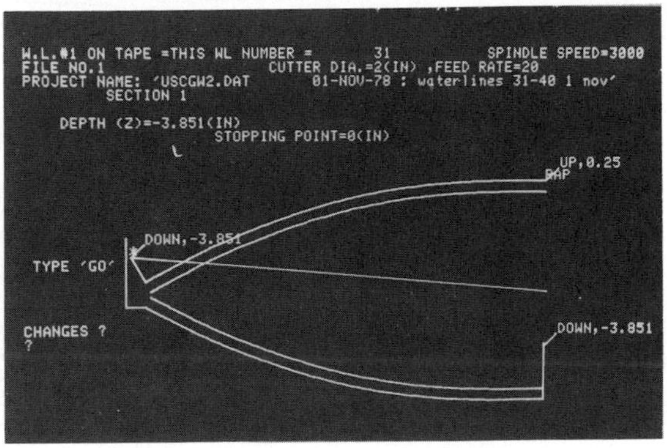

Figure 12. N/C program ship floor display.

Upon completion of milling the model surface is defined by the interior corner of the machined cut. During machining approximately .ØØ4" is added to the model for hand finishing. The model is then transferred to the wood shop for final hand finishing. The model maker runs a sharp pencil along each one of these corners. No templates are used. The model is finished by cutting away the excess wood to the pencil lines which precisely define the surface.

7. SURFACE ACCURACY

After the model is finished it is measured using the machining center connected to the Tektronix as before. This system is used as a three-dimensional automatic digitizer. A sensor, consisting of a modified mechanical distance indicator, is mounted in the tool holder of the machining center. A program, running in the Tektronix, controls the motion of this sensor. When the sensor touches the surface, an interrupt to the Tektronix is generated. When the interrupt is received the surface point is recorded on magnetic tape. Once the model has been completely digitized the data is transferred from the Tektronix tape back to the PDP 11/45 and displayed on the Picture System for comparison with the original lines. This provides a check on the manufacturing accuracy as well as base line data on the shape of the ship model actually tested. This operation is shown in Figure 14.

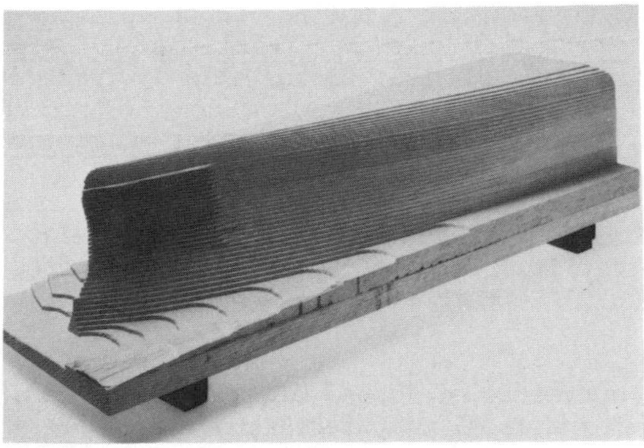

Figure 13. Milled B-Spline Surface for the Ammunition Ship of Figure 4.

Figure 14. Completed Model Being Digitized.

8. CONCLUSIONS

A system for designing ship hull surfaces and using the results of that design to manufacture an end product has been presented. The use of the resulting ship hull surface need not be limited to the specific application discussed here. It can also be used for more detailed manufacturing requirements, e.g. bulkhead design, plating, etc. It can also be used further in the design process, e.g. calculating hydrodynamic characteristics, hull dynamic (sea keeping) characteristics etc. Several such analysis programs have been implemented or are planned for the future. In a small way, the system illustrates an integrated design and manufacturing system.

REFERENCES

[1] Yuille, I.M., The Forward Design System for Computer Aided Ship Design Using a Mini-Computer, RINA, Paper No. 9, Spring Meeting 1978

[2] Munchmeyer, F. C., Schubert, C., and Nowacki, H., Interactive design of fair hull surfaces using B-splines, Computer Applications in the Automation of Shipyard Operations and Ship Design IV (ICCAS '82 - Annapolis), pp. 183-188, North Holland, 1982.

[3] Izumida, K. and Matida, Y., Ship hull definition by surface techniques for production use, Computer Applications in the Automation of Shipyard Operations and Ship Design III (ICCAS '79 - Strathclyde), pp. 95-104, North Holland, 1979.

[4] Stroobant, G. and Mars, D., Ship hull form fairing, Computer Applications in the Automation of Shipyard Operations and Ship Design IV, pp. 177-181, North Holland, 1982.

[5] Rogers, D. F. and Satterfield, S. G., B-spline surfaces for ship hull design, Proceedings SIGGRAPH '80 Conference, pp. 14-18 July 1980, Seattle and Computer Graphics, Vol. 4, No. 3, July 1980, pp. 211-217

[6] Rogers, D. F. and Satterfield, S. G., Dynamic B-spline surfaces, Computer Applications in the Automation of Shipyard Operations and Ship Design IV, (ICCAS '82 - Annapolis), pp. 189-196, North Holland, 1982.

[7] Rogers, D. F. and Adams, J. A., Mathematical Elements for Computer Graphics, McGraw-Hill, New York, 1976.

[8] Rogers, D. F., B-spline curves and surfaces for ship hull design, Proceedings SNAME, SCHAD '77, First International Symposium on Computer Aided Hull Surface Definition, 26-27 September 1977, Annapolis, Maryland

[9] Munchmeyer, F. C., The Gaussian curvature of Coons biquintic patches, Proceedings of ASME Century 2 International Computer Technology Conference, 12-15 August 1980

[10] Dill, C., "An Application of color graphics to the display of surface curvature," Proceedings SIGGRAPH Computer Graphics, Vol. 15, August 1981, pp. 153-161.

[11] Forrest, A.R., "On the rendering of surfaces," Proceedings SIGGRAPH '79, Computer Graphics Vol. 13, August 1979, pp.253-259.

[12] Dill, J.C. and Rogers, D.F., Color graphics and ship hull surface curvature, Computer Applications in the Automation of Shipyard Operation and Shipyard Design IV (ICCAS '82 - Annapolis), pp. 197-205, North Holland, 1982.

[13] Satterfield, S.G. and Rogers, D.F., A procedure for generating contour lines from a B-spline surface, to be published.

[14] Heap, B. R., Algorithms for the production of contour maps over an irregular triangular mesh, National Physical Laboratory Report, NAC 1Ø, February 1972.

[15] Rogers, D.F., Rodriguez, F., and Satterfield, S.G., A simple CADCAM system for the design and construction of towing tank models, 17th Annual Meeting and Technical Conference of the Numerical Control Society, 27-3Ø April 198Ø, Hartford, Connecticut.

INTERACTIVE TECHNIQUES FOR 3-D SHADED GRAPHICS

Tsu Yuan Shen
Engineering Manager
Lexidata Corporation
755 Middlesex Turnpike
Billerica, MA 01865 U.S.A.

ABSTRACT

Interaction with 3-D shaded graphics has become feasible by incorporating local hidden surface removal and visible surface shading capabilities in the raster display system. The Lexidata SOLIDVIEW system not only reduces the response time from minutes to seconds, it also provides powerful 3-D interactive techniques. This paper will describe some of these techniques:

1. 3-D Cursor
2. Sectioning
3. Surface Picking
4. Translucency
5. Contouring
6. Light Source Manipulation

These added capabilities coupled with traditional graphic techniques will greatly affect the man-machine interface of the next generation graphic systems.

By the end of the decade, their use will be widespread in such applications as 3-D medical and geophysical data interpretation, CAD/CAM, animation, technical illustration, architecture, and molecular modeling.

1. INTRODUCTION

The visualization of a three-dimensional (3-D) solid model by displaying its shaded color image on a CRT screen has proven valuable and necessary. Recent interest in solid modeling for CAD/CAM has demanded the display of a realistic image of the model under design [1]. Faster and better visualization of the design is required, not only to provide a natural man-machine interface, but also as an important presentation tool to help communicate design concepts among engineering, marketing, and manufacturing. Solid modeling systems have begun to become of a significant commercial importance lately. By the end of the decade, their use will be widespread in such applications as mechanical design, 3-D medical and geophysical data interpretation, animation, technical illustration, architecture, and molecular modeling. The growth will be driven by the technology of raster display systems, and the emergence of super-minicomputers that will meet the computational and display requirements cost effectively.

The quest for a realistic computer graphic presentation has long been a major field of research in computer graphics. While some very impressive pictures have been produced, the process in generating shaded images is often considered a passive off-line task, since a single shaded color image typically takes several minutes to hours.

To display a shaded image of a model, the visualization process is required. This involves the conversion of the data representation of the model into display information on the CRT, including 3-D geometry transformation, clipping to viewing volume, removal of hidden surface and shading of visible surfaces [2,3]. The conventional approach is to let the host computer process all steps for the shaded image generation, and at the end of the process, pixel data is sent from the host computer to a raster display's frame buffer. The resultant image is always created in the same manner: scanline-by-scanline appearance on the CRT from top to bottom.

The approach with SOLIDVIEW, however, is to remove hidden surfaces and shade visible surfaces in parallel with geometry operations. The host computer does the numerical tasks for which it is best suited (transformation clipping) while the raster display processor does pixel processing which it does better than the host (hidden surface removal and visible surface shading).

Display generation is reduced from minutes to seconds and for the first time, the user can interact directly with the shaded model display. As a further advantage over the previous approach, the display image begins to appear as soon as the host computer has transformed the first surface element, and the user can view the incremental construction of the image.

2. DISPLAY TECHNOLOGY VS. INTERACTIVE TECHNIQUES

Interactive graphics is one of the most natural means of communicating with a computer. The user dynamically controls the picture's content, format, size, or color on a display surface by means of interactive devices [3]. The interactive techniques are usually derived from the available input device and display technology. Most of the current interactive techniques derive from the use of stroke refresh displays which provide a dynamic display via manipulation of the refresh list buffer. Techniques like 2-D cursor positioning, rubber banding, dragging, etc. are direct results of refresh list manipulation. The DVST display technology provides incremental drawing capability without any refresh buffer. Write-through mode was provided to emulate cursor tracking.

While raster display technology with frame buffer has emulated successfully most of the interactive techniques offered by other display technologies, it has also introduced additional techniques based on manipulation of the frame buffer (BITBLT) and color look-up table [4]. Three dimensional display buffer structure has been proposed for interactive visualization of CAD surface models [5].

This paper will describe some of the techniques for 3-D shaded images as a result of the SOLIDVIEW display technology, which incorporates both intensity and depth information in the display processor.

3. SOLIDVIEW[tm]

Lexidata's SOLIDVIEW is the first commercial display system which provides local hidden surface removal and visible surface shading capabilities. With these time consuming and memory-intensive burdens removed from the host computer, the result is a 3-D shaded graphic display system fast enough for interactive application. SOLIDVIEW incorporates both intensity buffer and depth buffer under the control of a powerful local display processor. The host computer or any front-end processor does geometry transformation and clipping while the display processor does pixel processing.

Data Types

SOLIDVIEW accepts 3-D points, vectors, horizontal lines, and polygons as input data. The host computer has to provide a polyhedron description of a solid model for visualization. This representation is actually a hollow shell representing the volume taken up by the object. It is also necessary for the host to provide the surface normal of the polygon for constant shading, and the polygon vertex normals for either Couraud or Phong shading.

Hidden Surface Removal

The image-space depth-buffer algorithm is used to remove hidden surfaces in SOLIDVIEW. For each pixel on the display screen, the depth information is kept for the current visible surface. The polyhedron representation of the solid object allows the host to perform back-face elimination which reduces the number of polygons that have to be processed by the SOLIDVIEW.

Shading

SOLIDVIEW provides three types of shading for a polygon: constant, intensity interpolation, and normal-vector interpolation. They differ in the number of variables that are linearly interpolated across the face of the polygon. Constant shading has zero variables that are interpolated, as each pixel comprising a polygon has the same value. Intensity interpolation varies the pixel value of a polygon as a single unit, or scalar. Normal-vector interpolation breaks the pixel value into two parts, each of which is linearly interpolated across the face of the polygon.

The constant shading is the fastest of the three as there is no interpolation involved. The disadvantages are that the polygon facets that approximate a surface are readily distinguishable. The Gouraud shading smooths out polygons so that they appear as part of the surface. The Phong shading interpolates two variables which allow for light source manipulation. More memory planes are required in the intensity buffer to use it effectively. The value stored at each pixel location in the intensity buffer is not the color intensity, but the index to the color look-up table. Proper loading of the look-up table is required to decode each pixel and to give it the correct color and shade.

4. 3-D INTERACTIVE TECHNIQUES

The SOLIDVIEW approach has several unique interactive features that are not possible with other methods of display. This section will describe some of the most useful and effective techniques for 3-D shaded graphics.

3-D Cursor

The use of cursor as visual feedback for positioning and pointing has proven to be extremely effective in a regular display system. For interactive 3-D shaded graphics, it is natural to provide a 3-D cursor. The cursor will have depth information associated with it. Any portion of the cursor that is behind or inside a shaded object will not be visible. By using appropriate input device such as a 3-D joystick, the cursor can be moved and rotated in the 3-D image space. This feature is possible due to the phantom draw capability of the SOLIDVIEW. It conditionally update the intensity buffer based on the depth comparison and without modifying the depth data. The shape of the cursor is defined by the host. It can be any wireframe object constructed by 3-D vectors. Visually, the operator will see a dynamic 3-D wireframe object interact with static shaded objects. It can be used to define viewing positon, pick a surface, define sectioning plane and simulate tool path simulation.

Sectioning

Partial pictures are used constantly in traditional drafting environment to reveal detailed design information. Most of the current solid modeling software has the capability of providing object space sectioning. Due to the characteristics of SOLIDVIEW, incremental construction of solid object is a natural process. The operator can stop the drawing process at any instance to have a snapshot view of a partially constructed object.

Image space z-sectioning has been implemented on SOLIDVIEW. A plane parallel to the screen can be defined such that all objects in front of the plane will be removed. Care should be taken to ensure proper display of the new faces created by sectioning. If the backfaces are eliminated, one will see through the cut objects and detect objects behind them. If the back faces are made flat and constant shaded, cut objects appear solid. If the back faces are smoothly shaded, things look hollow, as they appear to be the curved backside of the object. Doing smooth shading with the same color as the front faces results in ambiguous looking objects, but smooth shading with another color separates the front and the back surfaces and is especially effective when looking at none-closed surface.

Surface Picking

There are two techniques to implement picking with minimal host computation. The objective is to select a 3-D object out of the host database by picking a visible point on the screen.

The first technique involves assigning a unique color label to each object. In this way the pixel value at the picked location not only points into a section of the color lookup table to determine the object's color, but also into the database to determine which object has been selected.
The second technique does not rely on using a unique color label for each object. Instead, the intensity and depth buffer data at the selected pixel is stored elsewhere and erased. The whole picture is then retransmitted one object at a time. After each individual object is sent, the intensity and depth values of the picked location are read and compare with the stored value. If they have the same values, the object that was just sent was the object that had been selected.

Translucency

SOLIDVIEW provides another type of surface variation akin to a "screen door" effect. This allows a user to define a spatial pattern to modulate the otherwise opaque surface display. This type of translucency results in which details inside the solid model can be made partially visible. Multiple layers of translucency can also be achieved by adjusting relative pattern properly. By combining 3-D cursor, surface picking and translucency capabilities of SOLIDVIEW, the user can step through a complex design interactively.

Contouring

Contouring is the result of the intersection of two surfaces. This is another example of the conditional draw capability of the SOLIDVIEW. It compares the value in the depth buffer for a particular pixel with the new data. If they are equal, then the intensity buffer is updated with the new color. This technique is particularly useful to check interference between objects.

Light Source Manipulation

In order to interactively manipulate light source, Phong shading technique has to be used. The SOLIDVIEW interpolates two variables, X and Y components of the surface normal. The light source orientation has to be decoded through the color look-up table. Reloading the look-up table is required for a new light source orientation. In order to achieve "sunrise and sunset" effect, copies of pre-computed look-up table values have to be loaded constantly. This is basically a look-up table animation technique.

5. CONCLUSION

SOLIDVIEW's local hidden surface removal and visible surface shading capabilities greatly reduce host computer loading and provide the speed for interactive solid modeling applications. SOLIDVIEW's special features add speed and flexibility to any application involving 3-D shaded images, and its ability to work in parallel with the host computer provides instaneous feedback for the user. Thus, SOLODVIEW does for 3-D application what existing display technology has done for 2-D -- it handles the task of generating and displaying the shaded images, it relieves from the host the burden of dealing with individual pixels and it provides the local power needed for interactive applications.

6. ACKNOWLEDGEMENTS

The work described here is part of the product development effort at Lexidata. Members of the project team whose contribution is gratefully acknowledged are: Melinda Shebell, Mary Schongar, John Ford, Joseph Marella, and William Stronge.

7. REFERENCES

1. Requicha, A.A.G., Voelcker, H.B., "Solid Modeling: A Historical Summary and Contemporary Assessment", IEE Computer Graphics, March 1982.

2. Newman, W.M., Sproull, R.F., Principle of Interactive Computer Graphics, McGraw-Hill, 1979.

3. Foley, J., van Dam, A., Fundamentals of Interactive Computer Graphics, Addison-Wesley, 1982.

4. Shoup, R., "Color Table Animation", Computer Graphics, Volume 13, Number 2, August 1979.

5. Atherton, P., "A Method of Interactive Visualization of CAD Surface Models on A Color Video Display", SIGGRAPH Proceedings 1981.

Chapter 2
Graphics Standards and 3D Models

DEVICE INDEPENDENCE AND INTELLIGENCE IN GRAPHICS SOFTWARE

James R. Warner
President
Precision Visuals, Inc.
6260 Lookout Road
Boulder, CO 80301, U.S.A.

One of the most challenging problems facing graphics systems designers and integrators today is the ever-growing influx of new, sophisticated graphics display devices offering a broad range of capabilities. While such devices give users efficient, cost-effective ways to produce the exact graphic output they need, they bring with them the on-going problem of software portability. Designers who can find ways to ensure that their systems are device independent, that is, will run on new devices with little or no modification, will have a definite advantage in developing graphics application software.

Device independence implies that a single application program will produce similar, perhaps identical images on more than one graphics device. For example, a systems designer might develop an application on a storage tube, even though the application will eventually be targeted to a beam-directed or color raster display. Graphics can be viewed and altered at an interactive graphics terminal, with eventual hard-copy output routed to a plotter or microfilm recorder. In short, device independence means that graphics application software is not bound to a particular manufacturer's equipment.

A device-independent application program, then, needs to be compiled only once. At execution time, the user chooses the particular device or devices to be run with the compiled program. Later, the user may decide to run the application with other devices--without recompiling.

There are basically two kinds of graphics devices: passive and active. Passive devices include plotters, microfilm recorders and scanline displays. Active devices include storage tubes, directed beam refresh displays, and raster frame-buffer displays.

Device-independent programming requires the application program to target graphics output commands and input requests not to the devices themselves but rather to a "virtual graphics device" that represents the combined capabilities of all the various kinds of graphics devices, both passive and active. The virtual device interface links the device independent routines and the device managers. A device manager is a library of subroutines that interprets the commands generated by the device-independent routines and converts these commands into the required device-dependent instructions necessary to drive the device.

TWO INTERFACES...INTELLIGENT AND SIMPLE

Virtual device interfaces, however, can be simple or intelligent. A simple interface can be described as representing "the intersection of all capabilities," while an intelligent interface can best be described as representing the "union of all capabilities." Each type has inherent advantages and disadvantages.

THE INTERSECTION OF ALL CAPABILITIES

Many of the device-independent packages on the market today use a virtual command vocabulary that represents the "intersection" of the capabilities of all graphics devices. In general, this amounts to the ability to draw a line and perhaps define color. Any other capabilities that the package offers are simply mapped into stroke primitives by the device-independent code. If the package offers area fills or character generation, for instance, complex algorithms in the device-independent code must be used to determine the actual moves and draws required to gain the desired result on the target device.

The advantage of a device interface based on moves and draws is that device managers can be quickly and easily developed, since they do not need complex mapping procedures. This gives systems designers and integrators the ability to respond quickly to their customers' needs.

Unfortunately, these simple device managers are unable to utilize the sophisticated hardware capabilities of many of the new graphics devices entering the marketplace. What's more, they increase the processing necessary by the host computer and also increase the communication bandwidth from the host to the device. Another problem is that the algorithms that must be executed as part of the device-independent code to handle such capabilities as area fills, character generation, or graphics input cannot be downloaded into today's intelligent graphics devices or satellite processors capable of handling them.

THE UNION OF ALL CAPABILITIES--DEVICE INTELLIGENCE

Another, more practical approach is the "union" of capabilities of all graphics devices. Under this approach, the interface is moved closer to the application program and the vocabulary of commands sent to the device manager is increased. The device-independent routines assume that each device can do everything. Wherever possible the device manager uses the hardware features of the device to produce the required output and ignores unsupported functions (for example, color on a monochromatic display). If the hardware cannot perform a particular function, it is simulated in software. A good example is the crosshatching of polygonal areas on devices that do not offer hardware area fills.

There are a variety of advantages to the union of capabilities approach. Not only does it allow users to take advantage of the hardware features of their devices, thus increasing graphics output speed, but it decreases the communication from host to device. The net result is that users don't have to wait a long time for pictures to be drawn on an interactive device.

In addition, software using this approach can be run on a distributed mode on intelligent processors that may serve as a front end to the devices. And because the approach allows for smaller device-independent programs, it reduces the amount of host computer time necessary.

A possible disadvantage to this approach is the increased complexity of the device manager. Each device manager must interpret and process a rich command vocabulary that is often beyond the capabilities of the target device. The device manager for a plotter, for instance, would require algorithms to simulate area fill by shading and simulate dashed lines by using a stroking pattern. Color lookup tables and graphics input commands would be ignored on the plotter. Though this added complexity can increase the amount of time required for a systems designer or integrator to develop the necessary managers for his clients, the net result is a large increase in user flexibility and efficiency.

DEVICE INTELLIGENCE AND DISTRIBUTED PROCESSING

The concept of device intelligence fits well with the growing move toward distributed processing and intelligent workstations. Until recently, graphics software systems were entirely resident in a large, centralized mainframe computer. The device-independent routines were closely intertwined with the graphics data structure and the device driver or drivers and loaded into the system as a huge task with the user's application program.

Today, however, the picture is rapidly changing. The increased intelligence of the new graphics hardware, coupled with the sophisticated networking capabilities of the latest generation of computers, allows distribution of graphics software among different tasks or even different CPUs, thus bringing significant increases in processing efficiency.

In Figure 1, we see the topology for a distributed, device-independent graphics software network. Such an approach is ideal for small, fixed-memory minis or micros, since the application program runs with the device-independent routines in a single task, which can be easily overlaid. The device drivers, however, reside in their own separate tasks or CPUs and can run concurrently.

To the network, the segment storage node looks like a device manager. The node maintains a segmented display file data structure representing all segments created within the application program. A segment is basically a collection of output primitives, the fundamental commands that define objects in a 3D world coordinate system: moves, lines, text, polygons, and markers. The individual images of one or more segments are what create the picture that is finally displayed.

All communication in the network is handled by the network manager, routing messages in the form of virtual device opcodes and parameters among the various nodes. Message buffers in the manager contain fields in which the called node can return status information or data to the calling node for device inquiry or graphics input.

The metafile generator node, which functions like a pseudo device manager, allows users to build a "time-independent" picture file of the graphics output that would normally be sent immediately to a device and displayed. The pictures stored in this library can be accessed and manipulated later by a special translator program and output to any graphics device.

While various other nodes and functions can be built into this system, it is important to remember that it is the sophistication of the virtual device interface that determines how much of the device-independent software can be distributed among different tasks. In short, it is only by using intelligent device managers that system designers and integrators can take full advantage of the many benefits of device independence.

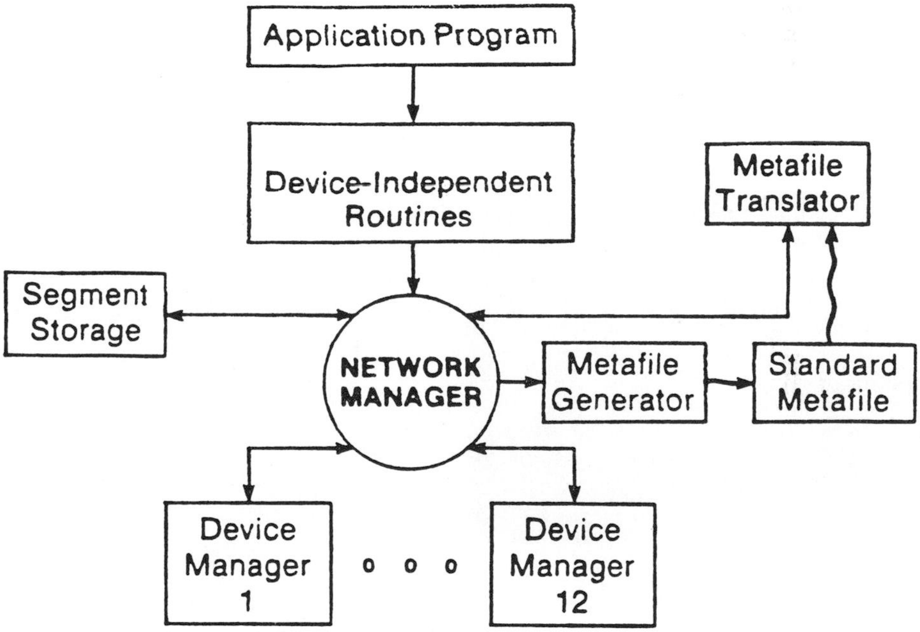

Fig 1 Device-manager support functions, metafile generation, and segment data structure management are performed by subordinate "area" nodes which can be implemented as separate overlays or tasks in limited-memory systems. In a distributed processing environment, these subordinate modules can run on separate CPUs or in intelligent terminals.

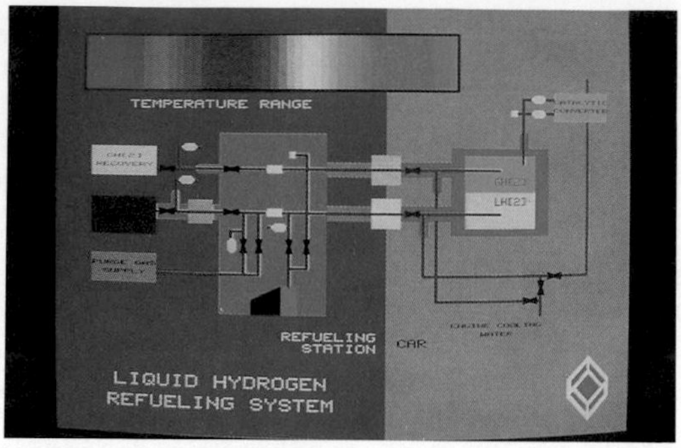

Fig 2 Process control diagram drawn on the Chromatics 7900 using DI-3000. All regions are filled using firmware. The "pipes" are drawn using thick lines. Note the different hardware text sizes. Colors may be changed dynamically to show changes in the Refueling System. Communication from the host computer to the graphics device is kept to a minimum allowing for rapid image update.

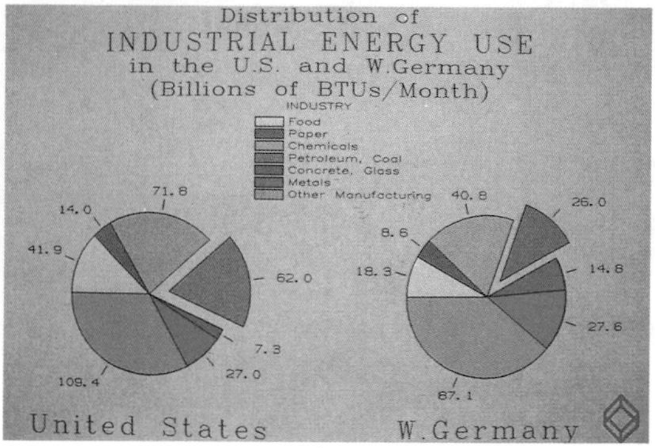

Fig 3 Business graph output to the Applicon Plotter. All text is drawn using software characters and the sectors are filled in hardware.

Fig 4 Same program output to the Xerox 350 color slide system. Note the use of publication quality text for annotation.

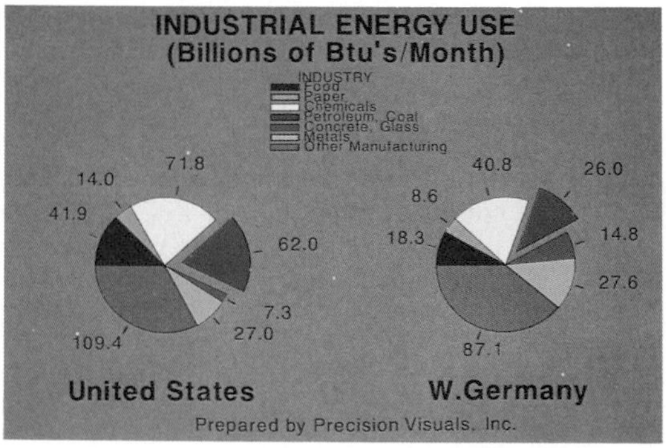

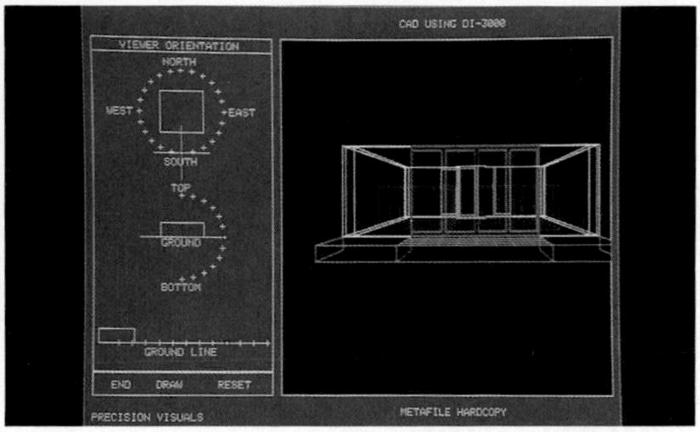

Fig 5 Device-independent computer-aided design program with output to the Raster Technologies Model One.

Fig 6 Device-independent graphics output to the Xerox 350 color slide system.

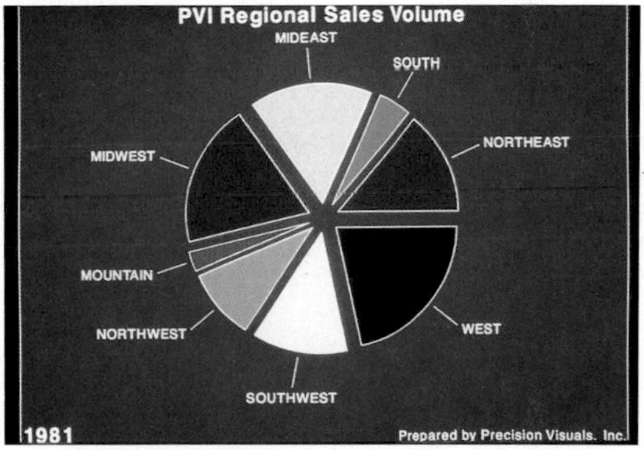

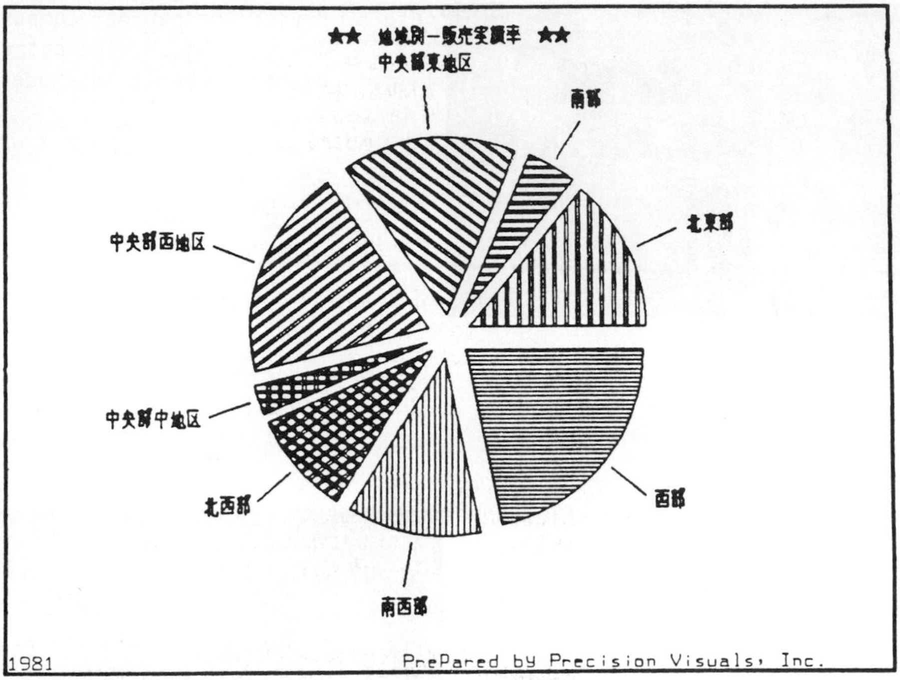

Fig 7 Another example of device-independent graphics output. This example is a hardcopy from the Tektronix 4000 series using DI-3000's Kanji character set.

IMPLEMENTATION OF THE GRAPHICAL KERNEL SYSTEM (GKS)

Yasuyuki Suzuki
Research and Development Dept. Computer Services Corporation
17th Fl. Sumitomo Bldg., 2-6, Nishi-Shinjuku
Shinjuku-ku, Tokyo 160-91, JAPAN

Abstract

There have been strong calls recently for graphics standards because of the need for portability in graphics programs and programmers. Existing graphics packages have depended upon the devices and so there has been little portability of graphics application programs between different hardwares. It is for this reason that several device independent graphics standards have been proposed. Of those, the Graphical Kernel System (GKS)[1,2] has become the draft international standard of the International Standard Organization (ISO) , and is likely to become the first graphics standard in 1983[3]. In order to evaluate the function of the GKS (and of course , to actually use it in the development of some graphics systems), we have implemented a graphics package based on this standard. There are two things we will discuss in this paper after introducing the GKS. They are how we implemented the graphics package , and the problems that exist with graphics standardization.

1. The Graphical Kernel System

The Graphical Kernel System (GKS) specifies a set of functions for computer graphics programming . The GKS separates the display part from other parts (for instance, the transformation from 3 dimensional to 2 dimensional, or the model description of the display object). Only the display part is defined by this standard. Other parts are in the application area which is undefined. Further , graphical resóurces should be used only via GKS (see figure 1).

WORKSTATION: The GKS is based on the concept of abstract workstations which provide the logical interface through which an application program controls physical devices. A workstation has zero or one display surface, and zero or more input devices. A GKS implementation has a workstation description table for every type of workstation. They describe the capability and characteristics of each workstation.

GRAPHICAL OUTPUT:
In the GKS, graphical output is built up of basic pieces called output primitives of which there are six kinds.

POLYLINE:
A set of connected lines defined by a point sequence.
POLYMARKER:
Symbols of one type centered at given positions.
TEXT:
Character strings.
FILL AREA:
A polygon which may be hollow or filled with a uniform color , pattern , or hatch style.
PIXEL ARRAY:
An array of pixels with individual colors.

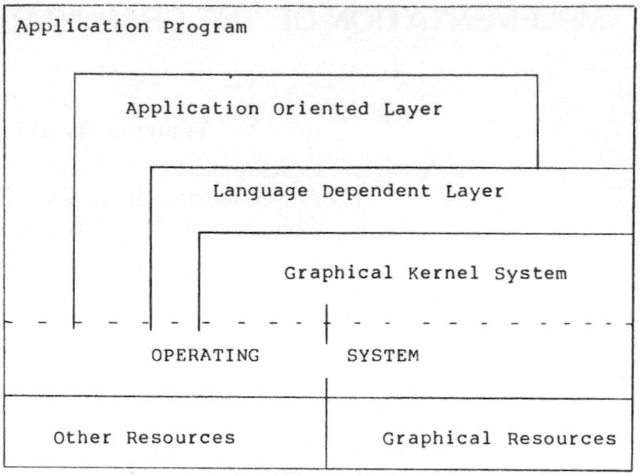

Fig.1
Layer model of the GKS

GENERALIZED DRAWING PRIMITIVES (GDP):
Special geometric workstation capabilities such as curve drawing.

GRAPHICAL INPUT: Graphical input in the GKS is classified into five varieties according to the type of its logical input value. They are called input classes. The five input calasses and the logical input values they provide are:
LOCATOR:
Provides a position.
VALUATOR:
Provides a real number.
CHOICE:
Provides an integer number.
PICK:
Provides a PICK status, a segment name, and pick identifier.
STRING:
Provides a character string.

There are also three modes for graphical input.
REQUEST:
The GKS waits until the input is entered by the operator.
SAMPLE:
The GKS returns current logical input value without waiting for an operator action.
EVENT:
If an input occurs, its logical input value is kept in the GKS- controlled event queue, and when there is an input request from the application program , the GKS returns the oldest value in the event queue.

COORDINATE SYSTEMS AND TRANSFORMATIONS: The GKS has the following 3 coordinates. These are all 2 dimensional orthogonal coordinate system. World Coordinates (WC) is used by the application programmer.Normarized Device Coordinates (NDC) is used to define a uniform coordinate system for all workstation. Device Coordinates (DC) , one coordinate system per workstation ,is representing its display space coordinates. Two transformations are applied to an output primitive enroute from the application program to the display surface. Normalization transformation maps the boundary and interior of a window in WC into the boundary and interior of a viewport in NDC (see fig. 2). Workstation transformation maps the boundary and interior of a workstation window in NDC into the boundary and interior of a workstation viewport in DC (see fig. 3).

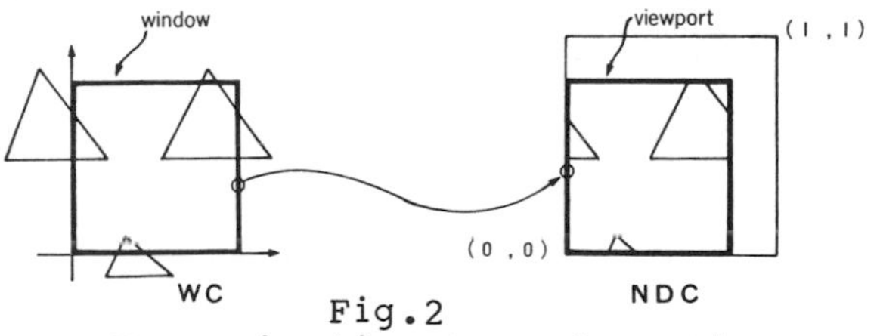

Fig.2
Normarization transformation

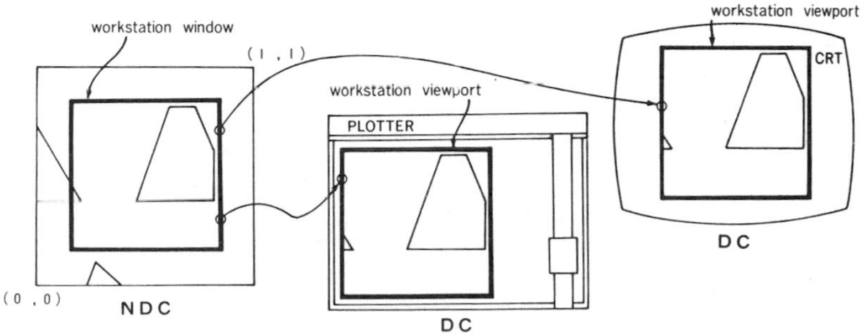

Fig. 3 Workstation transformation

SEGMENT: Segment is a collection of output primitives that can be manipulated as a unit. It may be transformed (see fig. 4 - a,b) , made visible or invisible, deleted, renamed, copied (4 - c) , ordered front-to-back (4 - d) and so on.

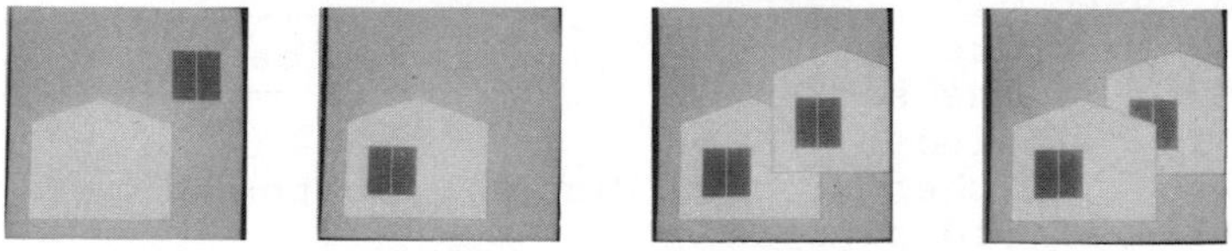
(a) (b) (c) (d)

Fig. 4 Segment facilities

METAFILE: The GKS provides an interface to sequential files called GKS Metafiles (GKSM's). They can be used to transport graphical information between systems.

2. Implementation of the GKS

The current system follows the GKS version 6.6. The system we used had an extremely small main memory of 64 K bytes. All the functions could not thereby be supported.

Several subset levels has been defined in the GKS so that when people are implementing the GKS and the capability of the object system is insufficient they will not implement an arbitrary standard dialect.(Fig. 5) Our system is based on subset level 2a. This is the reason for our calling this system GKS 2a. Subset level 2a is the one which fullfil the GKS without the input functions. GKS 2a can be divided into five blocks. (Fig. 6) If the six functions of the parts of the Device Driver which depend on single devices are rewritten , they can be converted to other types of devices. The GKS Common Block contains the basic common routine such as clipping and matrix calculation . GKS0, GKS1, and GKS2a contain respectively the functions of subset levels 0,1, and 2a. The application programmer can choose one block from these three according to the area necessary for the program and the balance of functions.

Level 0:
  Minimal capabilities.
Level 1:
  Passive output.
Level 2a:
  Passive output and segment storage , no input.
Level 2b:
  Passive output and simple input , no segments.
Level 3:
  Passive output , simple input and segment mechanism.
Level 4:
  Full set of GKS capability

Fig.5
GKS levels (version 6.6)

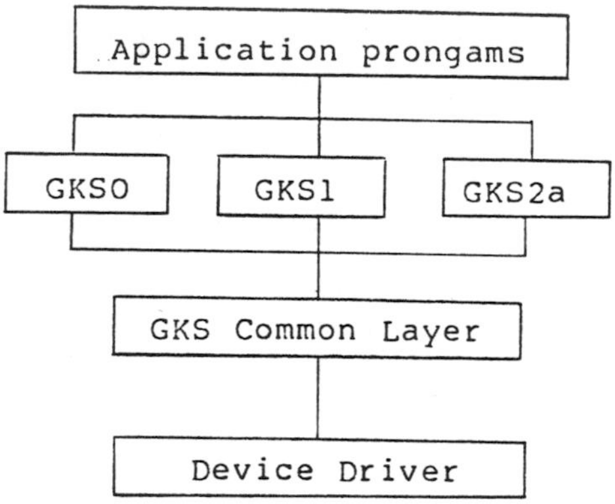

Fig. 6 Components of GKS2a

There are several things which we noticed when we actually used GKS 2a. First is that the segment functions serves no purpose. The segment is used together with the input functions when interactive processing occurs. It is no used in batch processing when there is no input device. If the segment function is included at implementation , then the input function should also be included. Next is the slow speed of GKS 2a. The problem here is that not much consideration was given to efficiency when implementing GKS 2a. It is not appropriate to think that efficiency can be sacrificed to achieve standardization. Meaningless standardization should be avoided. Finally, it was troublesome to define the attributes of each type separately when drawing several types of lines. This problem can be overcome by increasing the number of default attributes. Apart from these matters this is an easy graphics package to use, and has a high level of functions.

We plan to use what we have learned to begin transporting the GKS to a 32 bit super mini-computer in April , 1983. At that time all the functions of the final version, except for the asynchronous input , will be supported.

3. The use of GKS2a

The following sample program (fig.7 - a) illustrates the use of GKS2a functions. And fig.7 - b is the output of the sample program.

```
C
C  SAMPLE PROGRAM
C
C   A batch job generates three triangles which are hollow and
C   filled with a uniform color and pattern.
C
      REAL       POS1(2,3),POS2(2,3),POS3(2,3),COLOR(3)
      INTEGER    HOLLOW,SOLID,PATERN,WHITE,RED,GREEN,PURPLE
      INTEGER*1 IARRAY(8,8)
      DATA COLOR / Ø.7, Ø.Ø, 1.Ø /
C  set coordinates of points
      DATA POS1 / Ø.Ø5,Ø.3Ø,    Ø.3Ø,Ø.8Ø,    Ø.25,Ø.ØØ /
      DATA POS2 / Ø.35,Ø.3Ø,    Ø.6Ø,Ø.8Ø,    Ø.55,Ø.ØØ /
      DATA POS3 / Ø.65,Ø.3Ø,    Ø.9Ø,Ø.8Ø,    Ø.85,Ø.ØØ /
C
      HOLLOW = 1
      SOLID  = 2
      PATERN = 3
      WHITE  = 1
      RED    = 2
      GREEN  = 3
      PURPLE = 4
C  open GKS
      CALL GOPNGK
C  open workstation
      CALL GOPNWS('DISPLAY ',3)
C  set color representation ( PURPLE is a non default color index.)
      CALL GSTCRP('DISPLAY ',PURPLE,COLOR)
C  activate workstation
      CALL GACTWS('DISPLAY ')
C  set interior style
      CALL GSTIST(HOLLOW)
C  set fill area color index
      CALL GSTFIX(RED)
C  fill area
      CALL GFLARE(3,POS1)
C  set interior style
      CALL GSTIST(SOLID)
C  set fill area color index
      CALL GSTFIX(GREEN)
C  fill area
      CALL GFLARE(3,POS2)
C  set interior style
      CALL GSTIST(PATERN)
C  set color index array
      DO 1Ø I = 1,8
      DO 1Ø J = 1,8
         IARRAY(I,J) = PURPLE
         IF(I.EQ.J) IARRAY(I,J) = WHITE
   1Ø CONTINUE
C  set pattern
      CALL GSTPTN(IARRAY)
C  fill area
      CALL GFLARE(3,POS3)
C  deactivate workstation
      CALL GDEAWS('DISPLAY ')
C  close workstation
      CALL GCLSWS('DISPLAY ')
C  close GKS
      CALL GCLSGK
      STOP
      END
```

Fig. 7 Sample program — (a) source list

Fig. 7 Sample program — (b) output

4. Application for 3-Dimensional Graphics

There is a rather high degree of freedom in 3-dimensional handling with the GKS, for three dimensional model description and three dimensional to two dimensional trasformation are not defined. We tested several methods, principally using the surface model. Many CAD systems do not carry out perspective transformations. In this case, handling is possible at almost the same level of complexity for 3-dimensions as for 2-dimensions. Figure 8 shows how a clip in two dimensions was done by simply ignored the Z axis. When the concept of the point of view is also considered the problem became a little more complex. Singularity arises when there is no clip in 3-dimensional space. On the basis of the GKS we have developed a package for rotation, scaling and shift in three dimensions, for clipping for three dimensional polygons and for perspective transformation. Fig. 9 - a,b,c,d show examples of use of this package. The GKS had no problems whith three dimensional display.

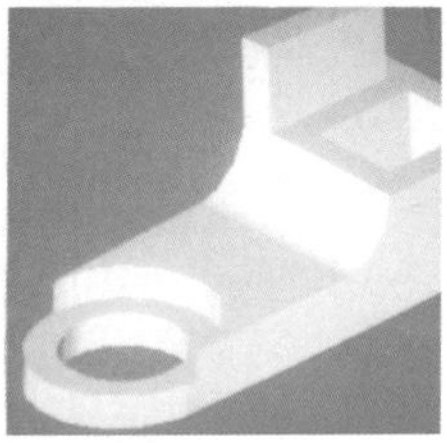

Fig. 8
Simple 3D graphics

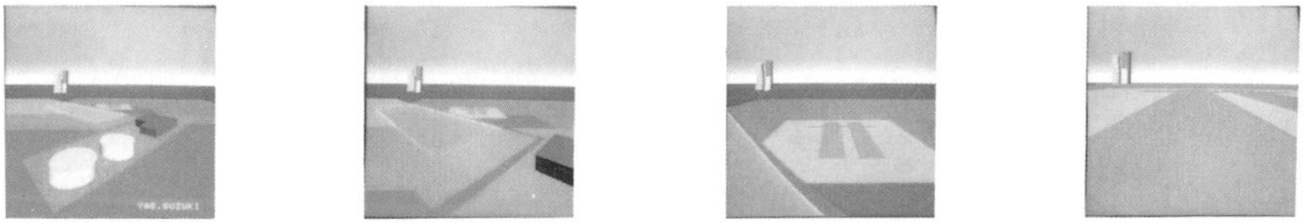

(a) (b) (c) (d)

Fig. 9 Examples of use of the 3D package

5. Problems of Standardization

Matters which the GKS leaves untouched are the standardization of the Metafile and of three dimensional section. The former is likely to be resolved soon , which the latter presents great difficulty. The attitude of the GKS is that three dimensional handling - that is , three dimensional model description and transformation into two dimensional - is possible by various means according to the objectives, and this should be included in the user area. This attitude is correct providing that the processing is done by the software. A new possibility is for graphics display in which the transformation from the three dimensional description to the two dimensional one is done by the hardware. At present these devices are few in number and do not have such great problems , even if standardization has been sacrificed for efficiency. It is obvious ,however, that as VLSI technology advances, high-performance displays will become very cheap and popular. The question remains whether, at that time, the standardization of these devices can be ignored. Herein lies the necessity for three-dimensional standardization. While the two dimensional standards clearly distinguished between model description and display, this is not acceptable for the the three dimensional. Because for the user sees the transformation with the hardware and the software as beeing absolutely the same, the original three dimensional description must be completely defined. This three dimensional description does not mean model representation for real three dimensional objects but only for display. Untill now,we have not distinguished these two types of description. Because we have not actually known how to describe real three dimensional objects perfectly. And treatment of the three dimensional part alters according to the application. So, the real three dimensional model can not be standardized. But if we can divide these two types of description , it will be possible that three dimensional representation for display is standardized. Since it is difficult to solve these problems, we should not decide three dimensional part so soon. But we should begin these discussion from now on.

6. Conclusion

Since the main topic of this paper has been the implementation of the GKS , the discussion of the problems with standardization has not been carried very far. Several problems did became clear in the relatively small GKS system which we developed. The minor problems dealt with in section 2 have been resolved. On the other hand , the major problems described in section 4 will need to be widely discussed over many years to come.

Acknowledgements I am gratefull to Dr.Ohsuga of the Institute of Interdiscriplinary Reserch, Faculty of Engineering, University of Tokyo, for giving me helpfull advice and suggestions.

References

1 ISO/DIS Information Processing Graphical Kernel System (GKS) Function Description version 6.6 1981

2 ISO/DIS Information processing Graphical Kernel System (GKS) Function Description version 7.0 1982

3 GKS The First Graphics Standard IEEE CG&A July 1982

4 A Discussion of Software Standards Computer Graphics World August 1982

A DESCRIPTION AND EVALUATION OF VARIOUS 3D MODELS

Brian A. Barsky

Berkeley Computer Graphics Laboratory
Computer Science Division
University of California
Berkeley, California 94720
U.S.A.

ABSTRACT

Parametric curves and surfaces have been defined for a long time in mathematics, and used extensively in engineering and more recently in computer aided design. In computer graphics outside of CAD, they have been used from simple object models with a few patches to 3-D animation models with several hundred patches.

In spite of all this activity, they still look a little forbidding to most people in computer graphics. This paper attempts to address this problem by describing the motivations, properties and references for the most common types of parametric curves and surfaces.

1. Introduction

In the last decade, it has become apparent that the use of straight line segments and planar polygons to approximate curved lines and surfaces has limited the state-of-the-art in computer graphics. Even with the most sophisticated continuous shading models, polygonal techniques generally result in visually objectionable images. Mach bands are apparent at the borders between adjacent polygons, and there is always a telltale jagged, polygonal silhouette. Also, polygonal methods often require excessive amounts of storage and the "resolution" at which a polygonal database is stored is fixed independent of the eventual display, as opposed to curved surface techniques in which the resulting image can be computed to whatever level of detail the situation demands.

Early work by Coons[13, 14, 19] and Bézier[9, 10, 11] introduced the use of non-linear parametric polynomial representations for the *patches* which are stitched together to form such *piecewise* curves and surfaces, establishing their viability. More recently, Riesenfeld[22, 21] has advocated the use of B-splines to represent such polynomials on the grounds of greater flexibility and efficiency.

Parametric B-splines have many advantages. Among these is the ability to control the degree of continuity at the joints between adjacent curve segments, and at the borders between surface patches, independently of the order of the segments or the number of control vertices. However, the notion of parametric first or second degree continuity at joints does not always correspond to intuition or to a physically desired effect. For piecewise cubic curves and bicubic surfaces these parametric continuity constraints can be replaced by the more meaningful requirements of continuous unit tangent and curvature vectors. Doing so introduces certain constrained discontinuities in the first and second parametric derivatives. These are expressed in terms of *bias* and *tension* parameters called beta1 and beta2,[4, 5] and give rise to *Beta-spline* curves and surfaces.

The motivations, properties and references for the parametric Hermite, Coons, Bézier, B-spline and Beta-spline curve and surface formulations will be described. The parametric representation has many desirable properties including the capability to allow multiple valued curves or surfaces and independence from the coordinate system. Similarly, functions other than polynomial formulations (with the possible exception of trigonometric functions to represent circles, ellipsoids and spheres), are too costly to compute with little gain in power to justify the cost; and of course theoretically any curve can be approximated to any tolerance by polynomials (with some customary analytical caveats).

2. Curve and Surface Formulations

2.1. Hermite Interpolation and Coons Surfaces

Hermite interpolation is specified by a set of points and derivatives to interpolate. In the cubic case, these derivatives are first derivatives, and the resulting curve has continuity of position and of first derivative ($C^{[1]}$). In particular, let $\{P_0, P_1, \ldots, P_m\}$ be $m+1$ points to be interpolated and $\{P_0^1, P_1^1, \ldots, P_m^1\}$ be the corresponding values of the first derivative vector. Parametrically, the ith curve segment is described as the parameter u varies. Specifically, a curve segment can be written as

$$Q_i(u)=\sum_{j=0}^{1}\sum_{k=0}^{1} g_{jk}(u)P_{i-1+k}^{j}$$

The functions $g_{jk}(u)$ are the cubic Hermite basis functions

$$\begin{aligned} g_{00}(u)&=2u^3-3u^2+1 \\ g_{01}(u)&=-2u^3+3u^2 \\ g_{10}(u)&=u^3-2u^2+u \\ g_{11}(u)&=u^3-u^2 \end{aligned} \tag{1}$$

which can be written in matrix form as

$$[g_{00}(u)g_{01}(u)g_{10}(u)g_{11}(u)]=[u^3u^2u\,1][H] \tag{2}$$

where :

$$H=\begin{bmatrix} 2 & -2 & 1 & 1 \\ -3 & 3 & -2 & -1 \\ 0 & 0 & 0 & 0 \\ 1 & 0 & 0 & 0 \end{bmatrix}$$

One of the first methods for surface representation was proposed by Coons.[13,14,19] The basic idea is to create a surface by blending four boundary curves. A simple Coons surface can be expressed as

$$Q(u,v)=\sum_{i=0}^{1} f_i(u)P(i,v)+\sum_{j=0}^{1} f_j(v)P(u,j) \\ -\sum_{i=0}^{1}\sum_{j=0}^{1} f_i(u)f_j(v)P(i,j)$$

or in matrix form

$$Q(u,v)=[f_0(u)f_1(u)]\begin{bmatrix} P(0,v) \\ P(1,v) \end{bmatrix} \\ +[P(u,0)P(u,1)]\begin{bmatrix} f_0(v) \\ f_1(v) \end{bmatrix} \\ -[f_0(u)f_1(u)]\begin{bmatrix} P(0,0) & P(0,1) \\ P(1,0) & P(1,1) \end{bmatrix}\begin{bmatrix} f_0(v) \\ f_1(v) \end{bmatrix}$$

Here P(u,0), P(u,1), P(0,v), and P(1,v) are the boundary curves; P(0,0), P(0,1), P(1,0), and P(1,1) are the corner points; and $f_0(t)$ and $f_1(t)$ are the blending functions (see Figure 1). Note that the blending functions must satisfy $f_i(j)=\delta_{ij}$, where δ_{ij} is the Kronecker delta. This simple Coons surface does not constrain the cross-boundary derivatives; thus, it is not possible to ensure continuity higher than positional when using composite surfaces.

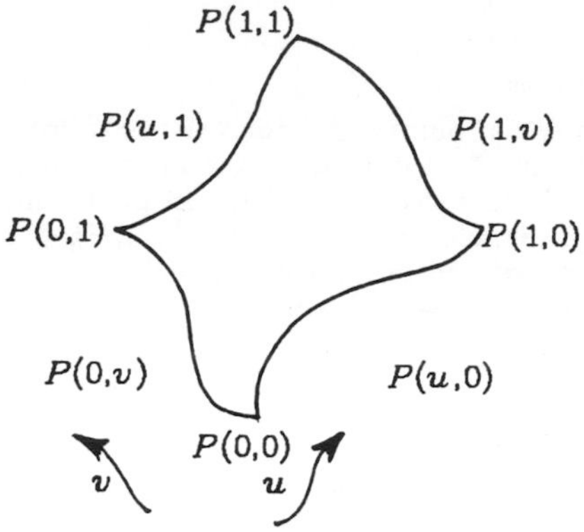

Figure 1. Boundary curves and corner points for a Coons surface.

For first derivative continuity this method is extended so that the user is able to specify the cross-boundary derivatives. This requires four blending functions, $g_{00}(t)$, $g_{01}(t)$, $g_{10}(t)$, and $g_{11}(t)$. The surface is now written

$$Q(u,v)=\sum_{i=0}^{1}\sum_{r=0}^{1}P^{(r,0)}(i,v)g_{ri}(u)+\sum_{j=0}^{1}\sum_{s=0}^{1}P^{(0,s)}(u,j)g_{sj}(v)$$
$$-\sum_{i=0}^{1}\sum_{j=0}^{1}\sum_{r=0}^{1}\sum_{s=0}^{1}P^{(r,s)}(i,j)g_{ri}(u)g_{sj}(v)$$

or, in matrix form:

$$Q(u,v)=[g_{00}(u)g_{01}(u)g_{10}(u)g_{11}(u)]\begin{bmatrix}P(0,v)\\P(1,v)\\P^{(1,0)}(0,v)\\P^{(1,0)}(1,v)\end{bmatrix}$$
$$+[P(u,0)P(u,1)P^{(0,1)}(u,0)P^{(0,1)}(u,1)]\begin{bmatrix}g_{00}(v)\\g_{01}(v)\\g_{10}(v)\\g_{11}(v)\end{bmatrix} \qquad (3)$$
$$-[g_{00}(u)g_{01}(u)g_{10}(u)g_{11}(u)]$$
$$\begin{bmatrix}P(0,0) & P(0,1) & P^{(0,1)}(0,0) & P^{(0,1)}(0,1)\\P(1,0) & P(1,1) & P^{(0,1)}(1,0) & P^{(0,1)}(1,1)\\P^{(1,0)}(0,0) & P^{(1,0)}(0,1) & P^{(1,1)}(0,0) & P^{(1,1)}(0,1)\\P^{(1,0)}(1,0) & P^{(1,0)}(1,1) & P^{(1,1)}(1,0) & P^{(1,1)}(1,1)\end{bmatrix}\begin{bmatrix}g_{00}(v)\\g_{01}(v)\\g_{10}(v)\\g_{11}(v)\end{bmatrix}$$

where

$$P^{(a,b)}(u_i,v_j)=\frac{\partial^{a+b}P(u,v)}{\partial u^a \partial v^b}\Big|_{u=u_i,v=v_j}$$

While the Coons formulation is useful and very general, it requires the specification of a great deal of data that lack intuitive interpretation. One way to simplify equation (3) is to use the following boundary functions:

$$P^{(0,s)}(u,j)=\sum_{i=0}^{1}\sum_{r=0}^{1}P^{(r,s)}(i,j)g_{ir}(u) \qquad (4)$$

$$P^{(r,0)}(i,v)=\sum_{j=0}^{1}\sum_{s=0}^{1}P^{(r,s)}(i,j)g_{js}(v)$$

Substituting equation (4) into equation (3), the three terms are now equal, and thus equation (3) reduces to

$$Q(u,v)=\sum_{i=0}^{1}\sum_{j=0}^{1}\sum_{r=0}^{1}\sum_{s=0}^{1}P^{(r,s)}(i,j)g_{ri}(u)g_{sj}(v)$$

or in matrix form

$$Q(u,v)=[g_{00}(u)g_{01}(u)g_{10}(u)g_{11}(u)][P]\begin{bmatrix}g_{00}(v)\\g_{01}(v)\\g_{10}(v)\\g_{11}(v)\end{bmatrix} \tag{5}$$

where

$$P=\begin{bmatrix}P(0,0) & P(0,1) & P^{(0,1)}(0,0) & P^{(0,1)}(0,1)\\ P(1,0) & P(1,1) & P^{(0,1)}(1,0) & P^{(0,1)}(1,1)\\ P^{(1,0)}(0,0) & P^{(1,0)}(0,1) & P^{(1,1)}(0,0) & P^{(1,1)}(0,1)\\ P^{(1,0)}(1,0) & P^{(1,0)}(1,1) & P^{(1,1)}(1,0) & P^{(1,1)}(1,1)\end{bmatrix}$$

The blending functions have to satisfy

$$g_{0i}(j)=g_{1i}{}^{(1)}(j)=\delta_{ij}$$

$$g_{1i}(j)=g_{0i}{}^{(1)}(j)=g_{0i}{}^{(2)}(j)=g_{1i}{}^{(2)}(j)=0$$

These conditions are satisfied by the cubic Hermite basis functions that were given in equations (1) and (2).

2.2. Bézier Curves and Surfaces

Recall the binomial distribution from probability theory and statistics. The probability of exactly i successes in m trials, where the underlying probability of success is u, is

$$B_{i,m}(u)=\binom{m}{i}u^i(1-u)^{m-i}$$

where $i=0,1,\ldots,m$ and $0\le u\le 1$. (6)

Consider now a *control polygon* formed by the ordered sequence of *control vertices*,

$$[V_0,V_1,\ldots,V_m]$$

The probability $B_{i,m}(u)$ can be related to these vertices by considering the following game. The player starts at the vertex V_0. With probability u, he or she moves to the next vertex, and with probablility $1-u$ stays at the current vertex. Then $B_{i,m}(u)$ is the probability of being at the vertex V_i after m trials. From this, the expected position after m trials must be

$$Q_m(u)=\sum_{i=0}^{m}B_{i,m}(u)V_i \tag{7}$$

In addition, since $B_{i,m}(u)$ is a probability density function,

$$\sum_{i=0}^{m}B_{i,m}(u)=1$$

The polynomials $B_{i,m}(u)$ are called *Bernstein polynomials*, and they form the *Bernstein basis* since they are a basis for the vector space of all polynomials with degree at most m . The expression (7) for the expected position can also be viewed as a Bernstein approximation to the sequence of control vertices. This expression is a weighted average of the $m+1$ control vertices, with the Bernstein polynomials being the weighting factors, and defines an mth degree Bézier curve.[9, 10, 11] Note that each polynomial is nonzero over the entire domain $0 \le u \le 1$, which is why there is global, not local, control.

Consider now the cubic Bézier curve. This means that $m=3$ and there is a control polygon consisting of the four control vertices $[V_0, V_1, V_2, V_3]$. From equation (6), the Bernstein polynomials for this case are

$$
\begin{aligned}
B_{0,3}(u) &= (1-u)^3 = -u^3+3u^2-3u+1 \\
B_{1,3}(u) &= 3u(1-u)^2 = 3u^3-6u^2+3u \qquad (8) \\
B_{2,3}(u) &= 3u^2(1-u) = -3u^3+3u^2 \\
B_{3,3}(u) &= u^3
\end{aligned}
$$

These polynomials are plotted for $0 \le u \le 1$ in Figure 2.

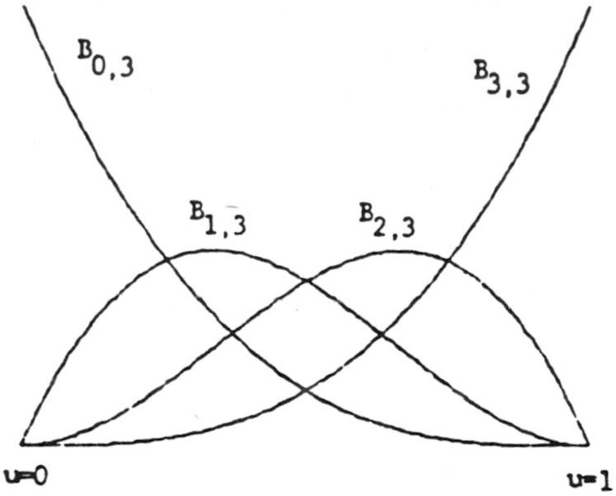

Figure 2. The cubic Bernstein polynomials for $0 \le u \le 1$.

Combining equations (7) and (8), the Bézier curve is

$$Q_3(u) = (1-u)^3 V_0 + 3u(1-u)^2 V_1 + 3u^2(1-u) V_2 + u^3 V_3 \quad (9)$$

These equations can be recast in matrix notation. From equation (7), the curve can be expressed as

$$Q_3(u) = [B_{0,3}(u) B_{1,3}(u) B_{2,3}(u) B_{3,3}(u)] \begin{bmatrix} V_0 \\ V_1 \\ V_2 \\ V_3 \end{bmatrix}$$

From equation (8), the polynomials can be written as:

$$[B_{0,3}(u) B_{1,3}(u) B_{2,3}(u) B_{3,3}(u)] = [u^3 u^2 u\, 1][B]$$

where

$$B = \begin{bmatrix} -1 & 3 & -3 & 1 \\ 3 & -6 & 3 & 0 \\ -3 & 3 & 0 & 0 \\ 1 & 0 & 0 & 0 \end{bmatrix}$$

From (9), the curve can be rewritten in the following matrix form:

$$Q_3(u)=[u^3 u^2 u\,1][B]\begin{bmatrix} V_0 \\ V_1 \\ V_2 \\ V_3 \end{bmatrix} \qquad (10)$$

The original motivation in the development of the Bézier formulation was based on the relationship between the derivatives of the polynomial and the edges of the control polygon. From (9) or (10), it can be readily verified that

$$Q_3(0)=V_0$$
$$Q_3(1)=V_3$$
$$Q_3^{(1)}(0)=3(V_1-V_0)$$
$$Q_3^{(1)}(1)=3(V_3-V_2)$$

This shows a strong relationship between the control polygon and the Bézier curve. The curve begins at the first vertex (V_0) and ends at the last last vertex (V_3) and is tangent to the control polygon at these vertices.

A Bézier surface is a tensor product of Bézier curves. It is defined by a set of control vertices, in three-dimensional x-y-z space, that is organized as a two-dimensional graph with a rectangular topology. A point on the surface is a weighted average of these control vertices:

$$Q_{m,n}(u,v)=\sum_{i=0}^{m}\sum_{j=0}^{n} B_{i,m}(u)B_{j,n}(v)V_{ij}$$

or, in matrix form

$$Q_{m,n}(u,v)=[B_{0,m}(u)B_{1,m}(u)\cdots B_{m,m}(u)][V]\begin{bmatrix} B_{0,n}(v) \\ B_{1,n}(v) \\ \vdots \\ B_{n,n}(v) \end{bmatrix}$$

where

$$V=\begin{bmatrix} V_{00} & . & . & . & V_{0n} \\ \vdots & \vdots & \vdots & \vdots & \vdots \\ V_{m0} & . & . & . & V_{mn} \end{bmatrix} \qquad (11)$$

In the case of $m=n=3$, this is the bicubic Bézier surface, where the basis functions are those defined in equation (8). Comparing the matrix formulations in equations (5) and (11),

$$HPH^t=BVB^t$$

From this, expressions can be derived for the elements of the P matrix in terms of the control vertices so as to produce an identical surface. Specifically,

$$P=H^{(-1)}BVB^t H^{(-t)}$$

which evaluates to

$$P=\begin{bmatrix} V_{00} & V_{03} & 3(V_{01}-V_{00}) & 3(V_{03}-V_{02}) \\ V_{30} & V_{33} & 3(V_{31}-V_{20}) & 3(V_{33}-V_{32}) \\ 3(V_{10}-V_{00}) & 3(V_{13}-V_{03}) & 9(V_{00}-V_{10}-V_{01}+V_{11}) & 9(V_{02}-V_{12}-V_{03}+V_{13}) \\ 3(V_{30}-V_{20}) & 3(V_{33}-V_{23}) & 9(V_{20}-V_{30}-V_{21}+V_{11}) & 9(V_{22}-V_{32}-V_{23}+V_{33}) \end{bmatrix}$$

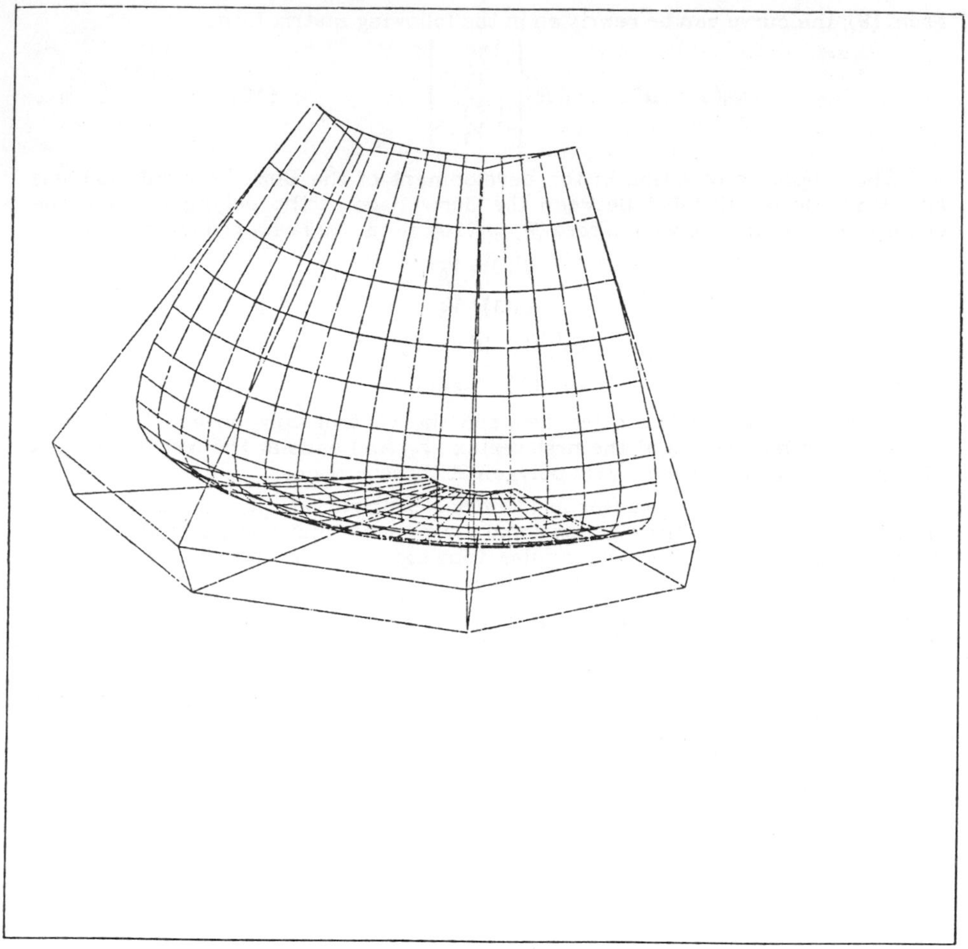

Figure 3. A control graph with its corresponding Bézier surface.

The following properties of Bézier curves and surfaces should be noted. They have axis-independence, the variation-diminishing property for curves, the convex hull property, global (not local) control, and limited ability to ensure continuity between adjacent curves and surfaces.

2.3. B-spline Curves and Surfaces

Splines were first introduced by Schoenberg[24, 16, 17] and are named from the devices used by draftsmen and shipbuilders to draw curves. A physical spline is used much like a French curve to fair in a smooth curve between specified data points. It is held in place by attaching lead weights called "ducks". By varying the number and position of the ducks, the spline can be forced to pass through the specified data points. A flexible ruler constrained to go through some points will follow the curve that minimizes the strain energy between the points.

If the physical spline is considered to be a thin elastic beam, then the Bernoulli-Euler equation can be invoked. For small deflections, the first derivative term in the curvature expression can be neglected, and thus the curvature can be approximated by the second derivative of the assumed curve. Assuming that the ducks act as simple supports, it can be shown that the solution to this functional calculus problem is a piecewise cubic polynomial, continuous up to its second derivative at the fixed points.

A spline is defined analytically as a set of polynomials over a knot vector. A knot vector is a vector of real numbers, called knots, in nondecreasing order; that is,

$$\mathbf{u}=[u_0, u_1, \ldots, u_q]$$
$$\text{such that } u_{i-1} \le u_i, \quad i=1,\ldots,q$$

A spline of order k (degree k-1) is defined mathematically as a piecewise (k-1)'st degree polynomial that is $C^{[k-2]}$ continuous; that is, it is a polynomial of degree at most k-1 on each interval $[u_{i-1}, u_i)$, and its position and first k-2 derivatives are continuous.

The i'th B-spline basis function of order k (degree k-1) for the knot vector $[u_i,\ldots,u_{i+k}]$ will be denoted $N_{i,k}(u_i,\ldots,u_{i+k};u)$ and can be expressed as the following recurrence relation:

$$N_{i,k}(u_i,\ldots,u_{i+k};u)=\frac{(u-u_i)}{(u_{i+k-1}-u_i)}N_{i,k-1}(u_i,\ldots,u_{i+k-1};u)+$$
$$\frac{(u_{i+k}-u)}{(u_{i+k}-u_{i+1})}N_{i+1,k-1}(u_{i+1},\ldots,u_{i+k};u)$$
$$\text{for } u_i \le u < u_{i+1} \tag{12}$$
$$\text{and } N_{i,1}(u_i,u_{i+1};u)=\begin{cases} 1 & u_i \le u < u_{i+1} \\ 0 & \text{otherwise} \end{cases}$$

In words, equation (12) means that the B-spline of order k in the i'th span is the weighted average of the B-splines of order k-1 on the i'th and (i+1)'st spans, each weight being the ratio of the distance between the parameter and the end knot to the length of the k-1 spans. Note that the computation of $N_{i,k}(u_i,\ldots,u_{i+k};u)$ involves all the knots from u_i to u_{i+k}, but no others, as it should since the width of support is k spans.

Curry and Schoenberg[16] showed that the $N_{i,k}(u)$ are indeed a basis, so that any spline of order k or less defined over a given knot vector, can be expressed as a linear combination of B-spline basis functions defined over the same knot vector extended at both ends by k-1 arbitrary knots.

The only restrictions on the specification of the knot vector are that the same value cannot appear more than k (the order) times and that the knots must be in nondecreasing order. When the same knot value occurs more than once, this is called a **multiple knot**. Specifically, u_i is a knot of multiplicity M if

$$u_i = u_{i+1} = \cdots = u_{i+M-1} \qquad \text{where} M \leq k$$

The continuity at this knot is reduced by M-1. Since the continuity at a knot would otherwise be $C^{[k-2]}$, this means that, in general, the continuity at a knot is $C^{[k-M-1]}$, where M is the multiplicity of the knot. For example, a cubic spline (k=4) usually has continuity $C^{[2]}$; a triple knot (M=3) would produce continuity $C^{[0]}$ at that knot. Thus, discontinuities are easily introduced in a spline curve.

Although the values of the knots are so unconstrained, an especially useful special case is that of **uniform** knot spacing, where u_i = i.[2] For the case k=4, this generates the canonical uniform cubic B-spline basis function :

$$N_{i,4} = \begin{cases} 0 & u < u_i \\ u_0'^3/6 & u_i \leq u < u_{i+1} \\ (-3u_1'^3 + 3u_1'^2 + 3u_1' + 1)/6 & u_{i+1} \leq u < u_{i+2} \\ (3u_2'^3 - 6u_2'^2 + 4)/6 & u_{i+2} \leq u < u_{i+3} \\ (1 - u_3'^3)/6 & u_{i+3} \leq u < u_{i+4} \\ 0 & u_{i+4} \leq u \end{cases}$$

$$\text{where } u_j' = u - u_{i+j}, j = i, i+1, \ldots, i+3$$

An important observation is that the shape of these basis functions are identical, independent of i; that is, all the $N_{i,k}(u)$ are translates of each other.

From the basis functions it can be noted that there are less than k nonzero basis functions at the extreme values of u. In order to consistently have k nonzero basis functions (except at the knots themselves), a slightly modified version of the above knot vector is used. This knot vector has uniform knot spacing with the first and last knot value each repeated k times.

This case closely resembles the behaviour of Bernstein polynomials (Bézier curves), and if no interior knots are presented in the knot vector, the B-splines specialize exactly to Bernstein polynomials. The corresponding knot vector is:

$$[00 \cdots 0 \quad 11 \cdots 1]$$

$$k \text{ times} \quad k \text{ times}$$

To see this, note that equation (12) reduces to

$$N_{i,k}(u) = uN_{i,k-1}(u) + (1-u)N_{i+1,k-1}(u)$$

where

$$N_{i,1}(u) = \begin{cases} 1 & u_i \leq u < u_{i+1} \\ 0 & \text{otherwise} \end{cases}$$

which is the recurrence relation for the Bernstein polynomials.

As with Bernstein polynomials and Bézier curves, B-spline basis functions can be used to approximate a sequence of control vertices. This expression is again a weighted average of control vertices; specifically,

$$Q_k(u) = \sum_{i=0}^{m} N_{i,k}(u) V_i$$

where the knot vector is:

$$[u_0, u_1, \ldots, u_q]$$

Since there are m+1 control vertices in the control polygon, and each control vertex has a corresponding basis function, there are m+1 basis functions. Moving through the knot vector, each basis function is nonzero over a successive set of k+1 knots. Thus, k+m+1 knots define m+1 basis functions that correspond to the m+1 control vertices. From this, it can be seen that the uniform knot vector with multiple end knots is

$$[\underbrace{00 \cdots 0}_{k-1}\ \underbrace{01 \cdots r}_{m-k+2}\ \underbrace{rr \cdots r}_{k-1}]$$

where $r=m-k+2$. That is,

$$u_i = \begin{bmatrix} 0 & i=0, & \ldots, & k-2 \\ i-k+1 & i=k-1, & \ldots, & m+1 \\ m-k+2 & i=m+2, & \ldots, & m+k \end{bmatrix}$$

In the same manner that a Bézier surface was formed from Bézier curves, a B-spline surface is a tensor product of B-spline curves:

$$Q_{k,l}(u,v)=\sum_{i=0}^{m}\sum_{j=0}^{n} N_{i,k}(u)N_{j,l}(v)V_{ij}$$

Like Bézier curves, B-splines have axis-independence, the variation-diminishing property for curves, and the convex hull property. In addition, B-splines have the advantages of local control (since each B-spline basis function is nonzero on only k spans or $k \times k$ surfaces) and ease of maintaining high order continuity. The formulation of B-splines curves or surfaces can be given in a manner similar to equation (10):

$$x(u)=[u^3u^2u\,1][S]\begin{bmatrix} V_0 \\ V_1 \\ V_2 \\ V_3 \end{bmatrix}$$

where :

$$S=\begin{bmatrix} -1 & 3 & -3 & 1 \\ 3 & -6 & 3 & 0 \\ -3 & 0 & 3 & 0 \\ 1 & 4 & 3 & 0 \end{bmatrix}$$

And for the surface:

$$x(u)=[u^3u^2u\,1][S]\ [V]\ [S]^T\begin{bmatrix} v^3 \\ v^2 \\ v \\ 1 \end{bmatrix}$$

where [S] is as above, and [V] is the matrix of control vertices as in (11).

2.4. Beta-spline Curves and Surfaces

The Beta-spline is a powerful new curve and surface representation that has been developed expressly for computer graphics and computer aided geometric design. A Beta-spline is defined by a set of control vertices that governs the general positioning of the curve. The underlying mathematical formulation is based on the constraints of continuous unit tangent and curvature vectors. These fundamental geometric measures are more appropriate than traditional algebraic ones based on derivatives. The use of geometric measures also adds degrees of freedom that can be captured to provide further control of shape via two inherent shape parameters, beta1 and beta2, which control the *bias* and *tension* of a piecewise cubic polynomial curve, respectively.[4,5] For example, a Beta-

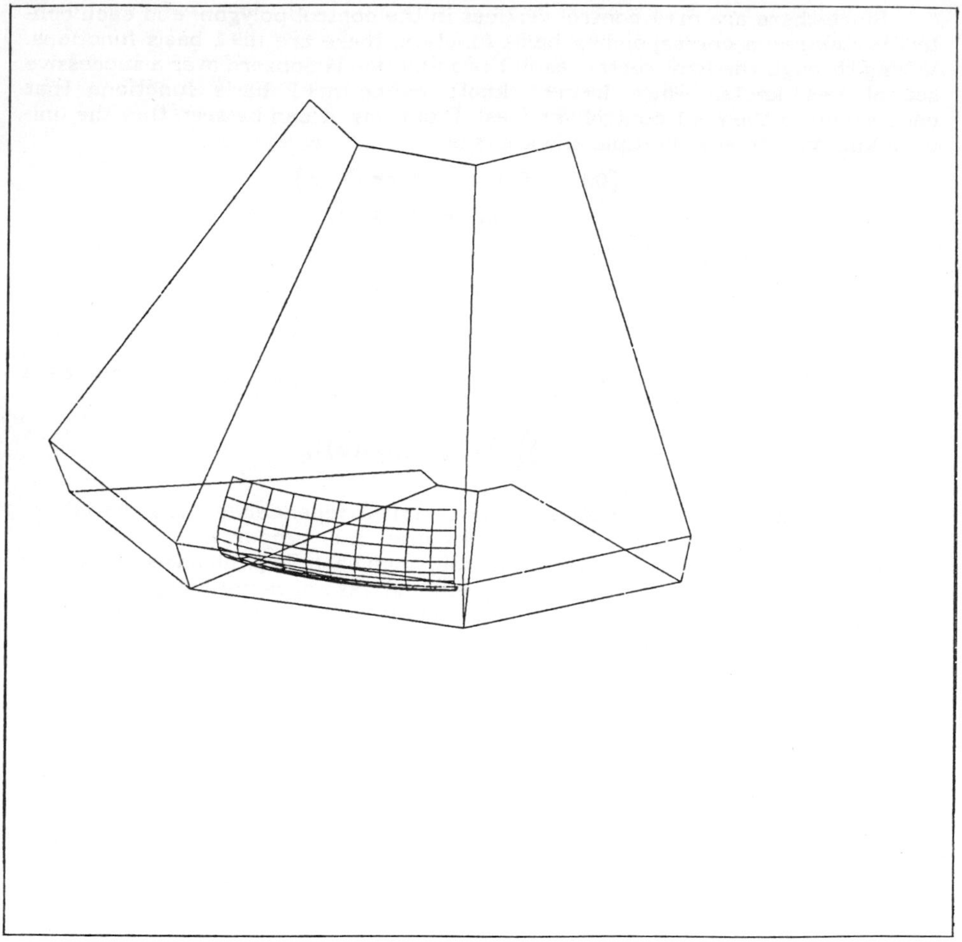

Figure 4. The B-spline surface defined by the same set of control vertices.

spline curve with high tension follows its control vertices more closely than a similar curve with low tension. Thus, the designer can lay down some vertices to get a rough shape and then modify the vertices and the shape parameters to refine it. The Beta-spline representation also has the important advantage of *local control*.

The effects of varying beta2, the tension shape parameter, are shown in Figures 5 and 6. Figure 5 shows a sequence of curves corresponding to increasing tension where each curve has a uniform tension value along the entire curve. Figure 6 is similar except here the tension value is altered at a point resulting in a curve whose tension parameter values vary along the entire curve.[7]

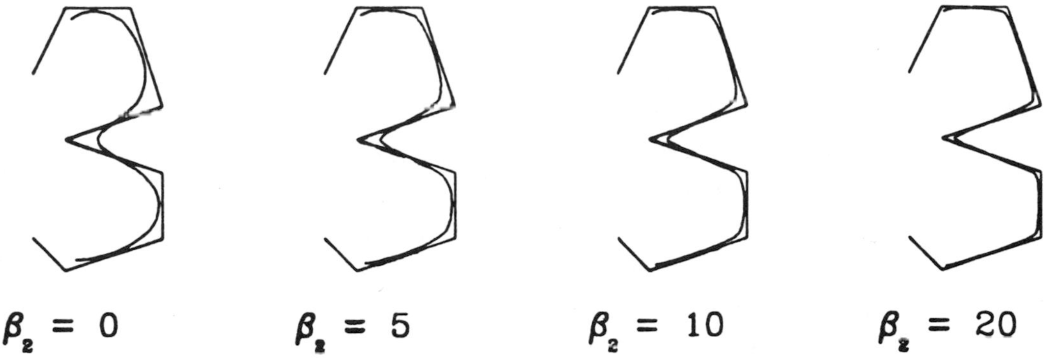

gure 5. Uniformly-shaped Beta-spline curves for different values of the tension shape parameter.

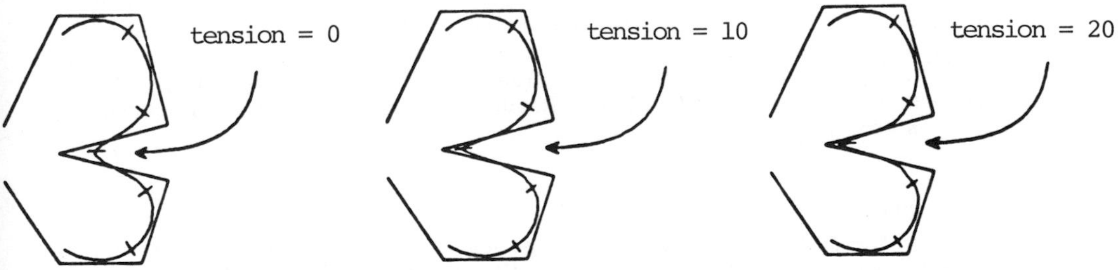

Figure 6. Continuously varying tension along a Beta-spline curve.

A Beta-spline curve or surface is specified by a set of *control vertices*. A point on the ith curve segment is a weighted average of the four control vertices $V_{i+r}, r = -2, -1, 0, 1$. The coordinates of the point $Q_i(u)$ on the ith curve segment are then given by

$$Q_i(u) = \sum_{r=-2}^{1} b_r(beta1, beta2; u)\ V_{i+r} \text{ for } 0 \le u < 1.$$

As the domain parameter u varies from zero to unity the ith curve segment is traced out.

The weighting factors are the scalar-valued ***basis functions*** evaluated at some value of the domain parameter u, and of each shape parameter beta1 and beta2.

The Beta-spline basis functions were derived in.[4,5] They are

$$b_{-2}(beta1, beta2; u) = 2beta1^3(1-u)^3 / delta$$

$$b_{-1}(beta1, beta2; u) = [2beta1^3u[u^2-3u+3]$$

$$+2beta1^2[u^3-3u^2+2] + 2beta1[u^3-3u+2]\ \ +beta2[2u^3-3u^2+1]] / delta$$

$$b_0(beta1, beta2; u) = [2beta1^2u^2[3-u] + 2beta1u[3-u^2]$$

$$+beta2u^2[3-2u] + 2(1-u^3)] / delta$$

$$b_1(beta1, beta2; u) = 2u^3 / delta$$

$$\text{where}\ \ delta = 2beta1^3 + 4beta1^2 + 4beta1 + beta2 + 2$$

A point on the $(i,j)^{th}$ Beta-spline surface patch is a weighted average of the sixteen control vertices $V_{i+r,j+s}$, $r = -2,-1,0,1$, and $s = -2,-1,0,1$. The mathematical formulation for the surface $Q_{ij}(u,v)$ is then

$$Q_{ij}(u,v) = \sum_{r=-2}^{1} \sum_{s=-2}^{1} b_r(beta1, beta2; u)\ V_{i+r,j+s}\ b_s(beta1, beta2, v)$$

$$\text{for } 0 \le u < 1 \text{ and } 0 \le v < 1.$$

3. Conclusion

Parametric curves and surfaces have been with us for a long time, and their use for object modeling in computer graphics (as opposed to computer aided geometric design) is still growing. There is sometimes, however, a reluctance to use them because it seems that the added power they give is more than offset by the complexity of their formulations and their computations. The purpose of this paper is to clarify their meanings and uses, and show how much they have in common behind the diversity of their formulations. The motivations, properties and references for the Hermite, Coons, Bézier, B-spline and Beta-spline curves or surfaces were given.

Acknowledgement

Many of the figures in this paper were generated when the author was at the Computer Systems Research Group at the University of Toronto with cooperation of Alain Fournier.

References

1. Robert E. Barnhill and Richard F. Riesenfeld, *Computer Aided Geometric Design*, Academic Press, New York (1974).
2. Brian A. Barsky, "A Study of the Parametric Uniform B-spline Curve and Surface Representations." In preparation.
3. Brian A. Barsky, "Algorithms for the Evaluation and Perturbation of Beta-splines." Submitted for publication.
4. Brian A. Barsky, "The Beta-spline: A Curve and Surface Representation for Computer Graphics and Computer Aided Geometric Design." Submitted for publication.
5. Brian A. Barsky, *The Beta-spline: A Local Representation Based on Shape Parameters and Fundamental Geometric Measures*, Ph.D. Thesis, University of Utah, Salt Lake City, Utah (December, 1981).
10. Pierre E. Bezier, "Mathematical and Practical Possibilities of UNISURF," in *Computer Aided Geometric Design*, ed. Barnhill, Robert E. and Riesenfeld, Richard F.,Academic Press,New York(1974).
11. Pierre E. Bezier, *Essai de definition numerique des courbes et des surfaces experimentales*, Ph.D. Thesis, l'Universite Pierre et Marie Curie, Paris (February, 1977).
12. Carl de Boor, *A Practical Guide to Splines*, Springer-Verlag (1978).
13. Steven A. Coons, *Surfaces for Computer Aided Design*, Technical Report, Design Division, Mech. Engin. Dept., M.I.T., Cambridge, Massachusetts (1964).
14. Steven A. Coons, *Surfaces for Computer-Aided Design of Space Forms*, Technical Report no. MAC-TR-41, Project MAC, M.I.T., Cambridge, Massachusetts (June, 1967). Available as AD-663 504 from NTIS, Springfield, Virginia.
15. Steven A. Coons, "Surface Patches and B-spline Curves," pp. 1-16 in *Computer Aided Geometric Design*, ed. Barnhill, Robert E. and Riesenfeld, Richard F.,Academic Press,New York(1974).
16. H. B. Curry and I. J. Schoenberg, "On Spline Distributions and their Limits: The Polya Distribution Functions, Abstract 380t," *Bulletin of the American Mathematical Society* **53** p. 1114 (1947).
17. H. B. Curry and I. J. Schoenberg, "On Polya Frequency Functions IV: The Fundamental Spline Functions and their Limits," *Journal d'Analyse Mathematique* **17** pp. 71-107 (1966).
18. Ivor D. Faux and Michael J. Pratt, *Computational Geometry for Design and Manufacture*, Ellis Horwood Ltd. (1979).
19. A. Robin Forrest, "On Coons' and Other Methods for the Representation of Curved Surfaces," *Computer Graphics and Image Processing* **1**(4) pp. 341-359 (December, 1972).
24. Isaac J. Schoenberg, "Contributions to the Problem of Approximation of Equidistant Data by Analytic Functions," *Quarterly Applied Math.* **4**(1) pp. 45-99 and 112-141 (1946).

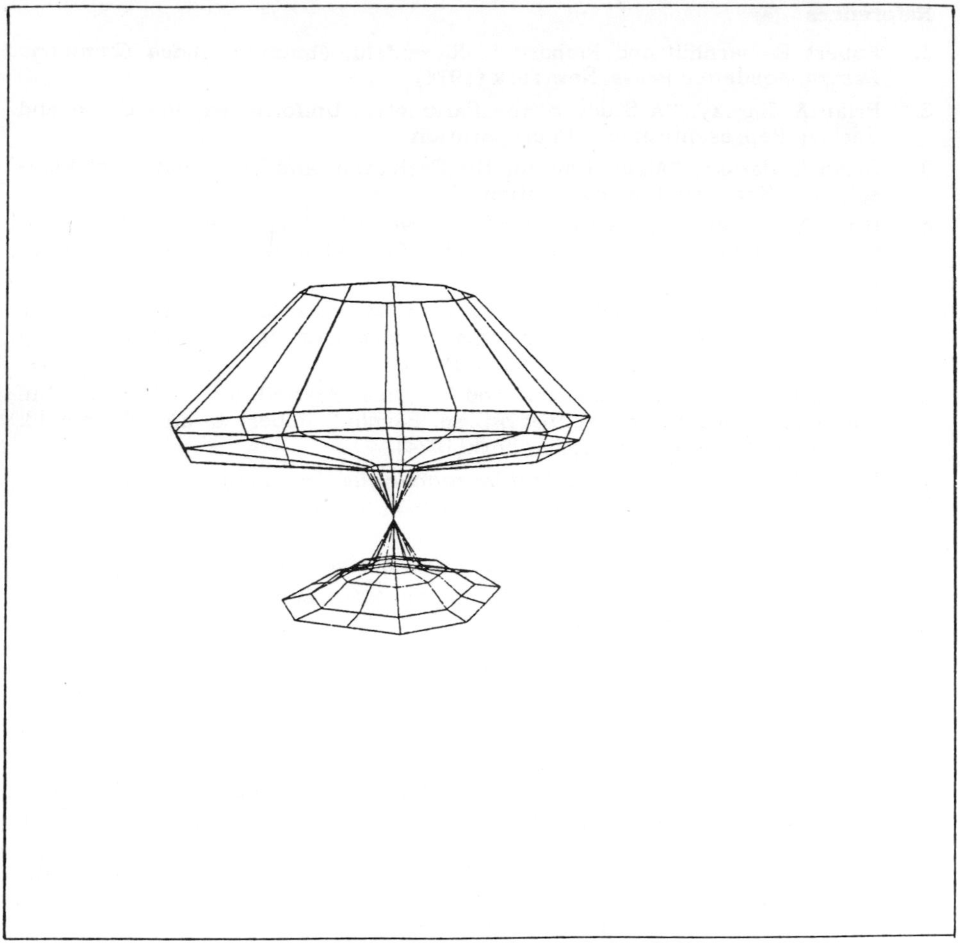

Figure 7. Control graph for a Bézier cognac glass.

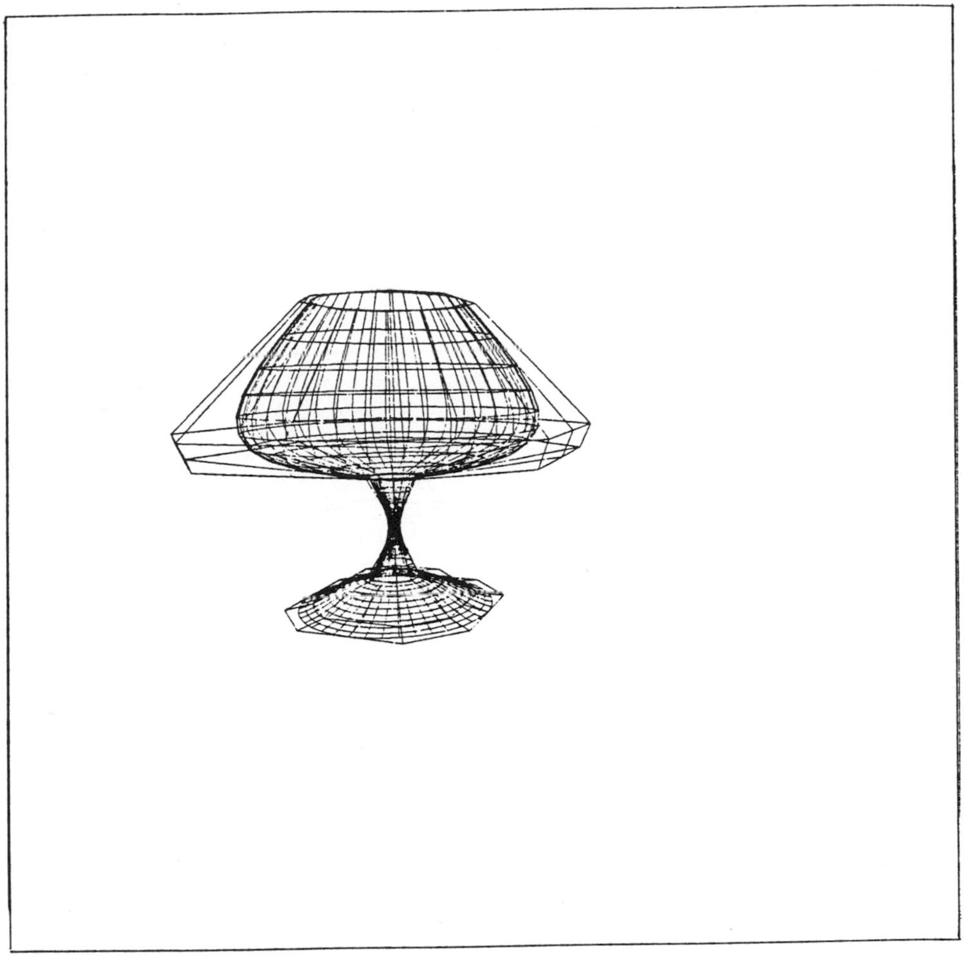

Figure 8. Bézier surface with its control graph.

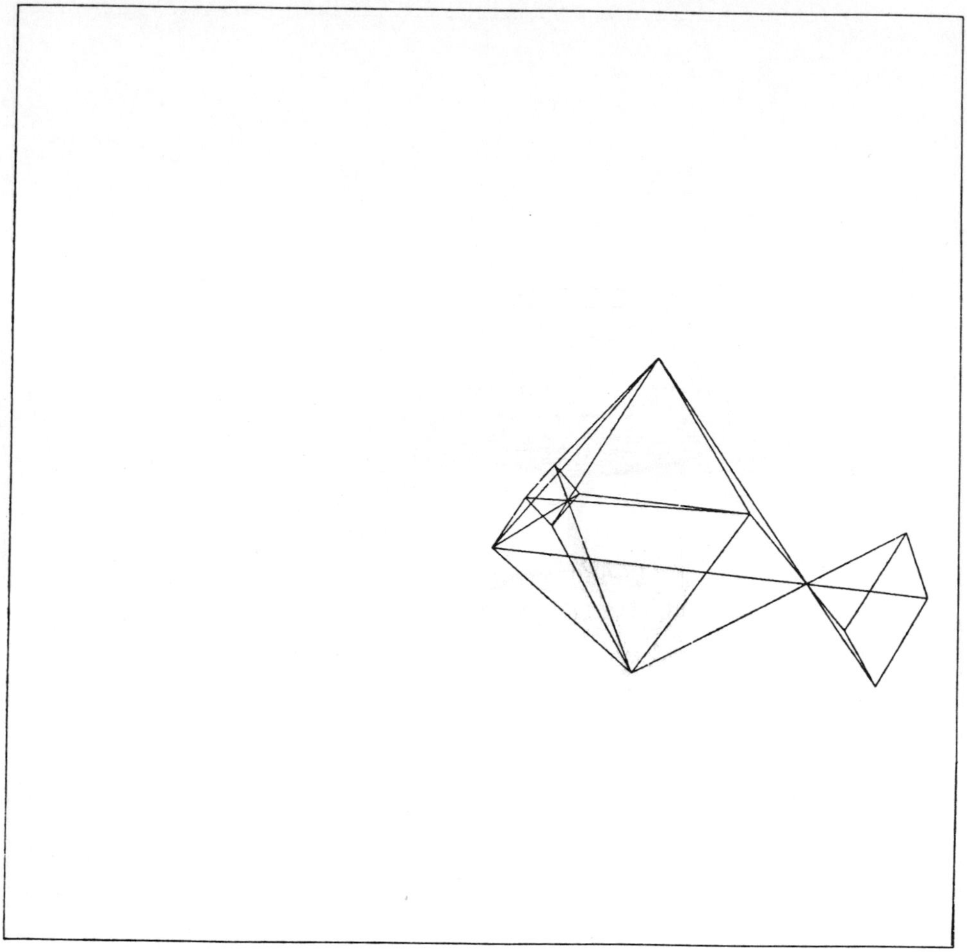

Figure 9. Control graph for the top of a B-spline wine glass.

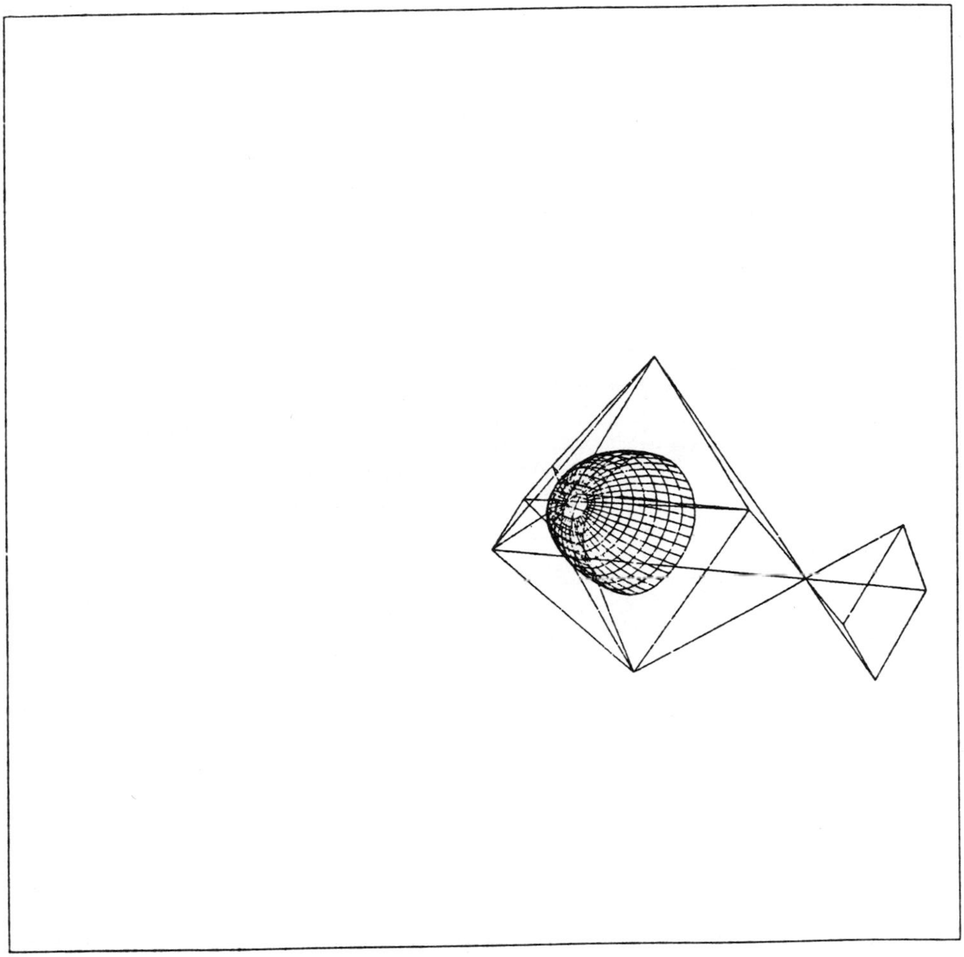

Figure 10. B-spline surface with its control graph.

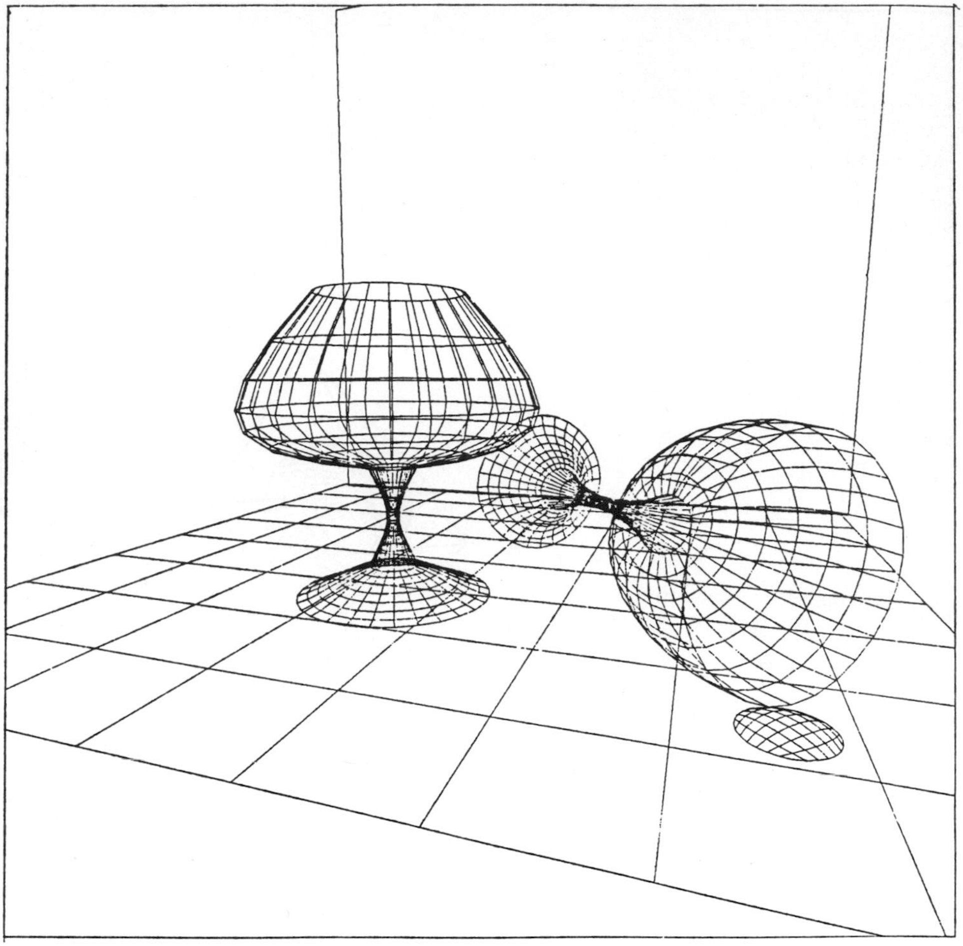

Figure 11. The entire scene composed of these glasses.

Figure 12. The same scene rendered on a colour raster display.

OCT-TREE ALGORITHMS FOR SOLID MODELING

K. Fujimura, H. Toriya, K. Yamaguchi
and T. L. Kunii

Department of Information Science,
Faculty of Science, University of Tokyo,
3-1, Hongo 7-chome, Bunkyo-ku, Tokyo 113
Japan

ABSTRACT

As an effective geometric modeling for 3-D computer graphics, we studied an oct-tree which utilizes space coherence of objects. By utilizing the oct-tree's properties we developed new efficient algorithms for performing geometric transformations and display operations. Especially, as our translation algorithm is combinatorial, its execution time depends on the number of nodes of given tree structures. Tree traversing algorithms for quick display are considered. A modified quadtree is employed in order to generate isometric 2-D image more quickly. By combining oct-tree representation and a surface model, we can rotate an object by an arbitrary angle without losing details of an object.

1. INTRODUCTION

The internal data structure is important for modeling 3-D objects in a computer. Various representation schemes have been proposed and were surveyed by Voelcker and Requicha [1,2]. Most existing systems use Constructive Solid Geometry (CSG) or Boundary representation. For example, PADL [3], GMSolid [4], and TIPS [6] use CSG representation while GEOMAP[5], ALPHA ONE [7], BUILD [8], EUCLID [9] and ROMULUS [10] use boundary representation. However, in these representations, object manipulations such as set operations, and display algorithms such as hidden surface elimination require huge amount of computation, because it is not easy to find whether a specific point is included in some object or not. Actually, the interference detection is performed by comparing a specified primitive with the other primitives, and it costs much computation time and memory space, as the comparison task can be achieved only by traversing more than million lines and points.

To overcome these problems, an oct-tree structure was proposed by Tanimoto [11]. As each oct-tree's node has numbered siblings, the comparison task is easy. Therefore efficient algorithms exist for display operations, especially for the hidden surface removal.

The oct-tree is an extension of 2-D quadtree proposed by Klinger [12]. Most of quadtree techniques such as set operations, rotation by 90 degrees and scaling by the factor of two are easily expandable to the oct-tree. All of these operations are algorithms linear to the number of nodes in the oct-tree.

Translation, rotation by arbitrary degrees, scaling algorithms and display techniques such as perspective, orthographic view, local shading, hidden surface removal, were developed and explained by Donald Meagher [13] and Louis J. Doctor and John G. Torborg [14].

Our contributions are a faster method of a translation algorithm and two new display algorithms. As to display algorithms, one of the algorithms is actually the improvement of a display method introduced by [14], and the other is a new method for an isometric view which is frequently used in engineering drawings. As to the translation, we introduced a gap translation which can save a lot of memories and time.

In section 2, the formal definition of an oct-tree is described. Section 3 is devoted to our new algorithms. In section 4, some problems of the oct-tree structure are discussed. Our solution is proposed in section 5.

Our system is implemented in the language C on the operating system UNIX* [15].

2. OCT-TREE STRUCTURE DEFINITION

The oct-tree structure is a tree structure which can be used to represent objects in the 3-D world. The oct-tree is a tree whose node has eight siblings called <u>octants</u>. This oct-tree represents a cube which is divided into eight disjoint cubes.

Each node has a flag. The flag has a value HOMOGENEOUS or HETEROGENEOUS indicating that the cube corresponding to the node is completely occupied by the object or partially occupied, respectively. If the flag has the value HOMOGENEOUS, it must be a leaf. If the flag has the value HETEROGENEOUS, at least one of its eight octants is not NULL where NULL means that the octant is empty. In our system, a color property is given to each leaf node. Other properties, such as a material type, density, luster can be added to each node. These properties may be used to display objects in more realistic way. The node HOMOGENEOUS which is actually a leaf has a color property. In order to reduce the number of leaves, the HOMOGENEOUS node may be pointed by many nodes. If the flag has the value HETEROGENEOUS, the node has function property called <u>FNODE</u>. This function property combines an oct-tree structure and a surface model, which is discussed in section 5. In our system the data structure of an oct-tree is called <u>TREENODE</u> which is defined as:

```
typedef struct node {
   int flag;
   int color;
   struct node *nodep[8]; /* These correspond to eight octants. */
   FNODE *fndp; /* function property */
} TREENODE;
```

Figure 1 shows an example of an oct-tree structure. The cube which corresponds to the root of an oct-tree is said an <u>entire universe</u>. The highlighted cube is represented by the highlighted path. This path is specified by the sequence 1-1-3, which is called a <u>node address</u>. The height of the oct-tree is called a <u>tree level</u> (as shown in Figure 1). In the oct-tree representations, in order to get the realistic view, complicated objects require very many small cubes with many tree levels. Available storage space and proceccing limit the maximum tree level. The limit of the maximum level is called a <u>physical resolution level</u>.

The part of objects which lies outside of the entire universe is not represented in the oct-tree structure. The oct-tree representation does not allow a 2-D object such as a plane nor a 1-D object such as a line. As a result, the intersection between two objects which touch each other is empty. Thus, the regularity of the objects holds automatically without any care. This is one of the virtue of the oct-tree representation. 3-D objects in the world coordinate system [-2**n,2**n]*[-2**n,2**n]*[-2**n,2**n] can be described in oct-tree representation freely, where ** denotes an exponential and n is <u>world resolution level</u>. In our system, the maximal value of n is currently equal to 10.

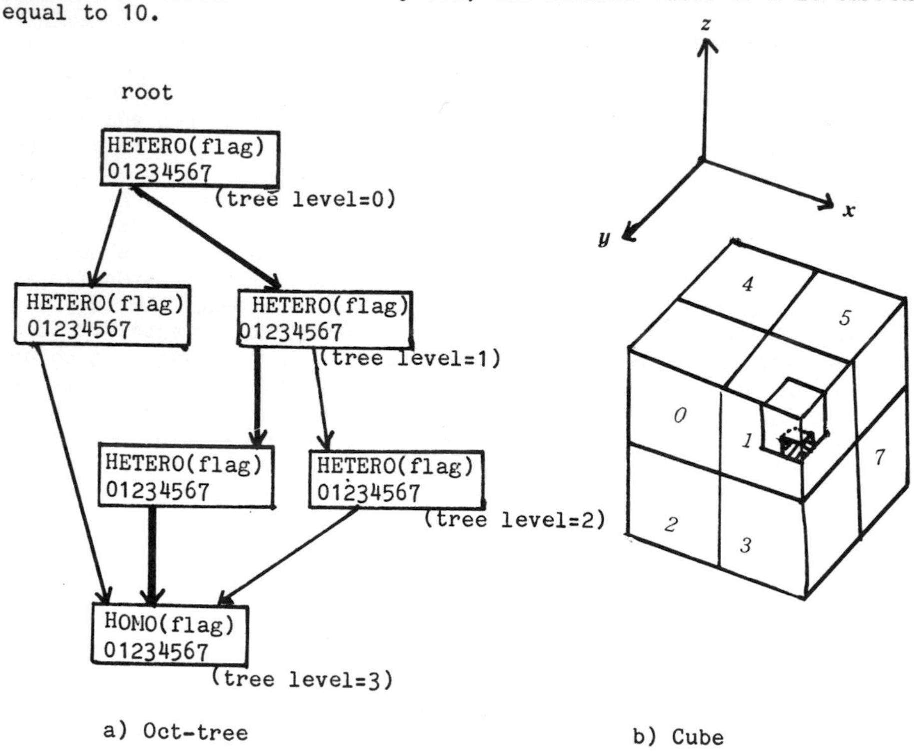

Figure 1. A cube addressed by the node address 1-1-3 and the correspond oct-tree structure.

3. ALGORITHMS

We now introduce a faster method of a translation algorithm and two kinds of display algorithms.

3.1 Translation

Let l be the translation distance. We decompose it into the sum of power of two as shown in the expression (a).

l=2**i1+2**i2+ ... +2**im   (n>=i1>i2> ... >im>=0) ---------(a)

We call (n-i1), (n-i2), ... , and (n-im) the translation levels, where n is the world resolution.

We can assume that the translation of a cube is carried out in the positive direction of the x axis without losing generality. If the maximum of the translation level n-i1 is smaller than the tree level, the resultant tree level is not changed by the translation. In this case, the translation can be performed by the permutation of octant numbers. Otherwise, the leaves of the input tree have to be divided as Figure 2. Thus, we have to treat these two cases separately. We define a gap as gap=(translation level)-(tree level).

We call the translation with a negative gap translation without a gap and the translation with a non-negative gap translation with a gap. We realize an arbitrary translation by the combination of translations with a gap and without a gap.

original node address : 0 - 1 (tree level = 1)
distance of movement : 256 (translation level = 2)
gap = 2-1 =1

new node addresses :
0 - 1 - 1
3
5
7
1 - 0 - 0
2
4
6

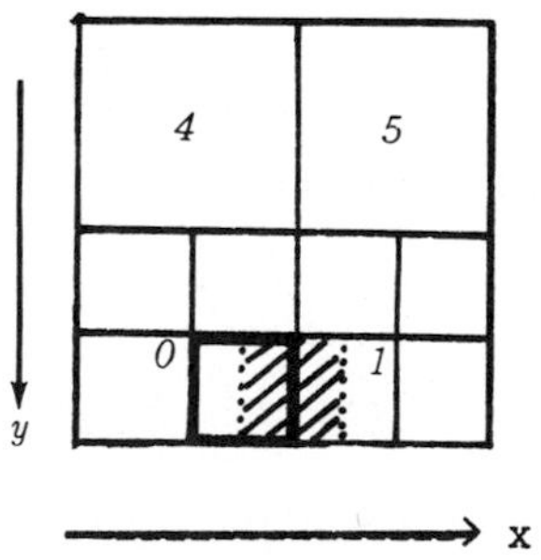

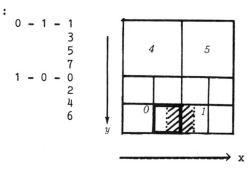

Figure 2. Translation with a gap(along with the x axis).

3.1.1 Translation without a gap

We define the sets S0 and S1 whose elements are octant numbers as shown below :

S0={0,2,4,6}, S1={1,3,5,7}.

At first, it is necessary to check whether a whole cube can be translated in the specified direction or not. This check is necessary, because the part of objects which goes out of the entire universe must be eliminated before actual translation. Otherwise, the part appears again in the reverse side of the universe. For this check, we test a node address from the translation level (obtained by the translation distance) the tree level 0 to see whether the node address contains an element of S0 or not. If all are elements of the S1, this cube cannot be translated, for it would be out of the entire universe by the translation.

The node address which is permitted to translate is modified from the translation level to tree level 0 until the element of S0 is found, by applying the permutation (0 1)(2 3)(4 5)(6 7) to the octant number in the node address. Figure 3 shows the sample translation.
According to the rule explained above, we modify a node address for each power of two repeatedly. The translation in the negative direction of x axis is accomplished by exchanging the role of the S0 and S1. In this way, the translation according to y or z axis is performed by using the set S2={4,5,6,7}, S3={0,1,2,3} or S4={2,3,6,7}, S5={0,1,4,5}.

Given node address is 0 - 1 - 1.
(tree level=2)
The distance of movement is 512.
(translation level=4)

original node address 0 - 1 - 1

0 - 0 - 1

new node address 1 - 0 - 1

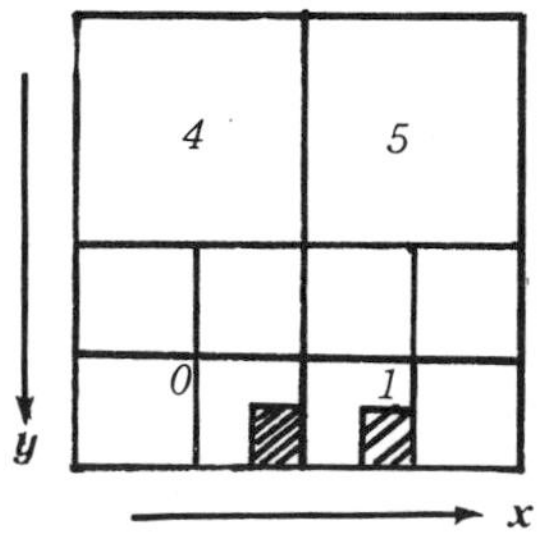

Figure 3. Translation without a gap.

3.1.2 Translation with a gap

As shown in Figure 4, a node address is changed into eight node addresses by the translation when the gap is 1. This translation is called translation with a gap 1. The rule of the change is characterized by the sets S0={0,2,4,6} and S1={1,3,5,7} that were defined before.

If the gaps are i1,i2,...,in, we call gap_i1_i2_..._in gap combination. When an oct-tree structure and the translation distance are given, the gap combinations is at first decided and then the node addresses are converted according to the gap patterns which is represented as tree structures shown in Figure 4. After the node addresses in the given oct-tree are converted, the resultant oct-tree is generated from the converted node addresses.

```
original node address   T - x - 0                 T - x - 1

gap combinations               gap patterns
                       (resultant node address for each gap combination)


gap_0                   T - x - 1                 U - y - 0


gap_1                   T - x - 0 - S1            T - x - 1 - S1
                              - 1 - S0            U - y - 0 - S0


gap_2                   T - x - 0 - S0 - S1       T - x - 1 - S0 - S1
                                  - S1                      - S1
                              - 1 - S0 - S0       U - y - 0 - S0 - S0


gap_1_2                 T - x - 0 - S1 - S1       T - x - 1 - S1 - S1
                              - 1 - S0            U - y - 0 - S0
                                  - S1 - S0                 - S1 - S0

          Notation
                T and U are nothing or node addresses
                x,y  { 0, 1, 2, 3, 4, 5, 6, 7}
                if x ∈ S0={ 0, 2, 4, 6} , y=x+1,
                   x ∈ S1={ 1, 3, 5, 7} , y=x-1.

          0 - S0 means 0 - 0  and  S0 - S1 means 0 - S1
                         - 2                     2 - S1
                         - 4                     4 - S1
                         - 6                     6 - S1
```

Figure 4. Gap combinations and patterns.

Seeing the resultant structure in Figure 4, we can find same forests appear repeatedly. Therefore, by sharing the forest, we can save memory as shown in Figure 5. When we modify the oct-trees into this representation, we have to be very careful not to destroy a part of the tree which is referenced by other nodes.

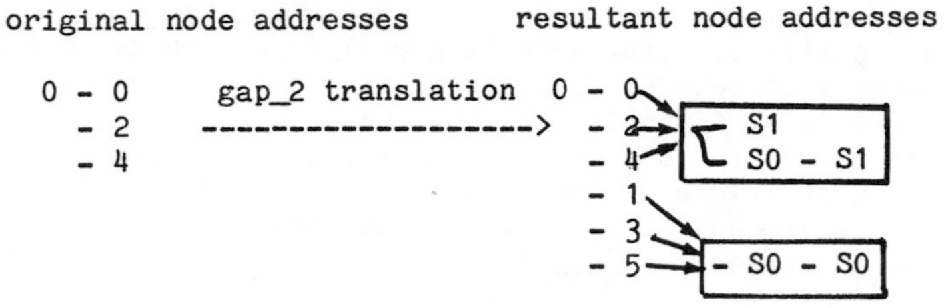

The number of nodes in the trees.

	node	leaf
Oct-tree with share	17	12
Oct-tree without share	31	108

Figure 5. Sharing sub-trees in the oct-tree representation.

3.1.3 Analysis

The translation without a gap is accomplished by the permutation of node address. This fact means that the translation algorithm is performed in the time linear to the number of nodes of the given tree, when minimum tree level is larger than the maximum translation level. As to the translation with gap, its execution time is dependent on the number of nodes of the given tree and the complexity of the gap pattern. The memory required for both of the translation algorithms depend on only the number of nodes of a resultant tree, if there is no need to decompose the original tree structure.

Another algorithm of translation was proposed by TANIMOTO in [11]. By this method, we must check 16, 32 or 64 cubes for each cube (i.e. node address) of given tree to determine which cubes are occupied by the resultant cube.

Compared with our method, it needs much computation and memory, especially when the object is moved in all the directions at the same time. The comparison is shown in Table 1.

The number of node.				translation	execution time		
original node		resultant node		distance	(second)		
node	leaf	node	leaf	(x , y , z)	(1)	(2)	(3)
1	1	1	1	(512, 0, 0)	0:11	0:01	0:01
1	1	3	8	(256, 0, 0)	0:13	0:01	0:01
1	1	11	36	(128, 0, 0)	0:30	0:01	0:07
1	1	43	148	(64, 0, 0)	2:01	0:03	0:48
1	1	171	596	(32, 0, 0)	8:25	0:23	7:41
56	8	52	8	(512, 0, 0)	1:21	0:10	0:11
56	8	32	8	(496, 0, 0)	10:26	0:11	0:12
56	8	36	8	(480, 0, 0)	7:44	0:08	0:08
56	8	40	8	(448, 0, 0)	5:30	0:12	0:12
56	8	44	8	(384, 0, 0)	3:40	0:11	0:12
56	8	48	8	(256, 0, 0)	2:30	0:11	0:12
56	8	44	8	(128, 0, 0)	3:27	0:11	0:14
56	8	40	8	(64, 0, 0)	4:36	0:11	0:13
56	8	36	8	(32, 0, 0)	6:10	0:11	0:14
56	8	32	8	(16, 0, 0)	7:44	0:11	0:13
56	8	28	8	(8, 0, 0)	9:34	0:10	0:12
56	8	64	36	(4, 0, 0)	11:32	0:15	0:19
56	8	14	8	(120,120, 0)	79:02	0:18	0:10
56	8	14	8	(56, 56, 0)	71:03	0:16	0:11
56	8	38	8	(128,128, 0)	5:32	0:17	0:12
56	8	32	8	(64, 64, 0)	10:01	0:19	0:15
56	8	26	8	(32, 32, 0)	15:15	0:16	0:11
56	8	20	8	(16, 16, 0)	24:00	0:17	0:11
56	8	14	8	(8, 8, 0)	35:10	0:17	0:10
56	8	72	50	(4, 4, 0)	59:07	0:26	0:20
56	8	42	8	(256,256,256)	5:05	0:31	0:12
56	8	35	8	(128,128,128)	12:10	0:28	0:12
56	8	28	8	(64, 64, 64)	32:02	0:26	0:12

(1) Translation by Tanimoto in [3].
(2) Translation with gap (our new method).
(3) Translation without gap (our new method).

Table 1. Comparison between our translation and TANIMOTO's translation.

3.2 View Function

Several display techniques using the quadtree were already introduced by L. J. Doctor [14]. We improve one of his algorithms, and get new one which requires calculation approximately as half as required before.

Moreover, we developed an algorithm for producing an isometric view which is frequently used as well as front, top and side views in engineering drawings. In our algorithm, we convert an oct-tree to a triangular quadtree as an intermediate 2-D structure for display purposes. The triangular quadtree divides the 2-D plane not into rectangles but into triangles as shown in Figure 6. Each triangle is divided into four small triangles, if necessary.

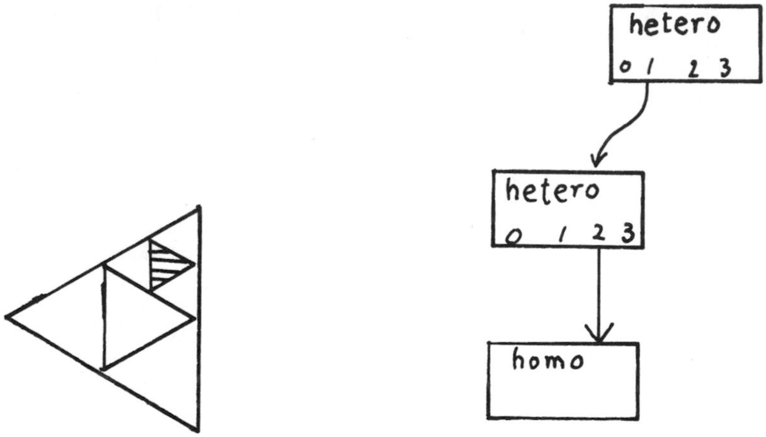

Figure 6. A triangular quad tree and its corresponding area.

3.2.1 Backward and Forward Processing

One way of making a quadtree from an oct-tree is called backward processing, because it makes at first the quadtree image which is fathest from the observer and then superimposes nearer image on the quadtree image. When we superimpose a nearer large simple image, the large complex image behind may be disposed. This situation is shown in Figure 7. The backward processing visits all the nodes of an oct-tree, even if a large cube hides small cubes.

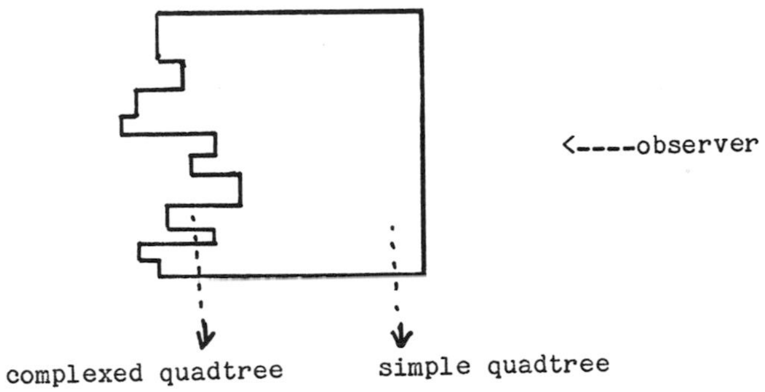

Figure 7. Forward processing.

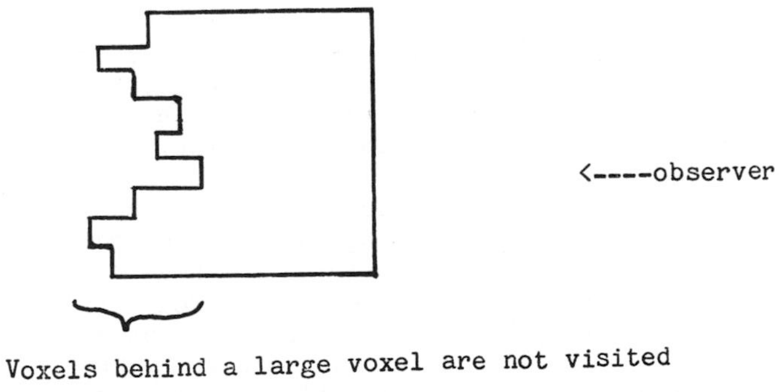

Figure 8. Unvisited parts in forward processing.

This suggests a better way of generating a quadtree from an oct-tree by processing the nearest image from a viewer first and then goes farther (Figure 8). By this method, small voxels behind a large voxel are never visited which is a major difference between our new method called forward processing. A comparison of the forward method and the backward method is shown in Table 2. The number of nodes visited in the course of displaying is shown in the table. This shows that the forward method is equal to the backward method in the worst case. For some oct-trees generated by the primitives, the former methods is two to three times better than the backward one.

primitives	backward	forward	ratio
cube	201	197	1.02
sphere	11017	6777	1.76
cylinder	1673	881	1.90
hectangular	457	273	1.67
	457	373	1.23
ring	2185	981	2.23
sphere			
(void inside)	5833	2865	2.04
hect.	5577	2513	2.22
cone	1129	965	1.17
	1129	345	3.27

Table 2. The number of nodes visited.

3.2.2 Isometric View

In this section, the algorithm to obtain an isometric view is described. In case of the isometric view, vertexes A, H and view point are aligned as is shown in Figure 9 (d). And a cube is seen as if it were a hexagon as in Figure 9 (c). Thanks to this geometric property, an efficient algorithm exists for producing the isometric view.

Similarly to the quadtree, each node except a root has an outdegree four, while the root of the triangular quadtree has an outdegree six. Highlighted area A in Figure 10 is a triangle in a hexagon from a 2-D geometric view point, which is a projection of four different octants of voxels as the 3-D geometry. If the octant 1 is not void, the image A is filled by the surface of the octant 1. There is no need to check octants 0, 2, ..., 7. Thus, this method also utilizes the forward method.

What is more effective in this case is that this orthographic view enables us to do this calculation in a simple and recursive algorithm.

Not only the strictly isometric view, but a little bit more general views are also possible by similar algorithms. Though all these projected cubes are composed of triangular quadtrees, outdegrees of roots are different. As the outdegree increases, the amount of calculation required also increases.

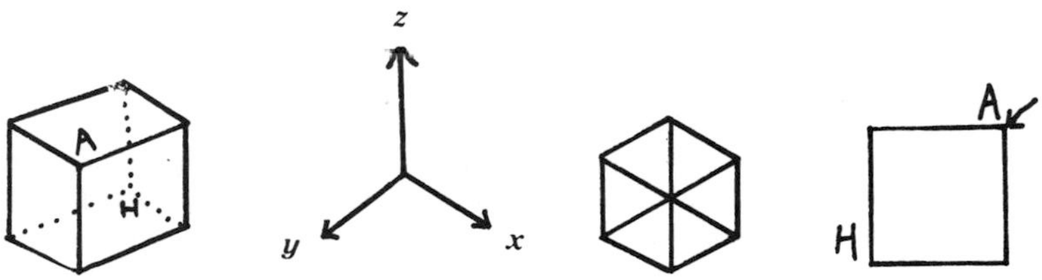

a) b) c) d)

Figure 9. Isometric views.

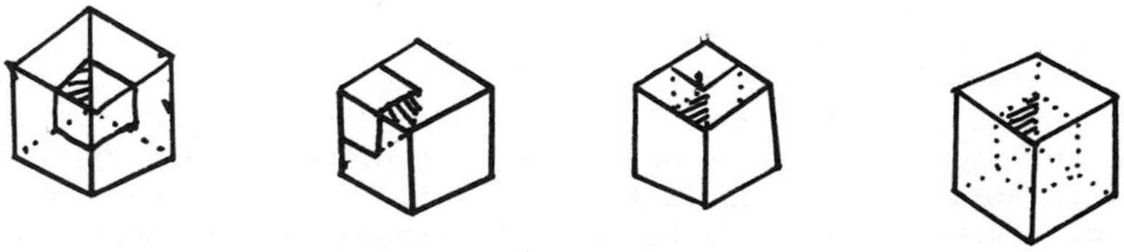

a) b) c) d)

Figure 10. Isometric views and a triangular quadtree.

4. PROBLEMS OF THE OCT-TREE

The oct-tree is an approximation of an object with smooth free surfaces by small cubes. It is intrinsic to this method that the encoded object entails some notched surfaces.

In order to avoid these jagged surfaces to be displayed, it is necessary to represent an object by a very deep oct-tree. Then, a complex object in considerably high display resolution requires very large data storage and a high speed processor. This means that the most important advantages of the oct-tree such as the processing speed and memory economy are lost.

5. SOLUTION

If we use the pure oct-tree structure for geometry modeling, we are soon faced with this problem. We are now building a new system that gives an answer to this problem, while keeping the advantages of an oct-tree.

Basic idea of this new method is to combine the oct-tree representation with a surface model (Figure 11). Suppose an object is defined by (f1 > 0 and f2 > 0) or (f3 > 0 and f4 > 0) We describe it by the following tree called a <u>function tree</u>.

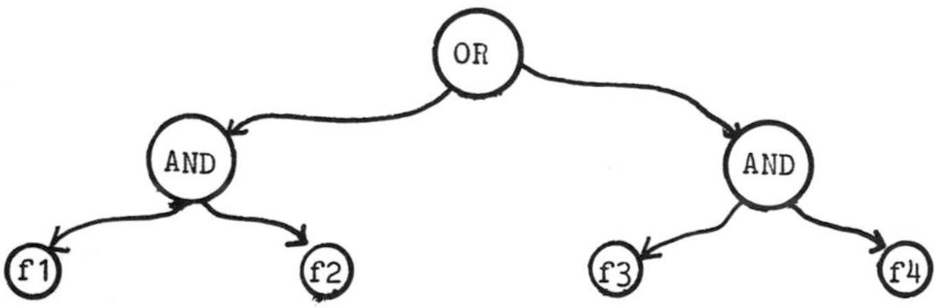

Figure 11. Function tree.

Most of the operations can be performed by consulting to the oct-tree structure, while operations such as rotation by an arbitrary angle or display operations can be done by the surface function associated with the oct-tree structure. In this representation, the very detail of the object is hold at each cube without loss of information. Thus, this operation enables one to rotate an object by an arbitrary angle without losing details of an object, which is impossible in the original oct-tree structure. When we use this functional representation, users can decide the trade-off between storage and resolution level. The set operations for this representation are already implemented. Other operations are now under development.

An oct-tree with function trees is described as follows.

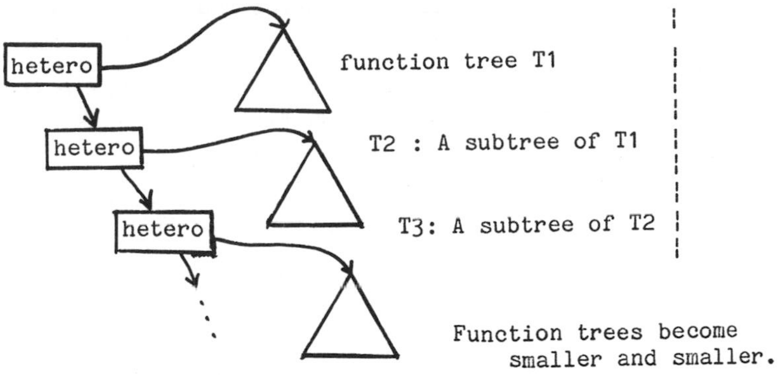

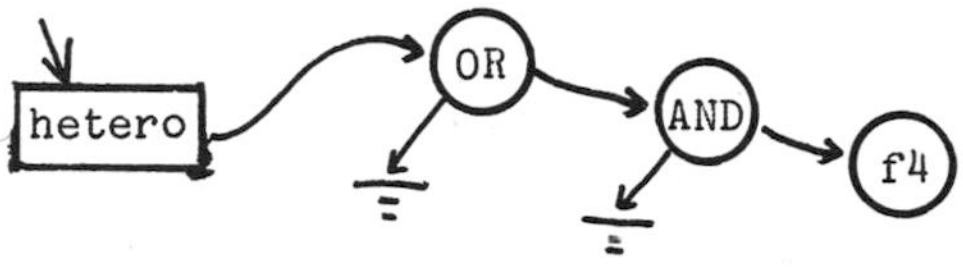

Figure 12. Combining the oct-tree representation with a surface model.

6. CONCLUDING REMARKS

In this paper, we have described some algorithms for computer graphics based on the oct-tree data structure. Here, we summarize our contributions.

1) A faster translation algorithm than ever is introduced.
2) A new display algorithm using triangular quadtree is introdeced.
3) A new oct-tree structure is introduced.

Its extension based on a new oct-tree will be discussed in future reports.

REFERENCES

[1] Requicha A.,
"Representation for rigid solids: Theory, methods and systems," Computing surveys, 12, vol 4., December, 1980, p. 437

[2] Requicha A. and Voelcker H.B.,
"Solid Modeling : A Historical Summary and Contemporary Assessment," IEEE Computer Graphics and Applications, March, 1982, p. 9

[3] Voelcker, H.B.,
"An Introduction to PADL:Characteristic, status, and rationale," Tech. Memo. 22, Production Automation Project, Univ. Rechester 1974.
[4] Boyse, J.W. et al.,
"GMSolid, Interactive Modeling for Design and Analysis of Solids," IEEE Computer Graphics and Apllications, Vol. 2, No. 2, 1982. p. 27
[5] Hosaka, M. et al.,
"A Unified Method for Processing Polyhedra, Information Processing, '74" North-Holland, Amsterdam 1974. p. 768,
[6] Okino, N. et al.,
"TIPS-1 Technical Information Processing System for Computer Aided Design, Drawing and Manufacturing," Proc. of PROLAMAT '73 1973.
[7] Cohen, E., at al.,
"Discrete B-spline and Subdivision Techniques in Computer-Aided Geometric Design and Computer Graphics," Computer graphics and image processing, vol 14., 1980. p. 87
[8] Hillyard, R.C.,
"The Build Group of Solid Modelers," IEEE Computer Graphics and Applications Vol. 2, No. 2, 1982. p. 43
[9] Bernason, Y.J. et al.,
"Automated Aids for the Design of Mechanical Parts," Tech. Paper MS 75-508 RME 1975.
[10] Veenman, P.,
"ROMULUS-The Design of a Geometric Modelling, in Geometric Modelling Seminar," W.A. Carter, ed., P-80-GM-01 CAM-1 1979. p. 127
[11] Jackins C. L. and Tanimoto S. L.,
"Oct-trees and their Use in Representing Three-Dimensional Objects," Computer graphics and image processing, vol 14., 1980. p. 249
[12] Alexandridis N. and Klinger A.,
"Picture decomposition tree data structures, and identifying direction symmetries as node combinations," Computer graphics and image processing, vol 8., 1978. p. 43
[13] Meager D.,
"Geometric Modeling Using Octree Encoding," Computer graphics and image processing, vol 19., 1982. p. 129
[14] Doctor L. J. and Terborg J. G.,
"Display Techniques for Octree-Encoded Object," IEEE Computer Graphics and Applications, July, 1981.
[15] Kernighan B. W. and Ritchie D. M.,
"The C Programming Language," Prentice-Hall,1978.

*) UNIX is a trademark of Bell Laboratory.

IMPLEMENTATION OF GEOMETRIC MODELLING SYSTEM: HICAD

S. Tokumasu, Y. Ohta, N. Nakajima
Hitachi Research Lab., Hitachi Ltd.
4026 Kuji-cho, Hitachi,
Ibaraki 319-12, JAPAN

INTRODUCTION

The geometric modelling defines a figure to a computer with structural descriptions. It is connotatively a technique of graphical operation, and denotatively a method to define figures in CAD/CAM technology. The structural description is to give a basic expression of a figure, and to define the internal expression which refers to the external figure . In order to accomplish this systematical approach, the structural description has to be systematically existed in computer, and the established system is so called geometric modelling system or geometric modeller. It is obvious that the process of CAD/CAM and graphical operation will be subjected to a modeller also whether a successful result is confirmed or not. It is why a modeller becomes such important to be considered. The first, it has difficulties to work on a system development for the present Neumann Computer. The difficulties are induced from the character of the machine that it recognizes objects in blind. Seconderly, it is almost impossible to consider most problems without knowing of the figure of the object in CAD/CAM (or applied numerical analysis). It is reasonable way to think that the application of computer is depended upon to obtain the efficient internal expression of the objected figure on the drafting procedures, the analyses of the performance, and the informating procedures for N.C. formulation,since our products exists on three—dimensional space. In this paper, from the stand point of views mentioned above, the newly developed geometric modeller HICAD is discussed.

2 GEOMETRIC MODELLING

Figure 1 shows an example of the internal description by BUILD, which is developed at Cambridge University, U.K. [1,4]

The internal data structure of a figure consists of two parts ; the one expresses topology, the structural side of the figure, and the other indicates geometry, which includes descriptions of the orientation, location, dimensions and so on. It is important for the characterization of a resulted modeller to implement and combine the topology and geometry. Although it is a common sense in geometric modelling, it should be noticed that a figure is abstracted by the numerical data as to the internal expression in computer graphics. Therefore, it sometimes cause to obtain irrational expressions. For instance, the klein bottle could be created, which is impossible to be appeared in the three—dimensional world, by a sophisticated expression ——The problem of the existence. An expression could be refered to several real bodies——Uniformity. Now, the modelling is found to be restricted with the mathematical condition due to the expression of the topology and geometry. Here, when the condition is satisfactory or satisfied, the model is said to be ` well—formed ` .It should be noted, in here, that the introduced data structure of the internal description is like a vessel of system. The next step of the modeller is how to construct the figure by applying the description. In general, the procedures were started from the vanity and the final object of the figure was constructed , hierachically. For example, vertexes are defined point by point and an straight line is drawn by connecting between the vertexes. The each step in this case is proceeded by a command to the computer. This command system (a set of commands which can be functioned as a modeller) is required to handle the data which the internal data structure demands. As it stands to be used, the command has to be constituted most efficiently. The abstract of the modeller can be determined by the internal data structure of a modeller and its command system given. At Introduction, the modelling was defined to give an internal expression to external for a figure. The function of an existed modeller also includes to draw outputs on CRT or Plotter, that is, to obtain one external expression from an internal data structure.

3 PREVIOUS STAGE OF GEOMETRIC MODELLING

There are many ways to realize the modelling. Indeed, many kinds of modellers have been introduced, thus far. These modellers were categolized and shown in Table 1 [1,2,3,4] . Herein, two dimensional model means a modelling method, which allowed to put an external description of a real figure onto a plane and the internal data structure is ordinarily existed in two dimension. The three dimensional model is a method which adapts the three dimensional space. The description is surely written in three dimension. The solid model in three dimensional modelling is mathematically constituted in detail and endorse the well—formed condition, consistently. But, the consistency makes the modelling complicated, and the command system become tight. It also tends to be criticized that the system does not have efficiency in memory and CPU operation. Moreover, since designers and product drafters like to expand their images freely on their designings, it does not become convenience for them. These listed reasons may remain the solid model in the college's cage or research insitute's hand, —— still yet, it does not get into the practical field. However, if the users limit the field of application of solid model, and pick only the handy part of the modelling, or more changes are admitted, the modelling will be very much functionally attractive. The solid model is also compared to wire frame model, surface model, and two dimensional model, which are established from the practical point of view. These three models did not care much in well formed condition, but chased the easy handling for the system, easy to use, and global utilities.The weak point of not—well—formed of these is obvious that the user has to determine whether well formed or not, possibly human makes mistakes as a result. Seconderly, the not—well—formed may cause to be imperfectly or non—operatable as a function of a system for hidden line process, cross sectional process, and intersectioned process, i.e., concluded to the lowering of function (disfunction). It must be noted that there is a way to explode the dead end. The conversational system made interactively among the figure and operator. On the Table 1, HICAD/2D and HICAD/3D are located by their functional field.

4 THE BACKGROUND PHILOSOPHY OF HICAD/2D AND 3D

As regards to various kinds of geometric modelling, it is known that each can show its ability in suitable circumstances. In this section, HICAD/2D and HICAD/3D are discussed from some points of view on the development.

(1) To be a specific purpose or to be a general purpose system

The system should be decided by taking account of the system properties; (a) easy to handle, (b) the efficiency of the system in memory and CPU operation, (c) the simplicity on development and maintenance of software and hardware for the system, and (d) the linkage of applications. Further more, neither of them will be absolutely better than the other in all of system properties. When an application is applied to a system, it will be better to employ an individual system. But, in order to expand the CAD/CAM to the integrated system and to apply in many fields of products, the general purpose system become prevailing especially in (a), (c) and (d). The weak points probably still remain for the application of a general purpose system. However, the technical environment is judged to recover sufficiently these weak points. The integrated environment of the computer engineering derived our final intention to conclude with the general purpose for the system developments.

(2) Two dimensional and three dimensional modelling

It is true and dare to accept that the three dimensional modelling can take care of the field of two dimensional modelling. And, it may be the way it should be. Our endeaver let two dimensional and three dimensional models be independent of their uses and purposes or functions as HICAD/2D and 3D, but, again, they can unit. HICAD/2D is the system for the GRADAS (a graphic system for design and manufacturing assistance by Hitachi) and includes conversational two dimensional system with global utilities in CAD/CAM.

(3) Specific geometric modelling

Modellings in HICAD/2D is sufficiently approved to handle the situations from the accumulated background (Wire frame modelling and Planer primitive modelling). In the case of the three dimensional model, as problems have been discussed in the preceding section, it is the best way to conclude with a modelling which includes the wire frame, the surface and solid models. Consequently, the wire frame model is obtained to appear on users' views. As water does not get along with oil , it is not easy to let the wire frame model and solid model co—exist without any special considerations. On this matter, another discussion wil be given in section 6.

(4) Conversational system or Batch process

In wire frame model, the user must determine well—formed for the expression. A conversational system realizes the necessary environment and generally solves the problems, well. It is reasonable for the application of the conversational system with these reasons. In HICAD, the menu command system was fully employed, which is succeeded from GRADAS, the conversational system. In case where an operation takes much CPU operation time, the command is able to be treated by the background part (Batch process).

(5) The linkage to user applications

In order to search for the general purpose, it should be equipped a modelling function which is compatible to a demand, without depending on individual applications. However, a modelling function does not go thus far to take it into account from a to z. Finally, the user interface system became available to utilize the HICAD. The user interface is a function system in which the user can intervene HICAD and exchange the data. On the other hand, the system management in maintenance became easy with an advantage of only one route existed, where the user can enter the world of HICAD.

(6) A system as a functional complex

Users demands highly general purpose system with matured functions in detail and a flexible systems in general. If our previous image system is accomplished, it is anticipated that the program will go over more than several hundred thousand steps, and it may cause to loose the functional ability. For this further problem, HICAD should be programmed to be operated under the operating system. It also should be structurally refined to function under the same level with operating system's operation. At present stage, the system is constituted as a functional complex which is the congregation of multiple functions, to be flexible for users' demands. Also, individually, applicable congregated functions can be arranged to any partial function comlex by the intergration. It ought to be remarked that the structure of the internal description is kept being unique. Therefore, the rearrangement of partial complex does not subject the whole system. It is a reason to be able to separate the HICAD/2D and 3D, individually, with this extended options.

(7) Development of tools for system development and maintenance

FORTRAN is chosen to be the basic programming language, but it does not function enough to describe the structure of the internal data structure (internal description) in complex. It was expectable to obtain unwished problems on the system management and maintenance, after the development. Therefore, a tool for solving these previous and futuristic problems was introduced into HICAD. It is named Flexible Fortran with Database Language (FDL). The FDL looks alike FORTRAN, but simillar to PL/1, functionally. The appearance of FDL contents the operations and functions of HICAD in needs.

Here, summerizing concepts of HICAD mentioned above, we have Fig.2 to show the configulation of HICAD diadic system. Further discussions will be held in next sections.

5 HICAD/2D

HICAD/2D was built to upwardly co—exist with conversational and two dimensional system developed presently, with the addition of following extended functions. It was made to improve its operation ability and efficiency.

(1) Catalogued function of the conversational operation

On the conversational environment, modelling is proceeded through the identified command input. This function automates similer operations by the catalogued operation procedure. The command become more sufficiently useful, if it is used with other following functions.

(2) Total parameterization of commands

It often happened in the actual modelling that the topology is the same, but the geometry is wished to be changed. Users experience the happening on each step of drafting and designing, or arrangement draft in drawings. This function permit to use variable format besides numerical format for input command parameters. Moreover, the geometry became able to be exchanged by appointing the dimension of figure. The figure drawn by this procedure is called parametric figure. When the hierachical relations are given to among figures, the parametric procedure is still able to be proceeded (see Fig.3,5).

(3) Automated hidden line elimination process among figures

Two dimensional modelling does not concerns of surface on figures. Thus, the hidden line elimination process is left to users. The hidden line elimination function automatically proceeds among the objected figures by pointing the top—bottom relation (on 2—dimensions), but the objected figures have to be the closed topologies due to the closed condition that defines as the surface. This function means to proceed the cutting and attaching procedures in conventional design room, automatically (see Fig.4).

(4) Display function of three dimensional view

Two dimentional modelling does not have a limit for expressions of the figure on display. Ordinarily, three dimensional figure is shown to express the object by orthogonal projection. This function makes three dimensional view of the figure appear during the process of the two dimensional modelling (see Fig.5).

(5) Linkage to HICAD/3D

Based upon the display function (4), data of a figure for HICAD/2D (means two dimensional data) are converted to the structural data for HICAD/3D (means three dimensional data).

(6) Apendix

More elements in varaiety were included such as elliptical and free curves (e.g.,Bezier curves) [5] .

6 HICAD/3D

HICAD/3D system is the three dimensional modeller which can proceed with HICAD/2D. In HICAD/3D, the wire frame modeller, the surface modeller and solid modeller are available for suitable choices to the user's purposes.

(1) Dynamic internal data structure

The data structure can take care of the most complex model, the solid. For example, two dimensional data structure can hold data of points, and edges, but three dimensional data structure has data of surfaces, also. In wire frame modelling, while the construction of only figures, unnecessary complexity should not be appeared, —— if surfaces can be neglected at the time, it should be left. If the correspond structure will be dynamically availlable to the complexity of the objected model, that is well generated.

(2) Automated yielding from wire framed topology to solid topology

In section 5, it is described that the wire frame and solid modelling has difficulty to co—exist. Avoiding the contradiction, this function presents to combine both naturally. Applying the graphical character of wire framed topology, the data of solid expression are converted from the data of wire framed expression, automatically. The inverse procedure can be carried out, easily. As a result, two of models are able to be handled on the same level, if it is required to, with the employment of this function (see Fig.6).

(3) High quality solid modelling function targeted to mainly local processing

The practical solid modelling is embarrassed with several problems. The first, the CPU recieves too much of load due to the complex automated process. Seconderly, the accuracy does not easily become acceptable due to the approximation of the curved surface by the polyhedron's surface (polygon patch), and it induced that the operative domain of curved surface is confined. An attempt was made to keep the practical accuracy by the three dimentional Bezier patch [5] . The apporoximation accepts the polyhedral trial to the curved surface, but reasonably obtains the information of surface within the tolerance for the practical use. Although it complicates the structure of internal descriptions and processing, either formated curved surface (e.g., cylinders and cones) or non—formated surface (free curved surfaces) is well expressed. In order to simplify the complicated processing, conversational process was extended, and the field of automated process were localized (see Fig.7).

(4) Conversational processing, mainly on wire framed modelling

HICAD/3D considers the conversational ability and emphasises the easy operations. Hence, the wire frame model comes ahead. The solid model and surface model become just like hidden in behind, and they are called out when they are needed. It could be outlined as: when cross section, intersection, hidden line elimination processes and area or volume calculations are needed, the solid or surface models will take places in stead of wire frame models. Also, the complicated internal data structure is only used for this kind of occasions.

(5) Apendix

The features of HICAD/2D will be added to the HICAD/3D in time, e.g., the catalogued operation function, and parametric function for commands, which will be taken into account by the solid model, first, for mainly solid model type's characteristic command. The extention of parametric function will strengthen the solid modelling as a much better modelling.

In Fig.8, some of output examples by HICAD/3D are presented, noting that all of the discussed matters on this paper are not included for output results in Fig.8.

7 IMPLEMENTION OF INTEGRATED CAD SYSTEM BY HICAD

In the heading section, we have put stress on key role of geometric modelling. Here, we can present a method to implement an integrated CAD system by introducing HICAD as shown in Fig.9. The implementation procedure in the figure has an additive feature. That is an integrated CAD system, e.g., global CAD system in Fig.9, grows up every time when the procedure goes from one local CAD system to other local CAD systems constructed or combined with, each of which shares the unique HICAD functions. This is because we have an idea that a system should get its growth by applying itself to the surroundings as human does.

8 CONCLUSION

The abstract of geometric modellings and our intentions are introduced on this paper. The geometric modellings will be the backborn of futuristic CAD/CAM , and excellent philosophy is necessary to develop a prevailling system. On Table 1, various kinds of modelling methods were evaluated by each individual appearance. In order to establish an integrated CAD system, it is important to know where the compromise should be done between the various modellings,with the opposed demands. For the development of new technologies, which breakthrough the contradictions between the modellings, it is another important point of view to know how to have reached to the point of the breakthrough. On this paper, those of two points were especially discussed for the geometric modelling system HICAD.

REFERENCES

1) I.C.Braid & C.A.Lang： Computer—aided Design of Mechanical Components with Volume Building Bricks, Proc. PROLAMAT'73, Budapest, (1973).
2) N.Okino, Y.Kakazu & H.Kubo： TIPS—1； Technical Information Processing System for Computer—aided Design, Drawing and Manufacturing, Proc. PROLAMAT' 73, Budapest, (1973).
3) M.Hosaka & F.Kimura： An Interactive Geometrical Design System with Handwriting Input, Information Processing'77, North—Holland, Amsterdam, pp.167, (1977).
4) A.Baer, C.Eastman & M.Herrion： Geometric modelling： a survey, Computer—aided Design, Vol.11, No.5, pp.253, (1979).
5) P.Bezier： Numerical Control, John Wiley and Sons, London, (1972).

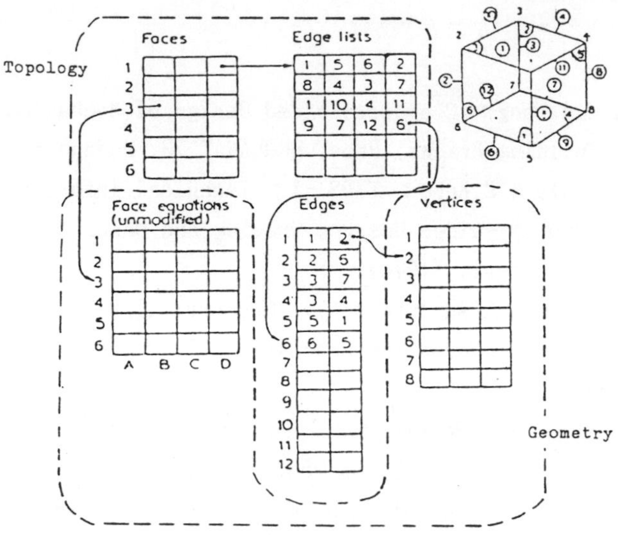

Fig—1. Internal data structure of BUILD

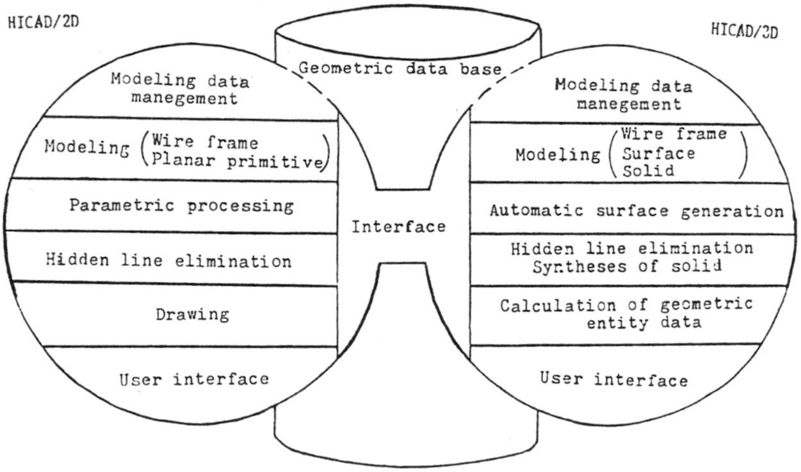

Fig—2. Configuration of HICAD diadic system

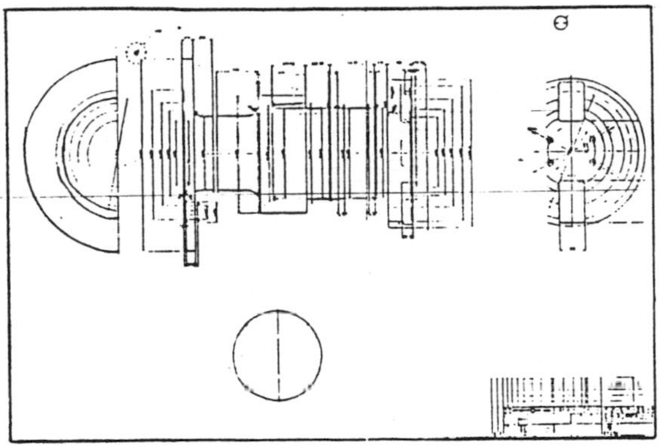

(3—1) Definition of parametric figures

Fig—3. Parametric operation

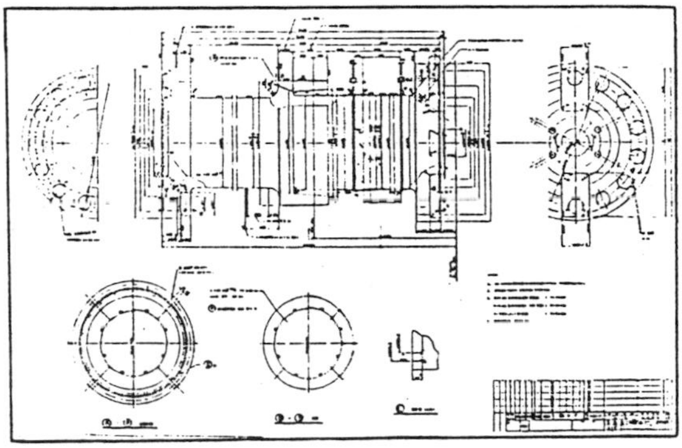

(3—2) Modification of (2—1) and drawing

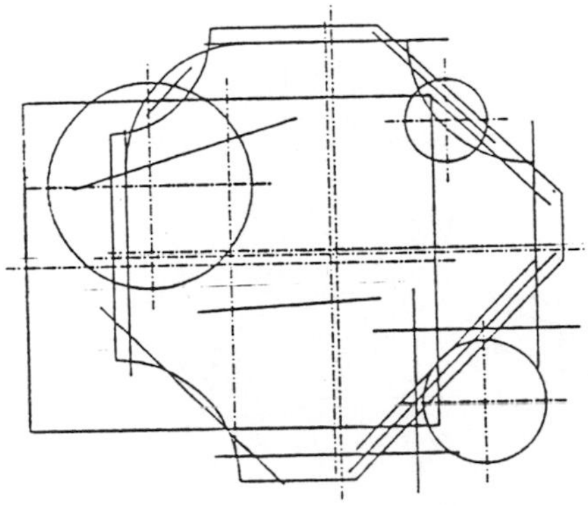

(4—1) Over lapped figures

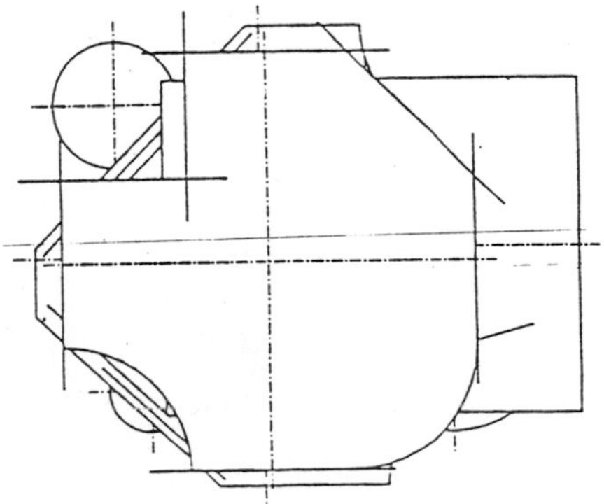

(4—2) Figures after hidden line removed

Fig—4. Automatic hidden line elimination

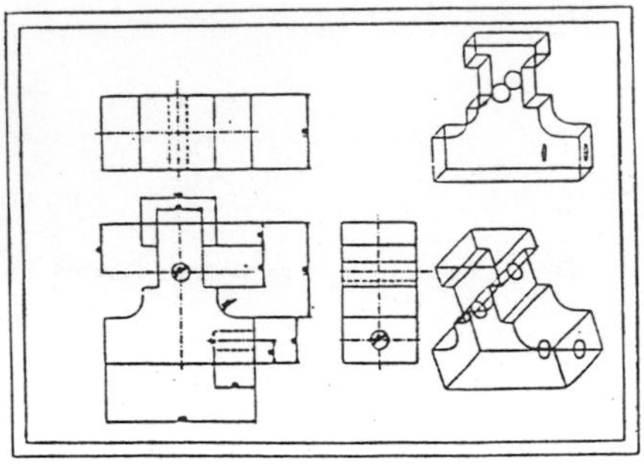

(5−1) Parametric 3D before modified

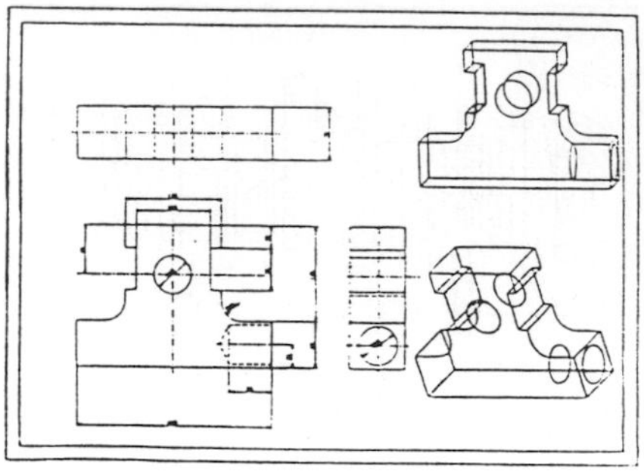

(5−2) Parametric 3D after modified

Fig−5. 3D−figures generation from 2D figures

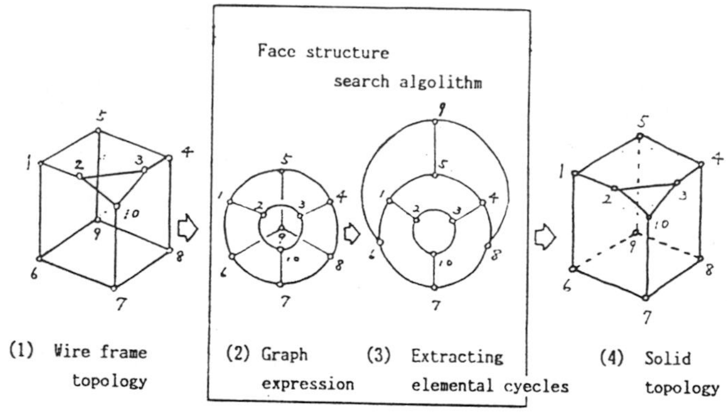

Fig−6. Generation of solid topology from wire frame topology

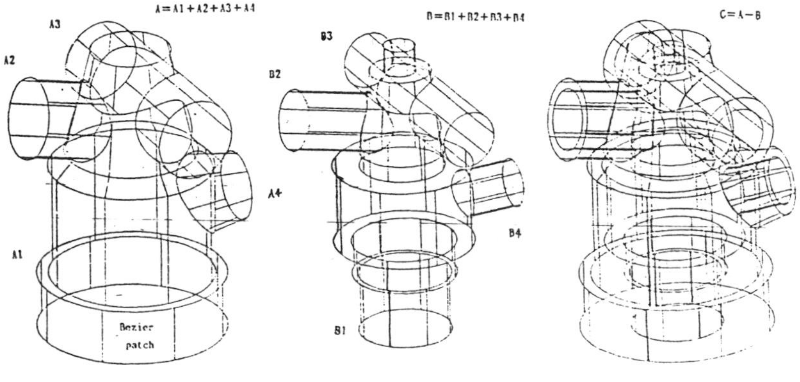

fig−7. Face expression by Bezier patches and solid operation

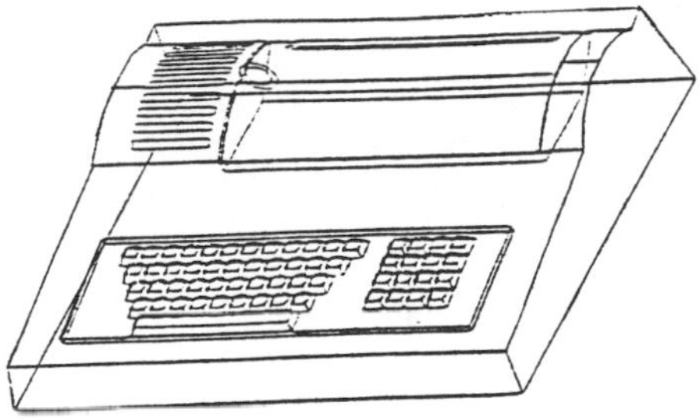

(8−1) Typwritter case (wire frame)

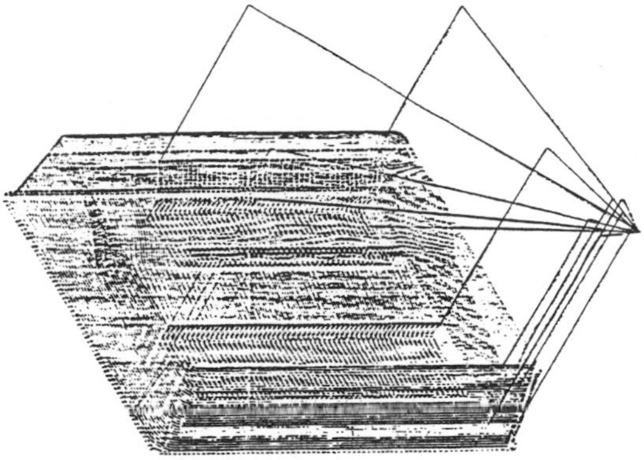

(8−2) NC cutter path for (8−1)

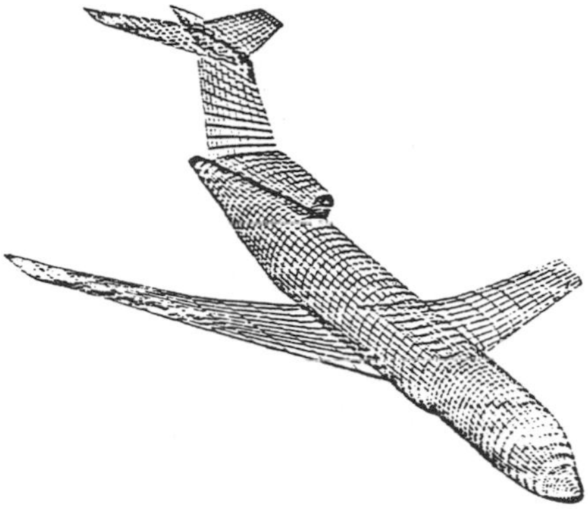

(8−3) Airplane (surface model)

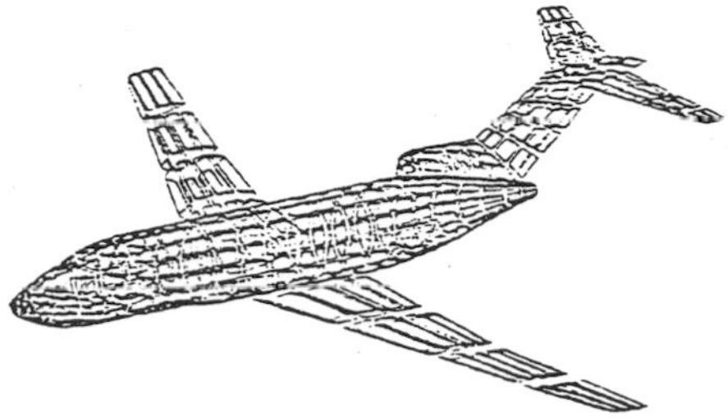

(8−4) FEM mesh generation for (8−3)

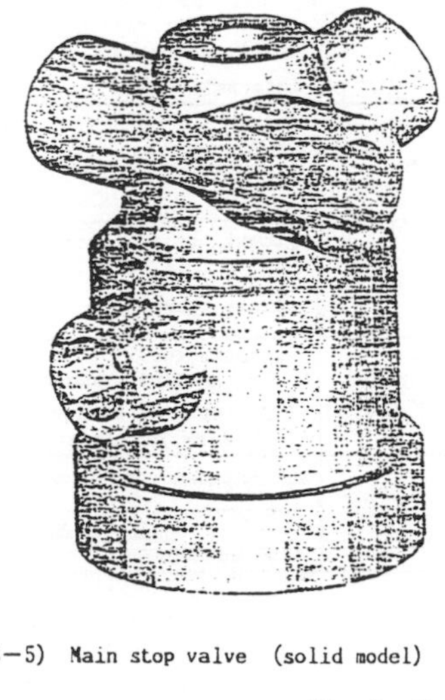

(8−5) Main stop valve (solid model)

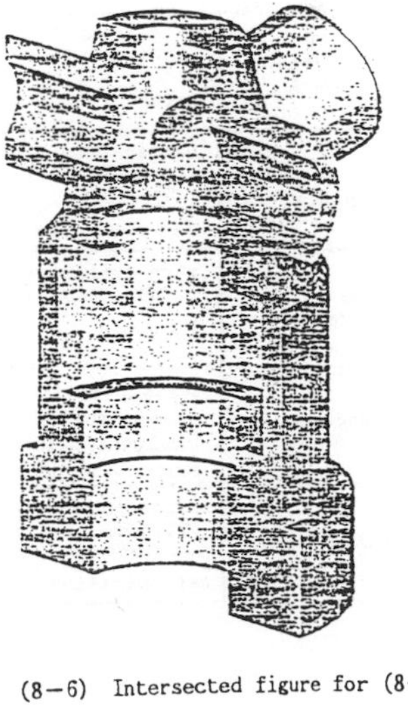

(8−6) Intersected figure for (8−5)

Fig−8. Modelling outputs by HICAD/3D

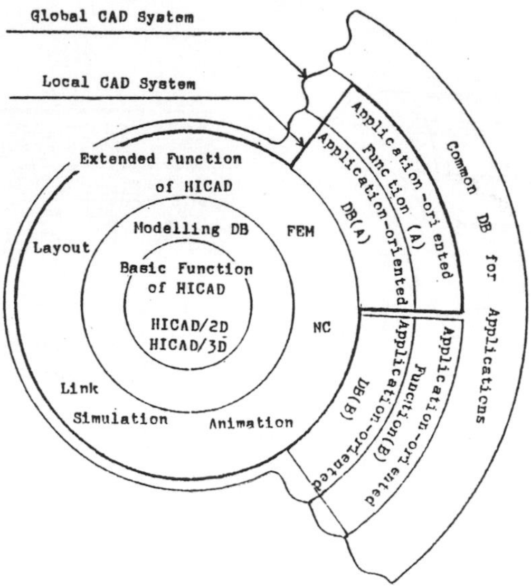

Fig-9. Implementation of Integrated CAD System

Table 1 Comparison of Geometric Modelling

Dime-nsion	Method of Model	Operation	Examples	Feature	HICAD
2D	Wire Frame Model	wire primitive (line,circle,spline) trimming	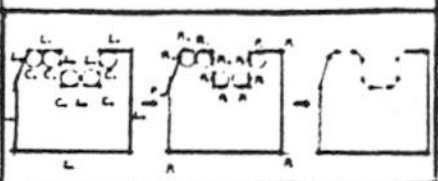	global applications in wide range; simple operations; interactive	HICAD/2D
	Planer primitive Model	planer primitive (rectangle,triangle, circle) set operation	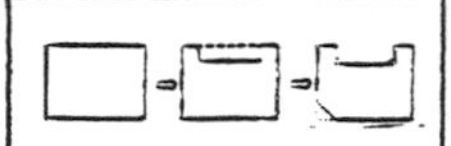	quick response	
3D	Wire Frame Model	wire primitive (line, circle,spline) trimming	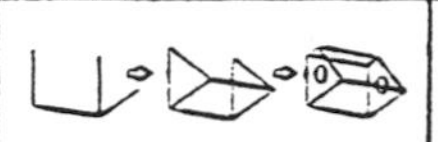	global applications in wide range; simple operations	HICAD/3D
	Surface Model	surface(revolution, sweep, rulled surace, sculptured surface) connection of surface		suitable for artistic design; difficulty of hidden line elimination	
	Solid Model	solids primitive(cubic, cylinder,cone,sphere, torus,revolution,sweep) set operation	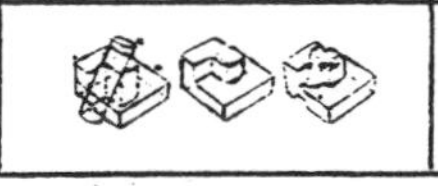	automatical operation; not prefered for artistic design; time consuming	

Chapter 3
CAD/CAM

COMPUTER GRAPHICS IN MECHANICAL ENGINEERING

Michael J. Bailey
School of Mechanical Engineering
134 Potter Engineering Center
Urdue University
West Lafayette, IN 47907, U.S.A.

INTRODUCTION

Computer Graphics is certainly one of the hottest technical subjects ever. One of the most interesting aspects of this topic is that it is seeping into such a variety of diverse, interdisciplinary fields. Computer Graphics is actually a member of the extremely broad study of *Information Management*. All fields need to manage information. Computer Graphics is such an important sub-category of Information Management because almost no area of study is exempt from the need to *visualize*. This is a common thread that transcends business, teaching, design, manufacturing, chemistry, physics, training, government, and even the social sciences. The universality of computer graphics comes from its use as a:

> "...window into a world. The world in which we deal may be real or fantasy, larger than a galaxy, or as small as an atomic particle. We may represent things that were, that are now, that will be, or that will never be."[1]

HOW COMPUTER GRAPHICS IMPACTS THE MECHANICAL ENGINEER

The need for computer graphics to visualize becomes even more pronounced when three dimensions are involved. Three dimensional design has always been a particularly difficult concept for the human brain to grasp. From birth, we have only been able to create and transfer three dimensional abstract ideas by rendering them on a flat 2D sheet of paper.

This is why the use of computers and graphics has hit the Mechanical Engineering field with such force. The very nature of the part design process is to conceive an abstract 3D idea, then gradually refine the idea until it is successfully through the manufacturing process.

A traditional method by which this can be accomplished is actually building a series of physical prototypes of the design and its refinements and testing them. This has always been costly and time-consuming. In today's highly-competitive and changing marketplace, expending that much time and money is a sure path to failure. But there is also more pressure on design quality. Today's world places a high value on reliability, safety, energy efficiency, appearance, and low cost to the consumer. The rapid growth of Computer Aided Design as a discipline indicates the necessity of using the machine as a partner to assist in the abstract thought processes associated with design.

Those who use computers discover that abstract thoughts are not compatible with the machine's way of doing business. Unfortunately, a computer can only store *numbers,* and not the original *ideas.* This forces the computer aided mechanical designer to be more explicit, and turn his problems into those which address *geometry.* This is the central focus of Computer Aided Mechanical Engineering. By creating a geometric model of a part on a computer, the designer turns his attention to creation and analysis of a *virtual part,* allowing faster and more flexible manipulation and study than what is possible with the physical part. The following three sections of this paper will discuss three aspects of the manipulation of this geometry and its application to computer graphics: geometric creation, display, and analysis.

THE MODELING OF ENGINEERING GEOMETRY

The oldest method of storing part geometry on a computer is *Wireframe storage.* This uses just the bounding edges to represent an object's solid geometry. For example, a rectangular solid would be stored as eight 3D points and 12 lines. No information about the enclosed surfaces is available. For certain applications, this works extremely well. Wireframe objects can be displayed rapidly and viewed from different angles, zoomed in on, etc. It is important to note that certain applications cannot be performed from this simple data base. Hidden lines can not be removed. Surfaces are required to hide lines and a wireframe object has no surfaces. Mass properties, such as volume, cannot be computed since wireframe edges have no volume.[1]

1. It would seem intuitive that one could determine the surface and volumetric information for a part given just its bounding edges. This is true for only the simplest of objects. For most others, the bounding edges do not *unambiguously* define a solid object. [2]

Computer-aided mechanical engineering has come a long way since then. What has finally evolved is the *Solid Modeler*. This produces a truly unambiguous data base from which to ascertain various pieces of information about the solid virtual part.

Primarily, Solid Modelers use a technique called *Constructive Solid Geometry (CSG)* or *Combinatorial Geometry*. Using CSG, one starts with a set of basic, or primitive, 3D shapes. These typically include blocks, cylinders, cones, spheres, and torii. They may be scaled and oriented in three-space and then combined using the Boolean operations of Union, Difference, and Intersection.[2]

Because geometry creation is so important to Computer Aided Mechanical Engineering, there has been a flurry of research and development in the area of interactive modeling using Computer Graphics. An example of this is the thesis research work of CADLAB graduate student Bill Charlesworth. His modeling system, Leo[3], runs on a Control Data Corporation CYBER 170-720, using an Evans and Sutherland PS300 for display and interaction. [3]

Leo gives the designer the flexibility to create and visualize geometry in a highly-dynamic 3D environment. A tablet-driven menu provides facilities to enter numbers, select primitives, orient them in three-space, and combine them. A bank of knobs is used at any time to scale the scene or view it from a different location. Figure 1 shows the primitives used to model a mechanical shifter on Leo.

During this object creation, Leo maintains a data base which is compatible with each of three commercially-available solid modelers which run on the CADLAB CYBER: ROMULUS, CDC SynthaVision, and TIPS-1. Each of the three evaluates the raw (primitives) design in a dramatically different manner. Figure 2 shows the results of the ROMULUS run from the raw geometry of Figure 1. Figure 3 shows the results of a TIPS run using the same input. It is helpful during the interactive creation of a solidly-modeled object to be able to dynamically display either one of these two geometric representations.

THE VISUALIZATION OF ENGINEERING GEOMETRY

While the Evans and Sutherland PS300 is an outstanding vector display device for visualizing wireframe representations of 3D solid objects, the most dramatic advances in the visualization of solid geometry have come from color raster displays. Color raster displays are not new. The 1960's and 70's brought forth a series of hidden surface display algorithms which took advantage of their unique capabilities. One of the most versatile which has found its way into the visualization of engineering geometry has been *Ray-Firing*. Very simply, a ray-firing algorithm fires a "bullet" from the viewer's eye, through an individual screen pixel, into the scene to be displayed. The program then determines which surface gets hit first, and assigns that color to the pixel through which the ray was fired. Progress

2. A good example of this is the placement of a hole in a block by subtracting a cylinder. The interested reader is referred to [2] for more details.

3. Named after a famous non-computer-aided designer, Leo DaVinci.

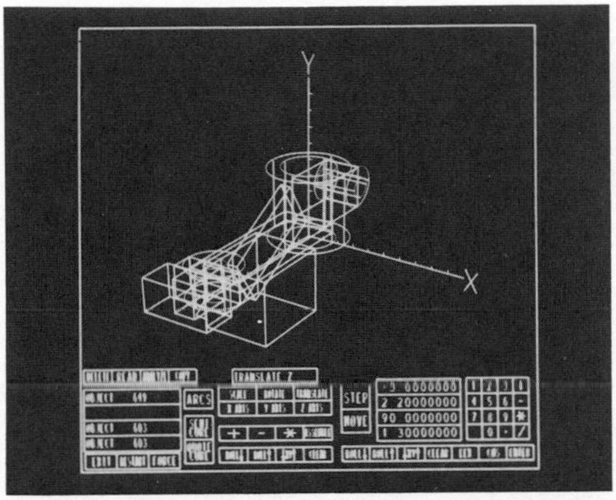

Figure 1: Raw Model of a Mechanical Shifter

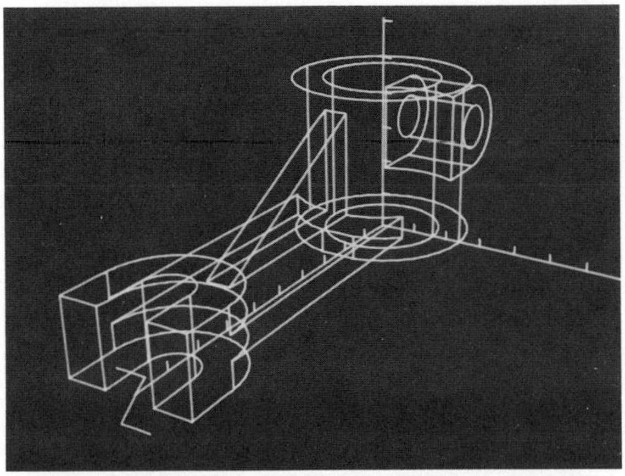

Figure 2: Shifter Bounding Edges Produced by ROMULUS

continues pixel-by-pixel until the entire image has been synthesized. Extensions to the algorithm provide for generation of advanced optical effects such as shading, shadows, reflections, and transparency with refractions.[4] [5]

4. For more information, see [4] and [5].

5. Ray-firing even has some interesting analysis applications. Mass properties can easily be computed by allowing the "bullet" to continue through the object rather than stopping at the initial penetration. If one assigns the fired ray a finite cross-sectional area, knowing where the ray enters and where it exits the object will yield the total volume swept by the bullet. Summing these over all rays will yield volume. Center of mass and moments of inertia are similarly obtained.

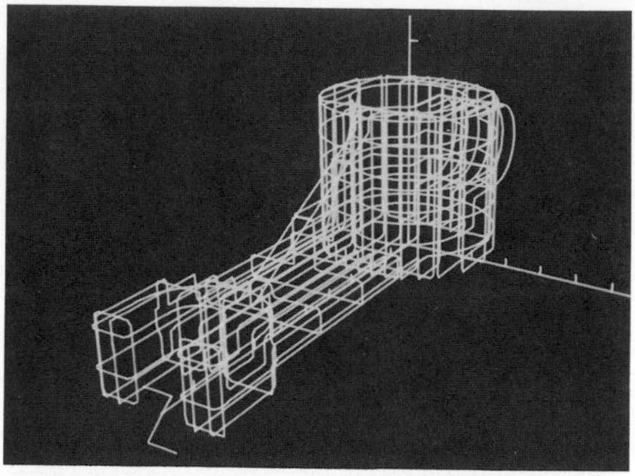

Figure 3: Shifter Interior Produced by TIPS

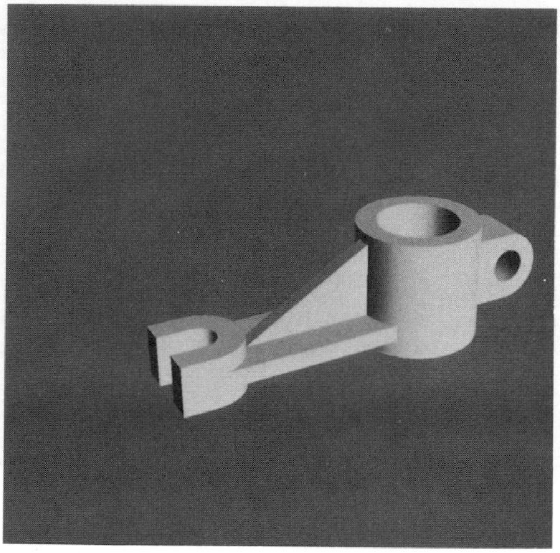

Figure 4: Shifter Display Produced by CDC SynthaVision

The important point is that a solidly-modeled mechanical part can be displayed with a dramatically high degree of realism. The goal of this kind of effort is to create a display from which the designers can extract as much information as if a prototype of the part was presented in a box with a glass front. The SynthaVision modeler uses a ray-firing algorithm. Figure 4 resulted when the shifter was run through CDC SynthaVision. The image in Figure 5 is the result of another ray-firing program, called SHADE [5]. SHADE examines the bounding-surface information produced by ROMULUS to derive the display. In Figure 5, a mirror has been placed under the part to view the underside. Also, some reflective qualities have been added to the part surface.

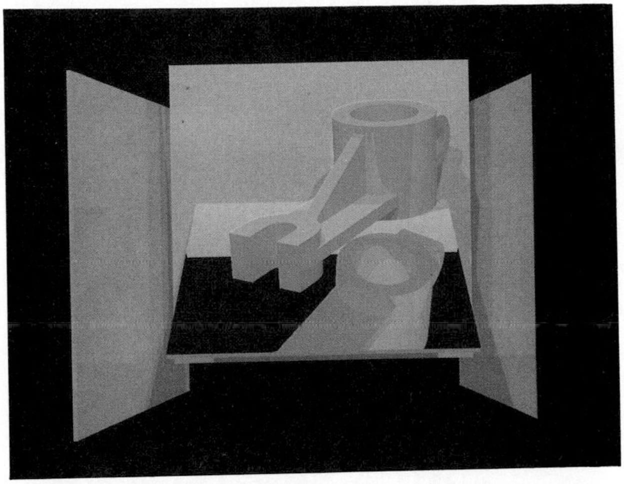

Figure 5: Shifter Display Produced by SHADE[5]

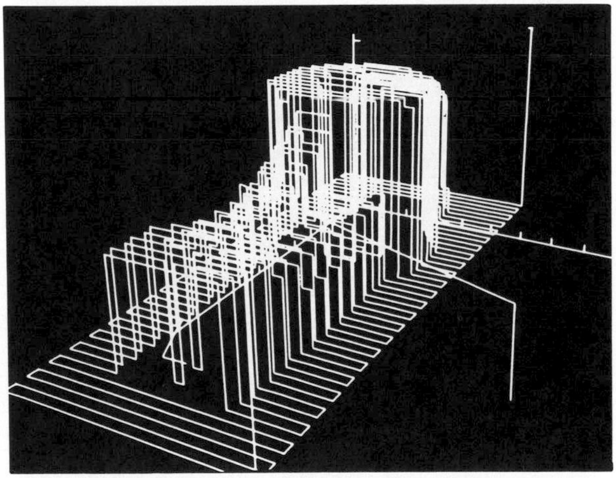

Figure 6: Shifter N/C Path

THE ANALYSIS OF ENGINEERING GEOMETRY

In some ways, Solid Modeling has been laboring under the weight of its own success. Because it has been used so effectively to generate realistic images, it has left the impression that image synthesis is its primary function. While this is indeed a useful application, Solid Modeling will only become cost effective for industry in general when it can be coupled with a variety of engineering *analyses*. These, too, are heavily incorporating computer graphics as part of the Information Management requirements to interpret the analysis results.

One major "analysis" is the actual manufacture of the designed part. Figure 6 shows another application of the TIPS modeler, the production of

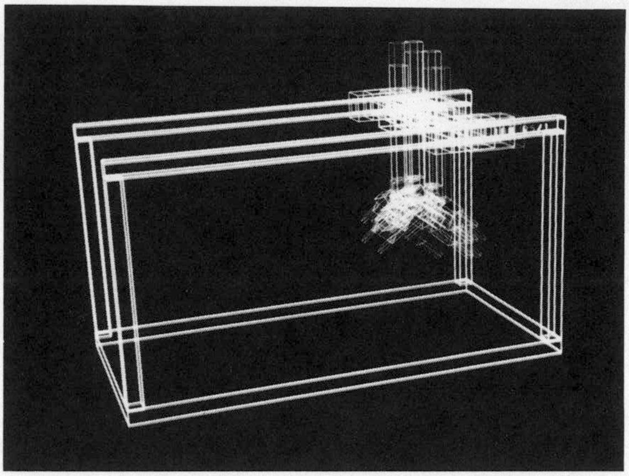

Figure 7: Dynamic Computer Graphics Model of an IBM Robot

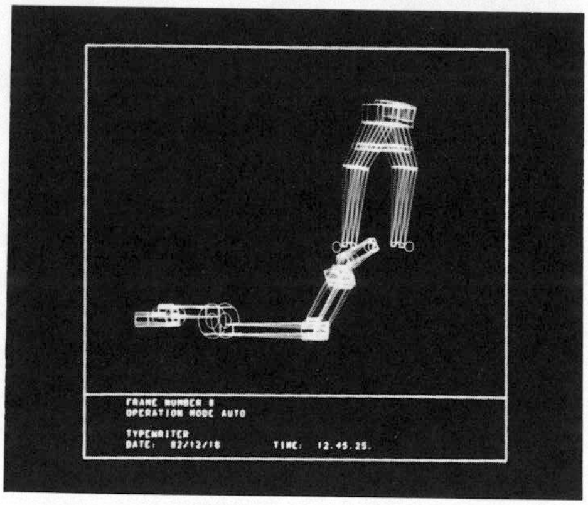

Figure 8: PS300 Animation of a Typewriter Assembly

an N/C tool path. Again, this has been displayed on the PS300 for examination. This can be overlaid with the display of the part itself and be verified for correctness.

One of the trends in the field of N/C will be the use of robots to perform more manufacturing work in addition to assembly operations. Computer Graphics is being used as an aid to this development. Figure 7 shows a moving computer graphical model of an IBM RS/1 robot which will be used at Purdue to perform machining tasks [6].

But there must be a fair amount of part-performance analysis long before manufacturing is reached. The very nature of the mechanical design cycle requires that as many iterations as possible be made on the design to attempt to obtain an "optimal" design in terms of whatever is being designed for: size, strength, appearance, speed, energy efficiency, weight, functionality, etc. Thus, it is necessary to analytically obtain as much physical information about the virtual object as is possible.

One area that lends itself very nicely to Solid Modeling is *Mechanical Dynamics*. Very often, one is interested in the interplay between parts in an assembly. There are commercially-available programs which will analyze the dynamics of mechanisms, but preparation of proper input is difficult at best, and inaccurate at worst. By tapping into a Solid Modeling data base, mechanical dynamics analyses can be run nearly automatically [7]. When such an analysis has been performed, the display qualities of computer graphics mentioned earlier can be used to animate the output. Figure 8 shows the animation of a dynamic mechanism on the PS300 display. The mechanism is part of the hammer assembly from a typewriter. By taking advantage of the PS300's dynamic and 3D capabilities, one receives a better understanding of the motion relationships between the typewriter actuator and the hammer.

CONCLUSIONS

The fervor of Computer Graphics has impacted Mechanical Engineering Design, and the field will never again be the same. As production requirements and pressures crest, graphics will be used in highly creative ways to solve the problems. The designers of the future will have a better mental "feel" for their designs -- a direct result of better visualization through Computer Graphics.

The trends for the future are closely tied to the trends in computing hardware: lower costs, faster computing speeds. Computing systems are becoming increasingly cost-effective for design use. The hardware trends will show better display capabilities, including more and cheaper 3D displays, and better methods of interacting with the designers.

Software trends will show more reliance on the Solid Modeling methods described earlier. More emphasis will be placed in the interfaces between Solid Modeling systems and engineering analysis applications.

There is abundant room for growth in these areas. Look for computer graphics to play a major part in that growth and in its rapid acceptance by industry. A heavy reliance on Computer Graphics today is still somewhat of an anomaly. In the future, it will become as commonplace as the use of a calculator is now, or the use of a sliderule was a generation ago.

ACKNOWLEDGEMENTS

The author acknowledges the following people and groups of people:

- The other members of the Purdue CADLAB research team: David Anderson, Director; the graduate students: Bill Charlesworth, Richard Crawford, Mark Feldman, Mark Henderson, Carleton Moore, Dave Plunkett, Candy Rush, Scott Staley, Steve Van Frank, and Warren Waggenspack; and the professional staff: Russ Boutell, Joe Cychosz, and Martha Schlegel.
- Control Data Corporation, for funding the CADLAB under Grant #81PO4.

REFERENCES

[1] Bailey, M.J. and Anderson, D.C., "Interactive Computer Graphics," Class Notes, Purdue University School of Mechanical Engineering August 1982.

[2] *Computer Graphics and Applications,* March 1982 issue.

[3] Charlesworth, William Wade, "The Interactive Creation and Manipulation of Solid Part Geometry," Masters Thesis, Purdue University, West Lafayette, IN, USA, May 1983.

[4] Whitted, Turner, "An Improved Illumination Model for Shaded Display," *Communications of the ACM,* June 1980, pp343∿349.

[5] Davis, J.E., Bailey, M.J., Anderson, D.C., "Projecting Realistic Images of Geometric Solids," *Computers in Mechanical Engineering,* Volume 1, Number 1, August 1982, pp6∿13.

[6] Henderson, Mark, "Hierarchical Feature Extraction from Solid Modelers," PhD Thesis, Purdue University, West Lafayette, IN, USA, December 1983.

[7] Rush, Candace, "The Mechanical Simulation of Solidly-Modeled Assemblies," Masters Thesis, Purdue University, West Lafayette, IN, USA, May 1983.

COMPUTER–AIDED DESIGN, ANALYSIS, MANUFACTURING AND TESTING TECHNIQUES AS APPLIED TO PLASTIC PART AND MOLD DEVELOPMENT

R. Rus Rodgers
Computer-Aided Engineering Marketing
General Electric Information Services Co.
20133 Waringwood Way
Gaithersburg, Maryland 20879, U.S.A.

ABSTRACT

In the past few years, manufacturers have turned to plastics seeking to maintain profit margins and market share. While plastics offer many advantages, they also present new complexities for product development and manufacturing. Current CAD/CAM and CAE techniques, developed with metal products in mind, are not adequate for engineered plastics. Computer-aided engineering techniques have now emerged for the specific design, analysis and production of plastic parts and their molds. These techniques will revolutionize the molding industry and involve the parts designer in the molding process. Substantial savings in the time-to-production, material requirements and production costs will result, in addition to significant improvements in part quality.

INTRODUCTION

The design and production of a plastic part and its mold has been a manual effort founded largely on the same concepts for metal mechanical parts and assemblies. The unique, complex design criteria and production requirements for plastic part molding is greatly dependent on individual experience and trial and error. There are now emerging a set of computer automated tools to assist the Plastics Industry in this effort. These tools include analysis software to simulate the plastic part and its mold in its real life environment, simulating polymer flow into the mold, resistant to forces, heat transfer, movement of mechanisms and the effects of vibration. Computer-aided design tools are available to reduce the manual effort currently required in the design process, and computer-aided manufacturing tools are available for control tooling equipment. These computer automated tools can be grouped into a Plastics Computer-Aided-Engineering (PCAE) approach to the design, analysis and production of plastic parts and their molds.

Recent experience in using CAE tools have shown their effectiveness in improving the design, quality and moldability of a part while at the same time reducing design, material consumption and production costs.

Material replacement studies for the automotive industry have shown that replacing plastics for metal is not just a re-evaluation of an existing design in which the dimensions and physical properties are changed. The optimum result is usually a totally new design starting with an evaluation of the function of the part and the forces it must resist. For example, the analysis of a trunk lid indicates that a "waffle" type reinforcement would give the best combination of weight and cost reduction as opposed to the beam or structural member design. The PCAE design tools allow the designer to rethink the design and produce a more cost effective solution in a timely manner, rather than just a re-evaluation of the existing design.

A major plastics design operation has been doing computer-aided mold analysis studies for several years. At first, they were only brought the critical problems where everything else had been tried and the part still could not be consistently molded. With the use of PCAE analysis tools, they now get simple and complex parts to analyze before the design is complete. Significant material and production cost savings are being realized through the use of PCAE tools.

A manufacturer has begun using the PCAE analysis tools on each of their new products. Prior to using PCAE analysis tools to study the plastics flow and cooling requirements, they prepared their drawings and specifications and sent them to the purchasing department who negotiated and interfaced with the vendors. They were never sure they were getting the optimum product in terms of cost, quality and functionality. Since using PCAE tools, they have found that they now can work directly with their vendors and modify the design of the part, if necessary, to improve its moldability. They are beginning to include in their specifications the runner design, gating requirements and molding temperature. If the custom molders will not guarantee the quality and moldability of the part under these specifications, they will "self-insure" the moldability of the part, but will be assured they have an optimum design that can be molded at high quality and for least cost.

THE PCAE CONCEPT

Figure 1 presents a schematic diagram of the PCAE concept; an interactive process with feedback loops to optimize the design and production through computer simulation before the first prototype mold and part are physically produced. The end result is an improved design, at lower cost which can go into production at an earlier date and at optimum production rates.

The concept of PCAE can be easily understood by following a typical scenario in the development cycle of a plastic part and its mold:

* The configuration of a plastic part will be done via a CAD/CAM System or an on-line computer graphics terminal. Various pre-defined shapes (e.g., cylinders, cubes, etc.) will be sized and combined to form a geometric model of the desired part. For example, a simple linkage arm might be made up of short cylinders and flat plates.

* This geometric model of the part will be transformed into a finite element model for structural analysis and test simulation. Deflection, vibration and movement will be displayed and actual test data will be incorporated into the simulated model of the part for improved simulation of actual performance. Modifications to the part design can be made in the geometric model as a result of this analysis to improve its design performance.

* The flow of the polymer into the mold cavity, defined by the part configuration, will be analyzed to minimize problems which might result from freeze off, flashing, packing, etc. Modifications to the part design will be identified to improve the polymer flow and reduce

material consumption before the physical mold is tooled. Various gating arrangements and runner systems will be analyzed. A runner and gating system will be selected and incorporated in the geometric model.

* The number of cavities in the mold and other financial considerations in part production will be evaluated to optimize the part and mold design for minimum cost.

* The mold core will be defined by geometrically subtracting the previously defined part and runner system from a solid block and then dividing this block into cavity and core halves through a planner disection.

* The cooling requirements of the mold will be analyzed to determine the number, size and location of cooling channels. These cooling channels will be incorporated into a geometric model of the mold. The optimum routing of coolent through the mold will be analyzed for the best combination of circulation of coolant, pressure and temperature necessary to balance the heat removal and minimize the cool-down time. In addition, cooling equipment specifications will be generated.

* The mold configuration will be completed by adding pins, pinholes and other standard mold base components to the geometric model. Specifications and a bill of material for these standard components will be automatically generated.

* The manufacturability of the mold and part can be analyzed to ensure the part can be produced and assembled into the final product. Financial tradeoffs and costs can also be reviewed and refined.

* Numeric control specifications for the cutting of each mold half will be generated through part programming and post processors. N/C program instructions will be fed directly to the N/C machine.

* Information will be generated for manufacturing operations and MIS Systems. This information will include bills of material, part specifications, quality assurance test data, etc.

* Engineering drawings will not be needed as geometric data can be transferred electronically between workstations. If necessary, drawings can be produced by CAD systems.

This scenario has been generalized to present the concept of PCAE and help understand the interrelationship of the various processes which are usually done independently and with significant manual effort. The benefits of using PCAE Tools, their uses and a description of these tools that are currently available follow.

THE BENEFITS OF PCAE

The use of PCAE tools can result in the benefits commonly sought by all manufacturing firms. These benefits and how they can be achieved through PCAE are:

* Improved part quality by being able to try a greater number of alternatives and select the optimum design before expensive tooling.

* Increased designer productivity through the use of automated design tools and the interfacing of these tools to analysis software.

* Lower material costs due to reduced material consumption as a result of analysis software.

* Increased production rates and hence reduced production costs through:

  - reduced mold cooling time as a result of analysis software

  - the automated generation of N/C machine control data.

* Lower material and inventory costs due to lower scrap loss and spare part inventory which results from improved part quality as a result of analysis software.

* Cost and weight reduction by replacing metal parts with plastic parts of equal or superior mechanical properties.

In addition, there is another significant benefit that can lead to greater overall sales and profits of manufacturing firms. This benefit is the reduced lead time and cost from part conception to part production as illustrated in Figure 2. This reduced lead time allows a firm to come to market with the product sooner and capture increased market share which is key to growth and higher profits.

THE USERS OF PCAE TOOLS

The benefits to be derived from using automated PCAE tools can be realistically achievable today and many firms are currently experiencing significant cost and time savings. These tools can be used by a wide variety of functions related to the design, analysis and production of plastic parts and their molds and by firms specializing in the plastics industry. For example:

* Product Designers can select the ideal mechanical properties and configuration from a wide range of alternatives.

* Raw Material Suppliers can use these tools to analyze more effective ways to use their engineered plastics.

* Part Suppliers can use these tools to improve productivity and quality plus reduce costs simultaneously.

* Mold Designers can use these tools to improve their mold designs and to lower their design costs. Significant savings in the cost of redesign and modification of molds that can be experienced with new molds can be realized through analysis software and computer simulation.

* Mold Producers can benefit as a result of the reduced manpower required to generate N/C data and hence by providing faster response to customer demands for new molds.

Raw Material Suppliers, Plastic Part Suppliers, Mold Designers and Mold Producers will find the use of these tools can increase the scope of the design and analysis services they provide their customers. They become more price competitive through reduced cost and improved response time. Being able to offer one's services and products quicker and at a more competitive price leads to more orders, greater sales volume and higher profits.

In the future, suppliers who do not use these tools may not be competitive and may, therefore, realize only a meager share of the market.

The final and most important beneficiary of CAE-in-Plastics tools is "End User of Plastic Parts" who assembles these parts into a final product and hence the consumer. In addition to benefiting from reduced cost and improved quality of the part from the above suppliers, the End User has the ability to do the complete design and analysis process internally. He can utilize these tools to work with the suppliers to solve design and production problems and improve part functionality. Historically, the End User has farmed out much of the design and analysis process. This effort is very labor intense and Design Engineers with the necessary skills and experience have not been available in sufficient quantity. This shortage will become more acute in the future, unless PCAE tools reverse this trend and allow the Design Engineer to increase his effectiveness and productivity in designing and analyzing parts plus take on additional responsibilities for the design and analysis of molds.

SCENARIO OF THE FUTURE

Currently, the PCAE tools are supplied by several vendors and are used independently. Interfaces between the various vendors are emerging. An integrated system with common data bases and automatic data flow will also emerge in the next few years. The Design Engineer will be able to sit at a work station designing the part and calling on analysis and test modules to simulate the part in actual production and operation. After necessary modifications are made and the Design Engineer is satisfied with the part design, the mold design and analysis can proceed in a similar manner. With the mold design complete, numerical control data can automatically be fed to the appropriate machining process and standard mold base components ordered.

Prototype part testing and mold production testing can feed back data to improve simulation models of the part and mold and thereby improve the part and mold designs. Bill of material and production information can automatically be fed to a Manufacturing Information System that can generate production schedules and work orders.

CURRENTLY AVAILABLE TOOLS IN PCAE

There are several tools available today to assist the Design Engineer in the design, analysis and production of plastic parts and their molds. Currently, the following vendors make available their PCAE tools and services through the General Electric Company.

* GE-CALMA - Stand alone, interactive graphics and computer-aided design and manufacturing systems. These systems aid the Design Engineer in the geometric modeling, design and drafting of parts and assemblies. CALMA's model-to-drawing concept allows engineers to work with 3-D models on a graphics display monitor and take those models to

2-dimensional production drawings in one step. Also available are pre- and post-processing finite element modeling software and numerical control capabilities. CALMA system can be interfaced to remote host systems to enable the Design Engineer to utilize complexed analysis software without manual generation of the required input data. CALMA has available finite element and numerical control, with mold base configuration software planned.

* GE-CAE - International (GE-CAE-I) - Finite element modeling and analysis, static and dynamic structural analysis, integrated mechanism analysis model simulation testing, fatigue simulation analysis, fluid flow and heat transfer analyses and other software developed by Structural Dynamics Research Corporation to assist the Engineer in the design and analysis of parts, mechanisms, structures and assemblies. GE-CAE-I is a CE/SDRC joint venture. Mold cooling analysis software is also available via time sharing.

* Plastics and Computers - Tooling Molding Cost (TMC) System for technical and economic analysis relating to thermo-plastic injection molding. The Systems assist in optimizing production and financial factors, such as selections of: number of cavities, molding equipment, production lot size, piece geometry and raw material types.

* MOLDFLOW, Ltd. - A scientific method of analyzing and predicting the flow of thermo-plastic materials into injection molds. The MOLDFLOW system assists in optimizing the design of the part, and hence the mold cavity, plus the design of the runner and gating system. MOLDFLOW analysis helps improve part quality and reduce molding problems like flashing, freeze off and warping.

* Applications Engineering Corp. - The MOLDCOOL System simulates the heat transfer events in plastic molds and assists the Design Engineer in selecting and placing cooling channels. The system also assists in determining the best coolant routing and cooling equipment requirements. The end result can be a reduced cooling cycle time resulting in greater productivity rates.

* General Electric Information Services Company (CEISCO) - Numerical control, manufacturing and general purpose software. Numerical control part programming (i.e., APT, ADAPT, etc.) and post-processing software generate N/C programs for most N/C machines. GEISCO also offers the MIMS package which provides data base management and reporting plus application software for MRP, BOM, Inventory Control, Production Control, etc. General Purpose software includes: Order Entry and Distribution Systems, Forecasting Systems and Accounting Systems.

* CAD/CAM Applications Division of Proto-Tel, Inc. - Turnkey minicomputer based system for Plastic Part design, mold design, mold filling analysis, mold cooling analysis, numerical control, viscosity testing and documentation.

CONCLUSION

PCAE computer automated tools are available today to assist the Design Engineer in the design, analysis and production of plastic parts and their molds. In the next few years, these tools will be the predominant methods used in the plastics industry. The benefits in terms of reduced costs and lead time plus improved productivity have been demonstrated and will lead to improved market share and profits for their users. A revolution is underway today that will be a standard within the Plastics Industry in five years.

COMPUTER AIDED MANUFACTURING OF MACHINE PARTS BY VOLUME BUILDING

Y. K. Chan

Dept. of Computer Science
The Chinese University of Hong Kong
Shatin, N. T.
Hong Kong

Abstract

A system of geometric modelling for the CAM of machine parts is described. The system is known as the MODCON system which stands for MODular CONstruction. The purpose of the system is (a) to facilitate the manufacturing of the 3-D geometrical machine parts with the aid of N.C. machining and (b) to generate data such as volume and centroid of the machine part manufactured. When using MODCON system, the machine part to be manufactured is defined as a series of simple volumetric modules which are merged together to from the whole shape required. This approach allows a wide range of 3-D shapes to be defined and N.C. machined with relatively few simple input instructions. Currently, the MODCON system is being applied to the CAM of EDM electrodes for dies and moulds in the forging and casting industry.

Introduction

The manufacturing methods predominently in use for the dies and moulds required for processes such as hot forging, casting, etc., involve such highly skilled, time consuming procedures as manual die sinking and/or pattern making, often in combination with electro-discharge machine (EDM). Numerically controlled (N.C.) machining of the dies or EDM electrodes, is an attractive alternative, as these highly skilled intermediate stages can be eliminated. However, the problems of pattern making, etc., are then replaced by those associated with programming the N.C. machine tools appropriately and for this a computer-based system will be necessary for all but the simpler shapes.

Computer based N.C. processing systems consist of several stages. Firstly, the geometry of the object to be machined must be suitably described and from this the required offset tool paths and cutting sequences are determined automatically. Finally the cutter location data is output in a suitable form, usually paper tape, for the N.C. machine to be used. Several alternatives are possible for the description of items such as forgings and castings for N.C. die manufacture. Firstly, computer based N.C. processing systems, such as APT or its subsets(1) could be used and the component geometry defined in terms of the lines and/or surfaces which make up this geometry. However, application of these systems to parts of some complexity, for example a connecting rod forging die, is not straight forward. Considerable programming experience is necessary and a lengthy part programme will result. Secondly, a number of so called 'sculptured surface programmes', viz. Polysurf(2) or Unisurf(3), have been developed, but again these are not straight forward to use and have significant disadvantages for objects such as forgings and castings, which exhibit abrupt changes in surface direction.

An alternative approach is to describe the geometry as combinations of commonly occurring volumetric modules or primitives, as has been adopted in a number of geometric modelling systems for the initial design of objects e.g. (4-6), which are under development. The basis of these methods is to define a series of basic primitives and then to from complex parts by employing shape operators on these, usually union (sumation), difference (subtraction) and intersection. In the systems developed at present, the primitives available are simple, for example PADL(5)(6). Consequently, application of these systems to forgings and castings, with fillets, edge radii and draft, may not be easy. However, this basic approach is a very useful one, and can be adapted more appropriately to forgings, etc., by including the features such as draft angle, edge radii and fillets, within the primitive definition. An additional advantage of this is that simple shape operators may be used also. This is the basis of the system described in this paper, which has been given the name MODCON(7). The aim has been to develop a relatively easy to use system for the geometric description of a wide range of forgings and castings, for producing N.C. tapes for the machining of EDM electrodes for dies and moulds.

Overview of the MODCON System

The MODCON system differs from most CAM systems in that MODCON is not a package in the form of absolute binary. MODCON has also a software front end, in the form of macros consisting of George 3 command strings, which act as an interface between a user and the system. The size of computer memory required in using the MODCON system varies from job to job and a simple job needs only a small computer memory requirement and very high run time efficiency. The backbone of the MODCON system consists of George 3 command string macros as well as a suite of six ANSI FORTRAN IV programs which have to be executed sequentially for every job.

In the MODCON system, the die geometry of the object to be machined is defined as a series of simple volumetric modules, which are combined together to build up the profile. This allows complex shapes to be defined and machined with relatively, few easy to use, input instructions. The system was designed initially for application to hot forging die manufacture and the volumetric shape features which can be defined are those found commonly in forging cavities, such as truncated cones, blocks with draft angles and edge radii, etc. However, the system can be used to describe other similar items, such as casting core boxes, dies, plastic moulds, etc.

The geometry is first defined using a series of primitive commands, each of which consists of a word, defining the type of element, followed by a number of parameters appropriate to the specific geometry of the particular shape feature. Currently 8 primitive commands are available, but these can be added to as required.

The specification of each primitive command defines an object having its own physical attributes and orientation relative to the origin as specified. The separate elements defined using the primitive commands are merged together during generation of the tool paths to machine the whole component. The transition surfaces between the elements are not defined on input as these are produced subsequently in the machining operation. A simple fillet of appropriate size can be obtained by a suitable choice of cutting tool and if necessary a larger blended radius can be specified. This approach is considered suitable, as the transitions in such items as forging cavities and casting moulds are not defined specifically, in general, but have only to be smooth blends between the main shape features, which can be readily produced during the blending process.

The object defined by the primitive commands are combined by MERGE commands, which select out the objects to be merged and initiate determination of the tool offset paths to machine these items separately. Subsequently, the overlapping regions of these separate tool paths are eliminated to give the tool paths to machine the whole object. The PARA commands contain details of the tool geometry and surface deviation tolerances, which allows the spacing between tool paths to be determined automatically to suit. The tool location data for the whole component determined after the merge operation is post-processed to give a N.C. tape to machine the object and/or a plot of the tool paths for visual checking. The system also has facilities for the generation of roughing cuts and generation of cross-sectional data.

Capabilities of the MODCON System

In any job run under the MODCON system there is a "directive session" in which a user issues commands to generate volumetric elements from standard primitives in the MODCON system and then shape operate previously created volumetric elements.

At the moment, the MODCON system can be used for:

(1) The 2 1/2 axis N.C. machining of the surplus material of a block of graphite using any pre-specified slot-drill, leaving an approximate male forging profile to to be machined accurately at the second stage of operation.

(2) The N.C. machining of the final shape of the male forging profile using any prespecified cutter. As the bulk of surplus graphite surrounding the male profile has already been removed during the first stage of operation, the cutter wear is minimized and the cutting speed is maximized.

(3) To produce a 3-D profile of the male forging in terms of lines and arcs on the x-y plane for discrete z-heights. This information can then be used to calculate the weight of the forging given the material density, moment of inertia about any given axis and also used as input to preform die design and roller die design programs.

Primitive Commands

The forging geometry is defined using a series of primitive commands for the individual shape features. Relatively few of these are required and the primitives have been chosen to correspond with those features found commonly in forging cavities. The primitive commands include:

(i) CYLI (Cylinder with edge radii and draft angle),
(ii) CONE (Truncated-cone vertical cylinder with edge radius and draft angles),
(iii) PLUG (Negative cone for cavity with draft angles),
(iv) ABLK (Block with edge radii and draft angles),
(v) DUMY (To define a region not violated by the cutting tool),
(vi) TORO (Segment of a toroid),
(vii) CURP (Segment of a circular ring with draft angle, edge radius),
(viii) CURN (Negative version of CURP).

In its present form, the MODCON system allows up to 9 shape features of a particular type to be defined in one job.

Each primitive command consists of a major word defining the type of object, followed by an integer from 1 to 9 identifying the particular object. This is followed by a number of parameters appropriate to the specific geometry of the particular shape feature. In each case some of the parameters included allow the basic shape to be modified to enable a range of shape features to be generated with a primitive command. Edge radii and draft angles found in forging shapes are included in the primitive definitions, whereas appropriate fillets are produced by the subsequent machining processes.

As an example, the primitive command for a cylinder (CYLI) can have up to 9 defining parameters as follows:

CYLI n, L, R, DAR, DAL, O_x, O_y, θ, SEP

where

L = Length of cylinder,
R = Radius of cylinder,
DAL = Draft angle, left-hand end (degrees),
DAR = Draft angle, right-hand end (degrees),
O_x, O_y = Position of cylinder from origin,
θ = Rotation of cylinder axis from x-axis (degrees),
SEP = Separation of two halves of cylinder parallel to cylinder axis.

The default values of these parameters are equal to zero. The draft angles and edge radii at either end of the cylinder are formed by generating an ellipsoid with appropriate major and minor axes. As an example the primitive command:

CYLI 7, 3Ø.Ø, 1Ø.Ø, 5.Ø, 7.Ø, 15.Ø, Ø.Ø, 9Ø,Ø

will result in the definition of a cylinder named CYLI 7, with dimensions and orientation as illustrated in Figure 1. The cylinder definition within the system allows ellipsoids at each end to be specified directly by giving the lengths of the minor axis rather than these being determined indirectly from the draft angels given. This is achieved by entering negative real numbers into the locations for DAR and DAL e.g. the command:

CYLI 7, 3Ø.Ø, 1Ø.Ø, -5.Ø, -7.Ø, 15.Ø, Ø.Ø, 9Ø.Ø

will result in a cylinder similar to the previous instruction but with ellipsoids on the ends having minor axes of 5.Ø and 7.Ø mm in length. It can be seen that by assigning the cylinder length to zero, it is possible to define spheres, ellipsoids, etc. However, it should be noted that spheres can be more readily generated from the CONE command, with better run-time efficiency.

The basic shape of the items defined by the primitive commands can be modified by the additional input parameters. For example Figure 2 illustrates the characteristic data for the CONE command, which results in the definition of a truncated cone for the basic shapes. The basic element is defined by the height (H), the upper radius (R_U), the lower radii (R_L) and the draft angle (α), with any three of these items being required in a particular case i.e. the commands:

CONE 4, VH = 40.0, DA = 45.0, UR = 10.0
CONE 4, UR = 10.0, LR = 50.0, DA = 45.0
CONE 4, VH = 40.0, UR = 10.0, LR = 50.0

all define the same object, namely a cone with 45 degrees draft angle and height 40.0 mm. The basic truncated cone shape can be modified by allowing the four quardrants of the cone to be separated in the X and/or Y directions (X SEP, Y SEPL, Y SEPR) and allowing a rotation relative to the origin (θ). Figures 3 and 4 indicate some of the range of objects which can be created from the CONE command. A sphere can be also from this command by H, R_L and R_E equal to one another. If R_E is not specified a default value of of 3.0 mm. is assigned.

Similar primitive commands are used for the other elements which may be defined and in this way wide range of shape features can be created from relatively few commands. The primitive command DUMY defines a rectangular block volume, which cannot be violated by the cutting tool. This is particularly useful for symmetrical components, for which one half (or quarter) only can then be defined and the final whole object produced by using the mirror image capabilities of the N.C. tape produced, but may somewhat increase the machining time of the final product.

Specification of Cutter Size

As the MODCON system is primarily designed as a Computer Aided Manufacturing system using a 2 1/2 axis N.C. machine, the tool offset must be taken into account when machining a component. Further, as a 2 1/2 axis N.C. machine is capable of reproducing a combination of straight lines and arc segments in the x-y plane, the surface accuracy of the constituent parts is only dependent on the closeness of the tool paths along the z-direction, i.e. widely spaced tool paths will lead to a rough surface with significant cusps.

The MODCON system allows the user to choose a tool (for N.C. machining) ranging from an end-mill to a ball-ended cutter. The general configuration of a typical tool used for N.C. machining in the MODCON system is illustrated in Figure 5.1. It can be seen that when the edge radius T2 tends to zero, an end-mill cutter is obtained (Figure 5.2). When T2 tends to the tool radius Tl, a ball-ended cutter is obtained (Figure 5.3).

Defining Resolution for N.C. Machining

The MODCON system also allows the user to choose the resolution of a constituent part to be defined by two parameters EPS and EPSEDG which represent the maximum height (normal to the surface of the primitive) of cusps remaining after the cutting operation (Figure 6). The parameters are included as it was found that if EPS alone was available, the edge radius (typically 3 mm) might not be cut properly. In practice, it is usual to make EPSEDG smaller than EPS. From the input values of EPS and EPSEDG, the number of z-increments for the cutter height is determined. The z-increments generated also depend on the characteristics of the cutter chosen for N.C. milling. In general, the number of z-increments is approximately inversely-proportional to the magnitudes of EPS and EPSEDG (Figure 6) and appropriately inversely-propotional to the magnitude of T2, the edge radius of the tool (Figure 5.1).

As an example, figure 6 shows the radial cross-section of a basic truncated cone. Also shown in Figure 6 are the cutter positions at 4 different z-heights indicated by Z_1, Z_2, Z_3 and Z_4.
The height of the cusp which remains uncut by the 2 cutter positions at Z_1 and Z_2 has a maximum value defined by EPSEDG.
The value of the cusp which remains uncut by the 2 cutter positions at Z_3 and Z_4 has a maximum value defined by EPS.
In the MODCON finishing-cut system, the values for Tl, T2, EPS and EPSEDG must be specified in the "PARA" command.

Merging of the Primitives

Only one shape operator is used in the MODCON system and this is called MERGE (with variants using similar algorithms for roughing cuts and cross section definition). This is possible because of the inclusion of cavity primitives in the system and MERGE is equivalent to the union shape operator in other geometry modelling systems. As a result of a MERGE command, the tool paths to machine the whole component are obtained by eliminating the overlapping regions of the separate tool paths for each primitive. For example, a typical instruction is as follows:-

MERGE CONE1, CYLI1, CYLI3, PLUG4

in which the primitives listed have been previously defined. Several MERGE commands may be used in a particular job, mainly to allow different tools or different surface deviation tolerances to be used for various regions of the final part.

A similar algorithm and input statement is used to generate roughing cuts to be used prior to the finish machining of the electrode shape. The correct variant of the algorithm is called up using a MERGEROUGH command similar to the MERGE statement above. The dimensions of the block of material from which the electrode shape is to be machined must have been supplied, together with the tool radius and the vertical spacing between each cutter pass, in a PARA statement prior to the MERGEROUGH command.

(a) Larger blend radii using the MERGE commands above, the transition surfaces between the various volumetric primitives are not defined on input, but are generated during derivation of the offset tool paths. A simple fillet of appropriate size is obtained by a suitable choice of cutting tool. In many cases this is sufficient, since the transitions in forging cavities are not in general, defined specifically, but merely have to be smooth blends between the main shape feature, with a minimum fillet radius value specified. However, in some cases a larger blend radius is sometimes required, for example between the big end and connecting piece of a connecting rod forging. It is possible to generate this blend region by using one of the primitives availble, but a facility has been provided, whereby a specified radius can be blended between the individual tool paths for any pair of primitives, by using a BLEND command in conjunction with the MERGE commands.

For example the commands:-

MERGE CONE1, CONE2, CYLI9
BLEND CONE1, CONE2, 25.4

will cause a 25.4mm radius to be blended between the individual tool paths of CONE1 and CONE2 , during the merging operation. At the intersection between CYLI9 and the other two primitives a fillet determined by the tool radius would be formed in this case.

(b) Allowance for shrinkage Hot forging dies are made oversize to allow for the shrinkage on cooling of the forging after processing. The usual allowance for steel forgings is one-sixtieth. This allowance can be made automatically in the MODCON system by entering a parameter at the start of the particular job. All of the primitive dimensions are then multiplied by an appropriate amount to allow for this estimated shrinkage. The default value for the shrinkage allowance is zero.

(c) Height above the die parting line of the last tool pass. A parameter may be entered at the start of a job called HDPLN, which gives a height above the die parting line below which the cutter is not allowed to go on its last pass. This is particularly useful for generating automatically the flash land on the finishing die electrode if required, although the appropriate width would have to be obtained by choice of a suitable cutter radius. The default value for this parameter is again zero.

Example of Shapes produced by the MODCON System

The MODCON system has been used to produce a wide range of electrode shapes for industrial forgings and castings, including cross arms, connecting rods, lever forgings and malleable iron pipe fittings. Figure 7 shows a lever forging together with the constituent primitives necessary to describe the shape. The spherical element is generated using a CONE primitive with the height, lower radius and edge radius all made equal to each other in the parameter list. Figure 8 shows the list of input instructions necessary for generation of both roughing and finishing N.C. tapes for this shape. The results obtained from these instructions are shown in Figures 9, 10 and 11, which show the rough machined shape, the finish machined shape and a plot of the finishing cut tool paths respectively. The transition surfaces between the elements are determined by the radii of the cutting tools used. Figure 12 shows a malleable iron pipe fitting, together with the constituent primitives necessary to build up the shape of the core for this casting (inside shape). This particular part was processed in two stages using two MERGE commands and the two DUMY primitives. This was necessary because a larger blend radius was required only on the left hand side of the CYLI3 and TORO2 primitives. The instructions necessary to finish machine this shape are as follows:-

```
STARTJOB 1
PARA T1 = 25.4/4.0, T2 = T1, EPS = 0.1, EPSEDG = 0.1
MERGE CYLI2, CYLI3, CYLI4, TORO1, DUMY1
BLEND TORO1, CYLI3, 3.68*25.4
MERGE CYLI1, CYLI2, CYLI3, CYLI4, TORO1, DUMY2
FINISHJOB 150 SECS
```

Figures 13 and 14 show the electrode shape and the tool-paths for this object obtained as a result of these instructions.

Figure 15 shows the electrode shape for an automobile connecting rod forging produced using the MODCON system. The geometric description of this particular object required the definition of 23 primitives in all. Advantage was taken of the symmetry of the forging and one half only was defined, with the complete shape being produced using the mirror imaging capability of the N.C. machine. The output for this particular part contained some 4300 N.C. instructional blocks, which results in a very long paper tape. For this reason the part was processed in two stages on independent jobs - firstly the outside solid shape was processed, followed by the cavities embedded in the big end and connecting piece. In this way two independent N.C. tapes are generated, consisting of approximately 3100 N.C. instructions and 1200 N.C. instructions respectively.

Figures 16 and 17 show the plots of the tool paths to machine the whole connecting rod shape, together with an indication of the primitives necessary to describe the overall object.

Concluding Remarks

The geometric modelling system MODCON has been developed mainly for the N.C. machining of EDM electrodes for the manufacture of dies and moulds, for such items as hot forgings and castings. The approach adopted in other modelling systems, viz (4-6) of defining volumetric modules or primitives which are combined freely to build up the whole object is used. The system differs from previous systems in that the primitive definitions include features such as draft angle, edge radii and fillets that are found commonly in forgings and castings. In addition, cavity, as well as solid, primitives may be defined. This enables an easy to use system, with a simple shape operator to merge the primitives to be developed. In its present form, MODCON is restricted to electrodes and other shapes which can be machined on a 2 1/2 axis N.C. milling machine, but this enables a high proportion of forgings and castings to be processed. A wide range of shapes can be defined and machined using relatively few easy to use input instructions.

REFERENCE

(1) "APT Part Programming", S. Hori, IIT Research Inst., McGraw-Hill (1967).

(2) "Polysurf: An interactive system for the computer-aided design and manufacture of components", A.G. Flutter and R.N. Rolph, Proc. CAD'76 Conf., London, p.150 (1976).

(3) "Numerical control - mathematics and applications", P. Bezier, J. Wiley & Sons (1972).

(4) "Designing with Volumes", I.C. Braid, Cambridge University Press (1973).

(5) "Geometric modelling systems for machine design and manufacture", C.M. Brown, A.A.G. Requiche and H.B. Voelcker, Proc. ACM'78, Annual Conf., Washington D.C. (1978).

(6) "PADL-2 : A Technical Summary", C. M. Brown, IEEE Computer Graphics and Applications (March, 1982).

(7) "A Perspective View of the MODCON System", Y.K. Chan, Proceedings 18th Design Automation Conference, p.179-188, Nashville, Tennessee (1981).

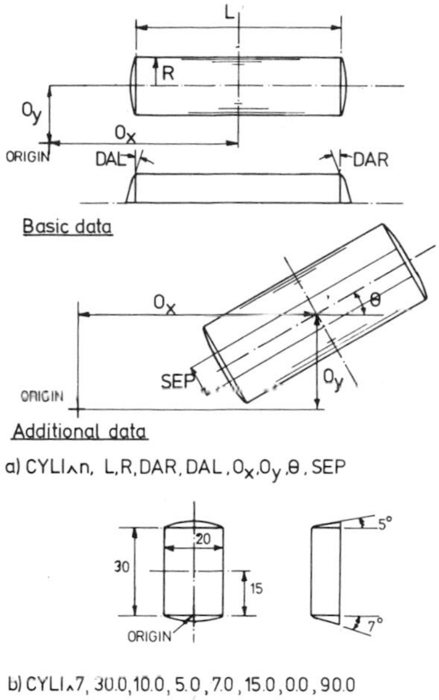

Figure 1(a) Primitive command CYLI and input parameters
1(b) Example of a cylinder using CYLI command

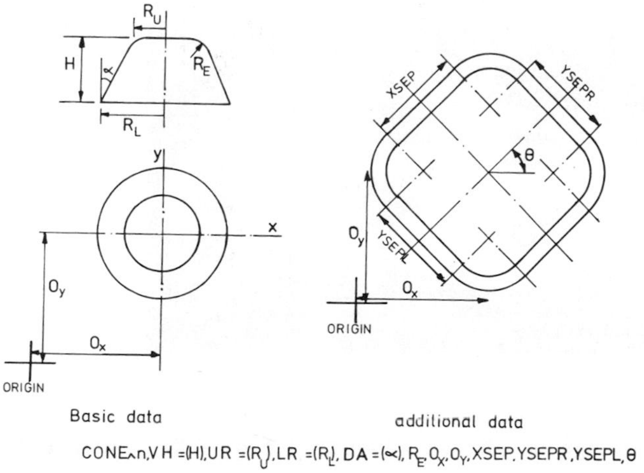

Figure 2 Characteristic data and input statement for primitive command CONE

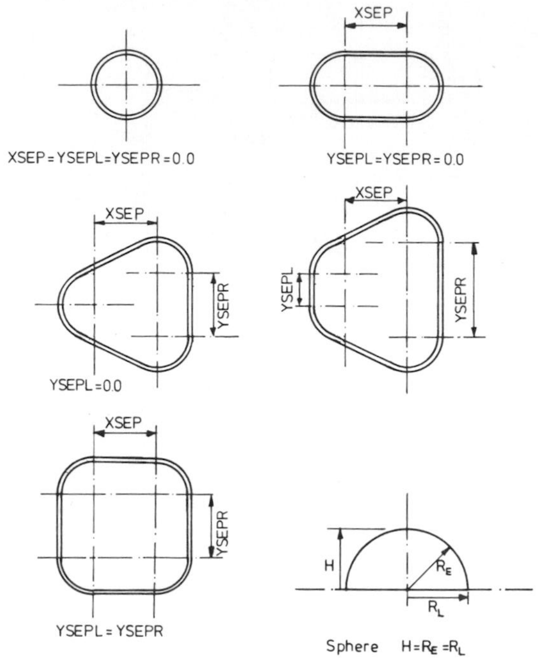

Figure 3 Modifications to the basic shape possible with primitive command CONE

Figure 4 Range of shapes generated from CONE primitive

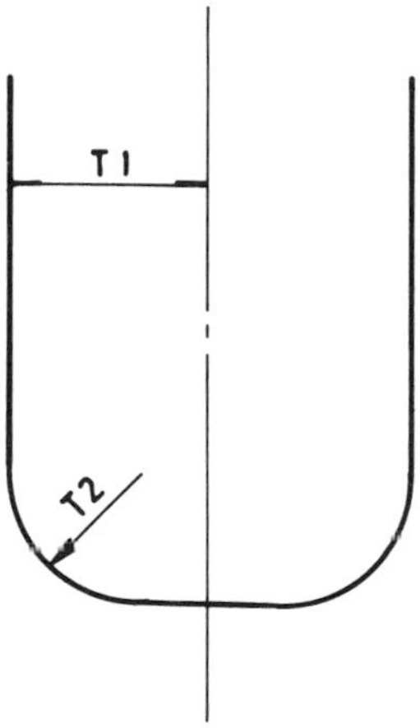

Figure 5.1
A typical cutter

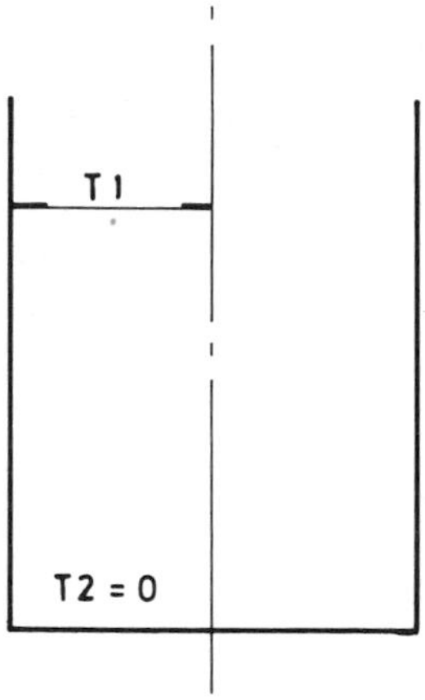

Figure 5.2
An end mill cutter

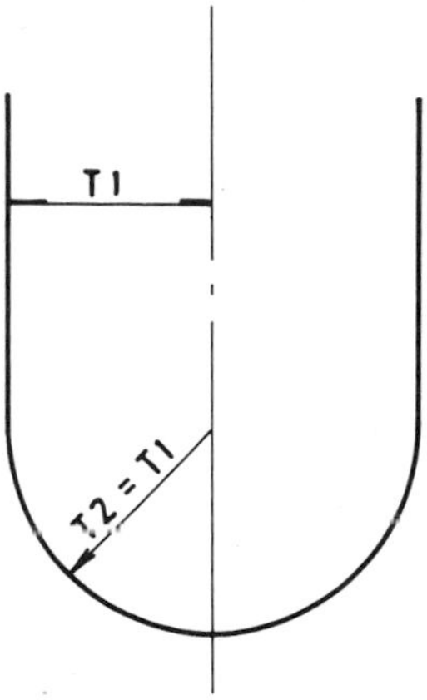

Figure 5.3
A ball ended cutter

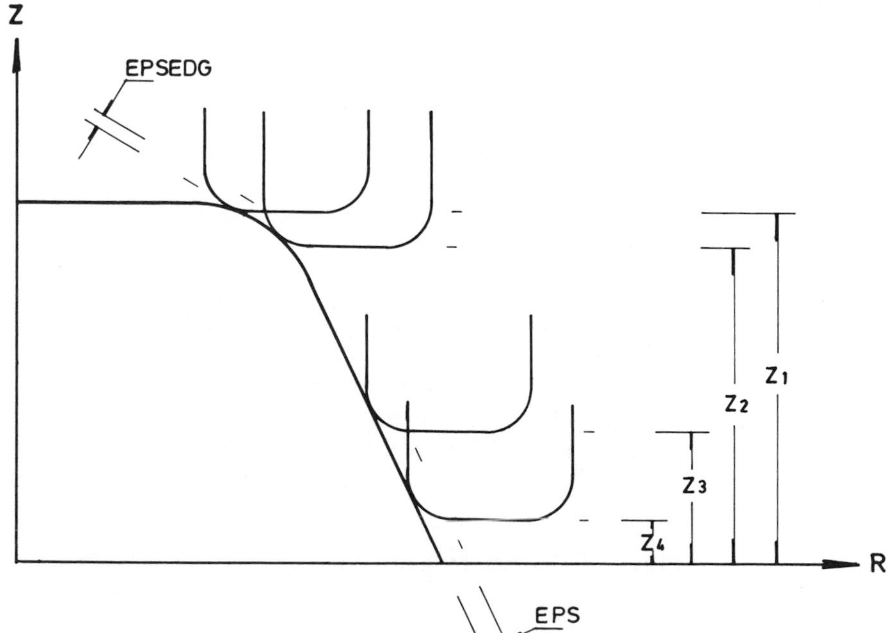

Figure 6 EPS and EPSEDG for an axisymmetric truncated CONE

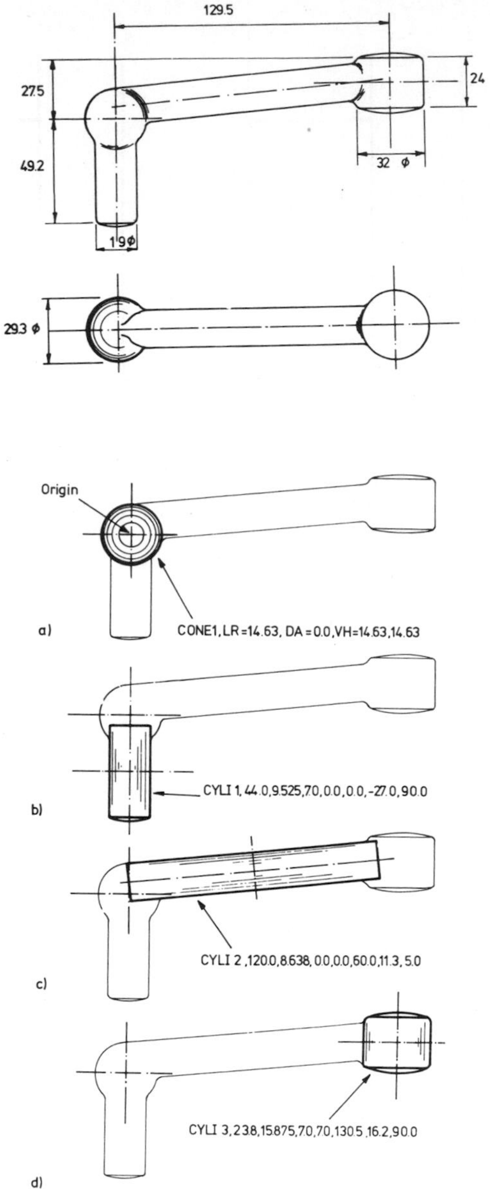

Figure 7 Lever forging and constituent primitives

```
STARTROUGH     1,XBMIN=-60.0,YBMIN=-70.0,XBMAX=200.0,YBMAX=60.0,ZINC=3.0
PARAROUGH      T1=25.4/4.0
MERGEROUGH     CONE1,CYLI1,CYLI2,CYLI3
FINISHROUGH    90SECS

STARTJOB       2
PARA           EPS=0.1,EPSEDG=0.1,T1=25.4/4.0,T2=0.5*T1
MERGE          CONE1,CYLI1,CYLI2,CYLI3
FINISHJOB      200SECS
```

Figure 8 Input data for roughing and finishing cuts for lever forging

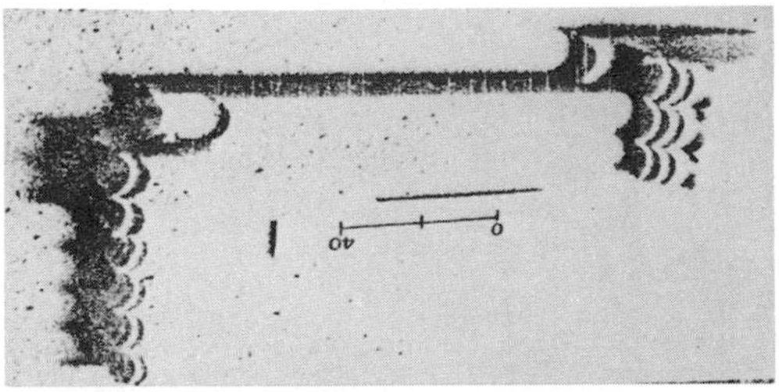

Figure 9 Roughing cuts for lever forging

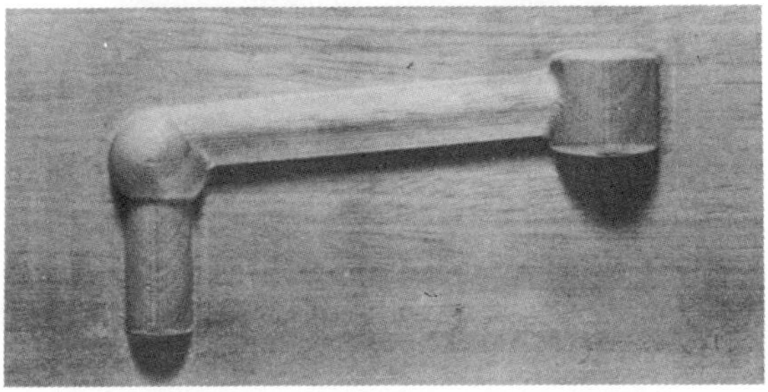

Figure 10 Finished lever forging electrode shape

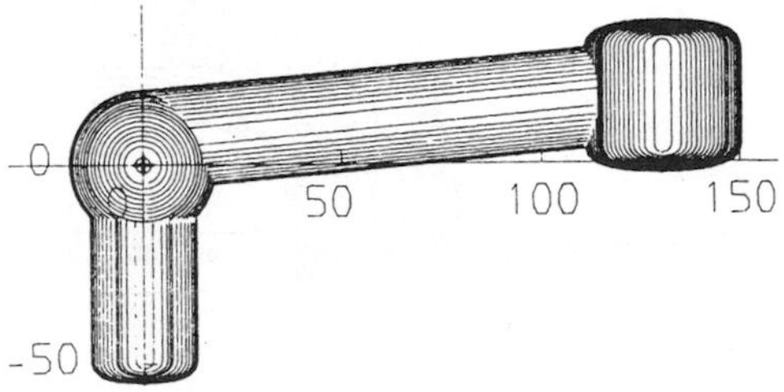

Figure 11 Plot of tool paths for finishing cuts on lever forging electrode

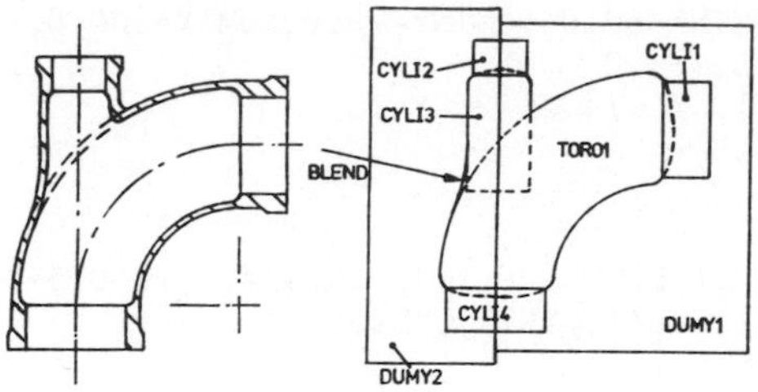

Figure 12 Malleable iron pipe fitting and constituent primitives for inside shape

Figure 13 Electrode shape for pipe fitting core mould

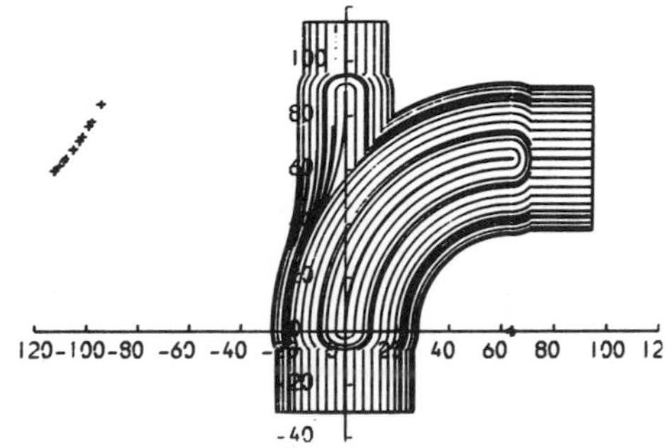

Figure 14 Tool paths of electrode shape for pipe fitting core mould

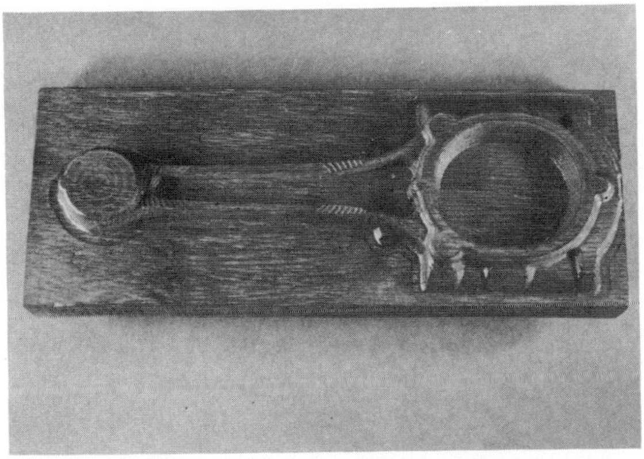

Figure 15 Connecting rod forging electrode shape machined using the MODCON system

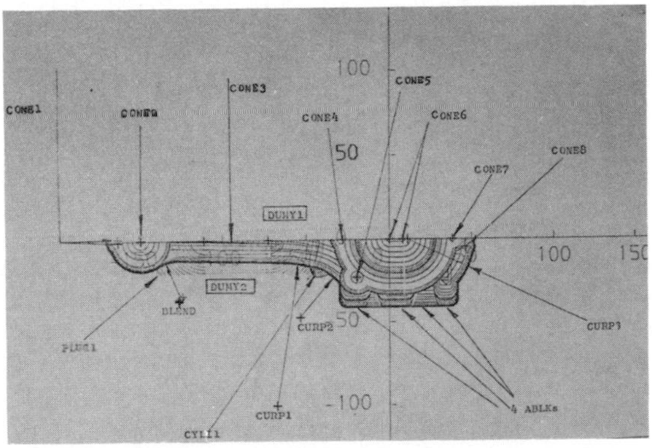

Figure 16 Tool paths for outside shape of connecting rod electrode

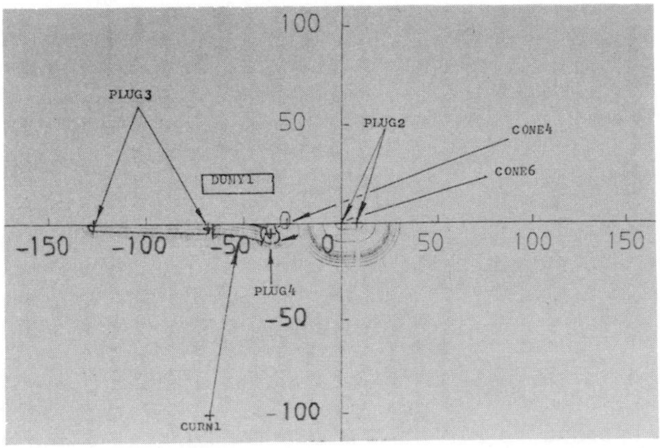

Figure 17 Tool paths for depressions in connecting rod electrode

COMPUTER-AIDED DESIGN OF PUMPS

Willem Jansen
Northern Research and Engineering Corporation
39 Olympia Avenue
Woburn, Massachusetts 01801
U. S. A.

Background

The design of centrifugal pumps has historically been based on experiments with hardware models. The pump geometry that showed the best performance was selected and used for various other applications. In the recent past designers have turned towards analytical methods that have been incorporated into software for batch processing on high-speed computers.

The requirements for centrifugal pumps have become more stringent in terms of power losses, reliability, cost and delivery time. These requirements are often contradictory and can only be resolved through the categoric application of appropriate design and manufacturing technologies. These technologies are multi-facetted and encompass two and three-dimensional fluid mechanics, finite element stress and vibration analyses, cavitation theory, and 5-axis N/C machining. Only Computer-Aided Systems' approach with adequate graphics for quick data assessment promise order-of-magnitude reductions in time and cost for the design and manufacturing of a pump that satisfies these current most stringent requirements.

COMIG - The Pump Design System

The primary developments that have allowed design methods of the future to be available today are interactive processing and display graphics (or simply "interactive graphics"). Their capabilities have given new expressions to the industry such as Computer-Aided Design and Manufacturing CAD/CAM. When applying their capabilities towards the design of pumps, a system such as the NREC COMIG system emerges.

COMIG, which is represented functionally in Figure 1 is an acronym for COMputer interface enhancement through Interactive Graphics. It provides for the detailed design of turbomachinery blading through the integration of many disciplines.

The central core is the data base (containing geometry of blade surfaces, etc.) that is generated during the hydraulics design procedure and can be modified when subjected to FEM stress and N/C machining analyses such that an acceptable compromise geometry is generated. Thus, the engineer can direct the flow of calculations to the modules that surround the data base. In this way the effect of a geometry modification made in one module can be assessed by entering the others.

COMIG is an extremely "friendly" system; that is, simple for the designer to use, even if he is not an expert computer analyst. When proper engineering judgment is applied, the resultant designs will be both efficient and reliable and capable of being documented and taken to prototype hardware rapidly. Figures 2a and 2b show excerpts of typical interactive commands.

Detail Design Philosophy

The detail design philosophy of COMIG embodies an iterative approach. That is, the designer sequentially modifies the blade geometry seeking to obtain optimal performance (in terms of efficiency and cavitation) while satisfying the requirements for mechanical integrity and manufacturing ease. In the centrifugal pump industry one distinguishes between a main pump impeller, where the fluid obtains its high pressure and an inducer where a small pressure is achieved at low speed to avoid cavitation. Both types of pump can be analyzed.

There are two major geometric factors affecting pump inducer and impeller performance: the shape of the pressure and suction surfaces of the blading, and the contours of the hub and shroud. That performance is determined primarily by the boundary-layer behavior, the extent of any separated flow regions, the intensity of the secondary flows and the minimum pressure occurring in the impeller to avoid cavitation. In general the designer uses velocity distribution along the blade surfaces to control boundary layer separation and flow losses, while he inspects pressure distributions along these surfaces to avoid cavitation. Nevertheless, it is through the manipulation of the blade geometry that the designer affects the velocity and pressure distributions and ultimately the performance of the design.

In particular, the effect on velocity distributions is considered most conveniently through the "loading diagram." The term loading applies loosely to the distribution of work or angular momentum along the blade camberline, and is a measure of the difference between the pressure and suction surface velocities as shown on such a loading diagram.

The iterative approach maintains flexibility by including the designer as an integral part of the design procedure. It both relies on and benefits from the skill and experience of the designer to produce a consistent standard of design for a wide variety of applications. For example, between two iterations he could run the blade vibration analysis to assure himself that the current blade will not exhibit any resonance problems.

The COMIG system can analyze any blade surface, whether it is cupped or rippled. However for purposes of ease of manufacturing, the blades are made to consist of straight lines. This allows the use of flank cutting with 5-axis N/C machines (Fig 3). It introduces a slight restriction, since now only three camberlines can be specified from loading considerations. The remaining blade geometry follows from the straight line specification. However, this restriction causes minimal loss in performance, in practice, while it improves the manufacturing process by order of magnitudes. For example the times to cut wheels with point milling or flank milling are 10 hrs and 45 min respectively.

A Sample Case

Specifications

The COMIG system was applied to an advanced pump, which had been designed a few years ago with a similar hydraulic analysis. Thus the sample is a recreation of the actual design, shown in Figures 13 and 14.

The pump is used as a fire fighting unit on board ships and oil drilling platforms. Thus, while standing on a deck it must be capable of drawing water from a level seven meters lower and provide discharge heads up to 125 meters. Moreover the pump was to be lightweight at less than 40 kilos. The volume flow is between 7000 and 11,000 liters per minute. The suction head and discharge pressure specifications lead to contradictory design rules. The required suction head depresses the inlet pressure to such levels that any appreciable flow velocity will drop the water pressure below its vapor pressure and cavitation which causes damage to the internal pump surface to occur. Thus at the inlet the flows must be kept slow. However, to achieve the high pressure at the discharge, the impeller must be rotating fast. Consequently, the inlet and discharge function must be separated with the inlet section (inducer) running at a slow speed of 2000 rpm, to achieve a low head rise without cavitation and the main pump running at 6000 rpm. The inducer and main pump are geared together, both driven by a 250 hp gas turbine. In the following, the inducer design, being the more interesting is given from start to finish.

Preliminary Designs

Preparatory to using the COMIG system for detailed design of the blading, the impeller's main dimensions have to be determined first. The NREC performance prediction program for pumps, PREDP (see Ref 2), was used for this purpose. PREDP utilizes a flow analysis with empirical loss formulations to predict discharge pressure and efficiency as a function of flow and rotative speed.

By generating various plots which indicate how design-point efficiency and geometry interact, the principal dimensions of the pump inducer were established from PREDP as:

Hub inlet diameter	=	53 mm
Shroud inlet diameter	=	230 mm
Hub exit diameter	=	188 mm
Shroud exit diameter	=	230 mm
Inducer length	=	190 mm

This inducer is thus an axial flow machine. The inducer length may be shorter at the hub or shroud than given above, subject to the flow analysis. The blade at the shroud and hub will be determined from hydraulic analyses in COMIG to take into account radial equilibrium of the flow between hub and shroud.

Detailed Blading Design

The steps in the detailed design of the inducer blading are described below:

1. The COMIG preprocessor is used to initially prepare the input file for the specification of blade geometry. The preprocessor contains many features to simplify input preparation, including an extensive series of prompts and help messages, digitizing and previewing capabilities for tabular data.

   A very brief excerpt from the interactive preparation of input is shown in Figure 2. It illustrates the prompting style of the preprocessor with response underlined, as well as the significant help available to the user on request.

   The β distribution at the shroud, where β is the slope of camberline, is an important element in specifying the shape of the pressure and suction surfaces. However, when starting a design such a distribution is not known. Nevertheless the designer usually knows what type of loading distribution he wants, and for this purpose he can use the PRELOD subset. PRELOD is one dimensional and must be checked later with the full set analysis.

   In the PRELOD subset of the preprocessor, a distribution at the shroud is calculated which corresponds to a prescribed blade loading. Since designers vary in their loading preferences, a number of different loadings are available to choose among: "optimum," linear, double-linear, and general. An optimum loading was chosen by the designer for the pump inducer with the resulting preliminary β distribution at the shroud (Fig 4) calculated by PRELOD. Figure 4 also shows the final values for β .

2. Next, with the input file prepared in Step 1, the geometric construction of the blading is conducted.

   This construction, as indicated in Figure 1, is conducted in the SPECIG module of the computing system. It provides information necessary for subsequent flow and mechanical analyses, manufacturing and finally inspection.

   A camberline with linearly tapered thicknesses from hub to shroud, is used to construct blading whose surfaces are formed by straight line elements.

3. The results of Step 2 (geometric construction of the blading) are examined interactively in the preprocessor, utilizing the COMIG Graphics Library.

   Both the 3D wire-frame graphics and the 2D plotting capabilities of the Graphics Library are used to examine the SPECIG results. As shown in Figure 5 the wire-frame graphics can present several views of the pump inducer blading together (as a mechanical drawing), or a single view at any arbitrary angle and magnification (as if one were holding the blade). In either case, the straight-line elements comprising the blades are readily apparent. Further as shown in Figure 6, one may view the blade passage rather than the blade itself.

4. Based upon the examination of Step 3, the designer may choose to proceed with a flow analysis, or return to modify the input file of Step 1 and reconstruct the blading.

   In the case of the pump inducer, with an experienced user, the design proceeded to the flow analysis.

5. The preprocessor is re-entered to assembly the input file for the flow analysis.

   This input file combines a specification of the operating conditions and other quantities needed to obtain a solution, with the previously constructed blade geometry.

6. With the input file prepared in Step 5, the flow analysis is conducted.

   The flow analysis, as indicated in Figure 1, is conducted in the BANIG module of the computing system. BANIG utilizes a quasi-3D flow analysis, consisting of (1) a two-dimensional streamline curvature analysis in the meridional plane, and (2) superimposed blade-to-blade analyses.

   In the streamline curvature analysis, the usual flow normals are replaced by quasinormals. These quasinormals, which are located at the discretion of the designer, lead to more informative and better-behaved numerical solutions.

   For the blade-to-blade solution, two analyses have been provided. There is an approximate analysis, which was used throughout the iterative design process for the pump inducer. A more exact finite-difference blade-to-blade analysis was utilized only when the iterative process approached its conclusion, to increase the confidence level in the predicted loadings.

7. The results of Step 6 (flow analysis) are examined interactively in the postprocessor utilizing the 2D plotting capability of the Graphics library.

   The 2D plotting capability provides for the automatic generation of 19 assorted plots from SPECIG and BANIG, without any user input necessary. However, if desired, the user is able to modify any of the plot parameters and to create custom plots, using any two variables in the plot file. In addition, there is an overlay capability, which the designer can utilize to directly compare the results of any two design iterations.

   As indicated in the design philosophy, attention in the flow analysis focuses on the velocity distributions in the passage. Of particular importance is the blade loading at the shroud. Figure

6 shows the actual pressure distribution obtained from the flow analysis of the blade geometry as modified from PRELOD. It shows that the blade surface is excellent at the entrance, maintaining the suction surface pressure well above the vapor pressure, thus avoiding cavitation. However, due to the length restriction, there is considerable loading at around 60 percent along the camberline and the analysis indicates negative pressures. At this point, the designer decided that he could have more blades and started new blades (splitters) at that point. This reduces the loading by a factor of two and raised the pressure above the vapor pressure.

8. Steps 1 through 7 are repeated as the blade geometry is systematically altered, until a satisfactory flow analysis is obtained.

   In the case of the pump inducer, only three iterations of the initial design were required to obtain a satisfactory flow analysis. As obtained utilizing the 2D overlay capability, Figure 6 provides a comparison between the initial and final pressure distributions, while Figure 8 shows that for the blade velocities at the shroud. It can be seen that the final design with the splitters eliminates the negative pressures near the middle of the camberline, and does not allow diffusion on the suction, or trailing surface until maximum loading is achieved.

   To check the off-design operation of the pump, other flows and speeds can be run. Figures 9 and 10 show the pressure distribution at 80 percent flow and speed respectively. Due to the incidence, low pressure and severe cavitation problems occur at the leading edge. Thus operation at those conditions should be avoided.

9. Once a satisfactory flow analysis has been obtained, the postprocessor is used to create a finite-element mesh for the blading and prepare an input file for subsequent mechanical analysis.

   Utilizing the 3D wire-frame graphics, Figure 11 illustrates the mesh which was automatically generated for the blading of the inducer pump.

10. With the input file prepared in Step 9, interfacing software is utilized to conduct finite-element vibration and, if necessary, stress analysis of the blading.

    Input files can be prepared in the postprocessors for either the ANSYS, NASTRAN (Ref 3), SUPERB (Ref 5) finite element programs.

11. If the mechanical analysis is unsatisfactory, the blading must be redesigned and Steps 1 through 10 repeated. Otherwise, the designer can proceed to the documentation and inspection of his design.

    Input files are available in COMIG to interface with both the Computervision and Applicon CAD/CAM systems for computerized mechanical drawings and other facilities they offer. Further, there are input files in COMIG to define the blading for the MAX5, APT, and COMPACT II numerical-control machining languages. No further instructions are needed for MAX5 (Ref 6) since it will automatically machine the pump inducer. APT and COMPACT II are generalized programs which require extensive N/C programming to arrive at final N/C machining instructions. Once the impeller is machined, the hardware can be inspected using an output data file from COMIG.

Conclusions

The design of both the pump inducer and main impeller was conducted on the NREC computing facilities, as represented in Figure 12. With the availability of a 5-axis machine, prototype hardware could have been produced within two weeks of the design request. Figure 13 shows the entire pump flow path while Figure 14 shows the pump in action.

References

1. An Interactive Graphics System for the Design of Centrifugal Machinery (NREC Report Nos. 1419-1 and 2), Northern Research and Engineering Corporation, Woburn, Massachusetts, 1981.

2. Program PREDP (NREC Report No. 1437-1), Northern Research and Engineering Corporation, Woburn, Massachusetts, 1981.

3. McCormick, Calib W., ed., MSC/NASTRAN User's Manual, MSC/NASTRAN Version 61, MSR-39, Macneal-Schwendler Corporation, Los Angeles, CA, February, 1981.

4. DeSalvo, G. J. and Swanson, J. A., ANSYS, Engineering Analysis System User's Manual, Volume I, Swanson Analysis Systems, Inc., Houston, Pennsylvania, 1979.

5. Mechanical Design Library = SUPERB, Part IV: User Information Manual, Control Data Corporation, Minneapolis, Minnesota, 1978.

6. Automated N/C Machining of Radial Turbomachinery (NREC Proposal No. 950-635), Northern Research and Engineering Corporation, Woburn, Massachusetts.

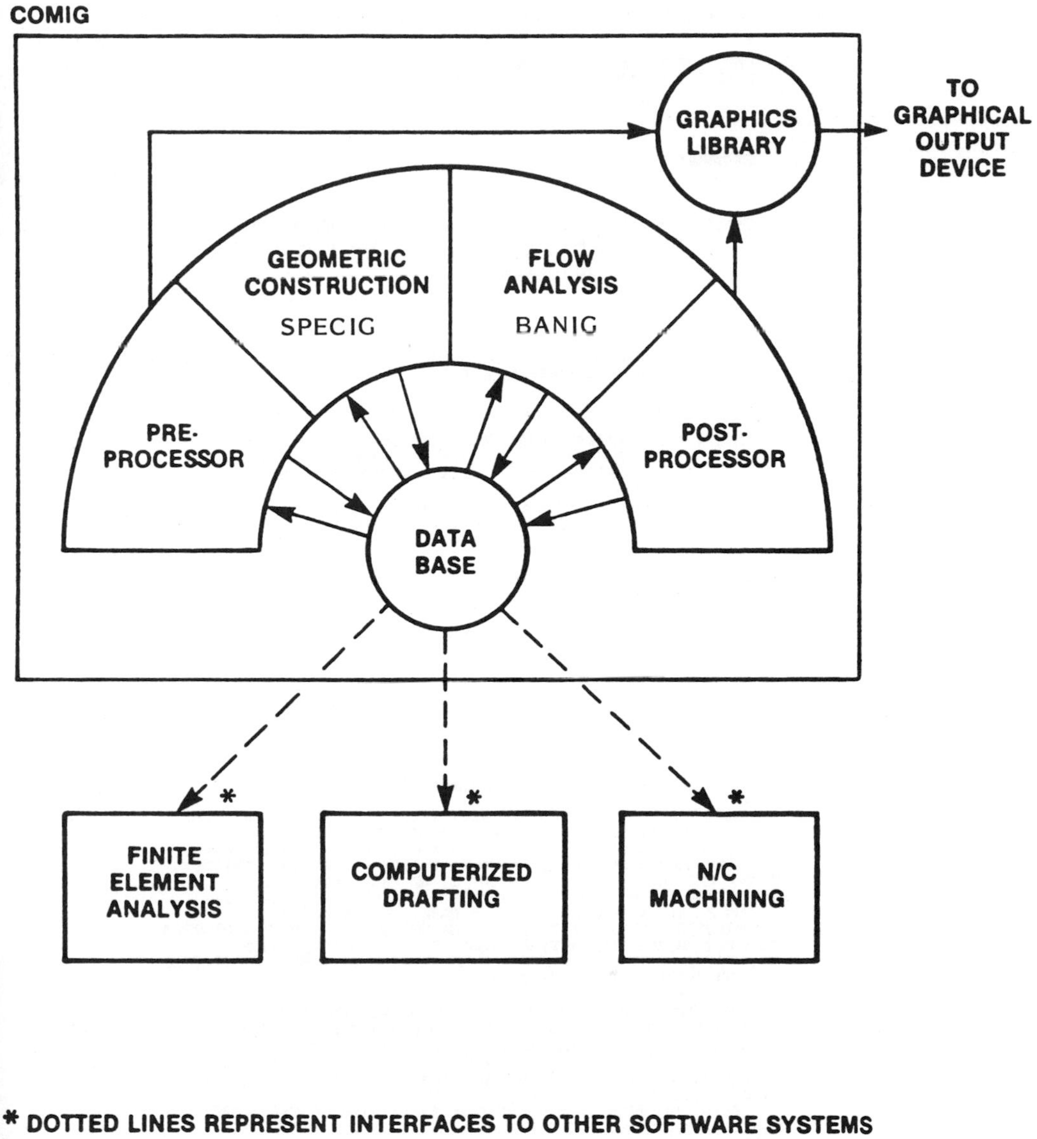

FIGURE 1 FUNCTIONAL REPRESENTATION OF THE COMIG PUMP DESIGN SYSTEM

```
*** WELCOME TO THE SPECIG INPUT DATA PROCESSING SECTION     ***

    TYPE " ? " FOR COMMAND HELP
    TYPE " H " FOR DETAILED HELP ANY TIME


    COMMAND:

GO
--
    ENTER: A DESCRIPTIVE STATEMENT (THIS MUST NOT BE OMITTED)
           THIS STATEMENT IDENTIFIES THIS RUN OF SPECIG AND
           WILL APPEAR AS THE TITLE ON ALL SPECIG RUNS.
           (MAX. OF 60 CHARACTERS),

PUMP INDUCER
------------
    ENTER: 0 FOR 2-D AND 3-D GRAPHICAL OUTPUT
           1 FOR NO GRAPHICAL OUTPUT

1
-
    ENTER: 1 FOR RADIAL BLADE SPECIFICATION
           3 IF ORIENTATIONS OF STRAIGHT LINE ELEMENTS ARE
             SPECIFIED AT THE SHROUD CONTOUR BY ALPHA-Z AND
             ALPHA-THETA DATA
           5 IF ORIENTATIONS OF STRAIGHT LINE ELEMENTS ARE
             SPECIFIED BY BLADE ANGULAR COORDINATES AT BOTH
             THE HUB AND SHROUD CONTOURS

HELP
----
```

FIGURE 2a TYPICAL INTERACTIVE COMMANDS

```
        *** ORIENTATION OF STRAIGHT-LINE ELEMENTS ***

    THE SPECIFICATION OF THE ORIENTATION OF THE STRAIGHT-LINE
ELEMENTS IS ESTABLISHED BY THE VALUE OF THIS INDICATOR.
THE FUNDAMENTAL PRINCIPLE IN THE BLADE CONSTRUCTION IS THAT
THE MEAN CAMBER SURFACE WILL HAVE STRAIGHT-LINE GENERATRICES.
IF THE DESIGNER ELECTS TO ENTER: 3, HE MUST KNOW AT THE
OUTSET THE DESIRED DISTRIBUTION OF LINE-ELEMENT ORIENTATION
(ALPHA-Z, ALPHA-THETA).  IN THIS CASE, THE REQUIRED
DISTRIBUTION IS SPECIFIED ALONG THE SHROUD CONTOUR. THE PROGRAM
THEN DETERMINES THE INTERSECTIONS OF THE LINES OF KNOWN
ORIENTATION WITH THE SURFACE OF REVOLUTION OBTAINED BY ROTATING
THE HUB CONTOUR ABOUT ITS AXIS.

    THE SECOND METHOD OF SPECIFYING THE BLADING (ENTER: 5), IS
FOR THE DESIGNER TO SPECIFY THE SHROUD AND HUB CONTOURS AND
THEIR RESPECTIVE ANGULAR COORDINATES OR BLADE ANGLES.  THE
ORIENTATION OF EACH BLADE ELEMENT IS THEN DETERMINED INTERNALLY
BY THE PROGRAM BY REQUIRING THAT EACH STRAIGHT-LINE ELEMENT
PASS THROUGH EACH OF THREE SPACE CURVES.
    THIS INDICATOR IS ALSO USED IN SPECIFYING IF THE BLADE
UNDER CONSIDERATION IS A RADIAL BLADE.  IF THE BLADE IS A
RADIAL BLADE, ENTER: 1.

    ENTER: 1 FOR RADIAL BLADE SPECIFICATION
           3 IF ORIENTATIONS OF STRAIGHT LINE ELEMENTS ARE
             SPECIFIED AT THE SHROUD CONTOUR BY ALPHA-Z AND
             ALPHA-THETA DATA
           5 IF ORIENTATIONS OF STRAIGHT LINE ELEMENTS ARE
             SPECIFIED BY BLADE ANGULAR COORDINATES AT BOTH
             THE HUB AND SHROUD CONTOURS

3
-
```

FIGURE 2b TYPICAL INTERACTIVE COMMANDS

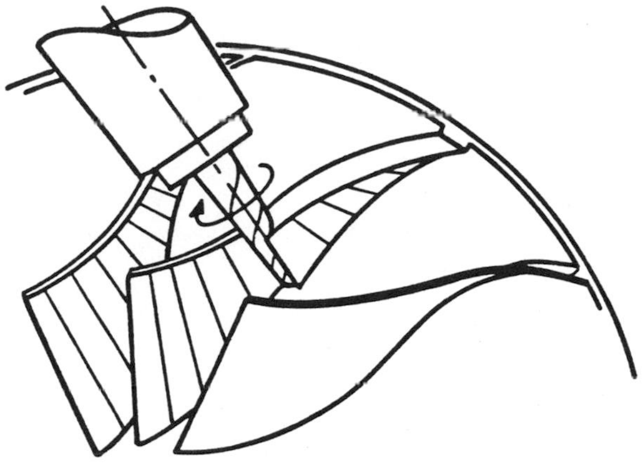

FIGURE 3 BLADE MANUFACTURING BY MILLING WITH CUTTER FLANKS. STRAIGHT-LINE BLADE ELEMENT CONSTRUCTION ALLOWS FLANK MILLING, THUS REDUCING MACHINING TIME BY AN ORDER OF MAGNITUDE COMPARED TO POINT MILLING.

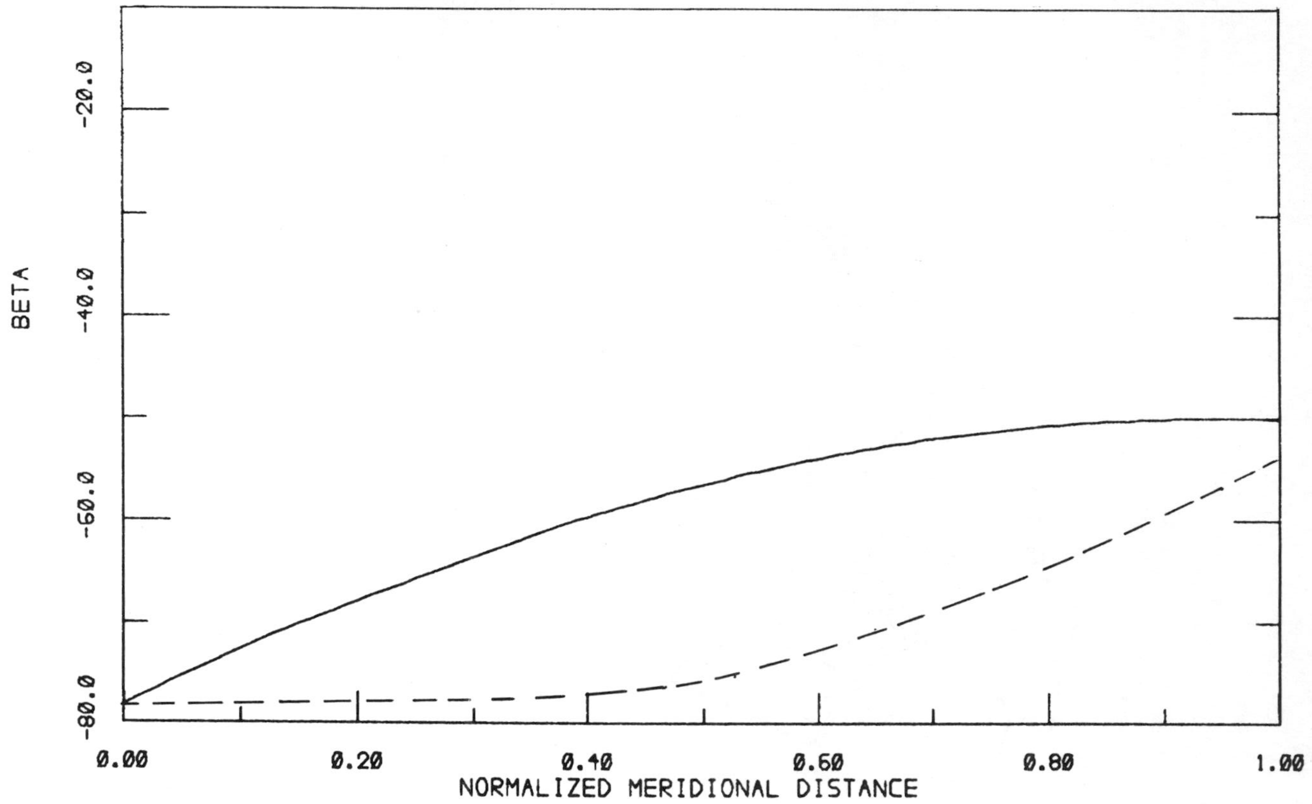

FIGURE 4 COMPARISON OF BLADE ANGLE DISTIRBUTION OF TWO RUNS. INITIAL RUN (FULL LINE) WAS DONE TO OBTAIN RANGE OF ANGLE. LATER RUN (BROKEN LINE) REFINES THE BLADE SHAPE FOR OPTIMAL PERFORMANCE.

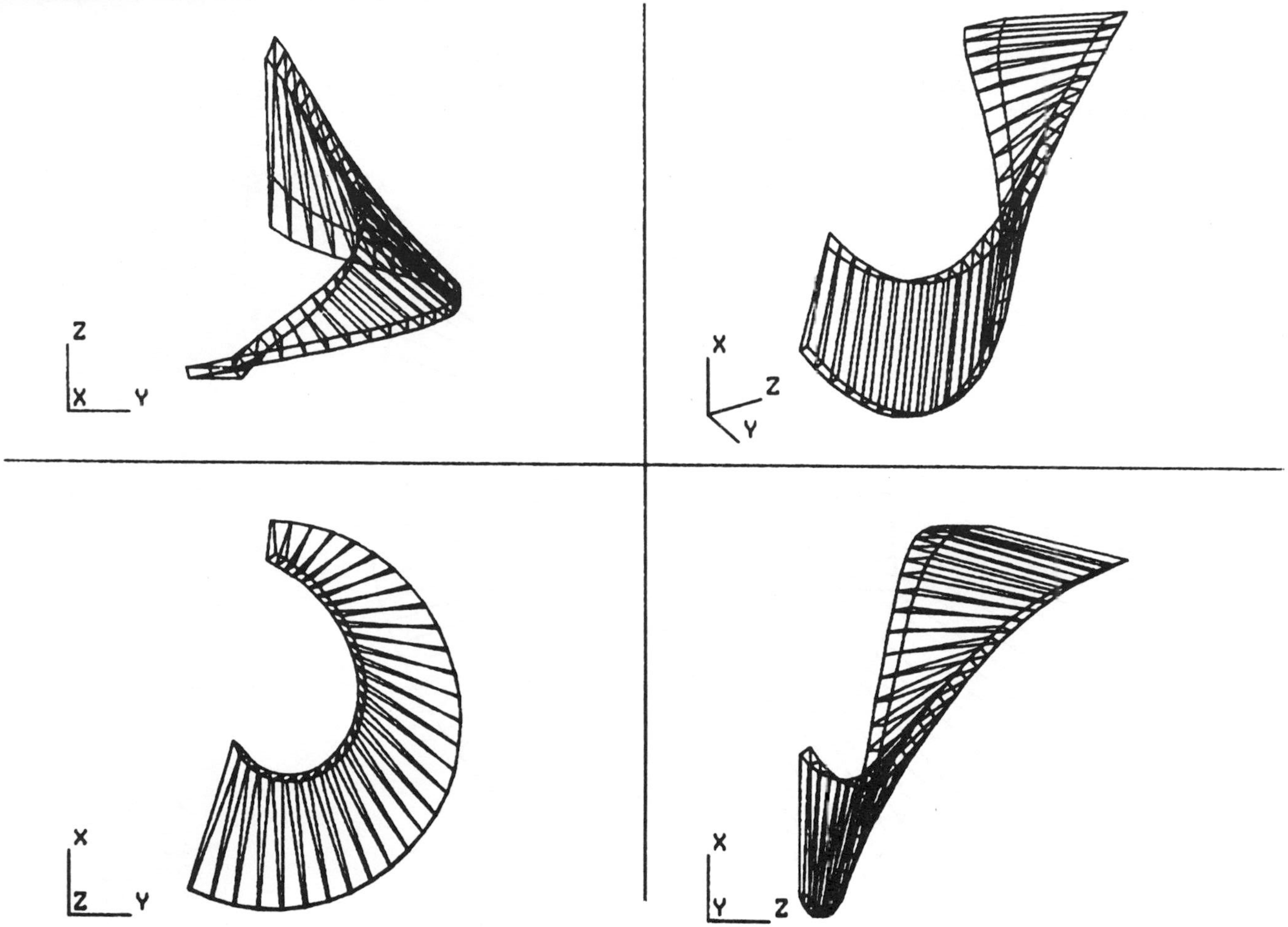

FIGURE 5 FOUR DIFFERENT VIEWS OF THE BLADE. THE SYSTEM ALLOWS FOR ROTATION, ZOOM AND PLOTTING OF THESE SECTIONS.

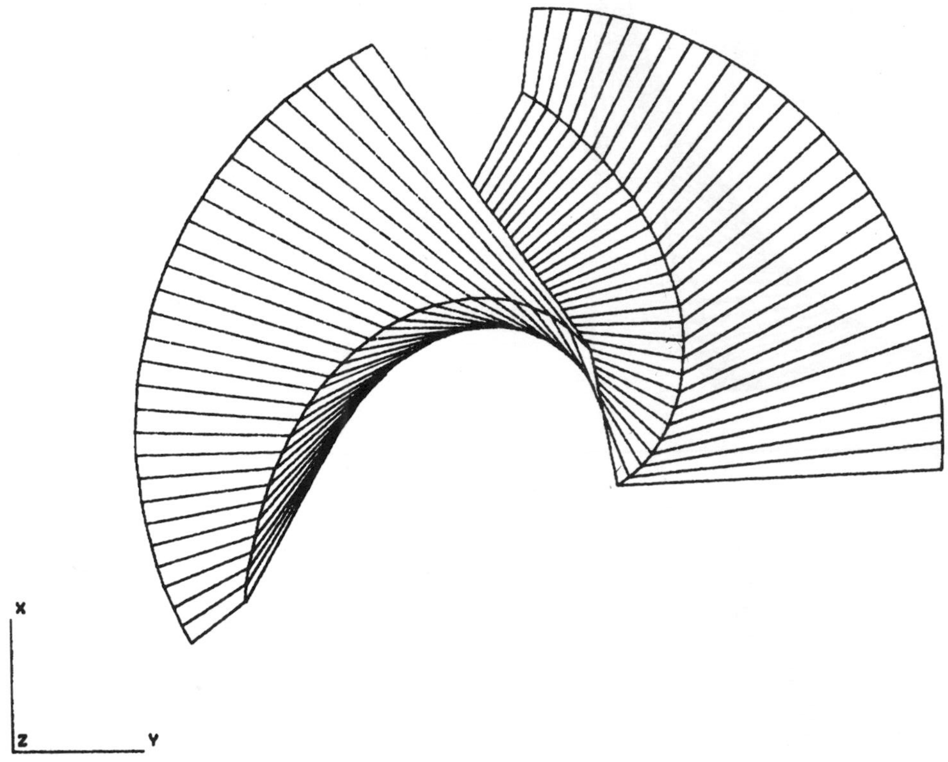

FIGURE 6 BLADE PASSAGE FORMED BY TWO ADJACENT BLADES. NOTE THAT HIDDEN-LINE REMOVAL IS IN EFFECT FOR IMPROVED CLARITY.

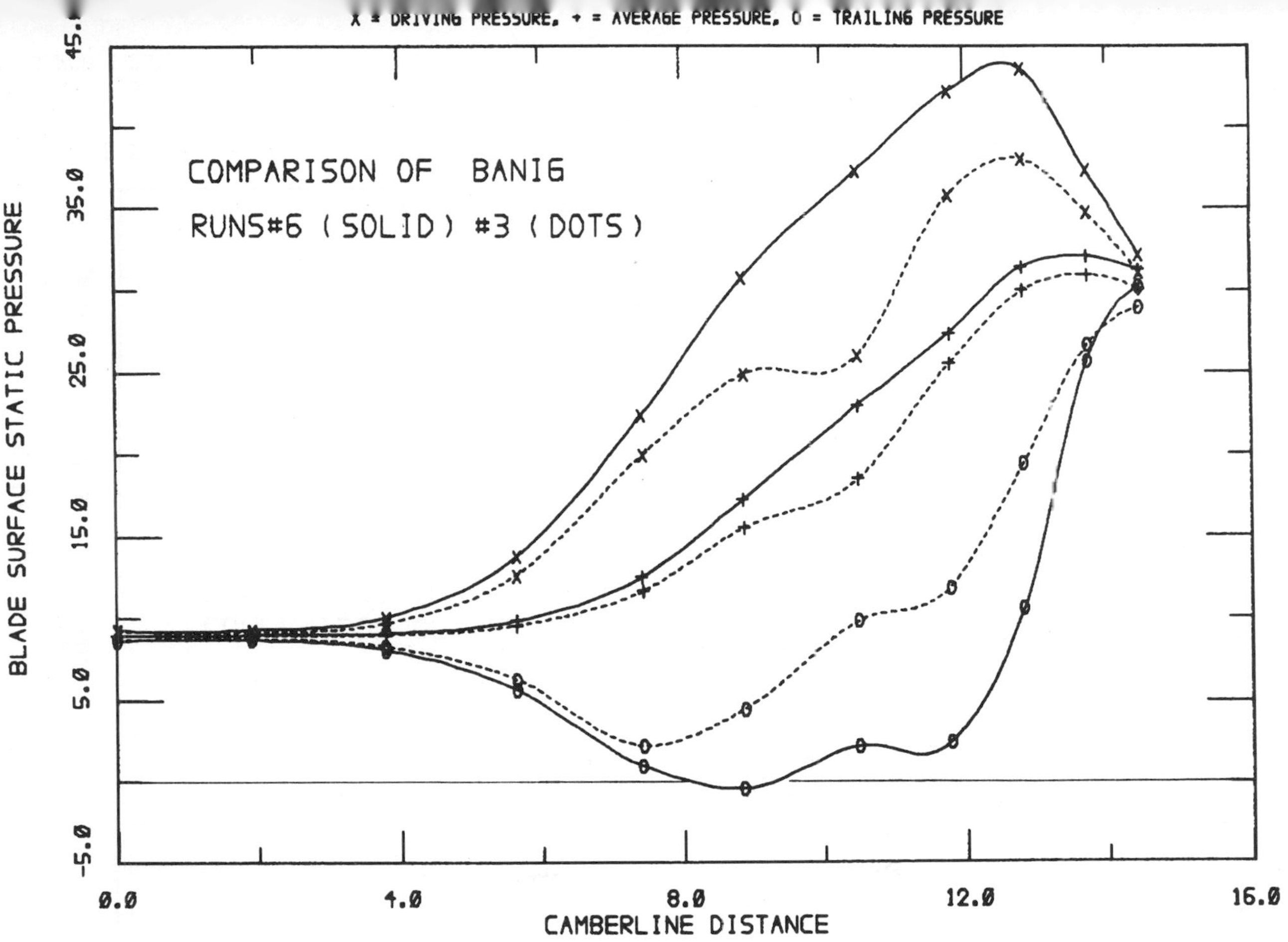

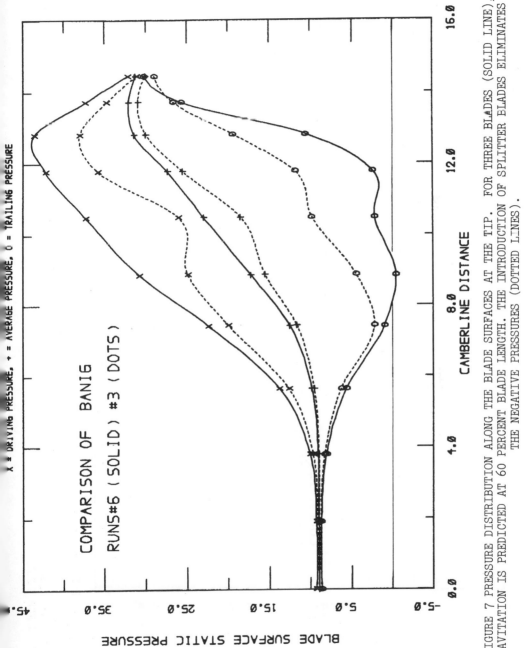

FIGURE 7 PRESSURE DISTRIBUTION ALONG THE BLADE SURFACES AT THE TIP. FOR THREE BLADES (SOLID LINE), CAVITATION IS PREDICTED AT 60 PERCENT BLADE LENGTH. THE INTRODUCTION OF SPLITTER BLADES ELIMINATES THE NEGATIVE PRESSURES (DOTTED LINES).

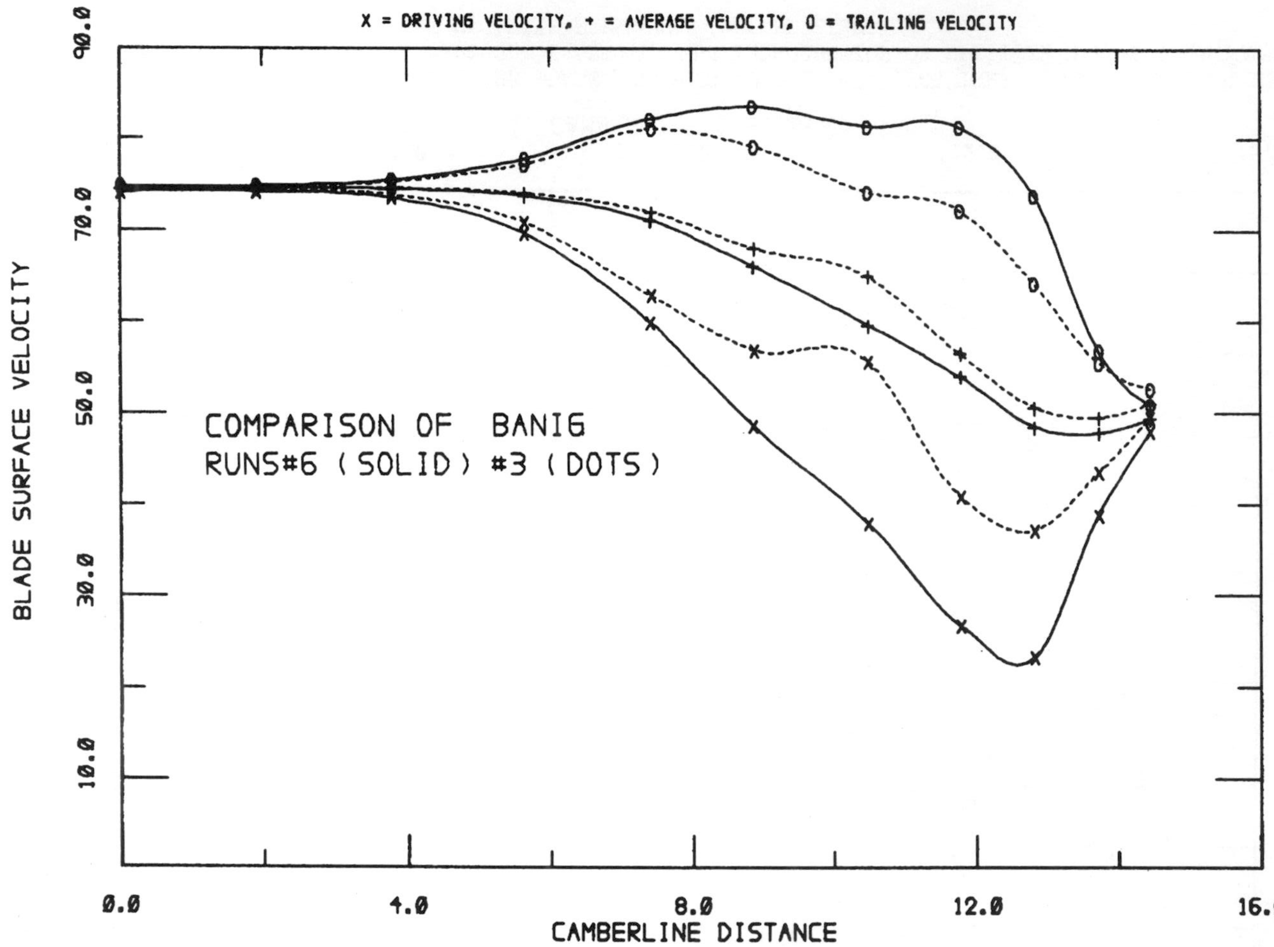

FIGURE 8 RELATIVE VELOCITY DISTRIBUTION ALONG THE BLADE SURFACES AT THE TIP. (SOLID FOR THREE BLADES, DOTTED FOR THREE BLADES AND THREE SPLITTER BLADES.) VELOCITY DROP ON SUCTION SIDE IS LESS FOR THE SPLITTER CASE, THUS INCREASING EFFICIENCY.

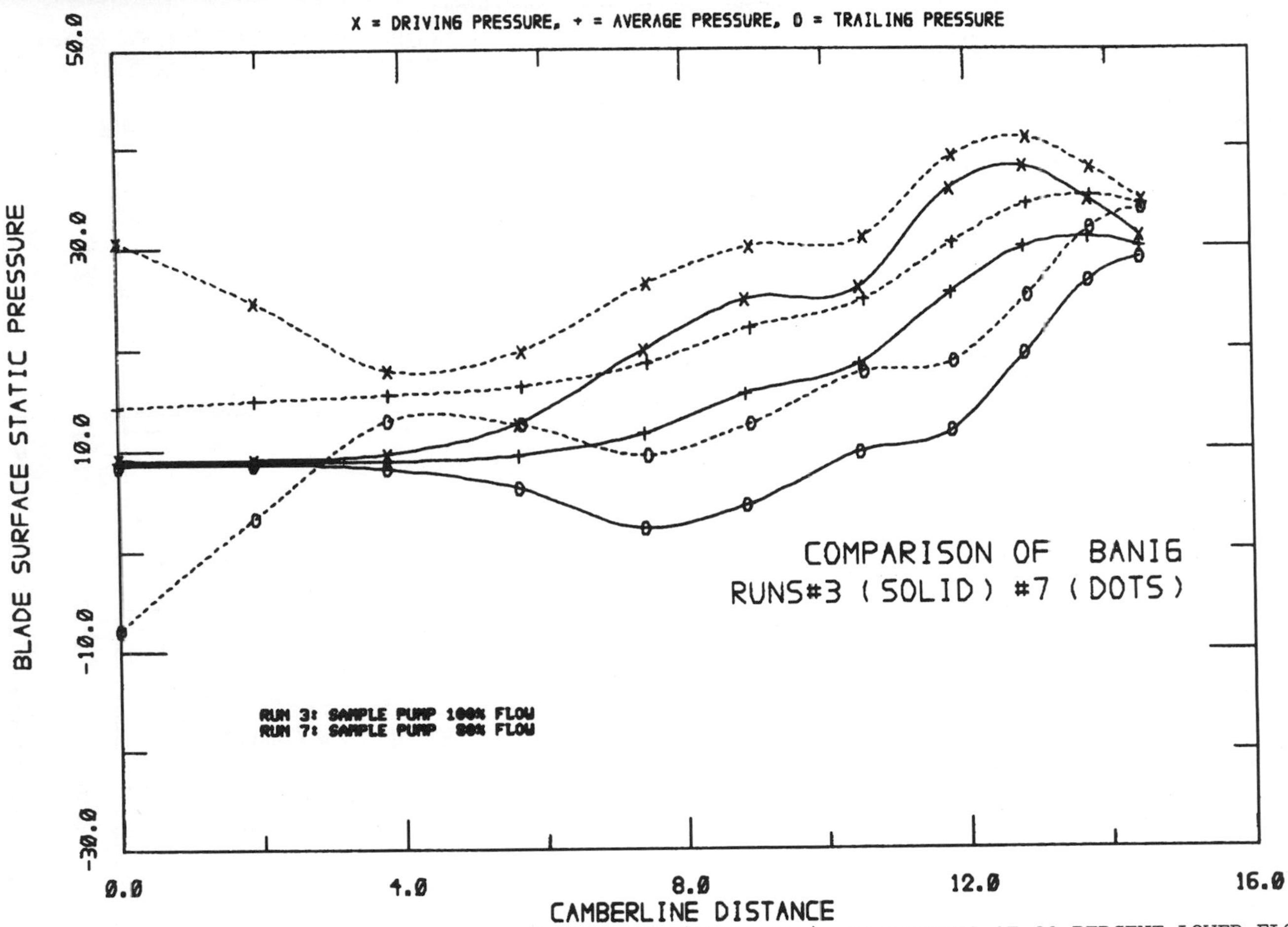

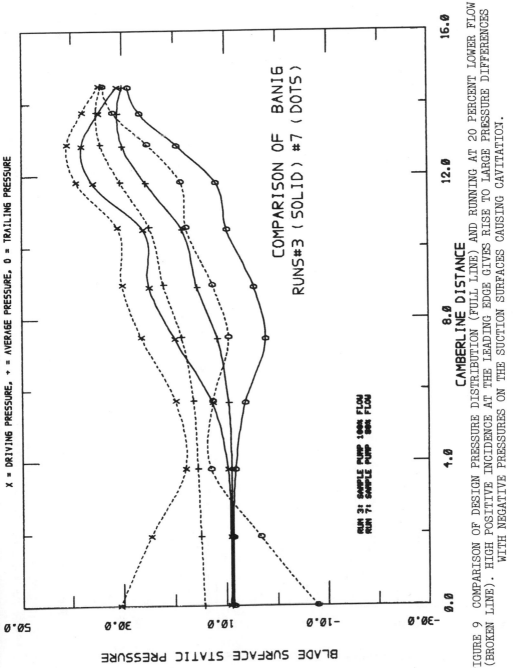

FIGURE 9 COMPARISON OF DESIGN PRESSURE DISTRIBUTION (FULL LINE) AND RUNNING AT 20 PERCENT LOWER FLOW (BROKEN LINE). HIGH POSITIVE INCIDENCE AT THE LEADING EDGE GIVES RISE TO LARGE PRESSURE DIFFERENCES WITH NEGATIVE PRESSURES ON THE SUCTION SURFACES CAUSING CAVITATION.

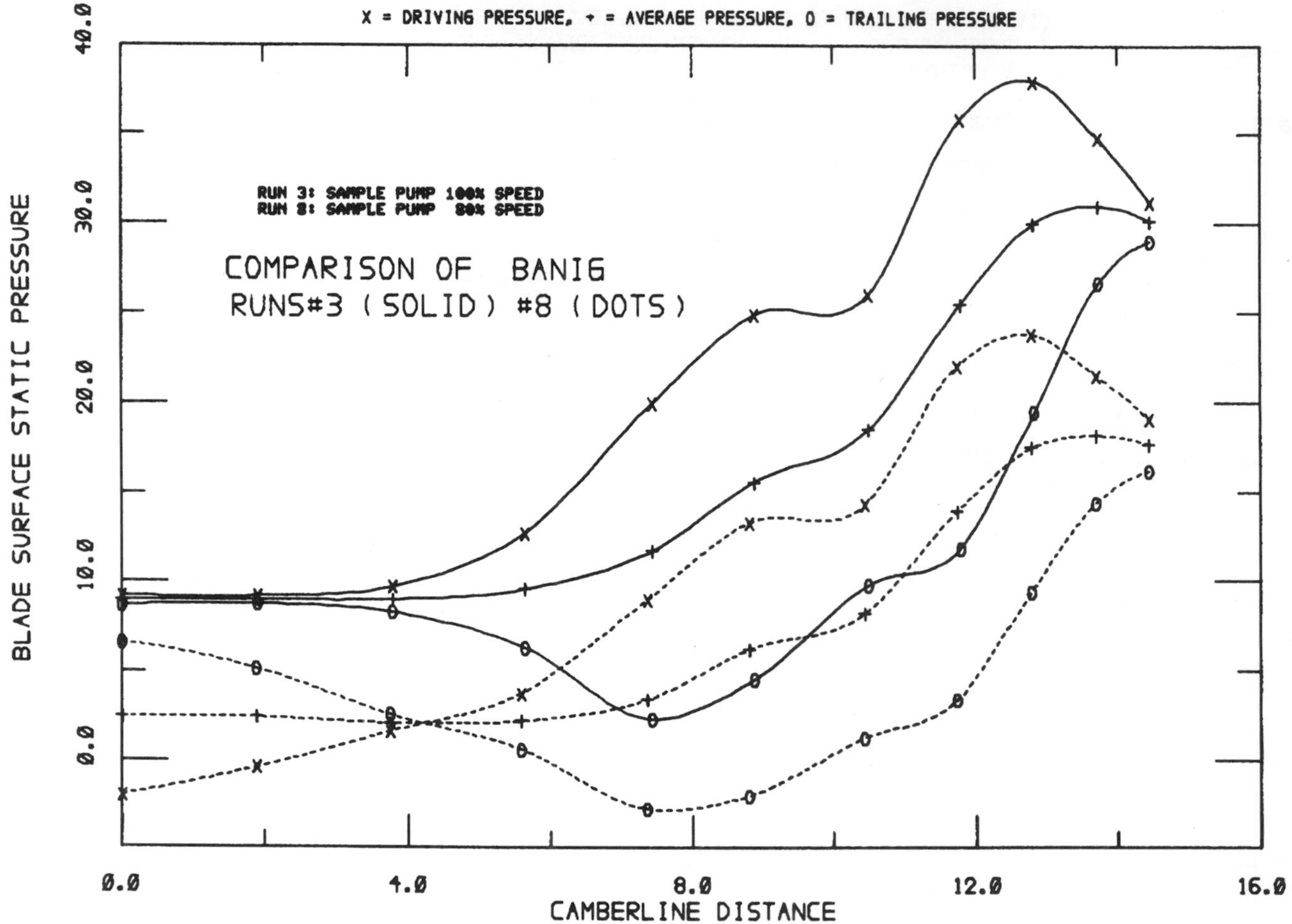

FIGURE 10 COMPARISON OF DESIGN PRESSURE DISTRIBUTION (FULL LINE) AND FUNNING AT 20 PERCENT LOWER SPEED (BROKEN LINE). HIGH NEGATIVE INCIDENCE GIVES RISE TO NEGATIVE PRESSURES ON PRESSURE SURFACES CAUSING CAVITATION.

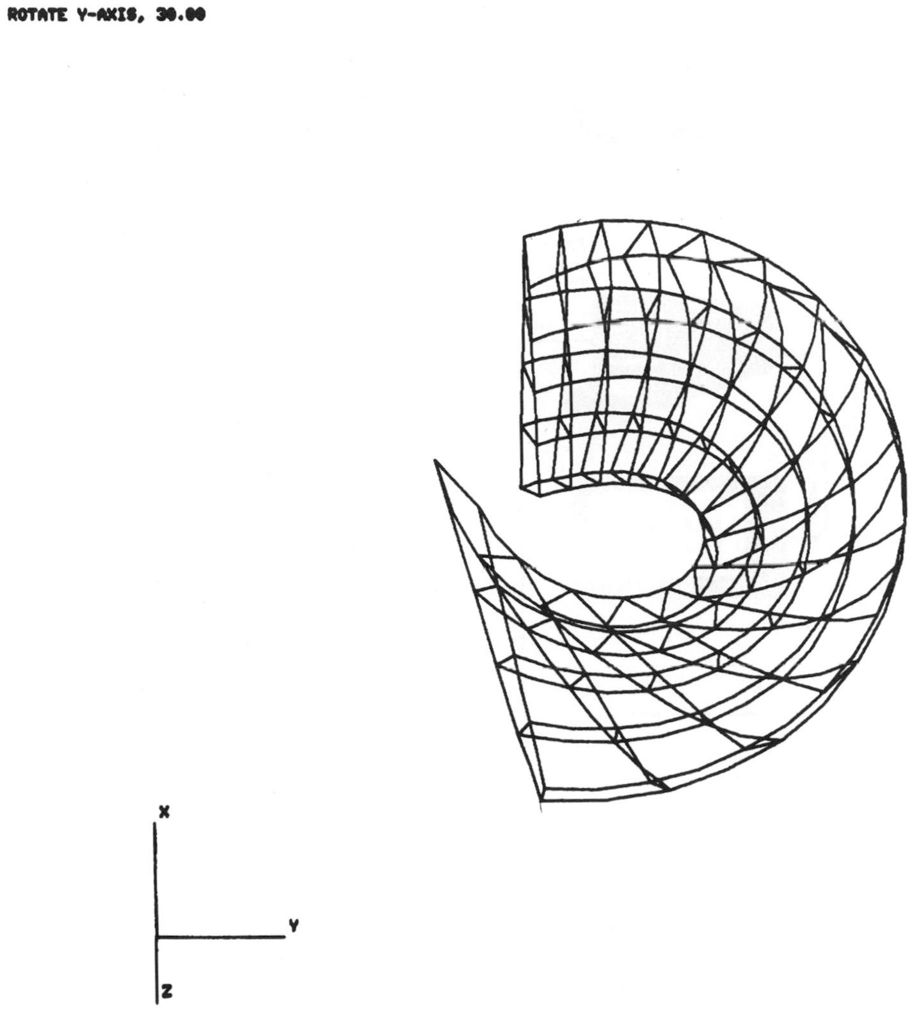

FIGURE 11 BLADE DIVIDED INTO A FINITE ELEMENT MESH, READY FOR ANALYSIS WITH NASTRAN OR ANSYS. MESH IS GENERATED BY POST PROCESSOR OF THE COMIG SYSTEM.

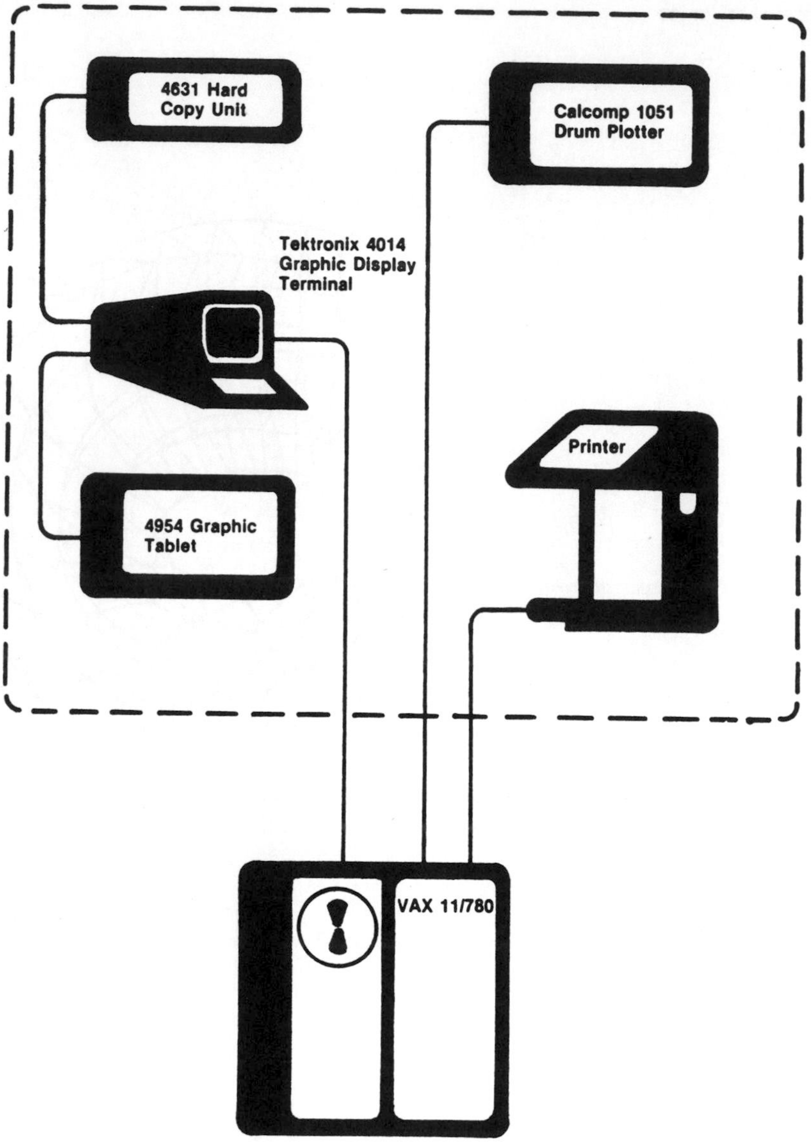

FIGURE 12 TYPICAL COMPUTATIONAL FACILITY FOR CONDUCTING INTERACTIVE GRAPHICS ENGINEERING ACTIVITIES.

FIGURE 13 CUT-AWAY VIEW OF THE TWO-STAGE PUMP. INDUCER IS ON THE RIGHT FOLLOWED BY RETURN DUCT AND MAIN PUMP. EPICYCLIC GEAR IS LOCATED BETWEEN INDUCER AND MAIN PUMP.

FIGURE 14 PUMP OPERATING ON A COAST GUARD BOAT. INSTRALLATION IS SELF CONTAINED WITH ENGINE, FUEL, CONTROLS, PRIMER AND PUMP IN ONE UNIT.

GEOMETRICAL ANALYSIS OF MASK PATTERN FOR VLSI AND ITS APPLICATION

A. Tsukizoe, J. Sakemi, and T. Kozawa
Central Research Laboratory, Hitachi Ltd.
Higashi Koigakubo, Kokubunji,
Tokyo 185, JAPAN

Abstract

An original definition is presented of four distances between two segments at any angle that are not uniquely-defined in plane geometry. A systematic method for generation of proper shapes for near-by regions within a fixed distance between segment sequences is also presented. These are indispensable for the checking of layout design rules pertaining to mask pattern data including diagonal edges.

Using this geometrical analysis, we have developed a high performance pattern checker, MACH (Mask Artwork CHecking program), that can detect all design rule errors and visualize them on a color graphic terminal. MACH performs well in VLSI pattern checking. This program has been applied to more than one hundred LSIs since April 1981.

1. Introduction

The demand for very large scale integrated circuits (VLSIs) is increasing year by year. To reduce the time necessary for errorless design of VLSIs, mask pattern data must be checked for every possible error before the time-consuming and expensive photomask generation process is undertaken. However, when VLSI data reach the volume of 1,000,000 or more, manual checking becomes not only tedious and time-consuming but also unreliable.

Consequently, many kinds of CAD systems have been developed and introduced. Amongst these, a pattern checking program, which detects design rule errors from among dense and complicated mask pattern data, is of especial importance.

Mask pattern data are represented by a simple closed loop of edges on a 2-dimensional plane. During the IC or LSI eras, mask pattern data included only a few diagonal edges. However, diagonal edges are now on the increase because of efforts to heighten pattern data density on a single LSI chip. This makes it absolutely necessary that mask artwork systems that include a pattern checking program be able to handle diagonal edges within a short run time.

A VLSI designer needs to check design rule error locations reported by a pattern checking program, and verify real error locations. Therefore, pattern checking program must not only be able to efficiently handle large amounts of data, but also detect all design rule errors without fail while reducing the number of false error indicators. If this is not possible, the designer can not rely on the program, and real design rule errors may often be overlooked.

In order to make it possible for a pattern checking program to accurately detect all design rule errors from among dense VLSI data including diagonal edges of any angle, the distances between two non-parallel segments that have previously not been uniquely defined in plane geometry must now be defined. To enable the designer to correctly judge to what exetent he should verify mask pattern data, the program must also display proper shapes for near-by regions that violate a specified tolerance value.

Recently, pattern checking programs providing good performance (2,000 ~ 3,000 figures per second) have been reported [1][2][3]. However, no report on performance good enough for mask pattern data of more than 100,000 figures has been made. Moreover, previous papers neither defined the distances between two segments at any angle nor described a systematic method for generation of proper shapes for near-by regions.

We have geometrically analyzed VLSI mask pattern. We have defined the distances between two segments at any angle that are to be measured by a pattern checker, and have developed a systematic method for generation of proper shapes for near-by regions that are to be output by the pattern checker. Using this geometrical analysis technique, we have developed a high performance pattern checker.

This paper presents the distances as defined in plane geometry, four distances between two segments at any angle, proper shapes for near-by regions, and application results for the geometrical analysis.

2. Geometrical Analysis of Mask Pattern

We took a look at uniquely-defined distances in terms of plane geometry. In our approach, distances between two points, d(P,P'), and between a point and a straight line, d(P,L), are defined (see Fig. 1(1)) as:

d(P,P')=((x-x')**2+(y-y')**2)**0.5 and

d(P,L) =|x*cosA+y*sinA-C|,

where (x,y) and (x',y') are co-ordinates of P and P', respectively, and the equation for straight line L is

X*cosA+Y*sinA=C (A,C : constants).

Points at a fixed distance from a segment can be defined based on these definitions, as shown in Fig. 1(2).

We define near-by regions, R, within a fixed distance, D, between segment sequences (see Fig. 1(3)) as:

R={(x,y)|d(P',P")≤D},

where $P(x,y)$ is any point in the interior of segment $P'P''$, and P' and P'' are any points on one segment sequence and the other, respectively. Segment $P'P''$, however, does not include any other points on two segment sequences. These are not proper output shapes for a pattern checker. First, processing of their generation would be very difficult and time-consuming. Second, their shapes are too complicated for clarification of all invalid distances between segments. Thus, transformation into more proper shapes is necessary.

3. Four Distances between Two Segments

We have undertaken the definition of four distances between two segments at any angle. We proceed to divide them into two classes.

Mask pattern data can be represented by polygons constructed from segment sequences. In manipulating pattern data for pattern checking, it is necessary to measure distances between two segment sequences or between two segments. Considering the complexity and speed of processing it is better to repeatedly measure distances between every pair of segments and generate a proper shape that indicates invalid distances between them, then to merge the shapes for all pairs of segments using an OR operation.

Consequently, we define distances between two segments at any angle, and both combinatorially and exhaustively analyze them. Let us consider the distances between two segments, P_1P_2 and P_3P_4.

Let H_i be the foot of a perpendicular from P_i onto $L(P_m,P_n)$, where $L(P_m,P_n)$ is a straight line passing through P_m and P_n. Also, if $i=1$ or 2 then $(m,n)=(3,4)$, but if $i=3$ or 4, $(m,n)=(1,2)$.

Let the distance between point P_i and segment P_mP_n, $d(P_i,P_mP_n)$, be the minimum $d(P_i,P)$ for any P in the interior of P_mP_n. That is, $d(P_i,P_mP_n)=d(P_i,H_i)$ if H_i is in the interior of P_mP_n. Otherwise, $d(P_i,P_mP_n)=\min(d(P_i,P_m),d(P_i,P_n))$. If $d(P_i,P_mP_n)=d(P_i,Q)$, we call P_iQ a distance-edge, where Q is H_i, P_m, or P_n.

We define the four distances between the two segments P_1P_2 and P_3P_4 as $d(P_1,P_3P_4)$, $d(P_2,P_3P_4)$, $d(P_3,P_1P_2)$, and $d(P_4,P_1P_2)$. (P_1,P_2,H_3,H_4) and (H_1,H_2,P_3,P_4) are linearly ordered on $L(P_1,P_2)$ and $L(P_3,P_4)$, respectively. There are 24 linear orders for each (P_i,P_j,H_m,H_n), where $((i,j),(m,n))=((1,2),(3,4))$ or $((3,4),(1,2))$. There are 84 possible combinations of linear orders of (P_1,P_2,H_3,H_4) and (H_1,H_2,P_3,P_4).

We assume that $L(P_1,P_2)$ is not at right angles to $L(P_3,P_4)$, and any intersection-point between $L(P_1,P_2)$ and $L(P_3,P_4)$ is not a point both in the interior of P_1P_2 and in that of P_3P_4, excluding P_1, P_2, P_3, and P_4. It is not necessary to check pairs of orthogonal segments. If $L(P_i,P_j)$ is at right angles to $L(P_m,P_n)$, neither segment P_iP_a connecting P_i nor segment

P_jP_b connecting P_j are at right angles to $L(P_m,P_n)$, where $a, b \neq i$ or j. Thus, violation data between P_iP_j and P_mP_n, even if it exists, can be detected by checking between P_iP_a and P_mP_n or between P_jP_b and P_mP_n. If an intersection-point exist between two segments, these segments can be dealt with after being cut at the intersecting point.

We also assume $d(P_1,H_1) \leqq d(P_2,H_2)$ and $d(P_3,H_3) \leqq d(P_4,H_4)$, without losing generality. By this assumption, the number of linear orders is reduced from 24 to 6 and the number of combinations is also reduced from 84 to 21.

Figure 2 shows four distances between two segments at any angle, with all cases listed. The number of distance-edges for one combination is 2, 3, or 4.

Next, we divide these distances into two classes. If (P_j,H_m,H_n) are on the same side with regard to P_i, and (H_j,P_m,P_n) are on the same side with regard to H_i, then we call P_i a free vertex. Otherwise, we call it a captive vertex.

We divide the four distances between two segments into basic distances and referential distances. If P_i is a captive vertex, we call $d(P_i,P_mP_n)$ a basic distance, and if P_i is a free vertex, we call it a referential distance. A minimum distance is included in basic distances. If P_1 is a free vertex and P_2 is a captive vertex, a half line passing through P_1 with terminal point P_2 has the same basic distances from P_3P_4 as segment P_1P_2 has.

4. Proper Shapes for Near-by Regions

Using the four distances, classified into basic and referential distances, we have derived a systematic method for generation of a proper shape that vividly indicates invalid distances between two segments of less than a specified tolerance value, D. However, the near-by regions within a fixed distance between segment sequences, as shown in Fig. 1(3), do not qualify as proper shapes. This is because they are too complicated for the designer to be able to recognize at a glance where and to what extent he should verify.

Up to the present, no paper has reported a method for generation of proper shapes for near-by regions on the basis of a distance definition for two non-parallel segments. Only one paper [2], though it has not described a distance definion, has mentioned output data for near-by regions. In that paper, a minimum distance between two segments was checked, and the two segments were output if less than a specified value. This method is very simple, but not adequate. This is because these segments do not vividly indicate to what extent the designer should verify them.

Our method for such a case is shown in Fig. 3. First, a minimum distance, $d(P_3,H_3)$, is checked. If it is less than D, an output shape must be generated.

It is generally easy to output a shape, $P_3P_4P_2H_3$, without checking the other distances, that is constructed from a minimum distance-edge and all captive vertices. However, in this method the shape merely assures that a minimum distance is invalid.

In our method all distances are checked for the purpose of indicating all invalid distances, not for indicating valid distances. For condition No. 3 in Fig. 3, all basic distances except the minimum distance are valid, and the basic distance-edge, that is the perpendicular, is moved parallelly. $P_4'H_4'$ is a segment parallel to P_4H_4 such that P_4' is in the interior of P_3P_4, H_4' is in the interior of H_3H_4, and $d(P_4',H_4')=D$. This segment can be easily obtained through proportional allotment of parallel segments. Referential distances are checked so that fine shapes can be output when adjacent shapes are merged.

Processing for generation of proper shapes for other cases is similar.

5. Application of Geometrical Analysis

We have developed a high performance pattern checker, MACH, that takes this geometrical analysis as a basis. Figure 4 shows the MACH system configuration. Input data are constructed from mask pattern data, DRL, and items to be checked. The DRL is a Design Rule Library described by the pattern operations [4] shown in Fig. 5. Thus, this MACH is independent of process technology and is applicable to both MOS and Bipolar LSIs. Mask data are represented by polygons of any angle and are classified into individual layers. Violation data are displayed on a color graphic terminal, electro-static plotter(ESP), or X-Y plotter.

The MACH consists of 4 subprograms:

(1) MACHV : Reads mask pattern data from the data base and transforms them into vector data;

(2) MACHC : Executes pattern operations following the DRL;

(3) MACHP : Outputs violation data as pattern checking results to the ESP or X-Y plotter; and

(4) MACHD : Displays violation data on the color graphic terminal. This program has more than 10 commands, such as enlarge and reduce. The VLSI designer can easily operate this system using these commands.

MACHV, MACHC and MACHP execute by batch processing. MACHD executes in the TSS mode.

The program is written basically in PL/I with some assembler language and cosists of approximately 75K lines of code. It runs on a HITACHI M-200H with a VOS-3 operating system. In practice, MACH has been applied to more than one hundred LSIs since April 1981.

Table 1 shows results from evaluating MACH for three manufactured LSIs. The amount of checked data was about 1,500,000 vectors, on the average. Our old program could not handle diagonal edges because the distances between two non-parallel segments were not defined. MACH can handle diagonal edges and detect all design rule errors without fail. Moreover, the execution time varies in proportion to the number of input data. Thus, MACH is quite effective for large amounts of mask data.

Figure 6 shows a space error display example. The hatched regions indicate locations that violate a specified tolerance value, D. Figure 6(2) shows a near-by region where both d(P,P') and d(Q,Q') are valid, and Figure 6(3) shows a near-by region where both identities are invalid. The dotted lines are edges selected in generating proper shapes for near-by regions between each pair of segments. The thin lines are generated to merge the shapes for all pairs of segments, using an OR operation. By means of this display, the designer can judge to what extent he should verify the mask pattern data.

In dimension-checking operations illustrated in Fig. 5(5), proper shapes are output for near-by regions using the systematic method mentioned above. These operations can be applied to decomposition of pattern data using pattern dimensions, such as widths.

6. Conclusions

We have defined four distances between two segments at any angle that are to be measured in pattern checking. Owing to our definition, pattern checking can effectively proceed without any real design rule errors lying in an LSI being missed. Moreover, this definition yields low-cost programming and high-speed execution of pattern checking.

We have also proposed a systematic method for generation of proper shapes for near-by regions that are to be output by a pattern checker. The shapes vividly indicate all invalid distances.

Using our geometrical analysis, a pattern checking program (MACH) has been developed. MACH can handle diagonal edges of any angle, detect all design rule errors, and display violation data in proper shapes on a color graphic terminal. The execution time varies in proportion to the number of input data, so MACH can perform well in VLSI pattern checking. This MACH has been successfully applied to more than one hundred LSIs since April 1981.

References

[1] P. Wilcox, H. Rombeek, and D. M. Caughey, "Design Rule Verification Based on One Dimensional Scans", Proc. of the 15th DA Conf., June 1978, pp. 285-289.

[2] D. Alexander, "A Technology Independent Design Rule Checker", 3rd USA-JAPAN Computer Conf., 1978, pp. 412-416.

[3] C. R. McCaw, "Unified Shapes Checker - A Checking Tool for LSI", Proc. of the 16th DA Conf., June 1979, pp. 81-87.

[4] T. Kozawa, A. Tsukizoe, J. Sakemi, C. Miura, and T. Ishii, "A Concurrent Pattern Operation Algorithm for VLSI Mask Data", Proc. of the 18th DA Conf., June 1981, pp. 563-570.

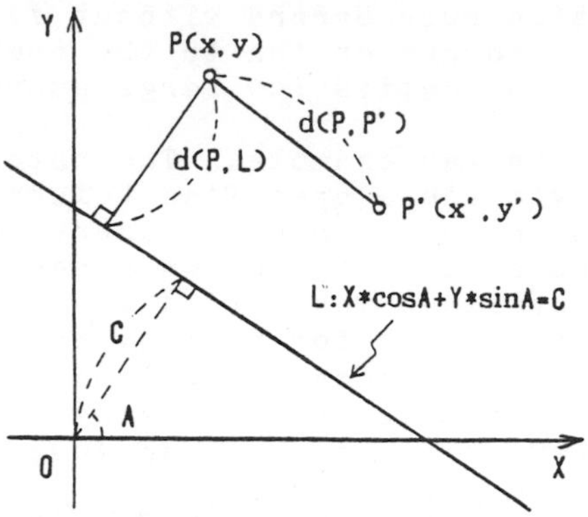

(1) Distances between two points and between a point and a straight line

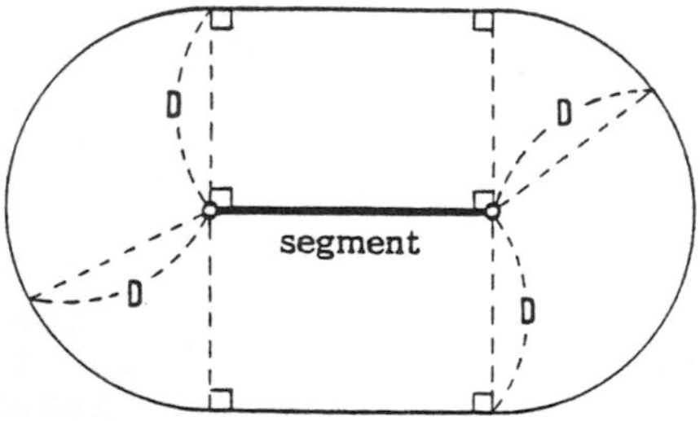

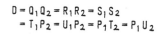

(2) Points at a fixed distance from a segment

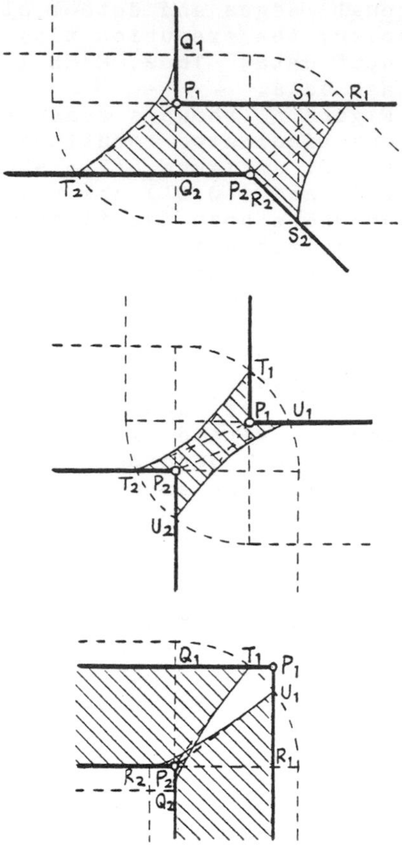

$D = Q_1Q_2 = R_1R_2 = S_1S_2$
$= T_1P_2 = U_1P_2 = P_1T_2 = P_1U_2$

(3) Near-by regions within a fixed distance between two segment sequences

FIG. 1. UNIQUELY-DEFINED DISTANCES IN PLANE GEOMETRY

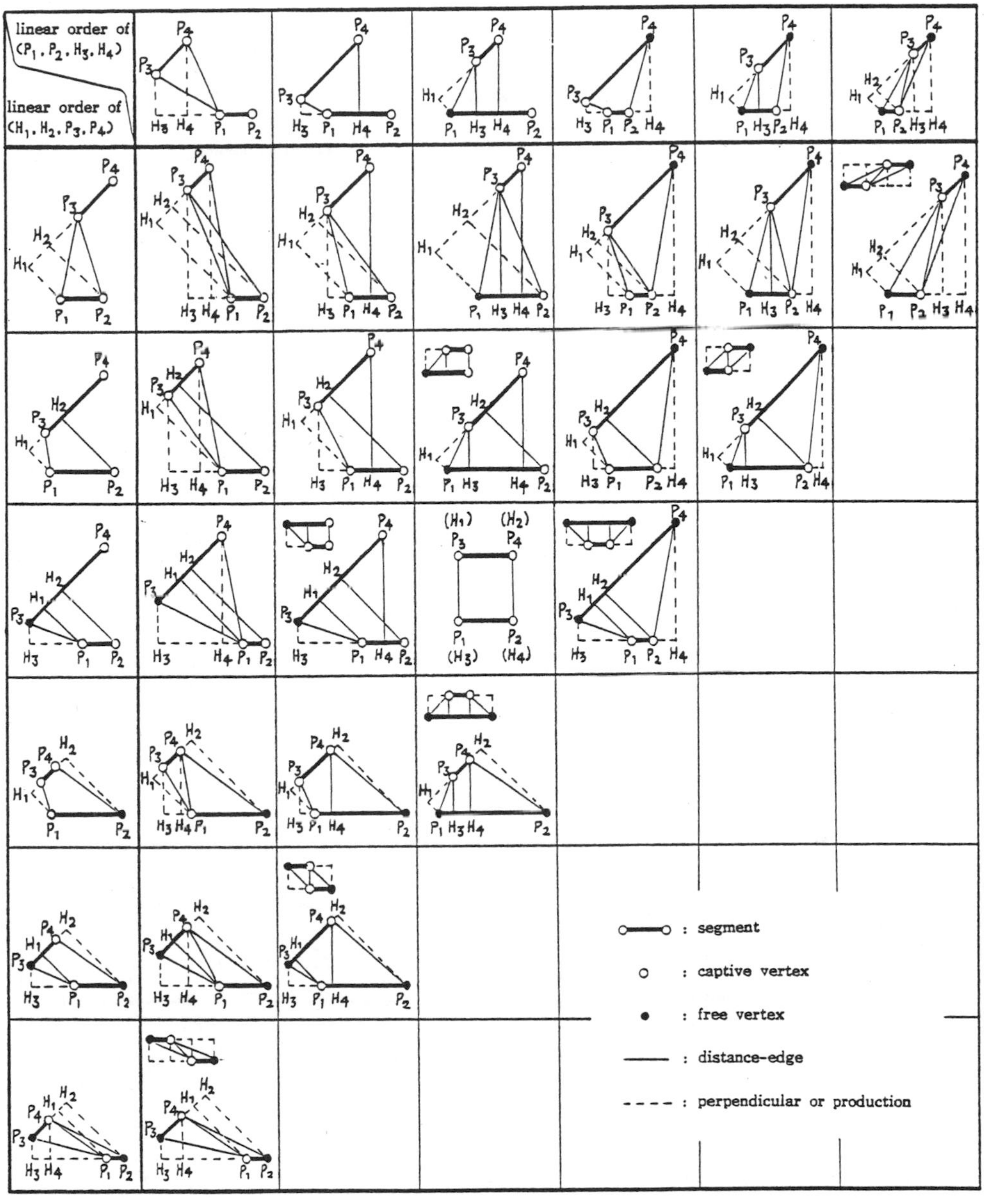

FIG. 2. FOUR DISTANCES BETWEEN TWO SEGMENTS

Four distances
between two segments

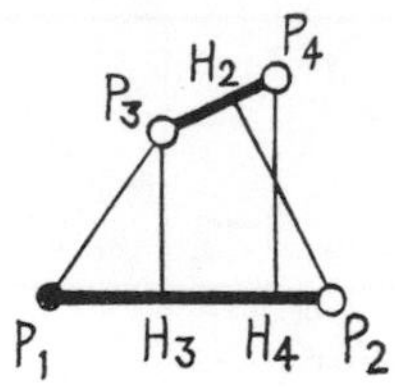

No.	Conditions		Edge selected
0	$d(P_3, H_3) > D$		None
1	$d(P_3, H_3) \leq D$	$d(P_1, P_3) > D$	P_3H_3
2		$d(P_1, P_3) \leq D$	P_1P_3
3		$d(P_4, H_4) > D$ & $d(P_2, H_2) > D$	$P_4'H_4'$ $(= D)$
4		$d(P_4, H_4) \leq D$ & $d(P_2, H_2) > D$	P_4H_4
5		$d(P_4, H_4) > D$ & $d(P_2, H_2) \leq D$	P_2H_2
6		$d(P_4, H_4) \leq D$ & $d(P_2, H_2) \leq D$	P_2P_4

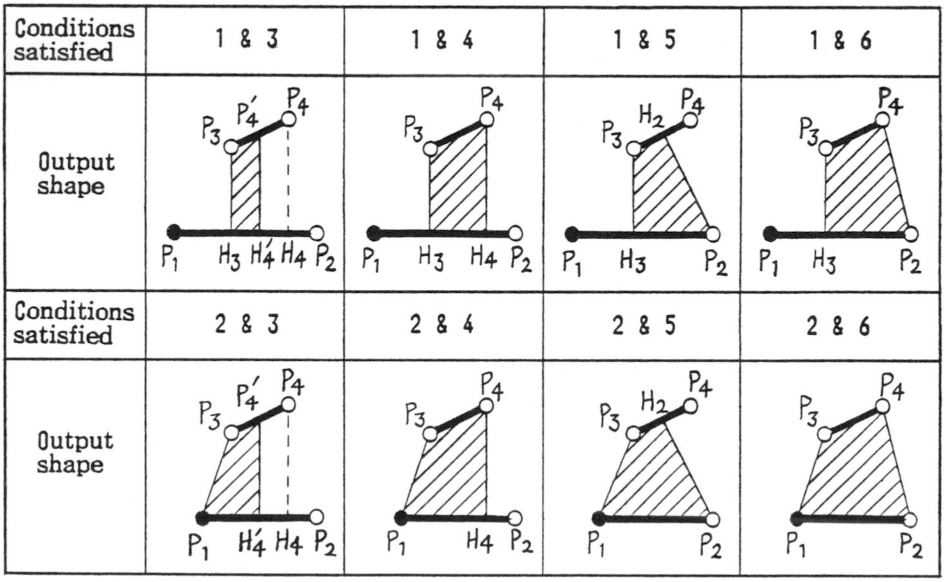

F I G. 3. PROPER SHAPES OF NEAR-BY REGIONS

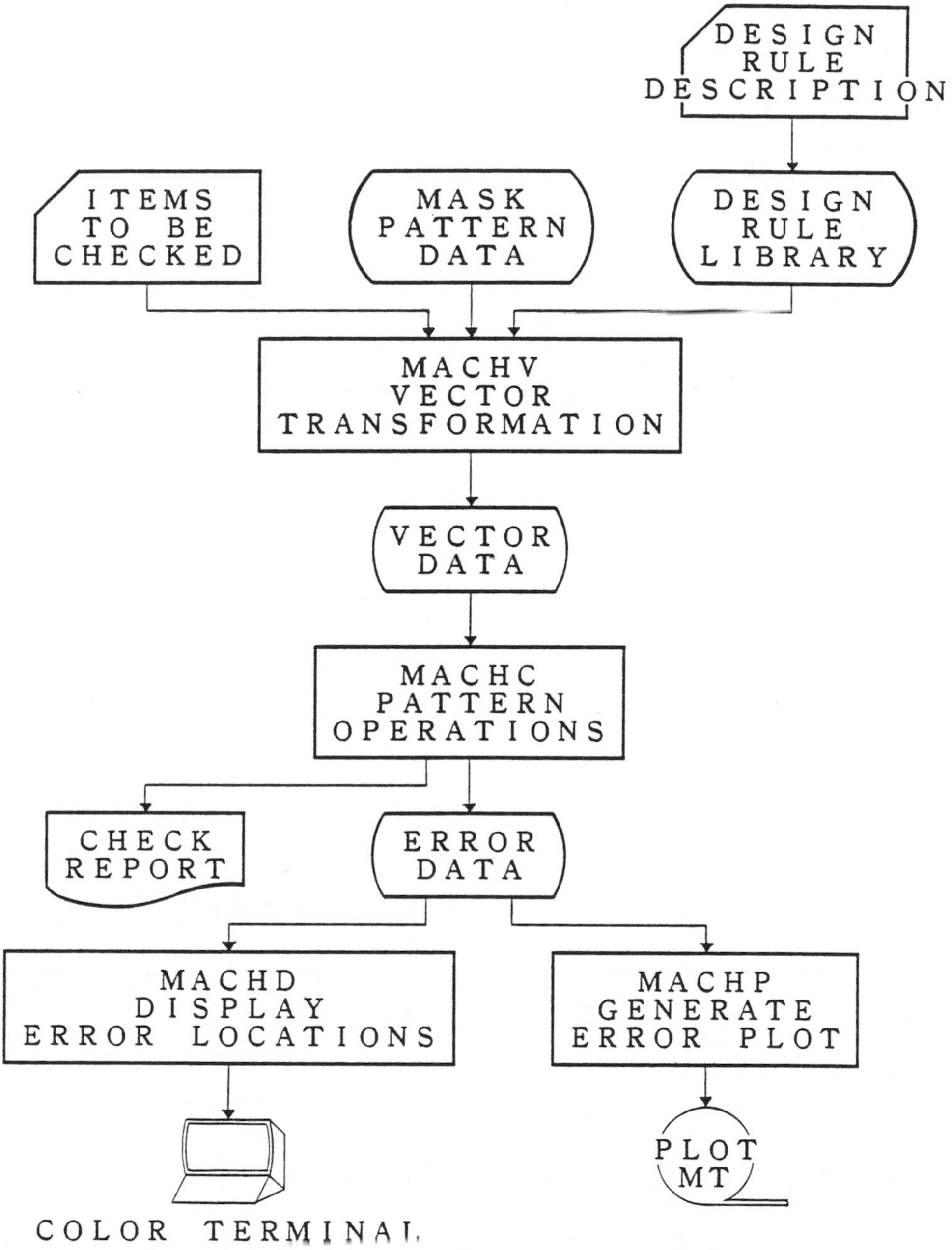

FIG. 4. MACH PROGRAM STRUCTURE

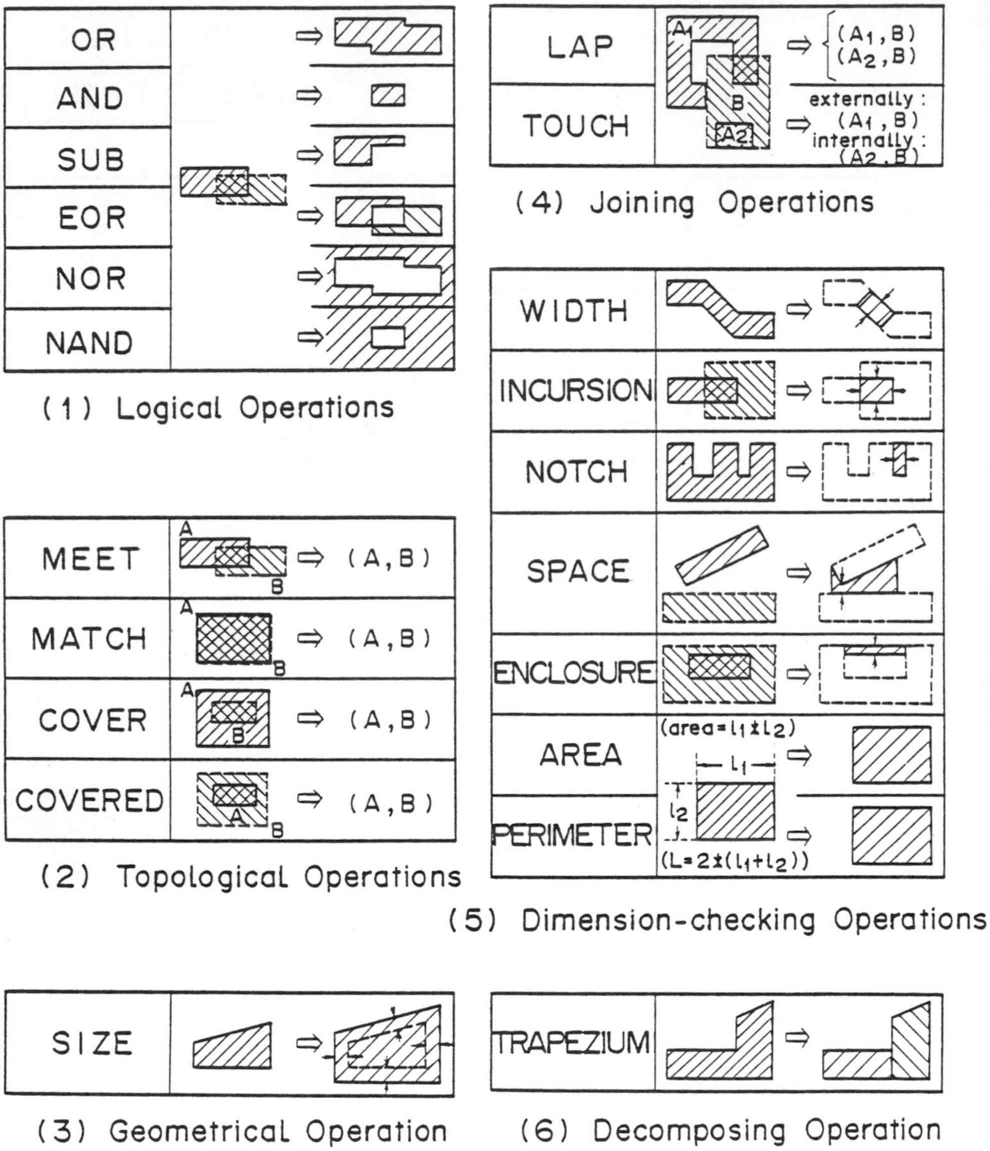

(A, A_1, A_2, B : Pattern Identifications)

FIG. 5. PATTERN OPERATIONS

TABLE 1. PERFORMANCE SUMMARY

PATTERN CHECKER	MACH	(OLD)
DIAGONAL EDGES	○	×
NO. OF OUTPUT SHAPES	264	210
DETECTING RATE (%)	100	80
EXEC. TIME COMPLEXITY (T : CPU TIME, N : NO. OF DATA)	$T \propto N^{1.0}$	$T \propto N^{1.2}$

$$\text{DETECTING RATE} = \frac{\text{NO. OF OUTPUT SHAPES}}{\text{NO. OF REAL DESIGN RULE ERRORS}} * 100$$

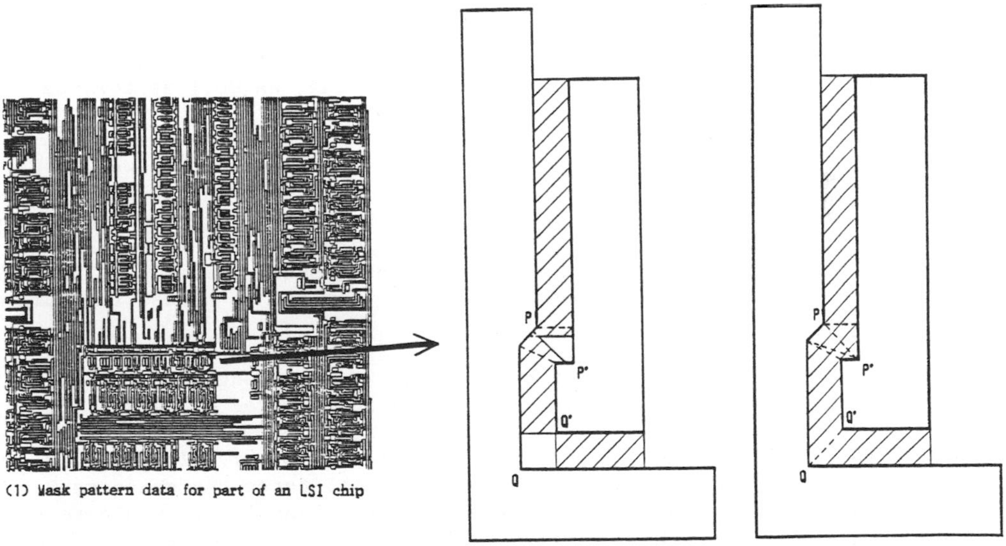

(1) Mask pattern data for part of an LSI chip

(2) d(P, P')>D & d(Q, Q')>D

(3) d(P, P')≤D & d(Q, Q')≤D

FIG. 6. EXAMPLE OF SPACE ERROR DISPLAY

HIGH-PERFORMANCE COMPUTER GRAPHICS FOR VLSI SYSTEMS DESIGN

Gene Chao
Metheus Corporation
5289 N.E. Elam Young Parkway, D-600
P.O. Box 1049
Hillsboro, Oregon 97123
U. S. A.

I. Introduction: The Evolution of Electronic Product Design

Since the invention of the planar transistor in 1959, the process of electronic product design has been rapidly changing. Two decades ago, electronics engineers were designing discretes and resistor-transistor logic gates into products totaling perhaps a thousand transistors. A decade ago they were designing 4- and 8-bit microprocessors and 1K and 4K RAMs into systems with perhaps a million transistors. Engineers today are designing with 16- and 32-bit microcomputers and 64K and 256K RAMs. Today's systems may contain 100 million transistors.

The skills necessary to design electronic products have followed this rapid pace. Two decades ago, engineers relied heavily on logic and circuit design. A decade ago the designer had to be skilled in firmware and software as well. Today, the necessary skill set extends in both directions: toward integrated circuit process and device understanding, as well as towards computer systems design.

The tools which electronics engineers use have followed suit as well. Figure 1 shows that scopes and DMM's were used to develop products based on discretes and SSI. MSI circuit complexities created the need for logic analyzers. LSI circuit complexities caused the microprocessor to be invented, and subsequently the microprocessor development system. Finally, a new generation tool, the VLSI development system, is required to access the full power of VLSI circuits.

The ideal VLSI development system would allow a design engineer to progress from product concept to packaged silicon chip in a matter of weeks. It would incorporate flexibility for the various semicustom (gate array) and custom design technologies (standard cell or full custom). It would follow a process such as the one in Figure 2, which facilitates the management of complexity and tracks and documents the project. Finally, it would rely heavily on high performance color graphics to allow the engineer to interact with the design process at each step.

II. The Trend Toward a Complete VLSI Development System

A. Current Tools

Within the past few years vendors have introduced a number of tools for VLSI design addressing different elements of the total design process:

1. Logic design tools
2. Layout design tools
3. Gate array design tools
4. Mainframe software packates

Logic design typically encompasses printed circuit board and hybrid circuit design as well as VLSI design. Logic design tools are represented by single-user networked systems costing \$50K - 100K and low-cost alphanumeric terminals with remote hosts. Turnkey IC layout systems generally support a handful of integrated circuit designers and cost \$250K - \$500K. Gate array tools are offered on a time shared basis by gate array vendors. Finally, large software packages are available only for mainframe or super-mini computers and the price is in the range of \$200K.

B. Trend Toward an Integrated Tool Set

In the past year, both computing power and VLSI CAD software have become sophisticated and cost-effective enough to allow a complete set of tools to be assembled. To the user, such an integrated set of tools represents the ability to streamline the VLSI systems design process by minimizing the number of organizations involved in the process. It also affords increased design and proprietary control of the product. In addition, control of a toolset with self-development capability allows the user to create new tools and customize tools for particular needs.

III. The Complete VLSI Toolset

A. Complete Set

A well integrated set of VLSI tools which can be conveniently accessed by the design engineer is needed to complete a VLSI design quickly and reliably. This tool set should be complete enough to support all the phases of the VLSI system design, from the concept all the way to the pattern generation (PG) tape used for mask generation. Ideally, the toolset needs to be flexible to allow the design engineer to select just the portions of the design process required by his particular design style. Table 1 shows a complete generic toolset.

B. Database Management, Documentation and Communication

The process of managing a complex development project is non-trivial. Writing system specification with functional block diagrams is an important first step, and is leveraged by good computerized textual and graphical documentation tools.

The communication and maintenance of project documentation is further enhanced by electronic mail capabilities. Development engineers are more effective if well-informed, and electronic mail is becoming widely accepted as a low-overhead means of communication.

Database management and configuration control augment designer productivity by providing record keeping assistance and visibility of changes.

C. Complexity Management Through a Disciplined Design Methodology

The increasing complexity of VLSI systems creates tremendous pressure for effective design methodologies. An incremental and hierarchical design methodology reduces the complexity that designers deal with at any given time. In addition, it increases interactivity by reducing the response time of graphics editors and design verification tools. A well-chosen set of design constraints will maximize design throughput time while sacrificing very little design efficiency, such as silicon area.

A well supported hierarchical design involves multiple levels of design detail nesting. Design analysis and verification tools operate much faster on highly regular hierarchical designs than on low regularly "flat" designs, simply because each unique cell is checked only once throughout a design hierarchy. The incremental characteristic of the tools means that cells are checked only if they have been changed. This feature avoids repeat checking which means that even in very large hierarchical designs, as minor changes are made, the effect of the change can be checked in seconds instead of minutes or even hours.

D. High Performance Graphics Computing Environment

High-performance color graphics capability is essential for an interactive design environment. This capability should be an integral part of the design system rather than an afterthought. A special-purpose graphics processor for high speed drawing and update is needed to provide designers with a highly interactive design environment. When a raster-scanned color display is used for the interactive human interface, a minimum of eight to twelve bits per pixel are desirable for display and manipulation of multiple layers of circuit topology. A high-bandwidth communication channel between computing system and graphics display is a must to minimize the designer's waiting time for the response from the computer. To be able to display not only physical layout and schematics but also textual information and node names on the same screen, a high resolution (1024 x 768) display is needed. Multiple windowing capability is convenient to display and manipulate several different forms of design information at the same time on a single display screen. The main computing engine, in the system cpu needs to be supported by a large main memory (expandable up to several megabytes) and a high speed on-line Winchester disk storage (minimum 30 megabyte) for fast disk swapping. When these physical memories are supported through a full virtual memory management, designers can run large programs quickly and conveniently. Floppy disk supports program update and software distribution.

System software required includes an operating system, (e.g., UNIX), network driver (e.g., Ethernet), and several popular languages (e.g. C, Fortran and Pascal).

A widely used O/S such as UNIX provides the users of the system with an instant access to a hierarchical file system, tools and utilities.

Hardware and software support for interfacing the system to other host computers (e.g., Digital Equipment VAX) will be also needed. A standard system bus such as the IEEE 796 Bus is attractive from the standpoint of supports a variety of industry standard peripherals and communication options.

Figure 3 shows a block diagram of such a system, and Figure 4 shows the λ750 stand-alone VLSI development system.

IV. Product Design with the Metheus λ750 VLSI Development System

The basic motives for the Metheus λ750 are to reduce time-to-market and to increase the integration levels used in products. Experience in the management of product design shows that time-to-market is a fundamental parameter in project cost, return on investment, innovation and quality. When the half-life of engineers on a project is exceeded by the project development schedule, it's very difficult to hold project costs or enthusiasm. Production and service costs are significantly impacted by integration levels. Increased parts count and interconnects not only add to manufacturing costs but decrease reliability and complicate serviceability.

A. Designing with the λ750

The design process typically begins with a written design specification. The Metheus λ750 supports this need with a powerful screen editor and text formatter, and a versatile graphics editor for line drawings.

Logic design is supported by a schematic editor and symbol creation editor for graphic design expression, a logic simulator and circuit simulator for circuit verification and analysis. A netlist comparator is used to compare logical and physical designs for connectivity verification or to compare different versions of logical or physical designs to each other.

Physical design is supported by five categories of tools: 1) Two editors, a physical layout editor and a symbolic layout editor, are included for physical design. 2) A router is included for wiring and cell interconnection. 3) A circuit extractor generates a netlist output from physical layout, and is used for design verification. An extracted netlist can be used to drive the simulators, the electrical rule checker, or the netlist comparator. 4) The design rule checker in the λ750 is an impressive state-of-the-art tool which is user-configurable to handle any combination of MOS design rules. 5) The system includes a PLA generator and optimizer for synthesis of programmable logic arrays and finite state machines.

The λ750 VLSI Design System includes a library of nMOS layout cells for full-custom design. In addition, CMOS standard cell libraries and design rules from several major silicon foundries have been adapted for use on the λ750.

Optional format interchange software is available to translate the λ750's Caltech Intermediate Form output to other popular CAD formats, and for input of design data from other systems. The λ750 internal database format is well documented and convenient for user written programs. In addition terminal emulation software is provided to allow the λ750 to act as a virtual terminal on remote host computers.

B. Color Graphics

A high resolution, interactive color display is crucial to the design process. While much of the computation and analysis that the λ750 performs does not require graphic output, the design process is best managed and understood by development engineers when block diagrams, logic diagrams, timing diagrams, netlist comparison and physical layout are easily accessed and compared.

The λ750 graphics engine incorporates several unique features developed for highly-interactive design applications. The graphics engine architecture supports powerful multiple window management, independent color maps for overlays, and extremely effective real-time pan and zoom capability.

The λ750's 19-inch color monitor displays 1024 x 768 pixels at a refresh rate of 33 Hz, using interlaced scan. This combination of resolution and refresh rate maximizes communication of design detail and minimize user fatigue.

Display graphics are handled by a bipolar bit-slice main processor and 12-MHz MC68000 which acts as a display list manager and preprocessor. Display memory is configured as a 16 bit-planes 1024 x 1024 pixels each. The 16 bit-planes are split into two sets of 8, each with independent color maps. At any one time 512 colors can be displayed out of a palette of 16.7 million possible shades.

The display engine draws vectors at a speed of 1 million pixels per second. Block transfers of pixels are accomplished at 4 million pixels per second, and polygons are FLASH-FILLed(tm) at 156 million pixels per second.

D. Fabrication -- Link to the Foundry

The first release λ750 VLSI CAD software set is minimal but complete allowing engineers to implement their designs in full custom VLSI chips.

Metheus is negotiating long term arrangements with well-proven silicon foundries to help the users of the λ750 with fast turnaround prototyping and production of VLSI chips. At least two foundry arrangements will be established to provide the users of the λ750 with multiple source fabrication. The CAD software in the λ750 will incorporate the design rules and technology parameters of the foundries. In additon, λ750 customers will be able to obtain a set of well-proven standard cells and update services directly from the foundries. More detailed information will be available when final negotiations with foundries are complete.

E. Design Example -- Program Source Address (PSA) Chip

Background

This special purpose control chip was designed by two experienced design engineers (Dick Blewett at Floating Point Systems and Myron White at Metheus Corporation). Both have extensive experience in digital system design using TTL and ECL components. A single PSA chip replaces 14 TTL MSI chips in a pipelined array processor for high speed floating point arithmetic operations. The chip generates a 4-bit address used to fetch the next executable program instruction from program source (PS) memory. The 4-bit chips can be connected in parallel to form any length address. Seven potential next addresses are calculated every 200-nsec clock period. One of the seven is selected for output as specified by the current instruction. The chip has 37 I/O pins including two power supply voltages (+5V, 0V). The chip contains approximately 2,000 transistors and the die size is 135 mil by 110 mil.

This chip was designed in one month using λ750 CAD tools. The chip was fabricated at a silicon foundry and is presently being tested. One interesting aspect of the PSA chip is that the design used PLAs and TTL replacement logic functions. The designers were able to inter-mix different design styles on a single design using PLA-like control structures as well as TTL-equivalent logic functions. Figure 5 shows a photomicrograph of the chip.

V. Applications

A. Initial

The λ750 VLSI design system supports full-custom and standard cell design. Its design tools are compatible with all MOS processes (both nMOS and CMOS).

Full-custom design is well-suited for new systems where architecture is flexible.

Standard cell design is most often used for TTL replacement. This design style facilitates product cost reduction by reducing package count in products. In addition, TTL replacement preserves a heavy investment in system software by preserving system architecture.

The λ750 guarantees each designer access to necessary computation power without performance degradation. The combination of high-performance interactive color graphics and hierarchical/incremental design methodology assure tremendous designer productivity.

For the design of a new proprietary architecture, the λ750 toolset provides total architectural flexibility. Applications that fall into this category include special-purpose display processors, data base machines, communication controllers, special memory devices land custom controllers. The advanced graphics computing architecture and complete toolset of the λ750 can support a design of up to 50,000 transistors in stand-alone mode without depending on an expensive host computer or central file server.

The λ750 system is designed to support rapid and correct system design, rather than to optimize chip area. With the λ750, designers save valuable engineering time and effort concentrating on effective system design instead of trying to minimize the size of the dice.

B. Future

As the technology advances, the complexity of the typical design will grow in the range of 100,000 - 500,000 per chip during the remaining decade of the 1980's. The system elements of λ750 such as system bus, disk storage, and main memory architecture are designed to support ever increasing complexity of VLSI system design. With the advent of the λ750, future applications of VLSI systems are not limited by the fabrication technology or design tools, but only by the availability of innovative product ideas.

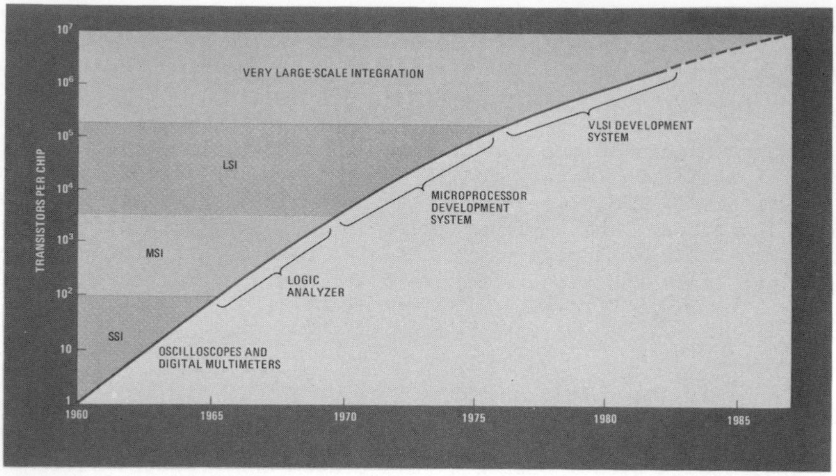

Figure 1. Design Aids evolve in step with chip complexity. A development system for very large-scale integrated circuits reflects the broad technology base supporting single-chip systems, from process technology to computer architecture.

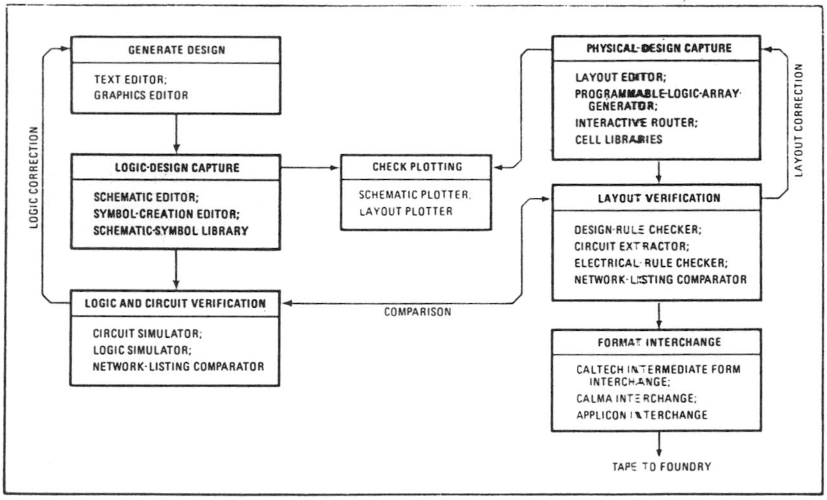

Figure 2. The complete integrated-circuit design process is supported on the workstation, from logic-design capture through mask specifications. A hierarchical methodology speeds execution of checking and comparing programs.

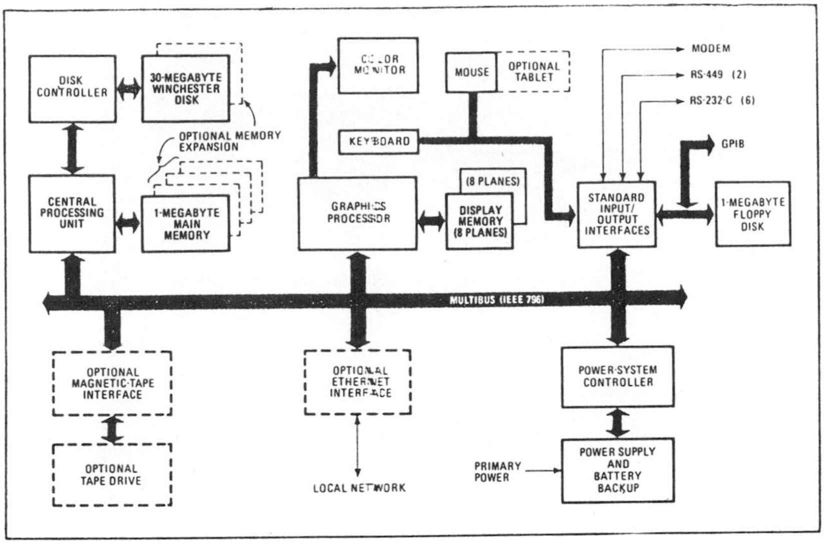

Figure 3. The λ750 workstation puts a 32-bit computer at the IC designer's desk. The Multibus-based system employs three 68000 microprocessors--two in the CPU and a third as a display-list manager for the bit-slice graphics processor.

Figure 4. The λ750 integrated stand-alone VLSI development system.

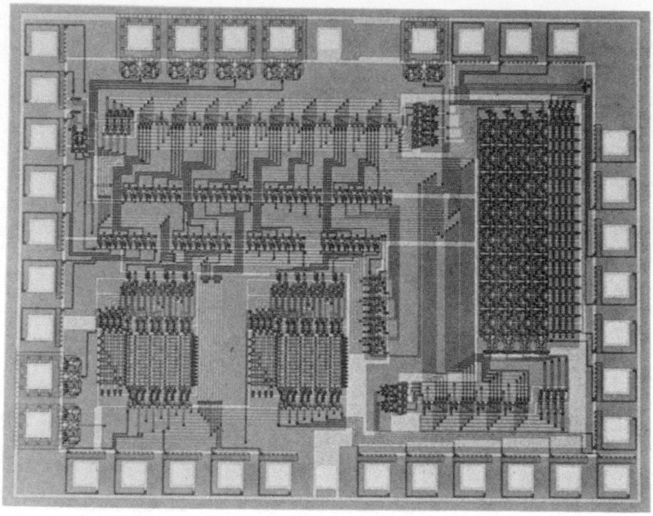

Figure 5. Photomicrograph of the chip.

EDUCATION AND TRAINING REQUIREMENTS IN CAD/CAM

Michael J. Wozny
Director and Professor
Center for Interactive Computer Graphics
Rensselaer Polytechnic Institute
Troy, New York 12181
U. S. A.

1. INTRODUCTION

The long term viability of CAD/CAM in industry dictates the balancing of short term training needs with long term educational growth.

The short term needs consist of training experienced designers to be proficient in the use of state-of-the-art CAD/CAM systems. Such training is generally rote in nature, with the objective of making the trainee productive as quickly as possible. Although such training has been easily accomplished in the past for artwork or drawing type applications, new directions in complete engineering workstations will require a deeper understanding of concepts.

CAD/CAM represents a continually evolving integration of computer and computer graphics into the complete design-production process. The objective of long term university programs is the education of students who can contribute to this integration process in a meaningful way. Such students will need to thoroughly understand CAD/CAM from all points of view: (1) as knowledgeable users of state-of-the-art computer-aided tools; (2) as innovative creators of the hardware and software components which make up the computer-aided tools; and (3) as systems integrators who can evaluate the impact of these tools on the total design-production process.

This paper discusses two programs at Rensselaer Polytechnic Institute which address both the short and long term training requirements of industry. The short term training effort involves the development of special hardware and software for a personal computer to be used as a low cost introductory operator training system. This effort is part of a large, industrially supported research program at the Rensselaer Center for Interactive Computer Graphics (See Appendix). The long term program consists of integrating computer graphics into the entire engineering curriculum in a fundamental way over all four years.

2. CHANGING THE TRAINING REQUIREMENTS

Until recently, the CAD/CAM market has been aimed at large companies. Large companies are able to justify sizable installations of CAD/CAM hardware and consequently, obtain thru the economy of scale, a lower cost per workstation. Many of these companies are able to justify their own internal training programs, also. (However, most are still having difficulty providing training on the new more sophisticated 3D software packages.)

This scenario is now changing due to the introduction of low cost ($100K range) stand-alone CAD/CAM workstations. The lower cost has attracted many smaller companies to CAD/CAM. In general, such companies are less sophisticated users (at least initially), commit all workstations totally to productions, and cannot afford training programs which cost 10% of their capital investment!

It is clear that a new approach to cost-effectve training is needed.

3. ROLE OF PERSONAL COMPUTER FOR TRAINING

The personal computer represents one method for reducing training costs while still maintaining a flexible approach to training. The personal computer is well suited for introductory training, such as learning which buttons to push.

Such systems are designed to be less complex than productions systems, and are therefore less intimidating. One can also program instructions modules directly into the system to monitor exercises and provide help as needed. For example, an exercise may consist of showing the trainee a partially completed problem, and then asking for the next step. The trainee's next step is then compared to all solutions stored, and a message is displayed evaluating his performance.

One can use voice synthesizers in place of written material so as not to lose concentration on the problem being solved.

Although the personal computer suffers from limitations such as execution speed, display resolutions, and memory size, it has enough capability to be a suitable training device.

4. ACTUAL APPLICATION

An IBM Personal Computer was used at Rensselaer to develop an introductory training system for CADAM™ [1,2]. (CADAM™ is a registered trademark of CADAM, Inc.)

A subset of the CADAM™ drawing functionality suitable for novice training was emulated using a layered software architecture. (See Figure 1). The lowest level of software emulates the basic CADAM™ graphics, I/O, and data manipulation functions. The next level of software represents thr CADAM™ functions and emulation drivers. The top layer represents the lesson controller and data file interpreter. This architecture allows additional functionality to be added in the future.

Both a light pen and a 32 button function box were interfaced to the personal computer.

This emulation operates exactly like an IBM 3250 terminal, right down to the font and character blast for light pen indicate, except more slowly.

The system is now being evaluated in an actual industrial environment.

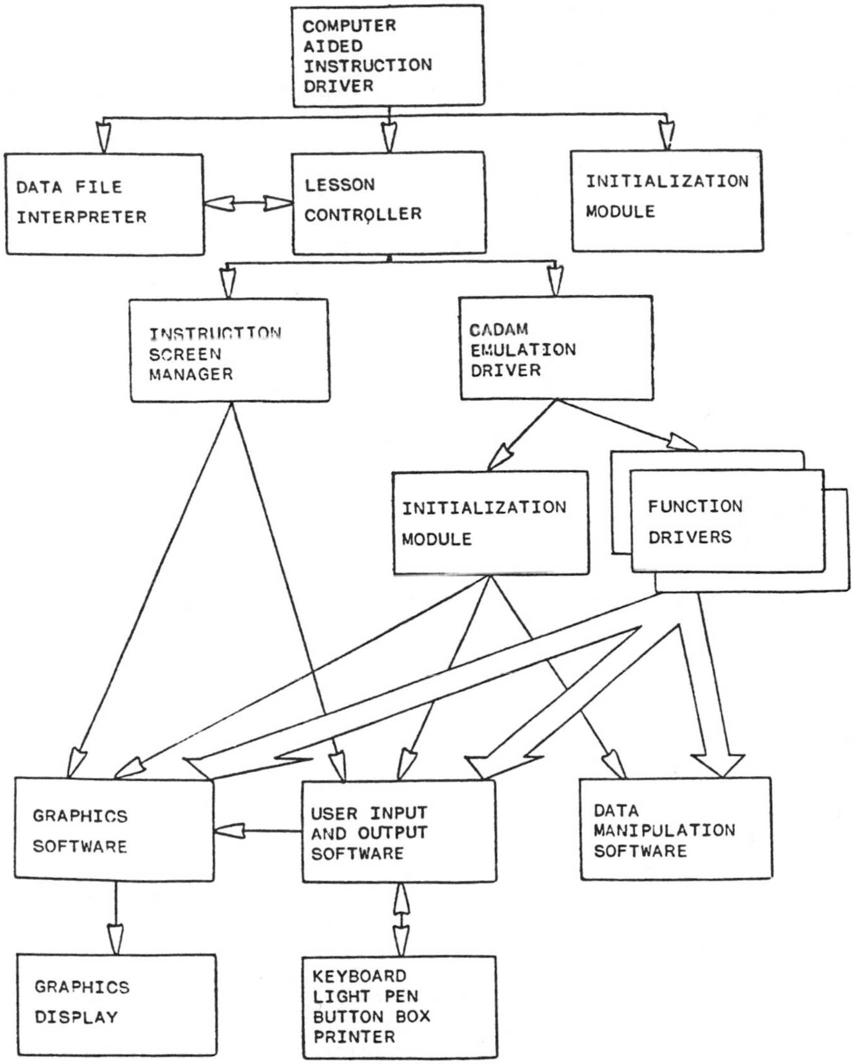

System Architecture Diagram
FIGURE 1

5. A RENEWAL IN ENGINEERING EDUCATION

The ultimate viablity of CAD/CAM as a means for improving productivity is directly dependent on the innovative capabilities of future graduates from universities.

The coupling of a visual graphics display with the computational power of the digital computer provides powerful assistance to the solution of complex problems in design and analysis. However, design - a major component in engineering practice - is the least tractable part of modern engineering education. Compounding this, the inituitive analysis base, provided through sometimes gross but necessary approximations, was rapidly disappearing from the curriculum as "exact" numerical solutions using time-sharing alphanumeric computers became the norm. Fortunately, the graphics system has the ability to provide the experience base for intuitive analysis through its ability to rapidly solve complex problems in which the problem variables can be readily changed and the results displayed visually.

Rensselaer has incorporated this philosophy into its entire engineering undergraduate program [3]. Tables 1 and 2 show the Fall, 1982 semester class usage. A total of 48 courses is listed, involving 1,500 students who used 19,000 terminal-hours of computer graphics time! These students will use graphics throughout their four year program at Rensselaer.

6. EDUCATION FOR CAD/CAM

In addition to the integration of computer graphics into the traditional engineering program, it is important to focus on CAD/CAM systems of the future.

Students should feel comfortable with ideas such as the solid model based professional workstation having a natural and realistic representation of the part design, and supporting integrated user transparent design methods, analysis routines, intelligent databases, management control, and manufacturing process capabilities.

It is clear that many aspects of design will be elevated from an art to a science by embodying in the design process more powerful methods for visualization, representation and change-oriented flexibiltiy, based on fast advanced color graphics and the power of a 3D geometric part modeling capability. In this environment, design and manufacturing process performance will be predicted by analytical methods prior to production of parts or products.

Students should also understand conceptualization in the design process and new design methodologies. For example, what can be done in the system to enhance the designer's ability to conceptualize a new design? What are the appropriate design descriptors so that an engineer can communicate ideas in a higher order terms? Why do we always start with points, lines, and arcs; why not flanges, brackets, and bearings? How far can we take the concept of parametric capabilities and generic shapes which can be manipulated in a design? How does one approach the problem of capturing and transferring experience to new designers, i.e., the concept of expert or knowledge-based design systems?

What should be done to facilitate the engineer's ability to communicate with computers for the purpose of improved effectiveness in the design process? How about better interactive devices for graphic displays to enhance conceptualization and decision-making, expecially in handling complex 3D objects or VLSI designs. The list of future directions is endless.

7. SUMMARY

This paper focused on two aspects of training and education for CAD/CAM, viz., near term operator training using personal computer, and long term professional growth in a modern university curriculum.

Both aspects are illustrated by on-going programs at the Center for Interactive Computer Graphics at Rensselaer. Training using the personal computer represents an industry sponsored project which is currently undergoing testing and evaluation. The education program involving computer graphics has received national attention.

8. REFERENCES

1. Koopman, Philip, "CADAM™ Training on an IBM Personal Computer", Master Thesis, TR-82019, Center for Interactive Computer Graphics, Rensselaer Polytechnic Institute, Troy, New York, December, 1982.

2. Curry, Margaret M., "CADAM™ Training on an IBM Personal Computer: Project Status Report", Center for Interactive Computer Graphics, Rensselaer Polytechnic Institute, Troy, New York, Internal Report, January 6, 1983.

3. Wozny, Michael J., "The Impact of Computer Graphics in Engineering Education: An RPI Perspective", Prepared for ASEE/NSF Compilation of Papers on the Impact of Advanced Technologies in Engineering Education. Center for Interactive Computer Graphics, Rensselaer Polytechnic Institute, Troy, New York, June, 1982.

9. ACKNOWLEDGEMENT

The author acknowledges Phil Koopman and Meg Curry for their work on the IBM Personal Computer based CADAM™ training system.

This work was supported under NSF Grant ISP79-20240 and other industry grants. This support is gratefully acknowledged. Any opinions, findings, and conclusions or recommendations expressed in this publication are those of the author and do not necessarily reflect the views of the National Science Foundation or any of the industrial sponsors.

TABLE 1 - FALL 1982 SEMESTER ACTUAL CLASS USAGE OF INSTRUCTIONAL COMPUTER GRAPHICS

Course No./Title (Faculty)	No. of Students	Total Sem. Term. Hrs.	Ave. Term. Hrs/Stud.
10243 Intro. Comp. Applic. in Architecture (Quadrel)	32	423	13.2
20114 Comp. Fund-Eng. II (Weidner)	116	488.4	4.2
20114 Self-Paced (Darling)	53	576.5	10.9
20220 Lumped Parameter Systs (Smith)	209	416.7	2.0
20220 Self-Paced (Smith)	64	112.4	1.8
20290 Engng. Project (Darling)	66	869.9	13.2
20243 Intro. Heat Transfer (Smith)	35	1.8	0.1(Demo)
20496 Adv. Mfg. Lab (Derby)	27	19	0.7
32665 Adv. Process Control (Arkun)	11	243.9	22.2
33654 Earth Structures and Slopes (Abraham)	9	63.1	7.0
33694 Readings in CE (Shephard)	4	131.4	32.9
34696 Topics in Electric Power Engng. (Nelson)	42	362.8	8.6
35202 Circuits and Electronics II (Carlson)	58	6.8	0.1(Demo)
35210 Electromagnetic Theory (Connor)	179	466.1	2.6
35451 Discrete Time Systems (Ponnathpur)	160	446.6	2.8
35471 Interactive CAD (Wozny)	70	7019.9	100.3
35475 Computer Graphics (Franklin)	142	3538.1	24.9
35479 Microprocessor Systems (Misra)	1	12.1	12.1
35640 Systs Analysis Techniques (Frederick)	30	62.5	2.1
35653 Information Theory and Coding (Pearlman)	8	19.7	2.5
37413 Designing with Composite Materials (Goetschel)	2	15.5	7.7
37442 Mechanisms (Derby)	34	435	12.8
37450 Mechanical Engng. Experimentation (Somerscales)	16	28.9	1.8
37496 Topics in Mechanical, Aeronautical Engng or Mechanics (Sneck)	47	623.3	13.3
37611 Kinematic Synthesis (Derby)	24	667.6	27.8
38611 Applied Atomic and Nuclear Physics (Block)	9	51.2	5.7
TOTALS:	1,448	17,102.2	11.8(Ave.)

TABLE 2 - Semester Independent Study and Course Preparaton Usage of Instructional Computer Graphics

Course		Terminal Hours
20294	Engineering Projects (2)	51.8
32645	Advanced Biochemical Engineering	154
33495	Mechanics of Particulate Materials	3.7
33634	Finite Element Methods	729.5
33645	Structural Dynamics	72.9
34688	Theory of Electrical Machines	23
34696	Topics in Electric Power Engineering	15.3
35210	Electromagnetic Theory	1.3
35427	Lasers and Optical Engineering	0.5
35441	Linear Systems	132.6
35475	Computer Graphics	162.9
35494	Readings in Electrical, Computer, and Systems Engineering	132.2
35498	Senior Projects (2)	128.7
35698	Master's Project	45
37211	Experimental Fluid Dynamics I	116.3
37461	Vibrations	63.2
37494	Individual Projects	31
37496	Topics in Mechanical, Aeronautical Engineering and Mechanics	3.3
37489	Senior Project	17.8
37699	Master's Thesis	3.9
38662	Critical Reactor Laboratory	42.2
97102	Naval Ships Systems I	4.1
	TOTAL	1,935.2

APPENDIX

Center for Interactive Computer Graphics: Equipment and Research

INTRODUCTION

The Center for Interactive Computer Graphics is an independent administrative unit within the RPI School of Engineering, maintaining a comprehensive university-industry computer graphics and CAD/CAM research program, in addition to an instructional program. The Center supports 25 full-time faculty/staff, and 30 graduate research students on a total annual budget in excess of 1 million dollars. The university-industry cooperative research program is funded by NSF and 34 participating companies.

EQUIPMENT

The Center maintains five computer systems and 61 graphics terminals valued at approximately 5 million dollars. The instructional/general research system consists of 2 PRIME 750's and 41 IMLAC Dynagraphics 4220 and Series II vector refresh terminals, with a Versatec electrostatic plotter and a CALCOMP 1051 4-color pen plotter; a Talos 40" x 50" Digitizing Board, and a Tektronix 4113 (640x480x4). The CAD/CAM research system consists of an IBM 4341 II mainframe, 2 IBM 3250 vector terminals, 3 IBM 3277 GA storage tube terminals, 2 IBM 3279 raster terminals, an Evans and Sutherland PS300, 2 Adage 4370 3D vector workstations, a Britton-Lee IBM 500 database machine and 4 IBM Personal Computers.

The raster graphics research system consists of a PRIME 500, 2 ADI Light 50 (512x512x8) raster terminals, a Sanders Graphics 8 (1024x1024x4), a Lexidata 3400 (640x512x12), 2 Raster Technologies Model I (512x512x24), a Tektronix 4113 (480x620), a Dunn 631 Camera System and an IMAPRO QCR35 Camera System.

The graphics hardware research system consists of an HP 1000 F-series processor with two HP 2648A graphics terminals, an HP 1310B vector display, and a Gerber IDS-80 turnkey system.

RESEARCH PROGRAMS

The University-Industry Cooperative Research program was established with industrial and NSF support to carry out research in computer graphics, CAD/CAM and engineering/manufacturing applications. The basic areas of research include:

- Graphics Systems (hardware, languages, standards, animation)
- Geometric Modeling (surfaces, solids)
- Analysis Interfaces (FEM, control systems, circuits)
- Databases (IGES, data exchange)
- Manufacturing Interfaces (NC, process planning)
- Applications

The basic structure of the program allows the results of all projects, except specific proprietary data, to be shared with all participating industries. Projects are defined jointly by the member company and the Graphics Center. Results include three formal reviews a year.

The research staff currently interacts with 34 companies on state-of-the-art problems. The comprehensive nature of the program and the compliment of equipment is unique among university-industry programs of this type.

DESIGN DOCUMENT GENERATION FROM ENGINEERING DATABASES

Fumio Nakamura, Atsumi Kimura

Systems Development Lab., Hitachi, Ltd.
1099 Ohzenji, Asao-ku, Kawasaki 215, JAPAN

Tadashi Takanishi

Tsuchiura Works, Hitachi, Ltd.

Kimio Arai

Software Technology Promotion Center
Hitachi, Ltd.

ABSTRACT

Compared with business applications, database concept was not widely accepted in engineering applications. Currently available are rather independent programs such as engineering calculation and analysis programs, and turnkey computer aided design systems which emphasize drawing. In recent years, however, active efforts have been being made to build integrated design support systems. Engineering databases play a key role for integration. Three types of data are included in engineering databases; geometric data, engineering data, and administration data. Engineering data includes several kinds of data such as design results and maintenance histories of completed products, design data for products being designed, reliability data, and design standards. It is accessed in a trial and error manner by engineers and has been least integrated into databases.

By retrieving and calculating engineering data, produced are design documents which are the most important output of designers as well as drawings. In the paper, we describe the features of design documents and the architecture of a design document generation support system.

1. Introduction

Recent progress in computer hardware has made it possible to apply computers to new applications. One of such new applications is data processing of ad hoc nature. White collars' jobs are a typical application of ad hoc nature: Focused on clerks' jobs are (general) office automation systems, focused on managers' jobs are decision support systems, and focused on designers jobs are computer aided design systems.

Current computer aided design (abbreviated into CAD) systems, however, are not real design systems but drawing oriented systems. Therefore, active efforts have been being made to build integrated design support systems since design process includes much more than drawing.[1-4] Database concept, called engineering databases, is essencial for integration. Engineering databases include three different types of data as follows:

(1) Geometric data -- holds three dimensional shape and attribute data of products, and drawing information which is a two dimensional projection of shape data. It has highly complex relationships among data items and requires high speed data access. Therefore, current general purpose databse management systems (abbreviated into DBMS) cannot fully manipulate the data structures from the performance point of view. Because of that, most present CAD systems access geometric data between main memory and secondary storage in simple ways, e.g. direct block access, and manage it as main memory data during one job, e.g. processing of a drawing, which lacks flexibility of data structure modifications, e.g. addition of new attributes, since they do not provide even data definition facility which all DBMS's provide.

(2) Engineering data -- includes several kinds of data such as design data, except geometric data, for products being designed, design results and maintenance histories of completed products, reliability data, and design standards. Among the three, it is least integrated into databases. Data access is made in an ad hoc manner with a wide variety of data selection conditions, while the data access traffic is usually low. So, the most important factor to select DBMS's for this data is the ease of use, which is the most significant feature of relational DBMS's compared with traditional ones.

(3) Administration data -- is data required for managerial applications such as manufacturing control and cost management. It is already implemented as on-line database systems using traditional general purpose DBMS's in a number of companies.

As above mentioned, data access patterns of the three types of data are quite differnt each other, and there are no DBMS's, at present, which can well handle all of the data. Although most present papers[3,4] still focus primarily on handling geometric data, (logical) integration of other two types of data is essential for construction of integrated design support systems. (We mean , by "logical integration", integration by more than one DBMS.)

We have now a project in Hitachi aiming to develop common tools, called **EASY** -- Engineering Activity support SYstems, which help construct engineering database systems, and are trying to implement engineering database systems at some factories by applying the tools. The largest tool is **EASY-DOC**, a design document generation support system, since design documents are the most important output of designers as well as drawings. Contrary to drawings, however, computer aided design document generation has not been frequently discussed. In this paper, we clarify the features of design documents and describe the architectural details of EASY-DOC.

2. Features of Design Documents

A typical page of a design document is shown in Figure 1. The following features can be derived from the figure: (The numbers one to six correspond to those in the figure.)

(1) Japanese or other statements appear.

(2) Formulas may be included.

(3) Also included are special symbols such as superscripts, subscripts, and mathematical symbols (root, integral, etc.).

(4) Tabular forms appear.

(5) Descriptive figures and graphs are included.

Page formats are composed by the above components. And usually, same page formats are used many times, with minor changes, for different products of same kinds.

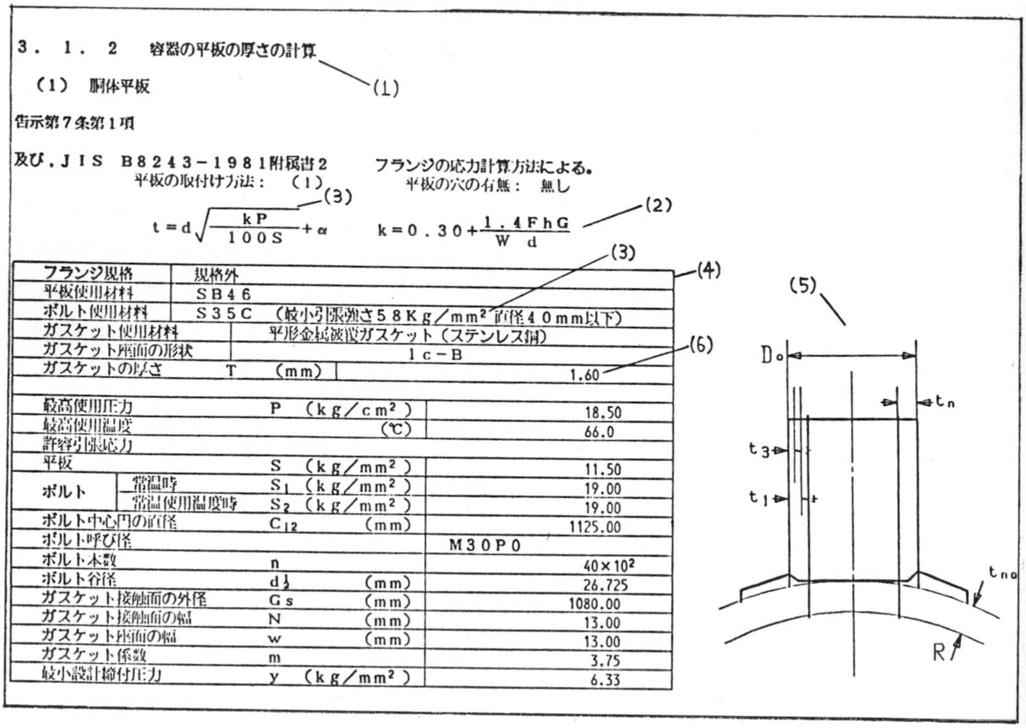

3．1．2　容器の平板の厚さの計算

（1）　胴体平板

告示第7条第1項

及び，JIS　B8243－1981附属書2　　フランジの応力計算方法による。

平板の取付け方法：　（1）　　平板の穴の有無：　無し

$$t = d\sqrt{\frac{kP}{100S}} + \alpha \qquad k = 0.30 + \frac{1.4FhG}{Wd}$$

フランジ規格	規格外		
平板使用材料	SB46		
ボルト使用材料	S35C （最小引張強さ58Kg／mm² 直径40mm以下）		
ガスケット使用材料	平形金属被覆ガスケット（ステンレス鋼）		
ガスケット座面の形状	1c－B		
ガスケットの厚さ	T （mm）		1.60
最高使用圧力	P （kg／cm²）		18.50
最高使用温度	（℃）		66.0
許容引張応力			
平板	S （kg／mm²）		11.50
ボルト 常温時	S_1 （kg／mm²）		19.00
ボルト 常温使用温度時	S_2 （kg／mm²）		19.00
ボルト中心円の直径	C_{12} （mm）		1125.00
ボルト呼び径		M30P0	
ボルト本数	n		40×10^2
ボルト谷径	d½ （mm）		26.725
ガスケット接触面の外径	Gs （mm）		1080.00
ガスケット接触面の幅	N （mm）		13.00
ガスケット座面の幅	w （mm）		13.00
ガスケット係数	m		3.75
最小設計締付圧力	y （kg／mm²）		6.33

Figure 1. A Page Example of a Design Document

(6) The different portions between products are variable fields whose values are set by the following manners based on design conditions and/or specifications.
- Retrieval from engineering databases or user files.
- Direct input by designers.
- Calculation on retrieved or input values.
- Calls of other programs.

(7) A design document consists of one or more pages. And document management including revision management is needed.

To accomplish the above, it is necessary to unite document processing ((1) to (4)), graphic processing ((5)), data processing ((6)), database management ((6)), and document management ((7)). EASY-DOC satisfies these features, especially (6) and (7) as we will discuss in next section.

3. Architecture of EASY-DOC

3.1 Overall Architecture

the overall structure of EASY-DOC is depicted in Figure 2. EASY-DOC has its own database, called document database, for document definition, processing, generation, and management. The structure of the database will be described in Section 3.2. The engineering database provides source data for variable fields whose values are decided for each product in document processing. These two kinds of databases are both managed by a relational database management system (abbreviated into RDBMS). The RDBMS provides SQL[5] (Structured Query Language) as data sub-language.

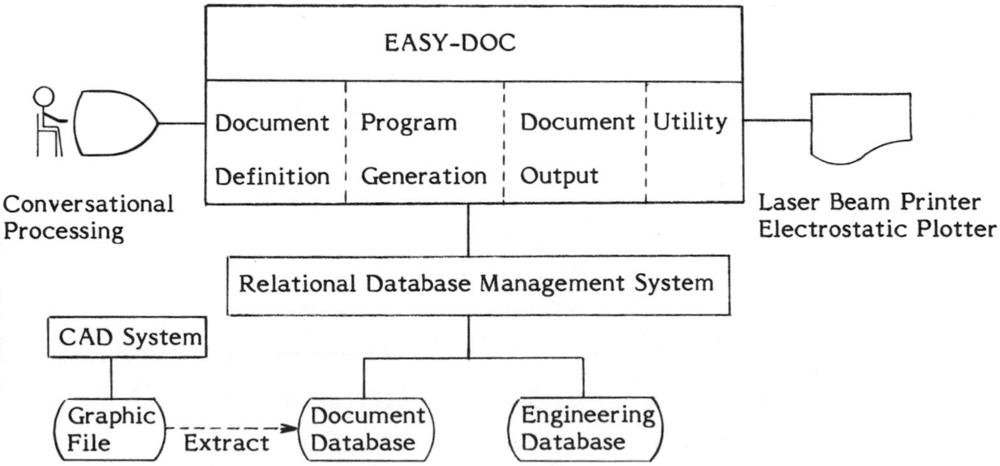

Figure 2. Overall Structure of EASY-DOC

The document definition function makes up document formats each of which consists of page formats like Figure 1. The program generation function will be discussed in Section 3.3. The document output function outputs document formats or generated documents to a laser beam printer or an electrostatic plotter.

3.2 Document Database

All information about defined documents and generated documents is stored in the document database whose principal entity sets and relationship sets are shown in Figure 3 using the Entity-Relationship model[6]. In a usual case, the document database is directly maintained only by EASY-DOC. Users indirectly access it through EASY-DOC. We will make a brief discussion on it. (Although we use the Entity-Relationship diagram depicted in Figure 3 for discussion, the actual database is of course represented as a set of relations, or tables in another word.)

(1) DOC-DEF holds overall document definition information. The definition is made in a conversational mode.

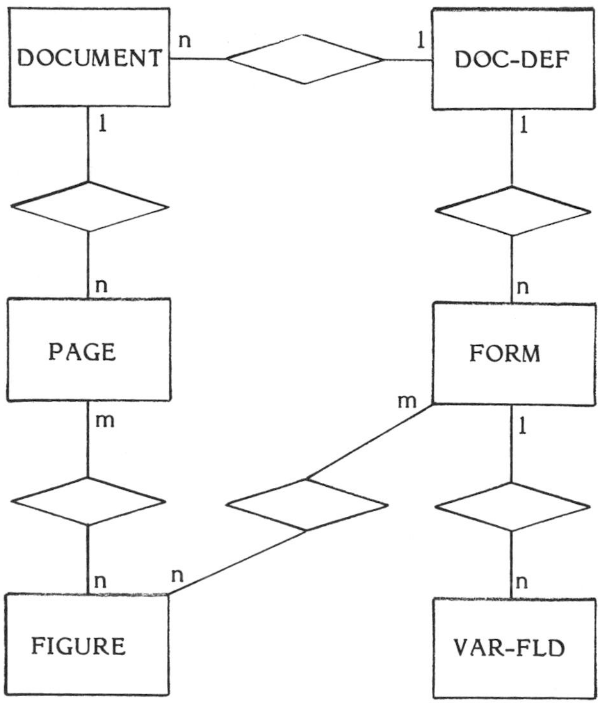

Figure 3. Main Data Structure of the Document Database

(2) FORM has page format information. A defined document consists of one or more forms. For each form, the following are specified and make up a page format as shown in Figure 1.

- Statements in Japanese or other languages are specified.
- Special symbols are defined as follows:

  $A^n \rightarrow$ A#SUP(n), $B_1 \rightarrow$ B#SUB(1)

  $x = \sqrt{(a+b)/(c-d)} + e \rightarrow x =$ %SQRT((a+b)/(c-d)) + e

  (The symbols "#" and "%" indicate control characters.)
- Tabular forms can be specified.
- Blank areas for figures and graphs are specified and the relationships between areas and figures are defined.

(3) VAR-FD holds information for variable fields. During the document definition, the following information is specified for each variable field:

- Name.
- Address and length in the form.
- Data type to receive.
- Display format.

(4) DOCUMENT holds information corresponding to each generated document from a defined document by setting variable field values. Furthermore, more than one document of the same kind for each product may exist. Namely, there can be revisions for each document.

(5) Each PAGE is constructed by setting variable field values in a form and by making minor changes to the form if necessary.

(6) FIGURE has information about figures and graphs to be inserted to forms and pages. It is extracted from graphic systems in plotter command form.

3.3 Program Generation

The presence of variable fields requires combination of document processing and data/database processing. The program generation function helps users easily write procedures which set variable field values. Users can write procedures using pseudo-codes the program generator provides. Pseudo-codes consist of FORTRAN, SQL, and the form control statements, and they may also directly include variable field names which are specified in the document definition. The program generator generates complete FORTRAN77 source programs with SQL statements from specified pseudo-codes by translating the form control statements and variable field names into appropreate FORTRAN procedural and declare statements as shown in Figure 4. It refers to the document definition information in the document database during the

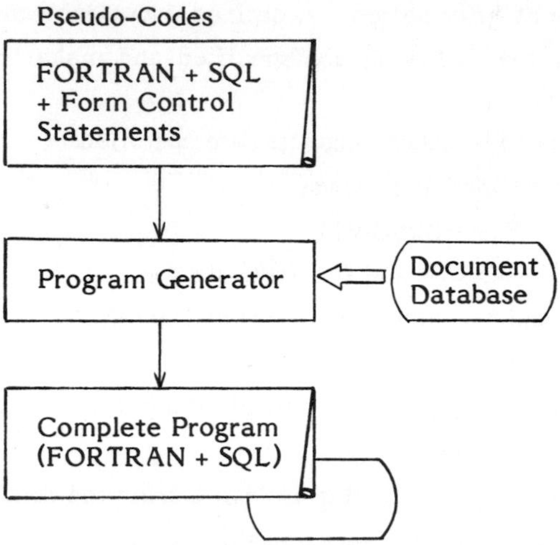

Figure 4. Program Generator

```
%OPEN   FORM1 ;
%GETF   ?A, ?B, ?C ;

EXEC SQL
  SELECT COL1, COL2
  INTO ?D, ?E  FROM  TBL1
  WHERE COL3 = ?A  AND  COL4>20
END EXEC

FORTRAN statements
           :
%LINK   PROG1 (?D, ?E, ?F) ;
%SETF   ?D, ?E, ?F ;
%DISPLAY   PAGE1 ;
%SAVE   PAGE1 ;
%CLOSE   FORM1 ;
END
```

(a) Pseudo-codes

Figure 5. An Example of Program Generation

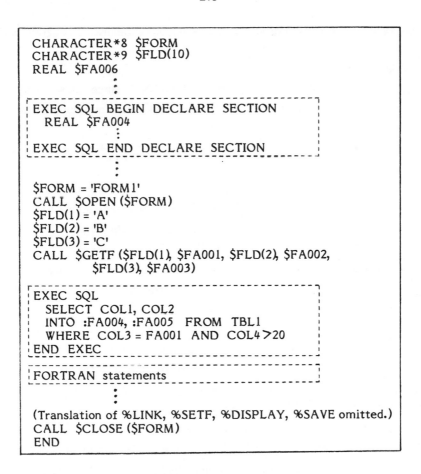

```
CHARACTER*8 $FORM
CHARACTER*9 $FLD(10)
REAL $FA006
        :
EXEC SQL BEGIN DECLARE SECTION
  REAL $FA004
        :
EXEC SQL END DECLARE SECTION
        :
$FORM = 'FORM1'
CALL $OPEN ($FORM)
$FLD(1) = 'A'
$FLD(2) = 'B'
$FLD(3) = 'C'
CALL $GETF ($FLD(1), $FA001, $FLD(2), $FA002,
         $FLD(3), $FA003)

EXEC SQL
  SELECT COL1, COL2
  INTO :FA004, :FA005 FROM TBL1
  WHERE COL3 = FA001 AND COL4>20
END EXEC

FORTRAN statements
        :
(Translation of %LINK, %SETF, %DISPLAY, %SAVE omitted.)
CALL $CLOSE ($FORM)
END
```

(b) Generated FORTRAN Program

Figure 5. An Example of Program Generation (continued)

translation process. An example of pseudo-codes and a generated program is shown in Figure 5.

(1) FORTRAN Statements

Pseudo-codes are primarily based on FORTRAN77 since most designers have familiality with FORTRAN and FORTRAN77 can well handle non-numeric data.

(2) Variable Fields

When the program generator encounters a variable field whose name is preceded by "?", it takes the following actions:

(a) It replaces the name by a FORTRAN variable name which begins with "$F".

(b) It generates a declare statement for the variable by retrieving the variable field definition information from the document database.

(3) SQL Statements

SQL statements may be written in the same forms as they appear in the host language FORTRAN77. They may include variable fields.

(4) Form Control Statements

These are special statements provided by the program generator for primarily form control such as open and close of forms, setting up variable field values, and display of pages to display terminals. The control statements begin with "%". There are ten kinds of statements.

(a) %OPEN makes a form ready to process.

(b) %CLOSE makes the form unable to process.

(c) %GETF is used to receive field values from a display terminal under guidance in conversation mode or as card image data in batch mode.

(d) %SETF sets up variable field values in the form. The values are edited corresponding to each display format defined in the document database.

(e) %DISPLAY outputs the generated page to the display terminal for confirmation.

(f) %SAVE stores the generated page to the document database.

(g) %GETP returns the number of pages already generated in the document.

(h) %SETP attaches a page number to the generated page.

(i) %LINK dynamically links to another program specified.

(j) %PUT outputs a message.

4. Concluding Remarks

EASY-DOC is now in detail design stage and will be completed by September 1983. Although the goal of EASY-DOC is a tight combination of document processing, document management, graphic processing, data processing, and database management, the combination with graphic processing is very loose now. So, it is our next target to integrate graphic processing into database management world. But it is not a short range target since the requirements for graphic data management completely disagree with the current database management technology as discussed in Section 1 and the full solution will not be brought in a short term in spite that many papers are published for the topic.[3,4]

References

1. Survey Reports on Engineering Database systems (in Japanese), IPA (March 1976, 1977, 1978).

2. A Survey Report on Computer Aided Engineering (in Japanese), JIPDEC (March 1982).

3. Computer-Aided Design, Vol.11, No.3 (Special issue on databases) (May 1979).

4. Encarnacao, J. (ed.): File Structures and Data Bases for CAD, Proc. IFIP WG5.2 Conf. (Sept. 1981).

5. Chamberlin, D., et al.: SEQUEL2: A Unified Approach to Data Definition, Manipulation, and Control, IBM J. Res. and Develop., Vol.20, No.6 (Nov. 1976).

6. Chen, P.: The Entity-Relationship Model - Toward a Unified View of Data, ACM TODS, Vol.1, No.1 (March 1976).

DATA COMMUNICATIONS, CAD/CAM GRAPHICS AND DISTRIBUTOR DESIGN CONCEPTS

Lewis D. Brentano

Dataquest Incorporated
19055 Pruneridge Avenue
Cupertino, California 95014
U. S. A.

ABSTRACT

The rapidly emerging CAD/CAM industry has impacted many areas of industry today. This paper investigates a future CAD environment called a distributed design concept. This concept is derived from market forces in the user community and will be important to the success of CAD/CAM and graphics vendors in the future. To melt the market requirements, vendors will need to implement strategies in data communications, data bases and graphics. This paper reviews the hardware and software aspects of these three components and presents the possible future scenarios for their application to distributed CAD/CAM.

INTRODUCTION

The Computer Aided Design and Manufacturing (CAD/CAM) industry is still in its infancy. It is a very small industry by standards of the computer marketplace. The revenues for the industry for the year 1982 are estimated by my firm at approximately $1.3 billion. Although this is a large growth from five years previous when the industry was under $200 million, it still is a very small percentage of the total computer business in the world today. As a case in point, the total yearly revenue of all CAD/CAM sales is equal to approximately 2 to 2 1/2 weeks of IBM's data processing revenues. There have been, however, many new entrants into this industry and it is expected to grow rapidly. The hallmark of the CAD/CAM industry has been its use of computer graphics; from its earliest conception until today it has used high-technology in the graphics area, and this is expected to continue. One feature of the computer aided design industry, however, has been its slowness in adopting certain new technologies in computers and graphics. The position of this paper is that this could well continue in the future in such areas as data communication and data bases. Cases in point for this argument would be the use of 32-bit mini-computers in the CAD/CAM environment. 32-bit virtual memory computers have been available since 1976. Computers by Perkin Elmer, Prime, and SEL were available in 1976 with 32-bit addressing in virtual or direct address mode. Digital Equipment announced a virtual memory VAX system in 1978. However, it was not until mid to late 1981 that any of the traditional CAD/CAM vendors started shipping 32-bit based systems and indeed it has not been until this past year, 1982, that there has been any large percentage of 32-bit systems shipped with CAD/CAM equipment. Another case in point is the use of raster graphics, more specifically, high resolution raster graphics. Such capabilities have existed for 1,000 line raster graphics to be used in conjunction with CAD/CAM systems since mid-1979, and at reasonable prices. However, it was not until 1981 that 1,000-line color and monochrome raster systems were available. The majority of systems shipped in 1982 will use such graphics devices.

In the area of data communiations and its impact on Computer-Aided Design and Manufacturing, it is likely that such history will be repeated and that most activity will be started in other sectors of the computer industry and implemented before CAM/CAM and graphics are integrated into local area and remote area networks. The import of this is that much of the activity and discussions about integrated manufacturing or factories of the future are pure speculation because the basic cornerstones of such implementations are beyond the current CAM/CAM systems capabilities. Such implementation will rely on data communications technologies that have both hardware and software aspects. Clearly though, end users are pushing for this integration concept.

This paper will discuss in detail the features that are needed for this communications cornerstone to exist and it will result in what might be called distributed design concepts. It is the position of this paper that the distributed design concept must exist before significant Factory of the Future or integrated manufacturing activities can occur. This paper will discuss these hardware and software technologies, review the market forces today to show what may happen in the future, and investigate the key elements that will be needed for graphics to contribute to this design concept.

In the area of hardware technologies there are essentially three aspects of the problem that must be reviewed. One is the data communications hardware that is used, the second is the graphics terminal or workstation used and the third is the central processors or the basic computers used. In the area of data communications hardware, the issues are the choice of hardware and environment in which the so called distributed design concept will be implemented. From a graphics hardware standpoint, the issue is how much local intelligence will be needed in the graphics equipment to meet the needs of this distributed design concept. The final hardware topic to be reviewed is that of the central processor. Basically, trends here are well defined as to what will be happening in the area of central processor development, but the key questions are how does the graphics and data communications hardware tie in with the central processor function, and is the central processor even necessary to attain distributed design capabilities.

Equally important in the realm of data communications, graphics and CAM/CAM will be the software technologies that are implemented. Areas here that are important are data communications, data bases, languages associated with the data bases, and the operating systems that control all of the various components. The issue of data communications software is unsettled primarily because there is no agreement or standard of any sort in areas of local area networks or remote networks. It is anticipated that in any distributed design concept the data base function will be a key component, since many users will be accessing a common data base, changing it and then sending that information to other users within a corporation. These activites will range from prototype testing, automatic testing, computer aided manufacturing (NC) to the basic manufacturing requirements planning capabilities for inventory control, production planning and shop floor scheduling. An associated software topic is that of the query language which will provide an environment which users with little or no computer background can access the required design information. This query language approach will also require accurate and reliable audit trail procedures to make sure that the history of all activity on a given project can be maintained and checked at any point in the overall design process.

These software aspects have direct impacts on the operating system that controls all aspects of the CAD/CAM environment. These operating system concerns will dictate the basic hardware architecture and structure of the CAM/CAM environment in the future. This paper will then review the need for integration that is developing in the industrialized environments in which CAM/CAM is being used today. Basic features of this need for integration are the fact that the amount of paper that can be generated by computer aided design systems with today's powerful graphics is literally overwhelming to the typical design process of even the major corporations, such as General Motors, Ford, Fujitsu, Hitachi or Toyota. The issue of retention will then be a major problem because computer aided design systems that are non-integrated can produce more paper, more drawings, faster than manual methods could in the past. The other need for integration stems from the future economic environment, in which many markets will be very competitive and demand better efficiency. The so-called basic industries--auto, steel, and rubber for example--clearly have great challenges ahead and the integration of the design process with analysis manufacturing, testing, production/inventory control will be necessary to achieve the required productivity. It is also true that the market needs are not necessarily voiced by all participants in the market place. Many end users do not always require sophisticated integrated manufacturing; for example, a local area network function for several graphics workstations is adequate to meet the needs of a $20 million design engineering company participates in small projects that have a short lifespan. However, the major companies in the United States do need this integrated capability and these companies produce the majority of goods in the United States. It is a fact that the top 20 percent of corporations in the world produce about 80 percent of the products that are purchased in the world. This indicates that there will be a tremendous market for the distributed design concept based simply on the volume of business that is generated by these leading companies. These large firms will require sophisticated local area networks as well as remote networks, since they are generally geographically dispersed. In fact these large firms will have an impact on the smaller companies, since many small companies subcontract work from the larger firms. In this case the distributed design concept would dictate that a smaller firm have some link to the larger firm's data base and Computer Aided Design system. This again will dictate a paticular type of graphics environment that is necessary for large and small companies alike and that will ultimately result in greater integration of CAD with the overall production process in any type of company in any country.

Market Forces

First we would like to review the market forces that are occuring today that will require the types of products that will be used in the distributed design concept. Two things stand out about CAD/CAM today. First, the number of engineers that are effected by CAD/CAM are very small today and second, most companies believe that this number will increase dramatically in the future. These two aspects, the small penetration today and the belief by many firms that penetration will increase dictates that the capabilities of CAD/CAM and graphics systems must advance also. The important feature here is that the graphics systems is the interface of the engineer or designer to the data base in the computer aided design system. Advances in graphics must necessarily then follow the requirements of the marketplace for CAD/CAM. The marketplace in 1982, at $1.3 billion dollars represents a total of 2,600 systems shipped this year, an installed base of systems of 7,800, with the number of graphics terminals shipped for CAD/CAM 9,518 in 1982, and an installed base of over 27,000 graphics units as of the end of 1982. This market size will increase in the future. It is felt by DATAQUEST that by considering two companies that are heavily involved in computer aided design and their future directions we can learn something about the market forces generated by companies using CAD/CAM.

The two companies are General Motors and Ford Motor Company. Recent estimates by General Motors indicate that approximately 25 percent of the engineers in their company that could use CAD/CAM are using it today. This small penetration still has accounted for over 1,500 graphics systems in use for CAD inside General Motors. Ford, on a somewhat smaller scale than General Motors, has installed well over 300 units just for automotive design and another 100 to 150 graphics units in place for other aspects of computer aided design of import to the company. Several things are common for both of these companies. The first is that the penetration is small, and the second is that there is little coordination today for all the different uses of these products, in other words, there is not always communication between different groups, even groups using the same computer aided design systems. A final point in common between these companies are that they are aggressively moving to address these problems. General Motors recently has developed a long-term plan for corporate computer coordination, the goal being to create a network and distribute design capabilities that will in turn lead to integrated manufacturing. GM does not anticipate that this will be accomplished quickly and they feel a timeframe of five years may be needed for this to occur. Ford also has taken steps to integrate the capabilities of all their systems, they are in the process of upgrading all CAD/CAM systems inside the company to 32-bit based mini-computer systems with standard networking and data base facilities that will tie all users into other 32-bit data base systems and also tie them into the other computers used by Ford in the analysis, testing, and other manufacturing aspects that are computerized today but cannot communicate to one another. Both companies feel that the key aspect for the success of this approach will be effective utilization of the graphics interface to the CAD/CAM system and the design data bases, freeing the engineers from having to learn very difficult, repetitious computer based languages. Indeed, simple commands are used to generate rather complex functions inside the network of the data base for both of these systems.

A closer look at the Ford system will give some idea of what future these market forces will shape for CAD/CAM and the distributed design concept. At Ford today, of the 300 units in place, 100 of the graphics systems are based on 32-bit machines. This network is composed of local and remote types of interconnections. A typical local network would be ten graphics terminals and five CPUs all on a local ring network with a very high speed, 8 Mhz communications link. Each node in the network, which is one CPU and two graphics systems, has local storage, local disk capabilities, and complete local processing power. A ring of five of these nodes would typically be used in one group for some type of automotive component design. Within a department it would not be unusual to see five or six such local networks in use by various groups. These groups work on a common data base that resides on a data collector processor. The data collector holds all final, signed-off drawings. These are the only drawings that can be accessed by other departments other than the originating one. Such data collectors are communicated to in a remote and interactive fashion by various local networks. The data collector then can communicate through remote links to other data collectors or other computers such as the large Cyber 7600 that Ford uses for structural analysis applications. Although all of the central processors in the network as it is configured could run such structural analysis programs, and could store all the data locally, Ford has chosen to control this so that security, access and protection rights are in place to assure that the proper design data is fed into the proper analysis program and that all activity is coordinated. The data collectors communicate to large mainframe types of systems for the analysis programs. All of the data, however, for such analysis is prepared at the local nodes in the network, using color graphics or high performance vector stroke refresh systems. Ford engineers are able to go from conceptual design to the actual data input used in the structural analysis, to the NC tapes; pre- and post-processing is carried out on these local nodes as is numerical control. Interactive parts programming and the generation of tapes can follow directly on the nodes or through the interaction with the data collector and the NC tape is then sent to the manufacturing floor. Ford's implementation shows the power of networking capabilities. In this particular case, engineers can stay within their department yet access resources that essentially circle the globe. Ford's networking today is implemented in the United States, activity is in various locations in Michigan, and communication takes place over many miles of geographical separation so that this is truly a mixture of local area networks and remote networks.

The approach undertaken at General Motors is slightly different in hardware architecture, yet very similar in the ultimate result that is planned in the company. Most of General Motors computer aided design is based on software that is run on their large mainframe systems with highly intelligent vector stroke refresh systems which are interfaced to users using remote networking facilities and local networking facilities so that the graphics terminals can be fairly close to the engineer or designer's physical location. A common data base is maintained on large mainframes, local storage is not available on the majority of the graphics systems. These graphics systems do have a fair amount of intelligence, however, because they are required to communicate at channel speeds to the host machine. A similar concept to the Ford approach is used in terms of separation of design from analysis, and although the capability exists for the designer to physically design everything and analyze everything without interruption or some other type of checking by the host, the procedures set up inside General Motors are such that design is done by one group, analysis by another and the common data base is accessed and controlled at the central site.

These approaches have one thing in common that has not been mentioned before and it is the fact that the users access times in the network configurations are interactive so that the communications are truly state-of-the-art, and perhaps even beyond current state-of-the-art. Interactive networking, local or remote, is required for the effective utilization of the CAD/CAM and graphics systems and the implementation of the distributed approach to design. To date, it is very possible to find excellent local area networks. However, the availability of interactive local area networks is somewhat more restricted and the availability of interactive remote area networks is very, very restricted. The ability of graphics vendors and CAD/CAM vendors to provide interactive capabilities in the networking area will be key to the succeess of these companies. For example, the ability of a graphics vendor to incorporate local area network processing and sufficient local processor horsepower to handle such local area network processing in a graphics terminal or workstation could provide a very important tool for engineers to become productive and for the manufacturer of this graphics hardware to become quite profitable.

HARDWARE COMPONENTS

Today's computer aided design appliations essentially look very much like islands of automation, and in some cases, simply very fast drafting machines. The uses of CAD at Ford and General Motors really are applications moving beyond this island concept to the emerging CAD of tomorrow which will feature workstation graphics systems that are very powerful, that have local intelligence, that generally will support local area networks, and in addition will allow remote interactive network access directly from the workstation or graphics system to other workstations or central processors. In the past such capabilities at a workstation level were felt to be very hard to accomplish at a reasonable cost, however, the one constant in hardware development over the past ten years that will continue into the future is the fact that the cost of processing is diminishing rapidly so that the requirements for central processor and memory that could be met only by very sophisticated equipment that was very costly two or three years ago, can now be met with perhaps a $5,000 to $10,000 item. The need for interactive remote data communications is one that generates a large requirement for memory and central processing power, in addition to the many fuctions that may be carried out at the graphics workstations. It will be no easy process to generate the type of graphics needed to support this distributed design concept, and indeed it is very likely that the graphics workstation will not replace a central host, but supplement it. The host will remain the repository of final design information and will be the central node of communication from the design to the other types of tasks that are necessary in the manufacture of any type of product.

Figure 1 presents a cost curve of graphics systems. Data for 1982 price/performance is the result of a survey[2] of 11 graphics suppliers. Products were rated in eight feature areas:

- o Viewable Resolution
- o Software Capability
- o Color Capability
- o Company reputation
- o Extras/Expandability
- o Refresh Rate
- o Zoom Functionality
- o Communications Capability.

Table 1 presents the results of this survey, in terms of overall performance and performance/price ratio. The methodology of this technique is based on earlier work by Leow and Nelson[5], that is modified with different weighting factors to account for CAD/CAM specific features. The 1984 price/performance trend line is generated based on the author's estimates of component price changes. This is evidence of a dynamic product environment that successful graphics companies must address and manage.These graphics systems essentially reflect a rapidly diminishing cost of memory and processor units used to produce high resolution, high band width graphics.

Looking at this cost curve one could change the subject or topic of the cost reduction from computer graphics to disk, or from computer graphics to central processors and have relatively the same type of performance available at similarly low cost. One result of the cost curve you see here is the fact that more power will be available to a local user. Another result of this cost curve will be the fact that there will be more users since it will be more cost effective today or in the future to purchase more graphics terminals. More graphics terminals will mean more data and this in itself will cause some problem, perhaps in the future. The larger number of users will also generate the need to store more data on line, much more in fact that had been thought of perhaps even two years ago. Here again this cost curve could be applied to the fact that there will be disks available for on-line storage of data that will be significantly less expensive than the options today[10]. It is very likely that optical disks, by the 1984-1985 time frame will be available, that will be on line and will cost up to 10 times less per megabyte of storage than the available technology today. We estimate that 50 E-size drawings for a typical mechanical product would fit on one megabyte of storage. It is obvious that 50 drawings is not a large number, and a tremendous number of megabytes of storage will be needed to handle the load of many more users, and many more projects using computer aided design. Optical disks in the neighborhood of 600 to 800 billion bytes of information will be available in the 1984-85 timeframe. This capability in turn will put a load on the data communications hardware since the CAD users will have the need for fast transmission of more data, over local or remote networks. Local networks frequently can run in the range of 8-10 megahertz, remote networks today really are limited to perhaps 19,000 to 56,000 bits per second transmission speed. Requirements for fast transmission really is a reflection of the need for good user interactivity at the graphics level, and this in turn will have an impact on the needs in the graphics workstation because even at the local area network speed of 8-10 megahertz along the cable, it is likely the overhead resulting from handling 50 workstations on such a local area network, could limit the effective transmission speed of usable data in the 100-200 kilohertz range. Such performance is not one that will give truly interactive response to graphics queries from the user to the remote disk. This indicates that the graphics workstation must advance to have a fair amount of local, interactive editing intelligence and storage in both disk and memory so that the user will be effectively using his resource and at the same time the data base will be maintained to reflect the most current activity and correct activity of the design.

Based on these market requirements, user activities, and developments in the hardware area, it can be seen that a hierarchy will exist for various types of processing and graphics within a distributed design environment. The hierarchy will start at the user location with high performance graphics capabilities on the workstation that will also have a local processor that handles more than just the graphics functions. It will control a disk, it will control a CPU, and will talk to a local area network. In addition, if such local area network does not have remote facilities, the graphics workstation will also have to talk to the remote interactive network at the same time. This will require significant horsepower in the area of central processing at the graphics workstation. Indeed, it is very likely that the 1985 graphics workstation will incorporate the horsepower of the moderate speed 32-bit mini-computer today. The next level in the hardware hierarchy will be a very powerful 32-bit, mini-computer system, four to five times the performance of today's available 32-bit high-end mini-computer systems. This performance will be needed to handle the data base activities of the local area networks that are plugged into the system as well as the remote networks with which this hierarchy will communicate. This second hierarchy will be required to maintan a data base that is extensive and large, and at the same time maintain a query language environment and handle communications overhead. It is unlikely that the horsepower required to carry out this large data base function can exist at the local workstation level, simply because of the number of users in the network and the amount of data that is archived that must be maintained and periodically checked for consistency and correctness. The third level of hierarchy would be a dedicated analysis or non-design machine. This machine may well run in the batch mode in which a job is started and upon completion, the pertinent results are fed back to a particular user through the network in this hierarchy. This third level in the hierarchy may also represent non-engineering functions, such as inventory control, production control, shop floor scheduling, and the like. These activities of course are derived from the design data base. This third level in the hierarchy is very likely to be more logical than physical, since the horsepower needed to carry out such functions is available today in super minicomputers or powerful mainframes, so the hardware in the second or third heirarchy are similar. The differentiation between these levels is due to usage of these resources by different disciplines, so the network configuration will be a logical heirarchy as much as a physical one.

In summary the impact of hardware advances on the distributed design concept will be very important and the key aspects of the hardware advance will be on the user of the CAD/CAM system. It is in this area that advances in computer graphics will be key to the entire distributed design concept. Computer graphics systems will require far more intelligence, more memory and networking facilities, for distributed design to take effect and for the integration of design, manufacturing, and analysis to occur. The various other developments in the area of processors and data communications hardware will make it easier for the graphics workstation of the future to handle all the various functions that are required, and in fact it is anticipated that simple board level options will be available to make a stand alone graphics workstation and implement it as a node in a larger local network and remote network environment. The key area that must still be addressed is the whole aspect of software to control this large and multi-faceted environment.

SOFTWARE CAPABILITIES

The problem existing for design in a distributed fashion really is solved by interaction of hardware, software and market forces. However, the crux of the solution to this problem will be the actual software environment in which a CAD system runs. Today it is very easy to move information from point A to point B. It is very difficult, however, to assure that it is correct, current and access to it is authorized. And it is important to make sure that the design engineer, design draftsman, or manufacturing personnel can use the system without a great deal of training. This ease of use feature is very important from the software viewpoint. It is certainly less technical than aspects of local area networks, however, it is nonetheless very important since a technically capable system that is hard to use will not be purchased by industry. In general the software aspects to be considered are data communications, data base management systems, and general operating system environments. Of course this software area must also address the concerns of the CAD/CAM product as well.

The first aspect of software to consider is that of data communication software. Data communication software could be broken down into many different areas, but for the purpose of this paper we will consider the aspects of local area networks and remote area networks. The area of data communications standards will be very important in the future. There is one problem today, however, in that there is no acknowledged standard. There are several systems that may be viewed as de facto standards, one would be Ethernet, the other would be SNA. It is unfortunate, however, that the basic structure of Ethernet and SNA are very different. Ethernet is what has been called a Carrier Sense Multiple Access or CSMA type of network. SNA on the other hand is what is called a token passing network approach. The CSMA approach and token passing approach are basically incompatible so therefore it would be likely to assume that one or the other might be adopted as the standard. However, in a standard development effort by the IEEE, a draft standard called IEEE-802 has been written for release as an official standard by mid-1983. Unfortunately the IEEE-802 standard incorporates both CSMA and token passing as standards because both are already in use. To further complicate the issues the standard also specifies two types of token passing: the ring network approach and the open bus approach. This allows for differences in hardware that have been brought out on the marketplace to date. In this environment it will be difficult for a given graphic vendor company to determine which approach should be taken. It should be noted in this regard that the token passing type of approach is one that has been adopted by IBM in its SNA, System Network Architecture system, and indeed it is very similar in concept to the CCITT X.25 standard. The CSMA approach is one that has been adopted by Ethernet. It is possible in the future to envision an Ethernet approach being used perhaps for a local network with the SNA or X.25 approach being used for the interactive remote network. It is important to note also that the X.25 is a recognized international standard adopted by many nations outside of the United States as the standard for remote communication. X.25 has been implemented by many vendors in hardware to date in the United States and is supported as well by IBM. Ethernet, of course, is very widely accepted and has a wide range of support from Digital, Xerox and Intel. Many new stand-alone workstation systems in the CAD/CAM arena feature graphics that also have Ethernet capability. This is not to say, though, that Ethernet is the final word in the area for software data communication and it is unlikely that a standard will be developed that could be applied and be used for all areas of computer grahics in the CAD/CAM environment and so it will be necessary for vendors to consider both options for the particular type of network access method that will be supported by a product. In any case the decision may be made easier by the fact that there will be board level products that simply plug into a particular hardware configuration, such as a graphics workstation, that would allow the system to act as an Ethernet system or as an SNA/X.25 type of system. The determining factor in which approach to take should be made based on the end user requirements of the CAD/CAM graphics systems and the overall CAD/CAM environment.

It is important to note today that much of the activity in products for local area networks centers on a concept that there will be perhaps 8-10 workstations per data base. In the opinion of the author this assumption is invalid and will only apply for the next year or so because as the cost curves come down the number of workstations that can cost effectively be purchased will increase inside a given company. There will be many more workstations per data base used in a given company or in a division of a company. Our estimate would be that 50 to 100 graphics workstations will exist per data base. This will generate a significant volume of work over a network. It will create a large transmission band-width requirement as well as an overhead load on all the processors involved in the network. It would then be logical to conclude that the networking approach that uses the least amount of overhead for data transmission over the network will be the most viable. At this point it is important to note that CAD/CAM graphics over a network, look very different than many of the end user environments for which these networking concepts were originally devised. Computer graphics and CAD/CAM frequently have large amounts of data that must be transferred in one direction, they are then operated on and passed back in the opposite direction for storage in the data base. The typical size of data that is passed over the network would be an entire drawing, a 10-20 thousand byte file that is passed to the graphics workstation, worked on and then passed back to the database. The impact then of having only 8-10 workstatins per data base as compared to 50-100 workstations per data base will be a significant increase in the load on the networking system and also on the data base management system. It would seem likely at this juncture then that a token passing type of approach would be most apropriate for a remote area network in which information is transmitted not very frequently but when it is transmitted, it comes in large volumes and could in fact be transmitted to various different workstations in a local area network.

The use of a local area network software that is most appropriate in this sort of environment is much more difficult to determine at this time. It is true that the SNA or X.25 approach can work in a local area network at high bandwidths, but some modifications would be necessary to the CCITT implementation. Several vendors in the computer arena have implemented such changes so that very high bandwidth local area networks can exist in an X.25 or token passing type of environment. The nature of computer graphics in the CAD/CAM environment is such that the decision to choose an Ethernet or an X.25 may not necessarily have to be made. Either one could function quite well in the environment in which the graphics workstation handles setting up vector lists and writing to the raster devices, and also handle some amount of local processing power, local disk, and local memory unrelated to the actual graphics function. Such architecture exists today and will continue to be developed to the point where it will be very cost effective to have CAD/CAM function on such computer graphics devices. Another issue in interactive data communciations then would be the interactive remote data communications in which information can be supplied from the certified data base to the authorized user at a local workstation with a minimum amount of time delay over geographically dispersed areas. In this case the geographical separation of the central host and the graphics workstations could be on the order of miles and so some type of communications over a leased line or voice grade telephone line will be necessary. With this being the case it would seem logical to conclude that an already implemented standard used by telecommunications companies around the world should be designated as the one most likely to be used. This would indicate X.25. However, the fact that the largest computer manufacturer in the world, IBM, has SNA as its standard will indicate some choice must be made by the particular vendor of hardware equipment. The General Motors scenario listed earlier in the paper corresponds to the IBM or SNA environment and the Ford scenario listed earlier also corresponds to the non-IBM CAD environment, so that a company who wishes to target a particular environment for CAD/CAM can choose between the SNA or X.25. It is interesting to note that under the SNA system it is possible to have support for the X.25.

In summary, in the data communications software area it is safe to say that computer graphics manufacturers who are putting together graphics workstations for CAD/CAM must consider carefully the environment in which their systems will be used and guarantee that support for interactive remote and local area networks will be available in the product as an option.

The second area of software activity to consider is that of the data base management system that is used to control all the distributed design activities. This is not a very simple task, primarily because with the larger number of users in the workstation network there will be large amounts of data, many changes and interrelation of the data that has to be carefully controlled so that the various design groups can access the most current information on their particular part. For example, it would be possible for a design organization to assign several design engineers to work on three or four sub-assemblies of a main assembly. It would be necessary for each of the design engineers to know when the assembly has been modified through an engineering change order and if that affected their sub-assembly. Conversely, it is necessary also for the project manager to be able to review the most current state of the overall assembly based on sub-assemblies finished by the design engineers. This currency of information is important and will be one of the major challenges to a good data base system in the distributed design environment. The currency of information has to be controlled and the control must function in a fashion so that the design engineer working on sub-assembly number one can be completely up-to-date on all the activities and materials that might be used in the overall assembly on a given project. At the same time it is necessary to consider concurrency of information and to avoid the conflicts that may exist if the overall assembly is being modified at the same time by two engineers each working on a sub-assembly. In this case, each user must be notified to wait until a given change that is more important than his activity has actually occured. The data base issues here involve currency of information from a time standpoint, but also concurrency of information from a multiple user standpoint. These are two of the key areas in the data base management system that have to be addressed for distributed design concepts to succeed.

The other major aspect of the data base environment that must be addressed in any adequate system for distributed design is the aspect of a query language. A query language should function to allow the design engineer to quickly recall information about a given part, sub-assembly, drawing, or project, without having to resort to a large amount of computer programming to access the data. The challenge here is to two-fold: one for the supplier of the distributed design system to make sure that he provides a query language that is suitable for the aspects of design that are carried on. Frequently, it will require key terms or key words to access information. A key word here might be a description of a part, a material name, or project number. Here the query language must also treat the issue of security and authorization so that access may be granted for information only, or access may be granted in order to add new information to an already existing design. This query language must also be easy to use and should function in the environment of the graphics system. The use of alpha-numeric type of keyboards and so on will be necessary in general to extract the information from the data base; so the graphics systems in this environment must have some alpha-numeric capability that permits the designer to quickly access information without leaving the graphics mode of his CAD/CAM operation.

This is a brief review of the data base issues in terms of software for distributed CAD/CAM. A more thorough investigation would be a topic for another complete paper. Suffice it to say that much activity has gone on in the area of data bases today, particularly the IPAD organization, and the ICAM, both sponsored by government agencies. In the case of IPAD, NASA, the case of ICAM, the U.S. Air Force. The intent of both groups is to discover what type of data base is needed to adequately represent design environments in which engineers would operate. There is so far no real agreement as to what particular standards could apply. The CODASYL standard, for example, is in use throughout the world for commercial data base activity and may apply to

CAD/CAM. However, other issues exist, such as should hierarchical or relational data bases be used or networked and hierarchical or combinations of all three. The issue is still not resolved. A key issue will be handling the overhead involved in providing fast, interactive response to the engineering user at his graphics workstation. A final note on data base software is that it is generally a large user of computer resources. Central processor and IO activities are heavily impacted by a large, comprehensive data base that has many keys and a query language. Care must be taken to configure the system properly for user turn-around in an interactive fashion.

The data communications and data base aspects of the distributed design environment put severe challenges on the operating system, as does the computer aided design software itself. This software is generally CPU intensive and generates heavy I/O loads just to load the program and handle the data arrays. The type of environment that must be supported by the operating system will be multiple user with very large programs, and with multiple processes. Multiple processing will stem from the data base and data communications needs, as well as the need to run peripheral devices such as printers and plotters, as well as the CAD graphics environment. It is anticipated that an off-loading of the operating system will be effected by the use of the very intelligent graphics workstations. However, the need for a central controlled data base and data communiations load will necessitate a central host either in the form of a dedicated central processor or some type of file server system. The need to support multiple users, multiple processes, heavy IO and CPU intensive programs with rapid reponse, would indicate that operating systems such as those that are used for large mini computers today would probably be the most effective. For example, Digital's VMS, Prime's Primos, or the MULTICS Environement from Honeywell might well be the best solution. A modified UNIX system that could handle multiple processing effecitvely while the same time handling heavy IO loads would also be appropriate. The operating environment will be very important to efficient use of all the resources in the system. The operating system has to handle the overhead involved in all of the above functions and assure good user response. It is not possible at this time to indicate which operating system will be the best, but it is likely that virtual memory systems that are multiple user, multiple tasking oriented, are probably the best approach. UNIX can certainly qualify with enhancements beyond some of the various extensions that have been applied by Bell Labs or University of California at Berkeley.

An ancillary issue that should be addressed here also is the use virtual memory. In many cases vendors have indicated that virtual memory is not necessary because central processor memory prices are so low that it is not be necessary to worry about virtual addressing and that direct addressing of the memory is. While this is valid it is very likely that the virtual memory approach will be used in the future. Direct addressing does not lend itself well to multi-task, multi-process environments and when it does work in that fashion, can put a tremendous overhead on the system. A typical CAD/CAM system with solids modeling, could easily take up two megabytes of programming space and data space could account for another several megabytes in central processor memory. This total of perhaps 5 to 8 millions bytes of information certainly would tax the capabilities of non-virtual systems which directly address the memory. It would indicate that in some cases if the distributed design concept were to use direct memory addressing, it would need 8Mbytes of memory on a graphics workstation. It is unlikely that the cost effectiveness of this approach would appeal to many organizatons in the distributed environment.

In summary, the key software requirements for the distributed design environment are in three areas: data communications, data base management systems and the operating system of the overall environment. It is anticipated that the distributed design environment would include local area networks communicating among various graphics workstations with a central host or file service running the overall data base system. This environment is conducive to using currently available operating systems with suitable extensions to avoid unnecessary overhead due to multiple-processing, multiple-tasking. In addition to UNIX, these include various virtual memory systems, that are in use today, are suitable systems from DEC, Prime, Honeywell, Apollo, Data General, or IBM.

CONCLUSION

The preceeding has shown the aspects that must be considered in computer aided design technology for a distributed design concept to occur. It is very likely that the advancements will happen, indeed many of them are currently available and are being fine-tuned into more cost effective solutions. It should be pointed out however that not every user of a computer aided design system will need the complete distributed design concept that includes local area networks, remote area networks and centralized, interactive, query language-based data base management system. DATAQUEST estimates that by 1985 there will be in excess of 104,000 graphics workstations available for use by engineers. It is very likely that this would account for over 400,000 designers using the systems since frequently more than one designer will have access to the graphics system during the normal course of the work day.

Table 1 presents DATAQUEST forecasts for the size of the marketplace in terms of number of systems, number of workstations and total revenue from 1977 through 1987. These aggregate statistics are the result of surveys[1] of vendors in all areas of CAD/CAM. The following 20 vendors were part of this survey:

Applicon
Auto-trol
Avera
Calma
Computervision
Digital Equipment Corporation
DAISY Systems
AM Bruning
IBM

Intergraph
Gerber Systems
MCAUTO
Prime Computer
Perkin Elmer
Sperry Univac
Telesis
Vector General
VIA Systems
Sanders/CALCOMP
Mentor Graphics
Racal-Redac.

The aggregate results have been further broken down in Tables 3 and 4. Table 3 presents the estimates for the number of CAD/CAM systems installed on a yearly basis by each company through the end of 1982. Table 4 presents the number of graphics workstations installed, on a yearly basis, by each company through the end of 1982. These three tables all indicate a segmentation among vendor companies. One, the "cluster" segment, of companies that supply both the central host and local intelligence workstations, and the other segment, the "workstation" segment, is composed of companies that supply a highly intelligent workstation that can communicate in a local or remote network to a particular host. Based on survey results, the first segment is composed of Applicon, Calma, Computervision, IBM, Intergraph, MCAUTO, Prime Computer, Perkin Elmer, Sperry Univac and Racal-Redac; the second segment is composed of Avera, Auto-trol, DAISY Systems, AM Bruning, Gerber Systems, Telesis, Sanders/CALCOMP, VIA Systems, and Mentor Graphics. The opinion of the surveyed companies was that both segments would grow in excess of 30% and that the workstation segment would show explosive growth of over 60% per annum through 1987. The tables reflect that the vendors believe more workstations than central processors will be shipped from 1982 to 1987, and this seems to corroborate the move to two segments of the CAD/CAM market that are linked via advanced data communications. (In these tables individual company forecasts for 1983 to 1987 have been deleted by request of survey respondents.)

It is likely that anywhere from 35 to 45 percent of the systems installed will be used in a distributed design environment. The remainder of systems will exist in smaller firms that will use four or five terminals and some type of local area network functions which do not require the sophisticated operating system and data base management that would be used in the larger organizations. It is likely that such a small company may have need for batch remote access to other larger systems. For example, a tooling manufacturer for Ford Motor Company may have two to four graphics workstations running a mechanical design and a numerical control system. This company would occassionally need inputs from the Ford Motor Company and it may be desirable to have Ford transmit these over a remote batch hookup to update the small company's data base for design and numerical control on a periodic basis. It is not necessary to have interactive networking in this case. Conversely, when a job is finished at this company's shop, it would be desirable to send information back to the Ford system in a remote batch environment as well. The impact of this future scenario on the design arena means that computer graphics suppliers will need to make sure that their products can cover a range of applications. It is very likely that the companies that can provide the ideal graphics workstations for the true distributed design environment will be able to address the needs of the smaller firms that require only a sub-set of the overall system that is necessary in the larger environment. It is clearly a high growth area in terms of the number of workstations, whose population will be increasing at a compound annual growth rate of 63 percent.

In the distributed design approach the graphics workstations will need to exist in a local area network environment. This could be Ethernet or some type of token passsing networking scheme, such as a localized X.25 or the SNA approach adopted by IBM. In addition, the aspect of a distributed data base would have to be addressed. It is likely that this would not affect the graphics workstation component of the design system, but rather the file server or central host environment component. Computer graphics can contribute significantly to ease of data base access by providing good and friendly user facility and in addition having certain graphics and non-graphics attributes built into the workstation so that a program is not always required to access the remote data base. It will be necessary for the graphics workstation to have the capability to support local data bases. This data base capability would be a subset of the larger distributed design data base and must incorporate the same user interface and security procedures that would be used on the large system. In this regard the computer graphics industry must look carefully to what standards are being used in data base environments. It is likely that the best way to accomplish compatibility with the larger design data bases is simply through a query language that is comparable to the remote data base, and is easy to learn how to use.

In looking at the 35 to 45 percent of companies that will require a distributed design system we see a development that might be called a cluster environment. A cluster environment is one that has a large mini-computer, or mainframe host communicating through a local area network to a large number of computer graphics workstations in a particular building; for example, a design building at Ford Motor Company or General Motors. The large number of terminals in this case would number somewhere between 50 and 100, the large central host may in fact be several machines in a tightly coupled network; however, the commonality of data base and the access to the data base will be transparent to the end users on the graphics workstations. This cluster concept would then allow a completely distributed data base to function with the user concerned only about his tasks and the management of the data base system worrying about the integration of all the components of the individual users. Such cluster concepts today exist in certain electronics companies in which all electronic and mechanical aspects of the design of a computer, its controllers and the chassis are maintained on central data base machines that communicate to distributed graphics or design workstations. In this case design is only one aspect of the total product development and manufacturing process, and so can be partitioned off to the different CAD workstations. Further observations that support this cluster concept is the fact that most engineering organizations today are fairly well defined, in the sense that design, analysis, prototype testing, prototype manufacture, final manufacture and inventory and production control issues are addressed by separate organizations or departments within a large division. It is unlikely that each division would let the other division use its computer resources, so a central data base machine must be maintained. In addition it is a good idea from the standpoint of protection of data and consistency of data that a central host concept exist. For certain departments such as analysis in which large non-linear analysis programs may be required that can easily use up the resources of a Cyber 7600, a Star 205 or a Cray machine, it is necessary that these machines be separate from the general design environment; but the design environment must still be able to communicate information such as the data files used to run these programs to the large super computers.

In another case, a design group may require the running of various programs that are CPU intensive, for example solids modeling. It would be likely that a designer would send his information to the program that creates the solids model on the central host and have it run in a batch mode; when completed the results would be sent to the designer at his workstation. In the meantime the design engineer has had the opportunity to work on other aspects of his design without waiting for the local graphics workstation to finish the solids modeling job. In the environment in which there is a graphics workstation it will not be able to handle the very complex numerical methods required for solids modeling. It would require perhaps an hour or two to generate a solid model. However, the central host could access the information to create this solid model and produce results perhaps in a quarter of the time compared to the local CAD graphics workstation. This environment is dictated as much by time management as by technology. The best use of time and the best use of equipment will dictate some trends here. It is unlikely that microcomputers will completely replace minicomputers for all engineering functions. The Cray machine has been developed to solve large complex engineering problems. And the mini-computer will still maintain a position to solve less complex problems, but problems which are still more complex than could be handled on micro-computer based graphics workstations.

A final observation that supports the concept of a centralized host that handles difficult tasks or large data base problems while at the same time existing in a local area network of CAD graphics workstations is that the development of software for solving engineering problems has always kept pace with the development of computer hardware. In the mid-60's the NASTRAN product was developed. This product was developed first on a IBM 7094, and as more powerful IBM systems came out, more sophisticated analysis techniques were built into the program. NASTRAN originally ran on a 7094 and now runs on the Cray[9]. If the analogy were that hardware advances would make software run on smaller and smaller machines, the NASTRAN system would only run today on the Apollo or the new VAX 11/730. This, however, is not the case since as hardware becomes available that runs faster and can do more things the user defines new software to take advantage to these new resources. The move from linear to non-linear analysis in electrical circuit simulation and structural analysis is one example of the utilization of available horespower to its maximum extent. There is no reason to assume that this will not be the case in the CAD/CAM environment of the future.

The final conclusion is that the future for computer aided design in a distributed environment will rest heavily on the ability of computer graphics to keep pace with the need of the user. These needs will include ease of use, local intelligence, local area networks, and local data bases for the individual user. In addition, the requirement will be for interactive remote networking to central systems that handle the data base and for remote access to the very powerful Cray class of machines for the occassional large analysis run that cannot be accomplished on anything other than the high performance computers. This overall architecture of a cluster system will apply to 35 to 45 percent of the installed CAD/CAM systems. A subset of this environment would apply to the smaller firms, and as the firm gets smaller, the number of users decrease, the subset itself becomes smaller and smaller. There is no question that the support for a local area network will be very important. The structure of this local area network could very well be a UNIX/Ethernet environment, but it could also be a central host-based token passing/packet-switching type of network that runs at very high speeds. There is, however, no clear cut choice today as to the local area network environment that will evolve and be the accepted standard. As for remote networking, it too must be interactive and should share some common traits with the local area network in terms of user interactivity and ease of use; however, the actual bandwidths speeds between units in this remote network will certainly be smaller. The typical local area network bandwidth of hardware is a 8-10 million bits per second. The actual achieved bandwidth will be a function of the operating system and the data communications software. In the area of the remote networking, speeds of 19,200 bits per second to 56,000 bits per second are available today. It is likely that this speed will increase as the technology in the area of data transmission increases, however, it will not come close to the 8-10 megahertz of the local area network for some time. For computer graphcis systems that exist in the Ethernet environment it would be well advised for these units to also feature support for one or more of the interactive remote networking facilities available today, such as X.25 or the SNA standard from IBM. While this may add cost, it will also add functionality; so that as hardware prices come down the user will obtain exceptional price performance whether he be from a small or large company.

It is evident that the challenges are many for the distributed design environment, but it is also equally evident that the hardware and software technology is available today to implement such a system. The cost effectiveness of such a system will require several years before it can be implemented widely; however, it can be done. The next step after that, of course, is the factory of the future. In this environment the final design and analysis results are passed through to prototype manufacture, prototype testing, those results are fed back into the design and analysis loop, those results then are fed back into prototype and so on. The result will be better communications among all groups making a product for a given company. The factory of the future concept means that a product goes from the back of a napkin to manufacture on the factory floor, and inventory control in the materials office of a given corporation. Before this is possible more advances will be needed. The first step towards the factory of the future and computer integrated manufacturing is the distributed design concept.

Table 1
1982 Graphics Performance Survey

Source: Dataquest Inc.

Vendor/Product	Performance Rating	Performance/Price Ratio
Metheus 420	57.1	2.72
Metheus 440	64.6	2.13
Ramtek 6412	78.2	3.12
Calcomp Vistagraphics 4300	86.2	3.07
CADLINC	80	4.0
Seiko D-Scan 2412	95.9	4.4
Megatek 7255	94	3.76
Ikonas	107.3	2.64
Lexidata GS8000	104.8	2.62
Lexidata 2000	81.5	7.4
AED 767	79.5	4.41

Table 2

REGION: WORLD WIDE

ALL COMPANIES

APPLICATION AREA: ALL

	1977	1978	1979	1980	1981	1982	1983	1984	1985	1986	1987	77-82 C A G	82-87 C A G
Systems Shipped	381	574	872	1317	1889	2600	4048	6211	9687	15875	25955	47	58
New Wrkstns Shipped	1099	1684	2832	4326	6378	8310	12624	20894	36146	56288	86859	51	61
A-O Wrkstns Shipped	97	141	260	479	814	1208	2291	3994	6631	10993	17864	70	71
Wrkstns Shipped	1196	1825	3092	4805	7192	9518	14915	24888	42777	67281	104723	53	63
System Retirements	49	71	95	130	188	277	393	578	860	1299	2033	40	49
Year-End System Pop	1343	1846	2623	3810	5511	7834	11489	17122	25949	40525	64447	43	52
Year-End Wrkstn Pop	3664	5309	8135	12533	19098	27667	41201	64032	103606	165707	262148	51	58
Annual System Rev ($M)	75	127	235	431	707	933	1332	1905	2701	3843	5486	69	42
Annual Service Rev ($M)	13	23	44	83	139	192	276	397	565	806	1134	74	43
Annual A-O/Upgrade Rev ($M)	8	13	29	66	128	188	285	429	616	887	1241	97	46
Total Annual Rev ($M)	96	163	308	581	974	1313	1892	2731	3881	5536	7861	73	43
Increase Over Prior Year (%)	39	71	89	88	68	35	44	44	42	43	42	(2)	2

Source: Dataquest Inc. Survey

Table 3
System Shipments By Company
1978-1982

Source: Dataquest Inc. Survey

	1978	1979	1980	1981	1982
AM Bruning	-	-	-	30	150
Applicon	73	126	166	160	150
Auto-trol	69	89	116	100	100
Calma	96	111	140	197	257
Computervision	151	271	427	552	609
Daisy	-	-	-	10	90
Gerber Systems	25	39	43	44	70
IBM	-	11	47	116	172
Intergraph	40	51	88	123	310
MCAUTO	-	5	31	69	87
Mentor	-	-	-	-	20
Perkin Elmer	-	-	-	-	25
Prime	-	-	15	37	75
Racal-Redac	50	100	150	240	260
Sanders/CALCOMP	-	27	38	50	58
Telesis	-	-	-	-	10
Others	70	42	56	161	157
TOTAL	574	872	1317	1889	2600

Table 4
Workstation Shipments by Company
1978 - 1982

Source: Dataquest Inc. Survey

	1978	1979	1980	1981	1982
AM Bruning				30	150
Applicon	258	501	675	670	640
Auto-trol	245	354	453	442	385
Calma	344	440	565	847	1016
Computervision	540	1077	1773	2387	2658
Daisy	-	-	-	-	90
Gerber Systems	88	152	172	183	166
IBM	-	56	277	753	1079
Intergraph	148	209	368	543	1100
MCAUTO	-	15	93	207	289
Mentor	-	-	-	-	20
Perkin Elmer	-	-	-	-	75
Prime	-	-	-	75	250
Racal-Redac	50	100	150	300	400
Sanders/CALCOMP	-	54	76	100	120
Telesis	-	-	-	-	10
Others	152	134	203	655	1070
TOTAL	1825	3092	4805	7192	9518

Figure 1

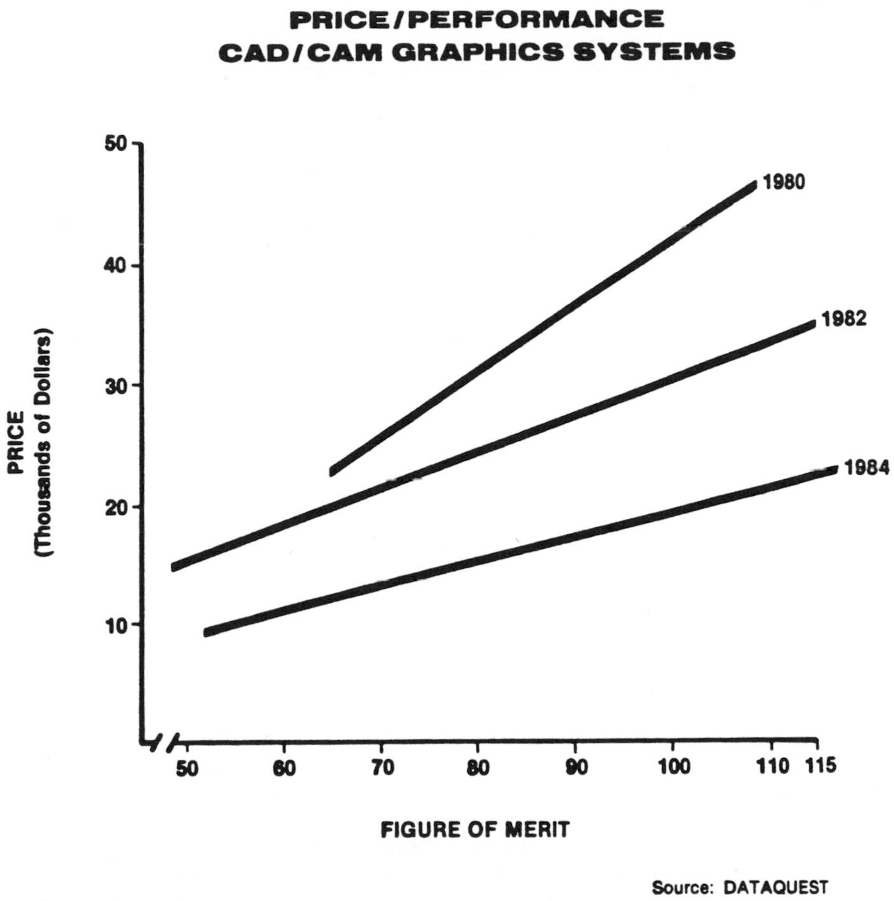
PRICE/PERFORMANCE
CAD/CAM GRAPHICS SYSTEMS
50
40
30
20
10
PRICE
(Thousands of Dollars)
1980
1982
1984
50
60
70
80
90
100
110
115
FIGURE OF MERIT
Source: DATAQUEST

References:

1. T.O. Gauhan, L.D. Brentano, M.E. White, "CAD/CAM Industry Service", Dataquest Inc., Volume I, Chapter 2, page 2.1-2, January 24, 1983.

2. Lewis D. Brentano, "New Performance Levels for Graphics Systems in CADCAM", Dataquest Inc., page 7, August 25, 1982

3. Victor Krueger, "Data Networking", Dataquest Inc., pp. 1-10, December 6, 1982

4. Keith Carlson, G. Funk, R. LeClaire, "Operating System Combines Local and Network Processing", Systems and Software, Hayden Publishing Co., pp. 65-71, September 1982

5. Hock Leow, T. Nelson, "Evaluating Raster-Scan Graphics Controllers", Computer Graphics World, pp. 65-71, May, 1982

6. Jack Conaway, "The Connection Between CAD and CAM", Proceedings: CAD/CAM Industry Conference, San Diego, California, Dataquest Inc., September 29 - October 1, 1982

7. George Shaw, L. Dannenberg, "The Role of Computer Companies in CAD/CAM in the 1980's", Proceedings: CAD/CAM Industry Conference, Dataquest Inc., San Diego, California, September 29 - October 1, 1982

8. Patrick deCavaignac, "Market Opportunities for the New Generation of CAD/CAM Companies", Proceedings: CAD/CAM Industry Conference, San Diego, California, Dataquest Inc., September 29 - October 1, 1982

9. Joseph Gloudeman, MacNeal-Schwindler Corporation, Correspondence on NASTRAN performance, July 1982

10. Ronald Price, "Applying Optical Mass Memory to the Storage of Engineering Drawings and Data", Proceedings: Symposium on Automation Technology for Management and Productivity Advancement through CAD/CAM Engineering Data Handliing, Santa Clara, California, November 3, 1982

COMPUTER AIDED ENGINEERING

Thomas H. Bruggere
Mentor Graphics Corporation
10200 S. W. Nimbus, G-7
Portland, OR 97223, U.S.A.

INTRODUCTION

The key to engineering success during the 80's will lie in the availability of more powerful and sophisticated Computer Aided Engineering (CAE) tools. This need is being driven by several discouraging trends which will force us to increase the effectiveness of engineers; the number of design engineers vs. industry needs, technological changes, product life cycles, product development cycles, product quality issues, and expense burden vs. capital equipment trade-offs.

Computer Aided Design (CAD) tools have greatly enhanced our ability to develop and manufacture complex electronic devices. However, most of these tools have been directed at "downstream" activities -- with few exceptions, design engineers don't benefit extensively from these CAD tools in their primary job functions.

In order to overcome this gap between the potential of technology and its practical use, tomorrow's designers will need an integrated set of CAE tools which address a wide variety of design tasks. These tools must be flexible enough to remain applicable as technology changes, and powerful enough to significantly improve the engineer's ability to do his job. Fortunately, many of the same technological advances which have contributed to the need for new tools have also set the stage for solution. This paper discusses the nature of these needed tools for the 80's, and which of the design engineering tasks are most likely to benefit from these new tools.

TRENDS

"As complexity grows, other aspects become important factors - for example, modeling and computer-aided design. Increasingly, we tend to experiment in a computer rather than in a furnace. Modeling is much more efficient and faster than making devices and measuring performance. It's becoming harder to live without CAD".

- Gordon Moore, Intel

The microprocessor revolution has dramatically increased the capability of sophisticated electronics products, but it has also greatly increased the complexity of many systems. This increased complexity has effected both the reliability and the product development times of new products.

Reliability has been affected because the more complex a product is, the more likely there is to be a design flaw. Further, the greater the number of parts the greater the statistical probability of failure of the product.

Product development times have been steadily increasing and can be expected to continue to increase in the coming years. At the same time, product life cycles appear to be compressing.

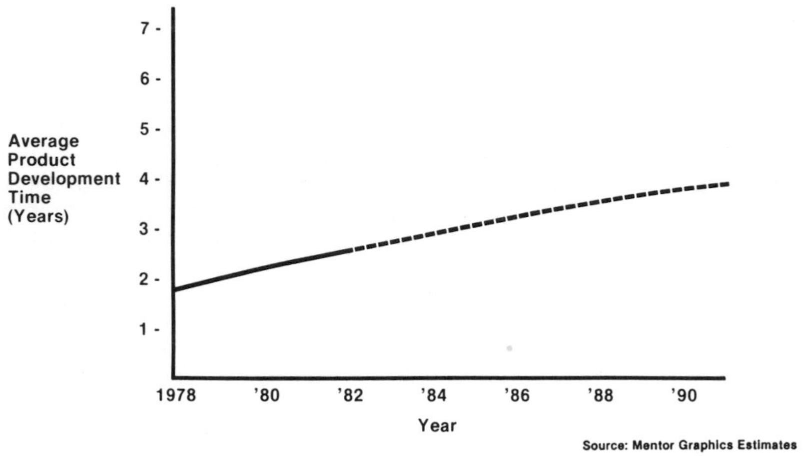

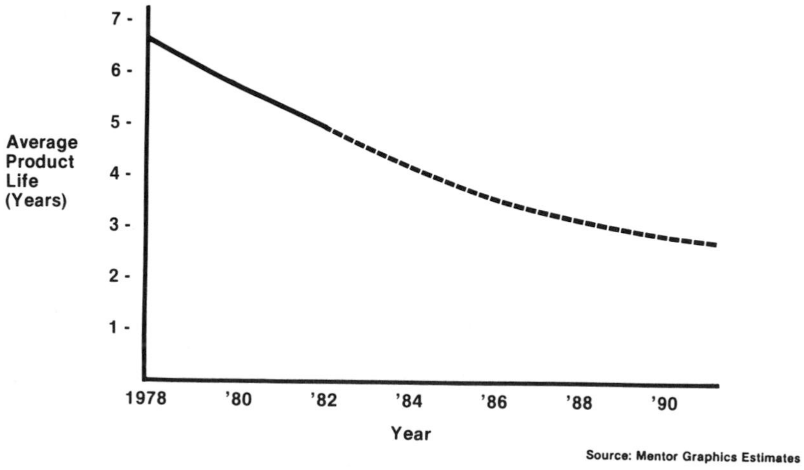

When these two curves cross, we have a situation where development of a new product must begin before the predecessor product has been put onto the market. This circumstance puts tremendous pressure on engineering productivity and time to market, and is very risky for a company since proper market feedback has not been received.

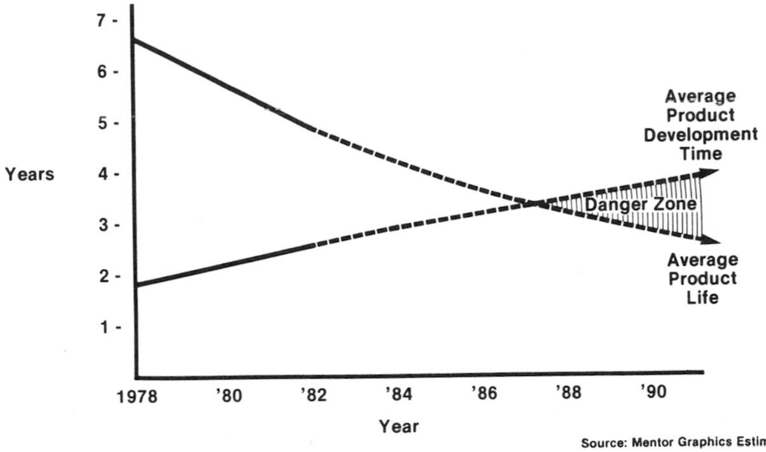

Source: Mentor Graphics Estimates

ENGINEERING PRODUCTIVITY

The coming decade is predicted to see a dramatic shortage of electronic engineers. A study by the American Electronics Associate predicts that the demand for engineers will exceed the supply by a factor of 3-1. This shortage means that companies will be forced to increase the productivity of then existing engineers if they intend to remain competitive.

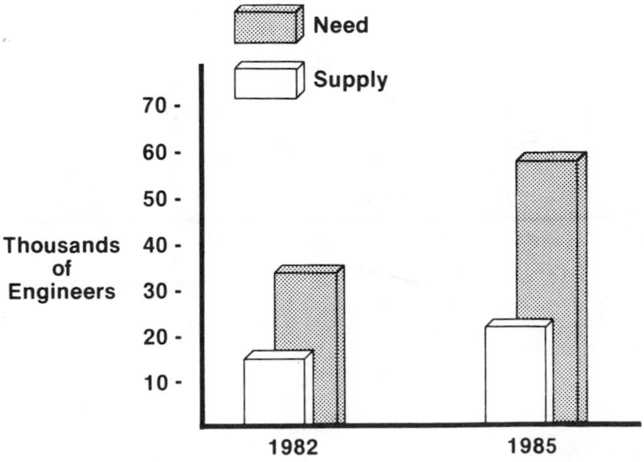

Source: American Electronics Association

Other industries which have been faced with demands for higher productivity have successfully used capital equipment to bridge the gap. In fact, the electronics industry is exceptionally low in its expenditures of capital equipment per employee. In order to achieve the required productivity by 1990, industry will need to spend as much in capital as it does in the expense budget for design engineers.

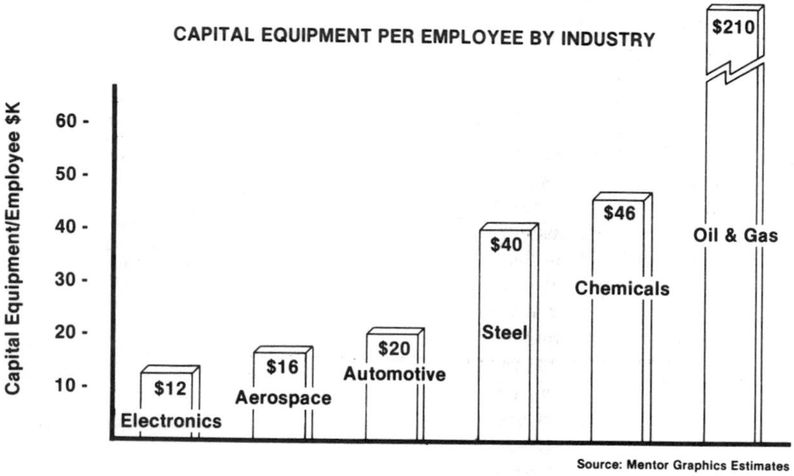

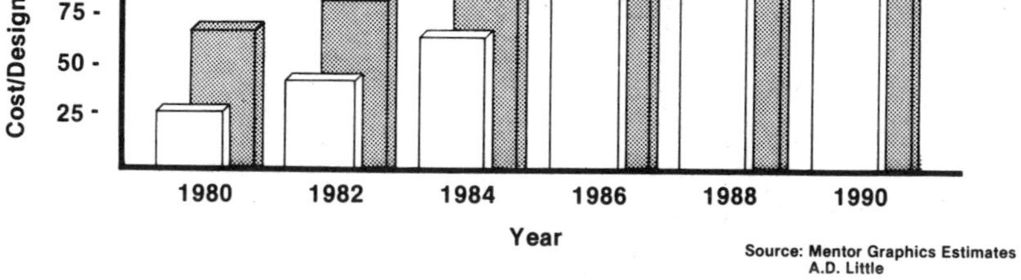

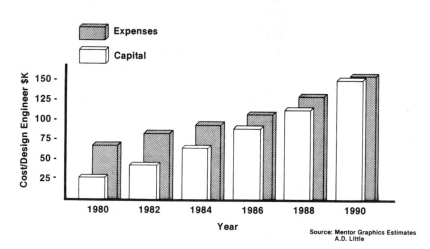

The electronics industry has already seen how capital expenditures for Computer Aided Design (CAD) equipment have dramatically impacted productivity and innovation in the physical layout portion of the product development process. The benefits of these systems have been decreased turnaround times, more effective processing of changes, higher quality input to manufacturing and greater product innovation.

What is needed now is an engineering equivalent to the traditional CAD layout system. In other words, a dedicated Computer Aided Engineering (CAE) system geared for the design engineer.

COMPUTER AIDED ENGINEERING (CAE)

In order to most effectively provide CAE tools for an engineer, it is important to first understand how engineers spend their time. Not surprisingly, the design process is only a part of what an engineer actually does during the day. Communicating, documenting, and planning are also important activities that occupy an engineer. A CAE system must address all of these tasks in order to increase engineering productivity.

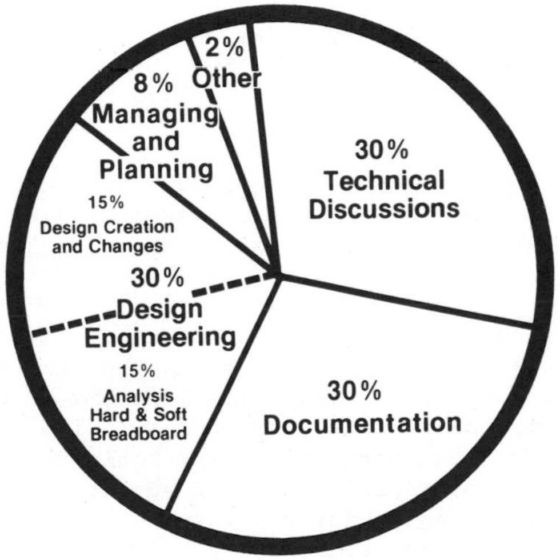

Source: Electronic Design Audience Survey
Mentor Graphics Estimates
Hewlett-Packard

The CAE system also must effectively integrate into the overall engineering process. It is important that the system augment the flow of activities and not cause significant changes to it. Such a system should effectively mirror the engineer's own work process as it is outlined below.

COMPUTER AIDED ENGINEERING (CAE)

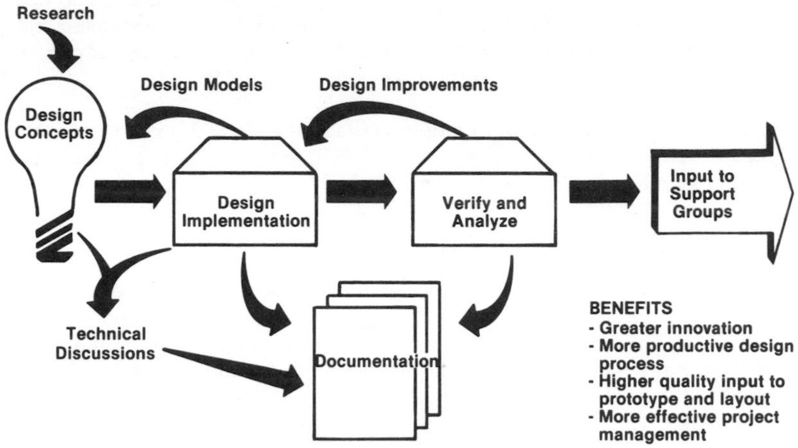

The benefits of such a system will be greater innovation, a more productive design process, higher quality input to the prototype and input process, and more effective project management.

CAE TOOLS

The tools required from a CAE system should be integrated into a central Data Base Management System. This DBMS is key to the system flexibility and should ideally be relational and provide view independence to the various applications programs.

The design capability should be flexible enough to allow either hierarchical, modular designs or flat designs. It should result in the creation of a data base which may then be processed by verification programs or by a physicalization system, or which may be formatted for transmission to external physical design systems or simulators. Ideally, logic diagrams should be able to be included in documents as figures or output on a plotter. The system should also encourage model replication and design sharing in order to most effectively lever productivity.

The design tools should be technology independent and therefore compatible with most design environments. The hierarchical design capability should be linked via the database to a functional simulator and other verification programs. Ideally, the simulator should be interactive and allow modeling at the gate level as well as of functional blocks. Graphical output from the simulator is also very useful since it allows an engineer to quickly understand the results of the simulation. One should expect the simulation to be done on the CAE system and not on an additional costly mainframe computer.

Other tools that should be available are a documentation system, project communications capabilities and programming aids. The documentation system should interface directly to the design database and should allow text and the current revision of a drawing to be combined directly into a document. Project communications tools should emphasize electronic mail and planning/controlling aids. Programming aid should include standard language compilers (Fortran, Pascal) and good editing and debugging tools. All of these tools complement the "other 50%" of the design process and should be considered as important as the actual design and analysis aids.

Finally, the system should be easy to use. Human interface technology has reached the point today where an engineer should expect to be able to learn to use a CAE system in less than one day. Phased learning approaches toward human interfaces probably give an engineer the best ease of use/ease of learning trade-offs.

CONFIGURATIONS

Traditional CAD systems have been timesharing configurations with a central CPU and terminals for the trained operator. This configuration suffers from severe multi-terminal degradation and is, hence, probably not appropriate for the engineering environment. A CAE system needs to encourage sharing of designs and documentation among large numbers of engineers, but this sharing is not possible on systems that can only support a few terminals, or whose response time is so poor that it becomes a nuisance to use.

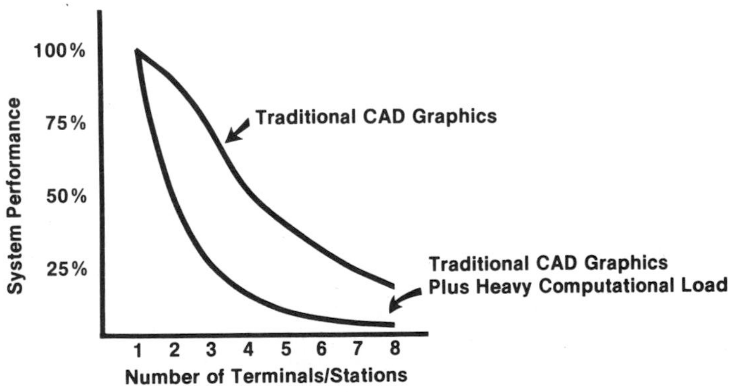

Sources: Computervision User Estimates
Mentor Graphics Estimates

For the CAE environment, the best approach is the distributed network architecture where each node is a standalone computer, but all nodes are hooked together over a high speed communication link. In this environment, the required sharing of resources is available, but additional nodes can be added without any performance penalty on the network.

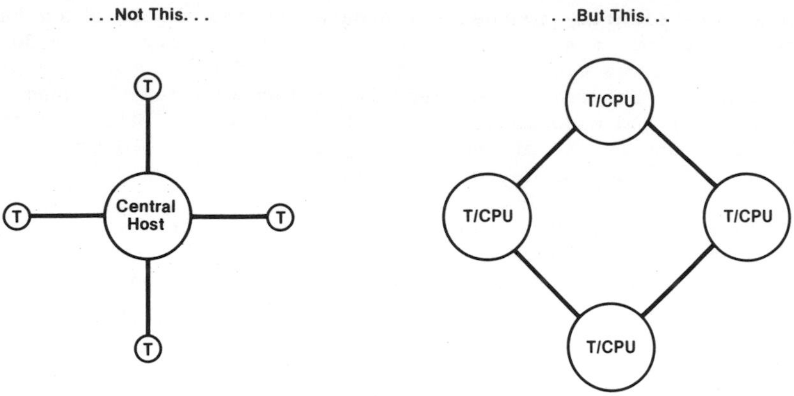

For processing capabilities, the dedicated CPU should ideally be a 32 bit machine with virtual memory capability. Virtual memory is important because of the size and performance requirements of the engineering design and analysis programs. For maximum flexibility, the system should be a general purpose computer with a multiprogramming operating system. This helps insure the system will grow with the needs of the engineering organization.

Primary storage of 3-4 megabytes should be available as well as secondary storage of 30-60 megabytes. A high resolution CRT is important, but it must be of a size that can fit conveniently into the engineering environment, perhaps similar to the common word processing display sizes. Finally, the system must support graphic input and output capabilities.

AN EXEMPLARY SYSTEM

An excellent example of the complete CAE system is Mentor's IDEA 1000 logic design and analysis system. It was developed with a clear understanding of the design engineer's job and what is needed to make that person more productive. The new system not only simplifies the engineer's typical design, analysis and changing tasks, but also aids him or her in project planning and managing, and in preparing documentation.

An appropriate mix of hardware and software, IDEA 1000 is the first totally integrated CAE system aimed at helping bench-level engineers create, capture, analyze, verify and document complex logic designs. It is targeted at engineers who design and document designs implemented in printed-circuit boards, VLSI, thick and thin hybrids and gate arrays.

Combining an Apollo Domain computer, its Aegis operating system, and six application software packages tailored for front-end design engineering applications, IDEA 1000 can be used as a stand-alone, self-contained engineering work station, or as part of a tightly linked distributed network with up to 200 separate nodes, or work stations. In the networking environment, the power of the entire system grows as each new station is attached. This is a major difference from mainframe-or minicomputer based systems, where additional work stations usually result in decreases in performance.

THE COMPUTER AIDED ENGINEERING (CAE) SYSTEM

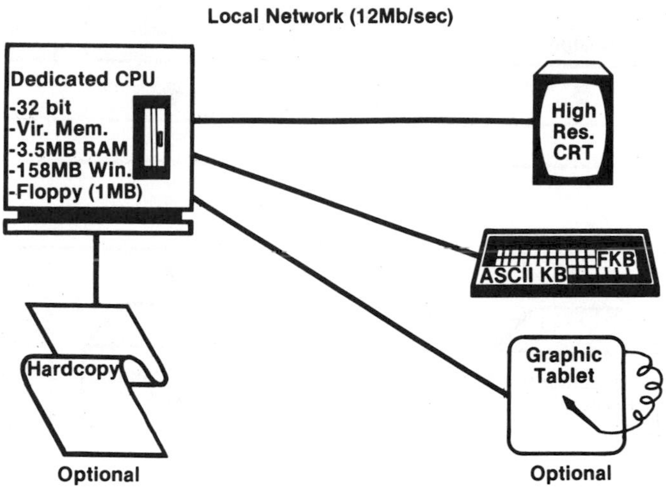

Because each IDEA 1000 contains its own central processing unit, along with multiprocessing-oriented software, system expansion is simple and can be accomplished without major changes in software. Networking in this easy manner, therefore, results in increased benefits in project management, documentation and communications among the design team.

IDEA 1000's software was designed to fit well with the needs of a typical project design team, and takes full advantage of the mainframe-like power of each microprocessor-based work station.

Central to the Mentor proprietary software is a full relational data base management system (DBMS) that provides both management and data base facilities. The management aspects include controls for versions, configuration, releases, concurrency, archiving and electronic mail. Users can be assured that they are working with the most recent version of the design, that changes made by one engineer are reflected to the rest of the project team, and that simultaneous access to a file is properly controlled.

The data base facilities provided by IDEA 1000 support typical design team approaches: Application programs can share data rather than require that each application program maintain separate and storage-intensive files. This approach to storage, retrieval and use of information enhances the performance of the system and furnishes high levels of data protection.

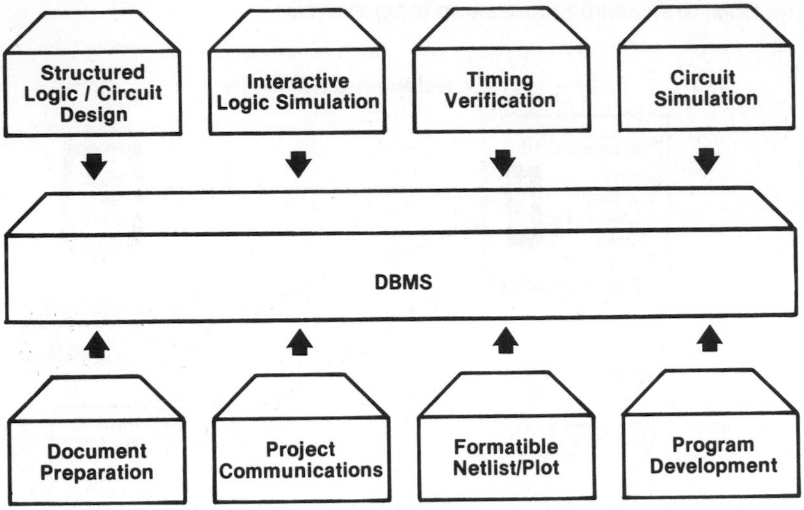

IDEA 1000's unique applications software include eight major programs.

Structured Logic Design (SLD) -- An intelligent graphics editor package that supports hierarchical design approaches, SLD eliminates the need for pencil and paper and allows designs to be captured at levels ranging from their entirety down to an individual part or cell. An intelligent editing system which understands the electrical connectivity of the circuit and provides considerable error detection at the early stages of the design, SLD, additionally, includes component files which contain a large number of attributes for each design component. Included in the component file is the capability to automatically access designs involving repetition; the component file can also store a mix of standard components for access to a wide range of alternatives, and needs only to create special circuitry if standard components are not available. Special circuitry developed in earlier designs can be entered as a component, so that designers need not continually "re-invent" approaches that have been successful in the past.

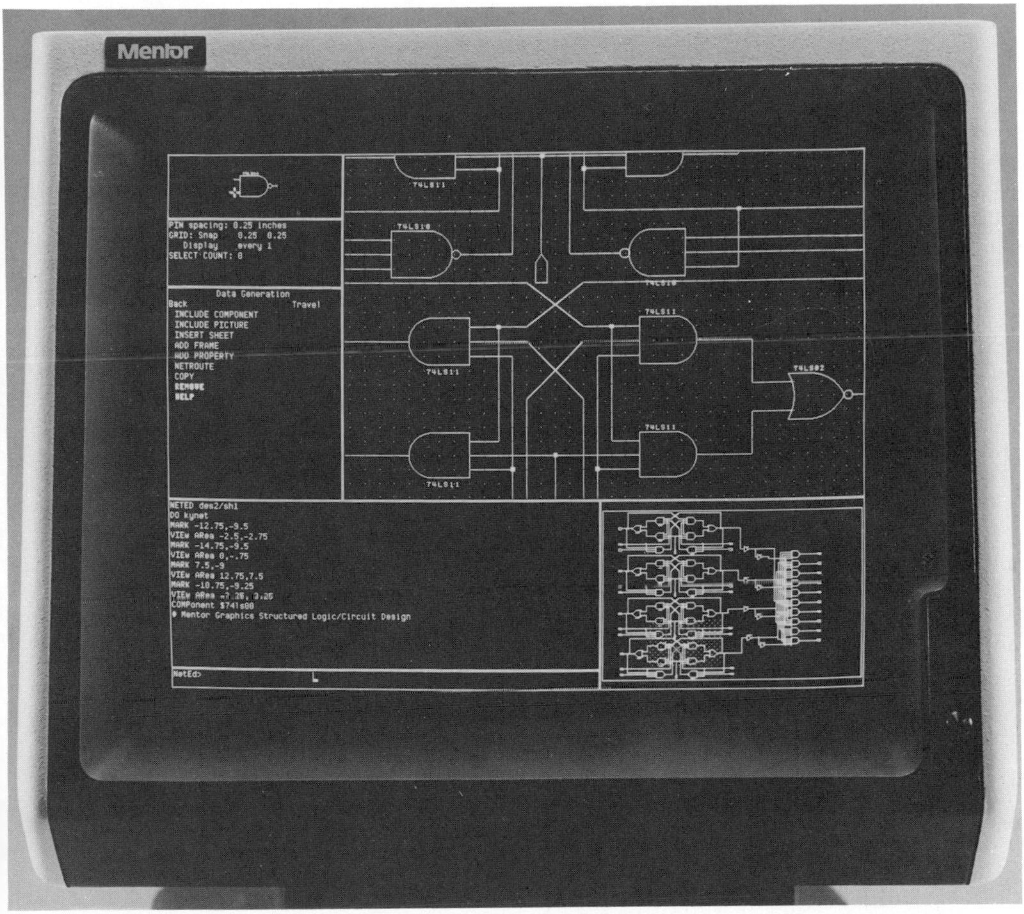

Interactive Logic Simulation (SIM) -- Designed to support both MOS and TTL logic, Mentor's SIM program simulates logic gates, RAMs, ROMs and PLAs; it allows a design to be "pretested" via the computer, before a prototype is built and substantial time and money invested, in order to determine design performance and identify any flaws or difficulties. SIM lets designers simulate portions of a design before it is entirely completed, resulting in the ability to identify potential design problems early in the process; SIM also avoids difficulties encountered in using earlier simulation programs. On the other hand, SIM works directly with the design parameters entered via the SLD program, so that logic input to the simulation program is as simple as a few commands. Designed for display options in formats most familiar to the designer, SIM outputs are similar to those obtained from a logic analyzer, an oscilloscope, or a development system; waveforms, or binary, hex, or octal tables. Finally, SIM has been optimized for high performance; with the IDEA 1000's microprocessor-based work stations, simulation is done primarily on the local station, permitting activity at other stations to continue.

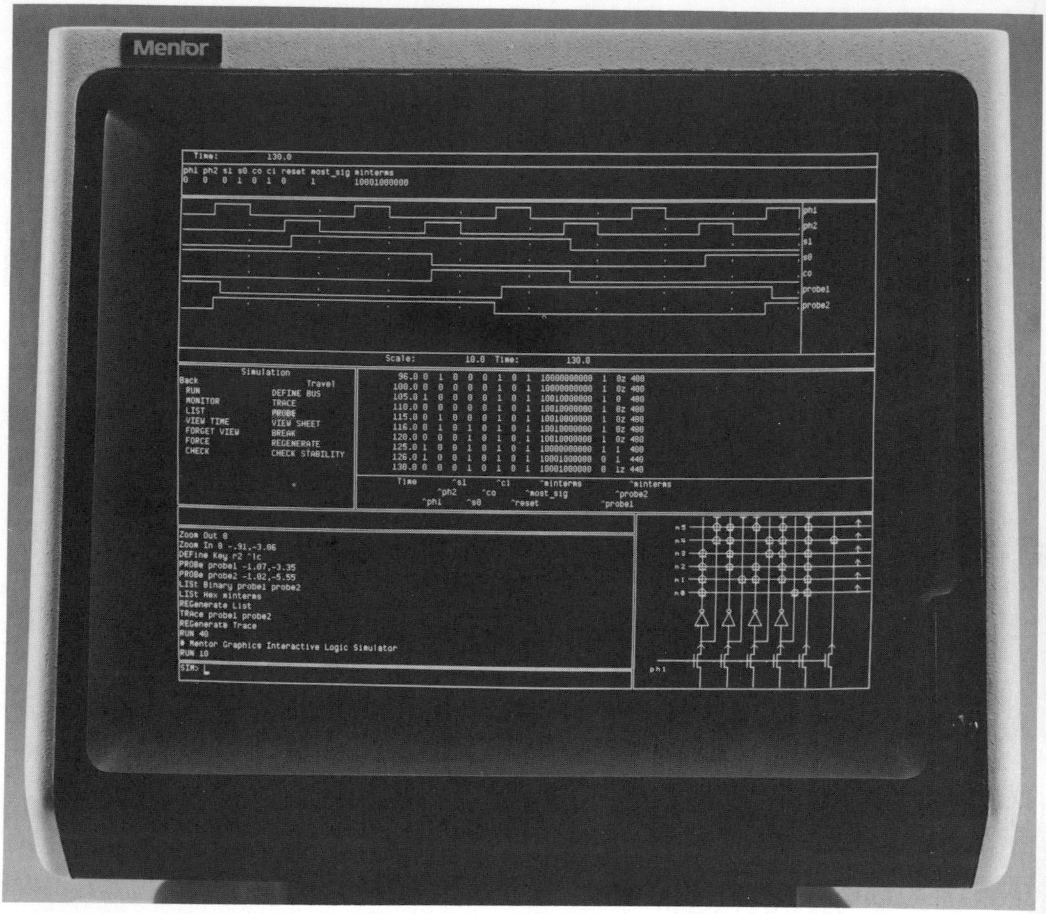

Timing Verification (TIM) -- The Timing Verifier allows the designer to ascertain if a circuit will function correctly when run at specified clock speeds. The timing verifier provides a complete list of errors which identify both the pin where the error occurred and the actual nature of the error. Also, waveforms of interest can be displayed graphically to enhance comprehension of their timing relationships. In addition, a schematic of the circuit under test can be called up, with pins containing errors automatically highlighted for easy identification.

The Timing Verifier takes all the circuit's signal paths through one complete machine cycle. This simulation of the time domain breaks the full cycle down into very small increments which allow as high a resolution as needed. During execution, the Timing Verifier works with timing characteristics for each signal. These characteristics are expressed in one of two basic formats. The most common is a format which describes the signal as "changing" (in transition from one logic state to another) or "stable" (logic state transition completed). The other is a format that describes the signal in terms of actual logic value (1 or 0), and also in terms of rising and falling edges.

Circuit Simulation (CSM) -- An enhanced version of SPICE, this package allows the engineer to do interactive circuit simulation directly off the design data base. In addition to the standard SPICE features, CSM includes interactive graphical output which dramatically aids the interpretation of the analysis.

Project Communications (COM) -- This applications software package consists of a series of communications utilities to keep members of the design project team informed of progress, and to provide electronic mail facilities.

Project Documentation (DOC) -- Designed to eliminate many of the clerical tasks of project documentation, DOC is constructed with a series of word processing routines that can update documentation during the design process, rather than do the entire documentation task at the end of the design cycle. Complete documentation can be done through the work station itself, integrating both text and graphics. If desired, employing manuals or technical writers, typesetters, graphic artists, and the like can be eliminated and design documentation can be produced entirely on the Mentor system.

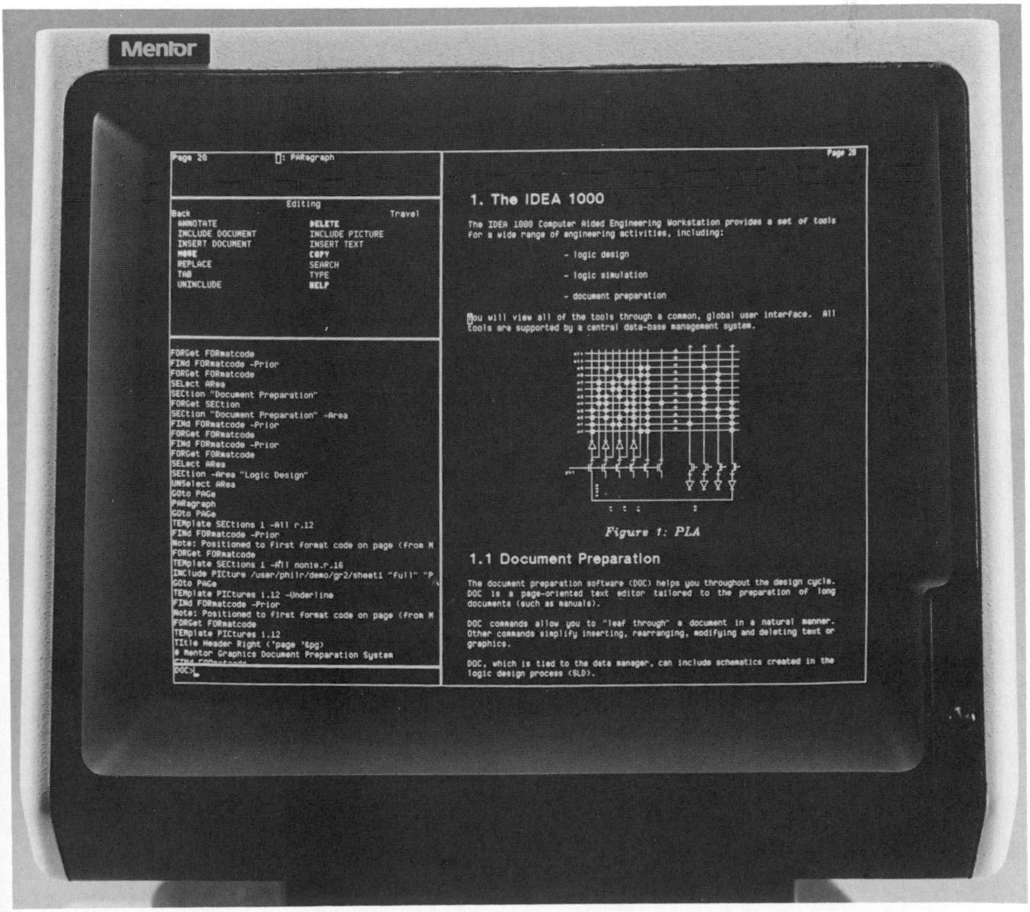

Outputs (OUT) -- OUT provides for completed and simulated design parameters to be passed to existing CAD/CAM or prototype construction systems in formats consistent with their requirements.

Programming Tools (PRO) -- To stimulate the use of the IDEA 1000 for a broad range of standard and custom design applications, PRO provides the capability for users to write their own applications programs in Pascal (standard) or Fortran 77 (optional) and still access the IDEA 1000's data base files. In addition, existing Pascal or Fortran programs can be converted to operate on the IDEA 1000.

CONCLUSION

Computer Aided Engineering capabilities will be essential in the 80's to companies who want to remain competitive and profitable. These systems increase productivity and allow engineering organizations to more effectively deal with increased complexity and decreased time to market trends. Yes, you do have a choice, but you would be ill advised to choose to avoid CAE.

COMPUTER AIDED DESIGN TRENDS IN THE 80' S

Camila Chaves Cortes

245 East 63rd St., Apt. #502
New York, N.Y. 10021, U.S.A.

> This century is but an episode in the life of human culture; it is clear that more paraphernalia of this epoch may be cast off than will survive into the next. Yet surely the computer will not. A solid state image will replace the chemical ribbon and cinema will eventually be interred in the archival museum. But computer and computer graphics will bring to mind the kind of tools that may characterize an age succeeding this century's age of the machine.
>
> -- John Whitney, Digital Harmony on the Complementarity of Music and Visual Art

ABSTRACT

The encoding and transmission of digital pictures dates back to 1921 when a transatlantic cable utilized a digital system with intensity levels and a teletype simulated a halftone. During the last thirty years the technology has evolved from the first computer driven CRT -- credited to the Whirlwind I at MIT in 1950 -- to countless home computers with graphic capabilities.

Great accomplishments from industry, military, research, and development laboratories as well as individual efforts have provided developments that today make the state of the art the most promising tool of the century.

A technology that has brough us the dreams of DaVinci, Pollock, Maholy-Nagy, and Duchamp, appeals to the senses because for the first time we can create the great elegance of motion, exactly as what happens in music.

We have always been able to see motion, but not able to re-create it. For the first time we can make patterns of motion; from geometrical equations we can create designs so rich and rewarding that the moving visual imagery of a culture may be recalled forever.

The time has come to revise and develop the guidelines that will reap the greatest benefits in all computer aided applications. The future lies in the principle that we must adapt machinery to people and their specific needs. In turn we can project an intelligent outlook in the process of man-machine communication that will accelerate the course of history.

As an artist/designer I faced some of the frustrations embedded in certain systems. I wished to find out how some of my colleagues perceived their systems, and to that purpose, I surveyed some of their experiences. As a result, I have formed some opinions on what I perceive to be computer aided design trends in the 1980s. Computer aided design is still relatively new and there is a great deal to be done to enhance individuality. Individuality is an asset to the process of creation and requires greater input and thought.

INTRODUCTION

This paper presents an overall picture of computer aided design trends in the 1980's. The emphasis lies in the different uses, processes, training, economics, applications, packaging, support, and productivity in the systems. Hardware and software applications are explored. Selected graphic applications are also addressed to provide a more complete picture of the market. However, the emphasis is upon the benefits that will develop in the computer graphics industry.

Many of the visuals and graphics that are part of these presentations depict some of the projects that are contributing to and determining the behavior and future of computer graphics and to a great extent, are shaping our existence.

Major objectives of this study are:

1. To provide a source document for the different areas where computer graphics in design is used.
2. To profile the aesthetic, education/training and practical considerations in computer graphics.
3. To review some of the major applications of software and hardware.
4. To identify and describe key forces and trends reflecting this market's future growth.
5. To identify some of the ongoing demands and expectations of individuals looking towards computers.

SCOPE

The data, projection, observations and conclusions are based on:

1. Survey
2. Review of trade journals, associated publications, independent studies, reports and conferences.

An emphasis was placed on data and information provided by key persons associated with computer graphics.

The visual information was provided by a variety of vendors, an effort of their marketing support people. I extend my special recognition and my gratitude to all the contributors in helping to make this an effective study.

SURVEY

A survey was mailed along with a cover letter and a self-stamped envelope to a sample of 100 users of computer graphics systems that include:

1. Electronic graphics users, including the three major television networks in New York City;
2. Users of Time-Life teletex system, "The Video Group";
3. Major computer animation facilities in the New York area and in California;
4. Users of business graphics systems in New England and Washington, DC from a list provided by Scott Weil of ISSCO (a provider of computer graphics services);

5. Users of computer graphics systems in Canada and the U.S. from a list compiled by Bob Auster;
6. Users of personal computer graphics systems, Genigraphics and Xerox, whom the author knows in the New York area.

ANALYSIS OF DATA OBTAINED FROM SURVEY

Thirty-five responses were obtained from the 100 surveys solicited. The data for ten of the eleven questions was tabulated and is presented in graphic form designed by InterChart of New York (see appendices). Question eleven has been categorized according to responses.

COMPUTER AIDED DESIGN IN THE 80's

Questions 1, 2

There is a definite picture emerging in the computer aided design world in the 80's. It is interesting to note that the majority of professionals are relatively new to the field, about half having between one and three years of experience and the other half, between four and seven years. Roughly fifty percent of these users employ a stand-alone unit, and the other half use a mainframe system.

Question 3

The commercial TV industry dates back to the early 1950's and absorbs the largest portion of applications and electronic imaging in advertising, TV news, or on air graphics.

Animation, the second largest application, is an industry with promising byproducts, such as the use of computer graphics to carry a story line, that will enhance aesthetic appeal to the communications media. A system compatible with video is in demand. Animation facilities are developing, advance 3-D packages -- some with solid modeling. Others create synthetic imagery with polygonal data base, wire-frame and object simulation. All kinds of special effects are seen in advertising, TV, and in feature-length films such as Tron and Future World.

Filmmaking both in the areas of animation and television production is making breakthroughs in visual and audio-digital techniques, and special effects. The industrial use of computer aided graphic design films is just now being tested. When will computer-aided design documentary filming begin?

Slide making is a large portion of the computer aided design in the 80's. Slides are widely used in business graphics. According to the Frost & Sullivan Report, business graphics, which cover transportation, manufacturing, general services, education, government, communications, industry and financial sectors, provided a revenue of $273.2 million. The same report cites a world-wide revenue of $35 million in slide making. Slide making is used for all types of corporate presentations. There is no system in the market that can produce an "audiovisual presentation" with diverse special effects and time at a cost-effective price. Slides are used as the standard output media for most presentations. Because of its multiple uses it is necessary to define those catchy terms -- management graphics, information graphics, financial graphics, business graphics, boardroom graphics.

The application of layout and design, one of the main reasons for the existence of graphic design, is to avoid confusion in the arrangement of different elements of copy. The survey indicates that more than a fourth of the systems incorporate some type of layout and design capability. The field of electronic publishing in videotex and teletex have already established format, layout and design capabilities. Extensive research must be done in this area, especially in incorporating grids and using flexible menus, yet some type of uniform key layout is needed, where all the elements of graphic design come into place. How many of the systems have and make use of the appropriate typefaces that could easily integrate in a menu tablet? Remember typefaces are aesthetic, and informative; they stimulate and have the capacity to communicate, to make written memory possible. They are accessible and can be licensed. The market is divided into different segments: there is a growing awareness in the office environment to communicate with type by integrating typesetting with word processors; and impact and non-impact electronic printing. By the end of 1983 some imaging systems will have typesetting capabilities incorporated that will generate both text and graphics. Specific screens with size and function such as one for newspaper format is not yet available. In fact, the number of word processors expand daily at an exponential increment and so does the quantity of information that "cries out for graphic interpretation".[1]

Computer aided drafting applications are used by over 22% of the surveyers. These applications are bound to grow, especially in small architectural firms, which comprise the bulk of the business. A benefit is that it solves the problem of employee turnover. From another point of view the demand for space allows for the growing number of plotters attached to macros used to develop overlay graphics systems for doing floor plans for multi-residential housing and office planning. For many users CAD software is rapidly replacing tools like templates, ellipses, etc. and has extended into the manufacturing process, creating a significant progression in CAM (computer aid manufacturing). Today CAD software capabilities provide any desired view, automatic cutting of sectional views of the model, including partial cutaway versions. All in color and with shadows as a result offering the precision needed in manufacturing. Future software developments

---

[1] Myers, Ware, The Need for Graphic Design Interpretation, Computer, July 1981.

will bring textures, new images and other representations. A significant amount of CAD is done through solid modeling and apply to processes in conceptual design, engineering analysis, engineering drawings, manufacuturing and technical publications.

According to data provided by Eric Teicholz of Graphic Information Systems in Cambridge, Massachusetts, labor intensive drafting phase of drawing accounts for 50% of the drawing's cost. It is in this drafting phase that the greatest savings can be achieved using CAD. Comparing typical manual and CAD drawings figures include:

Typical Drawing	Manual	CAD	Saving
C drawing	10 hrs.	3 hrs.	7 hrs.
D drawing	16 hrs.	4 hrs.	12 hrs.
E drawing	50 hrs.	20 hrs.	30 hrs.

The checking phase of design is still best to be accomplished with the known established A/E (Architectural/Engineering) reprographic methods. A/E firms are selecting low cost computer aided design and drafting systems rather than the traditional larger (mini and large-computer) systems because they are easy to use and therefore diminish the learning curve. At the same time many design firms have specialized design and drafting needs that justify a low-cost system.

Some software capabilities (mostly in electronics) are less expensive and without sacrificing power.

In a report by International Data Corporation (Framingham, Massachusetts) a terrific growth for low-cost CAD systems is projected, where sales of low-cost systems in 1981 were only 5% of total CAD. By 1986 they will account for 20%. The areas where low-cost CAD systems will be available are: architecture, electronics, printed circuitboard design, integrated circuit board, mechanical design and purchases by educational institutions.

Free-form drawing and fine art are 11.4% of the computer aid applications. A whole new dimension in art is available through the different imaging systems and software capabilities. But no significant effort has been made to bring systems to art schools or special creative environments, where the explosion of this media has promising contributions to make to the history of mankind. Soon a developed style equivalent to Duchamp, Escher, Calder or Lichtenstein will be attained with computer graphics.

More than 10% of the surveyers are now using computer aided printing. There is probably a lot more -- in conversation with George Alexander from Seybold Publications, electronic publishing currently generates 35 million dollars worth in the U.S. These figures hold for large-color imaging systems. Each system is about 1.5 million dollars, not including color separation. Electronic scanning dominates the field in figures cited by Richard Warner at Graphic Arts Expo 82, who stated, "Americans are doing 60% scanning, Europeans 75% and Japanese 90%."

A current figure of the number of sites with multi-format front end systems is about 45,000. This is a multiple terminal with slave typesetter (typesetting peripheral to a text editing system). On top of that there is a host of direct input systems that comes to 40,000 units. The trend is the emergence of systems which will handle all pre-press functions in an electronic environment. Publications, a growing field, is merging along with video.

Photography and package design both rate as 2.8% of the design applications in the survey. The uses of computer aided design have not been exploited in these and other areas. There is a need for a high resolution electronic still camera that will be able to process film onto plates and provide immediate hard copy to handle news pictures electronically. The greatest potential benefit of photography is in the saving of darkroom time and materials. In communications dealing with photos in electronic form means they can be readily telecommunicated. In art photography offers an innovation in manipulating form. Understand that computer aided design is important to people when you make it important to them. As far as these two applications and many others not mentioned, I quote <u>The New York Times</u> of May 5, 1982 in an article "Management Gospel Gone Wrong":

> "Some businesses are to be harvested for their cash....This approach breeds caution through an overdependence on analytical detachment."

Question 4

Reflects ease in operating the computer systems. Over 55% claimed to have an "excellent" system to operate, while for 44% a "good" rating was given. Overall, rating and evaluating users' systems are a positive experience in effect because these individuals have pioneered their own systems.

Question 5

The reliability of hardware is rated excellent by 27%; 45% rated good; and poor close to 10%. We are now experiencing a breakthrough in hardware and hopefully the fifth generation of computer-integrated chips will represent the most cost-effective creation in the computerized world. Like a multiprocessor optimized to perform repetitious processing at high speed, with clean processor/task definition. On the other hand, the development of intelligent workstations from the standpoint of users and application developers with high configurability and network configurability.

Products that go beyond function to embody aesthetic qualities and functional design which appeal to the individual needs, tastes and sensibilities are part of the hardware of the 80's.

Technical support and maintenance was rated excellent by an average of 35%; over one fourth rate it good; and the other fourth rate it fair.

The role of technical support and maintenance is a stimulating force, necessary when required. The beauty and effectiveness of training occurs when one learns and understands thoroughly what a tool can do.

There is a lot to be desired in the area of documentation. On examining the data, there is a clear correlation between the documentation of those users with the greatest number of years in the field and those with little experience. The one user with over 12 years has excellent documentation. Those with 4 to 8 years of experience are in the excellent and good brackets, with one exception who had poor documentation. A lot of problems and time consumption will be avoided and systems will be used if the right documentation is provided. In turn, many new applications will make use of this information.

Designing software implies hierarchal structure and limited data modules which can be easily compiled and tested individually so that all errors are handled at the appropriate time. At the same time paper documentation can originate at one place. The endproduct is a list of errors and, once software goes into production, there is no need to alter it -- meaning savings! Here is where the need for manpower will play a great role in the 80's. Testers can be trained under the assumption that:

> ...good programmers are such bad testers that the need for an independent test organization has been recognized.[1]

Question 5

Close to three-fourths of the responses claim that the computer does what it is expected to do, with 8% indicating it does even more than expected. This is the challenge of the 80's, a challenge where numbers can come into play. Systems should be designed with the least amount of effort and energy, in the most interesting and fun way. Other than a tool that makes calculations and computations, it should be stimulating. The user gets to see the effect of the tool in systems that appeal to the senses and enhance perception.

Question 6

At this moment computers are improving at a very fast rate. This decade will begin to experience the words of Steve Coons -- a computer graphics pioneer. "We find nothing alarming about a Da Vinci, an Einstein, a Heifetz or a Gauss. But the specter of a machine, a computer, much more imaginative and creative than any human is to many people bitterly alarming. Nevertheless, such a machine is entirely possible. That is because a computer can become self-improving, a kind of adaptive behavior that is something like a self-

---

[1] Experience With a Software Test Factory, Budd, Majora and Sneed.

induced and accelerated evolutionary process."

Productivity has improved for 71% of the users. With microcomputers entering the world of human feelings, productivity will boost. At all levels such as the case of music and voice synthesizers, the same is achieved with video and paint systems and all its functions in the development of kinetic art. The technology becomes a reflection of a new society, a new culture: Autonomy. Is this not what built the great empires throughout history? Productivity leads to creativity which in turn breeds inventiveness.

For 69% quality has improved with the computer system. Film media has all the quality available, if resolution is within range of 1025 pixels or above. The 80's demand better hardcopy output such as a graphic arts quality printer and it is time for a reasonably priced quality color laser plotter.

Question 7

More than half of the surveyers evaluated graphic application packages "good". The standardization and support of tool packages, device independent software and system software distribution will characterize the history and evolution of computer graphics.

Question 8

Results indicate that more than a third of the users write their own software while one third work with programmers and the other third buy package programs.

Looking at software from the creative side -- the visual world -- the scope of the future demands an interface of some type of universal visual communication. In the world of film, architecture, and graphics, mapping communication is visual. Writing and typing do not make sense yet the creation of images and symbols in connection become logical information. It is time that some type of visual communication becomes the accepted thought. Just in the way it happens in transportation: a green light means go...

In question 9 the human interface, the highest priority of technology, is rated, and demands that the 80's be a colorful decade!! The majority of the users are using color display terminals and many have more than one terminal. Most of the displays are 512 x 512 resolution, but there is an increased use of higher resolution which provides clarity. There are many display professors with extremely fast display writing speeds that are important for user interaction. The codes described above could be in color and for those color-blind individuals the use of texture is available. The light pen and function keys are the accepted methods of inputting data and on the average they are rated good.

Since Ivan Southerland's development and study on light pens and tablets, there have been remarkable innovations.

Yet the light pen remains the same. What if the light pen was equipped with several electronic keys? What if the light pen had more than one point? How many built-in functions would be possible? Or some type of a combination of a mouse and light pen. The uses of the tablet have been explored by Xerox Star System.

A very useful interface is a universal specialized colorful keyboard that features key-sequencing; numerous menus could be integrated in a logical form according to each application.

As demand grows this decade will recognize a lot of new design features and innovations.

Question 10 is an actitudal response in which more than a third consider the computer an idea machine. In essence the computer is an innovative tool where the creation of images brings a whole visual world. In the survey more than two-thirds of the responses state that the computer expands art/design education. To quote John Whitney:

> The organization is the information, indeed. I wish to propose that so far as the educational process is concerned, so far as art is concerned, we have hardly begun to comprehend the possibilities for meaningful reordering by the graphic image in the structure of time. We just do not know what media lie ahead nor what the message capacity will be. But we may well be well disposed to explore energetically these possibilities of structure in art information.[1]

---

1 Whitney, John, Digital Harmony, McGraw-Hill Publications, 1981.

The last part of question 10 refers to the projection that the computer will eliminate as many jobs as it creates. Only 9% answered. The 80's clearly emerge as the transformation age from an industrial society to a computerized information society. In any stage of social evolution some needs disappear as others emerge.

Question 11 solicits the opinions and needs of some of today's and tomorrow's users of computer aided design systems. I have categorized them in order of urgency. Information and education; effectiveness; cost performance; systems integrated to mainframes and future demands.

There were 18 responses to question 11. The description of an ideal system as far as features, users' interface, capabilities and looking ahead ten years. These opinions are quoted and range from different backgrounds. From small studio designer to a CIA program implementation. I have selected the outstanding ones and those that best describe and represent the majority of the statements.

1. Need of education/information

I do not know anything about any of this!

Sensuous curves and capacity for speech, never say "no"

2. Effectiveness

The speed necessary to complete difficult graphics in a short amount of time because we have to meed deadlines

Every time I write a new program, or modify an existing one, or mentally or formally propose features to upgrade our system,

Future Integrated Visual Communication System

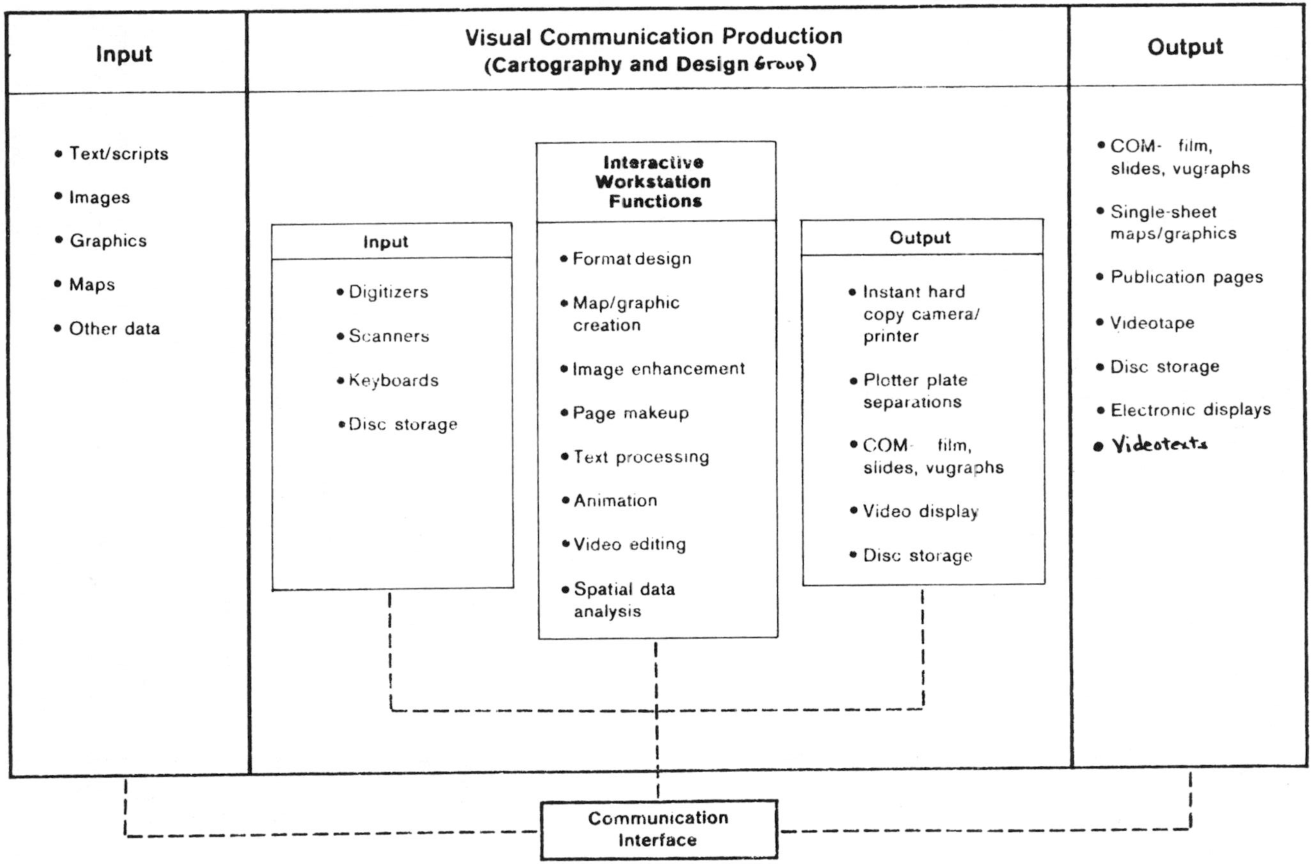

Unclassified

my concept of an ideal system changes. I think that generally, programmers grow along with the system, and hence there can be no ideal system since it is always in a state of progress

The computer will be the main source for communication and advertising

Certainly with more than one machine for a TV graphics operation

No user programming per se except for entering parameters, data, and organizing choices. Highly interactive. Most scenes compiled in real time

Software: understands my language, flexible, unlimited typefaces help with design suggestions

More versatility in storage pac

New programs written that will replace most of the supplies that we now use for making graphics

3. Cost performance

I would like to see low-priced raster scan systems capable of 3-D simulation (an evolution of the flight simulators made by E&S)

Higher resolution at lower cost
Lower cost peripherals

The Cray 10 computer for $100.00

4. System integrated to a mainframe

Totally integrated and network systems

A graphic terminal on every desk connected to a mainframe and access to electronic mail

The ideal communication system will be totally integrated visual communication system linked to the mainframe computer as shown on the enclosed diagram (see diagram on page 13)

5. Future demands

Real time continuous shading with all rendering capabilities: textures, shadows, unlimited detail with holographic output

Better displays (70mm film recorders, 3-D displays, large screens, lines video)

A 3-D database sculpting system where you carve out databases within a 3-D space, with a light pen and tablet type of device

This system is used to drive motors on animation stand. More motor drive capability, faster action and direct interface with video

More than half of the users have excellent application packages. Cross-tabulating the data shows that 50% write their own programs; 30% do not write their own software; nearly 10% modify the packages; and 10% work along with other programmers. In any discipline communication is the basis because it integrates all the different components in a way that specifies details and concrete concepts.

> In the designing application software we should understand and communicate in the ends-user's dialect. This means not only using a jargon appropriately, but also understanding the common experiences that underlie the group's dialect such as metaphors for such experiences into our communication.[1]

If application packages are to be successful the developments of the process should consider the logic of the machine as opposed to the reasoning of humans where emotions play a large part. In the book The World Challenge

---

1 Heckel, Paul, Designing Software for People, The New York Times, May 5, 1982

by Jean-Jacques Servan-Schreiber, he states

> ...software, the 'immaterial' part, the part that can be composed only by human brain, is the heart of the matter. It has been lagging far behind. It is in the realm of developing software, which commands computers and robots, that the whole future lies. Without waiting for their successors of the fifth generation, the present microprocessors are already establishing a computerized society. Under the guidance of human ideas, which alone can nourish software and, beyond that, the entire environment, the new social fabric is being built.

Cross-tabulating this data clearly shows that those who write and those that do not write their own programs do improve their creativity, productivity and quality above average. Certainly this correlation is higher if the time is taken to organize words, use modules and test them so quality control is achieved.

PERSPECTIVES

The 80's will bring powerful inexpensive microcomputers, low-cost systems, intelligent workstations, better application programs, better interfaces yet before this is done the knowledge should not be confined to experts and elites. A demand for teachers in the computer aided design field is vital to facilitate the transition. It is time to train teachers. As far as I know there is only one course in the U.S. that teaches data presentation techniques with computer aided graphics -- it is at the Harvard Business School. Other courses will have to come into play because graphic data is used in the sciences and arts. There are demands on education at all levels. They should be met in the 80's if a transition and acceptance of the technology expands at the present rate of growth. A revenue of 14.6 million dollars in 1980 was generated in the educational sector of business graphics as quoted from Frost & Sullivan Report by Dr. Carl Machover. Education constitutes 3% to 5% of business graphics and will grow 32% up to 178 million by 1980, with the purchase of equipment -- raster, refresh, store, electrostatic, printer, plotter, ink jet, line, service bureau, time sharing consultants and other.

Education can easily be achieved by building user guides in program structures and running a hard copy which one can always update, and providing visually, graphically structured manuals.

The category of effectiveness can best be summarized in the words of Mr. Hayesin, Managing Our Way to Economic Decline, July/August, Harvard Business Review:

> ...The Japanese succeed because they pay attention to such basics as clean workplace, preventive maintenance for machinery, a desire to make their production process error-free and attitude that thinks quality in every stage in the production process. We must compete with the Japanese as they do with us: by always putting our best resources and talents to work doing the basic things a little better everyday, over a long period of time.

In the category of cost performance, there is a big cry for more memory at less price. If the economics make it feasible, why not? When will the Gutenberg printing process absorb and take advantage of digital technology to its maximum?

As a designer in the graphic design field I see a design center. A mainframe for large number of users. I perceive as the computer aided design integration system for the 80's. A local computer network of micros with integrated type and page makeup and color separation configurations. Interfaces with a couple of film systems such as recorders, hard copy units and a laser color printer. Video systems and palettes, computer animation motion control cameras that operate in a timeshare basis. Or just a coin slot operation in which anyone is free to walk in and try the technology. Videodisk, videotape and CRT displays. A software configuration simply by allowing existing software modules -- from operating systems to compiler data base management. The benefits are computer-to-computer communication, with data sharing and cost sharing on a guarantee service. The future demands should be met by the turn of the decade, where further research and development will have allowed for innovations such as holography, 3-D displays and automatic digitizers at affordable prices.

SUMMARY OF FINDINGS

The origins of any future prediction lies in the fact that whatever the creation be in a system, it should have flexible alternatives making things as simple as possible.

This requires intensive research regarding man-machine adaptability. In effect it will assure any user that the new tool is his and will only serve to aid him and his ideas. It is a tool and should not inhibit anyone at any point: if it is good for experts, then why not for neophytes? In the area of research and development, to make technology accessible one route is that of low-cost CAD/CAM systems that are specific in many applications like animation, graphic design, package design, TV graphics, etc. Concentration should gear to push forward technology and not to exploit it. A big step for mankind...

We must continue to expand our knowledge about humans and understand their particular needs in order to develop mutual cooperation with computer aided design systems. In the aesthetic and functional considerations of CAD there is potential for far-reaching changes in the structure of the labor market and the economy. The aspects of creativity and heuristics are just beginning to evaluate and provide options and solutions where information contributes infinitely to a variety of processes. The fact is that information and communication can be put to timely, practical use. The major source of growth is knowing how to use this information in the 1980's which is characterized by the development and understanding of disciplines like psychology, behaviorism, philosophy, computer science, sociolgy, etc. that will evolve dynamically compatible to reap benefits towards a new era.

REFERENCE

Brock, E., "Microcomputer Network Application in Banking," Compcon 81, San Francisco, Spring, 1981.

Brooks, Fred, The Mythical Man Month, Addison Wesley, 1975.

Dreyfuss, Henry, Designing for People, Viking, 1955.

Fourth Annual Frost and Sullivan Conference -- Assessment and Forecast of Computer Graphics - 1982

Hakansson, J., "The Sesame Street Computer Gallery: An Electronic Playground for Kids," Compcon 81, San Francisco, Spring, 1981.

Harkin, Arthur, "Projected Future Impacts of Ethnotronic Systems on Human Systems," Compcon 82, San Francisco, Spring, 1982.

Heckel, Paul, "Designing Software for People," The New York Times, May 5, 1982.

Masanori, Moritani, Getting the Best for the Least -- Japanese Technology, Sumul International, 1982.

Negroponte, Nicholas, Computer Aids to Design and Architecture, Petroceli Chartes, 1975.

Servan-Schreiber, Jean-Jacques, World Challenge, Simon & Schuster, 1980.

Thomas, S.C. & Carroll, J.M., Human Factor in Communication Systems Journal, vol. 20, Nov. 2, 1981.

Whitney, John, Digital Harmony, McGraw-Hill Publications, 1981.

APPENDICES

Graphics by InterChart, Inc., N.Y.C.

Computer Aided Design Trends in the 80's

Users of Mainframe & Free Standing Units

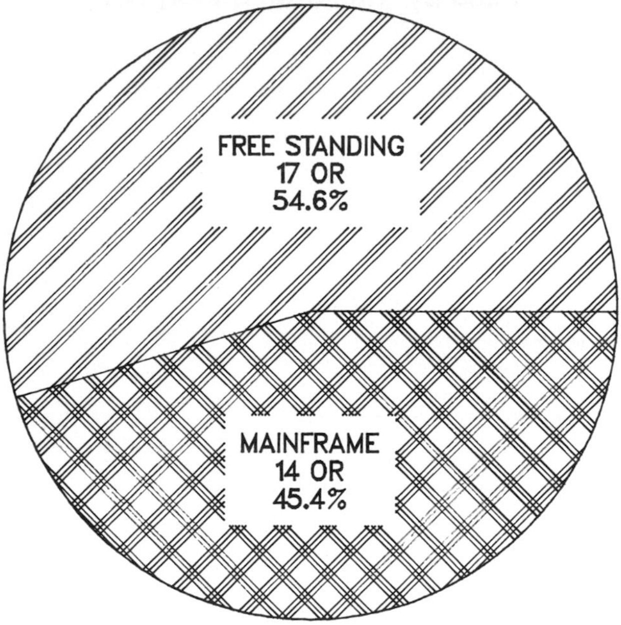

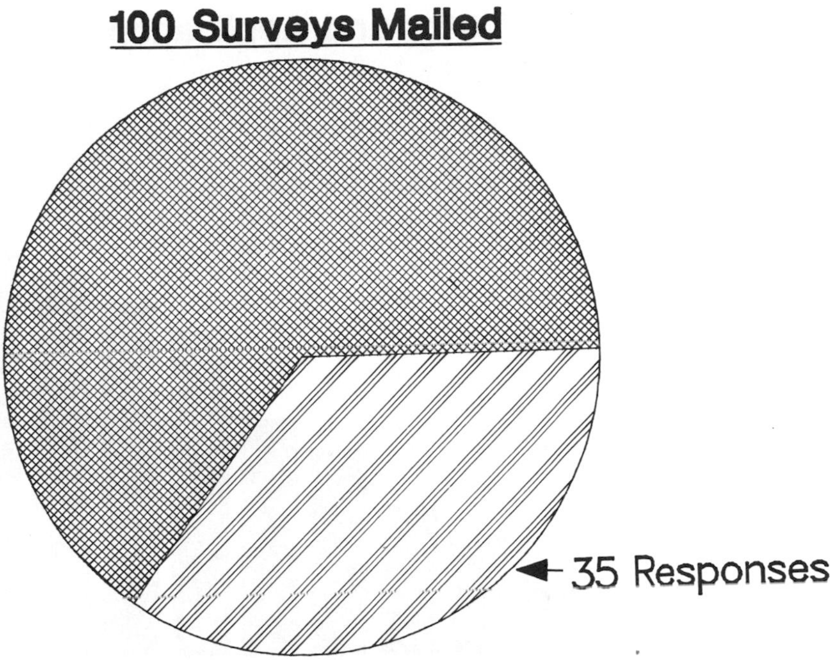
100 Surveys Mailed
35 Responses

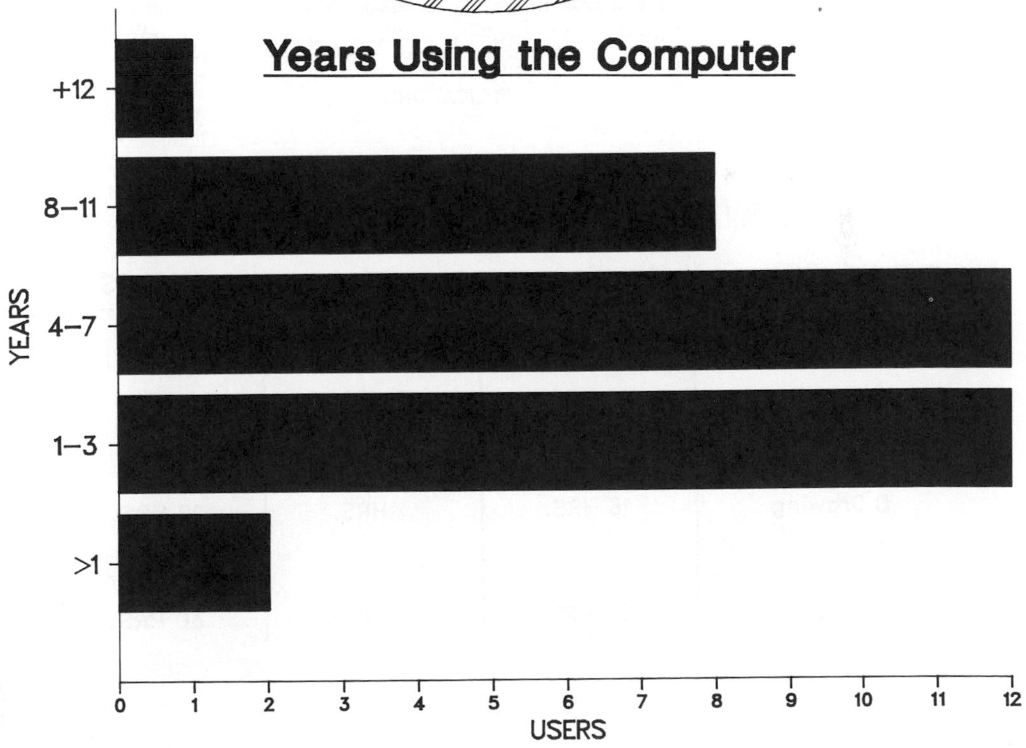
Years Using the Computer
YEARS
+12
8–11
4–7
1–3
>1
0
1
2
3
4
5
6
7
8
9
10
11
12
USERS

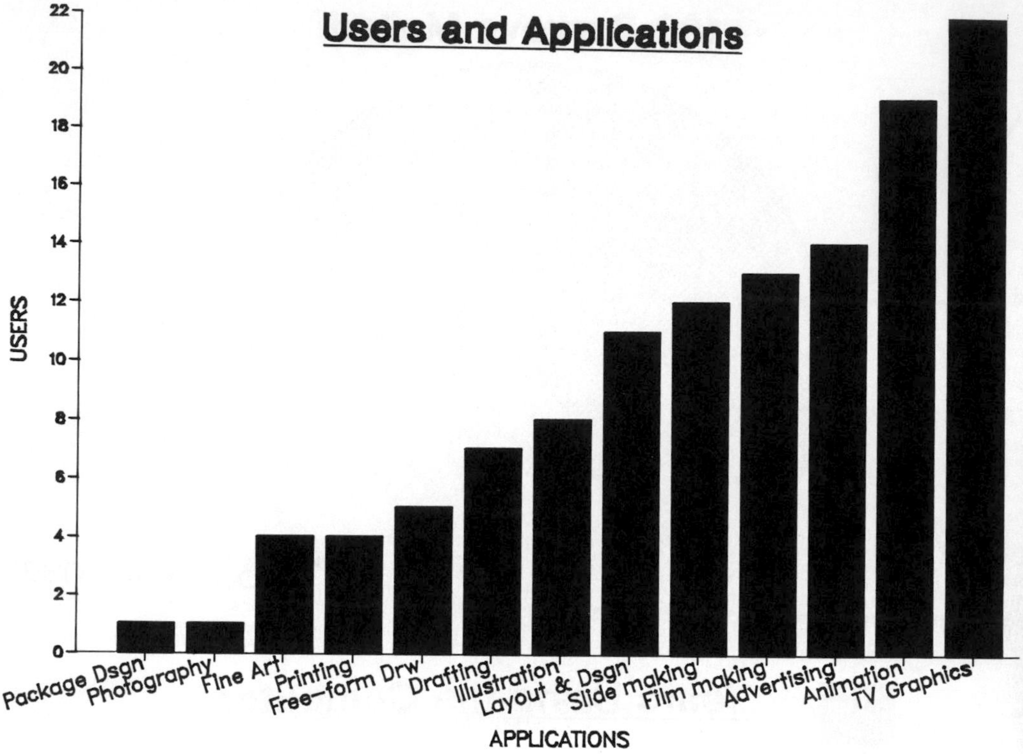

SAVINGS WITH CAD DRAWINGS

TYPICAL DRAWING	MANUAL	CAD	SAVINGS
C Drawing	10 HRS.	3 HRS.	7 HRS.
D Drawing	16 HRS.	4 HRS.	12 HRS.
E Drawing	50 HRS.	20 HRS.	30 HRS.

System Evaluation (Cont.)

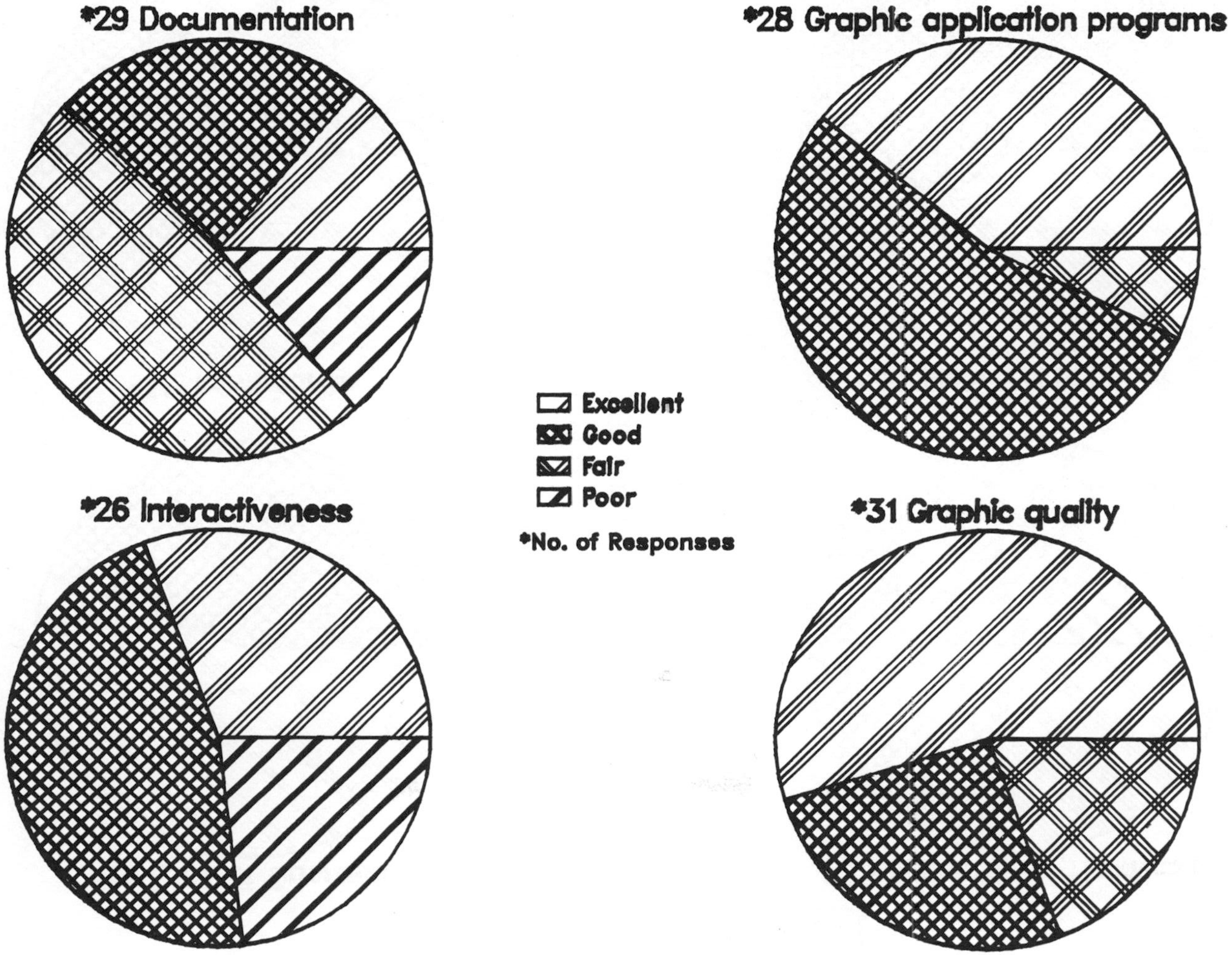

System Evaluation

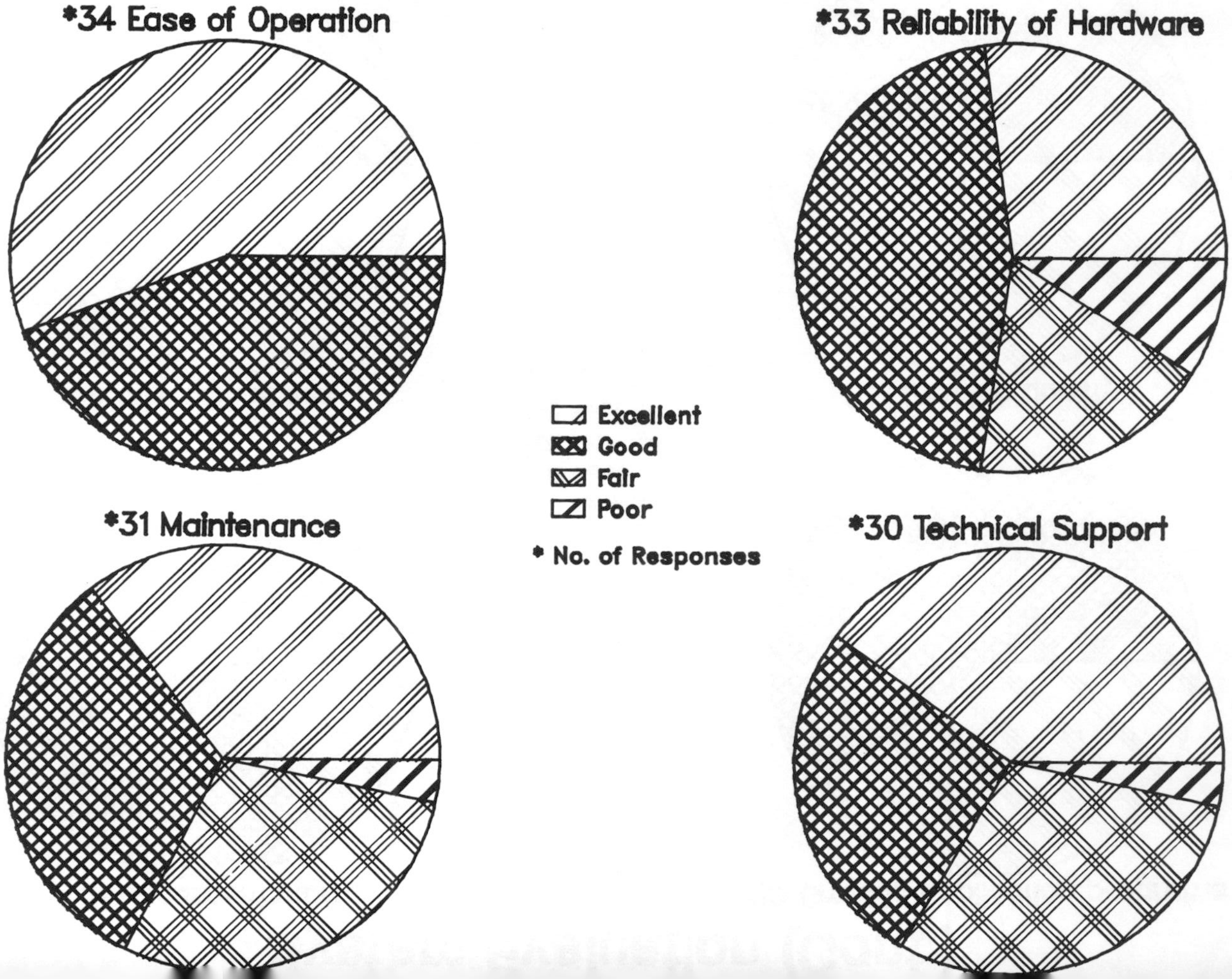

Expectations of Using the Computer

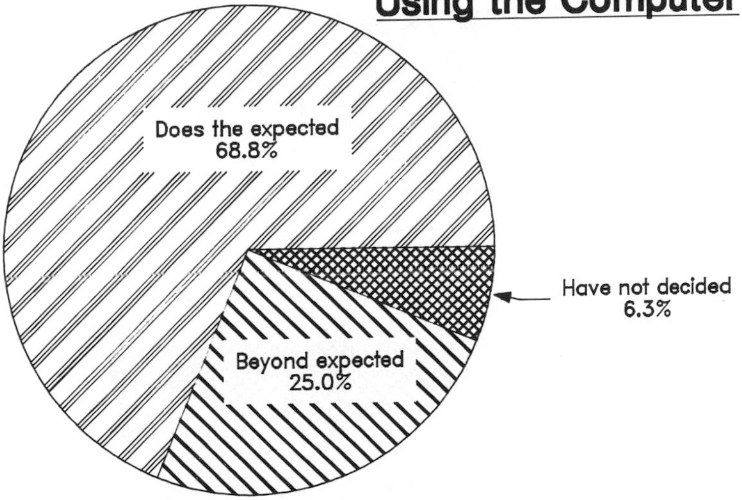

Rating for Improvement in Productivity, Creativity & Quality with the Computer

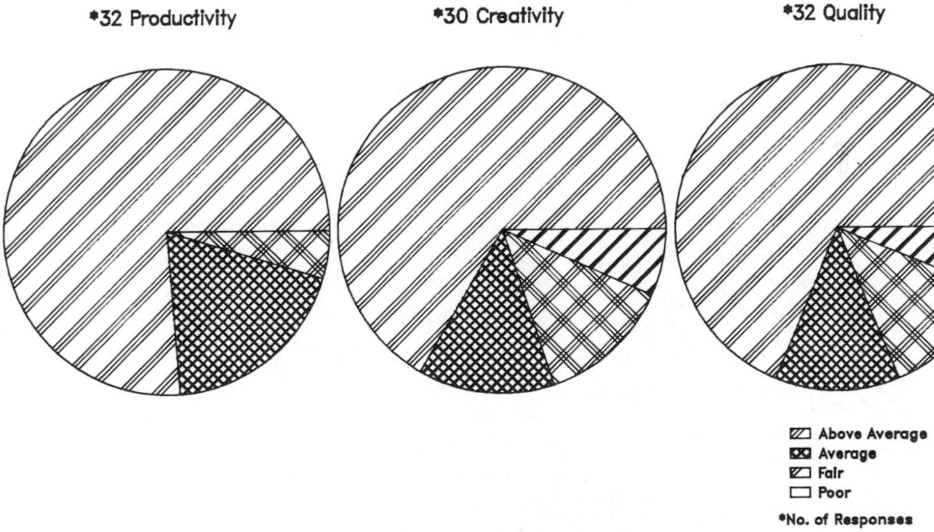

Application Packages Support Needs

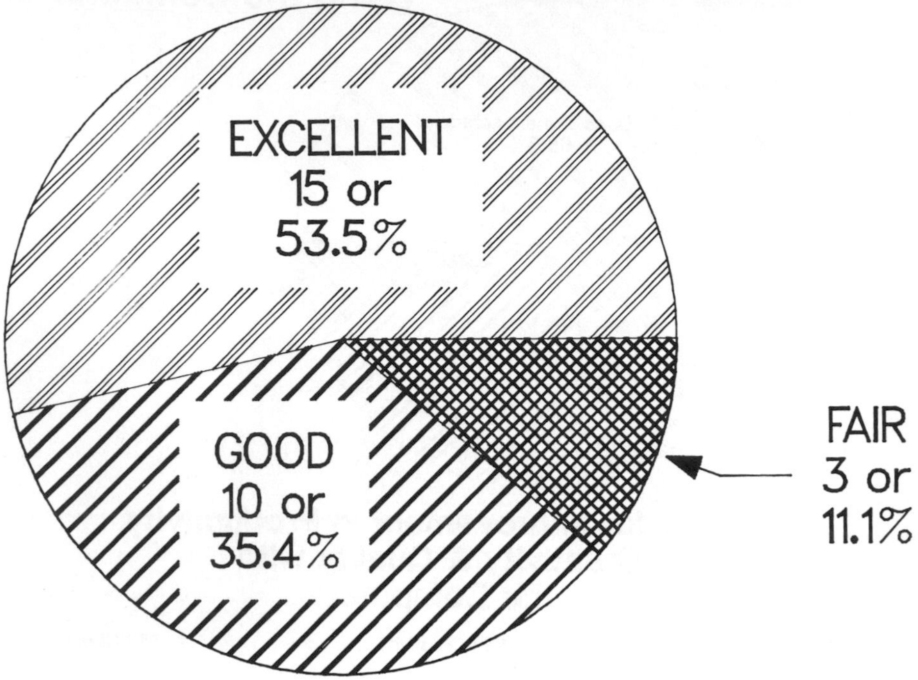

Software Writing

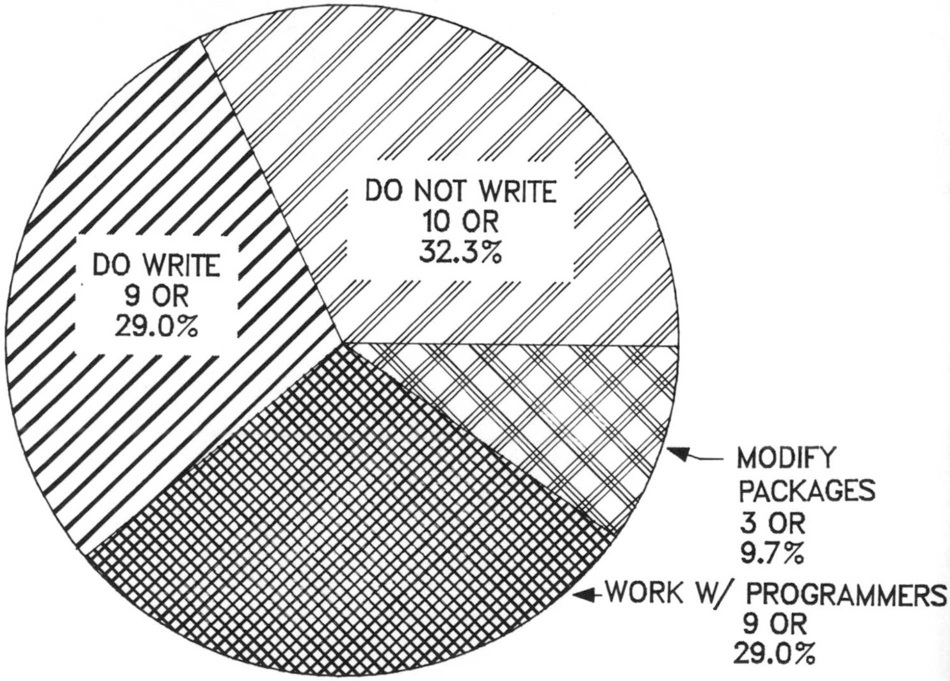

Interface Evaluation

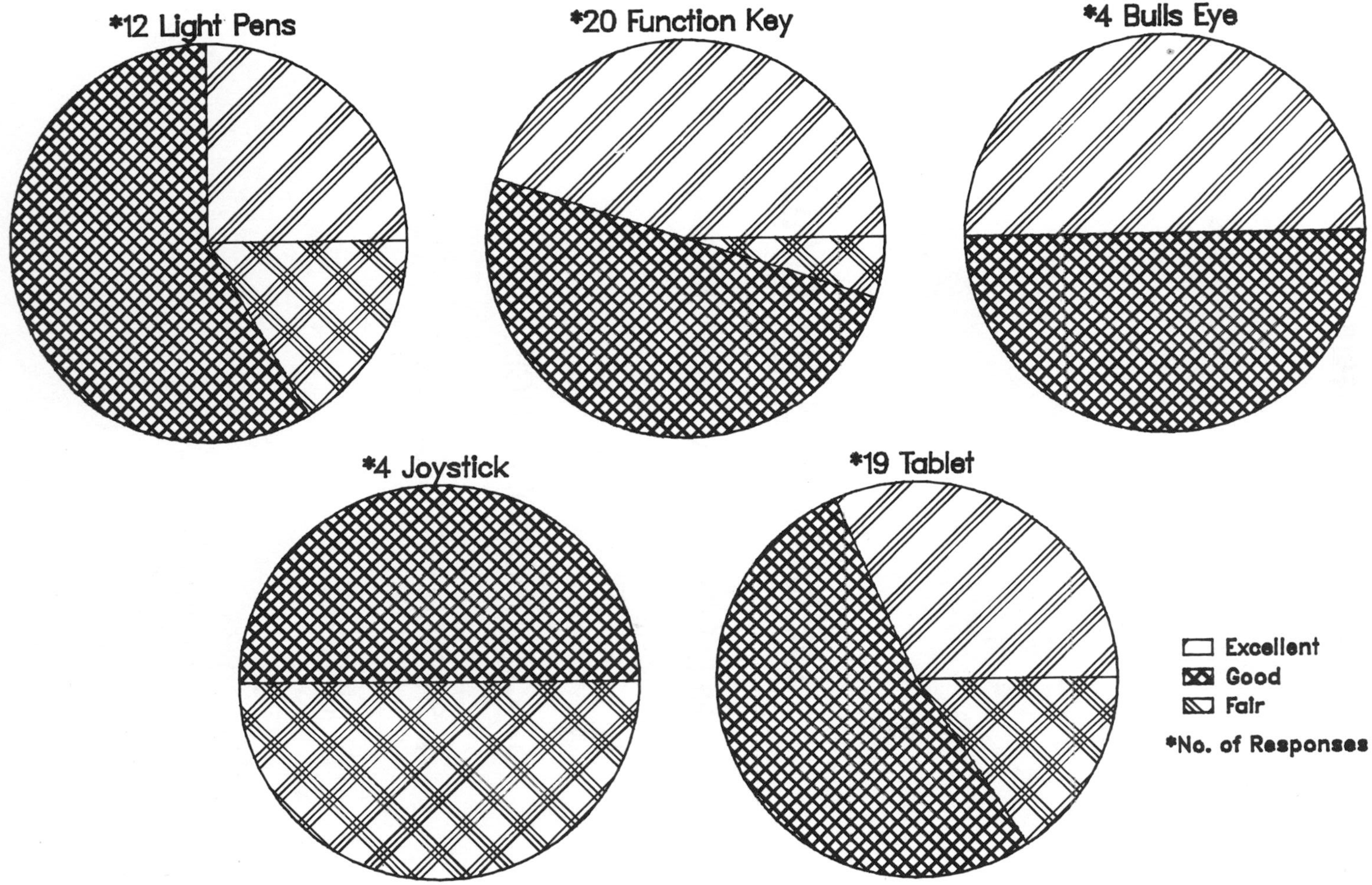

Terminal Users

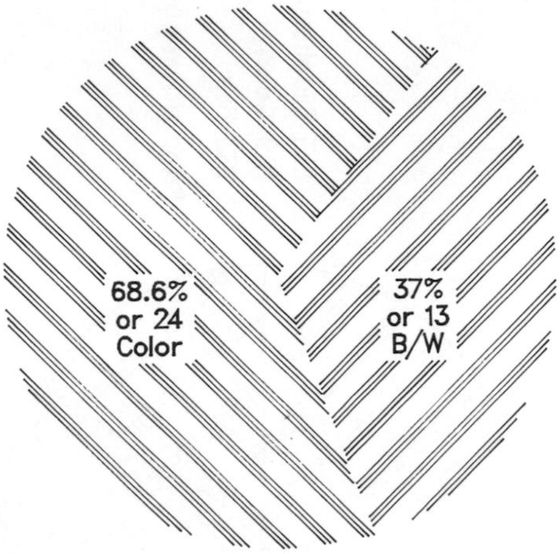

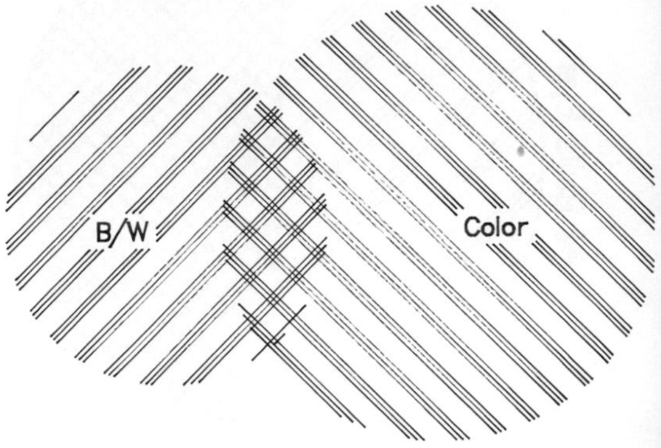

6 use both

DEMANDS IN CAD

1. NEED OF EDUCATION / INFORMATION
2. EFFECTIVENESS
3. COST PERFORMANCE
4. SYSTEM INTEGRATION
5. INNOVATION

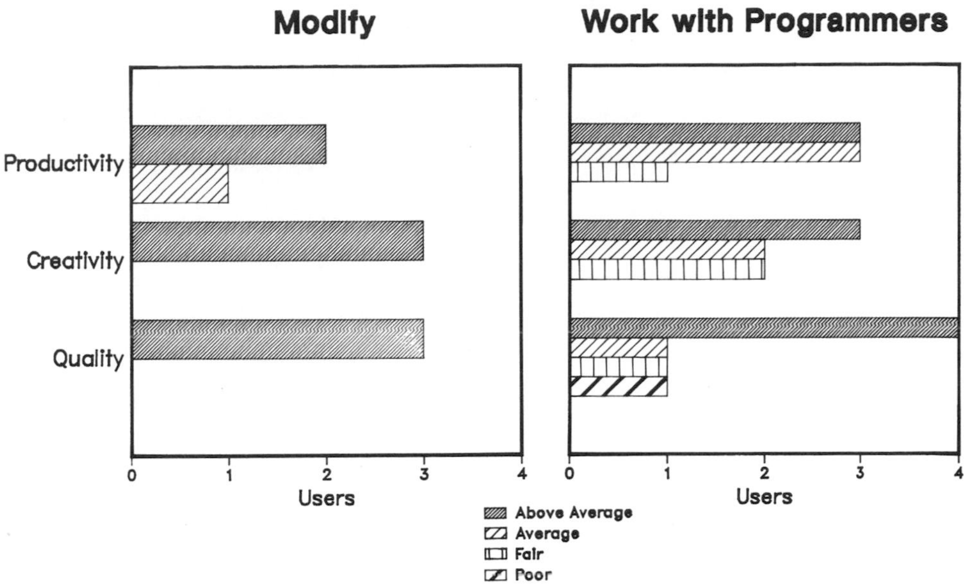
Modify
Work with Programmers
Productivity
Creativity
Quality
0
1
2
3
4
Users
Above Average
Average
Fair
Poor

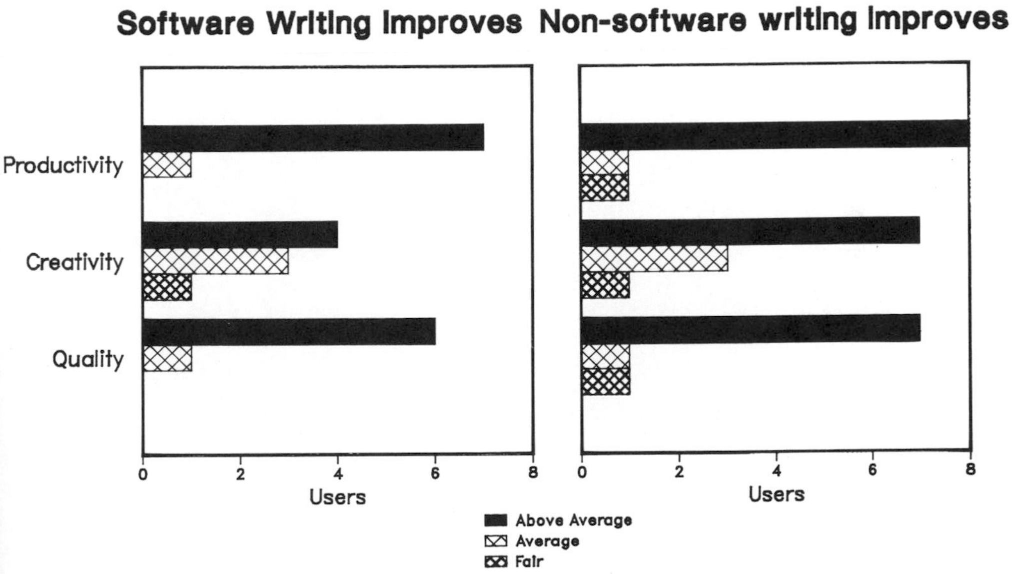
Software Writing Improves
Non-software writing improves
Productivity
Creativity
Quality
0
2
4
6
8
Users
Above Average
Average
Fair

Chapter 4
Office Automation

COMPUTER GRAPHICS FOR MANAGEMENT: PREREQUISITES FOR AN EFFECTIVE INTRODUCTION

Howard A. Spielman

Manager, Quality Assurance & DSS
Educational Services
Digital Equipment Corporation
12 Crosby Drive
Bedford, Massachusetts 01730, U.S.A.

ABSTRACT

The process of introducing computer graphics into an organization can have a critical impact on its acceptance and usefulness for management. Technical computer expertise must be coordinated with knowledge and skills from other areas: technical graphics expertise, the concerns of organizational development, and the needs and expectations of managers. This paper describes a study of the introduction of computer graphics within a fortune 200 company. The study surveyed the impact of graphics on five different levels of management. It identifies sources of resistance to the introduction of graphics as well as factors of positive influence in implementing the change. It also describes changes in management decision-making capabilities as well as the causes of sub-optimal utilization of graphics. Based upon an analysis of the issues raised in the study, the paper concludes with recommendations of prerequisites for the effective introduction of computer graphics for management.

INTRODUCTION

There is a developing mythology sbout computer graphics for management. To the uninitiated, its technical terminology sounds as Greek as the ancient mythology. But more importantly, its promised impact on management decision making is taking on such titanic proportions that to effectively live up to these expectations may require the mythological powers of zeus.

It has been observed, by Henry Mintzberg in the Harvard Business Review, that managers of today "are fundamentally indistinguishable from their counterparts of a hundred years ago (or a thousand years ago, for that matter). The information that they need differs, but they seek it in the same way - by word of mouth."(1) Why then, can't computer graphics deliver information in a new way and break this millenia-long tradition? This seems to be the thesis of Takeuchi and Schmidt in their article, also in HBR, "New Promise of Computer Graphics". Here they discuss "essentials for computer graphics," and assert: "Three resources are needed before a computer generated picture can appear for the user: hardware, data bases, and software." (2) This may be sufficient if "the user" has technical computer expertise but, as this study has found, few managers in a business environment meet this requirement. More than three resources are often needed before a computer generated picture can be effectively utilized by management.

Not only are these additional resources often essential; it hss been found that they are prerequisite for an effective introduction of computer graphics for management. The following case study and analysis will illuminate these issues.

THE CASE STUDY

The Introduction of Computer Graphics into the Organization

In late July the Controller of a division of a Fortune 200 company was invited to view three vendor exhibits at the Harvard Computer Graphics Week during a lunch hour. A member of the Controller's staff was attending the Graphics Week and, after three days of stimulating sessions, thought it would be easier to convey the content of the seminars if the Controller had some 'hands-on' experience with the available hardware and software. He came with several of his direct reports and spent about half an hour with each exhibitor. Not only was his interest piqued, but he also found that each of these vendors had already established a relationship with other divisions of his corporation. Their software was either currently installed in-house, on a trial installation, or about to be installed. By the next day he had already arranged to investigate the two systems installed elsewhere in the corporation (both of which were heavily color oriented), and initiated plans to bring the third vendor in for further consultation.

By the middle of August he had identified a financial manager, reporting to him, to spearhead the development of a computer graphics reporting system. Through his staff he prepared a variety of color bar chart, line chart, and pie chart transparancies on the two installed systems for presentation at a quarterly divisional management committee meeting. He assessed the reaction of management committee members to his presentation. He also reviewed the concerns of the third vendor, who stressed the issue of "graphics standards" and, taking a line from Henry Ford, asserted that their clients could have their graphs printed in any color they wanted, as long as that color was black.

The Controller called a meeting late in August that set the scene for the widespread introduction of computer graphics into the organization. He endeavored to get his peers from other divisions of the corporation to join him in his decision. When they appeared reluctant, he announced that he was going to begin adopting standards and working closely with the third vendor. Thus, barely one month after being introduced to computer graphics himself, the Controller made a decision to formally introduce computer graphics into his organization. While he did not know it at the time, within four months some of his reluctant peers would begin to adopt the same standards with software from the same vendor.

The month of September saw key meetings between the vendor and two of the Controller's staff to develop the standard formats to be used within the organization. Among the standards established, horizontal bars were to be used for the presentation of all item comparisons, variances, and ratios. Vertical bars would be used for time trends. The vendor also met with the Corporate Manager of the division, to whom the Controller reported. The vendor thus had personal contact with the highest officer of the division as well as one person on each of the next three organizational levels down.

October and November passed quickly as the software was adapted, the rest of the Controller's staff was introduced to the new graphics standards, and required hardware was acquired. By mid November, at the first quarterly divisional management committee meeting since the one in August, the first of the new graphs were presented. The next two months saw enhancements in the software, the standards, and the database.

In late January, just six months after the Controller's initial involvement with computer graphics for management, the first Monthly Report for the division was produced with graphical represnetation of almost all data. The Controller and Corporate Manager were quite proud of their achievement and thus produced additional copies of the report to be distributed to their peers in the corporation. It was in these six months that a computer graphics management reporting system was effectively installed.

There are a number of issues that must be addressed by users before the adopted graphics formats may be easily understood. Without entering into these interpretation issues, the following figures may be viewed as representative examples of the types of graphics used in the management reporting system described in this paper. They are typical of the type of matrix print output that is available to all users at this time. A higher quality graphics mode matrix printer (132 × 72 dots per inch) and laser printer output are enhancements planned for the near future. Figure 1 shows a typical statement of income. Figure 2 depicts a balance sheet, while the graphical representation of critical ratios is shown in Figure 3.

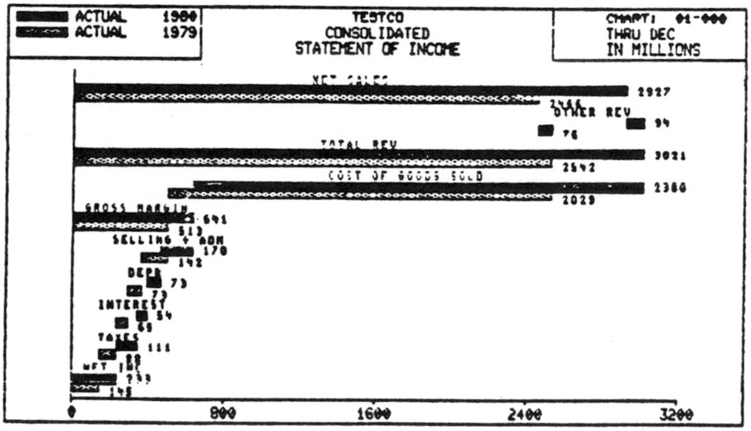

Figure 1

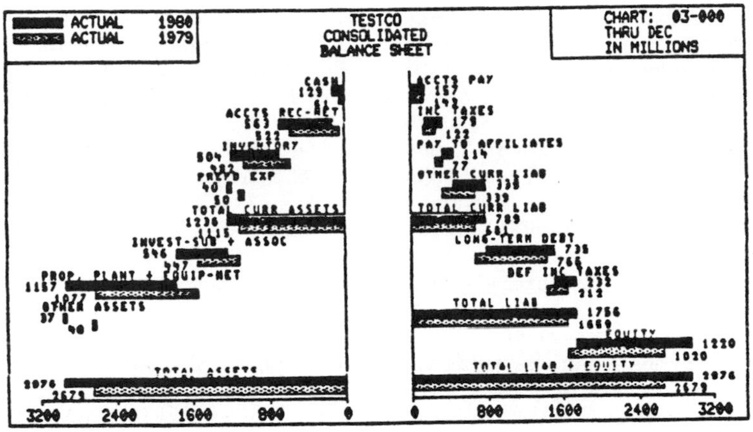

Figure 2

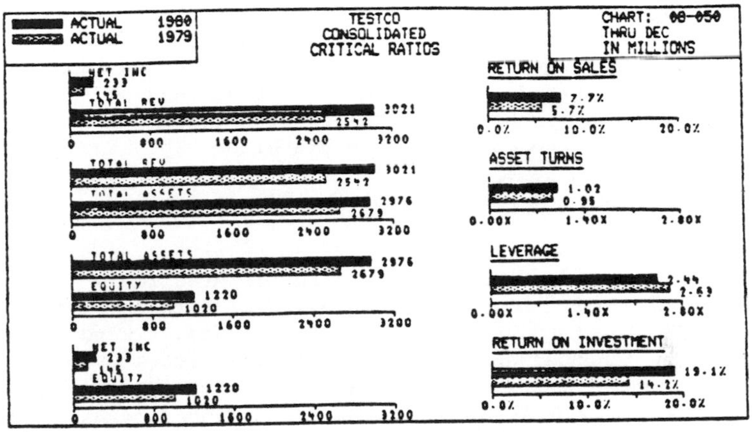

Figure 3

Analysis of the Introduction

The very first step in the introduction of computer graphics into an organization must be to ask the question "why?". It's not that there's a right or a wrong answer to this question. It's just that when those introducing the graphics are asked, they ought to have a clear and concise response that is meaningful to those who are impacted by this new graphics. In this case the answers came easily. The Controller had already been asking his financial analysts to prepare graphs, typically line charts, using manual methods. Having a computer generate these charts would probably improve the analysts' productivity. He was also concerned about the 'information overload' of vast tables of data and thought he might expedite management internalization of the data and possibly even improve the level of management decision making. These needs, so easily verbalized, were critical prerequisites to the Controller's 'hands-on' experience with the vendors at the Graphics Week. They also offered a real incentive to make the introduction of computer graphics work.

The mid-August management committee meeting tested some of these assertions. Response was generally favorable to the multi-color charts. A number of nagging issues arose though. Lack of standardization in both graphic structures and usage of colors caused more than a little confusion. At least one person who was color blind admitted that he could not understand a number of charts. Several managers wanted to distribute copies of the charts to their staffs, and found that the black and white photocopies could not be deciphered without the original color keys. With all of these seemingly negative issues relating to color, the Controller did not need much added incentive to consider the, potentially very large, total costs of all the color transparencies and color hard copies that would be proliferating.

We must remember though, that a raison d'etre of computer graphics in this environment was to address 'information overload' in regular monthly reports of tabular data. A precondition for effective graphics was thus large scale printing of a variety of charts in a short span of time. When a particular item was to be highlighted in a monthly or quarterly meeting, its standard chart would be pulled from the standard report, made into a transparency, and discussed. There would thus be little need for the typical 'presentation graphics' in this management decision making environment. All those present at the meeting would also be thoroughly acclimated to the previously standardized formats so that they could concentrate on the issues related to the data without first getting oriented to the presentation style and colors of the graphics. This too was thought to be a productivity enhancement. A compelling argument for graphics standards and two-color graphics was developing.

If the managers of an organization are going to use computer graphics in their decision making, then they must be prepared for a 'change'. Understanding the graphical representation of data is a 'change' from understanding the tabular representation of data. There is a growing literature on 'change' and this literature is clearly one of the resources that must precede "hardware, data bases, and software." Beckhard and Harris, in their book "Organizational Transitions: Managing Complex Change," speak of the "transition state" in the change process. For an organization entering this "state", and wanting to optimize the potential for success in the 'change', they suggest that "some considerations in determining the particular management structure are finding someone who:

1. Can have the clout to mobilize the resources necessary to keep the change moving. Usually in such a change situation, one is competing for resources with others who have ongoing work to do.

2. Can have the respect of the existing operating leadership and the change advocates. A great deal of wisdom, objectivity, and linkage may be needed in order to make the balancing decisions, e.g., how much resource to put into the new activity and at what pace.

3. Has effective interpersonal skills. A great deal of leadership at this time requires persuasion rather than force or formal power."(3)

There are various alternative structures for managing this state, that meet these considerations, and Beckhard and Harris discuss these in the ensuing pages. In the case study the considerations were substantially met and the change was instituted, though not without an undercurrent of concern on the part of a number of participants.

The discussion of the introduction of computer graphics into this organization has centered primarily on the Controller who was clearly the driving force in the change. Through the introduction process and beyond, though, a number of levels of management and staff were impacted by this change. A post-introduction survey studied the impacts in this case study.

The Impact of Computer Graphics on Management and Staff

The top level of the organization, the Corporate Manager, had a rather favorable reaction to the computer graphics reporting system. "I kind of like them, actually. Once you're used to them, you can see what you want. There's far more information on one page of graphics than with text." Why did he like them? "They are very useful to quickly see what's happening. I can identify problems as I switch from one organization to another." He seemed convinced that graphics reporting would be fully integrated into the decision making process: "We've got to use it to run the business." But, he did feel that the graphics lent themselves more to some types of data than to others: "Some things I was really impressed with. For example, ROA [return on assets - similar to Figure 3] I found extremely useful. It worked great for the balance sheet [see Figure 2], but maybe not for some other data."

Regarding the output, he said: "It's important to have high quality output, without high cost." Should we use color? "No, color drives up printing costs."

When asked how these standardized graphs were being received by managers outside of this division, he responded: "People are still having trouble with them. I made a presentation to the [corporate] management committee and it was a disaster." What about an educational program, then: "I want a presentation such that I don't have to educate people. The problem is getting people to spend time. My boss will not spend half a day on this. If a graph doesn't show him something right away, it's not a good graph." It should be noted, though, that the Corporate Manager spent better than two hours in an informal meeting with the vendor and the financial manager and technical staff person who set up the system and the standards. He thus had a rather good sense of the issues and the structure of the graphics reporting system. He could pass this on rather easily to his subordinates on the divisional management committee, but it was more difficult to pass it up to his boss and peers on the corporate management committee. He seemed to feel that this issue would resolve itself over time, as the graphical representation of data in these formats might evolve into more of a corporate-wide standard.

Members of the divisional management committee were generally in concurrence with the Corporate Manager. They seemed to feel that the graphics reporting system was useful and deserved a fair chance to prove its worth. One committee member from overseas said: "This is really superb. This is probably the best new management tool I've seen since I've been on the committee."

The impact of the new graphics reporting was felt most critically by the cadre of financial managers reporting to the Controller and each supporting a functional member of the divisional management committee. On their shoulders fell the burden of creating, analyzing, and interpreting the graphics.

The one member of this team who was involved most closely with the introduction of the graphics expressed his biggest disappointment as: "The training didn't happen right." He described some logistical and financial reasons for why some proposed training sessions were not offered and then continued: "Training is key, and I think there'll be problems because it isn't there." Already, he felt there were "people who were unhappy, not because of the graphics, or the standards, but primarily because of the way it was introduced" - without training. A particular example of this was that some people "can't see the virtue of the cuisinaire rod [or floating bar] format [see Figures 1 & 2], as opposed to item comparisons all beginning from the same baseline [see Figure 3]." He clearly felt the virtue of the adopted format, but then again, he had spent better than two weeks of total elapsed time in consulting with the vendor and discussing the issues. His peers heard the results of these deliberations from him and, as later interviews indicated, needed more of an opportunity to consider these issues.

He could easily find notable benefits to the program, though. "The graphics have allowed things to be put in perspective and to show relationships people haven't seen before." As examples he cited the graphical presentation of the balance sheet (Figure 2) for the product line and the key ratios broken into their component parts (Figure 3) to show effects on total performance. He was enthusiastic about these standard formats being considered for adoption by the Corporate Finance group for usage corporation-wide. He was asked if it might not be better to wait on achieving these benefits until proper training of the financial staff could be accomplished. He seemed to balance the immediate benefits that he perceived arising from the graphics, and the long-term potential for positively addressing training and internal political issues against the opportunity costs of waiting. He then responded: "You're probably better off to put graphics out and possibly confuse some people, - as long as [the Corporate Manager] pledges support.

At this point it is interesting to note a recent article, in the Harvard Business Review, by Rockart and Treacy: "The CED Goes On-line." Here they discuss several case studies and then identify four major themes in a simple model for "an information system for executives." Regarding the fourth theme, "...A support organization," they assert: "Finally, all the systems we observed depend on the provision of a high level of personal support to their executive users. This support is essential if those systems are to have a fair chance to demonstrate their full potential. Users require at least some initial training and ongoing assistance..."(4) As noted above, support is required in two directions. Not only does the executive user need technical support, but the technical personnel require executive support, for the success of the program. As we shall see, the request for 'at least some initial training and ongoing assistance' is practically a universal refrain from our user community.

Four peers of the above mentioned financial manager were surveyed. Interestingly, not only did they all have somewhat similar comments, but the tone of their reactions to the graphics all seemed to become more mellow, in a similar way, through the duration of the interviews. Some typical opening comments were: "Financial graphics are a waste of time. Personally, I find them confusing, and not worth the paper they're printed on." "I'm not very keen on financial graphics. I'm not sure they serve our purposes." "Financial graphics appear to be [designed] for analyses, but they don't facilitate analysis for me." "You want to talk about this garbage, I mean this stuff." This is not the type of reaction anyone responsible for the introduction of computer graphics for management would really like to hear. If the graphics are in fact so valuable to upper level management, what caused this reaction at lower levels, and what prerequisites could have been addressed to possibly prevent this? The issues seem to be political, educational, and logistical.

This team of financial managers is generally a closely knit group. It is only in retrospect that 'political' issues amongst them become visible. It has been asserted that there are seven stages in 'change': 1. shock, 2. disbelief, 3. guilt (change is perceived as a consequence of assessment of past performance), 4. projection (blame someone else), 5. rationalization, 6. integration (of change to one's own advantage), 7. acceptance. The change' literature also asserts that planning can greatly lessen the first four stages. In retrospect it can be seen that the timetable was so tight that little time was devoted to planning the introduction of this new graphics system, and therefore the initial reaction of shock and disbelief on the part of some financial managers is rather understandable. Once it became clear that the two levels of management above them definitely wanted the graphics management system, the reactions of guilt and projection could easily have followed for some. At this point, at the threshould of the stage of rationalization, the two most valuable commodities regarding this system became knowledge and resources. It seems to have been the effort to secure this knowledge and resources, this education and logistical support, that initiated all the 'political' issues. As one manager said: "It's only human nature, thinking you're going to be shown up."

The second issue, 'education', was addressed succinctly by one manager: "There was obviously not enough up front training. This was dropped on us and we were kept in the dark. The management report graphics goes to forty people and none of them have been trained in how to use it." Two other perceptive points were added by this manager as she said: "If you want something that looks cute and computer generated, then fine; ... maybe there's a political benefit." All seemed to concur that, six months after the decision to begin implementation, it was still not too late to begin training. Although, there also seemed to be a clear implication that it was someone else's responsibility to initiate it. Interestingly, none of the managers could vividly recall reading any of more than half a dozen journal articles and seminar papers, relating to the adopted graphics standards, that were available during the period of introduction. One manager internalized the concern for education on behalf of the group: "We should be able to publicly defend them (the graphic standards), but no one feels comfortable with that now. 'Logistical' issues seemed to center around the resources of hardware, time, and personnel. The current hard copy output device did not give very fine resolution, and this was mentioned continuously. (Interestingly enough though, there was a positive concensus regarding the software and its ease of use.) This problem would disappear as new hardware was on order and expected to arrive shortly. The time and personnel issues were not as easy to resolve. The new graphics were seen as an additional burden upon an already overloaded staff of financial analysts.

The survey was conducted shortly after each manager had completed producing their set of graphs for the monthly management report. A large amount of effort went into this that would not have to be repeated as, once the formats were set, all that would be needed in future months would be new data. High on the managers' wish list were software enhancements that would pull the data out of a database instead of requiring the analysts to key it all in. There was considerable concern expressed for the amount of ongoing support required. "There's not enough support for all, also not enough consistency in support." "There are very limited support resources. I don't have the luxury like [another manager] does of having someone to do graphs full time." A third manager expressed his concern most colorfully when he said: "These guys are high in pictures and we don't have any. That's because they have resources that we don't have."

The financial analysts interviewed supported their managers' perceptions of work overload. "I invariably get the data in late and I have all I can do to crank out the numbers and graphs too." But graphs are not new in the life of a financial analyst, as one analyst pulled out a whole sheaf of her hand drawn graphs from previous quarters. Distinctly different from their managers, though, a number of the analysts were given a one day seminar in the use of the software. There was general agreement that the seminar training was sufficient. They felt the software documentation was quite good. Also, some of the analysts had gone further and read the literature on the adopted graphics standards, and those who hadn't expressed great interest in doing so. Another distinction from their managers related to the applicability of the graphics to their level of data. While several managers expressed concern that the graphics were only useful on the management committee level but not all the way down to their subset of the overall financial picture, more than one analyst asserted: "Yes, it's good for both."

A 'postscript' to this discussion of the impact of the computer graphics on management and staff can be added here. Shortly after this survey was made, all of the financial managers reporting to the Controller organized themselves into a "graphics committee" to control the proliferation of charts in the management report. They felt they would thus assure consistency in presentation across all groups as well as have a peer review board for understanding the impact of any new charts. This action was seen by all as a positive measure. They clearly seemed to have passed through the "stage of rationalization" referred to above, and to have approached the last two stages of change: "integration" and "acceptance."

Overview of the Case Study

The clearest message arising from this case study seems to be the preeminent requirement to identify needs, set expectations, and then carry out thorough planning, training, and communication throughout the process of introducing computer graphics for management. Where resistance to the introduction of the graphics occurred, these would have alleviated it. Where these were integrated effectively they were a factor of positive influence in implementing the change. For those managers who receive the output of this process, it seems that those who receive some level of training perceive themselves to have enhanced decision making capabilities. The lack of training causes a myriad of organizational ills not the least of which is a sub-optimal utilization of the graphics output. Further research is now being conducted in an effort to quantify the impact of computer graphics on management decision making.

CONCLUDING RECOMMENDATIONS

Based upon the experience described in the above case study, the following recommendations can be made as prerequisites for the effective introduction of computer graphics for management.

1. Know why you want to introduce computer graphics for management.
2. Secure top management support for the project along with parameters such as: What are their needs and expectations? Is a pilot project required? Will color output be supported? How much of a budget is available?
3. Plan to cope with the impact of 'change' on the organization.
4. Be prepared to offer training, Training, and more TRAINING!
5. Address the issues of hardware, databases, and software.
6. Establish graphics standards for your organization with the assistance of experts in the field of graphic arts and the psychology of perception.
7. Set a reasonable timetable for achieving your goals. Include possible later enhancements such as automated data retrieval from a database.
8. Identify and schedule the resources required to meet the timetable.
9. Prepare a policy for the time when users request non-standard graphic formats.
10. Get management and staff at all impacted levels to 'buy in' to the standards, timetable, and resources allocation.
11. Introduce computer graphics for management while continuously communicating with all levels of the organization to catch any problems at the earliest possible point.
12. Prepare for success. Be prepared for calls from all over to see your graphic software in action. Be prepared for requests to come out of the woodwork - to use your hardware, databases, and software, ... as well as your expertise in identifying the other prerequisites for the effective introduction of computer graphics for management.

FOOTNOTES

(1) Henry Mintzberg, "The Manager's Job: Folklore and Fact," Harvard Business Review, July∿August 1975, p.49.

(2) Hirotaka Takeuchi and Allan H. Schmidt, "New Promise of Computer Graphics," Harvard Business Review, January∿February 1980, p.127.

(3) Richard Beckhard and Reuben T. Harris, Organizational Transitions: Managing Complex Change, Addison-Wesley, 1977, p.46.

(4) John F. Rockart and Michael E. Treacy, "The CEO Goes On-line," Harvard Business Review, January∿February 1982, p.85.

USING COMPUTER GENERATED GRAPHICS TO PRESENT FINANCIAL STATEMENTS

Irwin M. Jarett, Ph. D., C.P.A.
Chairman of the Board, Fingraph Corporation
960 Clock Tower Drive, Suite G
Springfield, Illinois 62704, U. S. A.
Howard W. Johnson, Digital Equipment Corp.
Merrimack, New Hampshire 03054, U. S. A.

Summary

This paper describes how the standard graphic presentation of financial statements eliminates the need to convert various currencies to a common currency for management control and financial comparison purposes. Once an acceptable operating template is defined, the financial data can be graphically presented and compared to the template in the original currency. Performance variances are readily identified between operations in various countries without conversion. (Obviously conversion is required for financial statement consolidation.) This powerful approach opens the potential for rapid dissemination of operating data and the accurate interpretation of the results graphically presented.

Problem

The comparison of operations between international corporations is one of the more difficult and time consuming financial analysis tasks. By the time the operations have been translated to a common currency, the exchange rates will have changed, and the relative values of the organization will have changed due to the different currency rate. Translation from one currency to another is time consuming, costly and, at best, approximate. But it must be done to make financial statements acceptable at best and hopefully more accurate. But the relative cost of an item may not relate to the revenue due to the timing of the purchase and the sale and the differing exchange rates. Differing inflation rates also add to the problem. The distortion could be significant and great care is taken to make sure that footnotes are accurate and the comparatives from one currency to another are as accurate as practical.

For this case study six corporations were selected to present annual comparative financial data in a standard graphic financial format. The six companies were Inland Steel Company; Digital Equipment Corporation; Hart, Schaefner and Marx; Matsushita; Nestle S.A. and Phillips Lamp Works. Inland; Digital and Hart, Schaefner and Marx are all American companies and their statements are shown in dollars. Matsushita is Japanese and the statements are shown in yen; Nestle is shown in Swiss francs; and Phillips in Dutch guilders. The data was taken directly from the annual reports or from Moody's report showing balance sheets, revenue and expenses, and ratio information.

Objectives

The objectives were:

A. To provide a readily recognizable set of patterns for each of the financial statements that would accurately picture the relationship between the components of the various statements, and

B. To describe the patterns that would be useful in comparing the operations of one company to the other without conversion to a base currency. Standard computer financial graphics were used to present the data without converting to a common currency. (1)

Discussion

An analogy might be appropriate. In medicine, CAT scanners are used to give a three dimensional perspective of part of the patient's body. The system works so that coordinates are identified by the scanner and these coordinates are given to a translator. If the coordinates were given to physicians only in numerical form little, if any, use could be made of the data. However, the data is taken one step further and translated into a graphic pattern of the organ and that pattern is presented to the physician. The pattern can be lifted one layer at a time to show different patterns within any perspective. When the pattern changes to something other than a correct pattern the problem is located.

Financial accounting is no more than a fiscal representation of a physical reality. In accounting, however, we only present the numbers without the translation to a pattern. Thus, the attempt here is to identify or establish the common financial patterns so that regardless of the currency, the relative importance of the parts will be accurately depicted. If this process works the patterns should be relevant regardless of currency. The importance of one activity to another should become clear without the need for a series of translations. For example, the relative value of the current assets to current liabilities ratio should be apparent simply by looking at the picture without computing it. Time series depicting the entire financial picture will be a multidimensional topographical representation of the growth and decay of a business, a picture never available to the business analyst.

The basic problem was finalizing the standard financial format to show a recognizable pattern; and a pattern clear enough to show the revenue and expense statements, the balance sheets and the critical ratios all on one page. It was necessary to put so much data on one page because too many pieces of paper or screens make it difficult and impractical to compare too many companies. It was found that using only the screens made it most difficult to make a financial comparison between companies or divisions and only when printouts were used did the use of the screen become valid as a support device, not the primary presentation media. For example, when the printed statements are available, any part of the statement could be shown on the screen, exploded and the comparisons could still be made because the printout would remain as a reference. After considerable effort, it was established that the picture resulting from the financial graphic standards would be comparable both visually and relatively, one company to the next, by utilizing standard window sizes and setting scales relevant to the size of the company. Though the scales would be different, the relative importance of one segment of the patterns to another would be shown. This approach automatically makes all size companies comparable in that the pattern becomes important and not the individual numbers. Also, it was not necessary to convert from one currency to another.

Examples of the six companies are attached, Exhibits 1 - 6. Please glance through them quickly without trying to read the numbers and look only for two points. First, look only at the difference in cost of goods sold and gross income for the various companies, and second for the different investments in fixed assets as a ratio to the overall assets. If you glance through the charts quickly those two patterns will become readily apparent.

The charts are read thusly: All subtotals and totals are shown at the axis; the bars add or subtract from one another just as a child would do by adding fraction blocks in kindergarten. Thus, the cost of sales bar is subtracted from the net sales bar leaving the gross margin or gross profit bar back to the axis. The darker bars are the current year, and the lighter bars are the previous year, so that in the statements you can compare one year to the next as well as comparing between companies. Once you have glanced through the various presentations, it is quickly apparent that the patterns are comparable between companies even though three of them use the dollar and the others use different forms of currency. The pattern is the critical point and it is clearly discernable.

Conclusion

The potential benefits from this approach are significant. Companies within the same industry can compare their relative performance across countries, a task which has been difficult, at best, in the past. Operating patterns can be seen quickly without having to go through the process of translating to a common currency. Inflation, for example, could be taken into account by the company for each country using a common base year. Thus the financial patterns could be seen with the influence of different inflation rates and differing exchange rates. The potential should be reasonably obvious.

Results have been presented at executive briefings under the sponsorship of the Harvard Computer Graphics Lab, at the A.I.C.P.A. Annual Computer Conference in Orlando, at the Illinois C.P.A. 1981 Accounting Show in Chicago in June and at the Harvard Computer Graphics Week '81. In all instances, the evaluations stated that this approach had extremely high relevance to the participants and that the patterns would indeed assist in comparing the operations of companies using different currencies.

It should be remembered that this project was not undertaken until after the financial standards had been identified. The standards eliminated a great deal of effort that might otherwise have taken place. As a matter of fact, the project probably could not have been successfully completed without having a set of financial standards upon which to base the project.

This process is highly transferable across continents, across industries, products and divisions. It could be used in almost any situation where there are different companies of different sizes, different operations and different currencies where it is important to see the relative importance of the components to the whole. These standard financial graphic patterns will set that relationship and a consistent presentation of those patterns will provide the analytical tools necessary to discern differences. These statements are based only on library research and empirical evidence, not on solid academic research. There has been only one formal research project to examine the usefulness of these patterns.(2) The potential appears to be large and the cry for research is significant. The Playfair Institute has been established to identify the research potential and to carry it out. Support is urgently requested.

Basically any good graphic computer equipment that can translate fiscal data to relevant patterns would be useful. The particular equipment used was a DEC PDP 11/34 with an LXY 11 hi-speed matrix printer and a GIGI graphic terminal. The software was developed for this application and took approximately six months in elapsed time and close to $1\frac{1}{2}$ years in people years to complete the software. Databases are standard financial statement presentations taken from the respective annual reports or from Moodys. Software for the application is available (with support) and the Proposed Standards were presented at the Harvard Computer Graphics Week, July 1981.(3)

(1) Jarett, Ph.D., C.P.A., Irwin M., "Computer Graphics: A Reporting Revolution?", Journal of Accountancy, May 1981, pgs. 46+.

(2) Jarett, C.P.A., Alex & Grudnitski, Ph.D., Gary, "The Effects of Using Computer-Generated Graphics to Present Financial Information", The Harvard Computer Graphics Week, July 27 - 31, 1981.

(3) Jarett, Ph.D., C.P.A., Irwin M., "Proposed Financial Computer Graphics Standards", Harvard Computer Graphics Week, July 27 - 31, 1981.

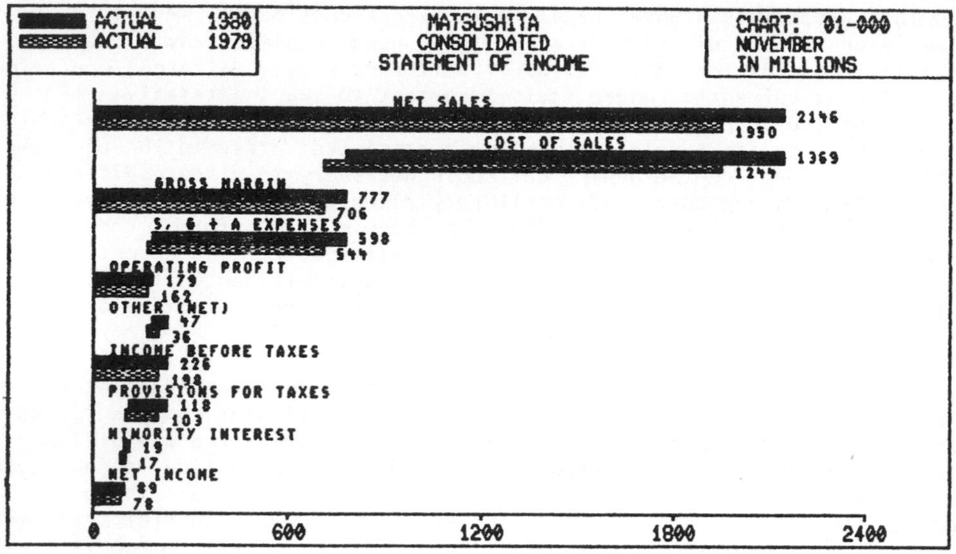
ACTUAL 1980
ACTUAL 1979
MATSUSHITA
CONSOLIDATED
STATEMENT OF INCOME
CHART: 01-000
NOVEMBER
IN MILLIONS
NET SALES
2146
1950
COST OF SALES
1369
1244
GROSS MARGIN
777
706
S, G + A EXPENSES
598
544
OPERATING PROFIT
179
162
OTHER (NET)
47
36
INCOME BEFORE TAXES
226
198
PROVISIONS FOR TAXES
118
103
MINORITY INTEREST
19
17
NET INCOME
89
78
0
600
1200
1800
2400

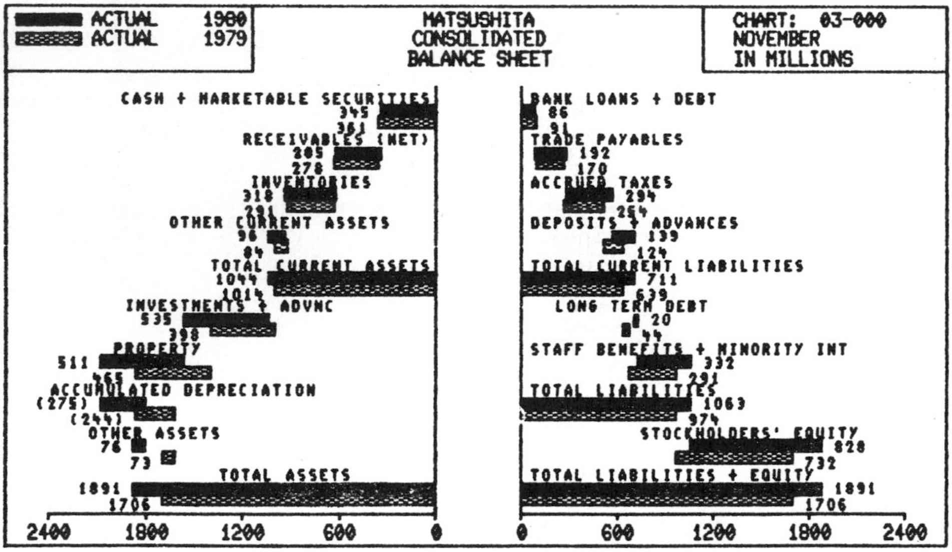
ACTUAL 1980
ACTUAL 1979
MATSUSHITA
CONSOLIDATED
BALANCE SHEET
CHART: 03-000
NOVEMBER
IN MILLIONS
CASH + MARKETABLE SECURITIES
345
361
RECEIVABLES (NET)
205
278
INVENTORIES
318
291
OTHER CURRENT ASSETS
96
84
TOTAL CURRENT ASSETS
1044
1014
INVESTMENTS + ADVNC
535
398
PROPERTY
511
465
ACCUMULATED DEPRECIATION
(275)
(244)
OTHER ASSETS
76
73
TOTAL ASSETS
1891
1706
BANK LOANS + DEBT
86
91
TRADE PAYABLES
192
170
ACCRUED TAXES
294
254
DEPOSITS + ADVANCES
139
124
TOTAL CURRENT LIABILITIES
711
639
LONG TERM DEBT
20
44
STAFF BENEFITS + MINORITY INT
332
291
TOTAL LIABILITIES
1063
974
STOCKHOLDERS' EQUITY
828
732
TOTAL LIABILITIES + EQUITY
1891
1706
2400
1800
1200
600
0
0
600
1200
1800
2400

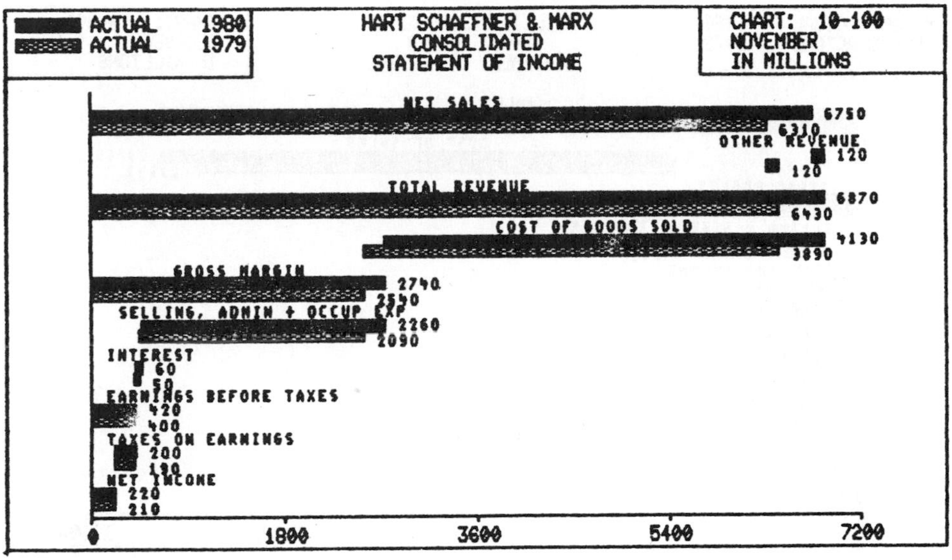
ACTUAL 1980
ACTUAL 1979
HART SCHAFFNER & MARX
CONSOLIDATED
STATEMENT OF INCOME
CHART: 10-100
NOVEMBER
IN MILLIONS
NET SALES
6750
6310
OTHER REVENUE
120
120
TOTAL REVENUE
6870
6430
COST OF GOODS SOLD
4130
3890
GROSS MARGIN
2740
2540
SELLING, ADMIN + OCCUP EXP
2260
2090
INTEREST
60
50
EARNINGS BEFORE TAXES
420
400
TAXES ON EARNINGS
200
190
NET INCOME
220
210
0
1800
3600
5400
7200

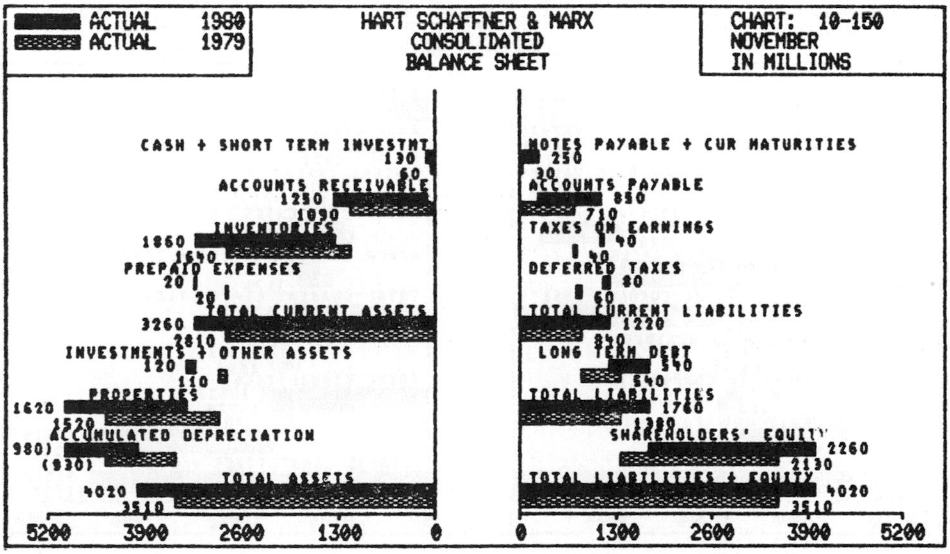
ACTUAL 1980
ACTUAL 1979
HART SCHAFFNER & MARX
CONSOLIDATED
BALANCE SHEET
CHART: 10-150
NOVEMBER
IN MILLIONS
CASH + SHORT TERM INVESTMT
130
60
ACCOUNTS RECEIVABLE
1250
1090
INVENTORIES
1860
1640
PREPAID EXPENSES
20
20
TOTAL CURRENT ASSETS
3260
2810
INVESTMENTS + OTHER ASSETS
120
110
PROPERTIES
1620
1520
ACCUMULATED DEPRECIATION
980)
(930)
TOTAL ASSETS
4020
3510
NOTES PAYABLE + CUR MATURITIES
250
30
ACCOUNTS PAYABLE
850
710
TAXES ON EARNINGS
40
40
DEFERRED TAXES
80
60
TOTAL CURRENT LIABILITIES
1220
840
LONG TERM DEBT
540
540
TOTAL LIABILITIES
1760
1380
SHAREHOLDERS' EQUITY
2260
2130
TOTAL LIABILITIES + EQUITY
4020
3510
5200
3900
2600
1300
0
0
1300
2600
3900
5200

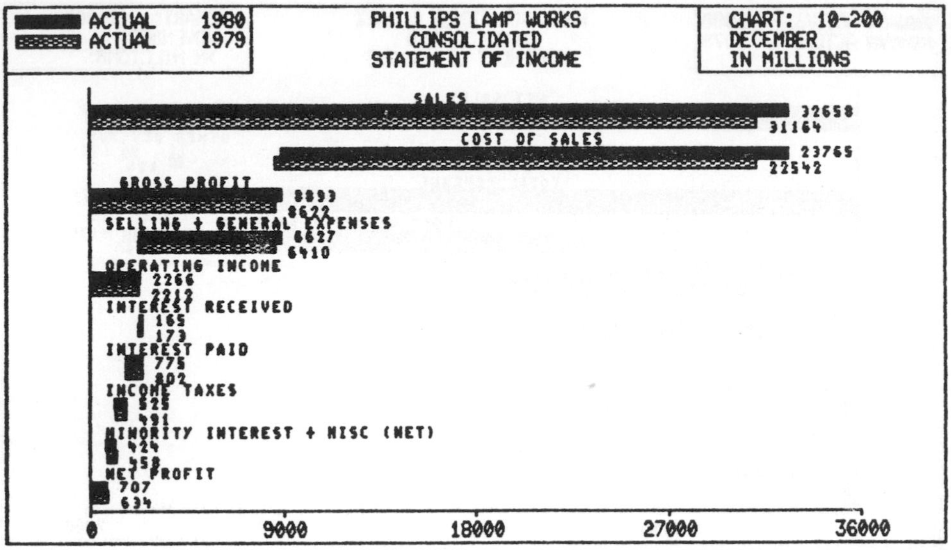
ACTUAL 1980
ACTUAL 1979
PHILLIPS LAMP WORKS
CONSOLIDATED
STATEMENT OF INCOME
CHART: 10-200
DECEMBER
IN MILLIONS
SALES
32658
31164
COST OF SALES
23765
22542
GROSS PROFIT
8893
SELLING + GENERAL EXPENSES
6627
6410
OPERATING INCOME
2266
INTEREST RECEIVED
165
173
INTEREST PAID
775
INCOME TAXES
525
491
MINORITY INTEREST + MISC (NET)
424
NET PROFIT
707
634
0
9000
18000
27000
36000

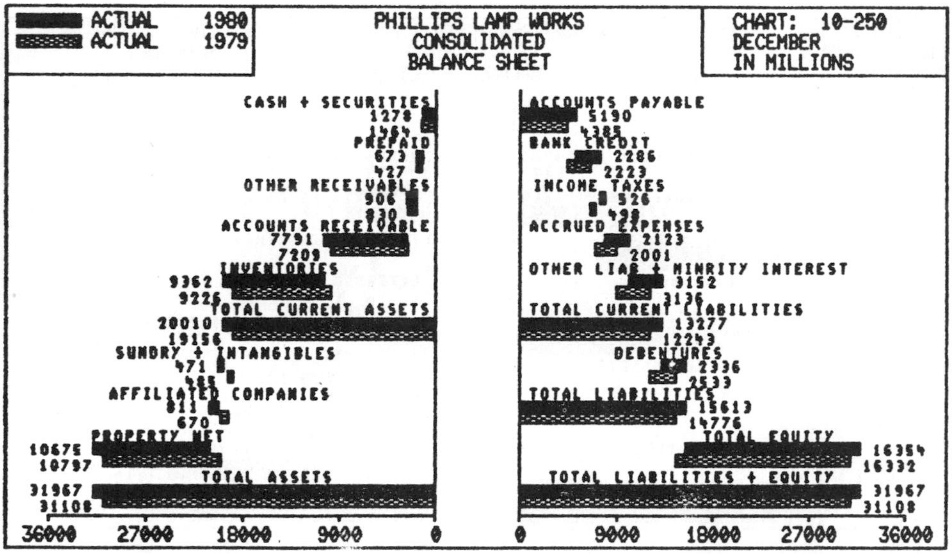
ACTUAL 1980
ACTUAL 1979
PHILLIPS LAMP WORKS
CONSOLIDATED
BALANCE SHEET
CHART: 10-250
DECEMBER
IN MILLIONS
CASH + SECURITIES
1278
PREPAID
673
OTHER RECEIVABLES
906
ACCOUNTS RECEIVABLE
7791
7209
INVENTORIES
9362
TOTAL CURRENT ASSETS
20010
19156
SUNDRY + INTANGIBLES
471
AFFILIATED COMPANIES
670
PROPERTY NET
10675
10797
TOTAL ASSETS
31967
31108
ACCOUNTS PAYABLE
5190
BANK CREDIT
2286
2223
INCOME TAXES
526
ACCRUED EXPENSES
2123
2001
OTHER LIAB + MINRITY INTEREST
3152
TOTAL CURRENT LIABILITIES
13277
12243
DEBENTURES
2336
2533
TOTAL LIABILITIES
15613
14776
TOTAL EQUITY
16354
16332
TOTAL LIABILITIES + EQUITY
31967
31108
36000
27000
18000
9000
0
0
9000
18000
27000
36000

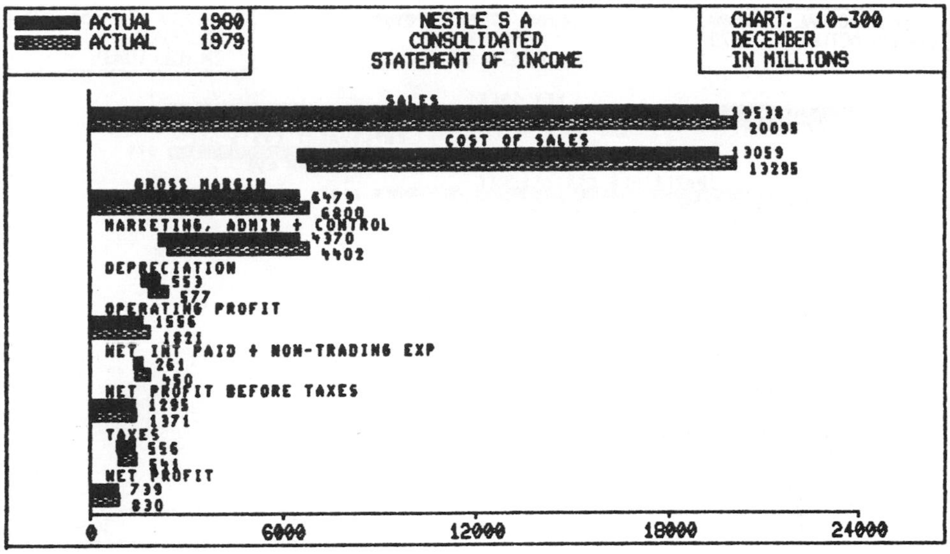
ACTUAL 1980
ACTUAL 1979
NESTLE S A
CONSOLIDATED
STATEMENT OF INCOME
CHART: 10-300
DECEMBER
IN MILLIONS
SALES
19538
20095
COST OF SALES
13059
13295
GROSS MARGIN
6479
6800
MARKETING, ADMIN + CONTROL
4370
4402
DEPRECIATION
553
577
OPERATING PROFIT
1556
1821
NET INT PAID + NON-TRADING EXP
261
450
NET PROFIT BEFORE TAXES
1295
1371
TAXES
556
541
NET PROFIT
739
830
0
6000
12000
18000
24000

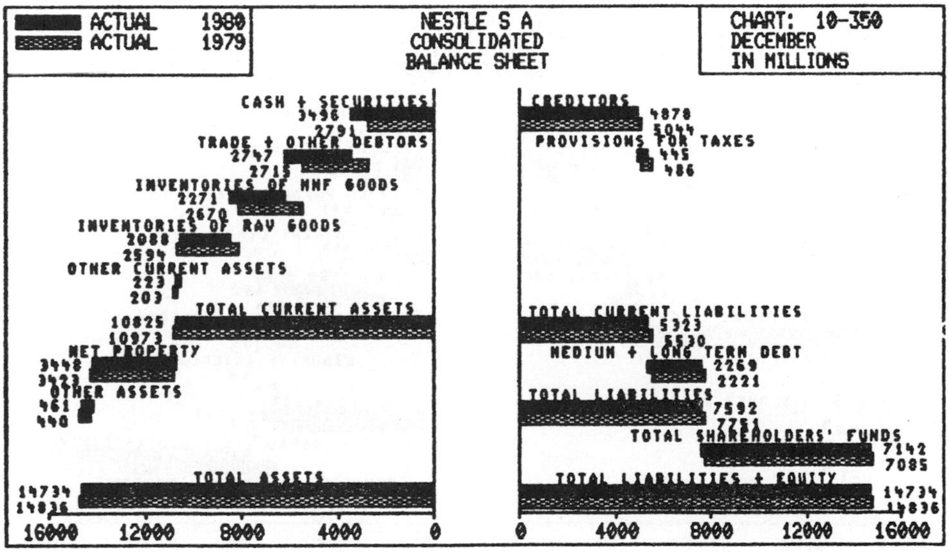
ACTUAL 1980
ACTUAL 1979
NESTLE S A
CONSOLIDATED
BALANCE SHEET
CHART: 10-350
DECEMBER
IN MILLIONS
CASH + SECURITIES
3496
2791
TRADE + OTHER DEBTORS
2747
2715
INVENTORIES OF MNF GOODS
2271
2670
INVENTORIES OF RAW GOODS
2088
2594
OTHER CURRENT ASSETS
223
203
TOTAL CURRENT ASSETS
10825
10973
NET PROPERTY
3448
3423
OTHER ASSETS
461
440
TOTAL ASSETS
14734
14836
16000
12000
8000
4000
0
CREDITORS
4878
5044
PROVISIONS FOR TAXES
445
486
TOTAL CURRENT LIABILITIES
5323
5530
MEDIUM + LONG TERM DEBT
2269
2221
TOTAL LIABILITIES
7592
7751
TOTAL SHAREHOLDERS' FUNDS
7142
7085
TOTAL LIABILITIES + EQUITY
14734
14836
0
4000
8000
12000
16000

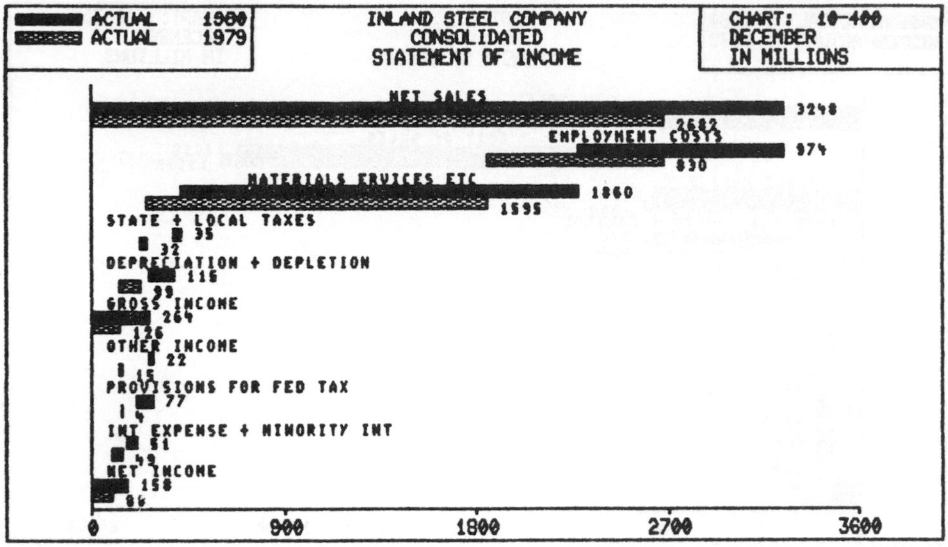
ACTUAL 1980
ACTUAL 1979
INLAND STEEL COMPANY
CONSOLIDATED
STATEMENT OF INCOME
CHART: 10-400
DECEMBER
IN MILLIONS
NET SALES
3248
2682
EMPLOYMENT COSTS
974
830
MATERIALS SERVICES ETC
1860
1595
STATE + LOCAL TAXES
35
32
DEPRECIATION + DEPLETION
115
99
GROSS INCOME
264
126
OTHER INCOME
22
15
PROVISIONS FOR FED TAX
77
4
INT EXPENSE + MINORITY INT
51
49
NET INCOME
158
86
0
900
1800
2700
3600

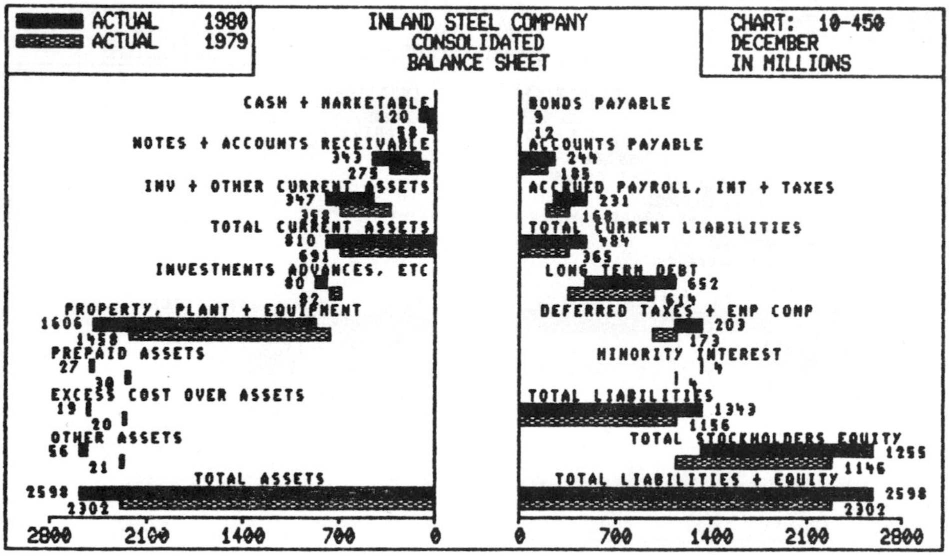
ACTUAL 1980
ACTUAL 1979
INLAND STEEL COMPANY
CONSOLIDATED
BALANCE SHEET
CHART: 10-450
DECEMBER
IN MILLIONS
CASH + MARKETABLE
120
58
NOTES + ACCOUNTS RECEIVABLE
343
275
INV + OTHER CURRENT ASSETS
347
358
TOTAL CURRENT ASSETS
810
691
INVESTMENTS ADVANCES, ETC
80
82
PROPERTY, PLANT + EQUIPMENT
1606
1458
PREPAID ASSETS
27
30
EXCESS COST OVER ASSETS
19
20
OTHER ASSETS
56
21
TOTAL ASSETS
2598
2302
BONDS PAYABLE
9
12
ACCOUNTS PAYABLE
244
185
ACCRUED PAYROLL, INT + TAXES
231
168
TOTAL CURRENT LIABILITIES
484
365
LONG TERM DEBT
652
614
DEFERRED TAXES + EMP COMP
203
173
MINORITY INTEREST
4
TOTAL LIABILITIES
1343
1156
TOTAL STOCKHOLDERS EQUITY
1255
1146
TOTAL LIABILITIES + EQUITY
2598
2302
2800
2100
1400
700
0
0
700
1400
2100
2800

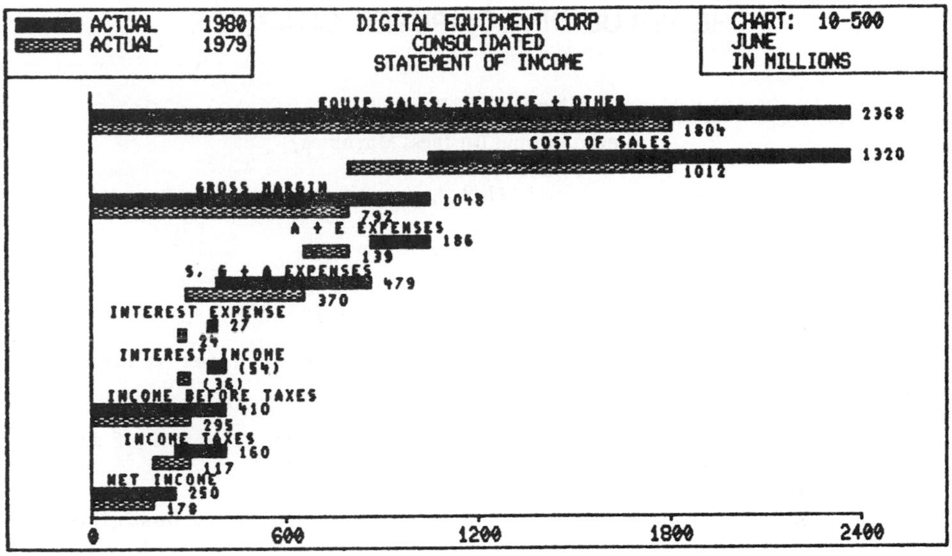
ACTUAL 1980
ACTUAL 1979
DIGITAL EQUIPMENT CORP
CONSOLIDATED
STATEMENT OF INCOME
CHART: 10-500
JUNE
IN MILLIONS
EQUIP SALES, SERVICE + OTHER
2368
1804
COST OF SALES
1320
1012
GROSS MARGIN
1048
792
A + E EXPENSES
186
139
S, G + A EXPENSES
479
370
INTEREST EXPENSE
27
24
INTEREST INCOME
(54)
(36)
INCOME BEFORE TAXES
410
295
INCOME TAXES
160
117
NET INCOME
250
178
0
600
1200
1800
2400

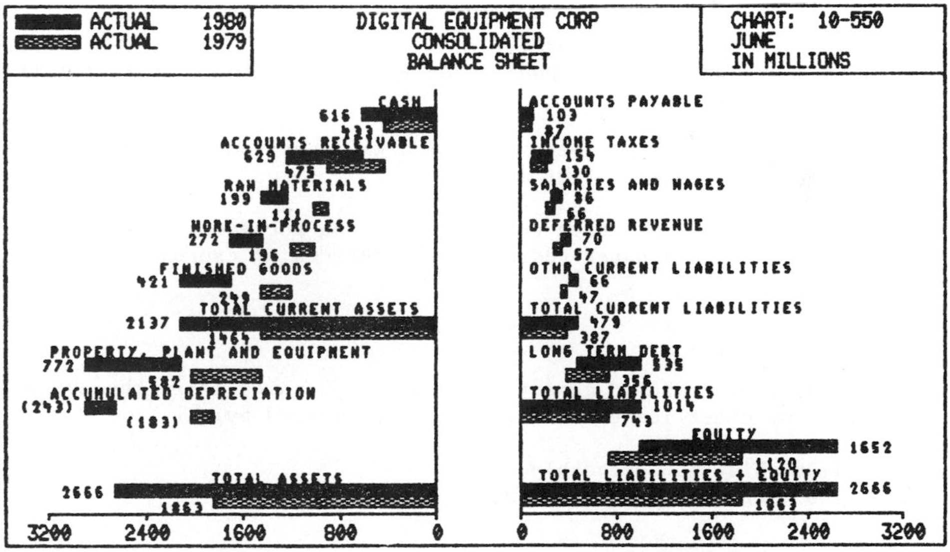
ACTUAL 1980
ACTUAL 1979
DIGITAL EQUIPMENT CORP
CONSOLIDATED
BALANCE SHEET
CHART: 10-550
JUNE
IN MILLIONS
CASH
616
433
ACCOUNTS RECEIVABLE
629
475
RAW MATERIALS
199
111
WORK-IN-PROCESS
272
196
FINISHED GOODS
421
249
TOTAL CURRENT ASSETS
2137
1464
PROPERTY, PLANT AND EQUIPMENT
772
582
ACCUMULATED DEPRECIATION
(243)
(183)
TOTAL ASSETS
2666
1863
ACCOUNTS PAYABLE
103
87
INCOME TAXES
154
130
SALARIES AND WAGES
86
66
DEFERRED REVENUE
70
57
OTHR CURRENT LIABILITIES
66
47
TOTAL CURRENT LIABILITIES
479
387
LONG TERM DEBT
535
356
TOTAL LIABILITIES
1014
743
EQUITY
1652
1120
TOTAL LIABILITIES + EQUITY
2666
1863
3200
2400
1600
800
0
0
800
1600
2400
3200

THE VALUE OF COMPUTER GRAPHICS

Donald J. Kostuch
International Business Machines
Boca Raton, FL 33432
U. S. A.

The value of computer graphics is largely unrealized.

Computer hardware exists to create images which transfer information to people accurately and in quantity.

Software is available to permit the convenient description of the information and messages we want to send.

What is yet required is the skill and planning tools to describe how to portray a message effectively, so that our audience will share our own understanding and feelings about a subject, or at least appreciate our position.

We need to understand the limitations and capabilities of:

- Human perception and memory.
- Computer graphics and publishing systems in producing effective, repeatable images.

Attention to the human side of graphics will overcome many of the physical and mechanical limitations.

We have much more influence over what goes on the media than how it is put there. This paper addresses the choices of expression and layout.

Text

The single, most abused aspect of computer graphics is in the use of text. Many otherwise excellent images are marred by:

- Text which is unreadable
- Too much or too little text.

Nearly every graphic needs some text to complement the image in order to create an unambiguous and lasting impression. What is often forgotten is the environment of the viewer and the limitations of the human optical system. The typical lower limit in size for the comfortable viewing of text is characters which subtend 17 minutes of arc. This value is easily maintained by ensuring that the maximum distance to the viewer is less than 200 times the size of an individual character.

This limit is important in two environments.

For group presentations measure the projected or printed size of the text characters and the distance to the furthest viewer. The ratio of these two numbers should be less than 200. For a conference room five meters long, the text should be 2.5 cm high. For an auditorium fifty meters long, 25 cm characters are appropriate.

For individual viewing, the age of the viewer becomes important. Up to age 40, the minimum focal distance is about 10 cm. Between the ages of 50 and 60 years, the minimum focal distance often reaches 100 cm. If we are to accommodate people in this age group, then text characters should never be less than 5 mm high.

Many images have far too much text which is of little value and only creates clutter. Excessive detail about scales, sources, titles and descriptions does not contribute to understanding.

The one piece of text that is often missing is the purpose, the message of the chart. Why was the chart drawn and presented in the first place? A spoken message is not always sufficient, and is not useful when the graphic is shown later without your presence.

The text on a graph should include:

- A brief but complete message, the intent of the graphic.
- About five labeled "tick" marks along a continuous, linear, unbroken scale which starts at zero. The two end points are often enough.
- A brief description of each set of data points or lines on the chart, near the line or data if possible.

Supporting Cues

The human perceptual mechanism is highly tuned to the detection of patterns and organizations. Many graphics fail to communicate because consistent and supporting cues are absent. Just as we search for supporting evidence before committing to a position, so our perception searches for supporting cues before accepting an image as "real."

When designing a chart, code a piece of information in at least two independent ways. Three ways is better.

For example, items on a chart may be simultaneously identified by distinct texture, color and intensity. Data points may be identified by both shape and color. Not only will the chart be more memorable, but it is more likely to usefully survive many generations of copying with only partial color fidelity or to black and white.

Color

The consistency of color rendition among various computer output devices is slight at best. Cathode ray tubes have a variety of phosphors. Color control electronics can vary and are subjective. Pen inks and printer ribbons come from a variety of sources with few objective standards. They are subject to aging both before and after use. A CRT is radiative, color additive device. Paper is absorbing and color subtracting media.

Right now there is little hope in predicting how a given color on one device will be portrayed on another device, or even the same device at a later time. While color can be used as a way of attracting attention and enhancing a graphic, other methods of coding the data should be included to assure understanding of the message when the color is missing or distorted.

Human Information Input

The production of a graphic must take into account the limits of human information input. Too much information, poorly organized, will choke off all input.

Once a concept or value is perceived, it is stored in "short term memory". This unit of information is often called a "chunk". The size of a chunk, the objective amount of information it contains, is determined by the rules the perceiver uses to organize the data. If the data fits into a well understood framework, a chunk can be very large. For example, your home address is one chunk (for you), "where you live", even though it may contain 50 or more characters.

If the data does not fit into any known organization, such as random digits, a chunk may be as small as a single character.

Most people can retain 5 to 9 chunks in short term memory. When this limit is reached, the data is either organized into an existing framework and moved to "long term memory," or it is discarded and forgotten.

It is incumbent on the creator of a graphic (or any other media) to evaluate the audience and their mental framework. The message and the data must be organized and presented such that short term memory is not overloaded with an excessive number of chunks. Each graphic must contain enough information to present a complete message which can be added to an existing mental framework without overloading short term memory.

Each graphic should contain one message or general concept based on five to seven chunks such as bars, pie segments, lines, etc. If your audience is familiar with the data, its organization and your presentation style, the charts may be more complex, but do not make this assumption lightly.

If you have more than one primary message, use additional pages and images.

Right/Left Brain Specialization

Many experiments with both normal human subjects and those with various brain pathologies indicate that most people have specialized functions relating to language (usually in the left hemisphere) and nonlanguage activities (usually in the right hemisphere).

The use of language, in particular writing, is a relatively recent development in human history. Previous to the wide availability of printing, language played a smaller role in the acquisition of information. Demonstration (for example, apprenticeship) and pictures were the rule.

The mechanization of information storage and distribution has now come full circle to the point where images again will play a major role in the transfer of information.

We can simplify the perception of organization and meaning of data by coding the data directly as size, shape, color, texture and arrangement which the right brain can perceive directly.

Each chunk encoded with text requires the left brain for interpretation, with some probability of error. The result must then be compared with the right brain perception to be related to the other elements of the image.

For example:

- The necessity to compare an image with a numeric scale. A better approach is to provide a known value for comparison rather than depending only on a scale.

- Complex encoding schemes and labels to identify data. Label the data element directly and proximately.

- Excessive text "noise."

  - Too fine a scale
  - Excessive description and detail
  - Numerical values

If such information is necessary, use separate pages or at least move it "out of the picture."

- Essential text placed "far from the action." Proximity is a strong cue for relations and organization.

In summary, use text only when the idea cannot be adequately rendered as a graphic element. The right brain relates graphics directly, text requires left brain interpretation. Use no more text then is needed.

Graphic Composition

An effective chart consists of a logical and coherent message supported by relevant data shown as an image portraying an unambiguous relationship with many supporting cues.

To be useful, a chart must have an underlying message or theme on which to base the choice of elements. Messages are simple and direct, such as good/bad, up/down, more/less, fast/slow. Anything more complex is often restatement of the data.

The data shown must be relevant to the message. Too much is overwhelming. Too little is unimpressive. Deletion of relevant data or inclusion of irrelevant data can be misleading.

The image chosen (a line, bar, circle, . . .) should be analogous to the dimensions of the data and easily perceived as a length, area, or pattern.

The image should be unambiguous. An ambiguous image has multiple interpretations due to insufficient or conflicting cues. This is the basis of illusions.

Keep data arranged logically, by value, alphabetically or whatever supports the message. Avoid parochial or arbitrary arrangement.

Use uniform scales for several charts of similar or related data.

Make important items "heavy," particularly the data and titles. Gridwork, scales and subtitles should be "lighter." Heavy means dark colors, thick lines, dark textures, and other techniques which lend "weight" to an image.

Avoid a large empty space unless it is a part of the message.

Avoid unusual scale factors. Scales which end with 1, 2, 5, 10, 20, 50, 100, are easier to interpret.

Observe traditional use of color, position, formats and other graphic elements by the audience. For example, Plus, good, is up. Minus, bad, is down.

Use one type font with varying weight and size. Print horizontally to avoid head twisting.

Consider the aspect ratio of the media to avoid loss of image elements near the edge.

Leave a margin about 5% of the image size.

Plan for the use of copiers to duplicate your chart. Lines which are too narrow won't copy. Lines which are too wide may "white out." Some colors will not copy, such as light blue.

Inks can bleed when plotting. Keep color fields separate.

Color vision has poor resolution. Do not use colors with fine detail.

Some color pairs have very low contrast, such as black and dark blue. They are difficult to distinguish.

Some colors "vibrate" due to a different index of refraction, such as bright blue and red.

Use simple texture patterns such as diagonal lines at a uniform angle. Change the weight, and spacing for variety.

Provide comparison cues such as familiar value.

Reserve depth for real or "pseudo-real" objects. The interpretation of depth as a numerical value is difficult.

Proximity and contact depicts a strong relationship. Separation indicates a lack of relationship.

The accurate interpretation of a logarithmic scale requires experience and familiarity. Use with care.

A suppressed zero scale may be difficult to interpret since it enhances the effect of changes in the values of the data.

The use of mathematics such as curve fitting can radically change the image and message of a set of data points.

Rate of change can easily be confused with absolute value, for example a chart of "percent increase."

A scale with insufficient range will cause the data to go off the chart, or show small changes as large fluctuations. Such an image may be out of proportion to its importance.

A scale with excessive range will crowd the data near the axis, giving it insufficient importance.

Reverse scaling, for example, minus upward, can easily invert the perception of the entire message.

Irrelevant shading can draw attention away from the data to space which is not relevant to the message.

Irrelevant summing of unrelated data may give it undue importance.

Irrelevant breakdown of related data may obscure relationships.

Obscuring or emotional images can direct attention away from the data.

Misleading codes such as a heavy, dark color for unimportant data may direct attention away from the significant data.

Conclusion

As with every advance in technology, the work has not been reduced, just changed in character. We must now learn a new method of communication which cannot even be called a language. It is more akin to art. This does not mean it is any less objective or accurate; indeed in some sense it may be more real then the text we are used to. Its application may not be obvious due to long disuse, but some rules can be learned and the effects can be powerful.

BIBLIOGRAPHY

Grandjean, E.

Fitting the Task to the Man
International Publications Service, New York 1981

Grimes, Jack

Psychology for User-Computer Interfaces
Siggraph (ACM) 1981

Rawlins, Mark

Figures Lie and Liars Figure
Siggraph (ACM) 1981

Schiffman, H. R.

Sensation and Perception
John Wiley and Sons, Inc. 1976

Szoka, Kathryn

The Standards of Graphics
Siggraph (ACM) 1981

Vinberg, Anders

Designing a Good Graph
Siggraph (ACM) 1981

Vinberg, Anders

What Makes a Good Graph?
Siggraph (ACM) 1981

COMPUTER GENERATED GRAPHICS... USER, DESIGNER, PROGRAMMER

Alice Bernhard

Bernhard Design
Box 242
RD 1 Hillcrest Lane
Rhinebeck, New York 12572
U. S. A.

Creating new products involves understanding and use of design methodology. This could begin with a study of the mental processes that lead to good solutions to problems. To look into what lies behind the special(ized) skills and intuitive methods is also recommended.

Design method includes special skills and intuitive methods. Which is the more desirable? Learning through study and/or the use of a teacher or attempts, which may be referred to experience, at the same time utilizing criticism or trials. For example, what is meant when a designer says something "works" as opposed to what does not work.

Is creativity taught and/or learned? Is it inborn? What is the aura and mystique surrounding design? ...or any design function? We hear that "it works!" or "the idea just came to me!" Is creativity subject to rational explanation? Design includes the evaluation of results, process and technique. Is this contrary to creativity?

Design responsibility includes the effect(s) of the design or solution on human behavior, i.e. poor, mediocre, good, better, best. In the creation of new products the many responsibilities include those of development, manufacturing and assurance.

Since office automation touches so many different tasks and people in all levels of business, the impact on development by team members makes questioning and understanding the responsibility of the design process imperative.

We should know who designs and how it is done in order to better select and work with today's creators and to better train tomorrow's designers.

The techniques of the computer in data processing deal with a variety of difficult and complex problems. Computer techniques include analyzing the problem and specifying exactly, step by step, the solution. This includes seeing and setting up rational, logical relationships.

The study of the techniques of computer solutions, which is problem solving, can help make the rationale of design process more easily understood. This includes systematic thinking about the design method. The organized method presents a stimulus and corrective to unaided thinking. This encourages a new clarity of thinking. Systematic thinking about the design or method is needed. To visualize and diagram are two aspects or techniques of the design method which also need to be understood.

RESEARCH.

To create new products much research is necessary. Due to the nature of office automation, research emphasis is not only on the technology and machines but on people as well.

Office Automation systems can provide a powerful mechanism for productivity increase and an improvement in the quality of work life. This is achieved by changing the fundamental nature of organizational information processing. Research on the impact of such office automation systems is needed.

Much can be gleaned from the knowledge of the implementation of computer systems. Research on the consideration of work design alternatives and the implementation process of such can help lead to guidelines for enhancing or minimizing the effects of office automation.

Implementors should take a broad view of the consequences of the new systems. Neither the long-term effects of altering the definition of "work" nor the consequences of new technologies at work are well understood. Some potential problems can be solved by treating the introduction of office automation systems as a problem in work design.

Research should help to provide more precise and adequate recommendations for the design of office automation systems so that through successful implementation they will contribute to improvements in organizational efficacy.

With research indicating that stress is a major problem in individual attitudes toward work, task structures and role definitions can be designed to both meet organizational objectives and configure the technology to support those work designs.

Regarding the individual's attitude, performance and health, research consideration should be given to:

1. Uncertainty about the system.
2. Operator autonomy over control of the work.
3. Machine pacing of work.
4. Monotonous and/or repetitive work.
5. Service work, i.e. responsibility for people rather than things.
6. Changed task interdependencies.
7. Overall workload.

DESIGN DEFINED.

Here the role of design is explained by a design consultant, which in this instance is a visual communication specialist with emphasis on computer graphics.

De'sign (di zin') v.t.
Defining DESIGN.

Definition:

1. To prepare the preliminary sketch or the plans for a work to be executed, especially to plan the form and structure of.

2. To plan and fashion artistically or skillfully.

3. To intend for a definite purpose.

4. To form or conceive in the mind.

5. To assign in thought or intention.

6. To mark out, as by a sign; indicate.

7. To make drawings, preliminary sketches, or plans.

8. To plan and fashion the form and structure of an object, work of art, decorative scheme, etc.

9. An outline, sketch, or plan, as of the form and structure of a work of art, an edifice, or a machine to be executed or constructed.

10. Organization or structure of formal elements in a work of art; composition.

11. A plan or project; a design for a new process.

12. Adaptation of means to a preconceived end.

13. An artistic work.

QUIZ.

Read the above statements. Put an "X" in front of those descriptions which you feel most accurately define(s) DESIGN.

The above statements are taken from the dictionary definition of DESIGN. All are correct. The purpose of this is to define and understand DESIGN. Design is all of the above and, simply stated, it is finding the best solution to a problem within certain guidelines and limitations.

SOLUTIONS.

Finding solutions involves much questioning. How can design solutions be best achieved? To find the best solution we need a method which requires systematic thinking and creativity. Again the question, is creativity taught/learned or inborn?

Information out of the subconscious into the conscious. Is creativity subject to rational explanation?

How can we teach/learn design skills? What lies behind the specialized skills and intuitive methods? Does this require a study of the mental processes that lead to good solutions to problems? Can we teach systematic thinking? What is the nature of thinking? How do we analyze thought?

In spite of today's hectic pace, now is the time to ask questions and begin to understand the hows and whys of what it takes, not only to create new office automation products, but to create successful ones.

DESIGN PROCESS.

Since design is the materialization of thoughts and ideas, the more clear the thinking at the time of inception, the clearer the visuals and script.

The steps in the process of design include the following:

1. The problem must be clearly identified and stated.

2. Information must be clear, precise, accessible, relevant.

3. Creativity takes information (research) and matches (relates) it to the problem. Concepts, actions, proposals as parts of a potential solution; each piece of information is weighed against the original statement of the problem. Each piece of information is considered valid/invalid according to its relationship/relevancy to the stated problem.

   note: therefore, the entire solution rests on a clearly stated problem.

4. Roughs or layouts of the proposed solution emerge.

5. They are tested as solutions or partial solutions from which the proposed solution is elicited.

6. Evaluation of the proposed solution begins. Steps 3-4-5 continue as a process within a process until the best solution becomes apparent.

7. Implementation of this solution takes place with the understanding that the solution is valid for only as long as the problem remains unchanged. When the problem changes, as all do, the solution is similarly affected and it is then necessary to re-initiate the design process.

With a new or fresh outlook, at any time, during any step, during the design process we may use particular guidelines and question our results or stage of design.

Is it... Simple?
Appropriate?
Functional?
Economical?

Efficient and effective use of time, energy and money are in direct proportion to the clarification of intentions and objectives stated at the outset. State the problem clearly! Changes after completion mean re-doing the job.

The design process is given here by a graphic designer as it is used, for example, for consultation and design in graphic presentations. However, given in this general manner, it is applicable to all design, including hardware and software products for office automation.

Not unrelated are the results of studies done in recent years to help the technical writer reach decisions regarding the best method of presenting specific data within a document.

Five skills that may be particularly useful to technical writers involve:

1. Doing a task analysis to find out how readers will use the document.

2. Careful use of language, particularly in the explanation of technical terms and complex procedures, with an awareness of the value of alternatives to prose.

3. Use of graphic and typographic presentation to help the reader grasp the underlying structure of the text.

4. Interpretation of behavioral research relating to the design of information.

5. Management of the document production process.

The complexities of technical writing need to be recognized, and organizations need to realize these and other such skills in the different members of a document production team.

The design consultant is one of the team members. For example, with the current demand for more clear, easy-to-use User Manuals for hardware and software application packages, this is especially important.

The process of design is an integral part of slide and visual presentations and also the CRT display screens of an application program. The process can be used for the actual slide or group of slides which make up the entire visual presentation. Similarly, it is used for the structuring of people, responsibilities, and interaction with the solution of how to physically produce the needed product.

There are many problems to solve within the one initially stated, to produce a visual presentation. Reviewing the design process can help the design consultant work with the manager who needs to compose a presentation. The process gives the two an important and common meeting ground. Similarly, the process of design is the foundation for the secretary and design consultant in visual communication.

FRIENDLY.

USER: One who or that which uses. Use: To put into service; make use of; apply to one's own purposes; a purpose for which something is used. Utilize.

FRIENDLY: Characteristic of or befitting a friend; like a friend; kind; helpful; favorably disposed; inclined to approve, help or support; not hostile or at variance. Friend: A person who gives assistance.

Define user-friendly. What is friendly language? Define language; define friendly. Whose language is being used? The language of the computer? The language of a person? ...a robot? ...the captain of the ship?

Why begin with a gross misconception? What is the image or picture that would be desirable for the end-user to have in mind while sitting at the terminal? Why not state the hierarchy of levels? CPU...software... subroutines?

We know a computer is fast, efficient, etc. Why not the language too? It can still be friendly in terms of color schemes, rhythm, smoothness, ease of use. Consider the size of screen and type. The variables become the use of color and space.

How much time does it take to read? How much energy (fatigue) to decipher the crowded display screen? Consider the process of design. Identify each level of design problem. What are the (design) aspects of each?

Questions are being used throughout this and other topics to emphasize the need for questioning, examining, discovering ...that is what creating new products is about and that is also what office automation is about.

EASE OF USE.

System planners are incorporating human-factors-engineering principles into the design of both hardware and software. The result of this is friendly or user friendly systems with ease-of-use features.

Labor is expensive. Computers are becoming relatively inexpensive. With more computer capacity available, programs can be written in natural-language commands. These are easier to use and remember, and contribute to developing friendly systems.

TRAINING.

Ease of use features, or the lack of such, become obvious during a training period. Although testing for possible difficulties should have been completed well before this stage, this is a situation for important feedback which should not be ignored.

Training should be carefully structured with the needs of the user being predominant. As with design, time and cost are main considerations. Training and classes may have to be scheduled in the evening, during lunch hour, weekends. They may be structured as mini-tutorials, workshops or courses from four to sixteen weeks in length.

Most important are flexibility and response to community needs. This is not only in terms of time and schedule, but the actual machine training. Businesses and schools can work together. There are many people with very limited skills and at the same time business offices are in need of help.

Business can inform schools of local industry needs, and as a team they can develop appropriate instruction. This is another important use of the design process. As with hardware and software product development, the extent to which the design process is successfully utilized determines the success rate of the class offering.

If the instruction and training are organized appropriately, this aspect of office automation--the use of automated office systems--can represent an upgrading of skills. In addition, job enrichment and increased status for clerical and secretarial workers can result. The more boring and repetitive jobs, such as filing, can be incorporated into other jobs, and may eventually disappear altogether.

Some easily overlooked elements should be considered in the planning stages of training sessions, i.e.

1. Professionals, especially those in executive management, are often reluctant to enter their own messages or operate their terminals.

2. Some executives do not know how to type and/or consider typing demeaning.

3. Younger people learn typing in school.

4. Many young people will grow up with a personal computer in the home environment.

5. Human factor implementations will continue at a rapid pace, i.e. use of a simplified keypad vs. a full keyboard.

COMMUNICATION DESIGN.

How can a designer of visual communication help? Here the designer describes the relationship of information to visual language to computer graphics.

Computer generated graphics is data processing technology combined with graphic capability. It is also the transmission of information. The latter is one concern of the graphic designer.

The computer accepts data in machine readable form. At the most basic of language levels, impulses are transmitted to the central processing unit, CPU. The CPU then performs the necessary functions or operations on the data.

Since the CPU/computer must have a comprehensible language, the data must be converted or translated by a programmer. A programmer has to write code to produce the binary on-off electrical impulses which make up the operating environment for the other programs.

The base software program which is a level above this must be written. It has a lot of code in it which enables another programmer to write an application program in another language which will operate because the base software interacts or communicates with it.

The program is written and structured also to communicate with the user. The user does not see all the code and steps that occur underneath the package which allows communication with the host system through the terminal.

The program support is written by a programmer who communicates in the necessary language. On every level there is a transmitting of information in a language understood by the sender and receiver, be it man or machine.

In the case of graphics, an application program (package) is written by a programmer in such a way that the base software supports the functions written in the application package which allows the construction of lines, shapes, and other graphic elements.

This graphic capability may be for drawing and/or text. Graphic means to give a clear, precise picture to convey an idea or make a statement, thus the transmission of information.

The term user-friendly is used to describe an application program used by a designer, without computer background. The programmer constructs it in a language which is easily understood and permits the designer to use the power of the computer without understanding the languages of the operating environment, the base software program or any other support programs or, for that matter, the programmer's language to write the actual program being used.

The users of this technology may be designers, analysts, executives, who most often are not programmers or traditional data processing persons. The user is interested only in the application of graphics for a specific need or needs, not the programming which goes into creating the package for someone's use.

Although the user is not involved with the operating environment or any other facet of the computer system, understanding at least on the described general level can assist the user. An example is the graphic designer when communicating needs or requirements to be included in the application package.

In the development of office automation products there is a new emphasis on interaction between user and creator. No longer should the user be unpleasantly surprised with frustrating stumbling blocks. No longer should the creator, i.e. the application package programmer, be allowed to work in the dark.

USER NEEDS.

If the user needs to see his profits/losses, debits/credits, inventory or some of the more intricate business functions, the need, if only for the language which will permit the communication with and through the application program. The particular program is selected according to the application need. In the area of business or presentation graphics, the program permits the user to extract from a data base and request information in bar, pie, line, chart form, etc.

Another application program permits the drawing of lines, shapes, values, colors for the creation of a variety of graphics from flow charts to traditional illustrations. This means working with pictures and not alphanumeric lists for the transmission of information.

If the designer needs to create original art instead of a chart or graph, an application program will be selected which permits drawing, text and drawing, or perhaps text only, depending on need.

A manual written for the user assists, as do some of the packages containing screens which explain commands, functions and give how-to instructions.

As the designer asks the program to permit the making of lines or circles, the potentially numerous internal communication levels which occur to make this possible are unnoticed. But the communication is "going on" unconsciously as does, for the most part, the visual communication.

The visual language in communication may be compared as "going on" in which the actual process and steps are similarly unnoticed. However, both are indispensible.

The correct organization of elements creates a structure of communication. This pictoral data is a product of computer generated graphics--visual communication.

Although we are almost always involved in some form of visual communication we are not usually aware of it as such. The lines, shapes, colors, etc. arranged in such a way as to communicate a particular message blend together much the same way as the words in our English language.

We speak and write our language, i.e. English, Japanese, etc. most of the time without giving it much thought. With the visual language, i.e. communication of information, which today is an industry in itself, we cannot afford to use it unconsciously.

Just as there are elements and principles of the English language to either learn or use correctly, the same is required to use visual language for optimal visual communication.

The Designer needs to assist in presenting information to both the Programmer and User in a way in which it can be an exciting, rewarding, synergistic experience for all concerned.

This is one aspect of Office Automation, computer generated graphics. With increased understanding and interaction among the Programmer, Designer and User, the design process may be more effectively utilized to meet the current needs of computer graphics.

INTEGRATION OF WORD PROCESSING AND GRAPHICS

Alexander Ames
Harry Lehrhaupt
General Electric Company
Space Systems Division
P.O. Box 8555
Philadelphia, PA 19101
U.S.A.

ABSTRACT

Production of technical publications must always overcome cost and time limitations. Device and CPU independent S/W exist that can be cost effectively integrated into a single system that will significantly aid in the production of technical publications.

INTRODUCTION

General Electric is currently working on a project to develop or identify for purchase a low cost system (less than $15K) that can integrate word-processing and graphics. The system will be used, at least initially, to generate all the requisite documentation for embedded software development projects. Anticipated annual savings at the GE Valley Forge plant alone are on the order of 50% or about $500,000.

The system generated by this project will allow engineers, secretaries or technical publications personnel to produce line art interactively on a terminal and integrate it with the text portion of a document. The system will be comprised of separate programs for laying out and drawing line art, for graphically specifying the contents of pages, chapters, and their inter-connections, and for displaying a document for user interaction.

It is a project requirement that the generated system be both CPU and output device independent, and that it integrate with current General Electric word processing capabilities (LANIER, GENITEXT and WANG) and output devices. The initial implementation will be for a VAX 11/780, an IBM 3033, and a low cost Motorola 68000 based microprocessor.

A standard well-defined link will be established between the software development organizations document generation capabilities and those of the publications organization. This feature is important as more and more of the documentation for projects is being generated as a by-product of the software development process with the aid of automated tools. In this manner engineers and programmers will be able to create parts of documents using various software tools on the development CPU, and pass it electronically to the publications processor. Further additions and modifications can then be made by publications personnel. If the software development organization needs to make further modifications, the organization may retrieve the document electronically and proceed to make the changes.

BACKGROUND MOTIVATION

Word Processing is beginning to experience general acceptance within General

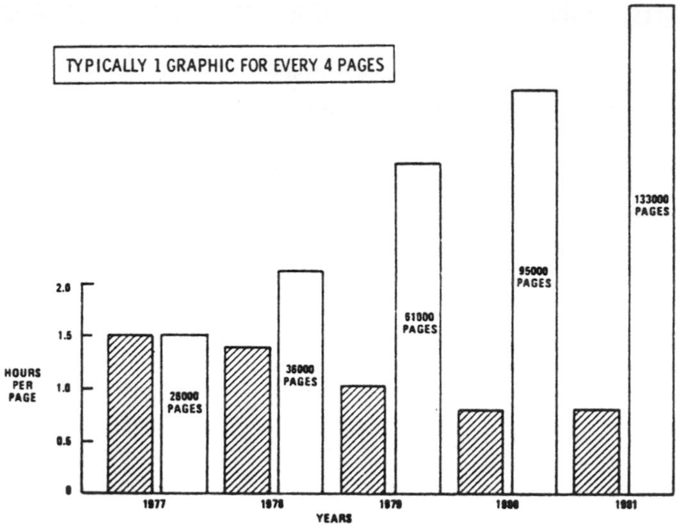

Figure 1.0. Enhancement of Productivity thru Word Processing

Electric, having proven repeatedly that it can drastically improve productivity in creating and maintaining documents. Figure 1.0 depicts the type of productivity gains GE has achieved through the use of word processing. While these savings are impressive, there still exists considerable potential for further savings through using additional office automation aids and making modifications to the current methodology for generating documents.

For example, Figure 1.0 took one and one-half hours of manual graphics arts time to draw and another two and a quarter hours to implement modifications generated by a series of reviewers. In the typical document, graphics represents one out of every four pages of the completed document. Line art is the main type of graphics generated in software development and engineering applications. It is also the type of graphic most amenable to computer automation.

Current Documention Generation Scenario

On a typical project, documents are generated as a joint effort by three classes of personnel: authors, secretaries and a publications organization. The class of "authors" includes managers, engineers, programmers and technical writers. They may or may not have access to software tools to aid them in preparing document segments. Programmers are the ones most likely to use software tools, since they are accustomed to working with computers and consequently do not find computers intimidating. Most frequently, authors create hardcopy drafts by hand and then turn them over to secretaries or the publications personnel for typing, hopefully on a word processor. After the document is typed, it is returned to the author(s) for corrections. Several interations usually transpire before an error-free version is generated.

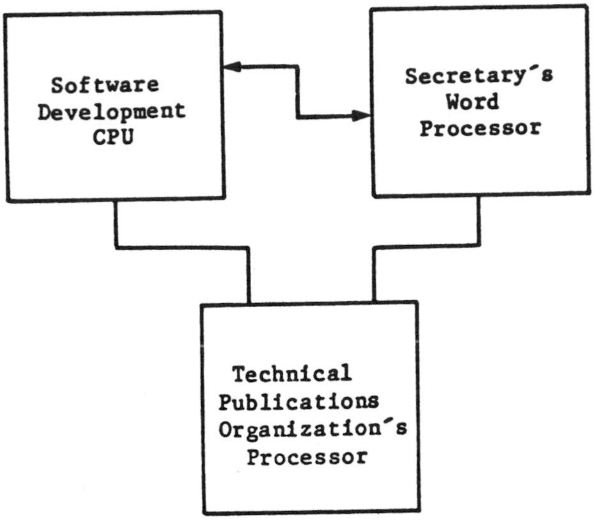

Figure 2.0. Network Interconnection Between Processors

Once the text has been entered and verified the line art must then be inserted manually. Insertions, modifications and deletions of text can easily cause a great deal of pain as page layouts have to be redone to reflect changes.

At some installations, various software tools exist to generate whole sections of documents[1]. The goal is to have a mechanism whereby these computer generated sections can be easily integrated into the document without the need for retyping the data or cutting and pasting the data into the appropriate sections of the document. One way of solving this problem is to have the processors used by each of the three classes of personnel hooked together in a network as depicted in Figure 2.0. Under this concept the software generated sections are mailed electronically from one processor to another. Unfortunately, the text processing commands for each of the processors are usually not compatable, varying in richness of capabilities supported as well as form. For example, one text processor may allow a choice of fonts and sizes while another supports only one. A command translation interface that takes into account these variances has to be written for multiple combinations of text processors.

The electronic transmission of graphics can easily absorb the communications path bandwidth, particularly if the graphic is sent via facsimile or in any other pixel-by-pixel fashion. We have previously noted that we expect one of every four pages to be a graphic. Fortunately, modern graphic software interface standards require a metafile concept, which permits the creation of a storable device independent graphic file. This file occupies less space than a pixel representation, and can be communicated electronically just as the text. It is this additional facility of the modern graphic standard that enhances its utility in the documentation facility.

Another problem that exists is that inter-vendor CPU communication capabilities, if they do in fact exist for a given pair of vendors, are usually fairly limited. So, while it may currently be possible to transmit files from one vendor's CPU to another, the transmission time for file of any appreciable size can be significant. Unless the communications link also supports error checking, data losses during transmission can also be a problem. The establishment of an efficient network protocol is an essential ingredient of the system being generated[7]

Multiple Author/Multiple Section Documents

On large projects, documents are seldom authored by a single individual. The writing tasks are broken down into specialty areas and assigned to appropriate personnel with one person having the responsibility of integrating the document into a cohesive whole. The biggest problem associated with having multiple authors on a large document, is the configuration management of the various sections. Usually the sections are interrelated and authors need to be able to access the most current version and must be notified when changes impact their sections. Using manual procedures, the document integrator must physically index, store and protect the document segments. He must also see how each documentation update impacts on both text and graphics in the integrated document (The effect on, the table of contents, the index, paragraph and page numbering and page layouts).

Automation will greatly ease the burdens of the document integrator. The documentation production system will have the capability of accepting a series of files with each file containing segments of the document (including line art) and be able to integrate the contents into a single cohesive document, while automating paragraph and page numbering, table of contents generation, index table building and headers and footers for the complete document. Control of the document segments will be achieved through the use of a configuration management system such as HLCS[8].

Line Art For Charts

Line art is not limited to documents. Presentation charts frequently contain line art and the time demands for generating charts is often more critical than for documents. The following paragraph describes a typical scenario for chart generation.

An hour or more is spent by the author preparing a neat drawing of a diagram, after which time it is taken to Graphics Arts. Accounting and control procedures (and possibly a waiting line) consume time, while turn-around in the Graphics Arts organization requires about a day. The graphics artist consumes about one and one-half hours to complete the artwork. The documenter can then present the diagram to a project review, with the inevitable response of "it's alright, but could you make just one change?" Editing the material typically requires an edit cycle be run on an average of one-and-one-half times on the original text or drawing.

Using the new system, the documenter will be able to sketch a diagram using the graphics capability of a desktop terminal. This sketching will permit the construction of icons, or graphic figures similar to flowchart figures, each of which may be selected and positioned, and then be given an interior or exterior label. Connect points may also be predefined, with the user able to select arrows, arrow direction and perhaps off page arrows for connecting lines. This sketching extension will support the generation of hierarchy charts, process flow diagrams, and other software design sketches.

During the initial learning period, a documenter will probably use as much time as before for the creation of the original graphic, selecting and positioning the icons, linking them with arrows or work flow path lines, making certain of their proportional sizes, centering them vertically and horizontally, and entering and editing the text in each icon. The savings are realized by the fact that the completed drawing may now be edited in much less time than the original, since the editorial changes do not require total reconstruction of the drawing.

Since the graphic may be directed to any output device, including graphics terminals, vuegraph cameras, or television projectors, the completed graphic can more easily be used in all kinds of presentations. Modifications to the graphics can even be made in real time during a review.

Importance of CPU And Device Independence

The integration of text and line art as a concept is not difficult or overly complex. The difficulty lies in the ability of the systems designer to acquire pieces which fit together to permit a coherent approach to documentation with the inclusion of graphics which satisfy customer needs in a cost-effective manner. Cost-effective integration of documentation requires software standards and device and host independence. Software standards linked with device independence ensure real long term economies, since the acquired software expertise and library can readily survive rapidly changing hardware technology. This survivability leaves the organization with a larger, more mature skill and knowledge base.

A core standard graphics software package is a must to limit the cost of training graphic programmers, and to take advantage of extensions built for modern graphic standard packages. A decision on which graphic interface to select is at this time particularly sensitive, since graphics software technology is at a crossroads forced by 1982 decisions on graphics software standards.

Graphics packages tend to be targeted at specific customers, such as CAD/DAM (CALMA/Apollo), slide generation (GENIGRAPHICS), or FEM (Finite Element Modelling - NASTRAN). Most of these computerized graphic systems are costly because they are device-dependent, task specific, and require a unique assembly or macro language, or a unique dialect of a higher-order language. Device-dependent software and graphic systems are vulnerable to change, and are quickly eclipsed by technology advances. Careful selection of a modern package may permit access to a wide variety of graphics technologies, including management graphics and CAD/CAM drawings.

Low Cost Driving Factor

The concept of Documentation Production Systems is not new. A number of systems are available for prices in excess of $100,000 - $400,000 for hardware and software to do the task - this is very nearly a workstation cost! The text formatting problem is relatively simple by itself, and work

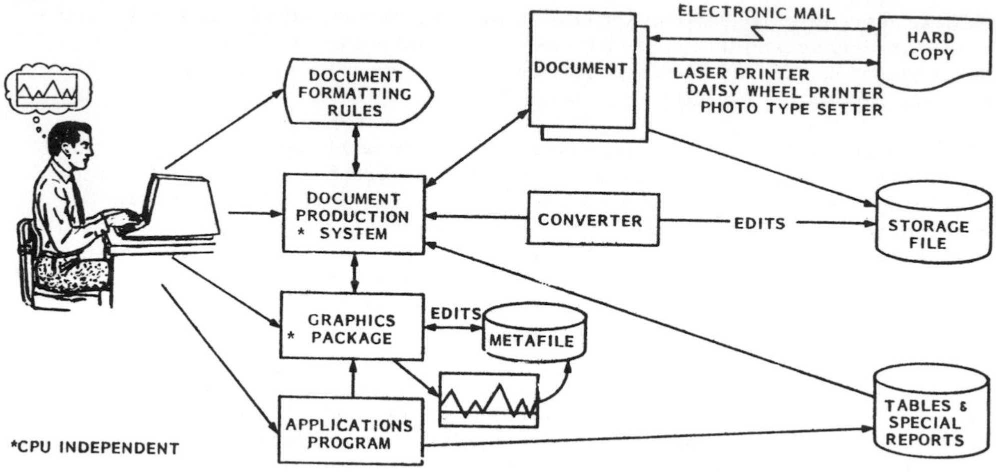

Figure 3.0. Document Production System Overview

stations can be acquired for under $20,000 which generate high quality formatted text output. Even integration is possible with $20,000 workstations. These inexpensive workstations, however, operate in a totally device-dependent mode, and offer neither flexibility nor portability.

DESCRIPTION OF DOCUMENTATION PRODUCTION SYSTEM

Integration of text and line art means that graphics and word processing are output to the same output media, both softcopy and hardcopy. The requirements include accepting the picture and text in some intermediate form, selecting the output device, formatting the text and the graphics so as not to violate each others' space, integrating the text and graphics within the one document, and outputting data in a form compatible with the selected output device. A program that performs this function is known as an integrator.

For convenience sake, any text formatter having a graphics inclusion capability is here called an integrator. The model implementation of an integrator used in this paper is the SCRIBE package from Unilogic, Inc. SCRIBE uses commands imbedded in the text for text formatting, and for the creation and use of picture space. In creating picture space, the user defines a picture label. This picture label is used in a picture table of contents (TOC), separate from the text TOC. The picture space reservation data and the name of the picture metafile is used to create the space, and draw and label the required graphic.

The integrator works as the "senior" software in the system, in that it formats the text, fits graphic space to each page, links the figure label to the figure table of contents, links the graphic space to its relevant

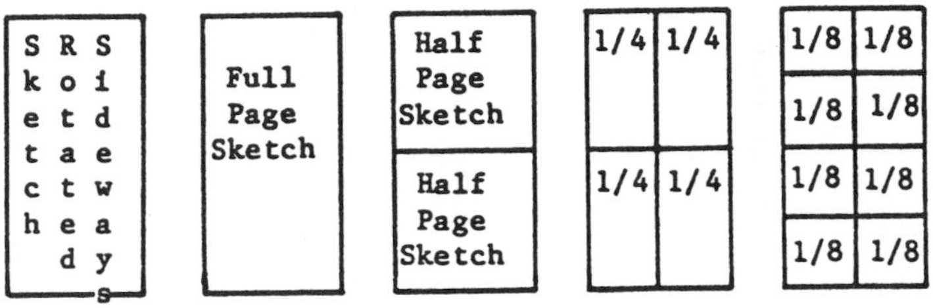

Figure 4.0. Page Layout Formats for Graphics Inclusions

text, and then permits the "junior" software to draw the graphic in the reserved graphic space. That is, the "senior" package converts all text into the appropriate format for the selected output device, reserving the space for pictures. Then the "senior" package permits the "junior" graphics package to fill each reserved graphic space with a graphic representation of the graphic metafile. The "senior" package has all responsibility for text formatting, for the graphic format and space reservation, and calling the "junior" package. The "junior" package inserts a single named graphic metafile into the assigned reserved area. The "senior" package calls the "junior" package for each and every picture required. Reserved areas may be unassigned; for new documents, the graphic may not yet be available, but the user wishes to see the draft copy with its picture space reservations blank.

Clearly, a single size of graphic is inadequate in this integrator; a complex CAD sketch and a bar chart require space appropriate to the complexity of each drawing. The space size selections are left in the hands of the integrator, assuming a fixed page size of 8 1/2 by 11 inches. The integrator will offer picture size formats of full page rotated sideways (base to the right), full page, half, quarter and eighth, fixed in position as in Figure 4.0.

The driving force of selections shown here is simplicity of interface with minimal complexity for the user. As the package matures, we may group eighth page graphics, say, as four figures on the bottom of the most convenient page, or center an eight page sketch in the upper half of a two column page, or permit a multiple-page-width foldout. But simplicity and workability must be a first concern.

There are three graphic interface functions we are asking the "senior" integrator package to perform: the interface must specify the user-selected picture reservation size (as in Figure 4.0 above) to the graphics package, the interface must specify the promixity requirements of the picture to the relevant text that the picture illuminates, and the interface must present the graphic metafile or the name of the graphic metafile to the graphic drawing package. Initially, the proximity selection will be limited to whether the graphic must be on the same page as the text, or whether the graphic may be floated to the next page. If the graphic may not be floated, an end-of-page may be forced on the text to keep the parts integrated. This kind of positioning and distance-to-end-of-page calculation remain the responsibility of the "senior" package, the integrator.

INPUT

```
@style(linewidth=40,spacing=1)
@make(article)
@majorheading(Merging of Text and Graphics)
@section(Introduction)
Commands are preceded with a @@ in column one
of the input page.  Spacing occurs according
to user defined defaults.
@Begin(enumerate)
Sample One

Sample Two
@end(enumerate)

@subsection(System Overview)
See Figure @ref(hypo) for an overview diagram
of the system.  The following sections will
discuss each of the main components in detail.

@Begin(figure)
@Picture(Size=1.5in,File="HYPO.PIC")
@Caption(System Overview)
@tag(hypo)
@end(figure)
```

OUTPUT

MERGING OF TEXT AND GRAPHICS

1. Introduction

Commands are preceded with a @ in column one of the input page. Spacing occurs according to user defined defaults.

1. Sample One

2. Sample Two

1.1 System Overview

See Figure 1-1 for an overview diagram of the system. The following sections will discuss each of the main components in detail.

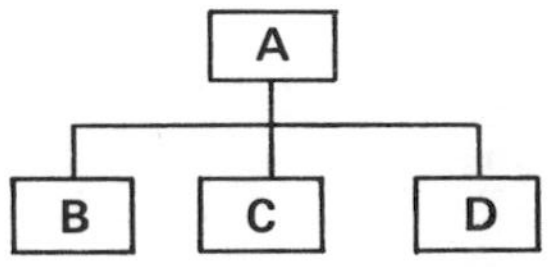

Figure 1-1. System Overview

Figure 5.0 Sample Scribe Inputs & Outputs

Figure 5.0 lists a sample CSRIBE input file and its corresponding output. All SCRIBE commands are preceeded with a @ symbol. The author begins his work session by identifying to SCRIBE via the "@make" command the type of document he wishes to create. The rules associated for each document are stored in a database and are referenced by SCRIBE when it formats the document. In the example depicted here the author has declared his document to be an "article". An "article" is defined to consist of major-headings, sections and subsections. The author does not have to concern himself with the formating rules of an "article". He simply precedes each majorheading, section and subsection with the appropriate command and SCRIBE takes care of sequencing, capitalization and spacing rules, and the creation of a tables of contents. Note also that a label can be explicitly assigned to a "Figure" which can be used for referal elsewhere in the document, and that the figure number is automatically assigned to the figure and all tagged references. Last, but not least, observe the use of the "picture" command to insert a previously drawn diagram directly into the document.

CPU And Device Independent

Both the integrator and the graphics packages must satisfy an identical subset of portability requirements. First and foremost, portability of the software must be a fundamental design element for an integrated graphics and word processing system. Proven CPU and device independence must be a fundamental selection criteria for both the graphics and integrator packages.

Portability must be proven on both input and output levels, for both the graphics and the integrator packages. The graphics package on each CPU must be capable of accepting input from any other graphics source, and each integrator must be capable of accepting input from any other text processor system. The graphics exchange will initially be limited to vector graphics in metafile form; the input number system must lie within (or be capable of interpolation into) the number system of the receiving device. Source selectability means accepting input from a graphic interface (e.g., CAD graphics plot file) via electronic mail, or from any device capable of generating, storing or transmitting 2D or 3D positioning data. Having read the data, the graphics package must then be capable of outputting the data to any display (softcopy or hardcopy), or to an electronic mail connection. This capability implies that the package can maintain information which the device may not support, such as colors, line styles or character fonts.

The integrator package also must prove its ability to input ASCII data from any alphanumeric display, and output to any hardcopy or softcopy display (graphic or alphanumeric). There are no established criteria for this transfer capability. Initially, this portability is defined as the acceptance or transmission of preformatted ASCII data, with some accompanying format commands (e.g., font change, font quality, page size, picture space, picture label, etc.).

Graphics Package Selection

The General Electric Space Systems Division (SSD) Data Systems Resource

Management (DSRM) organization, the organization responsible for developing this system, has reduced the field of graphics packages under consideration to two contenders namely:

1. BLOX Graphics Builder from Rubel Software. This is a core standard package that provides an interactive sketching capability. Cost is $6-8K. BLOX is a relatively new offerring that has been successfully hosted on only the VAX, though the vendor claims it is can be easily ported to other cpu's.

2. DI3000 with Grafmaker option from Precision Visuals Inc. (PVI). Core Standard package that provides an interactive business graphic capability but no interactive sketching capability. Cost is $12K. DI-3000 has proven portability to over 30 different CPUs, and to over 26 hardcopy and softcopy devices. PVI is projecting completion of a CALCOMP plot output interface by September 1982, as well as an interactive interface to charts and graphs. A CALCOMP input interface (for conversion of CAD graphics to the metafile form) is being considered.

Selection criteria included graphic language capabilities, adherence to a proposed graphic standard, performance, portability, quality and price.

No formal selection process has begun for the integrator package. A search was made for commercially available word processor candidates with a proven track record of integration, together with a record of portability. The only condidate which surfaced (in a superficial search) is the SCRIBE package from Unilogic, Inc. This package has proven portability to Three Rivers (PERQ), APOLLO, IBM, DEC (VAX) and Honeywell CPUs, and output capability to a variety of hardcopy and softcopy devices, including hardcopy to XEROX 9700, the DEC LA120, and some daisy-wheel printers, and softcopy to RETROGRAPHICS, VT125 and Tektronix 4014. Additional General Electric-owned CPUs and output devices are being identified to UNILOGIC as portability targets.

SUMMARY AND CONCLUSIONS

Graphics and word processing may be integrated at a relatively low cost by integrating existing software packages into a basic package that meets the basic documentation production needs of software developers. The benefits of such integration include cost effective editing of graphic line, improved response time of editing and publication of integrated documents, and the professional appearance of the integrated software documentation from proposal to delivery.

BIBLIOGRAPHY

1. John Arnon and Harry Lehrhaupt, "Software Documentation: An Automated Approach", Proceedings Trends & Applications 1982, IEEE, pp. 57-64.

2. "Computer Networks an Their Protocols", D. Davies, D. Barber, W. Price John Wiley & Sons, 1979.

3. Alan Paller, "Choosing the Right Chart - A Comprehensive Guide for Computer Graphics Users", ISSCO, Spring 1981.

4. "Status Report of the Graphics Standard Planning Committee", Computer Graphics Volume 13 Number 3 ACM SIGRAPH August 1979. (This is the complete Core Standard document as proposed to ANSI - (American National Standard).

5. Patrick Kenealy, "WP Software Advances Rapidly", Mini-Micro Systems, Vol. 15, No. 5, May 1982.

6. Wolfgang Harak and Wolfgang Postl, "Document Preparation by an Experimental Text and Facsimile Integrated Workstation", Proceedings Trends & Applications 1982, IEEE, pp. 81-87.

7. "Technical Aspects Of Data Communication", John McNamara, Digital Equipment Corporation, 1978

8. Harry Lehrhaupt, "Hierarchical Library Control System", Proceedings National Conference on Software Technology and Management, NSIA, October 14-16, 1981

9. Lansing Hatfield, "GKS and the alphabet Soup of Graphics", Computer Graphics Volume 16 Number 2 ACM SIGRAPH June 1982.

10. Steven Feiner, Sandor Nagy, and Andries Van Dam, "An Experimental System for Creating and presenting Interactive Graphical Documents", ACM Transactions on Graphics, Vol. 1, No. 1, January 1982.

11. Foley and Van Dam, "Fundamentals of Interactive Computer Graphics", Addison-Wesley, 1982

12. Richard Furuta, Jeffrey Scofield and Alan Shaw, "Document Formatting Systems: Survey, Concepts, and Issues", ACM Computing Surveys, Vol. 14, No. 3, September 1982

BIOGRAPHIES

Mr. Ames came to General Electric after 16 years with the Department of Defense. He began his data systems career in 1968, working primarily in graphics software development and graphics software and hardware acquisition. Mr. Ames published a paper on graphical analysis of a pseudo-random number generator and was graphics illustrator for a BYTE magazine article on computer graphics art.

Mr. Harry Lehrhaupt graduated from New York University with an M.S. in Mathematics. Since joining General Electric in 1973, he has managed several large software development projects. In 1981, Mr. Lehrhaupt was appointed Manager, Software Technology Systems Development in which capacity he has been responsible for introducing new software methodologies and tools into the Aerospace Business Group and has been serving as a focal point for software technology transfer within GE.

Chapter 5
Computer Animation

3D SHADED COMPUTER ANIMATION, STEP-BY-STEP

Richard Chuang
Glenn Entis

Pacific Data Images, Inc.
550 Weddell Drive, Suite 3
Sunnyvale, California 94086, U.S.A.

ABSTRACT

Computer generated animation for the entertainment industry is a rapidly growing area of computer graphics. Three-dimensional, shaded, color raster graphics offers many possibilities for exciting images and fast, flexible animation design. This paper is a step-by-step overview of how such a computer animated piece is produced, with particular attention paid to the tools and intermediate graphics generated in the production process.

One reason that computer generated animation is such a quickly growing field is that a lot of people are having fun making astounding images. The explicit goal of this paper is to provide an overview of how a computer generated animated television spot is produced. The implicit goal is to show that part of the fun and promise of computer animation is in the quality of the tools and the way in which these tools provide a flexibility previously unavailable to the animation designer.

Computers have already made a substantial contribution to the entertainment industry in the form of computerized motion-control systems, ink-and-paint systems, and computer controlled models. The animation discussed in this paper is computer generated, which means that all aspects of the image, including the objects, lighting, motion, and backgrounds, are synthesized entirely by computer.

The animated spot covered in this paper is an example of how a typical piece is produced in our studio, so we make no claim of universality. Nonetheless, this example should impart a sense of what producing computer animation is like.

The field of computer animation is young and growing quickly, so there are no veteran computer animation artists who know all the technical tricks from years of experience. Therefore, the computer tools discussed here were designed primarily to be used by a technical director working with a creative director or animation designer.

Several factors distinguish good from poor tools. Functionality (i.e., is the tool capable of doing the job in the hands of a trained user) is an obvious consideration. Another consideration is that given the choice between functionally equivalent tools, people generally choose the tool which is easier and more pleasant to use. Over time this implies that pleasant tools will be better understood by their users than tools whuch are functionally equivalent but painstaking to use. In other words, when given a choice people like to enjoy their work.

The remainder of the paper briefly describes some of the tools we use for the production of 3D computer animation. We start by describing the tools used to make things move. Next, we look at the tools which are used to build models. Given motion and models, the animator will want to preview the animation, so we next cover test shots, followed by the production of the final piece.

SCRIPT SYSTEM

We rely heavily on a script system for our animation design. Our script system is a special purpose graphics language which supports animation at a high level. The script system was influenced by many similar systems, most notably the LISP based ASAS (see [Reyn82a] for a description of ASAS). Our script is built on top of the programming language C (see [Kern78a]) and thus shares many C features. Specific goals for our script were simple syntax, default values for the entire graphic environment, support of complex modelling, transformations, and motion, and support of modular scripting. The data structures and file types used in the script are shared with other design tools in use, and provide a common ground on which all design programs communicate.

MOTION DESIGN

In 3D animation, choreography of objects and camera is the main job of the director and animator. We developed a motion design system to assist them in producing 3D animation. This system consists of several interactive and non-interactive motion design tools that set up each scene, and several methods for viewing each animation sequence.

The interactive motion design system utilizes a vector display to establish key frame positions of the camera and actors. The camera's view, focal length, and direction of view, along with the position and orientation of each actor is specified by the animator interactively. The key frames are then placed into an animation sequence, the computer generates the required number of positions for all the intermediate frames as specified by the animator. Mathematical control paths for both space and time can also be used to modify the transition of motions between key frames. Examples of key frame modification are camera tracking, easing in, easing out, and roll and pitch. For well defined motions, numerical paths can be entered manually or interactively. All motion specifications can interact with each other within the script of each animated scene. Combining numerical paths and key frames specifications is often used in animation.

Extensive use of paths simplifies the design tools needed for specifying complex motions. By using a simple description of motion in terms of motion paths, new animators can quickly learn the basics of 3D computer animation and later extend their knowledge to more complex scene choreography.

An animated sequence may be previewed in several ways. First a flip book approach can help animator view his design in the more traditional way. A sequence of frames is drawn in wireframe format into the 32 bit planes of the frame buffer. The animator, by using a pen on a digitizing tablet, can "flip" back and forth between the frames. This is equivalent to a flip book for viewing animation. By varying the rate of flipping, a animator can get a better feel of motion in time.

A second step is to film a wireframe pencil test of an animated sequence. This produces a display of the actual choreography. Motion tests can be done prior to having the actual actors in each scene. Stand-ins are often used for initial motion study.

Then finally the motion is viewed through a low resolution (256x256) animation in which the choreography of movements, lighting, and color are seen together before the final rendering. This low resolution animation is visually more helpful to an art director because a vector animation contains no information as to the color and mass of each scene. We are currently developing a vector motion editor that allows us to edit and preview complex animation sequences in realtime. But the choreography of a scene will still be done with key frames and paths, along with previewing in low resolution.

MODEL DESIGN

A designer has control over many characteristics of the objects to be animated, including geometric shape and size, color, surface quality, details, etc. (see [Newm79a] and [Fole82a] for introduction to these concepts). At some stages of the production very simple models, or "stand-ins", are used so the designer can get a feel for the scene or movement. At other stages different details of the models are required to complete and fine-tune the final piece. All this comes under the general heading of model design.

An animator may be called on to animate almost any kind of object, so it is important for the modelling tools to be flexible and fast. A prime objective of our modelling tools is to provide a graphics-oriented language that allows quick object definition and minimizes the need for custom software. The script system described in the above section on motion design is also used to build models. Most script values default to predefined values if not explicitly set by the animator, making simple object definition fast and easy. For example, if a 5-sided prism is required, the script command is:

```
prism 5
```

The unspecified prism attributes, such as color, radius, height, surface type, etc., all default to standard and/or previously set values. Other geometric primitives include spheres, cylinders, cones, pyramids, lathes, and arbitrary polygons. Quick specification of simple objects is useful for making "stand-in" objects. In the motion design of a complicated object the motion is often clearer and faster to compute if simple stand-in objects are used instead of the fully detailed final models. Since the script is the basis of the animation and modelling systems, all script primitives may also be used as the building blocks for more complicated models. Many models, such as buildings with multiple levels, windows, and doors, can be built by combining very simple geometric forms (Figure 1 - city).

When a simple geometrical approach won't suffice, a graphic model editor is used to draw the model. As the artist draws the model using a data tablet and interactive display, the computer stores the artist's drawing in a file. This information is converted into polygons which can then be used as model or model parts. For example, for a recent animation of complex calligraphy, there was no simple mathematical expression for the artwork to be animated. In this case, the most practical method of building the model was scanning the original art into the display memory with a video camera, displaying the image on the interactive display as a guide, then tracing around the scanned-in image to create the final model. Once defined, of course, this final model was available for display and animation from the script with a single command.

Rendering a computer graphics model means displaying it as a color solid object, with hidden surfaces removed and proper 3D shading. Once a model is defined, it can be rendered on the color display. Stand-in models are useful for the determination of color, placement in the scene, and scale. As in the case of motion design, the advantages of stand-ins are faster computation time and suppression of detail which may not yet be relevant to the current stage of design. An example of a scene of rendered stand-in models is shown in Figure 2 (polygonal "stand-ins" in still-life scene). The colors and final placement of the objects were determined using stand-ins, after which the final, detailed scene was created (Figure 3 - detailed still-life scene).

It is difficult to design a complicated object correctly on the first attempt, so a fast method of viewing objects in the design stage is desirable. In this system, any model may be previewed in color wireframe (Figure 4 - wireframe still-life scene). Such wireframes have the advantage of being quick to display and show the full structure of the scene. Wireframe drawings may also be plotted on paper for detailed planning and documentation.

Once models are created, they are rarely thrown away. Most computer animation studios build up the equivalent of a shopping catalog of models which are available for future work. The script system encourages modular construction of models from sub-parts. Each model is then given a name and saved in a model library. If a scene is made of several models, the script retrieves the necessary models from their libraries. Because each model is independently defined, the script can be used to isolate objects for documentation and detailed viewing.

When everything has been defined, the designer fully renders the model. The models or a group of models may be placed in any location. In addition, the camera may be positioned and aimed anywhere in the scene. Any number of light sources, of any position and color, are allowed; frequently a major portion of time at this stage of design is spent in adjusting the lighting and fine-tuning the color of the model. Subtle lighting effects, highlighting, and color balance can be adjusted to greatly enhance the strength of the final image.

Test Shots

Once a model or animated move is defined, it may be used any number of times in a variety of ways. This is particularly advantageous in the preparation of test shots; a script may be progressively refined and viewed in inexpensive test shot formats until everyone agrees that it is right.

The above section on motion design mentioned the use of "flip book" motion previewing and wireframe models. Combined, these two techniques offer a relatively cheap method of previewing the animation of an entire production. In traditional animation, a pencil test is the filmed sequence of raw pencil art shown at the normal animated play-back speed. For computer graphic "pencil tests", we use the script and models for the final piece, but draw each model in color wireframe rather than as a fully rendered image. A wireframe image may be up to several orders of magnitude faster to compute than a fully rendered image, yet the wireframe pencil test still displays the motion exactly as it will appear in the final work. Because the same script and models are used for the pencil test as for the final piece, the movement and models in the test are duplicatable. Thus misunderstandings and organizational overhead in the studio are reduced.

Test renderings are made at various stages of the animation so that the designer may view and modify the look of the models, coloring, lighting, and the general feel of key frames of the animation. Since test renderings are made from the same script and models as pencil tests and the final animation, it is simple to choose any frame from the pencil test and render it exactly as it will appear in the final image.

Usually the last piece of test footage is a low resolution rendered animation. This test has hidden surfaces removed, 3D shading, and is anti-aliased, but all at lower resolution than normally acceptable in a finished piece. In most cases, rendering frames at 1/4 the resolution (reduced to 1/2 both vertically and horizontally) gives everybody an excellent feel for the final film. Since resolution is closely tied to computing time, the low resolution test shot is still significantly cheaper to compute than the final image.

An important aspect of all test shots is the ease with which they are produced. In some cases, a motion test or rendered frame is available within a few minutes. Since everything is repeatable, the animation designer has precise control over what is to be changed and what remains the same. Imagine an architect who can refine a set of blueprints, build scale models from the blueprints, and then automatically have the building constructed directly from those blueprints.

Final Shot

After all necessary test shots have been completed and are agreed upon, the final animated spot is created. In our studio, this is usually 16mm film shot on a Dunn film recorder, but production directly to 1 inch video tape is also possible. A "Director's" language controls the frame rendering of the final scene from the animation script, and also controls the film recorder automatically. If multiple scripts are used, or if the scene requires images from outside sources to be matted with the computer synthesized images, the director's language also handles this. Rendering a single frame of a complex image may take a long time. Automation, at this point, becomes extremely important for the well-being and sleeping habits of the animators. The final spot then goes to the client, and all scripts, models, and selected intermediate images from the spot are archived in anticipation of future work.

Conclusion

This is a quick overview of our approach to the production of computer animation. The tools of our studio and the industry in general are new and improving rapidly. The goal of good tools is a good product, and in animation that still takes good designers and animators. However, as this paper suggests, tools which are responsive, flexible, and pleasant to use add to a designer's productivity by allowing the designer to think about the images rather than the detailed means by which they are created.

APPENDIX

Our current studio at Pacific Data Images was formed in early 1982. The objective of our small group, a total of three persons, was to produce computer-generated animation for the television and film industries.

The current animation system has been in development since the studio formed, and was completely designed and implemented in-house. The basic system was built around a small minicomputer, a PDP 11/44, and a 512x512x32 bit frame buffer, a DeAnza IP6400. At the end of 1982 we added to our facility a VAX11/750 minicomputer system, a DeAnza IP8500 frame buffer, and an IMI 500 real-time vector display station. All software was written in the programming language C under the UNIX operating environment. Our selection of UNIX and C was dictated by a desire for smooth development and growth. We also use low-resolution raster graphic terminals at our desks for design and preview. Animation is recorded onto film using a Dunn instrument camera and also placed directly on to one inch video tape.

The major software packages that we developed consist of a 3D modelling system, a script-oriented 3D animation system, a 3D motion editor system, a director/producer language system, an animation preview system, and an anti-aliased 3D rendering system. Our approach is to develop a state-of-the-art animation system that will accomodate growth. The ability of the software to be transported to newer and faster computers is essential in developing a productive and competitive animation capability. Modular design is critical in developing a transforming system. As new animation and image synthesis techniques become available, they will be integrated into the animation system with well-defined interaction.

For more information about our equipment and motion design, see [Rose82a]

References

Fole82a. James D. Foley and Andries Van Dam, _Fundamentals of Interactive Computer Graphics_, Addison-Wesley (1982).

Kern78a. Brian W. Kernighan and Dennis M. Ritchie, _The C Programming Language_, Prentice-Hall, Inc. (1978).

Newm79a. William Newman and Robert F. Sproull, _Principles of Interactive Computer Graphics_, McGraw-Hill, Inc. (1979).

Reyn82a. Craig Reynolds, "Computer Animation with Scripts and Actors," _SIGGRAPH '82_, Association for Computing Machinery (Summer 1982).

Rose82a. Carl O. Rosendahl, "A Tour through a Computer Animation Studio," _Harvard Computer Graphics Week Proceedings '82_, Harvard University (July 1982).

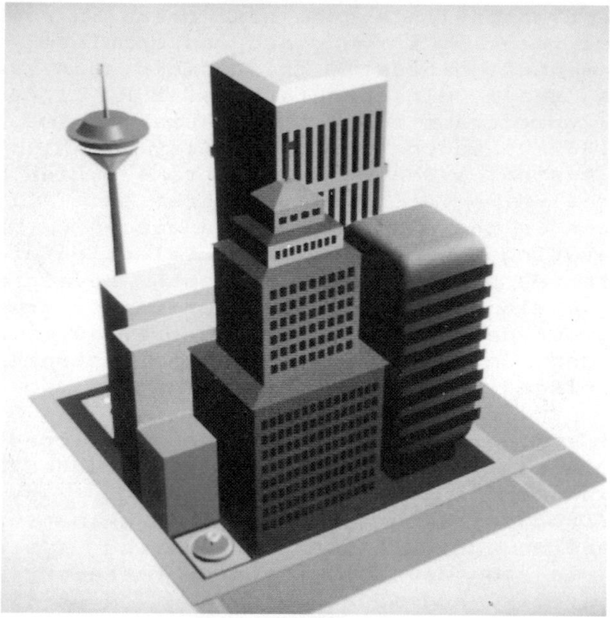

Figure 1 - CITY

Figure 2 - Polygonal Stand-Ins
Still-Life

Figure 3 - Detail Still-Life Scene

Figure 4 - Wire Frame, Still-Life

THE USE OF 3D ABSTRACT GRAPHICAL TYPES IN COMPUTER GRAPHICS AND ANIMATION

N. Magnenat-Thalmann
Département des Méthodes Quantitatives, HEC
5255 Decelles
Montréal, CANADA

Daniel Thalmann
Département d'Informatique
Université de Montréal
Montréal, CANADA

ABSTRACT

By introducing three-dimensional graphical types into PASCAL and by providing the means of defining any drawing with them, we obtain a powerful structured graphic language, called MIRA-3D.

These 3D graphical types, called figures, provide the following advantages to the programmer:

1) operations may be restricted to specific types; e.g. the angle between two planes may be defined, but not the angle between two spheres.

2) figures can be used as other types; e.g. we may define an array of cubes or a record with figure fields.

Because of the three-dimensional abstract graphical types, MIRA-3D is a very powerful tool for developing structured graphics programs. It also offers the advantages of PASCAL, GSPC and all the other graphical features. The system is reliable and may be easily moved to another environment. MIRA-3D has been used for a certain number of applications, including a three-dimensional computer animation film. The paper also discusses timevarying abstract graphical types, called actors and their impact in computer animation.

1. INTRODUCTION

A structured graphic language is not only a structured language with graphical procedure calls, but it has to provide a way of structuring data. As has already been shown, type-oriented languages offer a better way of checking data, and good data structures are just as important as good control statements. PASCAL [1] is a good type-oriented language and certainly the most popular one. It is possible to define new types based on existing types. By introducing three-dimensional graphical types into PASCAL and by providing the means of defining any drawing with them, we obtain a powerful structured graphic language.

In recent years, the abstract data type [2] approach evolved as an excellent means for design of quality software. We have defined abstract graphical data types [3] and introduced them as a graphical extension [4] of PASCAL for two-dimensional drawings. These concepts have been implemented with very positive results [5]. In this paper, we present our three-dimensional abstract graphical data types and their impact on computer graphics methodology. In the three-dimensional abstract data type approach, the design of an application programming system begins with its specification as a set of complex abstract data types. Then a refinement process is repeated until the standard graphical types are obtained.

These 3D graphical types provide also the following advantages to the programmer:

1) operations may be restricted to specific types; e.g. the angle between two planes may be defined, but not the angle between two spheres.

2) figures can be used as other types; e.g. we may define an array of cubes or a record with figure fields.

MIRA-3D is the three-dimensional graphical PASCAL extension which is based on the concept of 3D abstract graphical data types. MIRA-3D may also be considered as an almost complete implementation of the level-2 of the GSPC Core System [6,7].

It includes:

- three-dimensional vector arithmetic
- graphical statements
- image transformations
- viewing transformations: perspectives and parallel projections
- standard procedures and functions.

Section 2 of the paper discusses the most important features of the 3D abstract graphical data types.

A powerful set of three-dimensional graphical primitives has also been developed. We have emphasized three-dimensional graphical types such as: revolution bodies, cylindrical surfaces, conical surfaces, regular polyhedras or model surfaces like Coons, Bezier and B-spline surfaces. Section 3 presents the most important primitives and Section 5 shows a few examples, in computer animation. Section 6 briefly discusses latest developments in timevarying abstract graphical types. These new concepts are essential in computer animation.

2. 3D ABSTRACT GRAPHICAL TYPES

The most important tool in this graphical extension is the 3D graphical type: the <u>figure</u> type. This type is an abstract data type and has already been introduced in the 2D version. The syntax is described in Fig. 1. The word <u>figure</u> is a keyword. The formal parameter section, the declaration and the body are similar to the corresponding elements in a procedure.

To define a figure type, the following steps must be extended:

1) find the characteristics of the figure, which become the parameters.

2) find the algorithm which allows the user to build the figure with the help of the parameters.

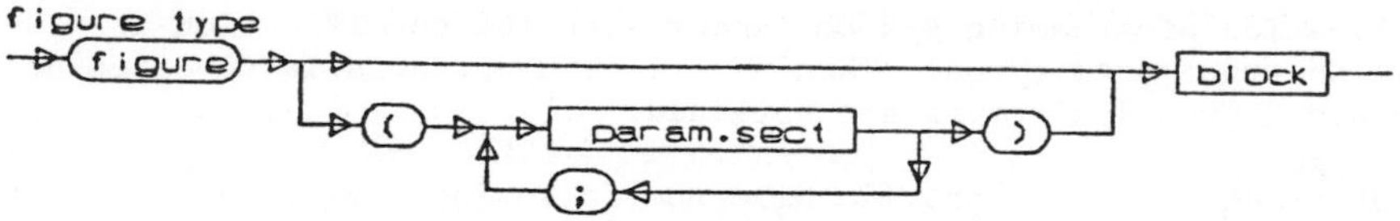

figure 1: Syntactic diagram of a graphical type

As in the 2D version, new statements have been introduced: moveabs, moverel, lineabs, linerel to draw vectors and include to define an existing figure as a part of a new one. Fig. 2 shows the definition of a tetrahedron type.

Attributes may be given to a figure; the most important ones are linestyle, intensity, linewidth and color. Graphical variables are defined as variables of graphical type. Four fundamental statements allow the user to manipulate these variables:

1) create <figure> (<actual parameter list>)
2) delete <figure>
3) draw <figure>
4) erase <figure>

The first operation creates the figure by giving values to the corresponding type parameters; the figure may then be drawn, erased or deleted.

A certain number of standard 3D figure types have been introduced, because they are frequently used. Some of these types are similar to the 2D ones e.g. SEGMENT, LINE, TRIANGLE, SQUARE, CIRCLE, ELLIPSE. For the last three, it is necessary to define the plane of the figure with respect to the normal vector plane.

The other types are typically, three-dimensional types:

i) the "box" defined by 4 vectors
ii) the "cube" defined by 3 vectors
iii) the "sphere" defined by its center c and its radius r.
iv) the "plane" defined by its 3 vectors
v) the three regular polyhedra:

a) type OCTAHEDRON = figure (CENTER,V,DIRECTION: VECTOR)
the octahedron is defined by its center, one vertex V and the direction of an edge with respect to the center.

b) type DODECAHEDRON = figure (CFI,CFA,V: VECTOR)
the dodecahedron is defined by its center CFI, the center of one face CFA and a vertex V.

c) type ICOSAHEDRON = figure (CFI,CFA,V: VECTOR)
the icosahedron is defined similarly to the dodecahedron.

Other interesting standard graphical types are discussed in the next section.

```
TYPE TETRAHEDRON = FIGURE(A,B,C,D:VECTOR);
                   BEGIN
                     MOVEABS A; LINEABS B,C,A,D,C;
                     MOVEABS B; LINEABS D
                   END;
```

Figure 2: The tetrahedron type

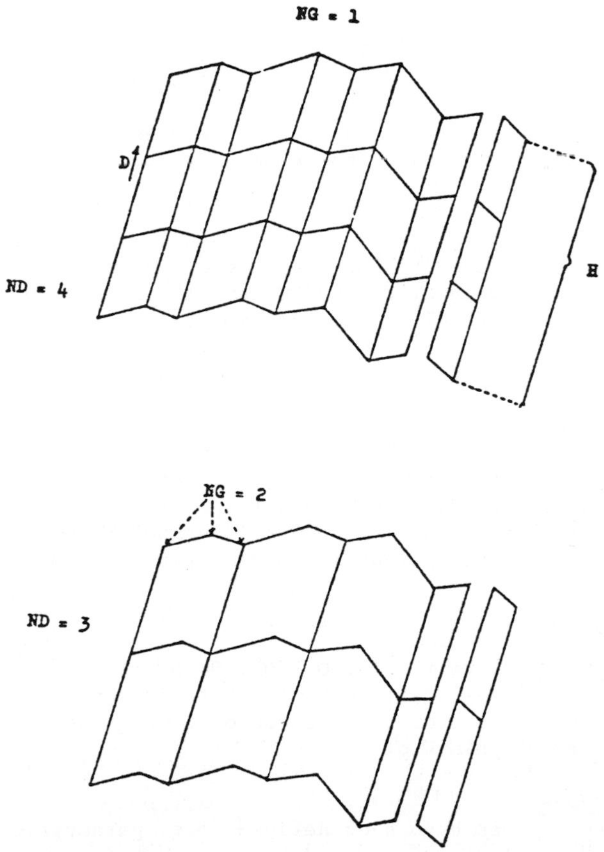

Figure 3: Cylinder parameters

The extension has been implemented by developing a preprocessor. This consists of a 6000 source line program in PASCAL developed on a CDC Cyber 173 and a D.E.C. VAX 780. The output is a standard PASCAL program. The runtime library is a 10 000 PASCAL source line library which is almost device-independent. However, the dependent part may be easily rewritten and has already been adapted for HP2648A, Tektronix 4027, D.E.C. GIGI and TELIDON terminals and for Hewlett-Packard plotters and differents printers.

3. SPECIFIC 3D GRAPHICAL TYPES

Apart of graphical types like boxes, spheres, cubes and polyhedra, the most convenient graphical elements are created by the displacement of a simpler graphical object. Among the different kinds of objects, we can emphasize the following ones:

a) the CYLINDRICAL type
<u>type</u> CYLINDRICAL = <u>figure</u> (F:FIG; D:VECTOR; H:REAL; NG,ND:INTEGER)
A cylindrical body is defined by the displacement of a segment of direction D and length H along a curve F; ND is the number of occurrences of F which are created; a line is created every NG points of F. Fig 3 shows the meaning of these parameters.

b) the CONICAL type
<u>type</u> CONICAL = <u>figure</u> (F:FIG; S:VECTOR; NG,ND:INTEGER; FRACT:REAL)
A conical body is defined by the displacement of a segment along the curve F, passing through S; ND and NG have the same meaning as for the cylindrical type and FRACT is the fraction of the segments which are represented. This feature permits the representation of truncated cones. Fig. 4 shows the role of the FRACT parameter.

c) The PARABOLIC CONICAL type
<u>type</u> PARACONIC = <u>figure</u> (F:FIG; S1,S2:VECTOR; P:REAL; NP,NG,ND:INTEGER)
This type corresponds to the CONICAL type, but instead of a segment a parabolic curve is moved; S1,S2 and W (a point belongs to F) must be in the same plane; P is the arrow of the parabolic curve and NP the number of points in each parabolic curve. Fig. 5 shows the meaning of the parameters.

d) The REVOLUTION type
<u>type</u> REVOLUTION = <u>figure</u> (F:FIG; D:LINE; NG,ND:INTEGER)
A solid of revolution is defined by the rotation of a figure F around a line D; NG is the number of occurrences of F which are created; a circle is created every ND points of F.

e) The SURFACE types
Different figure types have been defined: e.g. parametric surfaces, Coons surfaces, Bezier surfaces and B-splines surfaces.

Here is an example of giraffe which has been built using the previous 3D graphical types.

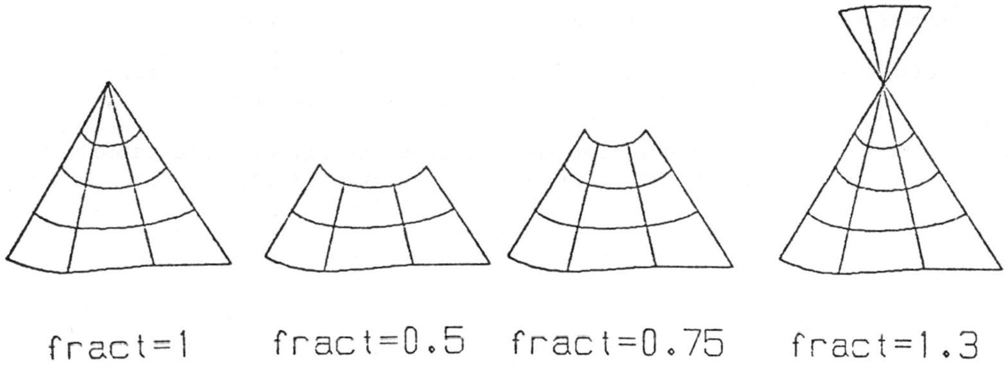

Figure 4: Truncated cones

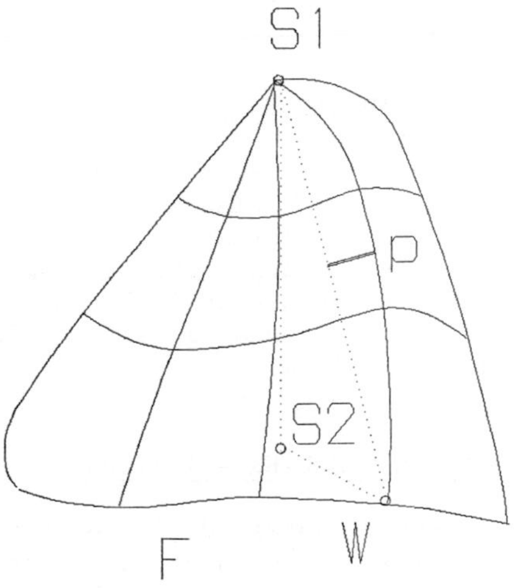

Figure 5: A parabolic cone

The giraffe type has been defined as:

```
GIRAFFE = figure (AXIS, ORIGIN, NECKORIG, TAIL:VECTOR; MOVEMENT:
                  INTEGER; NECKORIENTATION: ORIENTATION);
```

where AXIS is a vector that defines the giraffe orientation

ORIGIN is the origin of the new axis system

NECKORIG is the origin of the giraffe neck

TAIL is the vector that gives the tail direction

MOVEMENT is an integer that defines specific movements for the giraffe.

NECKORIENTATION is an array of three vectors defining the orientation of the neck that is divided in three parts.

The giraffe is modelized as it follows:

head..................box
neck..................serie of circular cones
thigh.................truncated elliptic cone
knee-cap..............sphere
foreleg...............cylinder
hoof..................two revolution bodies
tail..................a cylinder and a truncated cone

Fig. 6 shows different giraffes.

4. ABSTRACT GRAPHICAL TYPES WITH HIDDEN FACES AND SHADING

Figures can be also defined by faces. Such an approach allows the user to manipulate and animate 3D objects with hidden faces and 3D shaded objects. In the type definition, line vector statements like moveabs or moverel are replaced by vertices and face statements. The programmer has to define the different vertices and how the faces are built and the different colors that are used. Gouraud [8] and Phong [9] shading can be selected. Hidden faces are processed by a scan-line algorithm.

5. ABSTRACT GRAPHICAL TYPES IN COMPUTER ANIMATION

DREAM FLIGHT [10] is a 3D computer animated film of fiction which was completely produced by computer. It is the story of a creature living on a planet and dreaming that he flies across space like a bird and arrives on earth. Typical scenes of the film are located in Paris and New York (Fig. 7-8) others show natural scenes such as the sea (Fig. 9), trees (Fig. 10) or birds. The film has been developed using the MIRA-3D programming language to create the objects or motions.

To explain how static and dynamic objects are constructed, we take the first scene of the film as an example.

In this scene, Hipi is sitting in a forest at night and throws stones into a small pond. Hipi sees a bird and imagines that he is flying like the bird. This scene involves dynamic objects like Hipi, the bird and the waves on the top of the water. It also involves several static objects: stones, trees, the pond, the horizon and the spherical sky with stars.

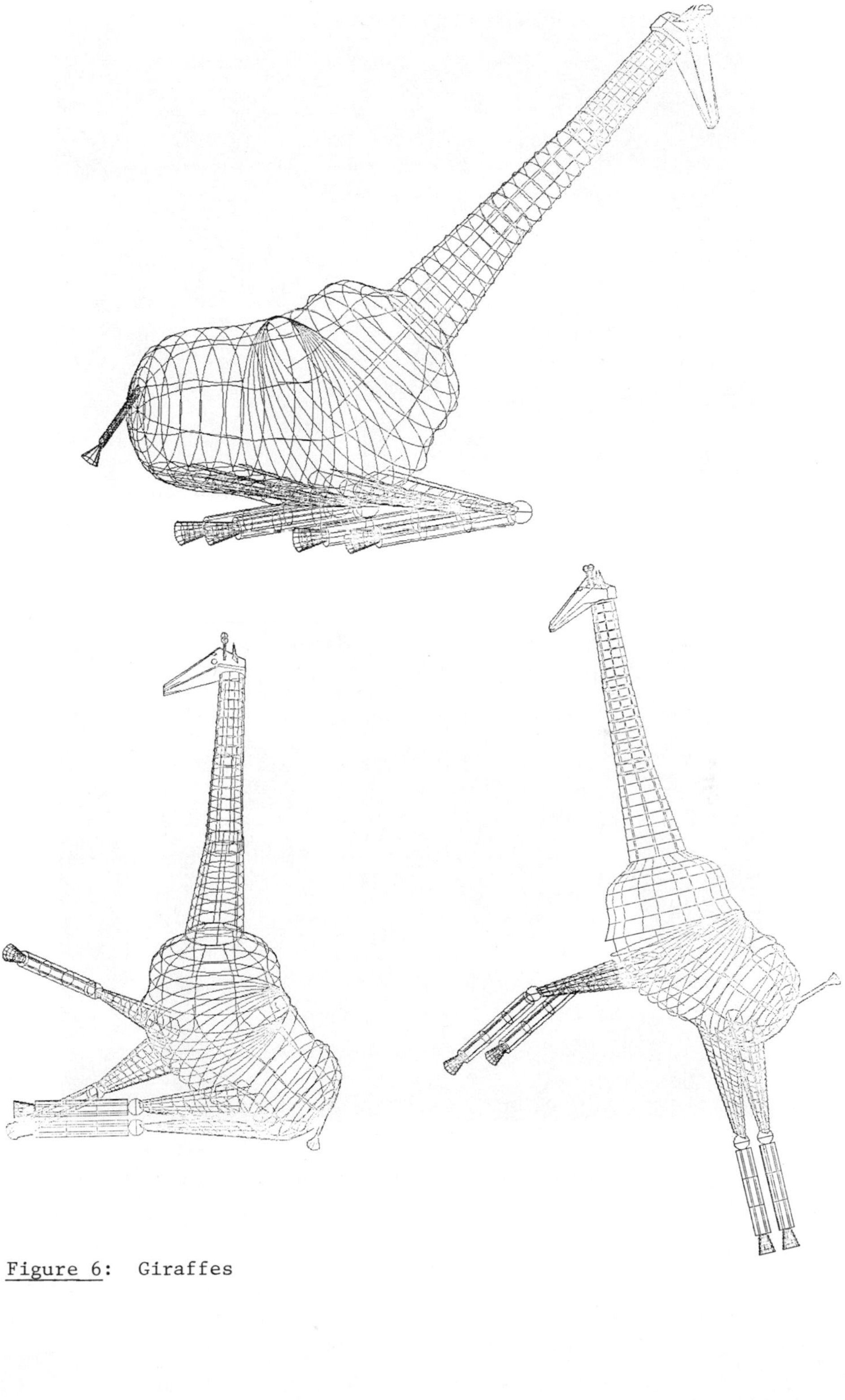

Figure 6: Giraffes

Figure 7: Arrival in New York

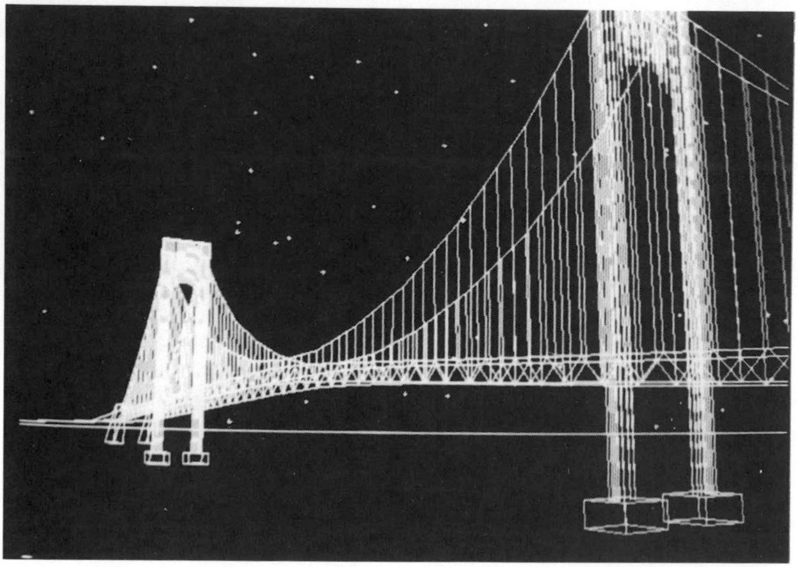

Figure 8: The Verrazano-Narrows Bridge

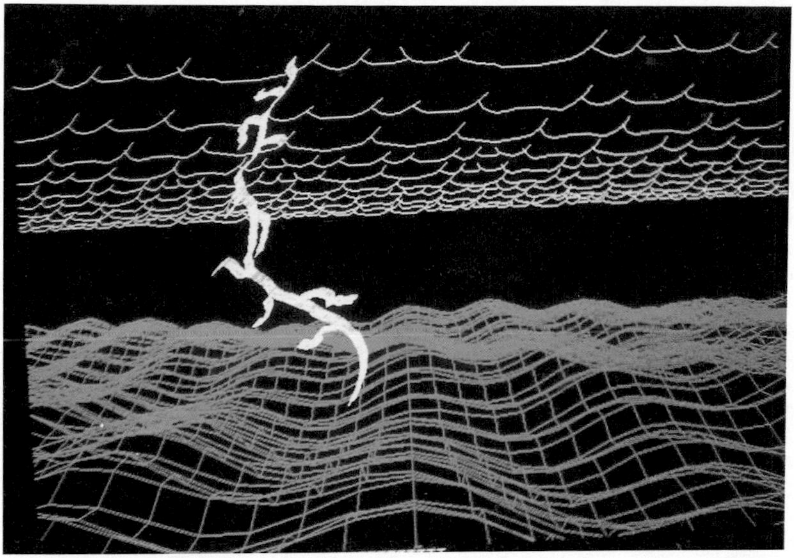

Figure 9: A thunderstorm

Figure 10: Sitting in a forest

A bird is represented by an abstract graphical type

```
type BIRD = figure (FRAME:INTEGER; H:HALFBODY; W:WING; C,D:VECTOR);
```

where H is the right halfbody, W the right wing, C the rotation center of the right wing and D the direction of rotation of this wing. As the right wing always starts in the maximal vertical position, it is only necessary to determine the angle of rotation downwards. This angle depends on the frame. We use for this a rotation with the acceleration/decelaration law. Figure 11 shows an excerpt of the code which is executed when a variable of BIRD type is created.

In this code, CYCLE is the number of frames required to make one wing flap up and down; FRAME is the current frame number; BETA is the rotation angle of the wing; ANGLEMAX is the maximum angle and FRAC the phase fraction. For example a bird is created and drawn according the following sequence:

```
procedure DRAWBIRD (FRAME:INTEGER);
var FIRSTBIRD:BIRD;
begin
   create FIRSTBIRD (FRAME, RIGHTBODY, RIGHTWING, C, D);
   translation (FIRSTBIRD, <<0, 0, FRAME * BIRDSTEP>>, FIRSTBIRD);
   draw FIRSTBIRD;
   delete FIRSTBIRD;
end;
```

The parameters in the <u>create</u> statement correspond to the parameters in the definition of the BIRD type.

Trees are also described by 3D graphical types:

```
type TREE = figure (var BRANCHES:TEXT; NBRANCHES:INTEGER);
                    POSITION:VECTOR; HEIGHT, LENGTH:REAL);
```

where BRANCHES is a file of kinds of branches, NBRANCHES is the number of branches, POSITION is the position of the trunk, HEIGHT is the height of the trunk and LENGTH the length of the branches.

A forest can be defined by the following declaration:

```
var FOREST: array [1..NBTREES] of TREE
```

6. TIMEVARYING ABSTRACT GRAPHICAL TYPES

To write a script (a program in an animation language), abstract graphical types like figures are very useful, but they don't have their own animation. For this reason, we have designed timevarying abstract graphical types. These types are called <u>actors</u> and variables of these types are only put into action during the animation loop. Fig. 12 shows an example of an actor type. It defines a square that is animated between the times T1 and T2. One vertex moves into the direction of the center with a constant speed V.

```
TYPE
  BIRD=FIGURE(FRAME:INTEGER; H:HALFBODY; W:WING; C,D:VECTOR);
      VAR
         RELATIVE:0..CYCLE;
         FRACTION,
         BETA    :REAL;
         W2      :WING;
         RIGHTPART,
         LEFTPART:FIG;
      BEGIN
        RELATIVE:=FRAME MOD CYCLE;
        IF RELATIVE > (CYCLE DIV 2) THEN
            RELATIVE:=CYCLE-RELATIVE;
        FRACTION:=(RELATIVE*2)/CYCLE;
        BETA:=LAW(ACCEDECE,ANGLEMAX,FRACTION);
        ROTATION(W,C,BETA,D,W2);
        UNION(H,W2,RIGHTPART);
        DELETE H,W2;
        SYMYZ(RIGHTPART,LEFTPART);
        INCLUDE RIGHTPART,LEFTPART
      END;
```

Figure 11: Excerpt of the BIRD type

```
TYPE
  STRANGESQUARE=ACTOR(A,B,C,D:VECTOR);
                TIME T1..T2;
                TYPE
                  TVEC=ANIMATED VECTOR(P1,P2:VECTOR);
                         VAL P1..P2;
                         TIME T1..T2;
                         LAW P1+V*(CLOCK-T1)
                       END;
                VAR VERTEX:VECTOR;
                BEGIN
                  INIT VERTEX(C,(A+C)/2);
                  MOVEABS A;
                  LINEABS B,VERTEX,D,A
                END;
```

Figure 12: An actor type

The moving vertex is defined as a "timevarying vector", the initial and the final positions are assigned by the <u>init</u> statement that is only executed when the actor is started. These timevarying abstract graphical types are now being introduced in MIRA-3D with other concepts like <u>decor</u> and <u>shoot</u> statements. Fig. 13 shows an excerpt of the BIRD actor type. Instead of the procedure DRAWBIRD shown in section 4, a bird has only to be initialized by the statement:

<u>init</u> <u>actor</u> FIRSTBIRD (H, W, C, D, 10, 16)

The bird is started at the time 10 and stopped at the time 16. Frames of animation are produced automatically and the bird can be synchronized with other actors.

7. CONCLUSION

Because of the three-dimensional abstract graphical types, MIRA-3D is a very powerful tool for developing structured graphics programs. It also offers the advantages of PASCAL, GSPC and all the other graphical features. The system is reliable and may be easily moved to another environment. MIRA-3D has been used for a certain number of applications, including a three-dimensional general-purpose interactive graphical editor and a three-dimensional computer animation film. In this latter case, the language provides us a powerful tool to generate patterns or movements that would not be possible with conventional animation or key-frame systems. Different examples of three-dimensional graphical types are used in this film. Hidden faces and shading have been also introduced in MIRA-3D. New developments in timevarying abstract graphical types have an important impact in computer animation.

8. ACKNOWLEDGEMENTS

This work was supported by the Natural Sciences and Engineering Research Council of Canada and the "Ministère de l'Education du Québec".

REFERENCES

[1] Jensen, K. and Wirth, N., "PASCAL User Manual and Report", Springer-Verlag, 1974.

[2] Guttag, J. "Abstract Data Types and the Development of Data Structures", Comm. ACM, Vol. 20, Nr. 6, 1977.

[3] Thalmann, D. and Magnenat-Thalmann, N., "Design and Implementation of Abstract Graphical Data Types", Proc. COMPSAC '79, Chicago, IEEE Press, pp. 519-524.

[4] Magnenat-Thalmann, N. and Thalmann, D., "A Graphical PASCAL Extension Based on Graphical Types", Software - Practice and Experience, vol. 11, 1981, pp. 53-62.

[5] Magnenat-Thalmann, N., and Thalmann, D. "Some Unusual Primitives in the MIRA Graphical Extension of PASCAL" Computers and Graphics, Pergamon Press, vol. 6, no 3, 1982, pp. 127-139.

[6] Committee of ACM/SIGGRAPH, "Status Report of the Graphic Standards Planning Committee of ACM/SIGGRAPH", Computer Graphics, 1979.

[7] Bergeron, R.D. et al., "Graphics Programming Using the Core System", Computing Surveys, ACM, 10 (1978) 4, pp. 389-444.

[8] Gouraud, H. "Continuous Shading of Curved Surfaces", IEEE Transactions on Computers", C-20 (6), 1971, pp. 623-628.

[9] Phong B.T. "Illumination for Computer Generated Pictures", Comm. ACM., Vol. 18, No 6, 1975, pp. 311-317.

[10] Thalmann, D. et al. "Dream Flight: A Fictional Film Produced by 3D Computer Animation", Proc. Computer Graphics '82, London, Online Conf., 1982, pp.352-367.

```
TYPE
  BIRD=ACTOR(H:HALFBODY; W:WING; C,D:VECTOR; T1,T2:REAL);
       TIME T1..T2;
       TYPE
         ANG=ANIMATED REAL;
               VAL 0..ANGLEMAX;
               TIME T1..T2;
               LAW ACCDEC(...)
             END;
         POS=ANIMATED VECTOR;
               VAL ORIGIN..UNLIMITED;
               TIME T1..T2;
               LAW BIRDSTEP*BIRDSPEED
             END;
       VAR
         TRANS      :POS;
         BETA       :ANG;
         W2         :WING;
         RIGHTPART,
         LEFTPART   :FIG;
       BEGIN
         INIT TRANS;
         INIT BETA;
         ROTATION(W,C,BETA,D,W2);
         UNION(H,W2,RIGHTPART);
         DELETE H,W2;
         SYMYZ(RIGHTPART,LEFTPART);
         INCLUDE RIGHTPART,LEFTPART
       END;
```

Figure 13: Excerpt of the BIRD actor type

3 DIMENSIONAL RECONSTRUCTION
A CASE STUDY OF A PERSPECTIVE PROBLEM

Judson Rosebush
Ditigal Effects, Inc.
321 West 44 Street
New York, NY 10036
U. S. A.

David Kushner*
Computer Math Inc.
98 Cuttermill Rd.,
Rm. 484, Great Neck, NY
11021, U. S. A.

One of the recurrent problems of computer graphics deals with perspective. The "forward solutions," that is the determination of a perspective projection or image from a 3D environment, has been known in the western world since the time of the ancient Greeks. The "backwards solutions," that is the reconstruction of a 3D environment from a projection or projections is a problem which is only solvable in certain cases.

Perspective drawing was known to the ancients and was a tool of the entertainment industry then as now. Perhaps the first recorded use of perspective is in the stage settings of Agatharcus, used by Aeschylus in presenting a tragedy (White, 1958). Vitruvius covered perspective in his book, De Architectura (23-25 BC). The artists of the Renaissance rediscovered perspective, possibly for wood inlay or intarsia (Tormey, 1982). Early writers include Alberti (1446), Ubaldo (1600), Desargues, Durer and Taylor (1715). As a branch of mathematics projective geometry evolved during the eighteenth century because of the needs of artists, engineers and scientists. In the nineteenth century Arthur Cayley formalized projective geometry using matrix notation.

The calculation of perspective in computer graphics follows much the same formulation as that used in traditional Renaissance perspectives. The pioneering work of Coons (1967) on digital graphics remains a standard reference.

The undoing of perspective, that is, the reconstruction of 3D environments from perspective projections requires that a certain amount of information be known about the 3D environment itself. The literature on this subject includes Burton (1973), Sutherland (1974) and a section in Rogers and Adams (1976).

Oftentimes, in computer graphics practice the information we are given is inadequate for a solution to be determined, or it does not contain enough precision for an accurate solution. A typical approach is for a computer animator to add information based upon common sense, aesthetic considerations, or rectifications. These solutions are customized for the application, and are based upon considerations unique to a problem.

Perhaps a case history of how we tackled and solved a "reconstruction" problem for a recent piece of computer animation provides an example of this process. The result is a generic solution for a special kind of problem.

ILLUSTRATION 1

We considered several solutions. Rotoscoping of action would not provide necessary precision. Our usual method of production--to create a synthetic road in 3D space and project it to 2D space provided no assurance the geometries would lock together. Witness tracking equipment to obtain camera positions was unavailable, and although a Burton style reconstruction was possible, we suspected the nature of the problem lent itself to a simpler solution.

Our conclusion was to employ a hybrid technique, one which employed defining a regular road grid in the original environment (but without measuring its relationship to an origin or camera position), digitizing a few selected points of the grid as it appeared in the photographic image, and then calculating the entire road directly--not reconstructing it in 3D space and projecting it, but calculating it as a 2D projection only. The nucleus of this procedure is an algorithm to calculate equal perspective intervals on a plane given the vanishing point, and two points on the image.

First, a grid was laid out on the set consisting of equally spaced squares. Illustration 2 is one of the sequence of motion picture frames of this scene.

ILLUSTRATION 2

The second step was to project each 35mm frame onto a coordinate table and digitize the vanishing point, along with two point pairs on each side of the road--point pairs that were visible on each frame throughout the duration of the shot. This is shown in Illustration 3.

ILLUSTRATION 3

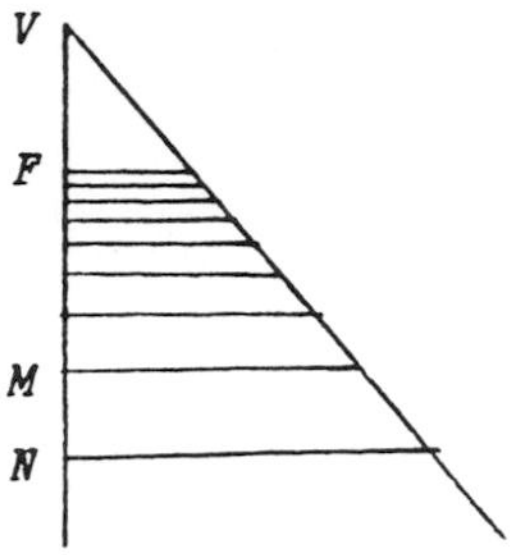

In Illustration 3 we call the point on the horizon, the vanishing point, V. We give it the coordinate (0), the origin. The point nearest to the camera (and always in the shot) we call N, and the next point away, we call M. These two points, along with V, are digitized. Our goal is to generate a complete sequence of coordinates for points going away from the camera to some arbitrary far point, F, or possibly to generate additional points that approach the camera.

Illustration 4 looks at the problem from the side.

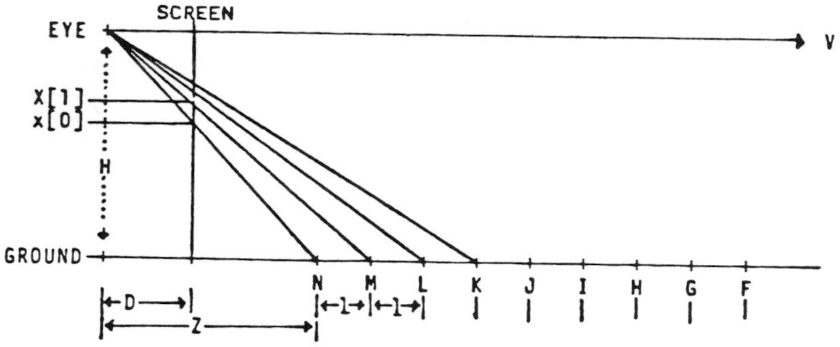

ILLUSTRATION 4

Notice that there are many cases of similar right triangles; in similar traingles the ratio of the legs are equal, in particular:

$$\frac{X[0]}{D} = \frac{H}{Z}, \text{ and } \frac{X[1]}{D} = \frac{H}{Z+1}$$

This formula can be rearranged and generalized. Using Iverson's (APL) notation:

$$(HxD) = X[I] \times (Z+I)$$

If we first solve for Z and HxD, we can then solve for any point,

$$(1) \quad X[I] = (HxD) \div (Z+I)$$

It is simple to find Z and HxD knowing X[0] and X[1], for we only have to solve three equations in three unknowns. The other two equations are:

$$(2) \quad (HxD) = X[0] \times Z$$

$$(3) \quad (HxD) = X[1] \times (Z+1)$$

Rearranging equations (2) and (3) so as to eliminate HxD,

$$X[1] = Z \times (X[0] - X[1])$$

or

$$Z = X[1] \div (X[0] - X[1])$$

Substituting equation (2) for (HxD) in equation (1),

$$X[I] = X[0] \times Z \div (Z+I)$$

Thus by direct definition we construct our algorithm.

```
POINTS: ω[0]×Z÷α+Z←ω[1]÷ω[0]-ω[1]
```

Where α is a vector of the sequence of points we want to solve for; the first point is N, the second point is M, etc. And ω is the Y coordinates of the two nearest points. This formula generates the coordinates of the sequence of points.

The results of this calculation may be seen in Illustration 5. This calculation is applied for each frame, that is V, N and M are digitized for each frame and the sequence is expanded. It is also possible for us to vary the technique and to widen the road, change the basic vertical interval, and install horizontal lines.

ILLUSTRATION 5

This solution provided us with a relatively smooth piece of animation that matched the original closely--much more so than a test in which we had rotoscoped and digitized all the points. A final operation was to presmooth the sequence of digitized points (V, N, and M) prior to the direct perspective calculation using a weighted average. This provided an excellent and convincing match. The car was inserted using traditional matte photography.

The director for the computer animation at Digital Effects was Jerry Kleiser. Animator was Donald Leich. Andrea D'Amico of ArtEfx, New York prepared mattes and artwork for digitization. Opticals were done by EFX, New York. The commercial director was Enrico Sannia, cinematography by Vittorio Storaro; the production company was Recta Films, Rome, and the client Opel.

Adler, Irving, A New Look at Geometry, The John Day Company, New York, 1966.

Aleksandrov, A. D., "Non-Euclidean Geometry," in Mathematics: Its Contents, Methods, and Meaning, the M.I.T. Press, Cambridge.

Coolidge, Julian Lowell, A History of Geometrical Methods, Dover Publications, 1963.

Coons, Steven A., "Transformations and Matrices," M.I.T., Boston, 1967.

Efimov, N. V., Higher Geometry, MIR Publishers, Moscow, 1980.

Eves, Howard, A Survey of Geometry, Allyn and Bacon, Boston, 1972.

Iverson, Kenneth E., Elementary Analysis, APL Press, Swarthmore, 1976.

Rogers, David F. and J. Alan Adams, Mathematical Elements for Computer Graphics, McGraw-Hill, New York, 1976.

Seidenberg, A., Lectures in Projective Geometry, D. Van-Nostrand Company, Princeton, 1962.

Sutherland, Ivan, "Three-Dimensional Data Input by Tablet," Proceedings of IEEE, April 1974. Reprinted in Kellogg S. Booth, Tutorial: Computer Graphics, IEEE Computer Society, Long Beach, California, 1979.

Taylor, Brook, Principles of Linear Perspective, 1715.

Tormey, Alan and Judith Farr Tormey, "Renaissance Intarsia: The Art of Geometry," Scientific American, New York, July 1982.

White, John, The Birth and Rebirth of Pictorial Space, Thomas Yoseloff, New York, 1958.

---

*Present Address

CBS Inc.
51 West 52 Street
New York, NY 10018

EXTENDED MEMORY USE IN THE ZGRASS GRAPHICS SYSTEM

Thomas A. DeFanti
University of Illinois at Chicago
Department of EECS
Box 4348 Chicago, IL 60680, U.S.A.

Computing has always been faced with the choice of optimizing for time (computer power) or space (memory). Real-time computer graphics is most likely the subset of computing that must choose between space and time most effectively. This paper describes in detail the evolved techniques of software memory management used by the Zgrass system to allow a slow (1.7mhz) Z-80 to be the processor for a useful computer animation workstation with at least 300K and up to 1472K bytes of memory. Conclusions will be drawn as to the applicability of these techniques to the new 16-bit microprocessors with memory management.

Background

The system being described here is formally called the Datamax UV-1. Since its software is called Zgrass, an earlier version of which is described in [1], we will refer to it as the Zgrass system. It actually started as a home computer graphics system in 1977 and later, after having been rebuilt for the cable television industry, became an artist's workstation for video production. The Zgrass system was developed to make people want to program by providing rich animated feedback with few initial barriers, yet give the user the ability to unravel layers upon layers of built-in sophistication when and if the desire arose. Rather extensive testing of the software has occurred at the University of Illinois at Chicago and the School of the Art Institute of Chicago where hundreds of art and engineering students have used it for the past several years and about 100 systems exist at this point. It is a system that encourages the writing of software tools as extensions to the command language and it makes possible the performance of real-time interactive visuals. Most of the systems are used by artists most of whom have become programmers over the years.

Difficulties of the Z-80

In 1977, the Z-80 was a rather advanced chip compared to the 8080, but in 1983, it is considered slow and primitive. In 1977, 64K bytes of memory was the limit for a personal computer; today we talk of megabyte ones. In 1977, one was lucky to have a macro assembler and a linking loader that worked. Now, assembler coding may be largely abandoned for programming in C.

The Zgrass Custom Chips

A research effort at Dave Nutting Associates, a division of Bally Corporation, produced in 1976 several custom integrated circuits to assist the Z-8Ø in making real-time color video at 32Øx2Ø1x2 bits per pixel resolution. A 1.7mhz Z-8Ø, of course, can barely do more by itself than drive the terminal this paper is being written on if it has to generate video. These custom chips which have been used in several coin-operated video games are still in production and were the basis for the home system called the Bally Arcade. The chips have the distinct advantage that they form a true bit-mapped frame-buffer and generate rather good NTSC video, a rarity in personal graphics systems then and now. These chips were very closely tied into the Z-8Ø so the development of Zgrass was locked in to both the chips and the Z-8Ø as well. Some 2Ø,ØØØ lines of assembler code had been written, so going to a faster processor was not possible; faster Z-8Ø's would not work with the custom chips. Thus, the only reasonable way to improve performance was to expand memory.

At the time of the BYTE article (198Ø), the Zgrass system had 16K of ROM, 16K of screen RAM, and 32K of user RAM. The ROM, later expanded to 32K, holds system code so the machine can run without booting anything from disk. The screen RAM uses 32 chips so it can be accessed 32 bits at a time in parallel to generate the video signal. The 32K user RAM is used for user programs, subpictures (called SNAPs), arrays, and so on. It is dynamically allocated and reclaimed in 4K or less blocks according to a highly tuned best fit algorithm. 32K is not much space for SNAPs, arrays and programs so the disk software was designed to be more or less an extension of user RAM.

Inexpensive 5" floppy disks are slow, however. The one we chose takes four seconds to go from track Ø to track 76. The use of the disk to store software tools and SNAPs works well but is slow since the disk has to seek quite often. Even winchester-type disks, although 2Ø times faster, still do an unfortunate amount of seeking. Since we were using the disk as extended RAM, it was an obvious step to load the disk into RAM and fetch out of it, so we did it. Of course, the Z-8Ø does not have memory management so the hardware was built rather straightforwardly and the software provided the flexibility needed.

The Current Memory Architecture of Zgrass

The system now supports 32K of ROM, 256K of screen RAM, 32K of user RAM and up to 576K of EPROM or 1152K of ROM. (An additional 32K of RAM is used to support a 64K CP/M (CP/M is a trademark of Digital Research, Inc.) system but it is not accessed by Zgrass so it will not be further discussed.) All the extra memory added is mapped into the address range 16-32K so that it can be accessed by the custom chips.

The custom chips have special features which are enabled by addressing the screen during writes to memory Ø-16K instead of 16-32K. Since there is always ROM at Ø-16K, this is not a waste of addressing space. When a write goes to Ø-16K, the data is manipulated by the chips according to an 8-bit value held in what the designers call "the magic register." The bits in the register, which you set by writing to a port, specify two extremely useful operations between the new data and the data on the screen: logical or and logical xor. They also allow the data to be shifted Ø, 1, 2, or 3 pixels before writing to the screen. The shifter is critical to the implementation of animations since pixels are packed four to a byte (2 bits/pixel) and laying a pattern down on non-byte boundaries would otherwise require pitifully slow shifting, masking and writing of each pixel in Z-8Ø machine instructions. The shifter does read-modify-writes and all the masking to make transfers to memory with shifts as fast as the logical function writes. Straight access to screen memory can be done by addressing 16-32K. Of course, reads from Ø-16K yeild instructions and data from the system ROM.

In the middle of 1981, memory prices dropped on 64K bit RAMs. Since we had 32 sockets for screen memory anyway, it was simple to modify the system to accept 32 64K bit RAMs to give 256K bytes of screen RAM. The difference in cost is about $2ØØ.ØØ. Changing the amount of memory by 16 times in any system profoundly affects its performance. The subject of this paper is describing just how profound the change is.

(Just for completeness, the second 16K of the 32K system ROM also overlaps the addresses 16-32K. The code in that 16K is constrained to never read or write screen RAM. All the graphics code is in the lower 16K or loaded into the RAM located at 32-64K.)

Keep It Obvious and Friendly

One of Zgrass's main tenets is "keep it obvious." Computer hardware tends to be devious and clever so keeping it obvious requires an astonishing amount of creative thought, testing and reworking. Yet, flexibility is also a primary goal, one more important to the user with a task at hand than anything else. Before explaining how the extra memory is used in detail, let us state it briefly:

The 256K of screen RAM can be used for:

a. sixteen screens, switchable instantaneously
b. four screens plus 192K disk cache
c. four screens plus panorama screen(s)

"Keeping it obvious" allows one to provide flexibility even if it is forced to be idiosyncratic by the hardware. Zgrass implements special device variables which are always set to default values on startup but may be altered by the user when the feature the variable specifies is needed. Specific to this discussion, $MW indicates on which screen of 16 the writes should be (e.g. $MW=5 means write on screen 5). $TV is set to the screen you wish to view on the television monitor. Clearly, you can be modifying one screen while viewing another, easily implementing double or even 16-buffered schemes. Thus, with a procedure not much different from changing the channel on a television set, users can have easy access to 256K of screen RAM. $MW and $TV are taken modulo 16 normally. However, when disk cache or panorama modes (b. and c. above) are enabled, $MW is taken modulo 4 to prevent accidental destruction of data.

The Disk Cache

The disk cache is setup by the DLOAD command which reads a whole floppy disk side into 12 of the 16 screens. Both floppies and winchester-type disks are formatted into 192K byte logical units comprised of 384 512-byte sectors. After DLOAD'ing, all subsequent reads and writes to that logical disk actually go to the cached memory. DLOAD.ZAP writes the disk back out again. The disk cache eliminates all seek time and transfers programs, arrays, SNAPs, and so on at memory to memory speeds (80K bytes/second at 1.7mhz clock rates). Of course, a disk file structure is not the optimal way to use RAM, but it has the distinct advantage that the modifications to the system to increase the user's RAM by sixfold only required a small amount of code to be added. More important though, the user has no problem understanding the disk cache, can move easily from a 16-screen system to a 4-screen system with disk cache. Furthermore, user backup is easy to do. If the 256K memory had been available when the system was designed in 1977, a different scheme might have been used, although given that the screen RAM is constrained by hardware to contain only data (the Z-80 cannot execute code out of it), the 256K memory would need special treatment anyway.

With the disk cache, a rather elaborate paint program was written in Zgrass by Copper Giloth to enable artists to draw and animate. The numerous modules are loaded and executed without perceptible delay based on menu choices of the user. Animations occupying about 1/4 the screen can be easily animated at 20 times a second.

Panoramas

The third option for using the screen memory is by building panoramas. This option was designed and implemented by Stephen Joyce, the author of most of the graphics code in Zgrass. The BUILD command allocates some or all of the last 12 screens as one or more "super screen." One can specify a single 3x4, 4x3, 1x12, 12x1, 6x2 or 2x6 super screen. A 3x4 super screen, for example, has dimensions 960x804, given that each screen is 320x201. Or, you can have several smaller super screens like two 2x3's or six 1x2's for example. The

DISPLAY command which ordinarily places SNAPs anywhere on any screen has an option to use a super screen instead of a SNAP as the source. The data is clipped to either the whole current screen (as specified by $MW) or a subset of the current screen set by the WINDOW command. Thus, a large image like a map may be viewed through a 320x201 or smaller window and you can roam around quite easily and quickly. SCALE is a command that works like DISPLAY except that it allows shrinking or expanding of the data while writing to the current screen. The PLACE command stores rectangular areas of the current screen on a super screen.

Following the next section on EPROM/ROM disks, an attempt will be made to justify which of these memory structures make sense in a system with lots of memory (like 68000's, PDP-11's and Z-8000's with memory management). Zgrass, of course, is an experiment in inexpensive graphics technology for personal access by artists and educators and, in such, provides many lessons to the designer of a new system.

EPROM/ROM Disks

The Zgrass system is ideal for the cable-tv operator who desires graphics better than those offered by teletext systems. Zgrass in this mode acts like a remote character generator with animation capability. Several problems had to be solved for this application, however. First, a suitable way to send commands and data had to be designed so that human operators would not be needed. This was not very difficult and was quickly done. Second, rotating memories like disks are simply not rugged enough for the environment of a cable head end block house. Cable TV equipment is designed for negligible downtime so a disk without moving parts had to be designed. Clearly, mass chip memory was the only answer.

The EPROM/ROM disk is configured as a board with 24 8K byte EPROMs (one 192K disk image) or 24 16K byte ROMs (two 192K disk images). For hardware simplicity, the maximum number of boards is three so a total of 576K EPROM or 1152K ROM may be installed. Picking 192K as the logical size once again allows the user to fully debug the package on a floppy, winchester-type or cache disk before committing to EPROM or ROM. Once the application is ready, it is a simple matter to transfer the whole disk to EPROM using a conventional EPROM programmer. ROM's, of course, have a much more involved manufacturing process. Once again, adding support for the EPROM/ROM disk required only a tiny increment in code given that this memory also resides in pages at the 16-32K address space.

Thus, it may be observed that this modest Z-80 system may be configured to have up to 1472K bytes of memory, all but 48K of it mapped into 16K pages at 16-32K.

Applicability to 16-Bit Systems

The Zgrass community eagerly awaits a higher-resolution system. A 640x480 screen requires 38,400 bytes/bit plane. To maintain the animation speed, a much faster processor is needed. Fortunately, Z-8000's, 68000's and PDP-11 chips are fast enough and also allow development of the software in the C language. Current work is proceeding on a VAX in simulation mode for several types of graphic display units. Faced at this point with a total re-design, what is worth keeping?

Without a doubt, the EPROM/ROM disk is a good idea. Rotating memories are simply unacceptable in poor environments where low-cost graphics may be needed. The EPROM disk is also quite a bit cheaper and much faster than disk drives. Its maintenance-free, operator-less operation is very desirable. It also fits right into a card rack using available power. These benefits, of course, are recognized by home video game manufacturers who supply software on ROM cartridges.

The disk cache is also a transferable concept. Creative users of a programmable system have no trouble dealing with disk files, if only to facilitate creation of libraries of software tools and images. Having disk images execute out of memory saves time and considerable wear on the mechanics of the disk drives.

The panorama idea also has validity in higher-resolution systems. Hardware support for choosing the window would be desirable so roaming around a large database could be done in real-time. Hardware scaling would also be quite useful.

User main memory, limited to 32K in the current Zgrass, should be much larger, in fact, expansion to any affordable size should be automatically supported. The current memory allocation and reclamation schemes are quite usable, however, and work well enough to be modified for much larger memory spaces.

It is also clear that multiple screens are important. Two screens allow double buffering; more allow animation. Although 16 have been very effective in Zgrass, a new system should provide for as many as the user can afford to buy. Five seconds of full animation at 12 screens per second (the speed of conventional animation on two's) requires 60 screens. Of course, at a resolution of 640x480x8 bits/pixel, 60 screens require 18 megabytes of memory. High resolution has its price, although, at current costs, 18 megabytes is not out of the range of studio broadcast television equipment.

Conclusions

This paper has narrowed its focus to memory paging techniques found useful in extending a Z-80-based graphics system to fully utilize a large memory space in a user-friendly way. Many of the techniques are directly applicable and desirable in systems having much greater memory addressing capability. Working on a small, low-resolution animation system with extensive memory has given insight into how to design higher-resolution workstations for artists, and much practice with delivery systems in situations applicable to videogames, interactive movies, education, public information displays and conventional television.

Reference:

[1] DeFanti, Thomas A., "Language Control Structures for Easy Electronic Visualization," Byte, Vol. 5, No. 11, November 1980, pp. 90-104.

Chapter 6
Graphic Applications

AUTOMATED CARTOGRAPHY

Allan H. Schmidt

Harvard University
199 Cambridge Turnpike
Concord, Mass. 01742
U. S. A.

SUMMARY

The preparation and use of maps has a long and remarkable history. However, during the last 20 years computer technology has begun to introduce major changes not only into the preparation of maps but also their use.

Part I of this paper begins with a brief description of the various applications of maps in terms of their uses and users. Part II sketches the procedures and resources traditionally involved in preparing a map. Part III discusses automated cartography objectives, processes and technological resources. Part IV concludes with comments regarding trends in the supply of and demand for computer generated maps in relation to data availability, new technologies, and future uses of maps.

I. Mapping Applications - Uses and Users.

Major categories of mapping applications include (1) geographic reference, (2) natural resource exploration and management, (3) land improvement, construction, and facilities management, and (4) analysis and display of economic and demographic data.

The use of maps as sources of information for geographic reference is their oldest and most fundamental use. Navigation maps are an example of geographic reference maps whether for use on land, water, or in the air. Other examples include geodetic and topographic maps which are used to record locational information required in the preparation of special purpose maps.

Natural resource exploration and management activities require the use of maps as an aid in locating, managing, and productively using natural resources for commercial as well as public purposes. Examples of such users include governmental agencies responsible for public land management and environmental protection programs as well as commercial firms involved in mineral or energy extraction as well as wood and paper production. Because of the small scale and high density of information, maps for these purposes are increasingly in the form of, or derived from, satellite imagery and aerial photographs. Climatological maps which contain data concerning air pressure, temperature, wind direction and velocity, precipitation, and cloud cover also can be considered natural resource maps.

Maps used for land development involving engineering, construction and facilities maintenance are necessarily at a much larger scale (smaller geographic area) than those used for natural resource exploration and management. Land development maps frequently include elevation contours to allow for terrain analysis and estimates of land movement (cut and fill), as well as vegetation, geologic, and hydrologic data which would affect construction activities. Construction maps record the location and type of man-made improvements built on or beneath the earth's surface. Land development activities within an urbanized area frequently involve preparation of engineering maps which include descriptions of public utility equipment such as telephone, electric, gas, and water lines. Such maps are essential not only for construction but also subsequent maintenance of these facilities. A related map use is as part of public records for land ownership. Land ownership maps supplement legal written descriptions of land boundaries. These maps are provided by land surveyors and assist in the identification of land boundaries for the property owner, land developer, builder, and tax assessor.

The analysis and display of economic or demographic data is another category of map use. Such maps are referred to as thematic maps because they are used to represent the geographic distribution of one or a small number of specific topics or 'themes.' Alternatively, a general reference map, such as would be found in a general purpose atlas, will usually contain numerous topics on the same map. Thematic maps are of growing interest for use in commercial market research as well as in governmental planning activities. They are used in a manner similar to that of military maps, that is they allow for the identification of problems or opportunities of interest to commercial firms or a governmental agency and provide a valuable source of information for assessing the effectiveness of current allocations of resources and assisting in the determination of where resources should be allocated in the furure.

II. Map Production

Preparation of a map involves the combination of several kinds of information. These include (1) locational data which provide a spatial reference frame and answer the question of "where," (2) geographic attribute data which describe various natural and cultural features or human activity patterns and answer the question "what," and (3) selection and placement of graphic symbols used to categorize and graphically portray geographic attribute data at their proper location on the map. When several different subjects are to be displayed on the same map, for example political boundaries, natural features, cultural features, and so forth, it is desirable to prepare a separate data base for each subject and then produce the final map as a layered composite of several different images for the same geographic area. The final product may be recorded as a graphic image on paper or film, displayed as a virtual image on a cathode ray tube, or saved as a digital data base for subsequent retrieval, manipulation, and display.

A. Locational Data.

1. Geodetic Control. Maps which accompany land records or are used in conjunction with land development activities must include reference to previously established ground control points. Such control points in the US are determined by the National Geodetic Survey and exist as monument markers with known latitude, longitude, and elevation. A local surveyor may then establish the position of other locations by measuring distance and direction from these known control points.

2. Boundaries. Political and administrative boundaries reflect regions of human activity and provide a geographic framework for partitioning a physical map, such as by nation or city. Federal, state, and local government

boundaries are well defined and provide not only location reference but also a regional definition for recording, analyzing, and reporting statistics regarding each region's economic and demographic characteristics.

3. Photogrammetry. Aerial photogrammetry provides a rapid and efficient means for acquiring graphic images of the earth's surface and are commonly used to produce maps. By use of multiple overlapping photographs and stereo triangulation devices, it is possible to establish precise x-y coordinate locations on the ground as well as their vertical elevation. Procedures used include the ability to correct for errors within the photos due to tilt, skew, and rotation of an airplane during the photographic process.

4. Map Projection. Although locational data may be recorded with great precision, the fact remains that the surface of the earth is curved whereas the surface on which a map is displayed is a flat piece of paper or film. The larger the geographic area the greater the curvature and therefore the greater the potential map distortion. Maps of small areas are relatively unaffected by such distortion. However, to correct for this distortion on a small scale (large area) map, geodetic coordinates are converted to rectangular cartesian coordinates by use of one of many possible map projection algorithms. The resulting map will not preserve true direction, shape, and equal area, but depending upon the projection chosen two of the three measurements may be preserved to varying degrees at specific locations on the map.

5. Map Scale. The scale of a map (the ratio of distance on the map to distance on the ground) is of critical importance in determining not only distortion introduced when projecting data describing a curved surface onto a flat surface, but also the information content of the final map. When a larger geographic area is included on a map of fixed size, it obviously becomes nessary to combine and generalize features on the map and delete detail. The relative precision of locations shown on a map also is reduced at small scales. It is for this reason that maps which are to be used for establishing or finding precise locations such as for engineering or construction purposes are at quite large scales. Conversely, for maps which are intended for navigation over long distances it is of greater importance to portray large areas on a relatively few map sheets and rely upon navigational markers to establish actual locations by visual or electronic means.

B. Geographic Attribute Data

Information which appears on a map typically is concerned with describing the earth's surface, physical features on or below the surface, or human activities which have ocurred at various locations.

1. Topography. The elevation or height of the earth's surface above sea level is typically shown on a map by use of contour lines, each of which describes a line of

constant elevation. The distance and value between each line may be used to estimate degree and direction of slope. Orientation and value of the lines also indicate the location of critical surface features such as peaks, pits, passes, pales, course lines, and ridge lines. Topographic maps also may be prepared as oblique views of three dimensional surfaces.

2. Natural and Cultural Features. Specific natural and man made physical features on or below the earth's surface may be included on a map to the extent that they serve a map's purpose or intended use. Natural features include not only topography, described above, but also rivers and streams, geologic and soil data, vegetation and wildlife, and other naturally occurring phenomena. Cultural features reflect the physical impact of human occupancy and include transport systems (roads, canals, railroads, airports, etc.) communication facilities, buildings, urbanized areas, agricultural areas, and so forth. The scale of a map will determine the detail possible and the intended use will influence the selection of features desirable for inclusion on a specific map.

3. Economic and Demographic Data. Information concerning human activity patterns typically represent measurements related to economic and demographic conditions and their change over time. Because such data is a description, or a measure of change for a group of individuals, it frequently cannot be represented on a map in the same manner as a physical object on the earth's surface. Due to the volume of data involved and the scale of a map, it is usually necessary to aggregate the data to a region prior to its display. The most common examples of such data is that collected by the US Census Bureau every 10 years concerning US population and housing. Numerous other governmental agencies also record data regarding their activities as does every commercial firm, for example concerning each customer, employee, and supplier. Since most such data includes street address and postal delivery (ZIP) code, it is necessary to aggregate the data to an area such as a city block, neighborhood, town, county, sales area, state, or other region appropriate to the purpose for which the data is to be interpreted.

C. Graphic Symbols and Conventions.

1. Position, Direction, and Scale. Position on a map is indicated by use of lines or tick marks which define x-y coordinates in terms of latitude and longitude, state plane coordinates, universal transverse mercator grid, or an abitrary grid imposed by the map maker. Orientation of a map has north at the top of the map by convention plus an arow or other symbol to point in the direction of true north. On maps intended for navigation, a second arrow will also be provided to indicate the direction of magnetic north, as would appear on a compass. The scale of a map may be given in one or more of three different ways. (1) A graphic measuring scale may be included with tick marks and numbers illustrating the ground

distance represented by the distance between tick marks on the map. (2) Comparable information may be provided by a statement which equates one inch or centimeter on the map with the equivalent ground distance in miles or kilometers. (3) A numerical ratio or fraction may be given which equates a unit length on the map with its equivalent distance in the same units on the ground.

2. Geographic Feature Symbols. The USGS is the primary governmental agency in the US responsible for creating and distributing cartographic products. The symbols which appear on a USGS map are used consistently for all USGS maps to describe geodetic, topographic, political, natural, and cultural features. Their topographic map series covers most of the US at a scale of 1:24,000 plus the remainder at 1:63,630 and is considered to be the standard reference maps series from which commercial and other governmental organizations produce other maps, such as for a city or state, at the the same or a smaller scale.

3. Thematic Map Symbols. In representing quantitative and qualitative information such as economic and demographic data on a thematic map, three basic types of symbols are used: dots of varying density, lines with various width and spacing, icons of various size and shape, and tones or color. The process of selecting symbols and assigning them to a set of quantitative data assumes that the data has been grouped into a number of classes or categories, each of which may then be represented by a specific graphic symbol. By limiting the number of different classes and therefore types of symbols, for example to 5 - 10, the data as displayed on the map has an opportunity to display spatial patterns which may be inherent in the data. Three dimensional symbolism also may be used to illustrate differences in quantitative values and eliminate the need for prior grouping of the data into a small number of classes. The resulting maps are usually more informative and have significant visual impact. However, it may be necessary to produce several such maps with views from different directions to fully examine the resulting data surface.

D. Graphic Media

For most applications, paper represents an economic and convenient media for recording, storing, and transporting maps. However, they are easily damaged and are unreliable if precise measurements are required due to paper's dimensional instability as a result of age and humidity.. For purposes of photographically reproducing a map, the dimensional stability and long life of Mylar and similar film materials make them superior to paper although at a higher cost. Film also allows for the superimposition of several different separation sheets to produce composite maps which retain their registration with one another.

III. Automated Cartography

A. Objectives.

The two major objectives of automated cartography are increased productivity and new utility. Increased productivity in the preparation of maps due to the use of automated cartography results for the reduction or total elimination of manual drafting operations and the substitution of electronic digitizing and computer generated graphic displays. The precision of computer graphic drawings, automated error detection capabilities, and associated standardization of procedures and therefore map products all contribute to the potential for an improved cartographic process and product. The greatest savings, however, result from the elimination of the need to redraw an entire map in order to incorporate revisions. The ability to maintain and continually reuse all or any part of a digital cartographic data base when adding new information is a significant savings over the continual redrafting of maps by manual methods.

New uses for maps result from the ability to manipulate a digital cartographic data base in a manner not posssible with purely graphic map products. Applications involving land subdivision design, land suitability studies, geological exploration, and commercial site location analyses involve the creation and interpretation of digital map products which go far beyond traditional capabilities and uses of manually prepared maps.

Automated cartography uses the capability of a computer to improve the productivity of cartographers responsible for the preparation of a broad range of map products such as those described in section I, above. In doing so, the traditional procedures and resources used in manual preparation of maps and described in section II, above, must be accomodated in a digital environment. The role of the cartographer as map designer becomes increasingly important in the process because although some traditional operations, such as redrafting of prior drawings are susceptible to automation, the increased range and application for which maps economically can be prepared creates many new opportunities for the use of maps. It also provides new tools and potential technical skills for professional cartographers. Although the changing role of cartographers is not an initial intent of automated cartography, it is a realistic result of the introduction of computers into cartography as it is into many other professions.

B. Process

1.Data Source Types. The primary sources from which cartographic data bases are prepared are either imagery, prior maps, or field notes. Imagery may be in a digital format such as a computer compatible tape obtained from remote sensing as with a satellite or a photographic image as with an aerial photograph. Alternatively, prior maps may exist as traditional prints on paper or film or in a digital format as a cartographic data base. Field notes include data obtained by a survey crew and could be used in either a digital or paper form depending upon the survey equipment used.

2. Graphic Encoding. Non-digital, graphic data sources such as maps or photographs are converted to a machine readable form by a digitizing process. Digitizing converts a graphic image into an equivalent numerical form which is recorded as a digital data base. The resulting data base may be organized either as a series of points and lines with x-y coordinate values for each vertex, or as a large matrix with a value for each cell. Point and line data bases are referred to as vector data bases. Matrix data bases are known as raster data bases to reflect the fact that they are usually processed sequentially by row, each row being contained in one raster of a cathode ray tube display. Raster data bases also may be used to produce vector data bases by extracting the point and line information which is implicit in an image recorded as a matrix of values.

Vector data bases are particularly well suited to applications where precise positional data is required, such as in land record or engineering maps. However, when geographic features are of primary concern, such as in natural resource exploration and land management, data is normally acquired in the form of an image stored in a raster data base.

3. Graphic Data Management. Creation of a digital cartographic data base implies use of the data base for more than a single point in time with associated maintenance and revision of the data. The data management activities involved necessarily require that the data be in a form and of a quality which will minimize costs of data management as well as subsequent retrieval, analysis, and display. As result, the data needs to be structured in a manner which allows individual components of the map to be added, deleted, or changed. In a vector data base, map components include point, line, and areal objects which have locational as well as categorical attributes. The ability and efficiency of data management becomes increasingly important as a cartographic data base grows in size and complexity. Retrieval and update operations require an efficient data base design which allows a data base to be accessed with flexiblity and efficiency. Flexibility includes the ability to construct, retrieve, and modify data for arbitrary geographic regions regardless of the map sheets which originally were used to define an arbitrary partitioning of geographic space. Efficiency requires that all such operations be possible quickly and with minimum computing resources and time.

4. Data Analysis. Automated cartography provides an ability to measure the current and potential future location and character of geographic features such as topography, natural resources, geology, land use, and socio-economic characteristics. Data which is aquired for several time periods

allow for time series analysis to detect and forecast change over time.

Topographic analysis includes determination of slope, aspect and orientation. Geolgic, soil, hydrologic, and vegetation data are also frequently included in studies of suitability of land for future use. Natural resource exploration for minerals, energy sources, and water are another example of applications which are heavily dependent upon the use of data derived from geographic data sources. Land management activities for natural resources in the public as well as the private sectors are using automated cartography to inventory, monitor, and develop timber, rangeland, recreation areas and agricultural resources.

Land records and related map products are being automated in several cities in a manner which will allow for the development of multi-purpose land data systems. Such systems have the potential for provididng substantial economies in the preparation and use of map products by numerous governmental and private organizations. Traditional development and use of map products by local governmental organizations involve substantial duplication of effort and exhibit a serious lack of standardization.

Similar capabilities are being develolped to support the creation of utility maps for one or more utility systems within a given metropolitan area. Such automated systems are capable of substantially improving the ability to create and maintain vital engineering drawings regarding the location and nature of a utility system's physical plant, both above and below ground. Given the description of a utility network, it also is possible to use that same data base in the context of a mathematical model to determine existing capacities and simulate future loading as well as to evaluate alternative modifications to the system in anticipation of changes in usage levels over time.

In the design of a new utility network, such as a cable television system, a schematic description of the network can be used to evaluate alternative routings and placement of specific components within the system to optimize and balance its performance. In this respect the use of network design tools appropriate for computer aided design of electronic circuits have their counterpart in the design of larger circuits, be they for electrical transmission, water systems, or highways.

5. Data Retrieval and Graphic Display. Computer graphic images are in themselves pictorial representations of numerical data. As a result, this data may be saved for subsequent use, either to produce additional computer graphic images of the entire file or of specific geographic "windows." Examples of subsets include an extracted region with the exterior deleted or a region with a smaller interior region blanked out. A superset would result from the combining of two or more data sets each obtained from a different map sheet but representing adjoining geographic regions.

In addition, a graphic data base may be updated to incorporate new information. Computer graphics also may be used to compare an original image with later information in order to detect the location and extent of changes that have occurred over time.

Although symbols are used to represent information visually on a computer generated map, the graphic symbols themselves need not be stored as part of a data base but may be defined as symbol tables in the computer software. The data base only would need to specify a location and its feature code. Text strings such as place names also may be displayed at specific sizes and with particular orientations which are determined at map display time rather than being prestored in the data base. This is particularly important for a data base used to produce maps at different scales or with different overlays of geographic features which may produce conflicts in symbol placement.

C. Hardware

1. Input Devices. Vector data bases are typically created by use of electronic digitizing devices. A map sheet is placed on a digitizing table and an operator traces the location of each line recording its x-y location ao individually selected points or as a stream of x-y coordinates. In addition to recording the geometry of each line, the operator also may use a keypad to enter an identifying code for each line along with other information such as the topolgical identifiers for end points plus left and right coboundary identifiers. Data produced by a digitizing device are stored on tape or disk for subsequent editing and organization prior to being stored as a data base.

Raster data bases normally are created using scanning devices which detect by optical sensors the reflectance of each x-y location on a map sheet as it passes through the scanning device. The resulting data is stored as a large matrix. However, for storage efficiency the matrix will normally be compacted by use of run length encoding or other techniques to reduce its size prior to being saved for future use.

Note that the above description of input device hardware assumes an initial map sheet which only contains black and white point, line, and area graphics. In practice maps are far more complex and include colors, special symbols, numbers and text strings as well. Such maps normally are the result of offset printing of several separation sheets, one for each color. Prior to its use with colored ink in a composite printing process, each separation sheet physicaly exists as a black and white drawing. Special symbols, numbers, and text strings also may be treated as separate data layers.

2. Central Processing Unit and Storage Media. Computing devices used for automated cartography tend to be of the 16 or 32 bit word length size due to the precision required for storing x-y coordinates plus the need to address large blocks of memory. Hard discs normally are used to store and

provide immediate access to cartographic data bases in active use. Magnetic tape serves as a backup or archival storage medium.

3. Cathode Ray Tube (CRT) Display Devices. Display devices used with automated cartography range from high resolution (4096 x 4096) vector storage tubes to medium resolution (512 x 512) raster refresh tubes. Applications requiring high resolution, real time displays, such as for air traffic control, would use vector refresh displays.

Color CRTs are particularly useful when several different types of information are to be displayed on the same image, in effect a color composite comparable to what might be produced by color separation plates in printing. However, on a color CRT opportunity exists to experiment with the visual interpretation resulting from use of different colors for a given set of data.

4. Paper or Film Hard Copy

The vast majority of automated cartography applications are intended to produce hard copy documents for subsequent interpretation and general use. These documents frequently will be larger than the image shown on a CRT screen and capable of containing more information. They may be produced on paper or film by pen plotters, laser plotters, ink jet plotters, electrostatic plotters, or any one of a variety of other computer driven drawing devices. In each case the resulting image may be in black or white or multicolored.

Photographic drawings also may be produced, essentially drawn with light on a photosensitive emulsion, from 35 mm to 24" x 36" or larger in size, as black and white or color images on paper or film.

D. Software and Data

1. Languages and Programs. The predominant language used for automated cartography is Fortran although other languages such as PL-1, APL, Pascal, and C are also used. The reason for Fortran's popularity reflects its common use in the scientific community plus the availability of standards. Input and output routines frequently are written in assembly language for greater efficiency.

The majority of automated cartography systems are sold as hardware and software combined. However, in the area of thematic cartography a number of programs are available from organizations such as the Harvard Laboratory for Computer Graphics, Geographic Systems Inc.(GSI), Environmental Science Research Institute(ESRI), and others. Combined hardware and software system vendors include large companies such as IBM, Intergraph, Synercom, Computervision, and Scitex, as well as newerer firms such as ESRI, GSI, Urban Systems Applications, Iconx, Geobased Systems, COMARC Design Systems, and ERDAS.

2. Data Bases.

a. Physical versus logical map data bases. Visual images are physical pictures. A physical map data base has a 1:1, direct correspondence to a physical picture except it is in digital form. Examples are (1) a bit map matrix used to produce a virtual display on a CRT, or (2) a simple vector or matrix data base resulting from the digitization of an image. In both cases, the physical data base contains only the information required to produce a physical picture by the direct substitution of graphic symbols for their data values.

A logical map data base has a different purpose, namely the logical and arithmetic manipulation of map information content such as the graphic objects and relations on the map. As a result, a logical data base benefits from the inclusion of information regarding the locational and geographic attributes of named graphic objects within the image and their logical relationship to each other, such as their topology. Given that information, it becomes possible to perform logical as well as arithmetic operations upon the graphic objects contained within a map data base. It is important to note, however, that the operations need not and should not be restricted to the pixel level. Far more valuable is the opportunity to include within the data base geometric, topological, and geographic attributes for higher order, named graphic objects such as lines and areas. These in turn may be aggregated to larger, complex objects which also would be described by their geometric, topological, and geographic attributes.

b. Coordinate Manipulation. Computer mapping involves three different coordinate transformations. Initial data base creation by use of a digitizer results in a data base expressed in terms of digitizer table cartesian x-y coordinate space. Because the source map document will usually include known geodetic coordinate control points in latitude and longitude plus a specified map projection, it is possible subsequently to convert the digitized data into geodetic coordinates by use of an inverse map projection algorithm. This is necessary for merging data derived from two separate but adjoining map sheets in order to treat the final data base as one continuous description of the earth's surface regardless of how many separate map sheets are used to create the total data base. At time of map display it is necessary once again to convert the coordinates, this time from geodetic to cartesian coordinates. This requires use of a map projection algorithm to produce coordinates which reflect the location of origin and min-max coordinates for the display device.

c. External Data Base Organization and Content. At time of vector data base creation (digitizing), there are many possible record and file structures which may be used. The most commonly used techniques involve the definition of coordinates for lines of varying length which describe continuous runs of x-y coordinates. The length of these runs are usually determined by the end points of a given line. The end points may be at the terminus of a line or at its intersection with one or more other lines. Each line will have an identification number as well as a feature code to indicate the type of information it represents. Other attributes of that line may be included as part of the same record or contained in a separate record keyed to the line by its identification number.

Procedures originally developed by the US Census Bureau and extended by others at the Harvard Laboratory for Computer Graphics and also at the US Geoogical Survey have introduced topological relations for lines as an explicit component of a cartographic data base. This is in addition to the essential description of spatial geometry for the lines (their x-y coordinates). Each record describes a line which is treated as though it were an 'arc' within a graph. End points of a line are defined by its terminus or the point at which it intersects two or more other lines. These end points are termed 'nodes' to distinguish them from 'points' at vertices intermediate to the end points.

The topology for each arc is described in terms of the connection its two end points have with other lines, plus reference to the two adjacent regions which lie on either side of the line. Connectedness is described by an arc's two endpoints (nodes) and their from/to relationship as determined by a clockwise cycling of the graph. Adjacency relations are based upon the identification codes for the regions to the left and right of an arc, relative to its from/to nodes.

One of the principal benefits which a topological data structure provides is the ability to automatically detect missing or extraneous nodes and lines resulting from the digitizing process. As a result, significant savings are possible in the cost of accurate data base creation. An additional benefit of a topological data base is its potential for geometric intersection and integration with other topological data bases.

d. Algorithms. Due to the large size of most cartographic data bases, it is desirable to use a "divide and conquer" approach when processing data. For example, it is often possible to segment the data by geographic regions as well as by geographic feature types. When a map can be decomposed and stored as a series of feature overlays, the amount of data which must be in active memory at any one time is reduced. It also is helpful to use local processing techniques which deal with the map in a step-wise fashion using a band-sweep approach. This allows for concurrent processing of input and output and efficient use of available memory. Such an approach requires that a file first be sorted on its x and y coordinates but it eliminates the need for random access files and allows the data to be processed in a sequential fashion.

Two operations used in the processing of cartographic data include line smoothing and line generalization. Line smoothing adds points to a line to achieve a smooth curvature. Line generalization selectively removes points from a line to reduce unnecessary detail in situations such as reduction of map scale or use of a display device with a resolution less than that of the graphic data.

e. Internal Data Structure. Cartographic data can be organizaed hierarchically with global descriptors for each file followed by header records for each arc with its summary statistics, extrema coordinates (x-y min-max) and topological identifiers. Detail records which contain the bulk of x-y point data may then be maintained separately in secondary storage. Geographic attributes for each arc also may be stored in this manner. Directories can be used to index the point and geographic attribute files to the header records. Similarly, graphic symbol files may be maintained separately for access at time of graphic output.

3. Geographic Attribute Data.

Geographic attribute data sources reflect the nature of the application and the map scale. Large scale maps of engineering projects such as utility maps acquire data attributes from the engineering drawings for a facility. Such maps necessarily are very precise in terms of location and feature attributes. However, the density of graphic information is relatively low.

Medium scale thematic maps, such as for an urbanized area, acquire attribute data from commercial and governmental records keyed to location by a geo-reference code such as a street address. Locations are less precisely defined than for engineering maps but with numerous attributes for each geographic feature.

Small scale, large region maps such as for natural resource exploration, make significant use of satellite imagery and aerial photographs to acquire multiple attribute information over large areas with location being less precisely defined relative to large or medium scale maps. Imagery, whether from satellite or aerial photographs, is a rich source of information especially concerning physical geographic attributes.

Economic and demographic data produced by commercial and governmental organizations are usually aggregated to predefined administrative regions. Unfortunately, the boundaries used are frequently unique to each organization therefore making comparisons difficult. For example, postal ZIP code districts, which could be used to summarize and display customer data for a firm, have different boundaries from census tracts for which total population data is available.

The ability to combine information from two or more sources, be they imagery, traditional cartographic sources, or various economic or demographic data bases is frequently desirable for applications such as land suitability studies or regional planning. However, because of the differences in geographic recording units for each data source, it is necessary that either (1) each source be used to produce separate graphic products with unique boundaries and these are manually superimposed for visual comparison, or (2) the cartographic and economic/demographic data available by administrative regions is recoded in terms of imagery pixels, thereby using pixels as a common unit of geographic analysis, or (3) imagery data available by pixels is aggregated to extract graphic patterns. These data zones may then be geometrically overlayed with one or more topological cartographic data bases and their attributes to produce a single composite data base composed of least common geographic units.

The alternative chosen is dependent upon the objectives sought and the resources available. They are described, above, in order of increasing cost and capability for subsequent analysis. The advantages associated with topological files over pixel files result from the preservation of predefined spatial objects, their boundaries, and their spatial relation to each other plus the ability to perform logical and arithmetic operations upon the data.

IV. Trends

A. Data Availability. The 1970's and 1980's have seen the beginning and rapid growth of digital cartographic data and related sources of geographic feature data. Current sources of such data bases include the US Census Bureau with data bases containing coordinate descriptions of major metropolitan areas by census tract and census block as well as US state and county boundary and congressional district boundary files. Several files also are available which contain x-y coordinate centroids for US counties and US places. All of the above files are distributed by the Census Bureau in Suitland, Maryland.

The US Geological Survey has for several years been developing and distributing digital data bases which describe patterns of land use and land cover at a scale of 1:100,000 for various sections of the US based upon aerial photographic interpretation. They are also in the process of developing digital line graph data bases at a scale of 1:200,000 with three separate sets of data: boundaries, transportation features, and hydrographic features. Elevation data in a matrix format is also available at a scale of 1:250,000. USGS data bases are distributed by the National Cartographic Information Center in Reston, Virginia. USGS digital data bases will be especially important because they will serve as national standard maps and provide the digital base maps onto which additional information will be added by others. Another federal agency, the US Soil Service, is in the process of creating digital descriptions of soil patterns accross the US based upon their soil maps.

Each of the above federal organizations have adopted a topological structure for their data bases. The specific formats vary, but each contains the essential information necessary for performing topological error checking and potentially, file integration.

NASA's Landsat satellite data collection system, now administered by the National Oceanographic and Atmospheric Administration, has its data products distributed by EROS Data Center in Sioux Falls, South Dakota. They have produced a continuous stream of multi-spectral scanner imagery, the latest of which, Landsat-D, is providing images with a pixel resolution of 90 feet on the ground. Use of Landsat imagery for natural resource exploration and management purposes continues to grow and include applications such as mineral, fossil fuel, and water exploration.

Multipurpose land data systems have been initiated in several metropolitan areas including Milwaukee, Wisconsin. and Philadelphia, Pennsylvania. These systems have begun to demonstrate procedures and capabilities required for governmental computer mapping systems on a city wide basis. Special purpose cartographic systems also have been developed in Nashville, Tennessee and Houston, Texas focussing upon multi-user public utility systems. Future developments of these and other municipal mapping systems will continue to grow as experience in their development and use accumulate and costs decline due to technological advances.

B. New Technologies.

1. Parallel processing. The development of parallel procesing capabilities with multiple processors will be of value for automated cartography applications where band sweep operations can occur simultaneously at several locations over a map. Image data bases as well as topological vector data bases will benefit from increased processing speed and the ability to handle larger and more complex sets of data with greater efficeincy.

2. High Bulk Data Storage Requirements. As the bulk of imagery grows due to the expansion both in number and resolution of image collection systems, there will be increased difficulty in satisfying storage requirements and a corresponding need to be able to preserve essential information contained within such images. Topological data bases created by automated extraction of graphic objects offer potential savings in storage as well as analytic interpretation.

3. Video Technology. The continual development of video recording, storage, retrieval, and communications suggests that optical data management will become increasingly important for all areas of computer graphics. High density optical recording with micro processor controlled image retrieval is likely to offer significant benefits, particularly given the availability of read/write video discs.

C. Future Uses for Maps. Technological capabilities in support of computer aided natural resource exploration and management undoubtedly will continue to grow as will demand for its use, particularly by energy exploration and commercial forest companies as well as developing nations. Agricultural and commercial fishing activities also benefit from an opportunity to monitor the status of agricultural crops and changes in fishing resources.

Business uses of computer generated maps have begun to offer new and valuable forms of information for market research purposes. The ability to display the location of current sales in relation to potential sales provides vivid and immediately useful information for evaluating effectiveness of current sales efforts, opportunities for additional sales, development of advertising strategies, and selection of sites for new stores.

Navigation maps have always been essential resources for travel by air, water, or land. However, future navigational systems are likely to use information obtained from navigational satellites. This data will be displayed on maps produced by digital cartographic data bases. The availability of portable graphic display devices, satellite receivers as well as cellular radio systems have the capacity to produce truly dynamic mobile maps. These devices will display the current position of the receiver in relation to roads, landmarks, or other identifying features regardless whether the receiving device is in a plane, boat, auto, or on an individual's wrist.

GRAPHIC DESIGN FOR COMPUTER GRAPHICS

Aaron Marcus
Aaron Marcus and Associates
1196 Euclid Avenue
Berkeley, California 94708, U. S. A.

ABSTRACT

Because computer graphics systems are capable of sophisicated displays of typography, symbols, color, spatial organization, and temporal sequencing, it is appropriate to seek principles for designing effective communication from the discipline of graphic design whose expertise lies in programming visible language. Examples of the author's work are cited to demonstrate how graphic design can improve three different types of computer graphics.

INTRODUCTION

From their very beginning, all computers were computer graphics systems, that is, they communicated with human beings by some means of graphic display. These devices might have been merely flashing lights, the revolving reels of a tape drive, or the simple alphanumeric characters of a line printer. Today, the means for portraying information to a human being are much more sophisticated. High resolution displays can portray sophisticated typefonts, three-dimensional structures, dynamic objects, and intricate color relationships.

Despite all of this increased capacity to display data, we nevertheless have the same fundamental tasks before us that we had from the very beginning. In fact, these essential goals of human communication have always existed, how can we attract people to information, how can we hold their attention, how can we facilitate their understanding, and how can we help them to remember what they have learned? Communication between computers and people takes place in three different phases. These might be called the three faces of computers: outer-faces, inter-faces, and inner-faces.

Outer-faces are the displays of information that are the final products of computation. They may consist of texts, tables, forms, charts, maps, and diagrams. They can be printed on paper, projected on a screen, or appear on the terminal screen. The people who look at this information may have very little knowledge of computers and the means of displaying information.

Inter-faces are the frames of command/control and documentation that the users of computer systems encounter. This human-computer connection allows the human being to understand and to manipulate the functional power of the computer system. Without this "handle" on the computer tool, the device is not effective. Inter-faces appear displayed on the glass screen or in printed texts. The users of computer systems may vary from the very naive user to a very skilled and sophisticated person.

Inner-faces are the frames of command/control and documentation that the builders and maintainers of computer systems confront. Like the other faces of computer systems, they may be static or dynamic, two- or three-dimensional, black-and-white or polychromatic, and high or low resolution. They depict programming languages, software tools, and operating systems.

Now that significant achievements have been made in the technical arena with regard to high-speed display of complex computer-generated images, it is necessary to be as inventive and sophisticated with the communicative quality of these displays. Most of the attention of computer science and technology has focused on the electronic communication that occurs prior to display on the glass screen or printed page. Computer graphics must improve the communication that takes place between the display surface and the human viewer.

SEMIOTICS, THE SCIENCE OF SIGNS

Effective communication requires greater attention to the semiotics [Eco, 1976] of computer graphics. Semiotics, the science of signs, calls attention to three dimensions of communication: syntactics, semantics, and pragmatics. In each of these dimensions, signs communicate to human viewers. The signs may vary from very representational, obvious "icons" to extremely abstract, conventional "symbols."

Syntactics is concerned with the visual appearance of signs and the relation of signs to each other. Here we ask, is a particular icon or symbol red or green, large or small, and near to or far from another. The visual syntax of signs may be loosely or carefully structured in any particular class of communications [Marcus, 1974]. When informational graphics is concerned, the specifications of visual syntax are usually precise.

Semantics is concerned with the relation of signs to the facts, concepts, structures, processes, or emotions being signified by means of the signs. Here we traditionally ask, what does this sign mean? Note that semiotics applies the term "meaning" to all three dimensions of sign communication. In the past computer graphics has given some limited attention to semantics, however, there is a realm of visual rhetoric which has not been fully explored. In using rhetoric one may take advantage of the value of exaggeration (hyperpole), partial signs standing for complete signs (metonomy), and other specialized figures of expression [Marcus, 1983c].

Pragmatics is concerned with how signs are produced and consumed. In this dimensions of semiotics we can ask, how expensive or difficult is it to display signs in a particular way, how legible will the signs be, and how appealing will they be? Computer graphics technology has usually been concerned with the practical aspects of achieving cost-effective displays of information. In a computer-intensive society, it also becomes reasonable to ask how different groups of people relate emotionally to, understand, and use visual displays of information.

VISIBLE LANGUAGE AND GRAPHIC DESIGN

Currently most information is displayed in verbal or alphanumeric symbolism. Computer graphics offers new opportunities to transform textual and tabular information into non-verbal formats of visible language. But what should these look like? What are the rules or principles for such transformations? Unfortunately, there is no science yet skillfull enough to predict generally how this should be done. To some extent the disciplines of human factors and applied psychology can assist the person faced with the task of designing frames of information. However, a single frame of information by itself has many inter-related aspects that exceed the more limited predictions of these scientific disciplines.

At this moment in the development of computer graphics it becomes appropriate to note the existence of a profession that is traditionally skilled in transforming facts, concepts, and emotions into visual analogies and to creating visual narratives. Graphic design is a discipline concerned with sign making, especially for visible language, the visual media of language expression. Graphic design utilizes typography, symbols (both representational and abstract), color, spatial organization or layout, and the sequencing of frames over time in order to achieve effective communication. Information-oriented graphic designers are sensitive to the complex requirements of the senders of information, the detailed structure of the content of the message, the nature of the communication medium, and the needs of the receivers of the message.

Once the mutual contributions of graphic design and computer graphics are understood, it would seem that a symbiotic relationship could exist between these two disciplines. Each could contribute to the design of end products or documents, to the user-oriented machine interface, and to the depiction of programs and control processes for builders and maintainers of computer-based systems. Computer graphics can design what happens behind the glass screen or before the printed document comes into existence, and graphic design can affect the communication that takes place between the display and the human mind.

For example, graphic designers can suggest changes to the appearance of texts, tables, charts [Marcus, 1980], maps, and diagrams based on precisely determined factors of legibility [Rehe, 1974] plus their professional expertise concerning readability or appeal. By establishing specifications for typographic changes from light to bold, by determining a clear spatial layout, by limiting the choice of colors [Marcus, 1982e], it is possible to build in useful, reinforcing reduncancy to the decisions about the appearance of all visual material.

Another example of the potential interaction lies in the design of online frames and offline pages for an information processing system [Marcus, 1982a,c]. The computer must help the user to learn complicated texts, to memorize functions, to make accurate decisions, and to build a clear conceptual image of the information processing system. By carefully structuring words, concepts, and images [Marcus, 1983a], these tasks are accomplished more easily in a legible and appealing verbal/visual environment. This is particularly important as computers are now used by people with varying educational, cultural, and psychological backgrounds. It is no longer appropriate to assume that one kind of interface can serve all kinds of people.

Finally, in the area of program depiction and computer system visualization, it seems likely that graphic design can assist in making the complexities of computer structure and processing more evident and more understandable

[Marcus, 1982b; Marcus and Baecker, 1982], just as graphic design has assisted in other areas of depicting complex subject matter such as global energy interdependencies [Marcus, 1981].

CASE STUDIES

In the next sections, the author presents some examples of his own application of graphic design to the products of computer science. The relevant design principles are described only briefly. Most of these projects have been documented in greater detail within the cited technical publications.

The Graphic Design of Outer-faces

In Figures 1 and 2 appear undesigned and designed default displays of simple line charts composed semi-automatically by Seedis, a large geographic database management system [McCarthy, 1982] developed at Lawrence Berkeley Laboratory. The second image shows a better use of available type sizes which makes the chart legible even at small reproduction sizes and which clarifies the hierarchy of titling. A more clearly organized grouping of typographic elements and a use of gray areas to emphasize portions of the chart add to the readability of the chart [Marcus, 1980].

Figures 3 and 4 show line printer and Xerox 9700 laser printer versions of 1980 US Census data as they appear in reports prepared by Lawrence Berkeley Laboratory for the National Technical Information Service (NTIS) [NTIS, 1982]. The design of the tables has reduced variations of positioning and indention to a minimum and has produced a design which can appear reliably both in fixed character width as well as variable character width presentations. Variations of size and boldness in the laser printer typography are used to clarify titling.

1

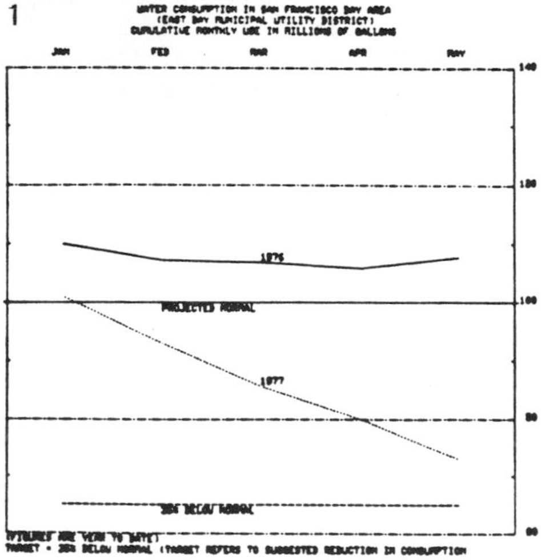

2

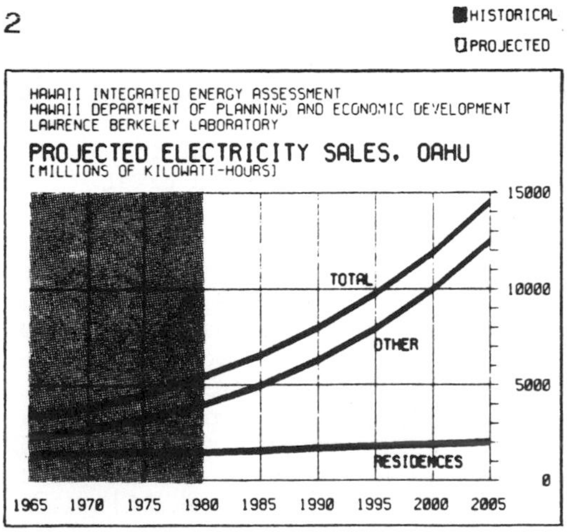

3

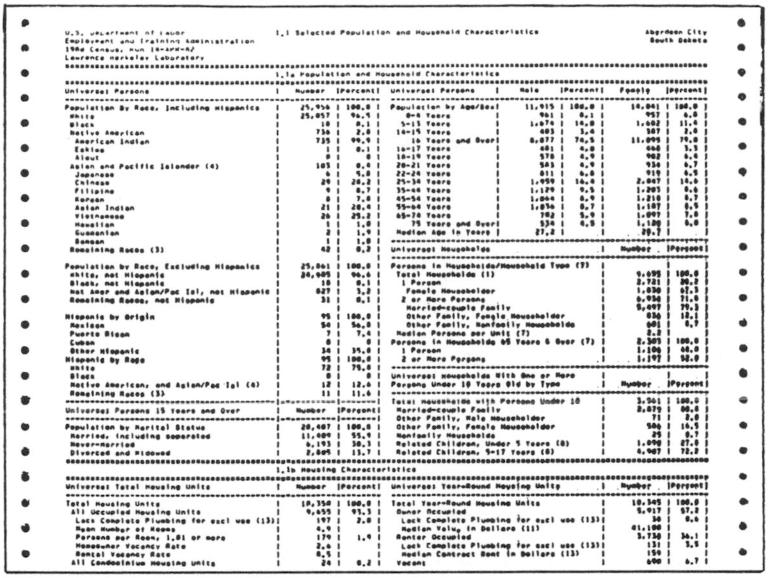
U.S. Department of Labor
Employment and Training Administration
1980 Census, Run 14-APR-82
Lawrence Berkeley Laboratory

1.1 Selected Population and Household Characteristics

Abgrdeen City
South Dakota

1.1a Population and Household Characteristics

1.1b Housing Characteristics

4

.S. Department of Labor
mployment and Training Administration
980 Census, Run on 6 Aug 1982
awrence Berkeley Laboratory

Report 1A: Population Characteristics
Table: Population and Housing Characteristics

Alaska

Population and Household Characteristics

Universe: Persons	Number	Percent
opulation by Race, including Hispanics	401,851	100.0
White	309,728	77.1
Black	13,643	3.4
Native American	64,103	16.0
American Indian	21,869	5.4
Eskimo	34,144	8.5
Aleut	8,090	2.0
Asian and Pacific Islander (4)	8,054	2.0
Japanese	1,595	0.4
Chinese	522	0.1
Filipino	3,092	0.8
Korean	1,536	0.4
Asian Indian	241	-
Vietnamese	383	-
Hawaiian	402	0.1
Guamanian	149	-
Samoan	134	-
Remaining Races (3)	6,323	1.6
opulation by Race, excluding Hispanics	392,344	100.0
White, not Hispanic	304,635	77.6
Black, not Hispanic	13,421	3.4
Nat Amer and Asian/Pac Isl, not Hisp (4)	70,893	18.1
Remaining Races, not Hispanic (3)	3,395	0.9
opulation by Origin, including all races	401,851	100.0
Hispanic	9,507	2.4
Mexican	4,615	1.1
Puerto Rican	965	0.2
Cuban	166	-
Other Hispanic	3,761	0.9
ispanic by Race	9,507	100.0
White	5,093	53.6
Black	222	2.3
Native American and Asian/Pac Isl (4)	1,264	13.3
Remaining Races (3)	2,928	30.8

niverse: Persons 15 Years and Over	Number	Percent
opulation by Marital Status	293,577	100.0
Married, including Separated	175,820	59.9
Never-Married	85,228	29.0
Divorced and Widowed	32,529	11.1

Universe: Persons	Male	Percent	Female	Percent
Population by Age/Sex	213,041	100.0	188,810	100.0
0-4 Years	20,040	9.4	18,909	10.0
5-13 Years	31,970	15.0	30,393	16.1
14-15 Years	7,517	3.5	6,825	3.6
16 Years and Over	153,514	72.1	132,683	70.3
16-17 Years	7,990	3.8	7,101	3.8
18-19 Years	8,005	3.8	6,678	3.5
20-21 Years	9,500	4.5	7,632	4.0
22-24 Years	14,686	6.9	13,272	7.0
25-34 Years	48,240	22.6	42,568	22.5
35-44 Years	29,561	13.9	24,461	13.0
45-54 Years	18,693	8.8	15,550	8.2
55-64 Years	11,080	5.2	9,633	5.1
65-74 Years	4,278	2.0	4,034	2.1
75 Years and Over	1,481	0.7	1,754	0.9
Median Age in Years	26.3		25.8	

Universe: Households	Number	Percent
Total Households (1)	131,463	100.0
1 Person Households	26,467	20.1
Male Householder	16,744	12.7
Female Householder	9,723	7.4
2 or More Person Households	104,996	79.9
Married Couple Family	80,344	61.1
Other Family	15,220	11.6
Male Householder, no Wife Present	4,948	3.8
Female Householder, no Husband Present	10,272	7.8
Nonfamily Households	9,432	7.2
Male Householder	6,543	5.0
Female Householder	2,889	2.2
Total Households w/ Persons Age 65+ (7)	8,878	100.0
1 Person Households	2,758	31.1
2 or More Person Households	6,120	68.9
Total Households w/ Persons Under Age 18	65,038	100.0
Married Couple Family	52,344	80.5
Other Family	11,766	18.1
Male Householder, no Wife Present	3,226	5.0
Female Householder, no Husband Present	8,540	13.1
Nonfamily Households	928	1.4

Housing Characteristics

niverse: Housing Units	Number	Percent
otal Housing Units (2)	162,825	
Total Year-Round Housing Units	154,171	100.0
Condominium Units	5,276	3.4
Lack Complete Plumbing for excl use (13)	18,773	12.2
Occupied Housing Units (1)	131,463	85.3
Median Persons per Unit (7)	2.6	
Homeowner Vacancy Rate	3.6	
Rental Vacancy Rate	15.4	

Universe: Occupied Housing Units	Number	Percent
Occupied Housing Units (1)	131,463	100.0
With 1.01 or more Persons per Room	13,225	10.1
Owner Occupied	76,663	58.3
Lack Complete Plumbing for excl use (13)	8,954	6.8
Median Value in Dollars (11)	75,200	
Renter Occupied	54,800	41.7
Lack Complete Plumbing for excl use (13)	4,717	3.6
Median Contract Rent in Dollars (13)	338	

For meaning of symbols, see Introduction. For footnotes and definitions, see Technical Notes.

The Graphic Design of Inter-Faces

The screens layouts shown in Figures 5 and 6 show undesigned and designed versions of the online inter-face for Seedis. In the undesigned version, note the unorganized appearance of groups of type and the inconsistency in the use of all capital letters vs. lower case letters. In the designed version, note the order of text blocks, the use of lines of hyphens, the regular use of lower case letters, and controlled tab settings. Capital letters are used in major titling and in the menu-prompt to identify the module in which the user is currently working. The screens are 80 characters wide by 24 lines deep, but information from the computer generally appears in character positions 21 through 80, while the user begins typing at character position 1. This helps to establish visually a separation in the dialogue between human being and machine [Marcus, 1982a, c].

5, 6

```
seedis
If you exit abnormally from SEEDIS, continue by typing
   @restore
   seedis
        Welcome to SEEDIS    VMS version 1.0
        Type  ?  for expanded menus
        Type  $  before VMS commands
(HELP,REVIEW,SUBJECT,AREA,AGG,DISAGG,
   PROFILE,DATA,DISPLAY,BUGS,NETSTAT,SHOW,QUIT): subject
Please select both data and a geographic area.
FORTRAN STOP
WELCOME TO THE SYSTEM.
YOU CAN ENTER

        EXPLAIN :TO SCAN KEYWORDS.
        SEARCH :TO LOCATE FILES CONTAINING KEYWORDS.
        QUIT :TO TERMINATE.

ENTER COMMAND OR ?COMMAND FOR MORE DETAIL.
```

```
                    ------------------------------------------------------------
                    WELCOME TO SEEDIS, VERSION 2.0
                    ------------------------------------------------------------
                    At any point in Seedis, you can type the following global
                    commands to get these services:

Input               Description
------------------- ------------------------------------------------------------
?                   list and describe commands in this menu
help                describe the purpose of this menu's commands
show                list and explain items to be selected
review              list current sessin status and history
cancel              delete current selections (depends upon context)
quit                return to previous menu
*<comment>          enter a comment in Seedis log

shortly.            Please stand by. Your menu prompt will appear

                    SEEDIS: area, data, display, profile
```

7

Figures 7 shows symbols from a high-resolution bit-mapped interface on a Three-Rivers Perq microcomputer graphics display. The interface is part of Metaform from Intran, Inc., a forms-design front end system for the Xerox 9700 laser printer. Because the complexities of the system are made available to computer-naive secretaries, pictographic light buttons use simple images to explain and reinforce the verbal mnemonics [Intran, 1982].

The Graphic Design of Inner-faces

The comparison of Figures 8 and 9 show undesigned and designed versions of C programs as they might be produced on a line printer and on a phototypesetter. In the typical undesigned version, fixed-width characters appear in a singe size and typeface. The source code is not easy to read because there is minimal expression of a typographic hierachy. In the variable-width designed version, spatial location, typographic and symbol hierachies, and additional commentary contribute to making a textual program depiction that is more legible and more readable [Marcus, 1982b; Marcus and Baecker, 1982].

Summary

Graphic design has improved visual communication in a variety of fields such as environmental signage [American Institute of Graphic Arts, 1974], diagrammatic communication [Herdeg, 1975], and governmental documents [Blackburn, 1977]. This same expertise has relevance to improving the "corporate" or "institutional" graphics of an information management system [Marcus, 1983a, d], cad/cam systems [Marcus, 1983b], or other computer graphics displays. By combining the expertise of graphic design with computer graphics, more humane as well as more cost/effective systems can emerge in the 1980's.

ACKNOWLEDGMENT

This article was prepared for presentation at Intergraphics 83, Tokyo, Japan, 11-14 April 1983, and appears in the *Proceedings* of that conference. The author acknowledges the use of illustrations from previous publications that originally appeared as technical memoranda from Lawrence Berkeley Laboratory.

REFERENCES

American Institute of Graphic Arts, *Symbol Signs*, U.S. Department of Transportation, Washington, DC, DOT-OS-40192, November 1974.

Blackburn, Bruce, *Design Standards Manuals*, Federal Design Library, National Endowment for the Arts, Washington, DC, 1977.

Eco, Umberto, *A Theory of Semiotics*, Indiana University Press, Bloomington, 1976.

8

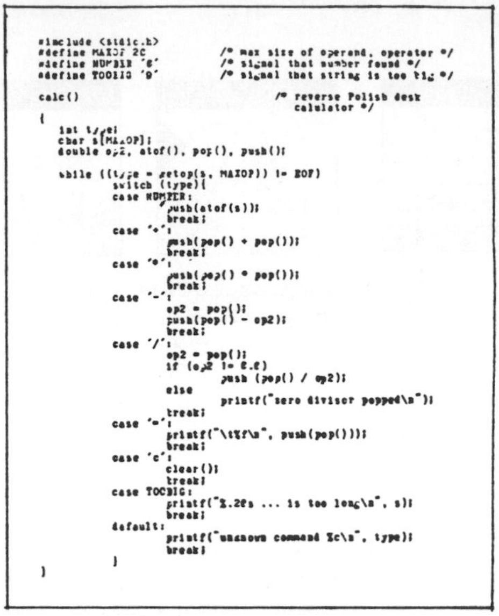

```
#include <stdio.h>
#define MAXOP 20                /* max size of operand, operator */
#define NUMBER '0'              /* signal that number found */
#define TOOBIG '9'              /* signal that string is too big */

calc()                                  /* reverse Polish desk
                                           calulator */
{
   int type;
   char s[MAXOP];
   double op2, atof(), pop(), push();

   while ((type = getop(s, MAXOP)) != EOF)
           switch (type){
           case NUMBER:
                   push(atof(s));
                   break;
           case '+':
                   push(pop() + pop());
                   break;
           case '*':
                   push(pop() * pop());
                   break;
           case '-':
                   op2 = pop();
                   push(pop() - op2);
                   break;
           case '/':
                   op2 = pop();
                   if (op2 != 0.0)
                           push (pop() / op2);
                   else
                           printf("zero divisor popped\n");
                   break;
           case '=':
                   printf("\t%f\n", push(pop()));
                   break;
           case 'c':
                   clear();
                   break;
           case TOOBIG:
                   printf("%.20s ... is too long\n", s);
                   break;
           default:
                   printf("unknown command %c\n", type);
                   break;
           }
}
```

9

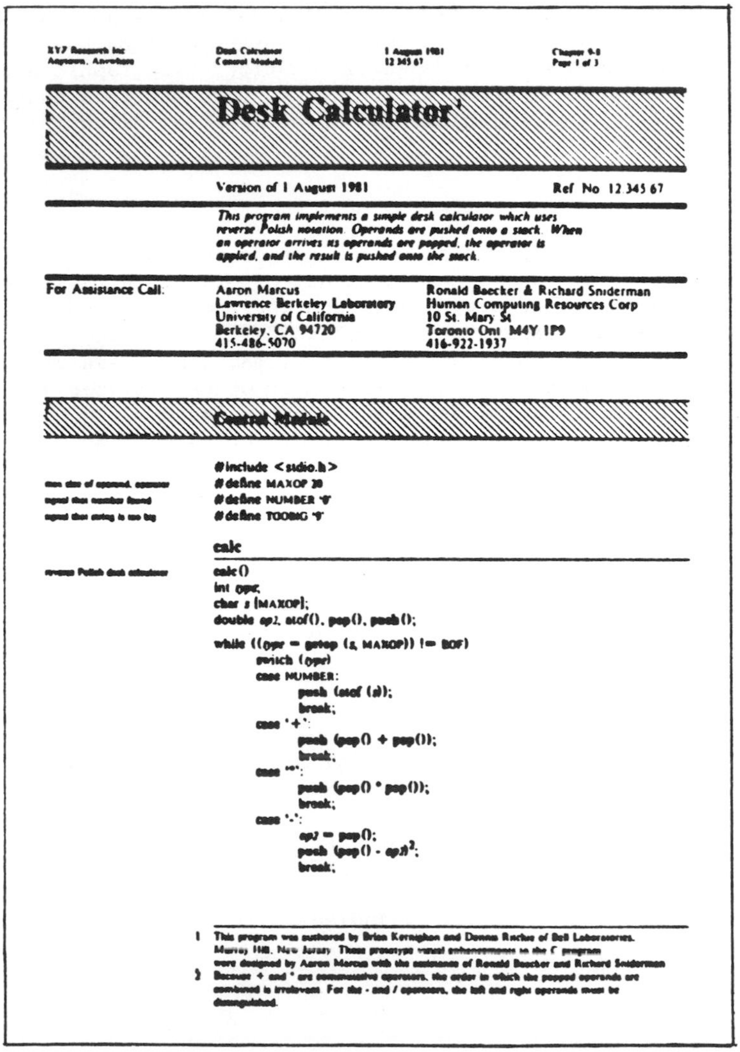

XYZ Research Inc
Anytown, Anywhere

Desk Calculator
Control Module

1 August 1981
12 345 67

Chapter 9-0
Page 1 of 3

Desk Calculator[1]

Version of 1 August 1981 — Ref No 12 345 67

This program implements a simple desk calculator which uses reverse Polish notation. Operands are pushed onto a stack. When an operator arrives its operands are popped, the operator is applied, and the result is pushed onto the stack.

For Assistance Call:

Aaron Marcus
Lawrence Berkeley Laboratory
University of California
Berkeley, CA 94720
415-486-5070

Ronald Baecker & Richard Sniderman
Human Computing Resources Corp
10 St. Mary St
Toronto Ont M4Y 1P9
416-922-1937

Control Module

```
                                   #include <stdio.h>
max size of operand, operator      #define MAXOP 20
signal that number found           #define NUMBER '0'
signal that string is too big      #define TOOBIG '9'
```

calc

```
reverse Polish desk calculator     calc()
                                   int type;
                                   char s [MAXOP];
                                   double op2, atof(), pop(), push();

                                   while ((type = getop (s, MAXOP)) != EOF)
                                           switch (type)
                                           case NUMBER:
                                                   push (atof (s));
                                                   break;
                                           case '+':
                                                   push (pop() + pop());
                                                   break;
                                           case '*':
                                                   push (pop() * pop());
                                                   break;
                                           case '-':
                                                   op2 = pop();
                                                   push (pop() - op2)²;
                                                   break;
```

1 This program was authored by Brian Kernighan and Dennis Ritchie of Bell Laboratories, Murray Hill, New Jersey. These prototype visual enhancements to the C program were designed by Aaron Marcus with the assistance of Ronald Baecker and Richard Sniderman.

2 Because + and * are commutative operators, the order in which the popped operands are combined is irrelevant. For the - and / operators, the left and right operands must be distinguished.

Herdeg, Walter, ed., *Graphis: Diagrams,* Graphis Press, Zurich, 1975.

Intran Corporation, "Metaform: Technical Documentation," Intran Corporation, Inc., 4555 West 77 Street, Minneapolis, MN 55435, 1982.

Marcus, Aaron, "An Introduction to the Visual Syntax of Concrete Poetry," *Visible Language,* Vol. 8, No. 3, 1976, pp. 157-173.

Marcus, Aaron, "Computer-Assisted Chart Making from the Graphic Designer's Perspective," *Computer Graphics,* Vol. 14, No. 3, 1980, pp. 247-253.

Marcus, Aaron, "Designing the Face of An Interface," *IEEE Computer Graphics and Applications,* Vol. 2, No. 1, January 1982, pp. 23-29.

Marcus, Aaron, "Paper and Glass: Graphic Design Issues for Software Documentation," *Proc. Software Documentation Workshop,* National Bureau of Standards, 3 March 1982.

Marcus, Aaron "Typographic Design for Interfaces of Information Systems," *Proc. Human Factors in Computer Systems,* National Bureau of Standards, 15-17 March 1982.

Marcus, Aaron "Color: A Tool for Computer Graphics Communication," in *Greenberg, Donald, Aaron Marcus, et al., The Computer Image,* Addison-Wesley, Reading, 1982, pp. 76-90.

Marcus, Aaron, *Managing Facts and Concepts,* Design Arts Program, National Endowment for the Arts, Washington, DC, 1983.

Marcus, Aaron, "Cad/Cam from the Graphic Design Perspective", *Proc. Symposium on Automation Technology,* 3-5 November 1982, Naval Postgraduate School, Monterey, California, 1983 in press.

Marcus, Aaron, "Visual Rhetoric in a Pictographic-Ideographic Narrative", *Proc. Second International Conference of Associations for the Study of Semiotics,* Vienna, 1979, Mouton, the Hague, 1983 in press.

Marcus, Aaron, "A Graphic Design Manual for Seedis," Technical Memo, Computer Science and Mathematics Department, Lawrence Berkely Laboratory, University of California, Berkeley, 1983 in press.

Marcus, Aaron and Ron Baecker, "On the Graphic Design of Program Text, *Proc. Graphics Interface '82,* National Computer Graphics Association of Canada and Canadian Man-Machine Interface Association, 1982, pp. 303-311.

McCarthy, John *et al.*, "The Seedis Project," Pub. No. PUB-424 Rev., Lawrence Berkeley Laboratory, University of California, Berkeley, August 1982.

National Technical Information Service, *Census Reports No. 1-7,* 5285 Port Royal Road, Springfield, VA 22161, 1982.

Rehe, Rolf, *Typography: How to Make it Most Legible,* Design Research International, Carmel, Indiana, 1974.

COMPUTER GRAPHICS TO SHOW OPTIMAL SMOOTHING AND TREND ADJUSTMENTS FOR EXPONENTIAL FORECASTS

David B. Hoffman
Ramachandran Bharath
School of Business and Management
Northern Michigan University
Marquette, MI 49855, U. S. A.

Carol M. Carlson
Computer Consultant
P.O. Box 74398
Fairbanks, AK 99707, U. S. A.

When simulating various demand conditions and then determining the best factors for both smoothing and trend adjustments in an exponential smoothing model, both the optimal values and the relative sensitivity of moving away from optimality are represented best using computer graphics. Transectional graphs are drawn using SYMVU, and contour maps are drawn using SURFACE II. The simulation is written in Pascal with an earlier version in BASIC.

INTRODUCTION

How do we achieve the best forecast of future conditions? This paper looks at the accuracy of exponential smoothing forecasts of various computer simulated hypothetical demand conditions. The accuracy of the exponential forecasts are calculated using different values for smoothing and trend adjustments with the changes in the sensitivity of forecasting accuracy presented both in tabular and computer generated graphical forms.

EXPONENTIAL SMOOTHING

Exponential smoothing is a useful forecasting technique. It is simple and responsive and is not complicated to calculate. When used, over time, each successive forecast builds new information on to the previous calculations. As exponential smoothing is used over time, each actual demand observation is retained in the determination of the new forecast but to a diminishing degree. This is referred to as "exponential decay" (Vollman, 1973). The exponential forecasting model can be adjusted to put more weight on more recent information and therefore cause the more historical information to be given less weight in forecasting the next period. This adjustment is called the smoothing constant.

In forecasting simulated demand, the smoothing constant (α) ranges from 0.0 to 1.0 in the forecasting equation:

$$F_{(T)} = F_{(T-1)} + \alpha\,(D_{(T-1)} - F_{(T-1)}) \qquad [\ 1\ ]$$

where: F(T) = Forecast for period T

F(T-1) = Forecast for the previous period (T-1)
D(T-1) = Actual Demand for the previous period (T-1)

α = Smoothing Factor

When α is close to 1.0, the calculated forecast is weighted toward the most recent past demand and when α is closer to 0.0, the forecast is based on data from many of the previous periods. What is the best α value to use in order to obtain the most accurate forecasts? That depends on the demand conditions. That is why several different conditions have been used in this simulation. They demonstrate the affect of the smoothing factor (α) on the accuracy of the forecast.

There tends to be some degree of inaccuracy in the forecasts from the model described in equation 1 because there is always a lag between the change in demand over time and the forecast. To compensate for this, a trend adjustment factor can be added to the exponential smoothing model. The trend can be represented as the difference between the forecast of period n and the forecast of period n-1. To diminish the affects of random variation in determining the trend, the principle of exponential smoothing can be applied to calculating the trend. A factor called beta (β) is used to represent the smoothing constant for the trend.

$$T_T = \beta\ (F_T - F_{T-1}) + 1\text{-}\beta\ \ (T_{(T-1)}) \qquad [\ 2\ ]$$

where:

T = Trend
β = Trend Smoothing Constant

Now, the forecast can be calculated using both the smoothing and trend adjustment factors.

$$F_T = \alpha D_{T-1} + (1\text{-}\alpha)\ (F_{T-1} + T_{T-1}) \qquad [\ 3\ ]$$

The β value can range from 0.0 to 1.0. If β is closer to 1.0, the new trend is weighted toward the change from the most recent previous forecast. When β is closer to 0.0 the trend is based on the trend values for many of the previous periods. The best β value to use in forecasting, like the best α, depends on the demand conditions. Different β values are also used in the forecasting simulation with some interesting results.

SIMULATED DEMAND

A computer simulation written first in BASIC and then Pascal is designed to simulate a time series of demand values which represent any combination of five possible functions: 1. a single sine wave, 2. a compound sine wave, 3. a ramp function, 4. a step function, and 5. a constant. The user sets the conditions of the time series by selecting from the five functions and then can also add a random disturbance, setting the standard deviation. Demand values are first computed for 210 periods and then forecasts is computed for each period (Torfin and Hoffmann, 1962). To start, the forecast for the first period, F(1) is set equal to the first period demand $D_{(1)}$, with the $T_{(1)}$ equal to 0.

The accuracy of the forecasts are measured by calculating the mean absolute deviation (MAD) for periods 10 to 210. Therefore:

$$MAD = \frac{\sum_{t=10}^{t=210} \left| F_i - D_i \right|}{200} \qquad [4]$$

The smaller the MAD, the more accurate the forecast of the demand over the 200 periods. The forecasts for the first ten periods are computed but excluded from the measure of forecasting accuracy. These ten periods are used to "run in" the model in order to eliminate most of the transient conditions.

The output from the forecasting program is matrix of MAD values for 81 different combinations of α and β used to forecast a particular set demand conditions.

The following seven demand conditions are simulated to evaluate the accuracy of the exponential smoothing model using a range of α and β values.

1. Sine wave with a sine frequency of 0.5
2. Sine wave with a sine frequency of 0.5 and a random disturbance with a standard deviation of 1.0
3. Sine wave with a sine frequency of 0.5 and a random disturbance with a standard deviation of 5.0
4. Sine wave with a sine frequency of 2.0 and no random disturbance
5. Sine wave with a sine frequency of 4.0 and no random disturbance
6. Combined sine wave with a sine frequency of 0.5 and a ramp with a slope increasing 0.5 every time unit. No random disturbance
7. Step function with a five unit increase after every fifth time period. No random disturbance

INTERPRETING THE TABLES AND GRAPHS

The accuracy of the forecasts of these seven demand conditions are presented in Figures 2 through 11. Each figure includes a table of 81 MAD values for the pairs of α and β values and also a computer generated plot which represents the range of α values on one axis, the β values on the second axis and the MAD values as the height of the surface.

SYMVU (from Harvard University's Laboratory for Computer Graphics and Spatial Analysis) is used to create a transectional plot for each of the seven tables of MAD values. In addition, SURFACE II (from the Kansas Geological Survey) is used to plot contour maps for three of the tables of MAD values. Figure 1 shows the steps taken to convert the forecasting simulation output to a graphical form. The table of MAD values produced for the 81 forecasts of a particular demand condition used as input to the graphics program along with the commands that control the graph to be plotted. These include the type of graph, special labeling and other parameters such as azimuth, width, length, height, and altitude. The graphics program creates a set of intermediate data points and other instruction which are used by the program controlling the plotter or CRT displays. Other examples of simulation output converted to graphs are in Hoffman and Carlson (1981). Producing the best view of a graph is often a matter of trial and error. The best view (azimuth and altitude) for one graph may be different for another.

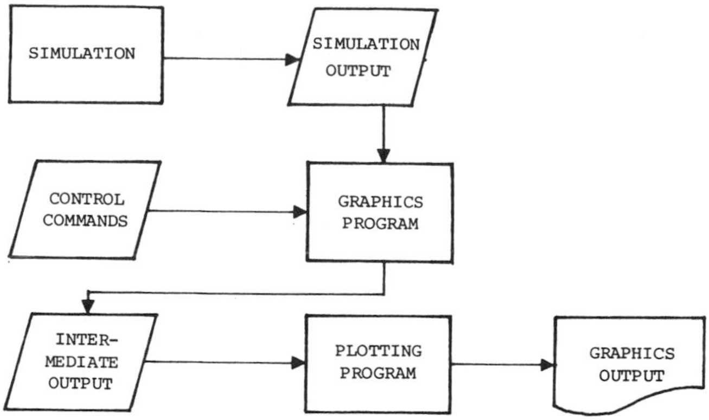

FIGURE 1 - PROCESS STEPS FOR PRODUCING GRAPHS

The main point we will address is the affect that changes in α and β have on the accuracy of the exponential forecasts. For each of the seven demand conditions there is an optimal or most accurate forecast based on a particular α and β value. In each of the seven tables of 81 MAD values, the most accurate forecast is represented as the lowest MAD value and the corresponding α and β values used to achieve that lowest MAD. The graphs provide a pictorial equivalent of the tables, with the lowest point on each graph showing the α and β that provides the best forecast. The highest point is the poorest forecast. The greatest advantage of representing this simulation output graphically is that the slope of the graphed surfaces represent the sensitivity of the changes in α and β will have in improving the accuracy of the forecast. The areas of the graph that are flat indicate that a change in α or β will have little or no affect on improving the accuracy of the forecast, given the particular demand conditions. Areas of the graphed surfaces that are steep, indicate that the accuracy of the forecast is more sensitive to changes in α or β .

RESULTS

In the first simulation, demand is represented as a sine wave with a frequency of 0.5. The best forecast is obtained when the exponential smoothing model uses a α of 0.9 and β of 0.8 (Figure 2). The lowest mean absolute deviation (MAD) is 1.66. The higher α value, regardless of β , provides a better forecast because the higher α follows the oscillations of the demand curve more closely. When the trend component of the forecasting model is deleted ($\beta = 0.0$) the forecast is more accurate as α is increased. This is represented as the front edge of Figure 2 and the left column in the corresponding table. As β is increased, using lower values of α , the forecasting accuracy decreases. When α is closer to 0.9, changes in β seem to have little effect.

ALPHA VALUES \ BETA VALUES	0	.1	.2	.3	.4	.5	.6	.7	.8
.1	3.3	3.43	3.56	3.72	3.89	4.08	4.29	4.54	4.81
.2	3.25	3.49	3.78	4.11	4.5	4.95	5.48	6.08	6.69
.3	3.09	3.37	3.71	4.09	4.5	4.89	5.19	5.33	5.27
.4	2.85	3.12	3.4	3.68	3.89	3.99	3.96	3.8	3.58
.5	2.59	2.79	2.99	3.14	3.19	3.15	3.03	2.87	2.71
.6	2.33	2.48	2.59	2.65	2.64	2.56	2.46	2.34	2.24
.7	2.1	2.19	2.26	2.27	2.23	2.17	2.1	2.03	1.96
.8	1.9	1.95	1.98	1.98	1.95	1.9	1.86	1.82	1.78
.9	1.73	1.75	1.76	1.75	1.74	1.72	1.7	1.68	1.66

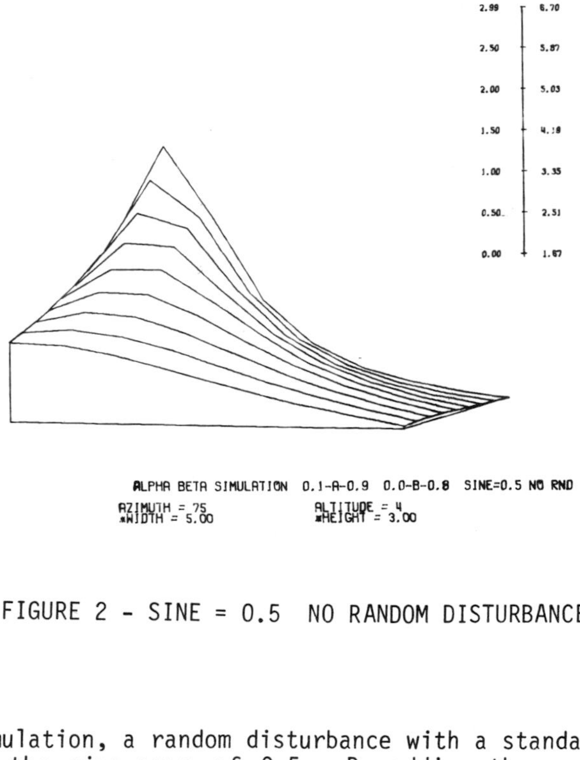

FIGURE 2 - SINE = 0.5 NO RANDOM DISTURBANCE

In the second simulation, a random disturbance with a standard deviation of 1.0 is added to the sine wave of 0.5. By adding the random noise, the accuracy of forecasts are decreased for all combinations of α and β but the overall shape of the surface is similar. (Figure 3) The best forecast is obtained when α = 0.9 and β = 0.8. The MAD is 1.98. The poorest forecast is 6.75, where α = 0.2 and β = 0.8. In the third simulation, the standard deviation of the random disturbance is increased to 5.0 (Figure 4). The α and β that provide the better forecast and the shape of the graph now change significantly. The MAD values are all higher because of the difficulty of forecasting against the random component of the demand and the best estimate is now when α is 0.1 to 0.5 and β is 0.0. Lower α values combined with higher β values produce a surface similar to demand conditions with less random disturbance however where α is larger, which represents a greater smoothing of the forecasts, there is an increase in the error regardless of β. The affect of changes in β, when α is small, are more pronounced than when α is greater than 0.5.

ALPHA VALUES \ BETA VALUES	.1	.2	.3	.4	.5	.6	.7	.8	.9
.1	3.35	3.49	3.64	3.8	3.99	4.19	4.4	4.64	4.9
.2	3.28	3.52	3.8	4.13	4.51	4.96	5.49	6.1	6.75
.3	3.13	3.42	3.76	4.16	4.57	4.99	5.33	5.48	5.4
.4	2.94	3.2	3.5	3.8	4.04	4.15	4.1	3.94	3.73
.5	2.71	2.92	3.13	3.29	3.36	3.32	3.2	3.05	2.9
.6	2.49	2.64	2.77	2.84	2.83	2.77	2.67	2.56	2.47
.7	2.31	2.4	2.47	2.49	2.47	2.41	2.34	2.28	2.22
.8	2.15	2.2	2.23	2.23	2.21	2.18	2.14	2.1	2.07
.9	2.02	2.04	2.05	2.05	2.03	2.02	2	1.99	1.98

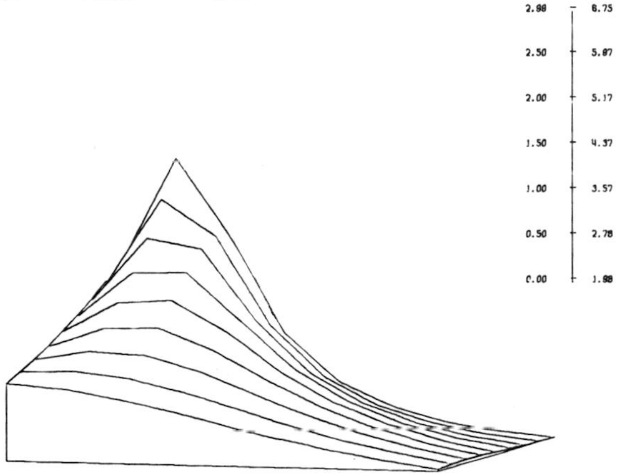

ALPHA BETA SIMULATION 0.1-A-0.9 0.1-B-0.9 SINE= 0.5 STD DEV = 1
AZIMUTH = 75 ALTITUDE = 4
*WIDTH = 5.00 *HEIGHT = 3.00

FIGURE 3 - SINE = 0.5 STANDARD DEVIATION = 1.0

ALPHA VALUES \ BETA VALUES	.1	.2	.3	.4	.5	.6	.7	.8	.9
.1	5.19	5.32	5.48	5.65	5.82	5.97	6.13	6.31	6.52
.2	5.22	5.38	5.57	5.78	6.02	6.28	6.62	6.98	7.36
.3	5.19	5.34	5.51	5.69	5.88	6.08	6.27	6.39	6.42
.4	5.21	5.3	5.42	5.54	5.65	5.72	5.77	5.78	5.76
.5	5.29	5.35	5.43	5.51	5.56	5.59	5.61	5.6	5.6
.6	5.42	5.47	5.52	5.57	5.6	5.61	5.62	5.62	5.62
.7	5.59	5.61	5.64	5.67	5.69	5.7	5.71	5.72	5.74
.8	5.77	5.79	5.8	5.81	5.82	5.83	5.84	5.86	5.87
.9	5.98	5.98	5.99	5.99	6 6	6.01	6.01	6.02	

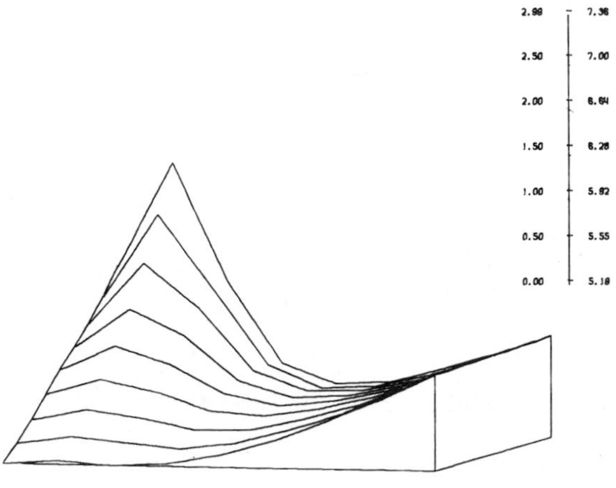

ALPHA BETA SIMULATION 0.1-A-0.9 0.1-B-0.9 SINE= 0.5 STD DEV = 5
AZIMUTH = 75 ALTITUDE = 4
*WIDTH = 5.00 *HEIGHT = 3.00

FIGURE 4 - SINE = 0.5 STANDARD DEVIATION = 5.0

A sine of 0.5 represents demand conditions which oscillate and cycle every 12.57 periods. This is similar to forecasting monthly demand which cycles approximately once every year. In the fourth simulation, the sine frequency is increased to 2.0. This means the demand cycles every 3.14 period. And when the sine is increased to 4.0 in the fifth simulation, demand cycles every 1.57 periods. Figures 5 and 6 respectively show the forecasting accuracy for various combinations of α and β when the sine is 2.0 and 4.0. The increased sine frequencies of 2.0 and 4.0 compared to 0.5 (Figure 2) show distinctively different surfaces. Changes in β now have almost no affect on forecast accuracy, and the lower the α , the greater the forecast accuracy. The view of the plots in Figures 5 and 6 are "turned" 30 degrees to better show the downward slope of the MAD values.

ALPHA VALUES	BETA VALUES .1	.2	.3	.4	.5	.6	.7	.8	.9
.1	3.37	3.37	3.38	3.39	3.4	3.4	3.4	3.37	3.35
.2	3.55	3.55	3.55	3.53	3.52	3.5	3.5	3.49	3.48
.3	3.73	3.73	3.72	3.7	3.69	3.68	3.68	3.67	3.66
.4	3.93	3.92	3.91	3.9	3.9	3.89	3.89	3.88	3.87
.5	4.15	4.14	4.13	4.13	4.12	4.12	4.12	4.12	4.12
.6	4.39	4.38	4.38	4.37	4.37	4.37	4.38	4.39	4.4
.7	4.65	4.65	4.65	4.65	4.65	4.66	4.67	4.69	4.72
.8	4.9	4.91	4.91	4.92	4.94	4.96	4.98	5.01	5.06
.9	5.14	5.14	5.15	5.16	5.18	5.2	5.22	5.26	5.3

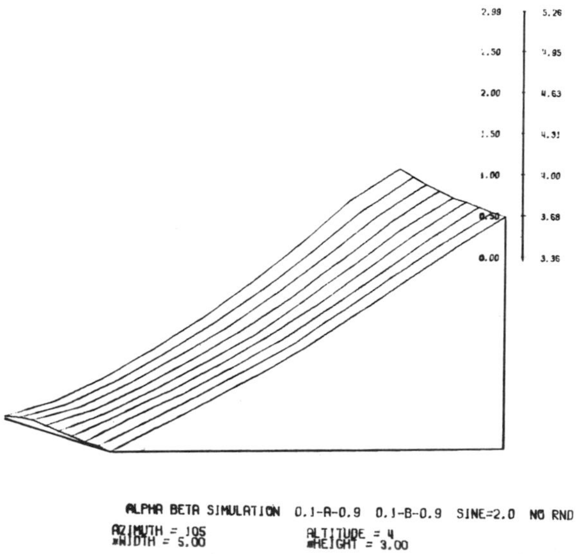

FIGURE 5 - SINE = 2.0 NO RANDOM DISTURBANCE

ALPHA VALUES	BETA VALUES .1	.2	.3	.4	.5	.6	.7	.8	.9
.1	3.37	3.36	3.35	3.35	3.34	3.34	3.33	3.33	3.33
.2	3.54	3.53	3.52	3.51	3.5	3.49	3.47	3.46	3.44
.3	3.74	3.73	3.71	3.69	3.67	3.65	3.63	3.62	3.6
.4	3.96	3.94	3.92	3.9	3.88	3.86	3.83	3.81	3.79
.5	4.21	4.19	4.16	4.14	4.11	4.09	4.07	4.04	4.02
.6	4.48	4.45	4.43	4.41	4.38	4.36	4.33	4.31	4.29
.7	4.77	4.75	4.73	4.71	4.69	4.67	4.65	4.63	4.61
.8	5.09	5.07	5.06	5.04	5.03	5.01	5	4.99	4.98
.9	5.43	5.43	5.42	5.41	5.4	5.39	5.39	5.39	5.39

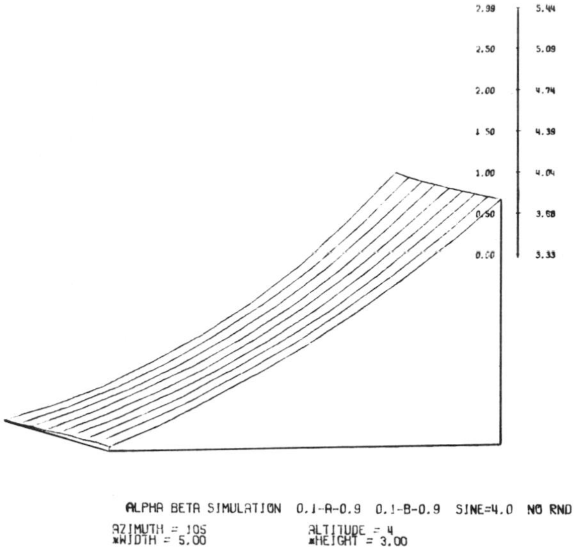

FIGURE 6 - SINE = 4.0 NO RANDOM DISTURBANCE

Just as the transectional graphs show information in a format different from the tables, Figures 7, 8, and 9 are included to show the advantages of another form of graph, the contour map. Figures 7, 8 and 9 are contour maps of the tables shown in Figures 2, 5, and 6 respectively. The α and β values are printed on the axes and the contour lines provide a picture of the changes in MAD for the combinations of α and β. On the major contours, the value representing the MAD are printed. The closer the contour lines, the more sensitive the MAD to changes in α or β. The contour maps provide equivalent information, but in a different form.

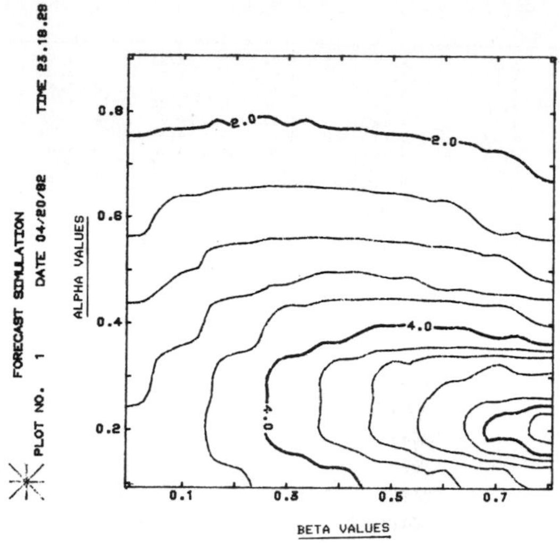

FIGURE 7 - CONTOUR MAP OF FIGURE 2

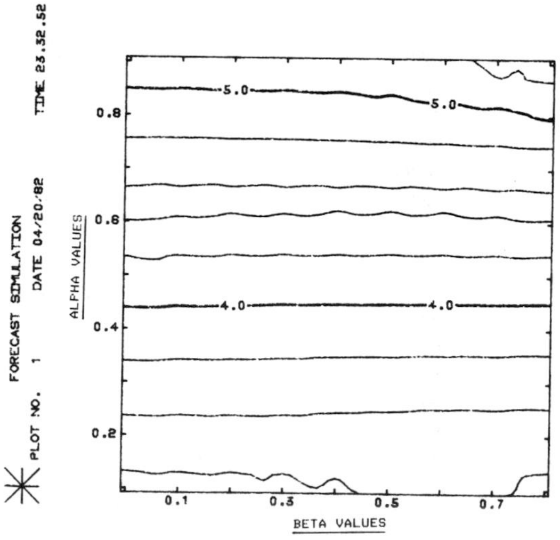

FIGURE 8 - CONTOUR MAP OF FIGURE 5

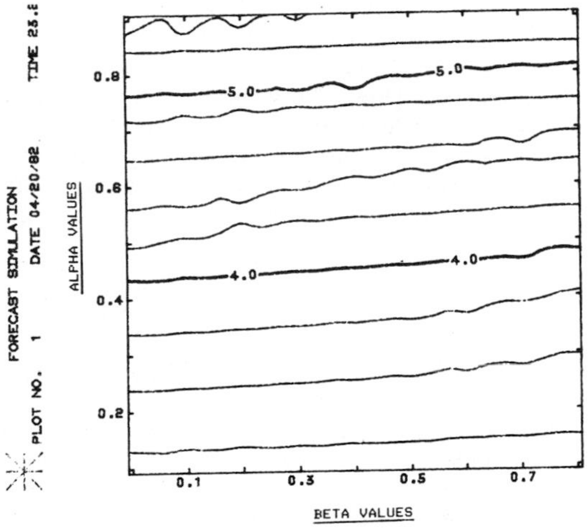

FIGURE 9 - CONTOUR MAP OF FIGURE 6

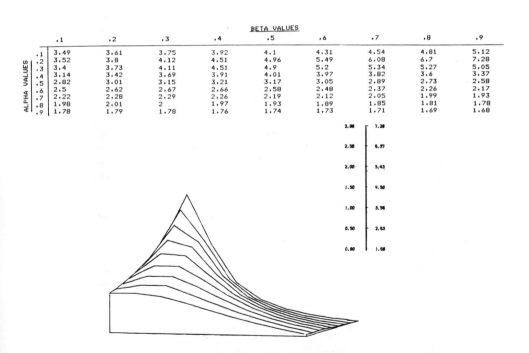

ALPHA VALUES	BETA VALUES .1	.2	.3	.4	.5	.6	.7	.8	.9
.1	3.49	3.61	3.75	3.92	4.1	4.31	4.54	4.81	5.12
.2	3.52	3.8	4.12	4.51	4.96	5.49	6.08	6.7	7.28
.3	3.4	3.73	4.11	4.51	4.9	5.2	5.34	5.27	5.05
.4	3.14	3.42	3.69	3.91	4.01	3.97	3.82	3.6	3.37
.5	2.82	3.01	3.15	3.21	3.17	3.05	2.89	2.73	2.58
.6	2.5	2.62	2.67	2.66	2.58	2.48	2.37	2.26	2.17
.7	2.22	2.28	2.29	2.26	2.19	2.12	2.05	1.99	1.93
.8	1.98	2.01	2	1.97	1.93	1.89	1.85	1.81	1.78
.9	1.78	1.79	1.78	1.76	1.74	1.73	1.71	1.69	1.68

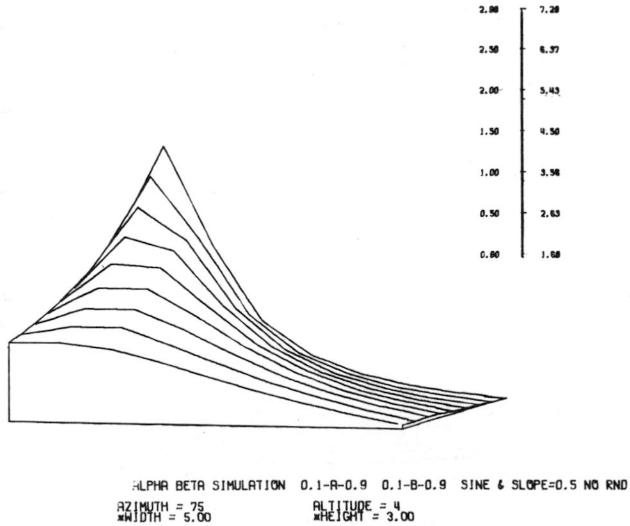

FIGURE 10 - SINE = 0.5 AND SLOPE = 0.5

Since the β adjusts the forecast by adding a trend component to the forecast, a slope of 0.5 was added to a sine of 0.5 in the sixth simulation to compare the affect. The previous simulated demand conditions really had no trend component. Figure 10 shows the MAD values for the combined sine and slope with values of 0.5. Because the forecast is smoothed when α is close to 0.1, the increasing trend component makes the forecast less accurate. When the α is closer to 0.9, increasing the trend component results in only a slight improvement in the forecasts accuracy.

The last simulated demand condition to be forecasted is a step function. Demand increases five units every fifth time period. Overall, this is an upward trend, however, the accuracy of the forecasts are noticeably different than with the previous conditions (Figure 11). Without a trend adjustment (β=0.0) an α of 0.1 produces a smooth forecast which is very inaccurate because it is always significantly lower than demand. The MAD is 9.84. When the trend is added to the "smoothed" forecast, when (α = 0.1, β = 0.8), the forecast tracks demand much more closely, thus a lower MAD of 1.52. When an α of 0.9 is combined with a β of 0.0 the forecasted line follows demand very closely. Except when α and β are very low, the values do not have a significant affect on the forecast accuracy. This is represented as the flat area of the graph.

ALPHA VALUES	BETA VALUES 0	.1	.2	.3	.4	.5	.6	.7	.8
.1	9.84	1.83	1.64	1.58	1.55	1.54	1.53	1.52	1.52
.2	5.01	1.59	1.54	1.53	1.53	1.54	1.55	1.56	1.57
.3	3.36	1.54	1.53	1.54	1.56	1.58	1.6	1.63	1.65
.4	2.52	1.51	1.52	1.55	1.57	1.61	1.64	1.68	1.72
.5	2.02	1.47	1.49	1.52	1.55	1.59	1.63	1.68	1.73
.6	1.69	1.4	1.43	1.46	1.49	1.53	1.57	1.61	1.67
.7	1.45	1.32	1.34	1.37	1.41	1.45	1.5	1.55	1.6
.8	1.27	1.24	1.27	1.29	1.32	1.35	1.38	1.41	1.43
.9	1.13	1.14	1.16	1.17	1.18	1.2	1.21	1.22	1.22

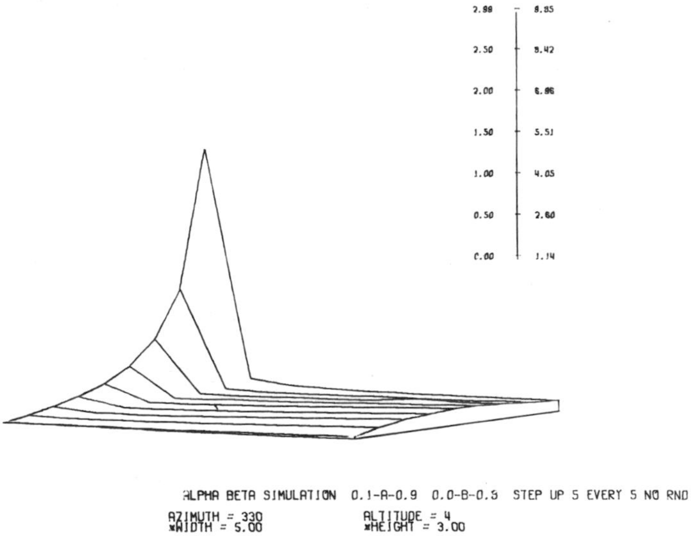

FIGURE 11 - STEP UP 5 UNITS EVERY 5 PERIODS

CONCLUSION

There are infinite combinations of demand condition which can be derived for study. These seven were chosen because they represent likely conditions, both with and without trend components and random disturbance. We find the results valuable in understanding that the sensitivity of changes in both the smoothing and trend adjustment variables of exponential smoothing are unique to the demand condition being forecast. The computer graphs are useful to help visualize forecasted results of the simulation. A logical extension of this process is to apply the forecasting to actual demand conditions. As demonstrated here, the graphics facilitate pattern recognition, which is the mental process of interpreting information. Graphic information speeds interpretation and decision making and reduces errors and through the use of graphics a "...much higher bandwidth man-machine communications..." (Foley and Van Dam, 1982, 6) is achieved.

REFERENCES

Foley, J.D., and Van Dam, A., Fundamentals of Interactive Computer Graphics, Addison-Wesley Publishing Co.: Reading, Mass., 1982.

Hoffman, David B., and Carlson, Carol M., "Using Computer Graphics to Interpret Simulation Output," Simulation, (August, 1981), pp. 59-64.

Sampson, R.J., SURFACE II Graphic Systems, Kansas Geological Survey: Kansas, 1978.

SYMVU Manual, Laboratory for Computer Graphics and Spatial Analysis - Harvard University: Cambridge, Mass., 1977.

Torfin, Gary P., and Hoffmann, Thomas R., "Simulation Tests of Some Forecasting Techniques," Production and Inventory Management, (2nd Qtr., 1968), pp. 71-78.

Vollman, Thomas E., Operations Management: A Systems Model-Building Approach, Addison-Wesley Publishing Co.: Reading, Mass., 1973.

APPLICATION OF INTERACTIVE COMPUTER GRAPHICS TO THE RESULTS OF ELECTROMAGNETIC FIELD CALCULATIONS

Ilhan A. Ince, Michael L. Barton, and James J. Oravec

Westinghouse Electric Corporation
Research and Development Center
1310 Beulah Road
Pittsburgh, PA 15235
U. S. A.

ABSTRACT

With the proliferation of modeling and analysis, computer systems engineers in all fields have experienced a great increase in the number and complexity of problems that they can profitably solve. Systems for processing the solutions to such problems have not, however, kept up and this has created a situation in which engineers have had to turn to methods that are less powerful and accurate than others that are available but provide output data in a form they can efficiently handle.

We present an interactive graphics post-processor designed as part of a finite element analysis system for electromagnetic field problems. We describe the ideas which are central to the design of a responsive interactive post-processor and explain some of the algorithms which have proven successful. Several examples are shown to illustrate the plotting and graphical results presentation capabilities of the post-processor.

1. INTRODUCTION

The ever increasing demand for larger, more reliable and more efficient electrical machines has necessitated the use of numerical methods; in particular the finite element technique. This, in turn, confronted the engineers with the problem of large scale data preparation (pre-processing) and result evaluation (post-processing).

In the last two decades the problem of data preparation has received world wide attention [1]. As a result, many good pre-processors are commercially available. On the other hand, the problem of result evaluation has not received the attention it deserves. As a result, many engineers have turned to methods that, while less powerful and less accurate than they would like, provide output data they can efficiently handle.

We present an interactive graphics post-processor -- WEPOSTS -- designed as part of a finite element analysis system -- WEMAP -- for electromagnetic field problems. WEMAP (including both analysis and post-processing) runs on a PRIME minicomputer. The graphics of WEPOSTS is based upon the Graphics Compatability System (GCS). Therefore, WEPOSTS runs on terminals supported by GCS. WEPOSTS is menu, command language driven and is self-supported by commands such as 'teach' and 'help'.

With WEPOSTS the user can interactively and selectively present the output data and derive engineering quantities from it. At his direction flux plots are available for in-phase and out-of-phase flux components. Plots showing

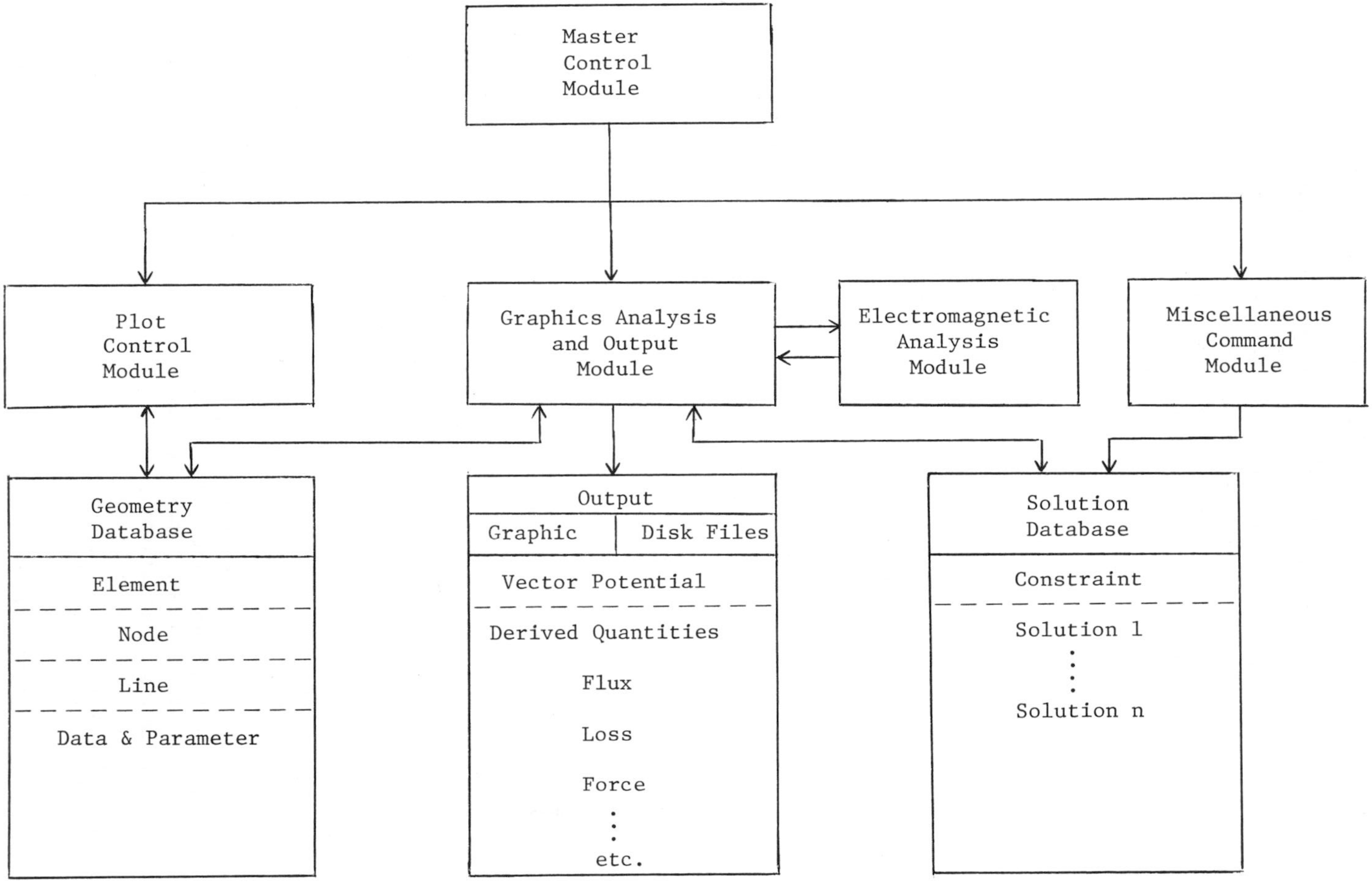

Figure 1. Post-processor structure

lines of constant magnetic saturation, loss density, and force density can be generated. The user may request field quantities of interest at points or over elements simply by pointing to the appropriate screen location. Upon specification of a line or an arc graphs showing the variation of the field components along the specified path are generated. Plots and derived quantities can be selectively sent to the screen or to a disk file. The FEM model and all derived plots can be viewed and manipulated in 3-D space by the use of commands such as 'view', 'orientation', 'window', and 'zoom'.

In the following section an overview of the structure of WEPOSTS is given. Next the philosophy and implementation of the user interface are explained and illustrated. We then describe the plotting and interface outlining algorithms and finally show how some of the user-directed calculations are executed and presented.

2. POST-PROCESSOR STRUCTURE OVERVIEW

The WEPOSTS post-processor acts as a design tool interface between the designer and design related electromagnetic entities. It allows the designer to exhaustively explore the implication of a given electromagnetic design.

The structure of the program can be seen from Figure 1. It has four modules: the graphic interaction and analysis, electromagnetic analysis, plot control and miscellaneous command modules. Each of these components is described below. The master control module acts as the interface between the user and the computer. The user communicates with the master control program either by keyboard commands or through a menu. The master control program interpretes the instruction and passes control to one of the lower level modules, thus coordinating their activities.

WEPOSTS utilizes two databases: the geometry database and the solution database. The geometry database is generated by the geometric modules (pre-processors). The solution database is generated by one of various electromagnetic analysis programs. Both databases are binary disk files and are transparent to the designer. To enhance the speed of interaction WEPOSTS only uses the databases for user inquiries and data retrieval. Upon user request output is generated either in the form of a screen tabulation and graphical displays, or in the form of formatted disk files.

3. USER INTERFACE

As in the use of any interactive graphics program the user interface is the most important element in user acceptability. Throughout the implementation of this interface we have tried to adopt a natural path of thinking and to generate a structure such that communication is done in terms of engineering design quantities. The final interface consists of command controls and on-line documentation.

Command Control Procedure

The method followed here is one of 'pre-programmed' functions to control operator dialogues, graphics manipulations and output. Macros are not allowed and functions are added as the necessity arises. The user has the option of communicating through keyboard command strings or by the use of menus. The pick and pointing actions are handled by the graphics tablet or other graphic input devices.

The command language is designed to conform to a tree structure. At every level there is a pre-defined set of commands to be allowed. Each command node may end up in another branch or in a leaf. At every level there are a set of pre-defined defaults which the user has the option of accepting or changing.

In keyboard input mode a given user command string is parsed into command sequences. These command sequences may include numeric values and/or alphanumeric command expressions of four characters or fewer. In the menu mode, the user creates the command sequences by selectively picking the appropriate command elements.

Once the parsing has occurred, the master control module command interpreter validates the first command element and passes the control to the appropriate submodule. This process is repeated until a leaf is reached. Upon encountering an error in a command sequence the interpreter informs the user of the error. Depending on the severity the user is either returned to the next higher branch or to the main command module. The only exceptions to this convention are the STOP command and the system break character (usually CTRL P). These are monitored at every level. STOP terminates the program execution. CTRP P terminates any graphic and/or computational process in progress and returns the control to the master control module.

For example, if the user enters the command:

```
FLUX LINE BMBPH
```

This is interpreted that the user would like to see the magnitude and phase variation of the flux density along a line to be specified. Flow of command transfer on a very simplified tree diagram is shown in Figure 2. It must be noted that tree branches have been terminated where a path is no longer to be followed. When the leaf is reached the graphic input device is turned on for the specification of the line. Requested entities are computed and plotted.

On-Line Documentation

At present WEPOSTS has three levels of on-line documentation. These are: 1) echo, 2) help, and 3) teach.

The echo feature echoes the arguments of any valid WEPOSTS command after the command is entered. If the user knows the command but has forgotten the arguments to the command, by entering the command followed by an empty carriage return, the program will echo the arguments required by the command. For example, if the user has forgotten the arguments for the FLUX command, the program responds as follows:

```
*FLUX
  <'NODE'/'ELEMENT'>
  <'LINE','BXBY'/'BMBPH'/'BNBT'>
  <'ARC','BXBY'/'BMBPH'/'BNBT'>
  <'MAXIMUM','MATERIAL'/'SOURCE','MATERIAL NO'/'SOUR NO'>
  <'CONT','NLINE','VALU'/'NOVALU','FAST'/'SLOW'>
```

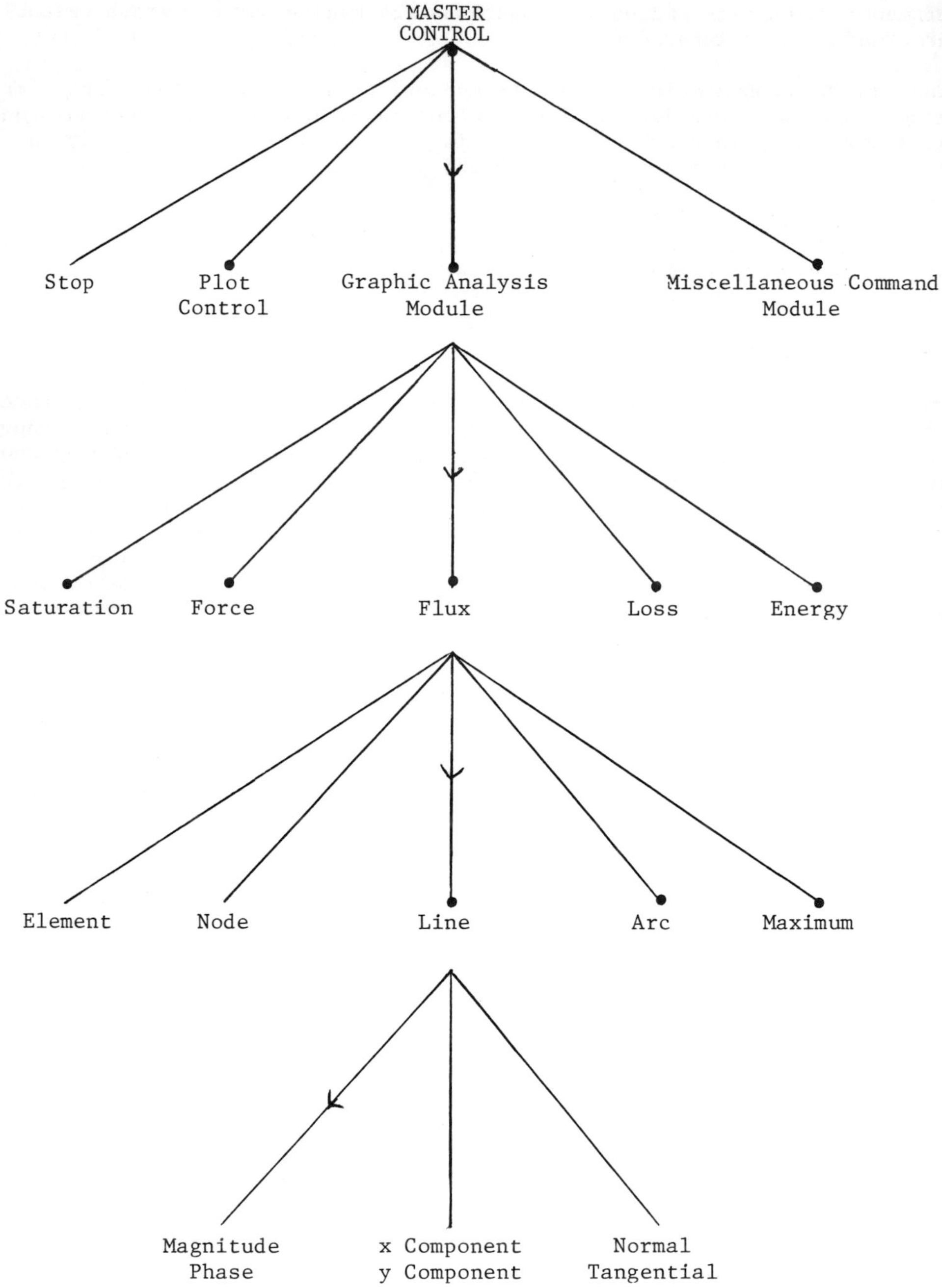

Figure 2. WEPOSTS command structure decision tree example.

The help feature is a more extensive on-line documentation. The command HELP followed by an empty carriage return will echo back all the valid commands in the WEPOSTS module. A HELP followed by a valid command will echo back the arguments to the command as well as a short description of each argument. For example, if the user enters help for the FLUX command, the echo would be:

```
*HELP FLUX
FLUX <'NODE'/'ELEM'>
   gives the flux density (electric field) at a node or the centroid
   of an element specified (by using the cursor).
   e.g.  FLUX NODE
FLUX <'LINE','BXBY'/'BMBPH'/'BNBT'>
FLUX <'ARC','BXBY'/'BMBPH'/'BNBT'>
   give an -xy- plot of the variation of flux density (electric field)
   along a specified line/arc.  The 'BXBY' option gives -x- and -y-
   components of the field along the line and is the default.  'BMBPH'
   option gives the magnitude and the phase variation along the line.
   'BMBT' option gives the normal and tangential field variation along
   the line
   e.g.  FLUX LINE
FLUX <'MAXIMUM','MATERIAL'/'SOURCE','MATERIAL NO'/'SOURCE NO'>
   gives the value of the maximum flux density (electric field) and
   its location in a specified material or source region
   e.g.  FLUX MAXIMUM MATERIAL 1
FLUX <'CONT','NLINE','VALU'/'NOVALU','FAST'/'SLOW'>
   gives isolines of the potentials.  NLINE is the number of lines and
   its default value is 15.  VALU/NOVALU option determines whether the
   isoline potential values are to be displayed.  Default is NOVALU.
   FAST/SLOW option determines the speed of the plotting.  Default is
   FAST.  SLOW option will give a slower but more precise plot.
   e.g.  FLUX CONT 23 SLOW
```

The teach feature is the most extensive on-line documentation. It takes the novice user through the commands and functions of the various WEPOSTS modules.

4. PLOT CONTROL MODULE

WEPOSTS provides the user with extensive control and flexibility of model plotting. A high degree of selectivity has been deliberately implemented. This, however, results in a rather large and complex set of control commands. A subset of the available commands is given in Figure 3. As can be seen, plot control commands are divided into two groups: the 'active' and the 'passive' plot commands.

Active plot commands are executed immediately after the command is given. These commands may be used to plot a single entity or a group of entities. They may be used to add selective additional information after a global model plot has been completed. The two special commands of this category are the ERASE and REDRAW commands. Both these commands will update any

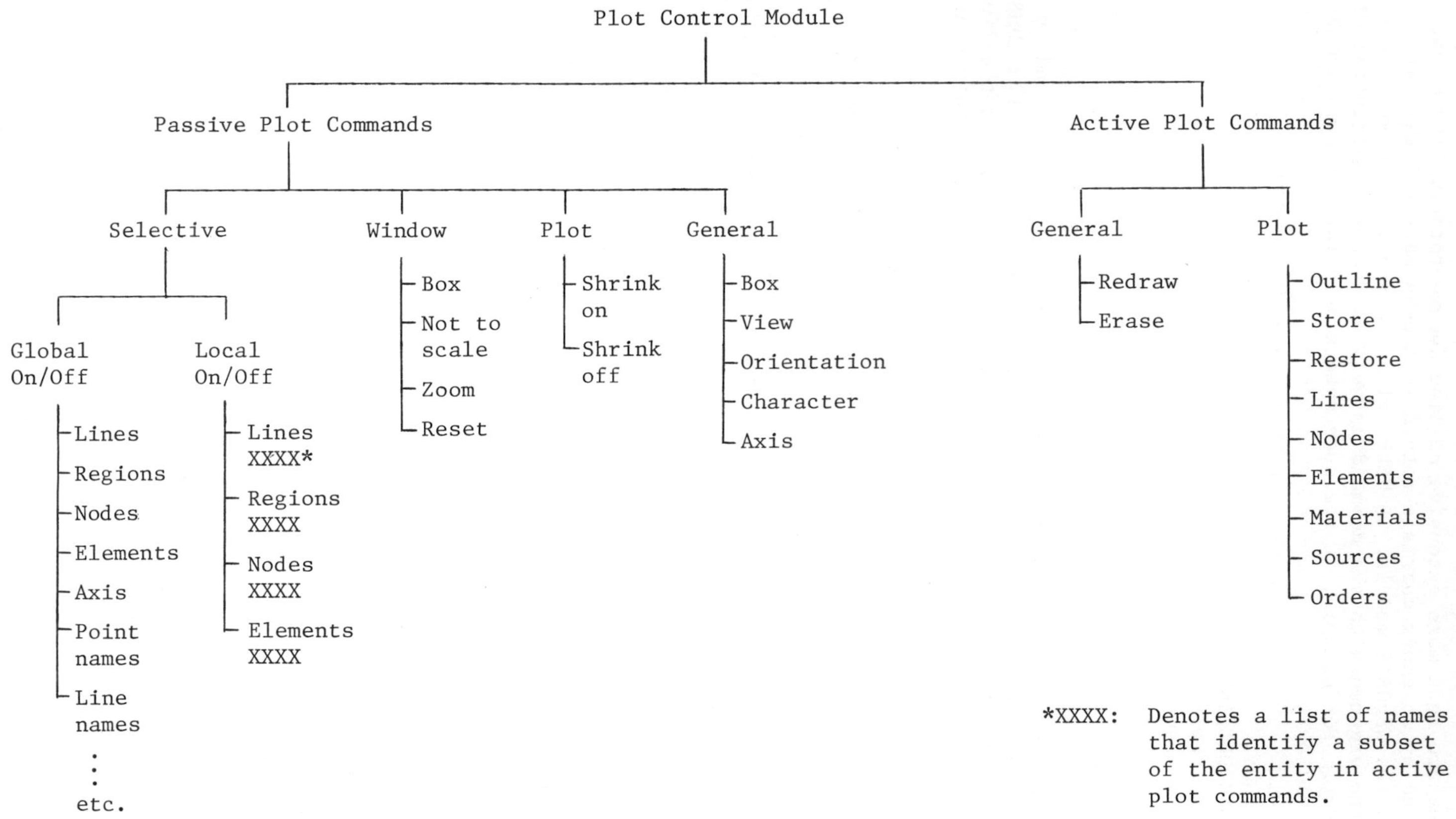

Figure 3. Most common commands of the plot module

plot parameters, e.g., windows, viewports, that may have been changed. The new parameters may be used the next time anything is plotted.

Passive plot commands control what is to be plotted upon the next REDRAW entry. As implied by their name, the selective plot commands control plotting of model components as well as item names. They can either be local or global. The WINDOW commands form the second major category and constitute different forms of zooming on a given area. BOX command is used to change the viewport.

5. GRAPHIC ANALYSIS MODULE

The display which gives the user the most immediate and satisfying feedback about the success or failure of the solution to his problem is undoubtedly the isoline plot showing equipotentials (for electric fields) or flux lines (for magnetic fields). This plot, though it usually provides none of the engineering quantities of interest, often gives the user the all important insight into some crucial feature of the design that he is analyzing; or it may make immediately apparent the fact that his model is missing some essential feature.

Plotting Problem Outline and Interfaces

The user of a finite element analysis package is generally an engineer who thinks about his problem in terms of its component parts rather than in terms of elements of any other analysis tool. The post-processor can cooperate with the user by displaying the results in ways most compatible with his expectations. A vital part of any display of the plotted results of the analysis over the problem region is the visual identification of subregions which have been identified as having distinct properties. These subregions may differ in their material properties or source values or they may have the same values but be given distinct identifiers by the user for some reason of his own. In any case the results plot will be more meaningful if these subregions are outlined, preferably in some way distinct from the lines which are going to be plotted to indicate the equipotential or flux contours.

One way to show these outlines would be to rely on the construction lines that the user generated during model construction. This method would be based on the assumption that the user treated each region that he regarded as logically separate as a separate region during model generation and assigned to each a unique material or source pointer. Clearly this will not always be true. A more important reason for not using this method to show material and source region outlines is that it provides no feedback to the user on what problem the analysis program actually solved.

To give the user a complete picture of where the source and material interfaces lie it is necessary to examine the problem data base and determine across which element edges material or source labels differ. These element edges can then be plotted and the result will be a picture of all of the subregions which differ in material or source label.

We have seen algorithms which perform this determination by comparing each side of each element with each side of every other element. If N is the total number of elements and K the number of sides per element the number of comparisons which must be made is the number of permutations of KN things taken two at a time. This number is

$$\frac{KN\ (KN - 1)}{2}$$

For a problem with 4000 triangular elements the necessary number of comparisons is nearly 72 million. Clearly this is not satisfactory.

Our algorithm for determining material and source interfaces is based on the following viewpoint: There are two ways to determine the interface between two types of material. One is to examine each pair of elements which share a common side and determine if the elements are of different types. The other is to form a list of all elements of one type and determine the set of sides which constitute the boundary of that group of elements. The first method (see above) requires an amount of work proportional to the square of the number of elements. The second method (which we use) requires each element to be examined once only and the amount of work grows linearly with the number of elements.

Our method starts by apportioning a fixed amount of memory into

$$(S - 1) + (M - 1) + 1 = S + M - 1$$

equals parts where S is the number of distinct source labels and M the number of distinct material labels in the problem (note that every element has a source and a material label). This memory will be used to accumulate lists of node pairs the union of which will constitute the outline for a particular source or material, or for the entire problem. The number of partitions is arrived at as follows: First we must draw an outline of the entire problem. Then we need to draw the outlines of only S - 1 sources (and M - 1 materials) because each piece of the boundary of the last source (or material) region will coincide with either the problem outline or the boundary of some adjacent source (or material) region.

The algorithm now proceeds by examining each element to determine its source and material labels. The node pairs constituting the sides of the element are added to the list of node pairs for that source and material and to the list of the total problem outline according to this rule: If the node pair is already in the list, delete it; if it is not in the list, add it. The operation of this algorithm can be understood as follows: Start with all of the sides of one element in the list. Take the next element of that type and add its sides to the list unless those sides coincide with a pair already in the list. If this happens that side is interior to the outline in question and so is deleted from the list. In the end only those node pairs which have been found only once appear in the list and the union of these pairs constitute the outline for that label type.

Several features of this scheme are evident: At no time until the algorithm is complete do the lists of node pairs bear any semblance to the desired outlines. Assuming a random ordering of elements the contents of the lists midway through processing will typically describe many disjoint shapes all contained within the eventual correct outline. For this reason it is impossible to plot outline segments as they are calculated since they are

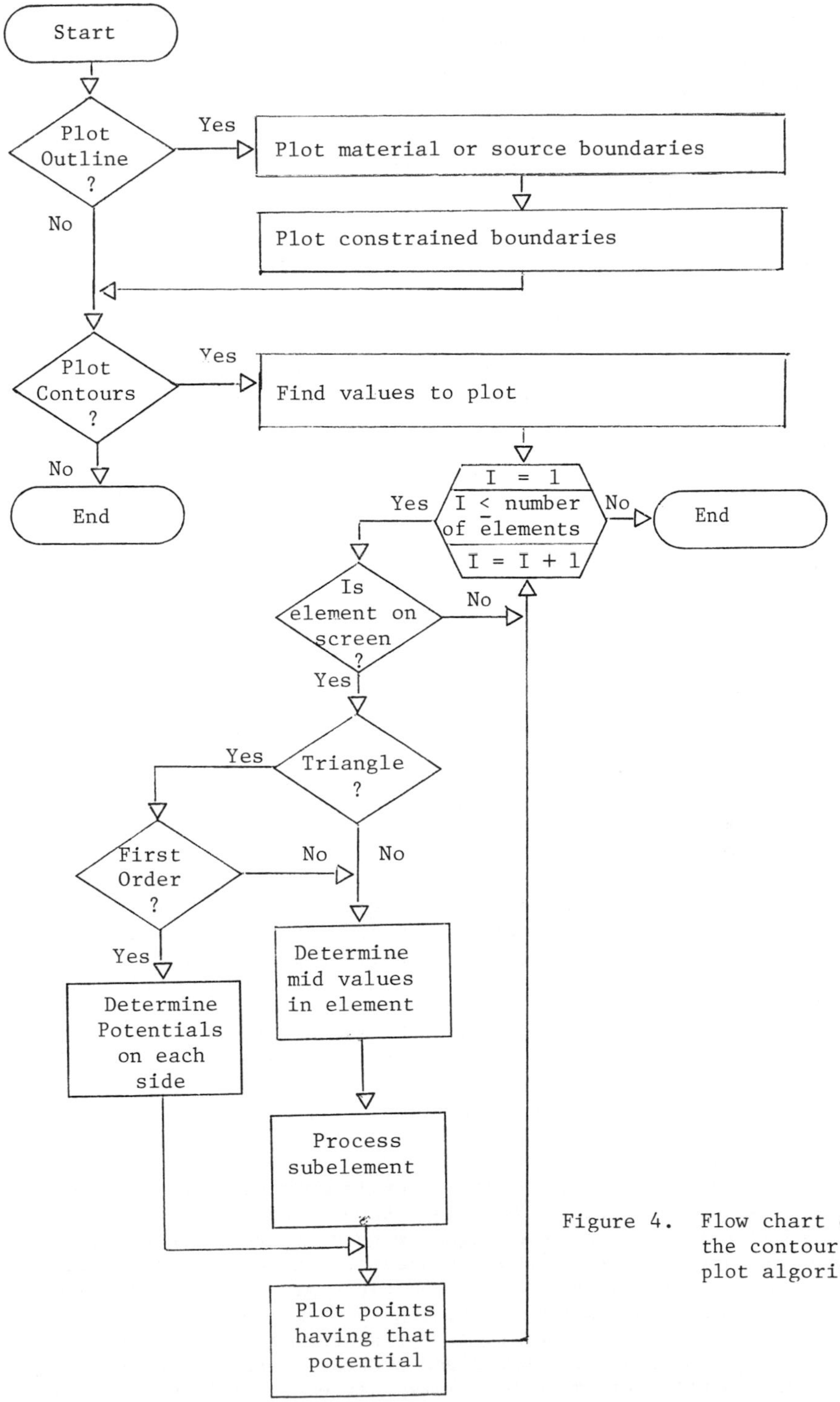

Figure 4. Flow chart of the contour plot algorithm.

only correctly calculated all at once when the method terminates. It is also very important to make the implementation of this method as robust as possible because if it fails for some reason the partial contents of the lists are generally useless. The most likely reason for failure is memory overflow since the lengths of the lists at intermediate times in the algorithms processing will generally be much larger than the final lengths of the lists and these lengths are hard to estimate since they are strongly dependent on the patterns in element numbering which are usually present as accidental side-effects of the adaptive model generation. In order to increase the efficiency with which we use the available memory the boundaries between lists are allowed to slide in either direction if one list fills up while a neighboring list has room left. The outlines are plotted with dashed lines with no attempt to avoid duplicate line drawing. To drive the graphics on a high-speed GCS supported terminal it is clearly faster to draw a line several times than to do the comparison checking to see if it is a duplicate. This priority might well change if a hard-copy plotter were being used.

Contour Plotting

First order finite element solutions are plotted by using the exact potential variation function (linear). The goal of the plotting algorithm for high order finite elements [3] is to capture all of the essential features of the solution without getting bogged down in attempts to solve for the roots of quintic (say) polynomials. A quadratic approximation to the behavior of the solution in subdivided elements provides a good compromise between accuracy and computational simplicity. The basis for such an algorithm for triangular elements is given in [2]. To the basic algorithm in [2] we have added the capability to plot solutions in dual order parallelogram elements [4] and a 'FAST/SLOW' option which controls the fineness of the element subdivision. 'FAST' (the default) generates a coarse subdivision and usually a good plot, adequate for most purposes. 'SLOW' generates a fine subdivision and a much slower, but generally perfect plot. A flow chart of this algorithm is given in Figure 4.

Figure 5 shows an electrostatic equipotential plot for one quarter of a coaxial electrode filled partly with an insulator with a relative permittivity of 3.0 and the rest with air. Figure 6 shows a magnetostatic flux plot for an induction motor with a highly permeable rotor and stator and current only in the stator slots. In the electrostatic plot (Figure 5) the elements are triangular with fourth order approximations. In the magnetostatic plot (Figure 6) the elements are triangles and quadrilaterals with cubic accuracy.

6. ELECTROMAGNETIC ANALYSIS MODULE

While the principle thrust of this paper is on the graphics involved in post-processing for finite element solutions, the techniques that are employed to calculate the quantities to be displayed have a major impact on the facility with which a post-processor can be used. The plot-generating algorithm is covered in the section on plotting. Most of the other calculations are based on numerical estimates of some derivative of the potential function (the gradient of the scalar potential or the curl of the vector potential). The speed and accuracy with which those derivatives are estimated will determine to a large degree the responsiveness of the system.

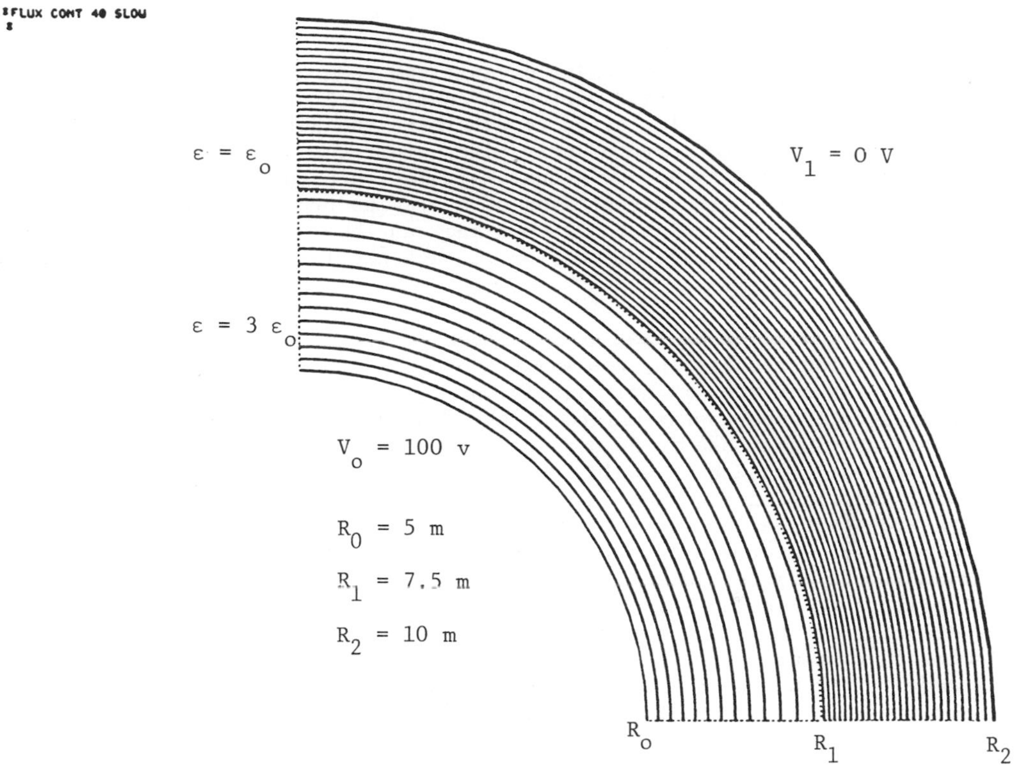

Figure 5. Electrostatic equipotential plot for coaxial cable.

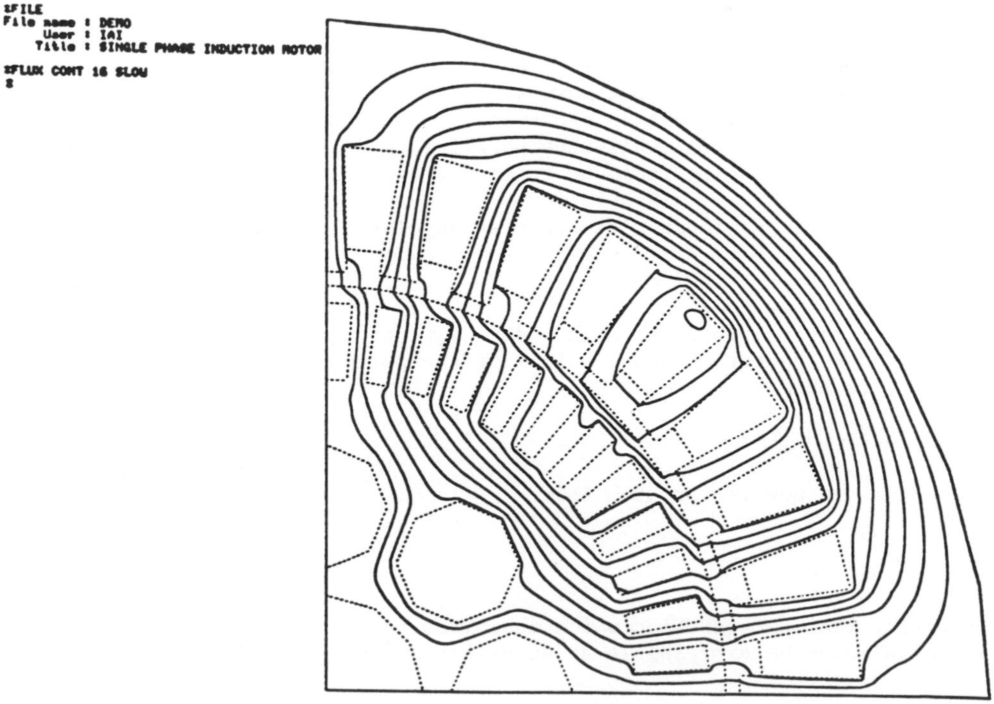

Figure 6. Magnetostatic equipotential plot for an induction motor.

Derivative Calculation

The main choice in how to determine derivatives from a set of potential functions defined on elements (and piecewise continuous) seems to be whether to do some kind of global calculation to determine the derivatives everywhere once and for all, or to compute derivatives element by element as needed. If the choice is made to do one global calculation a further decision involves whether to perform some kind of averaging procedure so that the derivative will be piecewise continuous and can thus be stored in a global array as the potentials are stored, or to save the locally defined derivative in each element.

Most application programs that we have seen do a global calculation and then average the results in some way. Averaging certainly requires less storage but in our view is only justified if it is indeed better to have a piecewise continuous approximation to the derivative quantity for all applications. We choose to do our computing on an element by element basis as needed, though we would have no quarrel with a system which did a global calculation provided that the results are stored directly by element so that the true derivative functions are always available. We have found that important information is lost when the discontinuities between normal derivatives in adjacent elements are eliminated. When the user asks for the derivative along a line or arc he gets feedback about the validity of the solution by observing the magnitude and directions of the jumps from element to element. The user can develop a good feel for the adequacy of his model after he has refined a couple of meshes, or increased the approximation order in the elements, and seen the dramatic reduction in the derivative jumps.

Derivative Calculation in an Element

In the analysis system that is most commonly used with the WEPOSTS postprocessor the user may select triangular or parallelogram elements (nonparallelogram quadrilaterals are subdivided transparent to the user). The approximating functions within the triangles may be of complete polynomial order from one to six [3] while the parallelograms are dual-order [4] with the orders again ranging from one to six.

The potential $\theta(x,y)$ in an n'th order triangular element can be written as

$$\theta = \tilde{\alpha}^n \underset{\sim}{\theta} \qquad (1)$$

where $\tilde{\alpha}^n$ is a row vector of n'th order Lagrangian interpolation functions and $\underset{\sim}{\theta}$ a column vector of nodal values of the potential. The x-derivative of $\theta(x,y)$ is then

$$\theta_x = \tilde{\beta} \underset{\sim}{\theta} \qquad (2)$$

where $\tilde{\beta}$ is the row vector such that

$$\beta_i = \frac{d\alpha_i}{dx} \qquad (3)$$

Now notice that the function which describes the derivative of an n'th order polynomial must be expressible as an n-1'st order polynomial. Thus,

```
%FLUX CONT
%FLUX NODE
  NODE      MATL      ER            ETHETA

   71        1     0.134E 02     -.888E-02
   74        1     0.118E 02     -.496E-02
   94        2     0.284E 02     -.102E-01
   45        2     0.225E 02     0.153E 00
   29        1     0.108E 02     -.347E-01
             2     0.322E 02     -.127E 00
   81        1     0.134E 02     -.745E-02
%ELEM NAMES ON
%FLUX ELEM
 ELEMENT       ER           ETHETA

   82      0.248E 02     0.477E 00
   67      0.271E 02     0.459E 00
   52      0.299E 02     0.472E 00
   21      0.111E 02     -.212E 00
   20      0.126E 02     -.230E 00
   17      0.126E 02     -.230E 00
%FLUX LINE
Please enter the BEGINNING and END points.
Is this line OK
Enter YES, NO, CANCEL
<YES
```

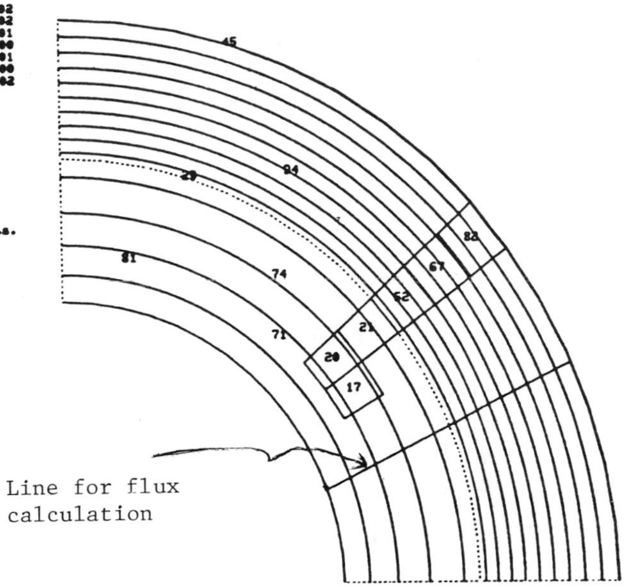

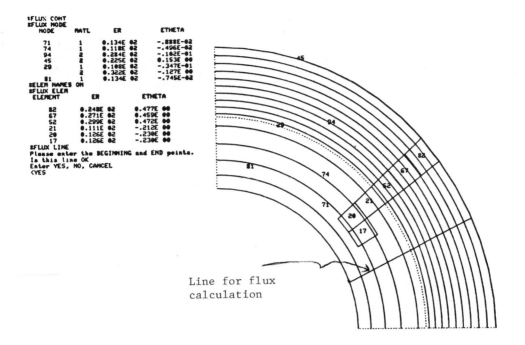

Figure 7a. 'FLUX NODE', 'FLUX ELEM' and 'FLUX LINE' examples.

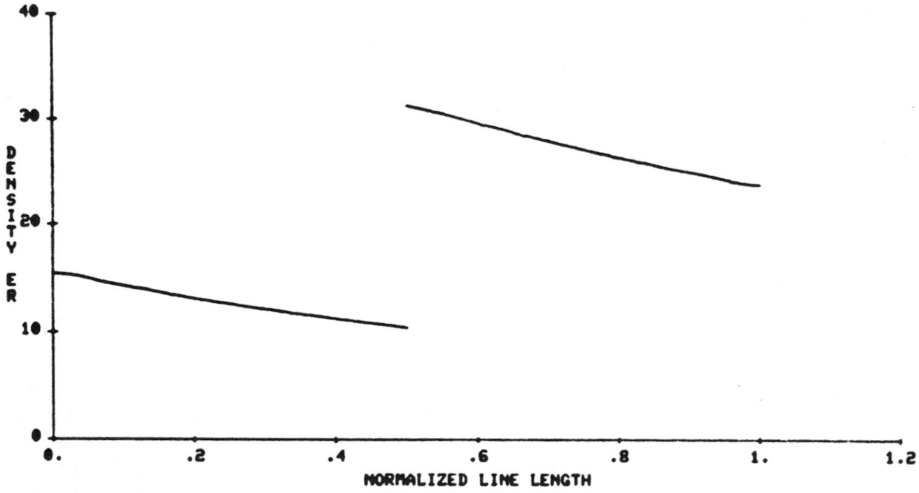

Figure 7b. Radial electric field along line of Figure 7a.

$$\theta_x = \tilde{\gamma}^{n-1} \underset{\sim}{\Phi} \tag{4}$$

where $\tilde{\gamma}^{n-1}$ is a row vector of n-1'st order Lagrangian polynomials and $\underset{\sim}{\Phi}$ is the column vector of the x-directed derivatives of the function $\underset{\sim}{\theta}(x,y)$. A comparison of equations (2) and (4) makes it clear that the i'th component of $\underset{\sim}{\Phi}$ is

$$\Phi_i = \sum_{j=1}^{N} \left(\frac{\partial \alpha_j}{\partial x} \bigg|_{(x_i,y_i)} \theta_j \right) \tag{5}$$

where (x_i,y_i) is the i'th node of an n-1'st order triangle and N is the number of nodes in an n'th order triangle.

Equation (5) leads to a matrix equation for $\underset{\sim}{\Phi}$

$$\underset{\sim}{\Phi} = D^{n-1,n} \underset{\sim}{\theta} \tag{6}$$

where

$$D_{ij}^{n-1,n} = \frac{d\alpha_j^n}{dx} \bigg|_{(x_i,y_i)} \tag{7}$$

The rectangular matrix D is a <u>differentiation matrix</u> [5]. A corresponding matrix can of course be defined for the y-directed derivative and similar derivations are available for parallelogram elements.

Efficient methods are available for the calculation of the differentiation matrices for each element and this forms the basis for all of our derivative based calculations.

Field At A Node

WEPOSTS allows the user to sample the derivative quantities by requesting, for example, the electric field intensity in an electric field problem at the node nearest the cursor position. (Electric field intensity is minus the gradient of the scalar potential.) WEPOSTS responds to the request by writing the node number selected at the node location and giving the components of electric field at that point. Figure 7a shows several nodes that have been selected on the coaxial cable problem and gives the electric field intensities. Figure 8 shows an example on the magnetic field problem.

When the user requests <u>nodal</u> derivative values it is clear that he actually wants <u>averaged</u> values so WEPOSTS calculates a weighted average of the value of the derivative function at the node in each element containing the node (the weights are the angles in each element at the node). Clearly the average must be computed separately over each different material incident to that node.

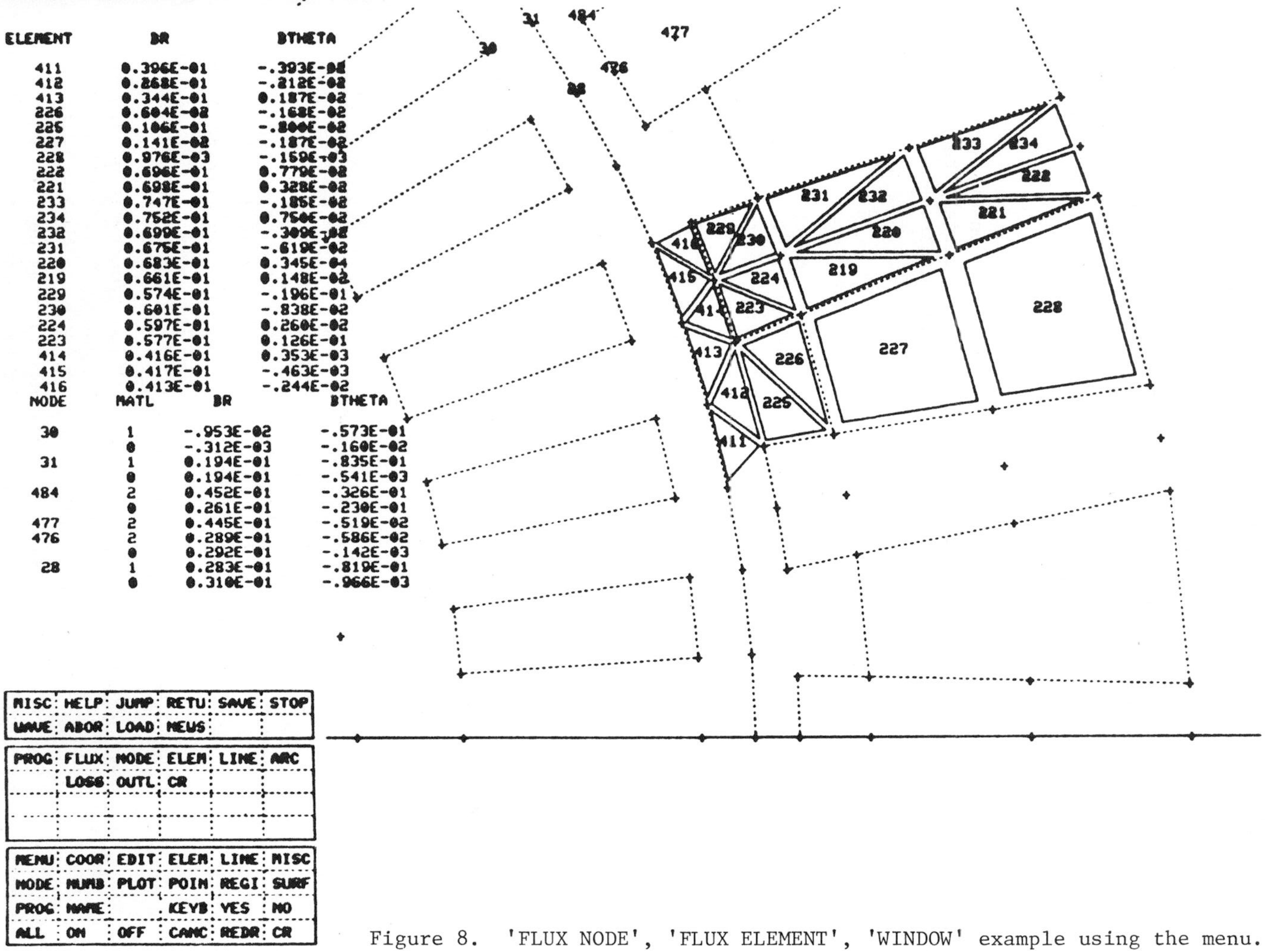

Figure 8. 'FLUX NODE', 'FLUX ELEMENT', 'WINDOW' example using the menu.

Field At An Element

Another sampling method is the calculation of field intensity in an element. Here WEPOSTS outlines the element which contains the cursor and gives the value of the field intensity at the centroid (see Figures 7a and 8). For elements of orders one or two the centroid value corresponds to the average value. For higher order approximations they will differ and the difference is another important measure of the local solution accuracy. WEPOSTS gives both values when they differ significantly.

If algorithms were used which generated a set of global derivative values at nodes by averaging over adjacent elements the generation of element-wise derivatives would pose a problem. Surely it is not right to give values of derivative in an element which involve potentials outside the element.

Flux Along A Line Or Arc

The estimation of derivative quantities along a user-generated line or arc is accomplished in WEPOSTS by determining the elements incident to the line and calculating the value of the derivative function (Equation (6)) at a sufficient number of points along the line segment within each element to capture the polynomial behavior of the function. For a triangular element of order n the number, m, of points at which the derivative is calculated is:

$$m = \begin{cases} 2 & , n = 1 \\ (n-1)^2 + 1, & n \neq 1 \end{cases} \tag{8}$$

The result of this calculation is a pair of graphs showing the components (x-y, r-θ, magnitude-phase, normal-tangential) of field or flux along the line or arc. Figure 7b shows the variation of radial electric field along the radial line in Figure 7a. The tangential field is zero. The true solution for E_r for this problem is (see Figure 7):

$$E_r = \begin{cases} V_o + \dfrac{V_o \ell n \dfrac{r}{R_o}}{\varepsilon_r \ell n \dfrac{R_1}{R_2} - \ell n \dfrac{R_1}{R_o}} & R_o < r < R_1 \\[2em] \dfrac{\varepsilon_r V_o \ell n \dfrac{r}{R_2}}{\varepsilon_r \ell n \dfrac{R_1}{R_2} - \ell n \dfrac{R_1}{R_o}} & R_1 < r < R_2 \end{cases} \tag{9}$$

The values in Figure 7b differ from the true solution by no more than 2% at any point. Figure 9a shows an arc selected for the magnetostatic problem and in Figure 9b the radial and tangential components of magnetic flux density are graphed. This is, of course, the air gap flux density.

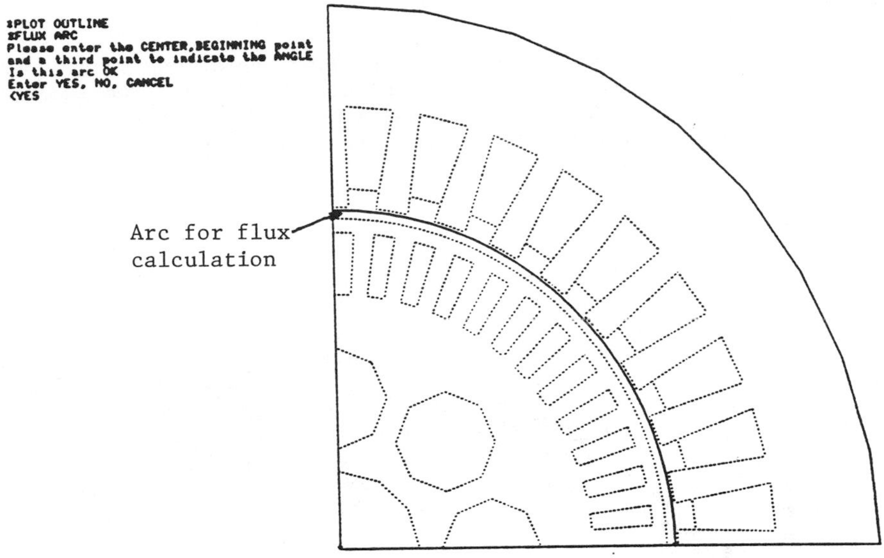

Figure 9a. 'FLUX ARC' example.

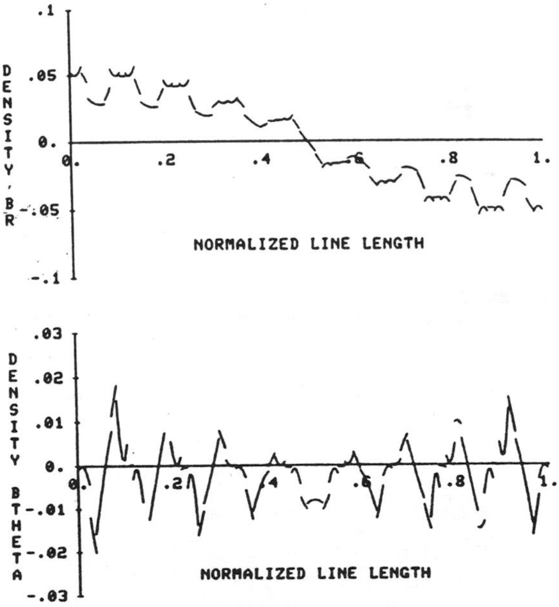

Figure 9b. Radial and tangential flux density graphs.

7. MISCELLANEOUS COMMAND MODULE

This module controls various commands controlling operations ranging from terminal configuration, to news service, to file handling. Two important facilities in this module are: ABORT, which enables the user to load in a new model, and LOADSL, which enables the user to load multiple solution files for the existing model.

8. CONCLUSION

WEPOSTS described above provides an electrical design tool which is tailored to the needs of the electrical designer. The graphical interaction is done in terms of standard design terminology. This enables the designers to use the computer as a friendly design tool rather than having to learn computer terminology. Its selective analysis and processing capabilities enable the designer to concentrate on the problem at hand rather than having to go through reams of irrelevant computer output. It thus allows electrical designers to use state of the art analysis and design techniques with maximum speed and efficiency. Furthermore, the interactivity and the speed of response enables the electrical designer to create and improve designs iteratively. WEPOSTS is a model example of a partnership between the computer and the electrical designer in effectively dealing with increasingly complex designs on the road to better performance and efficiency.

ACKNOWLEDGMENTS

The authors express their thanks to J. W. Morris, M. B. Newman, and J. R. Snyder for numerous technical discussions and for providing valuable pieces of code in an attempt to make WEPOSTS compatible with the Westinghouse pre-processor FIGURES II.

REFERENCES

[1] Morris, J. W., Newman, M. B., and Snyder, J. R., "FIGURES II Pre-Processor User Guide", Westinghouse Report 81-7E7-FIGTO-R1, 1981.

[2] Cendes, Z. and Silvester, P. P., "FINPLT: A Finite Element Field-Plotting Program", IEEE Trans. on Microwave Theory and Tech., Vol. MIT-20, #4, pp. 294-295, April 1972.

[3] Silvester, P. P., "High Order Triangular Polynomial Finite Elements for Potential Problems", Int. J. Engrg. Sci., 7, pp. 849-861, 1969.

[4] Barton, M. L., "Dual-Order Parallelogram Finite Elements for the Axisymmetric Vector Poisson Equation", IEEE Trans. on Magnetics, Vol. MAG-18, #2, pp. 599-604, March 1982.

[5] Cendes, Z. J., "A Finite Element Method for the General Solution of Ordinary Differential Equations", Int. Jrnl. for Num. Meth. in Engng., Vol. 9, 551-561 (1975).

HARD COPY AND COMPUTER GRAPHICS

Stephen R. Levine
Electronic Graphics Associates
841 Katrina Street
Livermore, CA 94550
U. S. A.

In the early days of computing, obtaining a hard copy of a computer graphics image was relatively easy since virtually all computer graphics images were generated on a pen plotter. Thus the "display" and the hard copy were one in the same. Although it was easy to produce the hard copy, it was often quite time consuming to finally obtain any acceptable results.

This was due in large part to the lack of feedback inherent in the method used to produce data to drive the plotter. Producing a computer-generated image/hard copy consisted of the following steps:

1. By hand, the user sketched the desired image on a sheet of graph paper. The coordinate system used was generally the coordinate system of the plotter itself. If a different coordinate system was used, they differed at most by only a scale factor. Before writing the display program, the coordinates of the sketch were converted (generally by hand) to the coordinates of the pen plotter.
2. The image, which consisted primarily of straight lines and text, was encoded into subroutine calls to a very primitive graphics library. The primary subroutines allowed the user to draw a line or plot a string of text and was intimately tied to the hardware device.
3. The program was run in batch on a mainframe and a plot tape was generated.
4. The tape was plotted and the results were delivered to the user (at least one day later).
5. Mistakes were corrected and the process repeated until a correct plot was made or the user gave up in disgust. It was often very frustrating to produce an absolutely error-free plot. These pens on the early pen plotters were not very good and often that 'final' correct graph was ruined because of a bad pen. The pen is still one of the weakest links in the plotting device.

Today, the concept of hard copy is quite different. Computer graphics is almost always first produced and edited on a display before any hard copy is made. Hard copy is not the only incarnation of the image.

COMPUTER GRAPHICS CATEGORIES

The computer graphics images to be recorded fall into the two general categories of vector or raster, depending on the techniques used to generate them. An image is a vector graphics image if the code that generates it produces a display list that causes a CRT beam or pen to 'randomly' trace out the desired picture.

A raster image has its data organized into rows or raster lines, each containing a number of picture elements or pixels. The data is always presented in this fixed order regardless of the image on the CRT. Thus, if no encoding of the image is performed, it would take the same amount of time to display or storage to store a simple raster image as well as a complex one.

RESOLUTION CONSIDERATIONS

The quality of the hard copy depends not only on the resolution of the hard copy device itself, but also on the detail provided in the data describing the graphic image. For vector graphics, this is the line width and the addressable grid upon which the image is defined. For example, if 16 bits are provided to store coordinates of vector endpoints, then the image could potentially have a resolution in excess of one part in 65,000 in X and Y. It's worth noting that there is no appreciable cost associated with describing pictures with fairly high resolution in vector format. Data described in this way could be drawn on pen plotters of increasing resolution with potentially more detail becoming noticeable.

For raster graphs, this is not the case. Ultimately, the picture must be stored as an array of pixels. A 512x512x8 bit pixel image requires more than 250,000 bytes of storage regardless of picture complexity. To double the resolution requires more than 1 megabyte to store the image. In this case there is an appreciable cost with increasing resolution, not only with the display, but also with the storage of the pictures itself.

HARD COPY CATEGORIES

There are many ways to classify hard copy devices. In light of the previous discussion, it would seem natural to classify them according to their ability to record vector or raster images. Another could be black and white vs. color. Here we choose to make a first order differentiation between hard copy devices according to whether toner, ink, etc., is applied to material such as a matrix printer; or whether the hard copy material itself changes according to heat or light such as film. In the first case, it is not possible to directly record a continuous tone image. Continuous tone can be achieved by techniques such as dithering.

The other category includes film recorders which allows for the direct recording of continuous tone images. These devices account for the high-resolution high-quality color images such as those seen in the recent Walt Disney movie TRON.

INK/TONER ON PAPER

PEN PLOTTER

As was mentioned earlier, the pen plotter was one of the first hard copy devices. With a pen plotter, it is only feasible to record vector images. Pen movement is controlled by display list commands. Plotting time is directly proportional to the number of elements in the display list. Higher resolution plotters do not run appreciably slower than lower resolution devices. Many of today's pen plotters have intelligence built in. Some of the key factors when evaluating today's pen plotters are as follows:

- Only records vector images
- Rotation, translation, scaling
- Multiple fonts
- Multiple pens
- Greater than 3G acceleration
- Curves, special symbols
- Priced from $650 on up

Because these devices can be very large (greater than three meters diagonal) and have very fine resolution (accuracy and repeatability of less than .001 cm), they can produce the highest quality images (measured in total resoluable lines in an image) today.

From a software point of view, the pen plotter presents some interesting problems. Although the basic commands that the hardware responds to are quite simple, the mechanical movements involved require an organization of those commands into an order which will drive the plotter in an efficient manner.

For example, suppose a set of commands was generated to draw a dashed line with every other dash a different color. The simplest and most straight forward software approach would move the pen from start to finish changing the pen color on every line segment. A faster, but more complex, method would draw the line from start to finish twice. The first pass would draw in the first color, leaving space for the second color. The pen would then return to the start, change pens, and then draw the second color. An alternative scheme would be to draw the first pass in the first color, change pens, and then draw the second color by drawing the line from finish to start, saving the amount of time it takes to return the pen to the start of the line. Depending upon where the pens are located, either of these last two methods could be the faster.

Thus it is clear that the mechanical nature of pen plotters imposes some very real device-dependent constraints on graphics software. If the application software is to optimally drive different pen plotters, the sophisticated device-dependent drivers must be written to order the plotter commands so as to minimize plotting times.

The remainder of the devices in the ink/toner or paper category are raster oriented.

IMPACT PRINTERS

The first graphics output from a computer was not from a graphics device at all but from an ordinary line printer. Low resolution graphics was emulated by the judicious placement of text on paper. Today, typewriter graphics is still used. One of the most visible applications is its use in concert with a digitizing TV camera to produce images of people for transfer to T-shirts.

Although character-printing line printers and typewriters are still heavily used for computer output, dot matrix impact printers are now used for graphic printing. They create images by the transfer of ink from a ribbon. This transfer is accomplished by the impact of moving wires arranged in a row. In some cases, there are up to 18 wires arranged in two parallel overlapping rows to provide high resolution. As a general observation, there appears to be no standard whatsoever as to the size of the printing matrix or the printing resolution. The state of the art today is nearly 300 dots per inch in the horizontal direction and 200 dots per inch in the vertical direction. Some printers have higher resolution in the vertical direction than in the horizontal direction.

A key point is that vertical resolution is affected largely by accurate paper movement, while horizontal resolution is controlled by mechanical head motion.

Color is provided by multi-color or multiple color ribbons. Almost all of the devices use subtractive color (yellow, cyan, magenta) so as to allow color mixing. This can provide eight colors (including white and black). By the use of dithering, over 100 colors can be provided. This is useful only in area filling as the dithering technique does not work on lines or characters.

From the application point of view, the user views the printer as a large matrix. There are two key points to be considered.

Since most of the software produces vectors, software (or hardware) must be provided to scan convert these vectors into a raster format for printing. Since the printer only makes one pass (except for color) all the vectors that appear on a line must be scan converted at the appropriate time. Since the application program more than likely does not do this, then a second pass must be made. All the vectors must be scanned into memory before printing can begin. Since the matrix can be quite large, this is a most time consuming process.

The second key point is that the resolution is not uniform in the horizontal and vertical direction. For an application program to drive a variety of printers requires that the required scaling be done in the driver's software or hardware. This mapping often gives results which vary considerably from device to device. Some standards in this area would help.

NON-IMPACT PRINTERS

INK JET/THERMAL TRANSFER

Although these devices are recently receiving a great deal of attention, ink jet technology has have been around since the mid-sixties. Ink is applied to paper in the form of drops either on demand or in a continuous stream where the drops are first charged and then allowed to strike the paper or deflected into an ink recycling system.

The color quality appears to be very high. Resolution of 240 dots per inch have been reported in laboratory models with with up to 150 dots per inch more typical in current devices. Color is provided by three or four colors (yellow, cyan, magenta, black). The image is painted either by moving the ink jets in typewriter fashion across the paper incrementing the paper on each pass, or wrapping the paper on a drum and moving the ink jets by a lead screw across the moving paper.

From a computer graphics perspective, the thermal transfer technology is very similar. It can be viewed as kind of a solid state ink jet. The ink is held on a ribbon and ablated off by heat. This technology appears to have all the advantages of ink without the mechanical problems of a moving liquid. It is, however, a very new technology with many unknowns. We will have to wait and see.

From a software point of view, the same considerations apply here as for impact printers.

ELECTROSTATIC/ELECTROPHOTOGRAPHIC

For some time now, the highest resolution non-impact printers have been of the electrostatic or electrophotgraphic variety. Resolutions of 400 dots per inch are available with more than 600 dots per inch demonstrated. In these devices, an image is laid down on a paper or film base in the form of a charge. Toner is then applied and fixed to the substrate. One can buy electrostatic printers that handle paper up to about two meters in width. Electrophotographics is currently limited to less than .3 meter. Laser technology promises larger, faster, and even higher resolution.

Color is achieved by three or four passes. The best resolution commercially available today is 200 dots per inch. There are in existence, however, printers that can produce near photographic quality. It is not clear that they will be available in the near future.

Because the number of pixels on a line can be quite high, the time required for scan conversion can be very large. If these printers are to go to even higher resolution with higher speed, more attention must be given to the scan conversion problem. In order to print a large complex engineering drawing onto an electrostatic plotter with software designed to plot on a pen plotter can require a prohibitive amount of computer time. The plotter manufacturer's need to address the total systems solution, rather than just the hardware issues.

FILM PRINTERS

The fundamental difference in this technology from the Ink/Toner System is that the image founding materials are initially present in the printing medium. In the case of film, the image is generated by exposing film to light and subsequently processing the film. Thermal printers also fall into this category. Here the image is "developed" by heat from a print head. There are two basic types of film recorders.

The first is similar to an electrophotographic recorder, except that the image from the fiber optic CRT (or laser) exposes film. These devices move film or paper and are really suitable for recording raster images. The facsimile copiers using thermal paper fall into this category.

For computer graphics applications, the CRT full frame film recorders are the most interesting. These devices use a small white phospher CRT, and a camera. Color is added by placing filters between the camera and the CRT. We can further separate these recorders into two categories, depending upon how the image is supplied to the CRT.

The first group could be called video recorders, as the input is a video signal from a CRT. In order to facilitate color recording, RGB inputs are provided. The recorder selects the proper filter and refreshes the image for the correct amount of time, according to the filter selected. Recorders are available to record signals up to 1,000 line resolution. These devices come with cameras that can handle film from 16 mm to 8" x 10." The recent introduction of instant 35 mm color film should make these devices very popular. They range in price from about $1,500 to $25,000.

It must be remembered that the limitation of the video signal is quite serious for high resolution recording. Video is analog in the X direction and digital in the Y direction.

For very high resolution film recording we turn to the digital input film recorders. For around $200,000 you can have a device that will produce full color, vector and/or raster images with more than 4,000 lines of resolution. These devices are capable of reproducing photographs that are indistinguishable from the original. Some of the major applications areas are presentation graphics, computer-aided design, phototypesetting, and computer animation.

CONCLUSIONS

As one can see, hard copy for computer graphics has been around for practically as long as computer graphics itself. Computer graphics hard copy manufacturers have been busy building faster, less expensive, and higher resolution recorders with what seems to be little regard for the software required to drive them. This can be seen by observing the number of different resolutions/formats available. Increasing the number of dots per inch by 20 percent does not necessarily produce a 20 percent higher quality image by simply scaling up the original data. In fact, the picture may look worse. It must be recognized that the software investment is considerably higher than the hardware cost. We need standards now. We cannot afford the cost to reprogram every time a new device is built. We don't want a new inexpensive printer to end up costing us a great deal of money.

APPENDIX

The following pages are sample output from a variety of devices.

1. ZETA four-color pen plotter

2. ENVISION dot matrix printer

3. VERSATEC 200 dot per inch electrostatic printer

4. IMAGEN laser printer (CANON printing engine)

5. PRINTACOLOR ink jet

6. XEROX color printer

7. DICOMED D48 color film recorder
   (See Page II, oposite of the title page.)

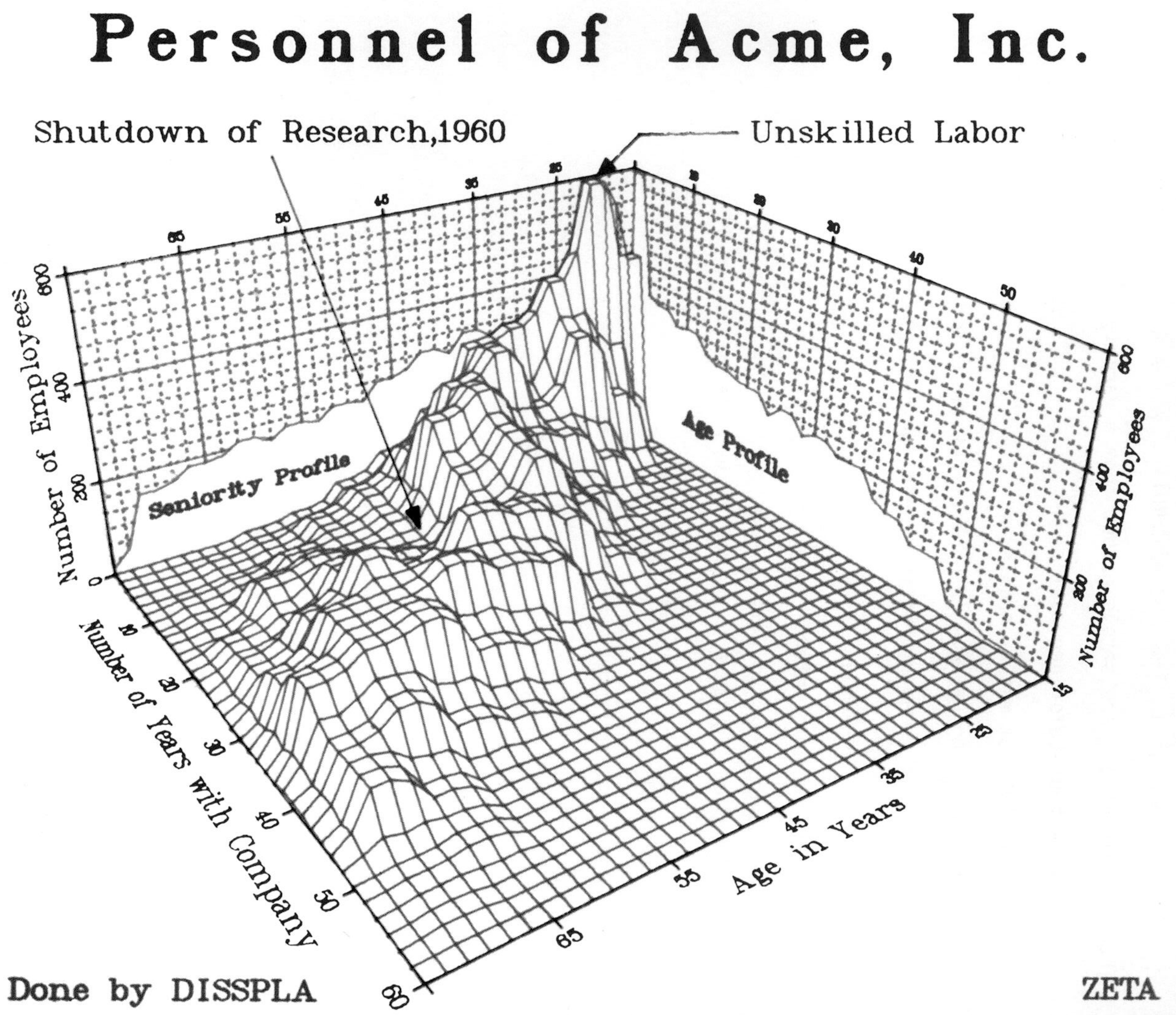
Personnel of Acme, Inc.
Shutdown of Research,1960
Unskilled Labor
Seniority Profile
Age Profile
Number of Employees
0
200
400
600
Number of Years with Company
10
20
30
40
50
60
Age in Years
15
25
35
45
55
65
Done by DISSPLA
ZETA

ENVISION ENVISION ENVISION ENVISION ENVISION ENVISION

ENVISION ENVISION ENVISION ENVISION ENVISION ENVISION

ENVISION ENVISION ENVISION ENVISION ENVISION ENVISION

ENVISION ENVISION ENVISION ENVISION ENVISION ENVISION

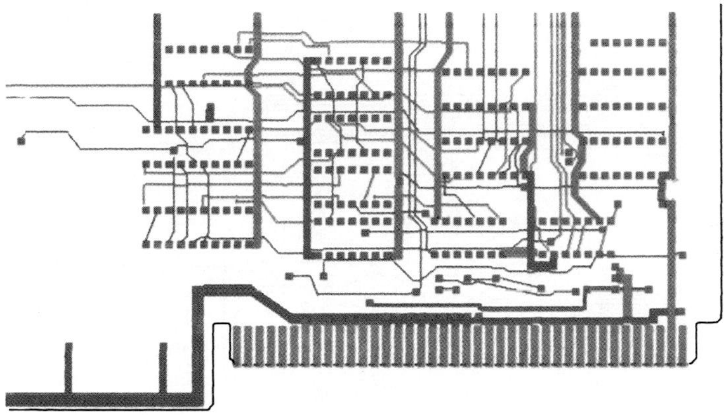

THE ENVISION 420: THREE PRINTERS IN ONE

The Envision 420 prints letter-quality text at up to 100 characters per second. These speeds are attainable because text is printed in a single pass of the high-speed 18-wire print head. Various character fonts are available and include Pica (bold and italic), Elite and Orator. Any of these fonts AND color can be programmatically mixed on a character, word or line basis.

When the need for high-speed draft printing arises, the Envision 420 easily shifts into 300 characters per second print mode. The Envision 420 eliminates the needs for a separate letter-quality printer for word processing and a high-speed printer for draft printing.

Dual 16-bit microprocessors provide the power needed to print high-quality, high-resolution color graphics at 360 by 144 increments per inch. The Envision 420's use of four color ribbon cassettes, which can be indepenently replaced, greatly extends ribbon life while providing crisp, sharp multicolor printing.

Envision 631 River Oaks Parkway, San Jose, CA 95134

Printed by the Envision 420 Color Printer

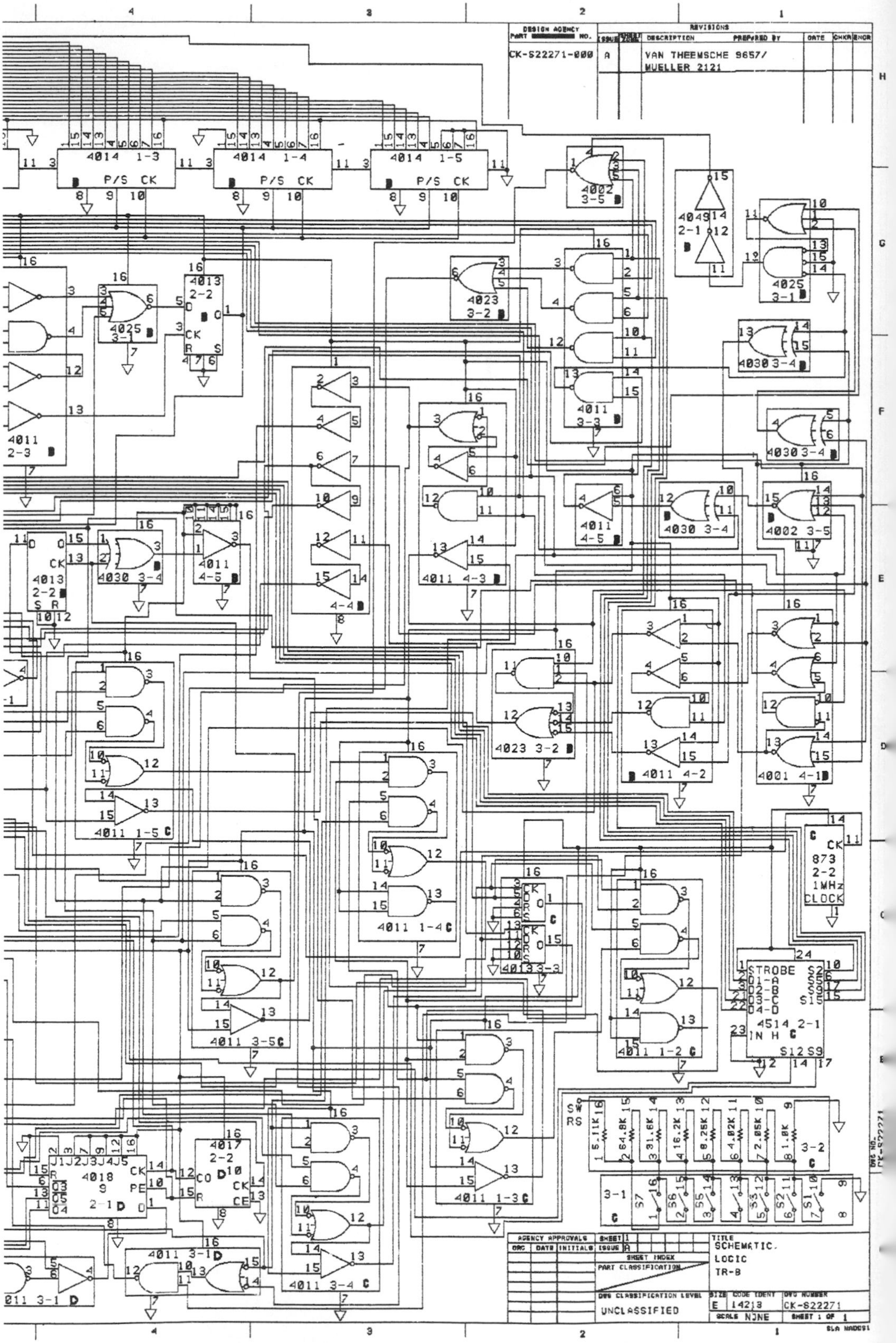
DESIGN AGENCY
PART [redacted] NO.
CK-S22271-000
REVISIONS
ISSUE
DESCRIPTION
PREPARED BY
DATE
A
VAN THEEMSCHE 9657/
MUELLER 2121
AGENCY APPROVALS
SHEET INDEX
PART CLASSIFICATION
DWG CLASSIFICATION LEVEL
UNCLASSIFIED
TITLE
SCHEMATIC,
LOGIC
TR-B
SIZE E
CODE IDENT 14213
DWG NUMBER CK-S22271
SCALE NONE
SHEET 1 OF 1

IMAGEN

IMPRINT-10

Sample Sheet

The difference between one typeface and another is often very subtle, it may be no more than a slight difference in the shape of the serif, the length of the ascenders and descenders, or the size of the x-height. But regardless of how small the difference, the typeface, and therefore the appearance of the printed page, will be affected.†

THE DIFFERENCE BETWEEN ONE TYPEFACE AND ANOTHER IS OFTEN VERY SUBTLE; IT MAY BE NO MORE THAN A SLIGHT DIFFERENCE IN THE SHAPE OF THE SERIF, THE LENGTH OF THE ASCENDERS AND DESCENDERS, OR THE SIZE OF THE X-HEIGHT. BUT REGARDLESS OF HOW SMALL THE DIFFERENCE, THE TYPEFACE, AND THEREFORE THE APPEARANCE OF THE PRINTED PAGE, WILL BE AFFECTED.†

The difference between one typeface and another is often very subtle; it may be no more than a slight difference in the shape of the serif, the length of the ascenders and descenders, or the size of the x-height. But regardless of how small the difference, the typeface, and therefore the appearance of the printed page, will be affected.†

To John Doe
Date mo/da/yr Time hr:min

MEMO

Mr. David Perlmutter
of IMAGEN
Phone No. 415/960-0714

TELEPHONED	RETURNED YOUR CALL
PLEASE CALL X	CAME TO SEE YOU
WILL CALL AGAIN	WANTS TO SEE YOU

would like to arrange a
demonstration of the IMPRINT-10

$$\Psi(P) = \frac{1}{4\pi} \oint_S \left(\Psi \nabla \frac{e^{ikr}}{r} - \frac{e^{ikr}}{r} \nabla \Psi \right) \cdot \mathbf{n}\, da$$

$$\Psi(P) = i\, \frac{Ak}{4\pi} \int_\sigma \frac{e^{ik(r+r_0)}}{r r_0} (\mathbf{e}_r - \mathbf{e}_0) \cdot \mathbf{n}\, da$$

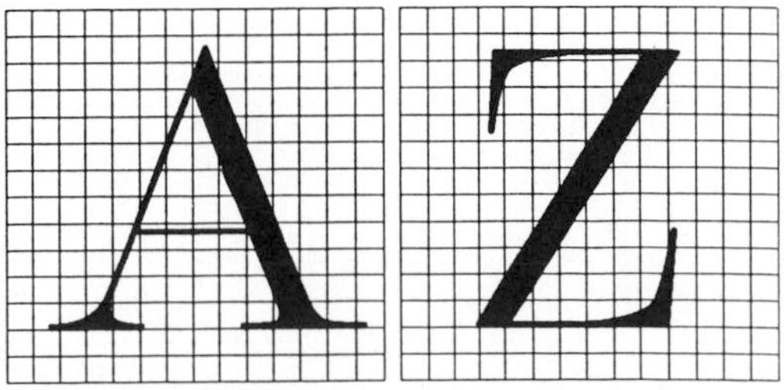

† **Phototypesetting: A Design Manual** by James Craig

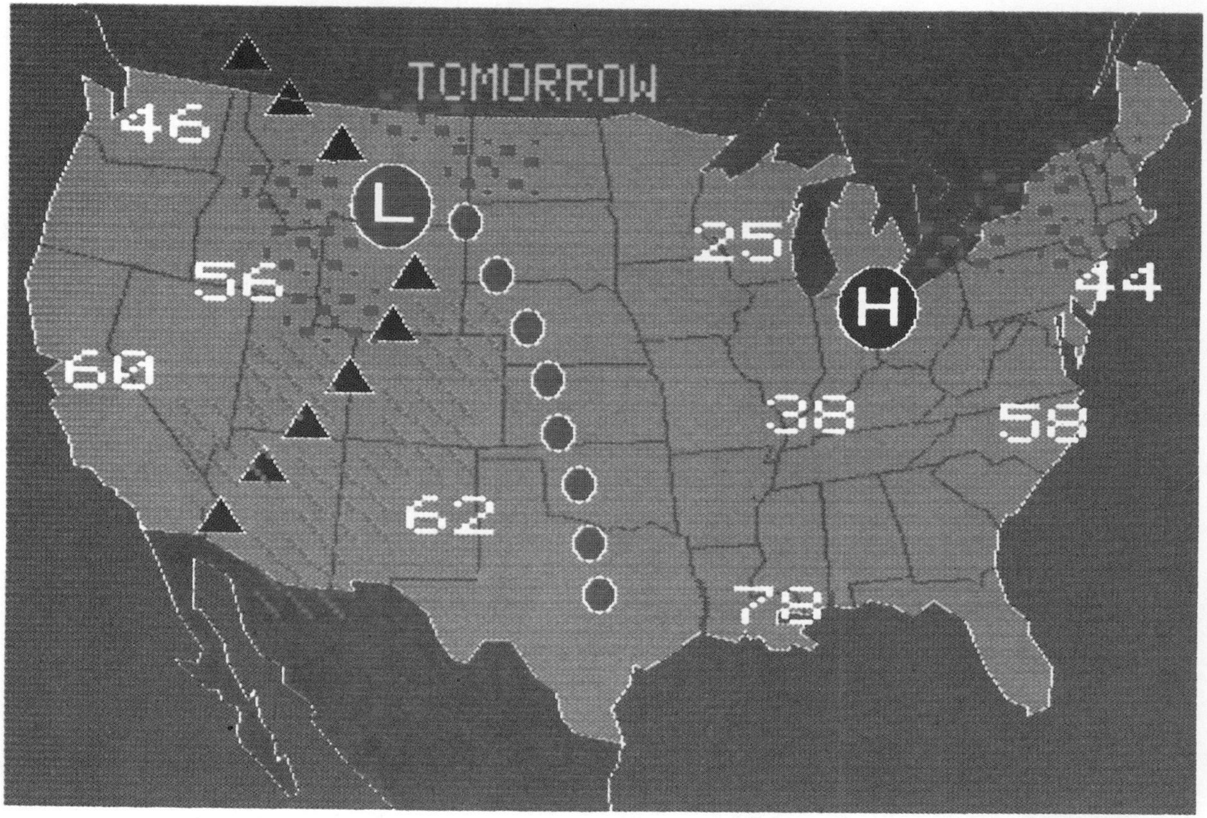

COLOR INK-JET BY PRINTACOLOR

SIMULATION OF A 5 STEP/PRIMARY COLOR CONE USING PATTERN FILLED POLYGONS

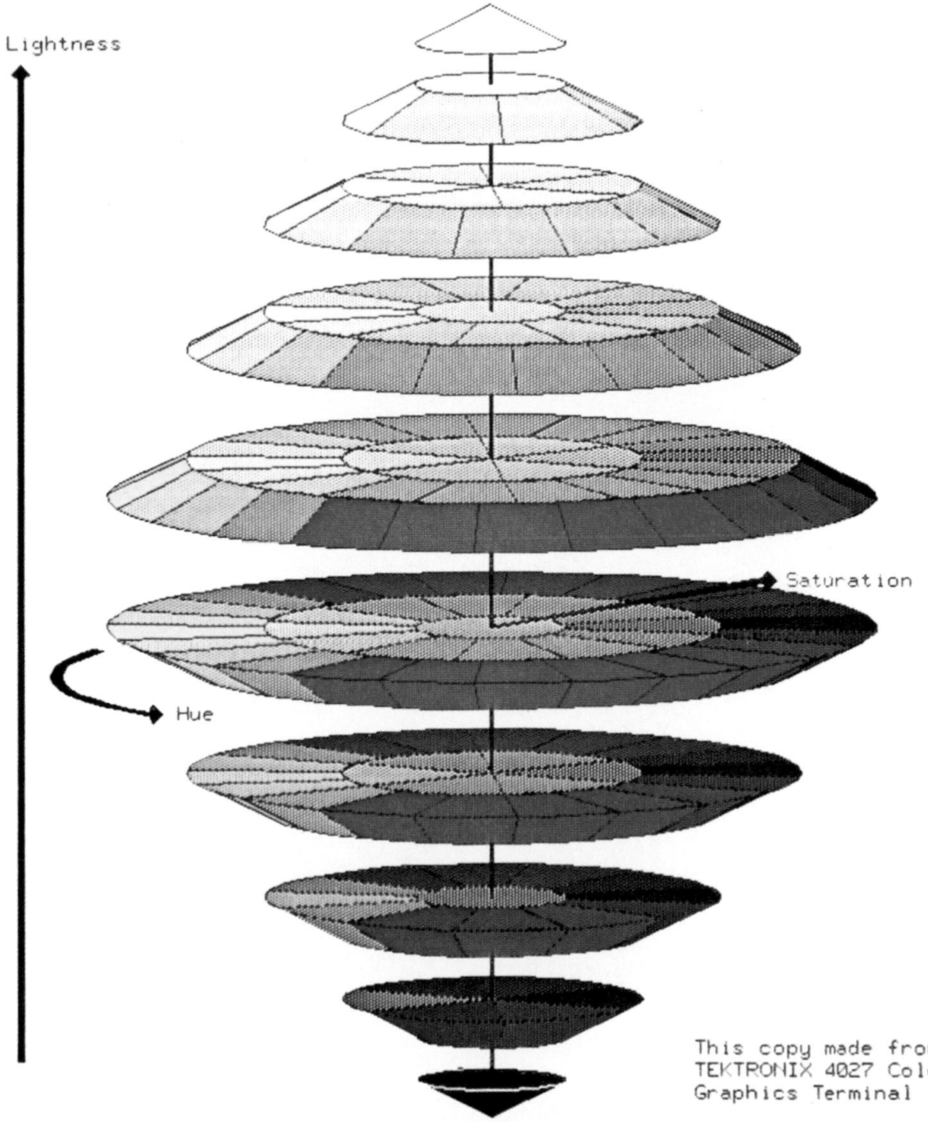

This copy made from a TEKTRONIX 4027 Color Graphics Terminal

Colors vary in Hue, Lightness, and Saturation. Hue is the attribute which makes it possible to classify color as red, yellow, green, blue or intermediates of these. Lightness is the attribute that can be described as ranging from black thru various grays to white. Saturation is the attribute that determines the degree to which a color differs from a white of the same lightness. Geometrically the family of colors can be described in terms of a double cone. Variations in Hue are represented around the circumference. Variations in Lightness are represented along the axis of the cone. Variations in Saturation are represented along the radii. The highest degree of Saturation is perceived for medium Lightness colors; as Lightness increases or decreases, the attainable Saturation becomes less. The attributes of Hue, Lightness, and Saturation exhaust the degrees of freedom of a color.

Chapter 7
Image Processing

A LANDSAT IMAGE DATABANK USING MASS STORAGE SYSTEM —"TSUKUSYS" IMAGE–BANK—

Takashi Hoshi
Science Information Processing Center
University of Tsukuba
Ibaraki 305, JAPAN

Kazuhiko Nakayama
Science Information Processing Center
Ibaraki 305, JAPAN

Abstract

The purpose of this paper is to give a comprehensive description of a databank consisting of image data which was extracted from the Landsat multispectral scanning system. The databank, which will be called Tsukusys image-bank, is intended to provide an environmental monitoring and image analysis in Japan. The conventional Landsat image data in the databank are stored in data cartridges on the mass storage system that permit on-line operations. The design consideration of the Tsukusys image-bank includes the following item : types of data structure, hardware resources and data processing for constructing the image-bank. The image-bank is under development as an experimental Landsat image databank at University of Tsukuba. We include in this paper a case study of application of the Tsukusys image-bank.

1. INTRODUCTION

As computers become cheeper and faster, processing of multiband and multispectral image data become easier. Landsat multispectral scanner data (M2S data) extracted by remote sensing may be as large a volume as 50 MB per scene. Object image area may be as large as 185x185 km2 per scene. Storage, maintenance and utilization of their image data at national level entail problems of quantity and quality of large amount of image data (P.N.Slater (1980)). A system for processing such a large amount of image data should be designed as an image databank based on database concepts. In this paper we will be concerned with design of Landsat M2S data image-bank for land analysis of Japan, which we call Tsukusys image-bank. We have actually constructed such image-bank for demonstrating its usefulness. We will describe an outline of the Tsukusys system (T.Hoshi and Y.Ikebe (1981)) in the sequel.

2. DESIGN OF IMAGE-BANK

Designing of Landsat M2S image-bank for land areas in Japan requires a carefull analysis of data structure of source data. We have decided to design Tsukusys image-bank with the assumption that the supervised method be used for point-by-point classification in the M2S data analysis. Therefore we will first determine kinds of source data at each image analysis step in order to apply the image analysis with the supervised analysis techniques (T.Hoshi (1978)). The source data are summerized in Fig-2.1. We will describe the source data at each supervised classification step in the below.

(a). Scenes which are to be objects of analysis are selected. Factors affecting the selection include location, time, amount of cloud and resolution in the observational image. The selection is usually done using catalogues and photographs (D.L.Light (1980)). In this image-bank the image information retrieval data is used in place of catalogues and photographs. This image retrieval data or files are referred to as "Reference Data".

(b). For a given scene at given time and location of observational image the corresponding data computer compatible tape (CCT) format is available from RESTEC and NASDA in Japan. This CCT data will be called "Image Data" or "Image File" in our image-bank.

(c). The area to be analyzed, which will be called study area, is selected from CCT data and is stored in a disk pack of DASD. This selection is done with the aid of 1:25,000 or 1:50,000 scale topographical maps and 1:200,000 scale geographical maps, where these maps are compared with images. Therefore full view color maps will be use for the images. In our image-bank these data or files making color maps is named "Color Map Data" or "Color Map File".

(d). The data for a given study area is pre-processed. This includes location identification, data conversion and noise removable, where for the location identification (G.Konecny (1976)) the coordinate (X,Y) of ground control points (GCP) have been selected and made available. This ground control point data or files are called "GCP Data" or "GCP File" in our image-bank.

(e). Sea and ground truth data are used for the determination of the nature of such items as river, lake, forest and urban area etc. These areas of surface object are assigned to classification items and have been termed as trainning areas or test areas. Classification data or files are called "Trainning Data" or "Trainning File" in our image-bank.

(f). Each pixel is assigned to corresponding classification item. The result is stored in disk pack.

(g). If the classification result is fit to the purpose of the analysis, classification map is produced with off-line color plotter from the data prepared at step (f). If social statistics data or administrative boundary data etc. needs be supplemented to the data prepared at step (f), the combined data will be created in our work. Only administrative boundary data will be combined in this research. These data or files are named "Combined Data" or "Combined File" in image-bank.

3. DATA FORMAT AND STRUCTURE OF IMAGE-BANK

In this chapter we will state data files in Tsukusys image-bank in detail. We will discuss the mutual relationships among these files for clarifying data structures in the image-bank.

Reference Files

At the head of CCT data there is a group of headers describing image data. We used this header group as reference data. The header group consists of three kinds of ASCII data: directory, header and annotation. These data depend on the format of Landsat image data and tape density. We decided to assign three records to a scene, considering the Band Interleaved by Line (BIL) format of National Aeronautics and Space Administration (NASA) and National Space Development Agency of Japan (NASDA). One record is 3,596 bytes long.

Image File

The format of Landsat M2S CCT data may be of Band Interleaved by 2 Pixels (BIP2), Band Interleaved by Line (BIL) or of Band Sequential (BSQ) types, as is shown Fig-3.1. Each format has its special feature for the purpose of utilization. We use the BIL structured in band unit direct file as image file because, by doing so, we can make the access efficiency of BIL and of BSQ equally easy.

Color Map File

Full view color maps should be in such a size as to be easily handled on desk, and should have enough resolution to make main patterns in the scene easily understood. Moreover, selection of M2S band applied to this color map should be done in such a way that no correlation among the selected bands exists. Having considered the conditions stated here, we require the Color map file to satisfy the following conditions.

(1) Data format should be the same as the output format of plotter and the data should be of binary code.

(2) The data should be compressed so as to give enough

resolution of the main patterns (patterns greater than 1 km2 should be displayed on color map).

(3) Yellow, cyan, magenta are assigned to band 4, 5, and 7 of Landsat data, respectively.

GCP File

Time and effort are needed to select GCP while map and images are being compared. For this reason it pays to maintain the previously analyzed GCP for the convenience of re-uses. On the GCP file coordinate values (X,Y) of the map and pixel positions (L,C) of the image have been made to correspond. In addition to these data, necessary header and helpful comments are added to GCP file. Details of header, comment and GCP data format are shown in Table-3.1.

Trainning File

Trainning areas are to be supervisor areas (B.L.Markham (1981)) and test areas for verifying classification result. The trainning areas and test areas are given in the form of rectangle in the supervised classification method. Under the condition just stated the Trainning files are structured in the form of card image file shown in Table-3.2.

Combined File

We take the data structure of administrative boundary data to be of Table-3.3. Drawing administrative boundary, the data is changed to chain structure. A chain data consists of chain number, point number, point coordinate (X,Y) and of node number, as shown in Fig-3.2. The areas included in the combination file of administrative boundary considered in this research are given by the area shown in Fig-4.2. The minimum unit for an area enclosed on graphic display by line plotting is towns and villages. These may be parts of larger cities or prefectures.

We designed each file and we analyzed overall data structure under the conditions stated so far. As a result,we were able to represent the data structures of image-bank in tree structure shown in Fig-3.3.

4. USED DATA CARTRIDGE FOR FILE STORAGE

Mass storage system (MSS) requires longer access time than disk storage system. However mass storage system (J.P.Harric (1975)) is more cost-effective when it is used to store a large volume of data only part of which is used at a given time. The analysis of Landsat image data gives one example of such situation. In this research, therefore, M2S data are stored in data cartridge of MSS according to processing on Fig-4.1. The contents of data stored in the data cartridges includes Landsat scenes of Hokkaido, Honshu, Kyushu and Shikoku. Fig-4.2 shows the areas of experiment in the Tsukusys image-bank, as hatched area. Reference files, Image files, Color map files and Combined files contain information on the total hatched area on Fig-4.2, while GCP files and Trainning files consist of only several scenes of Kanto areas at path 115 and row 35, for the purpose of experiment. Two data cartridges of mass storage system are allocated to one scene in each files, as shown in Fig-4.3. The computer system used for our experiment is a FACOM

M-200 system with IC memory size 32MB, DASD memory size 40 GB and MSS memory size 101.7 GB. The experimental MSS memory size is 10 GB.

5. EXPERIMENTAL RESULT AND DISCUSSION

Reference File

Reference files are organized as direct files so as to make addition of CCT data easy whenever this is necessary. However sequential files will suit better for information retrieval. For this reason direct files and sequential files are created as Ref-1 and Ref-2, respectively. Ref-2 file is updated once every half year. We construced ADABAS and FAIRS databases for information retrieval (T.Hoshi and K.Nakayama (1982)), using Ref-2 file, and we confirmed that we were able to retrieve each reference item accurately. Moreover, Ref-1 or Ref-2 file are a maintained in DASD for easy and fast access.

Image File

A complete set of M2S data containing the four lands of Japan shown in Fig-4.2 was written on MSS data cartridges and was output on a color display. The result confirmed correctness of our design of Image file.

Color Map File

Output size of the color pattern at our computer center is given approximately by 860x550 mm2. For this reason we determined full view color map size to be about 500x500 mm2. The color map will have title in the upper part, date of CCT observation and paths and rows in the lower part, all in Japanese. Such an example is shown in Photo-5.1. The Color map file is now in the working state.

GCP File and Trainning File

We developed a module which creates the GCP files previously defined (See Section 3.). The process of creating GCP file includes matching of GCP file in the ordinary topographical map for the given area ((for example, Kanto area)) with the corresponding points in the color display image, using trackball. We run a set of tests and confirmed that the GCP files is in the working state for the intended purpose. The module for creating Trainning file was constructed according to format shown in Table-3.2. Trainning files were then created.

Combined File

Administrative boundary data and Landsat M2S image data are overlaid on CRT by matching and departure. From this experiment, the structure for administrative boundary data may be taken to be of chain structure in the module. A example of administrative boundary data on color display is shown in Photo-5.2.

6. CONCLUSION

Landsat M2S data as useful, for environmental monitoring of the land areas in Japan where image analysis is an indispensable part in this use of these data. Construction of a computer system for the image analysis is influenced by quality of the database used. With this fact in mind we have been developing remote sensing analysis system Tsukusys. Especially constitutes databank for Landsat M2S data the bases for database of Tsukusys. Hence it may be safely said that the design of image-bank is a key factor for usefulness of Tsukusys in the feature use. Fortunately the Tsukusys image-bank proposed in this paper gives bright hope in the design of files in the image-bank. We will, elaborate this in the following.

(1) It was found that tree structure suits best for the description of Tsukusys image-bank structure by carefully analyzing image analysis process.

(2) As a consequence files in the image-bank are related high actually to each other.

(3) Landsat multispectral scanner image data for a scene and the corresponding sea and ground truth data are stored in the image-bank in an integrated manner. This storage mechanism makes data analysis easy and fast.

(4) Use of data cartridge for large volume data resulted in the saving of storage space,and permitted on-line operations on mass storage system.

(5) In Tsukusys system, Reference file and Color map file in image-bank may be used implace of Landsat scene catalogues and photographs. This considerably saves preparation time for data analysis.

(6) Color map can be drawn directly color map files.

(7) Existence of GCP files and Trainning files make repeated use of computer compatible tape data easy and fast.

(8) Each file except Trainning file in image-bank will use to unsupervised classification or per-field classification.

ACKNOWLEDGMENT

The authors wish to express appreciation to Dr. Yasuhiko Ikebe for reading the manuscript of this paper and giving suggestions for improvement.

REFERENCES

P.N.Plater (1980) : "Remote Sensing--Optics and Optical System --", Addison-Wesley, 1980.

Takashi Hoshi and Yasuhiko Ikebe (1981) : "Tsukusys, A Remote Sensing Data Analysis System", Proc. of Working Conference on Picture Engineering, 15th IBM Computer Science Symposium, No. 3, p.351-374, 1981 (in Japanese)

J.P.Harric et al (1975) : "The IBM 3850 Mass Storage System Design Aspects", Proc. of IEEE, No.63, 1975.

Takashi Hoshi(1978) : "Study on Identification of Ground Cover Types in Urban Area by Remote Sensing", Ph.D. Thesis of Kyoto Univ., p.70-118, 1978.

D.L. Light (1980) : "Satellite Photogrammetry", Manual of Photogrammetry, American Society of Photogrammetry, 1980.

G. Konecny (1976) : "Mathematische Modelle und Verfahren zur Geometrischen Auswertung von Zeilenabtaster-Aufnahmen", Bul, No.5, p.188-197, 1976.

B.L.Markham and J.R.G. Townshend : "Land Cover Classification Accuracy as a Function of Sensor Spatial Resolution", Proc. of 15th International Symposium on Remote Sensing of Environment, Vol.3, p.1075-1085, 1981.

Takashi Hoshi and Kazuhiko Nakayama (1982) : "Retrieval of Landsat Image Data in the Data Cartridge", Proc. of 8th Annual Conference on Remote Sensing, Society of Instrument and Control Enginners, p.151-154, 1982 (in Japanese).

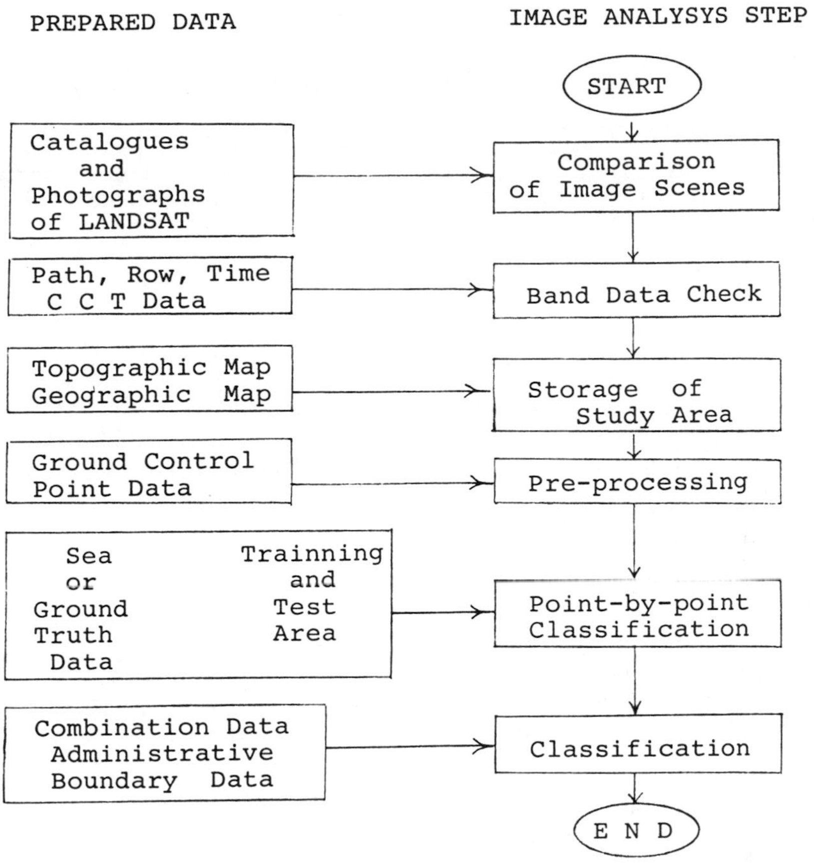

Fig-2.1 Each Step of Supervised Classification.

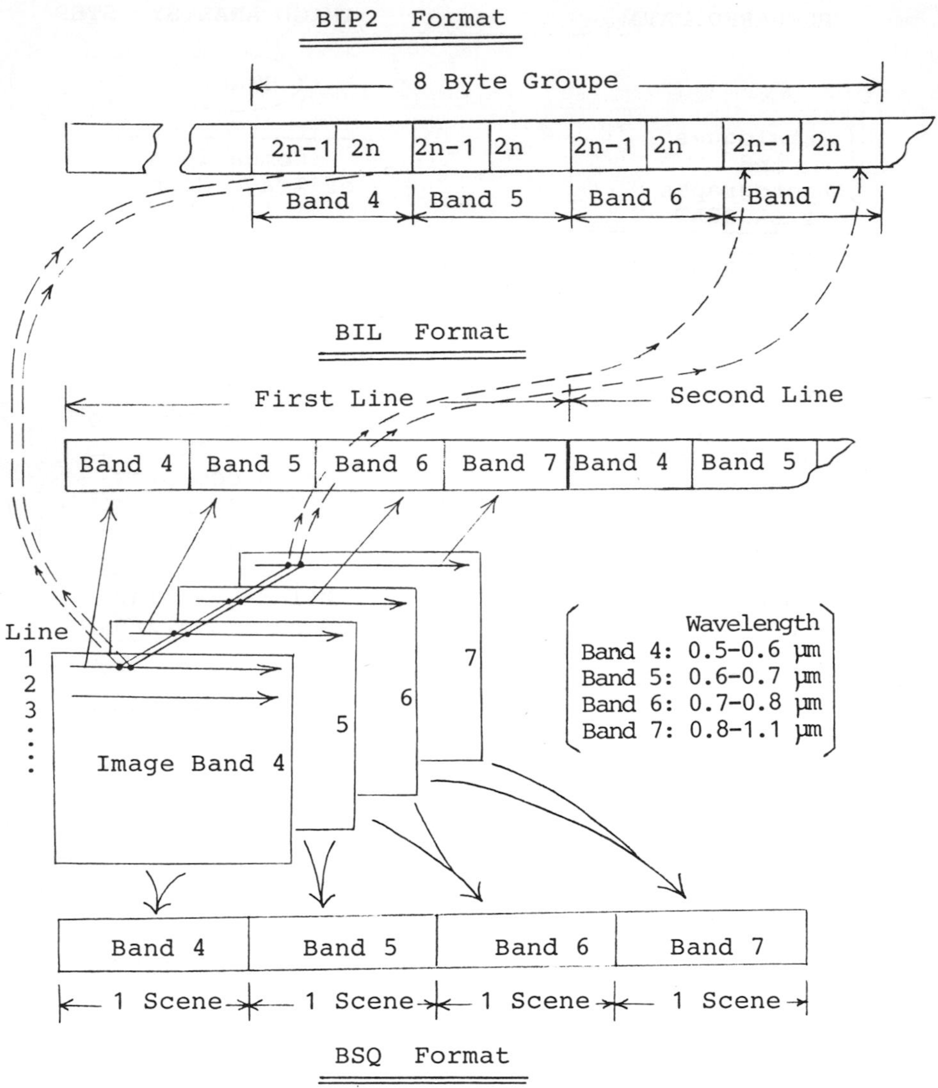

Fig-3.1 CCT Data Format Type

Table-3.1 GCP Data Format

```
....*....1....*....2....*....3....*....4....*....5....*....6....*....7....*....8
```

G	S	C	P,R	Y,M,D	N	STUDY	SMX1	SMY1	SMX2	SMY2

COMMENT OF MAKING FILE (NAME, BELONG, DATE, ...)

GMX	GMY	GOFC	GOFL	COMMENT OF G.C.P.

SYMBOL	FMT	CONTENTS	SYMBOL	FMT	CONTENTS
G	A4	GCP FILE NAME	STUDY	A10	STUDY AREA NAME
S	I2	STUDY AREA ID	SMX1,SMY1	2I10	STUDY AREA MAP
C	A6	CCT NUMBER	SMX2,SMY2	2I10	COORDINATE
P , R	2A3	PATH and ROW	GMX ,GMY	2I10	GCP MAP COORDINATE
Y,M,D	A8	DATA COLLECTION DATE	GOFC,GOFL	2F10.1	GCP FILE COORDINATE
N	I4	NUMBER OF GCP	COMMENT	A40	GCP POSITION etc

Table-3.2 Trainning Data Format

```
....*....1....*....2....*....3....*....4....*....5....*....6....*....7....*....8
```

T	S	C	P,R	Y,M,D	N	STUDY	SMX1	SMY1	SMX2	SMY2

SFC1	SFL1	SFC2	SFL2	COMMENT

COMMENT OF MAKING FILE (NAME, BELONG, DATE, etc)

TIC1,C2,C3	TIL1,L2,L3	RL	AREA	IN	COMMENT-1

SYMBOL	FMT	CONTENTS	SYMBOL	FMT	CONTENTS
T	A4	TRINNINT FILE NAME	COMMENT	A40	COMMENT OF STUDY AREA
S	I2	STUDY AREA ID.	SMX1,SMY1	2I10	STUDY AREA MAP
C	A6	CCT NUMBER	SMX2,SMY2	2I10	COORDINATE
P , R	2A3	PATH, ROW	SFC1,SFL1	2I10	STUDY AREA FILE
Y,M,D	A8	DATA COLLECTION DATE	SFC2,SFL2	2I10	COORDINATE
N	I2	CLASSIFICATION ITEM	TIC1,TIC2	2I5	TRAINNING / TEST AREA
STUDY	A10	STUDY AREA NAME	TIL1,TIL2	2I5	IMAGE COORDINATE
RL	I2	RECTANGLE / LINEAR	TIC3,TIL3	2I2	SAMPLING INTERVAL
AREA	A4	TRAIN. or TEST AREA	COMMENT-1	A38	COMMENT OF ITEM NAME
IN	I2	CLASSIF. ITEM NUMB.			

Table-3.3 Administrative Boundary Data Format

....*....1....*....2....

NI	SH	LS	RS	TG	DX	DY

SYMBOL	FMT	CONTENTS
NI	I4	MESH CORD
SH	I2	ISLAND CORD
LS	I4	LEFT POLYGON
RS	I4	RIGHT POLYGON
TG	I2	TAG CORD
DX	R4	LONGITUDE (Degree)
DY	R4	LATITUDE (Degree)

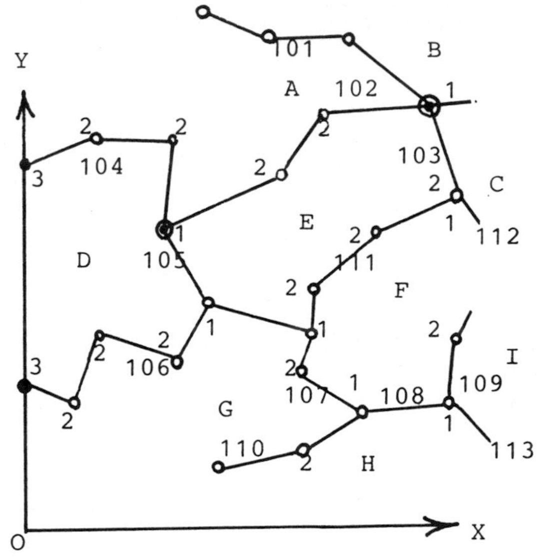

Chain Element	Symbol or Mark
Polygon :	A,B,C,........,I
Chain :	101,102,103,....
Node :	1 (◉ mark)
Point :	1,2,3 (◉,●,o mark)

Fig-3.2 Element of Chain Structure

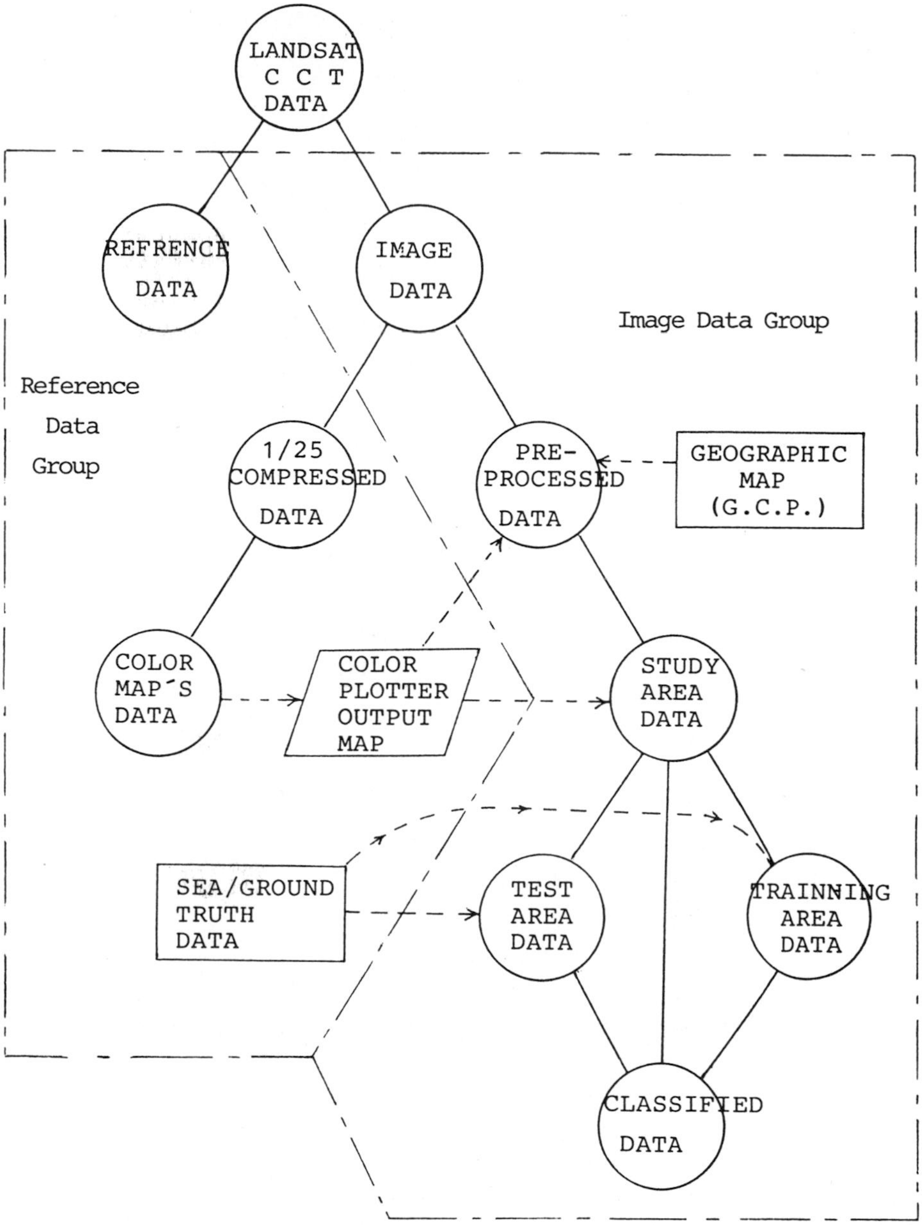

Fig-3.3 Data Structure of Image-bank

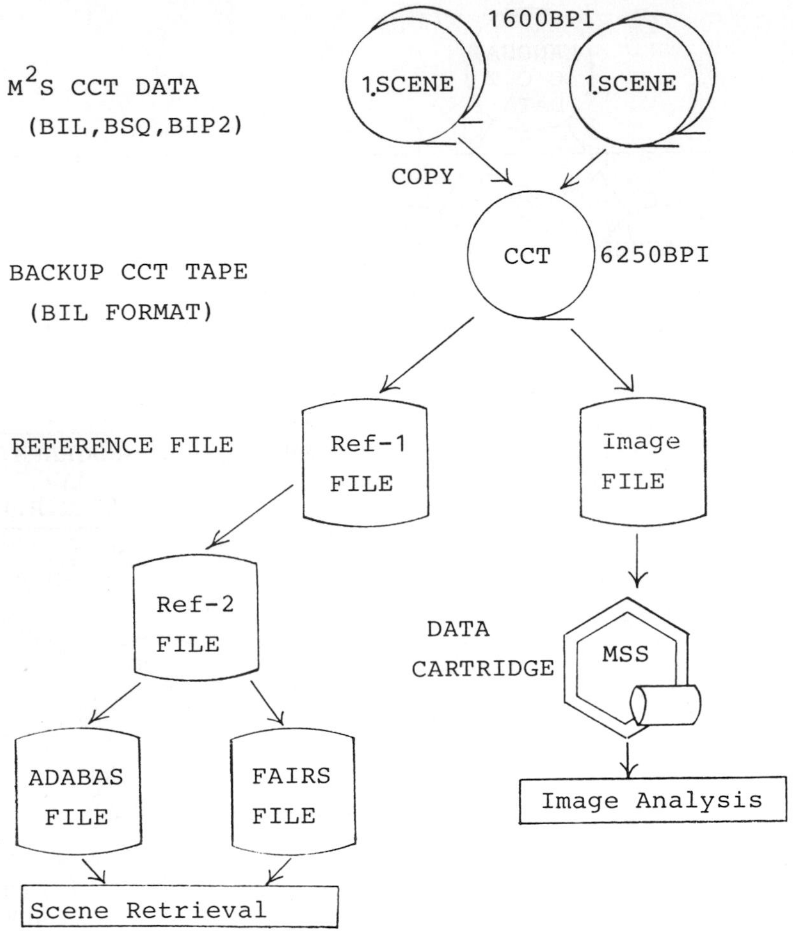

Fig-4.1 Data Processing for Reference File and Image File.

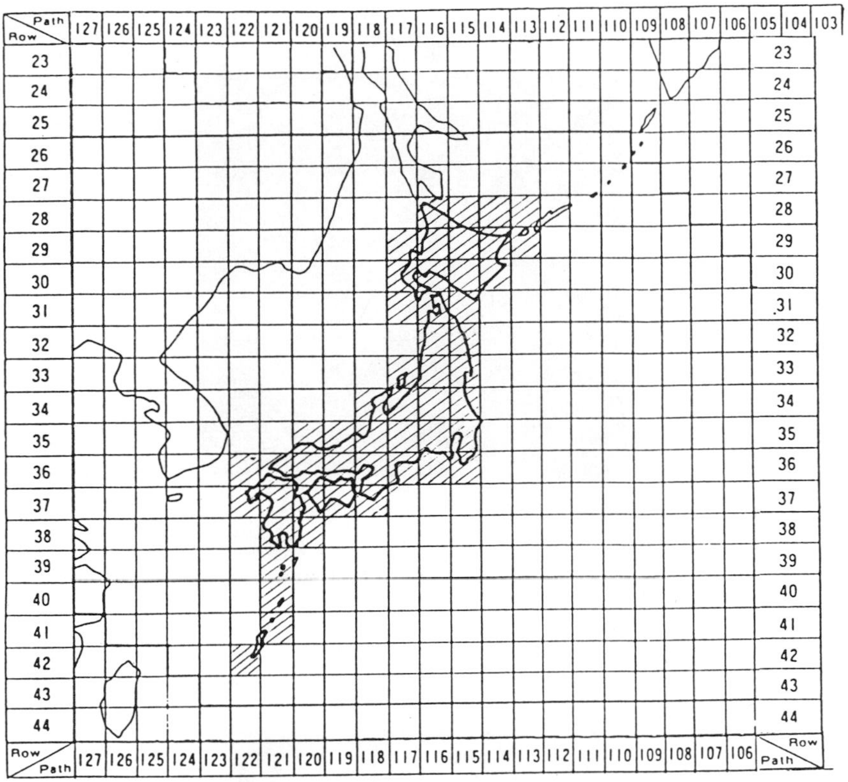

Fig-4.2 Image Scene Position in Image-bank.

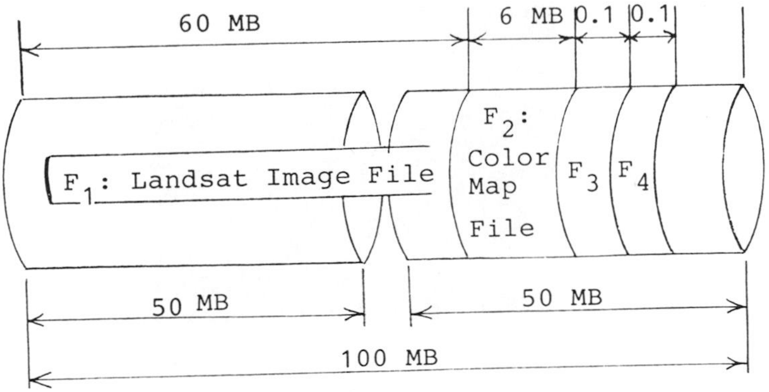

F_3: Ground Control Point (GCP) File

F_4: Trainning File

Fig-4.3 Each Stored Files in Data Cartridge.

Photo-5.1 Color Map at Tōkai

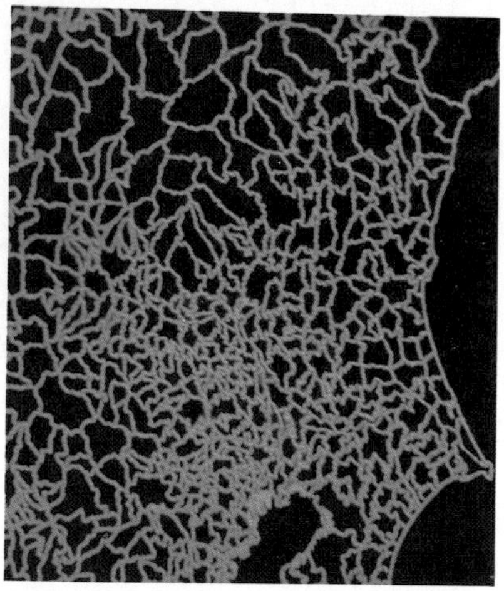

Photo-5.2 Administrative Boundary at Kantō

A RULE-BASED INTERPRETATION OF CONTOUR PATTERNS WITH CURVES*

Mitsuru Ishizuka, Masayuki Numao and Yasuhiko Yasuda
Institute of Industrial Science
University of Tokyo
7-22-1, Roppongi, Minato-ku, Tokyo 106, JAPAN

ABSTRACT

A method of rule-based interpretation of curved patterns is presented. A production system formalization which is one of knowledge engineering methodologies is employed to facilitate the systematic utilization of relevant knowledge including the model representation of object patterns and some of heuristics for efficient inference. To achieve a flexible matching between the model and observed pattern, a certainty measure is introduced in the interpretation.

1. INTRODUCTION

It seems that interaction between computer graphics and computer vision techniques is becoming important for the both areas. For example, the modeling of 2D and 3D patterns in the computer graphics seems to be useful for model-based pattern interpretation which is one of recent trends in the computer vision. The techniques of the computer vision or pattern recognition may be required in advanced interactive graphic systems.

Because the modeling and search (or inference) process are primary parts in the computer vision [1], the authors think that the methodology of knowledge engineering [2] facilitate the design of the vision system with respect to systematic knowledge utilization. This paper presents a production system approach [3], which is one of basic methods in the knowledge engineering, for the interpretation of curved patterns. A similar approach has been adopted in syntactic pattern recognition [4]; however, the approach of this paper provides a more flexible and more intuitive method for describing the patterns.

*This work was supported by Ministry of Education, Japan, under Grant-in-Aid No.57580019.

Figure 1 shows the schematic configuration of our vision system. The basic mechanism of the production system is symbol manipulation. In order to fully utilize this computational power, the system has been designed in such a way that two-dimensional image data are converted at first by a simple pre-processing into pattern primitives with attribute values. The pattern primitive, or simply primitive, is the lowest-level symbol from which higher symbols are inferred. The hierachical model of an object pattern is described with the use of rules along with some heuristic knowledge for the inference. These rules are stored in the rule base in Fig.1 and activated by the inference machine to verify whether or not a specific pattern exists in the image. The program of this vision system is written by using LISP except the pre-processing portion.

2. EARLY PROCESSING

Our objective in this study is to identify 2D silhouette patterns of several objects in the image. The models of these patterns are described in a rule format. Figure 2 exemplifies one of these patterns. No overlaping of the patterns is assumed at present. Unlike in subsequent model-based interpretation which proceeds in a distinctive way for each model, the following common processing is applied in early processing stages to the input image to yield intermediate symbols called segments. Figure 3 shows the overall process of pattern interpretation.

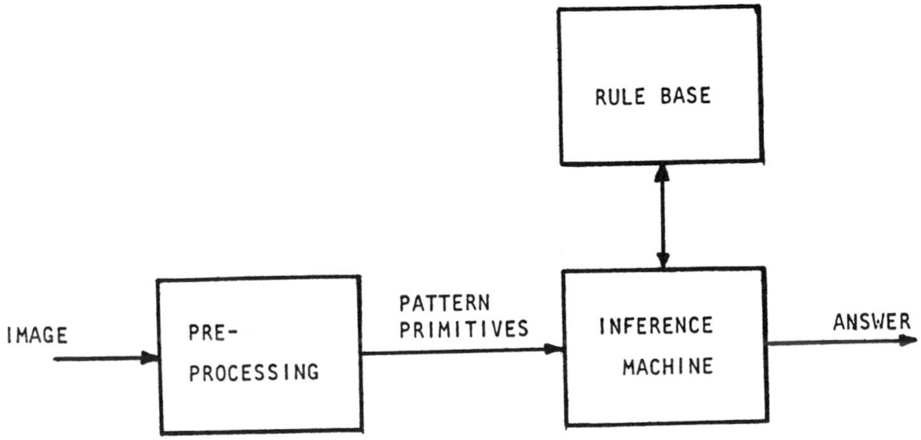

Fig.1 Schematic diagram of the vision system.

(2-1) Primitive Extraction

The input image containing grey level data obtained from a television camera is converted at first to a binary pattern by an appropriate thresholding. Then a chain-code string is generated by tracing the contour of this binary pattern. Using this chain-code string, the direction and curvature of the contour line is calculated at each point; the direction and curvature in this case are defined respectively as the direction toward the point apart by K=12 along the contour, and as the difference between the directions of the present point and the point apart by M=8. These definitions are not unusual in digital image processing; the parameters K and M have been chosen emperically so as to reduce noise effect without losing effective resolution.

A primitive is extracted from these data as a set of consecutive points having similar curvature. That is, tracing from one point along the contour, a set of consecutive points, the minimum and maximun curvatures of which are within a certain range, is find out to be the primitive. This process is repeated starting from each point on the contour. Each resultant primitive is given the positions (in 2D space and along the contour line) and directions of its starting and ending points and its average curvature as its attribute values. Then the primitives completely included in other primitive are deleted, though the partial overlapping of the primitives is permitted not to overlook neccesary information. Figure 2(a) illustrates some of the` extracted primitives, which are transfered to the inference machine for subsequent symbolic computation.

(2-2) Generating Segments

To reduce the amount of data for the model representation and the inference, the primitives having a continuous and similar property are assembled into a segment. A set of knowledge for this assembly process is written in a rule format and stored in the rule base. It is noted that the knowledge to be applied here is independent of object patterns whereas the knowledge specific for the object is required in later interpretation stages.

A pair of primitives, a pair of primitive and segment or a pair of segments is assembled into one segment (1) if the two are overlapped, or those end points are positioned closely each other and have almost equal directions, and (2) if the average curvatures of the two are almost equal. The primitive which has not been assembled with others becomes a segment by itself. The segment is given the positions and directions of its end points and its average curvature like in the case of the primitive. Figure 2(b) illustrates the generated segments.

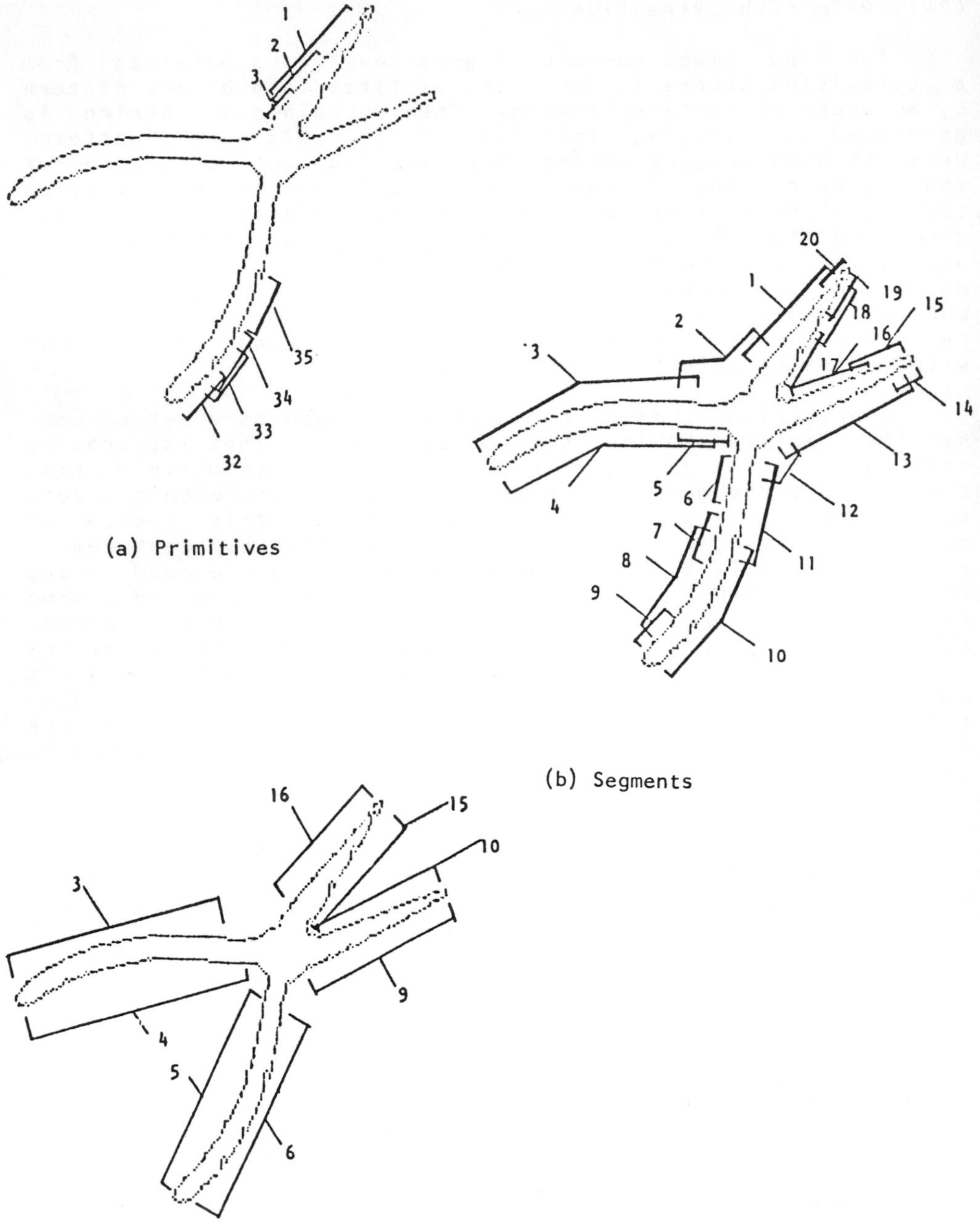

(a) Primitives

(b) Segments

(c) Sub-models

Fig.2 An example of hierarchical interpretation.

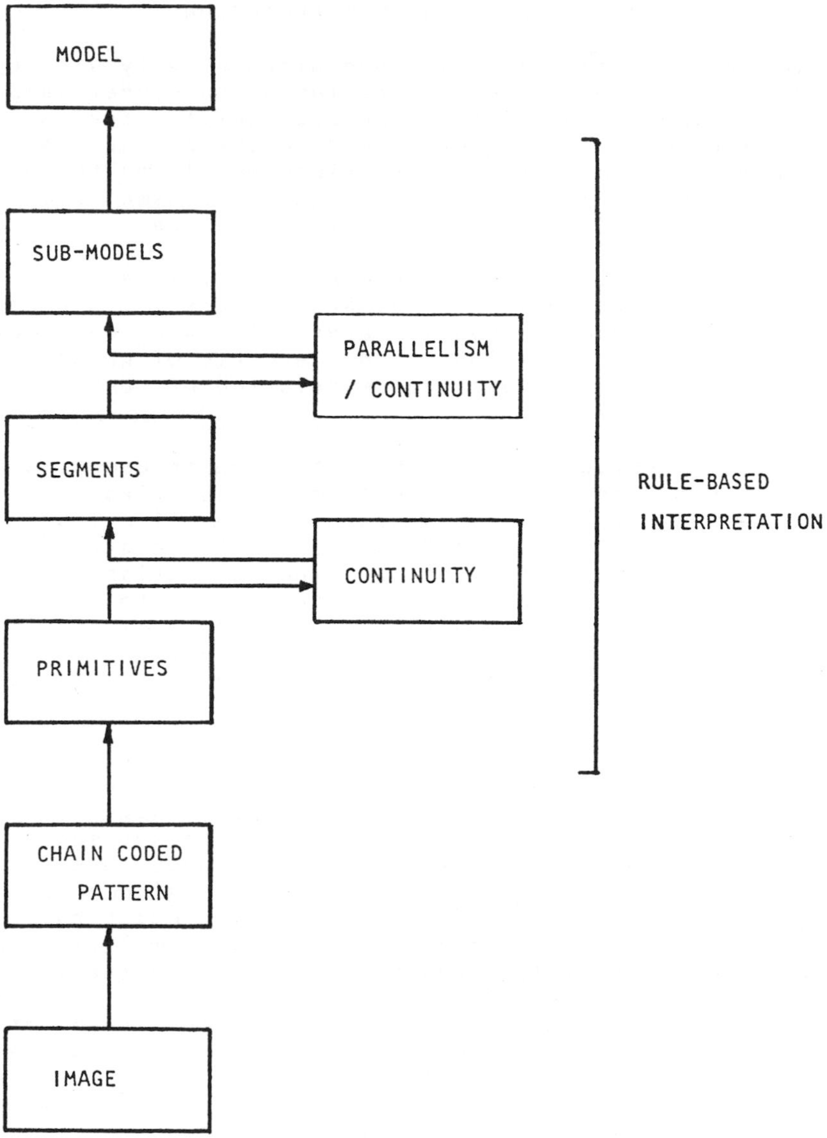

Fig.3 Process of interpretation.

3. MODEL-BASED INTERPRETATION

Each object model is described hierachically with the use of rules which include the declaration of sub-models and relations among them. Heuristic knowledge helpful for an efficient inference is also expressed in the rules. To realize flexible matching between the described model and the observed pattern, a certainty measure which plays the same role as that of truth value in fuzzy logic [5] is introduced.

For example, the object pattern of Fig. 2 called pincers can be described as shown in Fig. 4(a), where the pincers consist of four sub-models, namely handle-l, handle-r, pinch-l and pinch-r, the relations and lengthes of which are also defined. Figure 4(b) shows the description of one of these sub-models.

In this particular case, the inference proceeds as follows. First, the segments are further assembled with a certainty measure which allows an assembly condition looser than that of section (2-2). Let DS and DR be the distance between the segments and the difference of the directions of their facing edge points, respectively. Then the certainty measures CM(DS) and CM(DR) for DS and DR are assigned as shown in Fig. 5(a)(b), respectively. If DS is larger than 0, then min{CM(DS),CM(DR)} is given to a newly generated segment.

Second, a nearly parallel pair of the segments called arm pair is searched as a candidate for the sub-models, namely handle-l,r and pinch-l,r. The differences between the directions of the corresponding edge points of the two segments and the difference between the average curvatures are used to check the parallelism. Certainty measure assignments similar to Fig. 5 are employed to achieve flexible matching. As a result, the sub-models are generated as exemplified in Fig. 2(c) with attribute values and the certainty measure.

Finally, by checking the length and curvature of each sub-model and the relations of their connecting angles, the final object model is searched. The certainty measure always propagates in such a way that the minimum is taken when they are connected in cascade or parallel fashion.

If one final model is find out with the certainty measure larger than 0.7, then the inference process stops there and brings out the answer. If it fails to find such a model, then, in the present system, every final models are tried to match to the every combination of the segments and one gained the maximum certainty measure larger than 0.4 becomes an answer. This process may be improved by attaching a hypothesis generating stage which indicates possible object models by using simple features prior to the exhaustive search.

```
pincers
  handle-l
  handle-r
  pinch-l
  pinch-r
  ANGLE(handle-l,handle-r,pinch-l,pinch-r)
  LENGTH(handle-l,hancle-r,pinch-l,pinch-r)
```

```
(p=m1
 ($is$ state level submodel)
 ($is$ state flow lavelling)
 ($same$ submodel handle-l *va1)
 ($same$ submodel handle-r *va2)
 ($same$ submodel pinch-l *vp1)
 ($same$ submodel pinch-r *vp2)
 (or ($pincer-angle$ '*va1 '*va2 '*vp1 '*vp2)
     ($pincer-angle$ '*va1 '*va2 '*vp2 '*vp1))
 ($pincer-length$ '*va1 '*va2 '*vp1 '*vp2)
 ($set$ ($mask$ 'p=m3))
 ->
 ($add$ '(model pincers (*va1 *va2 *vp1 *vp2) *?CM))
 (setq haltflag t))
```

(a) Pincers

```
handle-l
  arml
  arm2
  PAIR(arml,arm2)
  CURVATURE(arml,arm2)
```

```
(p=l1
 ($is$ state level arm)
 ($is$ state flow labelling)
 ($same$ arm *vp1 *vv1)
 (eq 1 (mod *vp1 2))
 ($eval$ (add *vp1) *vp2)
 ($same$ arm *vp2 *vv2)
 ($arm-angle$ '*vv1 '*vv2)
 ($arm-curve+$ '*vv1)
 ($arm-curve-$ '*vv2)
 ($set$ ($mask$ 'p=l1a))
 ->
 ($change$ '(state n))
 ($add$ '(submodel handle-l (*vp1 *vp2) *?CM)))
```

(b) Handle-l

Fig.4 Model representation and their rule descreptions using LISP in which functions with '$' are implemented functions for this system and '->' is used to separate IF and THEN parts of the rule.

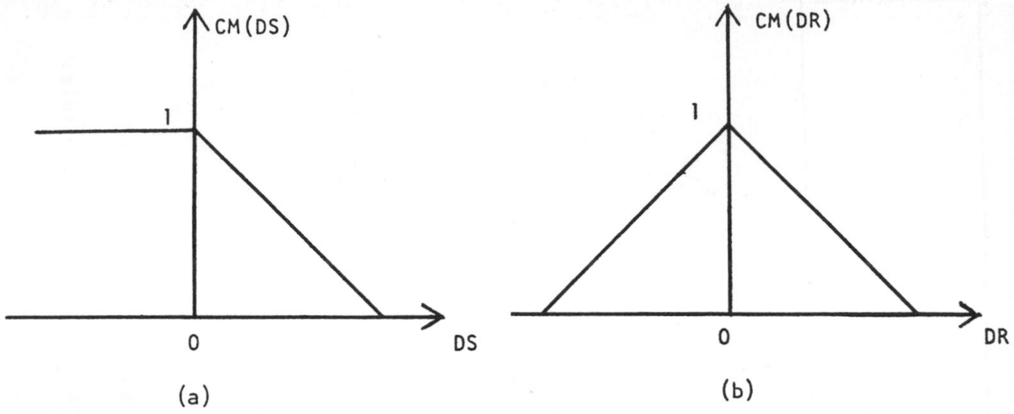

Fig.5 Examples of certainty measure assignment.

4. CONCLUSION

A method of the rule-based interpretation of curved patterns has been described. All the relevant knowledge except the pre-processing of section (2-2) is expressed in the modular rule format, which permits highly handling capability of the system design. The technique described in this paper may become useful in the advanced interactive graphic systems. Because the present inference speed is not satisfactory with the LISP running on a conventional computer (VAX11), the authors are now developing a new computer vision system based on frame-like knowledge representation, in which an efficient inference mechanism can be implemented [6].

REFERENCES

[1] H.G.Barrow and J.M.Tenenbaum, "Computational Vision," Proc IEEE, Vol.69, pp.572-595, May 1981.
[2] A.Barr and E.A.Feigenbaum ed., "The Handbook of Artificial Intelligence Vol.II," William Kaufmann Inc., Los Altos, 1982.
[3] D.Waterman and F.Hayeth-Roth ed. "Patern-Directed Inference Systems," Academic Press, 1978.
[4] K.S.Fu, "Syntactic Pattern Recognition and Applications," Prentice-Hall, 1982.
[5] L.A.Zadeh, "Fuzzy Logic and Approximate reasoning," Synthese, Vol.30, pp.407-428, 1975.
[6] M.Numao and M.Ishizuka, "Frame-Based Search System (FBSS) As a kernel of Vision Systems," submitted to 8th Int'l Joint Conf. on Artificial Intelligence.

A SPECIFICATION OF IMAGE PROCESSING FOR REMOTE SENSING

Yoshio Tozawa
Tokyo Scientific Center, IBM Japan
3-2-12 Roppongi, Minato-ku
Tokyo 106, JAPAN

ABSTRACT

A specification method of image processing for remote sensing is discussed using an example, that is SST (sea surface temperature) estimation from NOAA AVHRR data. This method of specification is a representation of data flow of image processing. Coordinate mapping and value mapping are specified independently. This specification is intended to specify the processing for operational use. This specification allows user to use many procedures which are written to implement some knowledge and to retrieve databases. The change of user decision may localized to a specification statement or a procedure. This suffices the requirement of operational use of remote sensing data.

1 INTRODUCTION

Remote Sensing is expected to widely applied to various applications such as environmental monitoring, regional planning, bio-mass, harvest, fishery, oceanography and so on. There are many case studies of various applications. However there seems to be some difficulties if we want to use these remote sensing technologies for operational use. We analyze and show what are difficulties for operational use by an example, which is estimation of sea surface temperature using AVHRR data of NOAA series satellites.

Remote Sensing is commonly understood as a technology to extract some information from data observed by satellites. Image itself gives us many information. We usually use much knowledge about images to interpret them. If we want to extract specific information among many other information, we expect machine to help us. Some information may be enhanced only by using low level image processing technique. On the other hand we have to integrate image data with other data or knowledge such as maps, ground truth or world models in order to extract information.

Our experience and many case studies tell us that we usually have to explore new image processing procedure for each image in the same application and that image processing highly depends on each individual image. In consequence, we felt interactive image processing system was necessary and many such systems are developed. These systems are very useful to investigate what kinds of processing are required for some application.

Now we have to think about operational use for given applications. Interactive system does not suit for operational use. We realize two stages.

First is the development stage where interactive system is essential and much experience is accumulated through case studies. Second stage is operational use where input data are automatically processed without human intervention or with less interaction. In this stage system has to be flexible and adaptable. We usually become learned much information about property of input images for operational use after the first stage. We need to teach knowledge about property of image and application for the second stage. A specification method proposed here intends to accomplish the second stage of remote sensing.

2 AN EXAMPLE OF ESTIMATION OF SEA SURFACE TEMPERATURE USING NOAA AVHRR DATA

In this section we describe what kinds of processing are required to estimate sea surface temperature from AVHRR (Advanced Very High Resolution Radiometer) data of NOAA series satellites. Table 1 shows characteristics of the NOAA AVHRR instruments. Some AVHRR (such as that of NOAA-7) have 5th channel, but some do not. 4th (and 5th) channel is sensitive to the thermal band. Fig. 1 is a 4th channel image of NOAA-6 AVHRR on 26th of April 1980. Fig. 2 is a sea surface temperature map processed from Fig. 1. 3rd channel is also sensitive to the thermal band, but sun light reflects in this channel in the daytime.

In order to estimate SST from AVHRR, the following three processing is required.
(1) Calibration
(2) Atmospheric correction
(3) Geometric correction

The data we receive is output of the detector. It is required to convert from output count of the detector to observed radiation (or brightness temperature) at the satellite. This process is called calibration. Characteristics of thermal infrared detector (sensitivity) is always changing. AVHRR provides us data for calibration in orbits. Those are output of space observation, output of the internal target observation and output of thermometer for the internal target. The manuals[1,2] describe how we can use these in-flight calibration data for calibration. But decision of parameters for calibration is still left to users. This decision may change according to the change of the characteristics of the sensor, required ac-

Table 1. Characteristics of the AVHRR instruments

Channel	Detector	Wavelength (μm)	Resolution at nadir	bands
1	silicon	0.58 -0.68	1.1 km	visible
2	silicon	0.725-1.10	1.1 km	near infrared
3	InSb	3.55 -3.93	1.1 km	infrared
4	HgCdTe	10.3 -11.3 10.5 -11.5*	1.1 km	thermal infrared
5	HgCdTe	11.5 -12.5	1.1 km	thermal infrared

* In the case of 4-channel system

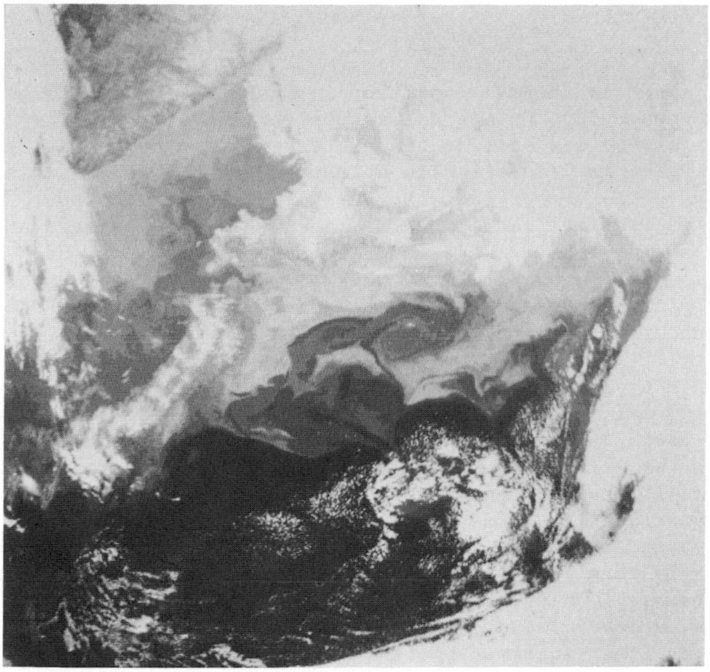

Fig. 1 Original thermal band image of NOAA AVHRR (April 26, 1980)

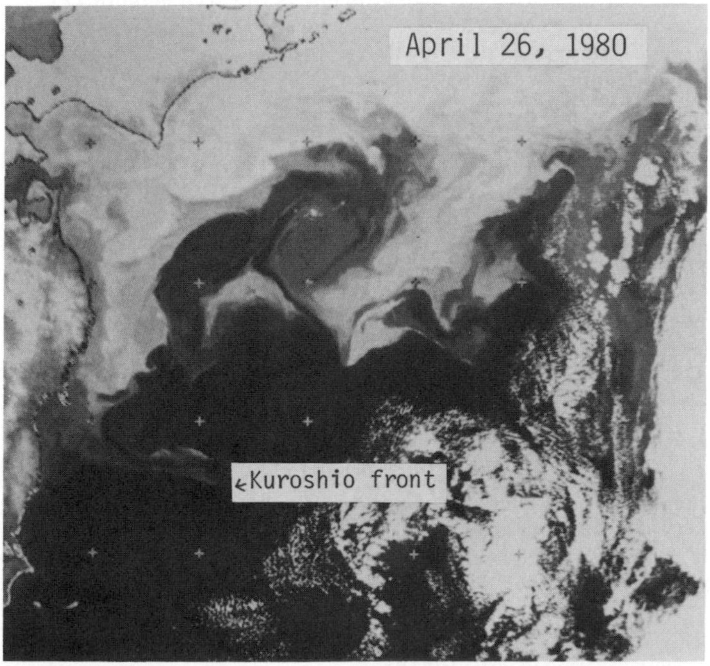

Fig. 2 Sea surface temperature map from Fig. 1

curacy or processing speed, resulting in the change of a program of calibration.

The sensor observes thermal radiation from the surface. Thermal radiation depends on emissivity, but we can assume that of water is very close to 1. So we can determine sea surface temperature if we know thermal radiation at the surface. Thermal radiation is attenuated by atmosphere mainly by water vapor. We have to correct the attenuation effect of atmosphere in order to determine the surface radiation from the radiation observed at the satellite. This process is called Atmospheric correction. Atmospheric correction is still open problem. Several models and methods are proposed. It depends on user to select the method of correction taking account of application, accuracy and availability of data.

Swath of AVHRR is about 2,800 km. Maximum of scanning angle is 55.4 degree. Original image has distortion due to scan angle, curvature of the earth and earth rotation. We want output image in accustomed coordinate system such as mercator. Mapping from original image to specific coordinate system is called geometric correction. We need to know the corresponding location (latitude and longitude) of each AVHRR pixel. Accurate geometric correction allows us to superpose many images and other data. This process is very important for such applications that monitor ocean dynamics or temporal change. In the case of NOAA satellites, every orbit is different each other. Geometric correction of AVHRR data requires orbital information. This information is not included in the satellite data but broadcasted by NOAA, which tracks the satellite.

SST estimation consists of calibration, atmospheric correction and geometric correction. Algorithms of these processing are essentially independent of each other. But parameters used in the processing are related each other. When we develop programs for these processing, we have to take care of relations among parameters. Structure of a program is determined by dependency of parameters.

3 DECISION IN DATA PROCESSING FOR REMOTE SENSING

In remote sensing we need much reference data or ground truth data other than satellite image. We sometimes feel that we could conclude with more confidence if some data were available. In atmospheric correction we would determine attenuation of radiance more accurately if we could observe distribution of water vapor by some other instruments. Adequate data is not always available. We sometimes have to use more inadequate data for reference of ground truth. We have to decide what kinds of data can be used for what. This decision depends on accuracy, application and other environment.

This decision should be done by user, and this decision may change according to the change of user requirements. An advantage of interactive system is adaptability to this change. In general, however, users of remote sensing are not experts of image processing, and they are not good at programming. They want to use Remote Sensing data operationally for their own objectives.

Key problems come from the following,

- Programs have to be developed to process Remote Sensing data,

- There are many decisions to be made by users,
- Decisions may change according to the change of requirements, and
- Programs are not flexible for decision change.

Users describe their requirements in their application terminology. But decisions are usually done in terms of parameters of image processing.

Decision in the calibration process affects accuracy and amount of computation. Two points (linear) calibration method is used for AVHRR data. Output of the sensor is converted to radiance by (1).

$$N = G*X + I \qquad (1)$$

where N: radiation

X: output of the sensor

G (gain) and I (interception) are parameters for calibration process. G and I can be determined by the response function of the sensor, output of space observation (SP_X), output of internal target observation (TG_X), temperature of internal target (TG_T) and a given parameter for each sensor (SP_N). Relation among these is written as the following.

$$G = (SP\_N - TG\_N) / (SP\_X - TG\_X) \qquad (2)$$

$$I = SP\_N - G*SP\_X \qquad (3)$$

$$TG\_N = TN(TG\_T) \qquad (4)$$

where TG_N is black body radiation from internal target detected by the sensor, and TN is a function from temperature to detectable radiation derived from the response function of the sensor. SP_N and TN depends on the detector (which is identified by the platform TIROS-N, NOAA-6 or NOAA-7 and channel number).

As we can see from (1), accuracy of N depends on that of G and I. G and I are time varying, especially in thermal bands. We want to know G and I at the time of X. In-flight calibration data contain only 10 samples of SP_X and TG_X at the time of X. If the variance of the detector is high, reliability of SP_X and TG_X using 10 samples is low. The more samples, the higher reliability. If we assume that characteristics of the detector does not change so rapidly, we can use more samples (say 50 samples) to calculate SP_X and TG_X. But if we want to collect more samples, G and I are slow in following the real time varying characteristics. In this case decision is to determine how many samples are used to calculate G and I.

This decision is based on the judgement about the characteristics of the sensor, time variability and variance. It is possible to assume that G and I are constant in a short time interval when the satellite passes over a particular area. This assumption reduces the amount of computation because once G and I are determined there are no necessity to re-calculate them. These decision should be made by user, and it is important for user to know what decisions are made.

Decisions become more complex in atmospheric correction. First of all we have to decide what model of correction we use. Each model requires different parameters. Even if a model is known good, it can not be used unless required parameter data are available. In our case we adopted McConaghy's method, where optical depth is empirically determined using sea truth data (sea temperature by ship). Attenuation by water vapor is directly calculated from optical depth, which is assumed to be proportional to the thickness of atmosphere according to scan angle. Sea temperature data by ships are available in sea truth database. Sea truth database is a relation SEATRUTH (DATE, TIME, LONGITUDE, LATITUDE, TEMPERATURE) and maintained for other objectives.

Next we have to select adequate sea truth for parameters. Quality of parameters affects the quality of output results. We have to decide database query condition to retrieve adequate sea truth. This condition has to be decided by users. As ships move slowly, there are rarely sea truth data at the just time when a satellite passes. It is possible however, to use sea truth within a few days because we can assume that sea temperature does not change in a few days. Of course there are some exceptions. If ocean front passes, sea temperature at a location may change a few degrees. Decision includes whether ocean front likely passes the location or not.

We need to know the brightness temperature at the satellite correspond to the sea truth so as to calculate optical depth. We have to point out the location of the sea truth in AVHRR image. Mapping from the geographical coordinate (latitude and longitude) to the location of AVHRR image is one of the geometric correction. The process of conversion from sensor output to brightness temperature requires calibration. Before we calculate optical depth from sea truth and brightness temperature, we have to check whether the points of sea truth are adequate or not. If the points are covered by cloud, we have to abandon to use the points for calculation of optical depth. This judgement is usually done by human in interactive system. For operational use, however, this judgement has to be done by machine.

Experts of this judgement use knowledge or experience about concerning area. This means that decision is changeable and system is required to have the facility to adopt a new decision procedure easily and to show users what decision procedure is used now.

In the geometric correction process, decision is made mainly on what method is to be used. In the case of NOAA satellites, we use orbital information for mapping. Decision includes approximate form of the mapping function, considering trade-off among accuracy, error and computability. The way of registration and resampling method also have to be decided.

In summary, there are many decisions in the processing for remote sensing. When we use the result of the processing, we have to know what decisions are made and what are effects. If some decisions become not to be suitable, decisions has to be changed. Decisions usually depend on applications, objectives or other environment such as availability of data or computing power. Therefore decision should be made by users. From this view point, requirements of data processing system are the followings.
(1) System has a facility for user to specify decisions.
(2) It is easy for user to know what decisions are made in the system.
(3) Decisions can be easily changed to follow requirements of users.
(4) Details of programming should be concealed.

4 KNOWLEDGE IN REMOTE SENSING

In order to extract information from remotely sensed data, we use much knowledge. Examples of knowledge in Remote Sensing are as follows.

· Neighboring pixels of a sea pixel are likely sea.

- Values of cloud pixel is saturated in visible channel and low radiance in thermal channel.
- The ground control points can be identified by peculiar features.
- Noise data can be

- Changing of characteristics of a detector is slow.
- Effects of many kinds of filters.
- What form of approximate function is adequate for geometric correction of near Japan area.
- How to select and evaluate good sea truths.
- Least square fitting method to determine optical depth.
- McConaghy's model can be used for atmospheric correction.

If we want to utilize some of this kinds of knowledge, we have to write programs. These programs represent knowledge and can be used in several application programs. These programs require their own parameters.

For example, McConaghy's model of atmospheric correction is regarded as knowledge. This knowledge is implemented as a function from brightness temperature to corrected temperature (or SST). Required parameters of this function are optical depth (OPTDEPTH and C), height of the satellite (H), height of atmosphere (ATMHEIGHT), radius of the earth (R) and scan angle.

We have to teach above knowledge to the system. We may use procedures to represent it. Representation of knowledge may be sophisticated and changed later. All applications that use the knowledge should take advantage of this improvement of representation. This kind of change should be localized. Some knowledge may constrain parameters for these procedures. It must be easy to see what kinds of knowledge are used. It is therefore necessary to specify procedure names and their parameters and how to chose them.

5 A SPECIFICATION OF IMAGE PROCESSING

The purpose of specification is to make it easy for users to see what kinds of processing are done with what parameters. It is specified what decisions are made and what kinds of knowledge are used. Details of programming such as physical format of data or execution sequence are concealed in the level of specification. Image processing has the following property.

- Uniformity of processing of pixel value over a given image.
- Independent process of coordinate calculation from that of pixel value.
- Locality of the elementary process.

Image processing mainly consists of how output pixel values are calculated and how the coordinate is mapped. Procedures as a representation of knowledge are applied to local subimage of a whole image. We have to teach machine how to handle these. What is required is a specification technique of control structure. Control structure of image processing determines which procedures are invoked with which parameters in what sequence order. Database may be searched in order to determine parameters.

Specification consists of input specification, output specification, coordinate mapping specification and output value calculation specification. Fig. 3 shows an example of a specification of simple image processing. Lowercase letters are key words known to the system. Capital letters are user defined name. Inputs are two images X1 and X2. Coordinate of these images are same. This is a very usual case in remote sensing. Most of

```
(1)  Input;
(2)   X1(*,*) index (I1,J1);
(3)   X2(*,*) index (I1,J1);
(4)  end;
(5)  Output;
(6)   Y(512,512) index (I2,J2);
(7)  end;
(8)  Coordinate;
(9)   I1 = I2 + (COLUMNSIZE(X1)-COLUMNSIZE(Y))/2;
(10)  J1 = J2 + (LINESIZE(X1)-LINESIZE(Y))/2;
(11) end;
(12) Value;
(13)  Y = (X3-X2) / (MX1-MX2);
(14)  X3 = FILT(SUBIMG(X1,I1-1:I1+1,J1-1:J1+1));
(15)  MX1 = MAX(X1);
(16)  MX2 = MIN(X2);
(17) end;
```

Fig. 3 Specification of simple operation and extraction

multi spectral scanner provide images of this type, that is, images of different bands of the scanner have the same coordinate.

Conceptual data flow of this example is shown in Fig. 4. The detail format of input (and output) image is not specified here. We assume that it is known to the system. We have to teach the format to the system. But this should not be done by users, and have to be specified other place. Lines (1) to (4) specify input. '*' means that image size of input is arbitrary. 'Index' is a key word and the same index (I1, J1) is used in both (2) and (3). By these statements the system can understand that X1 and X2 have the same coordinate. Index is mainly used to specify coordinate mapping. This example shows an extraction of center area of image. 'Columnsize' and 'linesize' are builtin functions. Our intention is independence of this process from input image size. (9) and (10) define the interpretation of the word 'center' using 'columnsize' and 'linesize' builtin functions, which are known to the system.

Lines (12) to (17) specify how to calculate pixel values of output image Y. Order of statement sequence is not important. Because this specification can be thought as a sentential representation of Fig. 4. Line (14) specifies that image X1 is filtered by FILT function and produces image X3. 'subimage' is a builtin function. 'subimage' builtin function extracts a small part of image and allows us to restrict our view in concerning area. First argument is the base image and second and third arguments indicate the location and the size to be extracted. In this case it is 3 x 3 filtering. Conceptually this specification produces a filtered image X3 as shown in Fig. 4. Most of interactive system produce a filtered image physically. However, there are no necessity to make X3 image in order to calculate Y in this case.

It is application or image dependent which type of filter is adequate. This is know-how or knowledge. We may continue to make efforts to improve output quality, resulting in exploration of a new filter. If we invent a new type of filter, this knowledge can be implemented as a function. Then

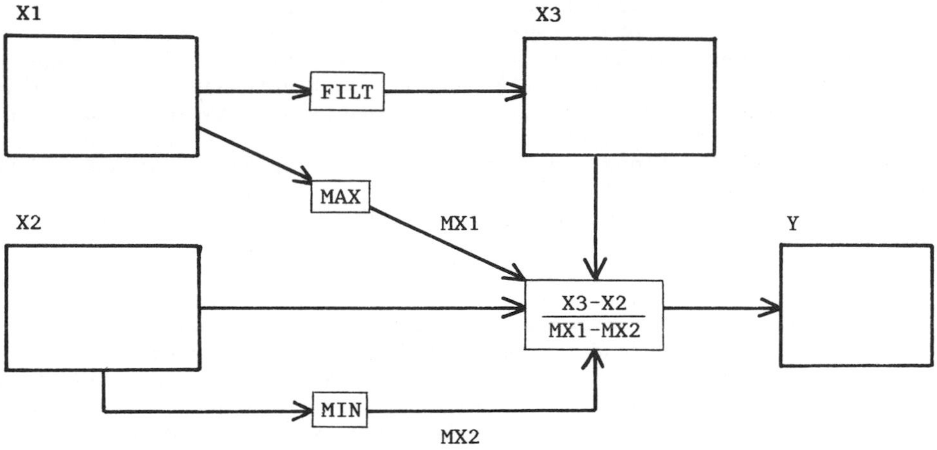

Fig. 4 Conceptual data flow of a specification of Fig. 3

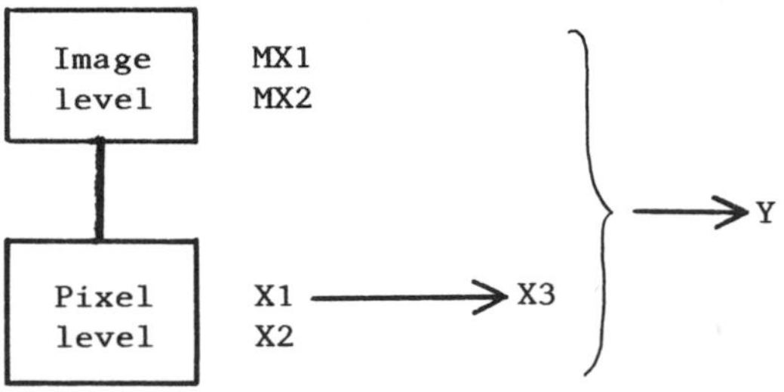

Fig. 5 Hierarchy of variability of variables in Fig. 3

we can change the function name of line (14) to use it. It is very easy to use new knowledge like this in this specification. 'MAX' and 'MIN' are user defined (or builtin) functions. 'MAX' finds the maximum value in image X1 and 'MIN' finds the minimum value in image X2. It is easy to see that we need at least two scans to produce image Y. In some interactive system, intervention at the end of each scan may be required. But if we specify like Fig. 3, system can understand the necessity of two scan and do it automatically.

Fig. 5 shows the hierarchy of variability of the variables used in Fig. 3. MX1 and MX2 are regarded as attributes of image X1 and X2 respectively, so they belong to the image level. This means these values are constant over an image. On the other hand the value of pixels of X1, X2, X3 and Y differs each other, so they belong to the pixel level. If MX1 and MX2 are necessary to calculate Y, system calculates MX1 and MX2 first because they are in the upper of the hierarchy.

Fig. 6 is an example of a specification of NOAA AVHRR data calibration process. Fig. 7 is conceptual representation of data flow of Fig. 6. '*' used for output images in line (10) means that the size of output image is the same of input. Lines (12) to (14) specify what database is used. This is a user view. In this case conversion functions between radiance and temperature which depends on the response function of detectors are stored in a database. The functions are retrieved specifying SAT = SATNAME and CH = CHANNEL (see line (23)). SAT and CH are field names in line (13) and SATNAME and CHANNEL are required input parameters defined in lines (6) and (7).

The number 2 in line (21) and (22) specifies a decision that we average 50 samples and we assume characteristics of a sensor do not change in consecutive 5 lines. If we find it not adequate to average 50 samples, it is easy to change. CHKAVR in lines (21) and (22) is a function to check whether the value of samples are reasonable or not and to average them. How to check reasonableness of samples is know-how that depends on the characteristics of noise on signal. Checking procedure is written as a function and registered as CHKAVR. If you want to change the way to check, you can either change the function name in the specification to use other function or modify the function procedure.

Fig. 8 shows the hierarchy of variability of variables in Fig. 6. G and I are in the level of line, that is G and I are constants in a line while column is changing. If it is possible to assume that G and I are constant in

```
(1)  Input;
(2)   X(2048,*) index (I, J);
(3)   SPX(10,*) index (I3,J);
(4)   TGX(10,*) index (I4,J);
(5)   TG_N(*)   index (J);
(6)   SATNAME;
(7)   CHANNEL;
(8)  end;
(9)  Output;
(10)  BT(*,*) index (I,J);
(11) end;
(12) Database;
(13)  FUNCS (SAT, CH, FUNCNT, FUNCTN);
(14) end;
(15) Value;
(16)  BT = NT(N);
(17)  N = G*X + I;
(18)  G = (SP_N - TG_N) / (SP_X - TG_X);
(19)  I = SP_N - G*SP_X;
(20)  TG_N = TN(TG_T);
(21)  SP_X = CHKAVR(subimg(SPX,*,J-2:J+2));
(22)  TG_X = CHKAVR(subimg(TGX,*,J-2:J+2));
(23)  (TN,NT) = select FUNCTN,FUNCNT from FUNCS
            where SAT = SATNAME and CH = CHANNEL;
(24)  SP_N = 0;
(25) end;
```

Fig. 6 Specification of calibration

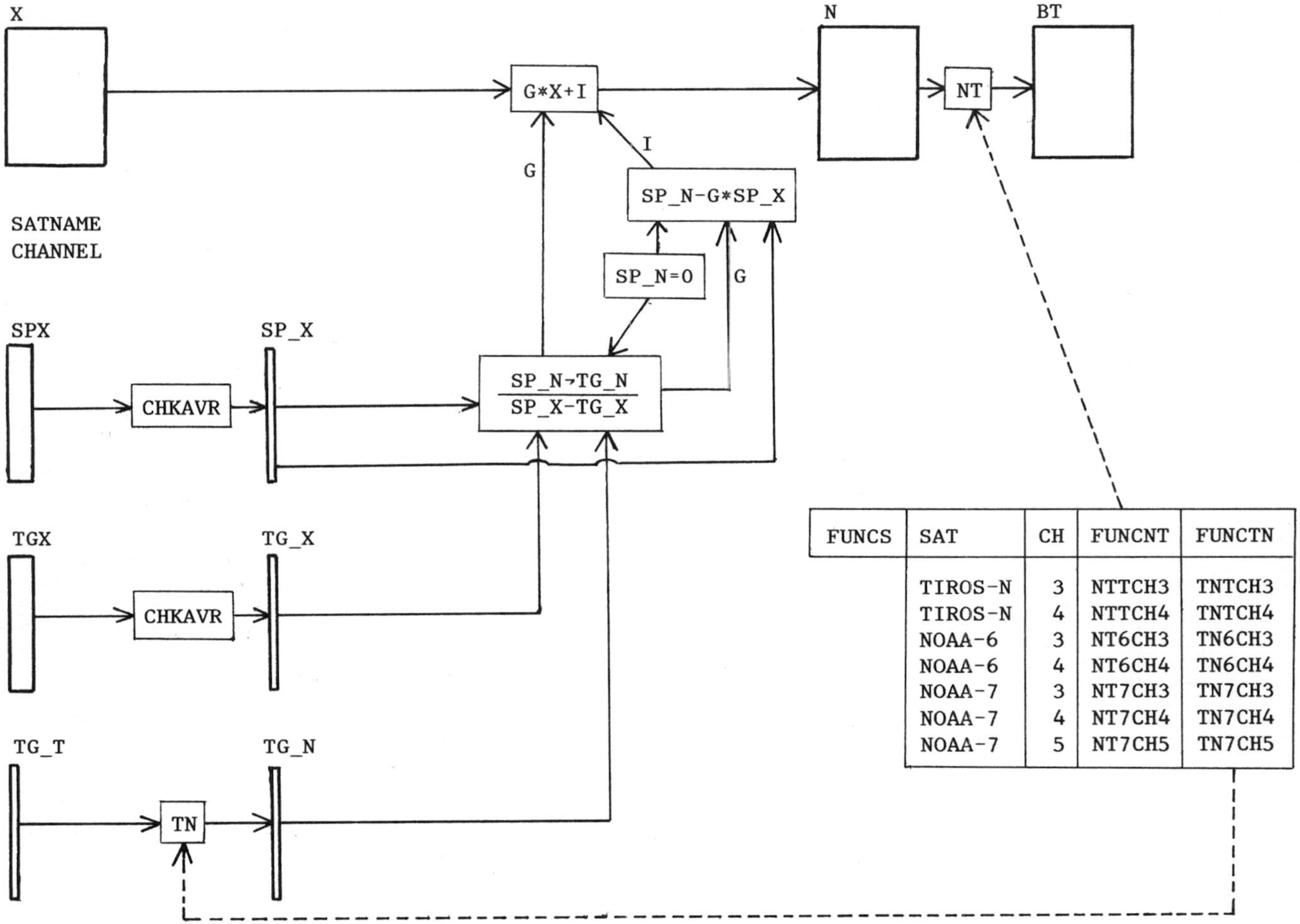

FUNCS	SAT	CH	FUNCNT	FUNCTN
	TIROS-N	3	NTTCH3	TNTCH3
	TIROS-N	4	NTTCH4	TNTCH4
	NOAA-6	3	NT6CH3	TN6CH3
	NOAA-6	4	NT6CH4	TN6CH4
	NOAA-7	3	NT7CH3	TN7CH3
	NOAA-7	4	NT7CH4	TN7CH4
	NOAA-7	5	NT7CH5	TN7CH5

Fig.7 Conceptual data flow of Fig. 6

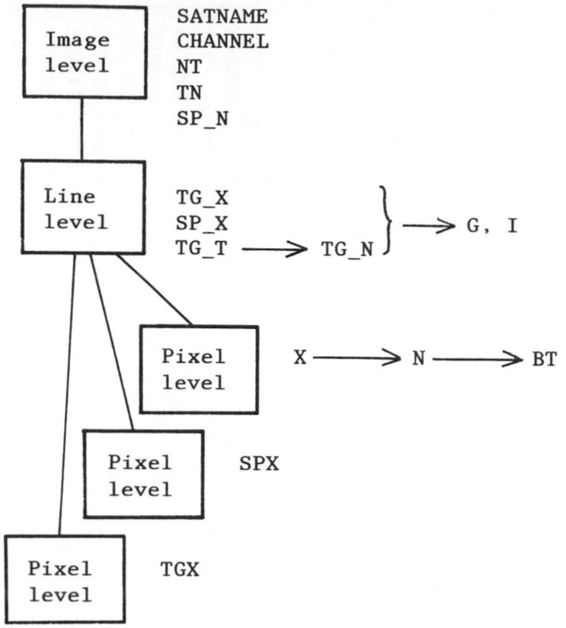

Fig. 8 Hierarchy of variability of variables in Fig. 6

a whole image, G and I can be regarded in the image level. If you judge to change from line level to image level, taking account of computation time, you can specify as the following in stead of the lines (20) to (22). In the following case 110 samples are used to calculate G and I. '*' in (20) and (21) means that it is the same size of base images. TG_T varies in every line, so TG_T is in the line level. But TG_T(6) can be considered in the image level, because it is a constant.

```
(20) TG_N = TN(TG_T(6));
(21) SP_X = CHKAVR(subimg(SPX,*,1:11));
(22) TG_X = CHKAVR(subimg(TGX,*,1:11));
```

Fig. 9 is a specification of geometric correction. The essence of geometric correction is calculation of input location (I, J) from given output coordinate (I2, J2). We use two functions NOAAGCOR and MERCATOR. These two functions are essential to geometric correction and independent of calibration and atmospheric correction. NOAAGCOR is a mapping function from (longitude, latitude) to the location of an AVHRR image. This function can be implemented independently without any concern about AVHRR. Decisions of form of the approximate function are included in the NOAAGCOR function, taking account of accuracy and computation time. MERCATOR is a mapping function to make a map of the mercator system. If you want to make a map of the other system, you may change the name of this. Ability to make combination of functions like this is a merit of a specification of image processing.

```
(1)  Input;
(2)   X(2048,*) index (I, J);
(3)   SPX(10,*) index (I3,J);
(4)   TGX(10,*) index (I4,J);
(5)   TG_N(*)   index (J);
(6)   SATNAME;
(7)   CHANNEL;
(8)   STIME;
(9)   ORBIT;
(10) end;
(11) Output;
(12)  BT(512,512) index (I2,J2);
(13) end;
(14) Database;
(15)  NTFUNC (SAT, CH, FUNCN);
(16)  ORBDATA (ORB,HEIGHT,PERIOD,INCLANGLE,CRSLONG,CRSTIME);
(17) end;
(18) Coordinate;
(19)  (I,J) = NOAAGCOR(LONG,LAT,H,R,T,INC,CLONG,CTIME,STIME);
(20)  (H,T,INC,CLONG,CTIME) =
       select H,T,INCLANGLE,CRSLONG,CRSTIME from ORBDATA
              where ORB = ORBIT;
(21)  (LONG,LAT) = MERCATOR(I2,J2,SCALE,R,LONGO,LATO);
(22)  SCALE = 2;
(23)  LONGO = 140;
(24)  LATO = 35;
(25)  R = ERADIUS(LATO);
(26) end;
```

Fig. 9 Specification of geometric correction with calibration

Parameters required are for geometric correction such as H, T, INC, CLONG, and CTIME, and information about output area such as SCALE, LONGO and LATO. Some of these are retrieved from the database (see line (20)), some are specified in the specification (lines (22) to (25)) and some are given as input parameters (lines (8) and (9)). LONGO and LATO specifies the center of output image. ERADIUS function calculates the radius of the earth at a given latitude. Value part of Fig. 9 is the same of Fig. 6, so it is omitted here.

Fig. 10 specifies atmospheric correction. Coordinate part are omitted because it is the same as Fig. 9. Conceptual data flow of atmospheric correction is shown in Fig. 11. As shown in Fig. 10 and Fig. 11, the sea truth database is searched. Result after the search of the database is a relation. Declaration of relations is given in lines (19) to (22). We need the values of BT which corresponds to the sea truth data in order to calculate parameters OPTDEPTH and C for ATM function (see line (36)). The values in BT that correspond to the sea truth are inserted into the attribute SAT of SEADATA1 relation. This process is specified in lines (39) and (40). This calculation is prerequisite to calculate OPTDEPTH and C by FITOPTDPTH. OPTDEPTH and C are in the image level (see Fig. 12). In consequence, the values of BT of these particular points are calculated before usual BT calculation.

Lines (41) and (42) calculates range of longitude and latitude for condition to retrieve sea truth used in line (38). CHKSEATRUTH is a procedure to implement knowledge to eliminate inadequate points (because of cloud cover or etc.) Input of this procedure is SEADATA1 relation which may con-

```
(1)  Input;
(2)   X(2048,*) index (I, J);
(3)   SPX(10,*) index (I3,J);
(4)   TGX(10,*) index (I4,J);
(5)   TG_N(*)   index (J);
(6)   SATNAME;
(7)   CHANNEL;
(8)   STIME;
(9)   ORBIT;
(10) end;
(11) Output;
(12)  SST(512,512) index (I2,J2);
(13) end;
(14) Database;
(15)  FUNCS (SAT, CH, FUNCNT, FUNCTN);
(16)  ORBDATA (ORB,HEIGHT,PERIOD,INCLANGLE,CRSLONG,CRSTIME);
(17)  SEATRUTH (DATES, TIMES, LONGS, LATS, TEMPS);
(18) end;
(19) Relation;
(20)  SEADATA(LONGS,LATS,TEMPS,SAT);
(21)  SEADATA1(LONGS,LATS,TEMPS,SAT);
(22) end;
(23) Value;
(24)  /* calibration */
(25)  BT = NT(N);
(26)  N = G*X + I;
(27)  G = (SP_N - TG_N) / (SP_X - TG_X);
(28)  I = SP_N - G*SP_X;
(29)  TG_N = TN(TG_T);
(30)  SP_X = CHKAVR(SUBIMG(SPX,*,J-2:J+2));
(31)  TG_X = CHKAVR(SUBIMG(TGX,*,J-2:J+2));
(32)  NT = select FUNCN from NTFUNC
           where SAT = SATNAME and CH = CHANNEL;
(33)  /* atmospheric correction */
(34)  SST = ATM(BT,OPTDEPTH,C,ATMHEIGHT,H,R,SCANANGLE);
(35)  ATMHEIGHT = 100;
(36)  (OPTDEPTH,C) = FITOPTDPTH(SEADATA);
(37)  SEADATA = CHKSEATRUTH(SEADATA1);
(38)  SEADATA1 = select LONGS,LATS,TEMPS from SEATRUTH
       where LONGS>=LONGL & LONGS<=LONGH & LATS>=LATL
           & LATS<=LATH & DATES>=DATE-3 & DATES<=DATE+3;
(39)  SEADATA1.SAT = BT(I6,J6);
(40)  (I6,J6)=NOAAGCOR(LONG,LAT,H,R,T,INC,CLONG,CTIME,STIME);
(41)  (LONGL,LATL) = MERCATOR(512,1,SCALE,R,LONGO,LATO);
(42)  (LONGH,LATH) = MERCATOR(1,512,SCALE,R,LONGO,LATO);
(43) end;
```

Fig. 10 Specification of Atomspheric Correction with Calibration and Geometric Correction

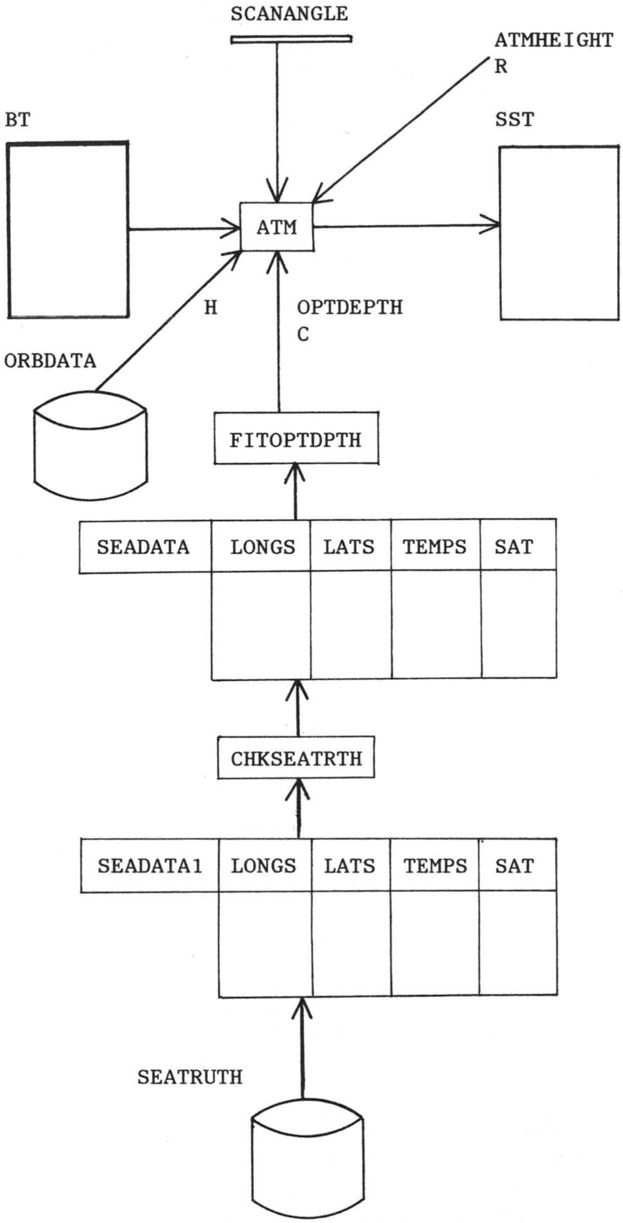

Fig. 11 Conceptual data flow of atmospheric correction

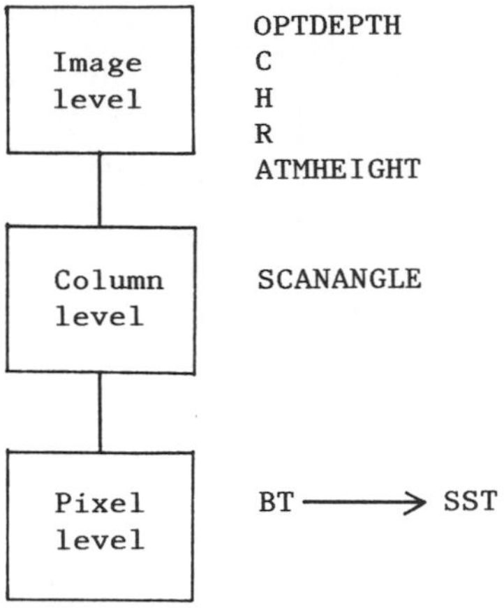

Fig. 12 Hierarchy of variability in atmospheric correction

tain inadequate points to calculate OPTDEPTH and C. SEADATA relation contains only good points FITOPTDPTH is a procedure to determine OPTDEPTH and C using say least square method.

As a matter of fact, atmospheric correction is very troublesome procedure, if it is implemented on interactive image processing system. It requires much intervention. The reason is that it is difficult to use knowledge (such as geometric correction or calibration procedure) systematically. The specification of Fig. 10 solves this problem. This specification can tell the system control structure of image processing. Calculation of BT in line (25) is invoked twice. First is in the image level at line (39), and second is in the pixel level at line (25) (see Fig. 12).

6 CONCLUSION

In order to use remote sensing data operationally, we need to avoid intervention by human. Interactive system is nod adequate for operational use. Interaction by human is not creative work. Basic information to judge can be considered in database or images. We have to teach a system how to use these information. Specification of image processing is a clue to solve this problem. In operational use, the change of environment affects the processing. Users who are not familiar with programming have to deal with this change.

We showed that a specification technique of image processing for remote sensing using an example of estimation of sea surface temperature from NOAA AVHRR data. This specification can be interpreted as conceptual data flow of image processing. It is therefore easy to see what decisions are made and what kinds of knowledge are used. If it is found that some changes are necessary, the change is usually localized in a specification or procedure.

REFERENCES

(1) Schwalb, A.: "The TIROS-N/NOAA A-G Satellite series", NOAA Tech. Memo. NESS 95, March 1978

(2) Lauritson, L., Nelson, G. J., Porto, F. W.: "Data extraction and calibration of TIROS-N/NOAA radiometers", NOAA Tech. Memo. NESS 107, Nov. 1979

(3) McConaghy, D. C.: "Measuring Sea Surface Temperature from Satellites: A ground Truth Approach", Remote Sensing of Environment 10:307-310 1980

(4) Tozawa, Y., Iisaka, J., Saitoh, S., Muneyama, K. and Sasaki, Y.: "SST ESTIMATION BY NOAA AVHRR and ITS APPLICATION TO OCEANIC FRONT EXTRACTION", Proc. of the second ACRS, NOV. 1981

(5) Japan Marine Science and Technology Center and IBM Japan Tokyo Scientifc Senter: "OCEANOGRAPHY FROM SPACE" July 1982 (In Japanese)

THE ANALYSIS OF LANDSAT (M2S) IMAGE DATA USING INTERACTIVE INFORMATION RETRIEVAL LANGUAGE SOAR

Yoshioki Ishii
Software AG of Far East, Inc.
2-7-2 Yaesu, Chuo-ku, Tokyo 104, JAPAN
Kazuhiko Nakayama and **Takashi Hoshi**
Science Information Processing Center
University of Tsukuba
Ibaragi 305, JAPAN

ABSTRACT

This paper presents an experiment to store and process the Scene Image data using ADABAS and SOAR. The Scene Image data (extracted by LANDSAT) is a set of Pixels. The data (Pixel records) is stored in ADABAS database. All attributes (Band 4, 5, 6, 7 and others) of the Pixel records are defined as descriptors (Retrieval keys). ADABAS automatically generates and maintains an Inverted List for each descriptor attribute.

SOAR considers the ADABAS database as a set of records, and provides comprehensive facilities for set operations against the Scene Image data. In the experiment, the Scene Image data is analyzed using these set operations.

When clouds are found above the earth surface where a survey is to be carried out, the corresponding Scene Image data cannot be used for analysis. Utilizing SOAR, the parts of the Scene covered with clouds are located and the cloud images are output to a terminal printer. By matching the output with the actual map of the Scene, the locations of the Scene covered with clouds can readily be obtained. This can prevent the wasteful efforts in performing the unfruitful Scene Image analysis.

Various representations on the Scene (for example, the shape of an island, the river, and even the contamination in the sea) can be obtained and output to the printer in similar ways. With SOAR, various sets of the Scene under different conditions can be obtained and set operations can be performed to map multiple sets. Thus surveys like how far the sea is contaminated by a river can easily be obtained using simple set operations.

As a confirmation check, real image output is obtained and compared with the various output obtained from the experiment. The comparison indicated that the output/map obtained from the experiment is of very high accuracy.

1. INTRODUCTION

The main objective of storing and administering information is for easy retrieval of the required information. For a certain "Entity", several attributes which describe the entity most appropriately are selected and values (characters or numerics) are assigned to each attribute. This forms a record and is stored in a database. One of the key roles of a DBMS is to find the records from a database which satisfy the various retrieval conditions.

However, very few existing database systems support the storage of image data in the database as well as the interactive specification of various retrieval conditions such as locating clouds against the image, or part of it, to find out the required image data location and ultimately output the data to a regular terminal.

For image data processing, a drum digitizer recorder, for example, is required for output. A remote terminal user must go to the place where data is stored for such processing. If after the user had the image output on a film or a paper, he found that the portion he wanted to study was covered with clouds, then all his ealier efforts would be in vain.

This paper presents an experiment to eliminate such inconvenience in image data processing. The image data used in the experiment is obtained by a Multi Spectral Scanner (M2S) which is mounted on the Satellite LANDSAT. The image data is stored in an ADABAS database, which has a function for automatic generation and maintenance of inverted lists; and inverted lists are generated for each attribute of Pixel, which is the smallest unit of image data. For data search, SOAR (designed by Y. Ishii), and interactive retrieval language to facilitate retrieval of ADABAS database, is used. The initial proposal for development of SOAR is based on the idea that data processing should be performed in the set oriented manner.

The experiment proves that ADABAS, which is accepted generally for its suitability in business applications, together with SOAR, the set oriented interactive language, are also very effective and efficient for handling of image data.

2. ADABAS AND SOAR

ADABAS (Adaptable DAta BAse System) was initially designed and programmed in 1969 by P. Schnell* of Software AG, West Germany and Version 1 was completed in 1970. It is not a result of a mere theoretical concept, but was accomplished through cumulative efforts to eliminate inconveniences in daily data processing.

It is also interesting to know that E.F. Codd proposed the relational model almost at the same time (1970) as the first ADABAS development, and that so many ideas formalized in the model are efficiently realized in ADABAS [1], [2].

SOAR (Set Oriented Architecture of Request) can serve as a user-friendly and powerful aid for developing information retrieval application systems.

SOAR was evolved from SOIR (Set Oriented Information Retrieval) [3]. SOIR Version 0.0 and SOIR Version 0.5 were completed in July, 1978 and in March 1979, respectively. They were first utilized for several experimental IR applications at JICST (Japan Information Center of Science and Technology). Terminal users could use SOIR to interactively create sets of records retrieved according to some requirements and freely manipulate them by means of various set operations. Finally, users could get desired data on the display screen. Through experimental usages of SOIR, it became clear that the core part of SOIR had to be reinforced to support more powerful data

---

* P. Schnell is president of Software AG, Darmstadt, West Germany.

search capabilities. Then Software AG of Far East started redesigning the overall architecture of the core part of SOIR, and developed a completely new version, which is named SOAR [4].

SOAR has various commands, which can be used via calls from host languages such as COBOL, PL/I, FORTRAN, and Assembler. An interactive SOAR language is also developed, which can be directly initiated from terminals. In the experiment, the interactive SOAR language is used.

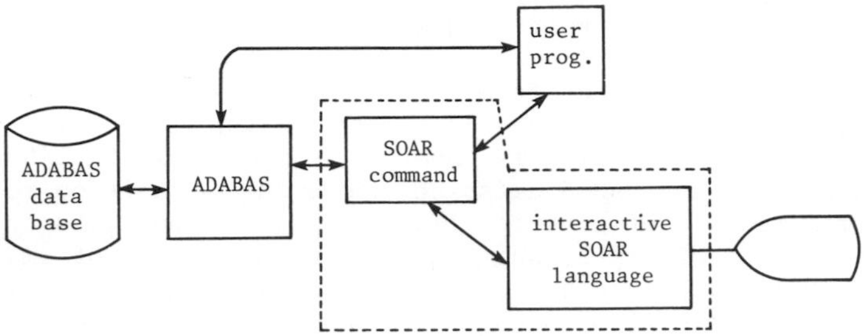

Fig. 1 ADABAS and SOAR Systems

Interactive SOAR provides the user with various comprehensive commands. These commands are very simple and easy to input. The commands are as follows:

(1) Set Generation
- $FIND .... Find Set
- $CONCAT ..... Concatenate Find Set
- $DEFINE ..... Define Set
- $SEARCH ..... Search
- $PCSRCH ..... Partial Criteria Search
- $COMPARE .... Compare Set
- $INDF .... Indirect Find Set
- $JOIN .... Join Set
- $SORT .... Sort Set
- $RELEASE .... Release Set
- $RENAME ..... Rename Set

(2) Data Read
- $READ .... Read Record to Screen
- $SKIP .... Skip Records
- $MAP .... Draw an Image

(3) Set Saving
- $SAVE .... Save Set
- $ACTIV ...... Activate Set
- $PURGE ...... Purge Set

(4) Service Command
- $SHOW .... Show Saved Sets
- $HISTO ...... Histogram
- ? .... Help

D,@ .... Control Output Information
L .... Screen Rolling

(5) Control Command
$FILE .... Declare File(s) or Set To Be Used
$OPEN .... Open DB
$CLOSE ...... Close DB

(6) Data Update
$ADD .... Add a Record
$UPD .... Update Field(s) Value(s)
$DEL .... Delete a Record

3. THE LANDSAT IMAGE DATA

LANDSAT scans the surface of the earth with the view range of 185km by 185km from the height of 915km, and orbits the earth in 103 minutes per revolution. LANDSAT travels along the Path as shown in Fig. 2 from top to bottom, and each time it revolves around the earth, the orbit (ROW) is shifted a little from right to left. Therefore, in every 18 days, LANDSAT focuses the same

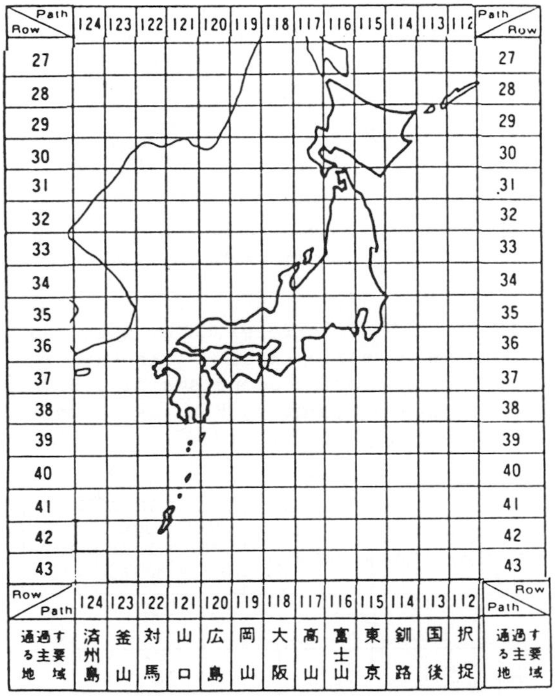

Fig. 2 PATH and ROW

spot of the earth. Each square portion is the area extracted by M2S on LANDSAT, and this is called a "Scene". For example, a Scene with Path 119 Row 36 can be drawn on a regular map as shown in Fig. 3. As readily recognized, the frame of Scene does not correspond to lattitude and longitude lines.

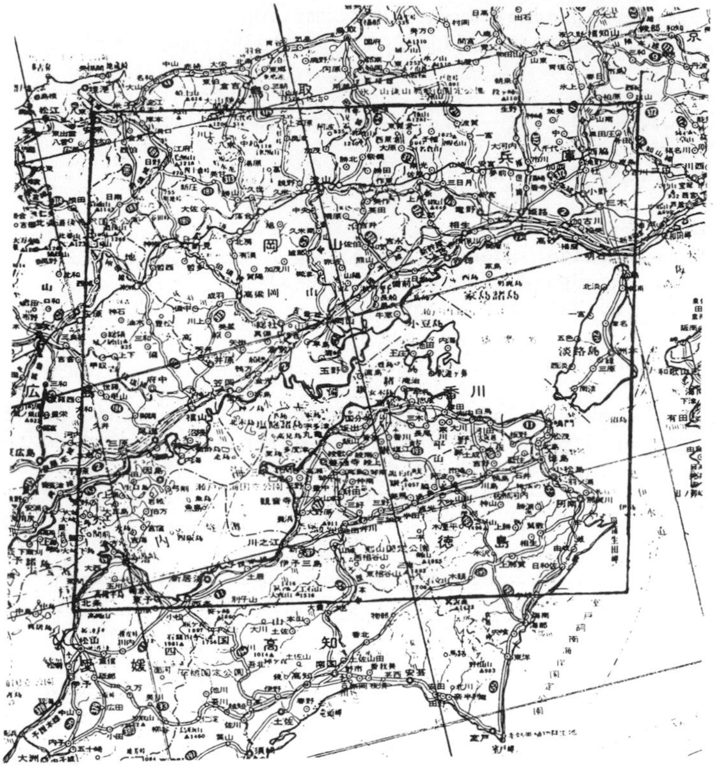

Fig. 3 Area Corresponding to a Scene
Extracted by M2S on LANDSAT

Data extracted by M2S on LANDSAT is received by a ground station and distributed to subscribers in magnetic tapes. This tape is called a Computer Compatible Tape (CCT) and its format comprises BIL, BSQ and BIP2. The format of CCT used in this experiment is BIL, as shown in Fig. 4.

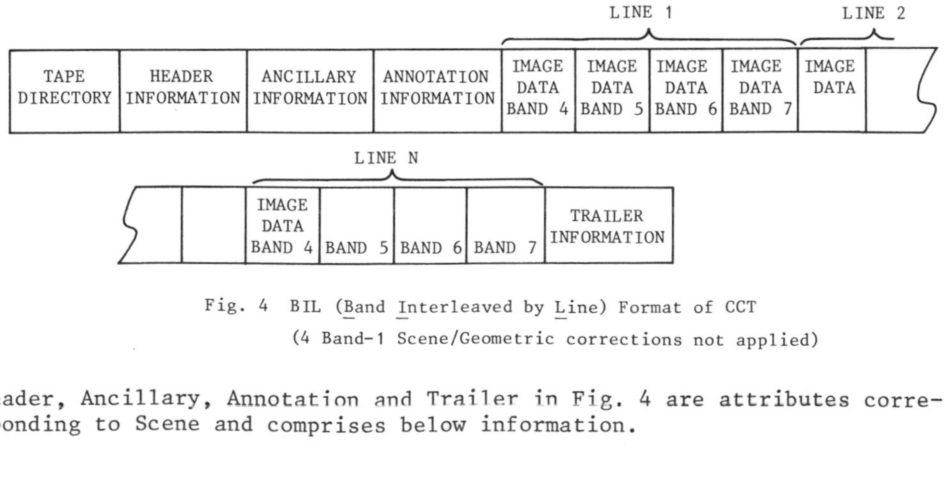

Fig. 4 BIL (Band Interleaved by Line) Format of CCT
(4 Band-1 Scene/Geometric corrections not applied)

Header, Ancillary, Annotation and Trailer in Fig. 4 are attributes corresponding to Scene and comprises below information.

. Scene recognition
. Description of the satellite
. Data on shooting time and World Reference System (WRS)
. Geometrical model for geometrical corrections
. Data for special usage, etc.

Image data is the image itself. The image is stored in digits by each line and Band.

M2S collects data by analyzing the reflected light from the ground and categorizing into four kinds of light. The light is recognized by naked eyes as green (Band 4), red (Band 5), and near infrared (Band 6, 7).

The computer recognizes and handles LANDSAT M2S image data as dots which have the "value corresponding to the brightness on the ground" called Pixel. One typical Scene extracted by M2S comprises 10,726,868 Pixels (3,596 horizontal Pixels x 2,983 vertical Pixels) per Band. The resolution capability corresponding to one Pixel is approximately 80m x 80m.

4. THE DATABASE

The data for the experiment consists of the Scene data provided by the National Astronomical Science Development Association (NASDA), in CCT with BIL format. The Scene data is edited by the Science Information Processing Center (the Center) of University of Tsukuba.

Each Scene comprises an index record (Header, Annotation, Ancillary, Trailer information) and the M2S image data. The generated database consists of the following:
(i) SCENE INDEX File (1 record per Scene), and
(ii) SCENE IMAGE DATA File (1 record per Pixel, and 1 file per Scene).

The SCENE INDEX file stores all information related to LANDSAT image data to be utilized in the experiment. SOAR makes it possible to retrieve this file at anytime from a terminal [5]. Thus, any person can easily find out from a terminal if the Scene he wants to use is stored in the Center.

The volume of SCENE IMAGE DATA is so large that it cannot be made resident in ADABAS database due to physical storage constraints. Therefore, SCENE IMAGE DATA file is normally stored in the Mass Storage System. For processing, an approach is devised in which, when the SCENE INDEX file is retrieved and a required Scene is determined, the SCENE IMAGE DATA file corresponding to that Scene will be restored into the database for utilization. Fig. 5 shows the overview of LANDSAT image database.

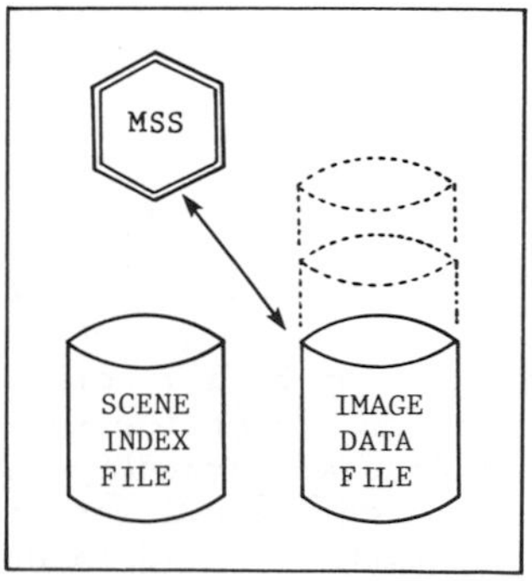

Fig. 5 LANDSAT Image Database

4.1 SCENE INDEX FILE

The SCENE INDEX file contains all index records of Scenes available at the Center. Each record corresponds to one Scene and contains various attributes which describe the Scene. Of the 162 attributes in the record, 47 are defined as descriptors (Retrieval keys). When this file is loaded into the database, ADABAS automatically creates inverted lists for the 47 descriptor attributes. The SCENE INDEX file stays resident in the database and the descriptors are used for retrieval of required Scenes.

The main retrieval keys of SCENE INDEX file are shown below:

. Path
. Row
. Date of shooting
. Types of geometric correction
. Ground station
. Latitude and longitude of center portion of Scene
. Others.

It only took 2 minutes to load this file to the database. When a new Scene is obtained, the corresponding SCENE INDEX record can be easily added to this file using the '$ADD command' of SOAR.

4.2 SCENE IMAGE DATA FILE

A SCENE IMAGE DATA file is a set of Pixel records for the particular Scene. CCT provides 10,726,868 (3,596 x 2,983) Pixels for one Scene, but the number is too large for the storage space currently available. So we decimated them by a factor of 5 along both the vertical and horizontal Pixels, and construct one file for a Scene with 422,676 (708 x 597) records. The decimated Scene is still accurate enough in comparison with the original one for processing.

An image data record consists of:

. two location factors of Pixel (Line and Column)
. five image elements of spectral Bands by M2S
  (Band 4 - Band 7 LANDSAT 2)
  (Band 4 - Band 8 LANDSAT 3)
. two attributes (one of them is reserved).

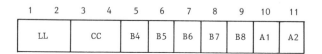

1 2	3 4	5	6	7	8	9	10	11
LL	CC	B4	B5	B6	B7	B8	A1	A2

Fig. 6 A Pixel Record (11 bytes)

Each Band can have value from 0 to 255. Using the Scene of Path 119, Row 36 (Refer Fig. 3) taken on November 30, 1979, for example, a zone with value 0 through 5 of Band 7 corresponds to water or shadow, and the one with value 29 through 127 of the same Band corresponds to cloud. The highest value of 255 indicates unscenery data. One of the two attributes, A1, contains the categorized information of each Pixel. It is obtained through the pre-examination of the data during the editing stage.

The A1 field of each Pixel record can comprise any of the characters, E, W, U, T, C and O. This is an attribute whose value is assigned before the Pixel records are loaded into the database, based on the judgement of each

Pixel record according to the below definitions:
E ... Edge (Band 7 = 255)
W ... Water (and shadow)(Band 7 = 0 thru 5)
U ... Uban (and field)(Band 4 = 15 thru 26 and Band 7 = 11 thru 25)
T ... Tree (Band 4 = 9 thru 11 and Band 7 = 12 thru 28)
C ... Cloud (Band 7 = 29 thru 127)
O ... Others

These definitions have been determined based on the experience of the third author (T. Hoshi).

Since the above conditions/representations vary according to the Scenes, the value of A1 for each Scene is determined by viewing the actual image of the Scene. The attribute enables the terminal users to estimate the area representation of each Band of Scene without viewing the actual image itself.

The two byte fields LL (line) and CC (column); one byte fields Band 4, 5, 6 and 7; as well as A1 are all defined as descriptors with inverted lists automatically created for each by ADABAS. At present the fields Band 8 and A2 contain no value. The time taken to load this file to the database is only 40 minutes.

5. ANALYSIS OF LANDSAT SCENE DATA

SOAR provides various set operation functions and makes it possible to interactively retrieve information under complex retrieval conditions.

5.1 RETRIEVAL FROM SCENE INDEX FILE

First we retrieved some required Scenes under a certain condition from SCENE INDEX file which is resident in the database. An example is shown below.

```
* TYPE COMMAND
$FILE INDEX;
$FIND PATH=119 AND ROW=36 AND YEAR=78 THRU 80
 AND MONTH=9 THRU 12;
$READ SCENE-ID YEAR MONTH DATE GEOMETRIC-CORRECTION.
```

SCENE ID	YEAR	MONTH	DATE	GEOMETRIC CORRECTION
119-36	79	11	30	NO

5.2 RETRIEVAL FROM SCENE IMAGE DATA FILE

When a Scene is selected by the retrieval as described in 5.1, SCENE IMAGE DATA file corresponding to the Scene is restored into the database, utilizing ADABAS Utility program. It took approximately 5 minutes for the restore.

5.2.1 RETRIEVAL OF CLOUDS LOCATION

In order to find out the existence of clouds in the sky, we first studied the values of A1. To facilitate it, HISTOGRAM Command of SOAR is used.

```
* TYPE COMMAND
$FILE IMAGE;
$HISTO % A1.
       NO. OF BASE-RECORDS 422,676
```

KIND OF VALUES		6
32.35%	136,758	T
24.36	102,979	W
18.19	76,925	O
14.16	59,862	U
7.44	31,476	E
3.47	14,676	C

The output shows the number of Pixels for each value of A1, and the percentage of each against the total. From the output, the number of Pixels for cloud is 3.47%. Thus it is clear that clouds did exist somewhere in the sky.

Next, we located the place of clouds as follows:

```
* TYPE COMMAND
$FIND KUMO A1=C;
$MAP KUMO=C LINE=1 COLUMN=1 FA=5 WIDTH=130 DEPTH=100.
```

The above commands mean first find a set of clouds (A1=C) and name the set as 'KUMO'. The location of cloud is represented by character 'C'. Next, obtain sampling for every five (FA=5) portion in both the vertical and horizontal directions starting from Line 1, Column 1, and print out the image on a printer with width of 130 and depth of 100. The set named 'KUMO' is saved in this session. It took only a few seconds to find the set and output the image. Fig. 7 shows the output. It depicts that clouds were found in several places in upper left, part of the top and bottom middle portion.

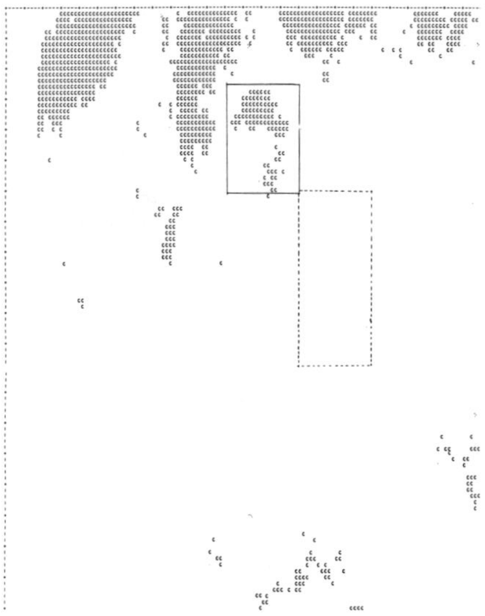

Fig. 7 Locations of Clouds

The area enclosed with solid lines can be expanded with the following command:

```
* TYPE COMMAND
$MAP KUMO=C LINE=60 COLUMN=300
     FA=1 WIDTH=100 DEPTH=100.
```

Any portion of the Scene can be expanded by changing the specification of Line and Column positions. The Scene used for this example is of Path 119, Row 36 and the actual image of this Scene has never been viewed. However, matching Fig. 7 with the map in Fig. 3, the viewer can tell that clouds were found above several places in the northern and northwestern parts of Okayama, western top of Tokushima and eastern top of Ehime, and that no clouds were found in any other places.

Similarly, the waters (seas) can be exclusively output on the terminal using the same approach.

5.2.2 OUTPUT OF ISLAND IMAGE

The map of Fig. 3 shows numerous islands. Since it has become clear that there was no cloud above the sea from the preceding processing 5.2.1, an image of Shodoshima Island can be obtained easily.

Islands are located in the sea. The sea is described with values 0 through 5 of Band 7, so we first created such a set and have it printed out. The portion corresponds to islands was output in white.

For processing, only the location where Shodoshima Island might be situated (Line 160 through 360, Column 350 through 480) is required.

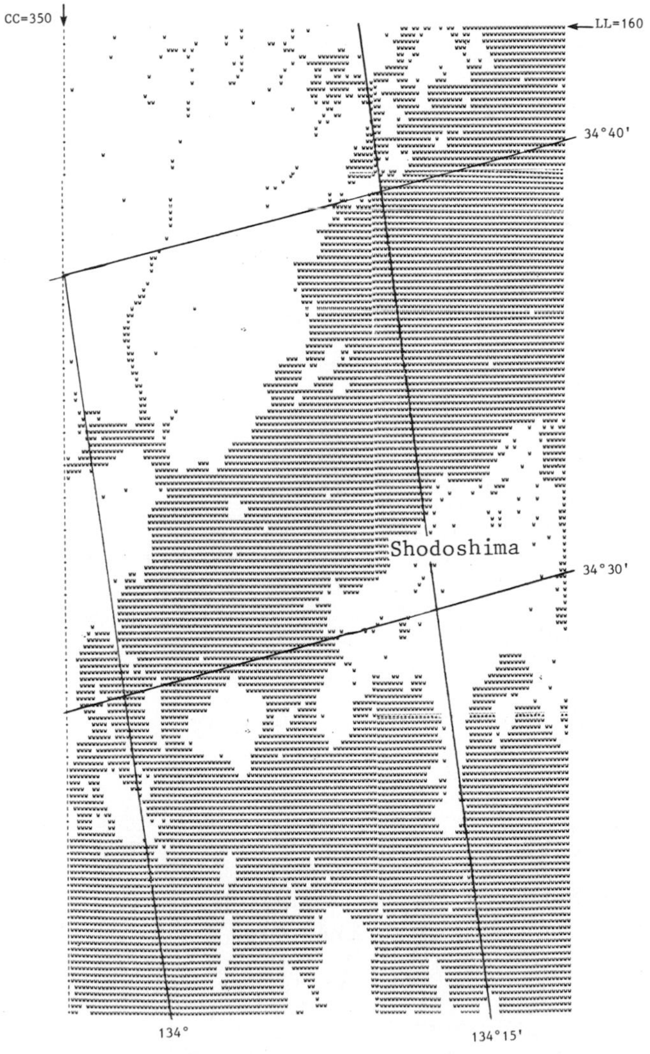

Fig. 8 Image of Shodoshima and Other Islands

```
* TYPE COMMAND
$FIND L2C4 LL=160 THRU 360 AND CC=350 THRU 480;
$FILE L2C4.
```

A set framed with dotted lines is named L2C4.

```
* TYPE COMMAND
$FIND UMI B7=0 THRU 5;
$MAP UMI=W LINE=160 COLUMN=350 FA=1 WIDTH=130 DEPTH=200.
```

UMI is a set name given to the sea surrounded by dotted frames. Fig. 8 shows that the image of the island is clearly depicted and the image of a river is also clearly displayed.

This image is not of reduced scale (FA=1).

On Fig. 8, the longitude and lattitude are entered, corresponding to the map (1:200,000) in Fig. 9. The map in Fig. 8 is elongated compared to the actual map because of the type face of the printer.

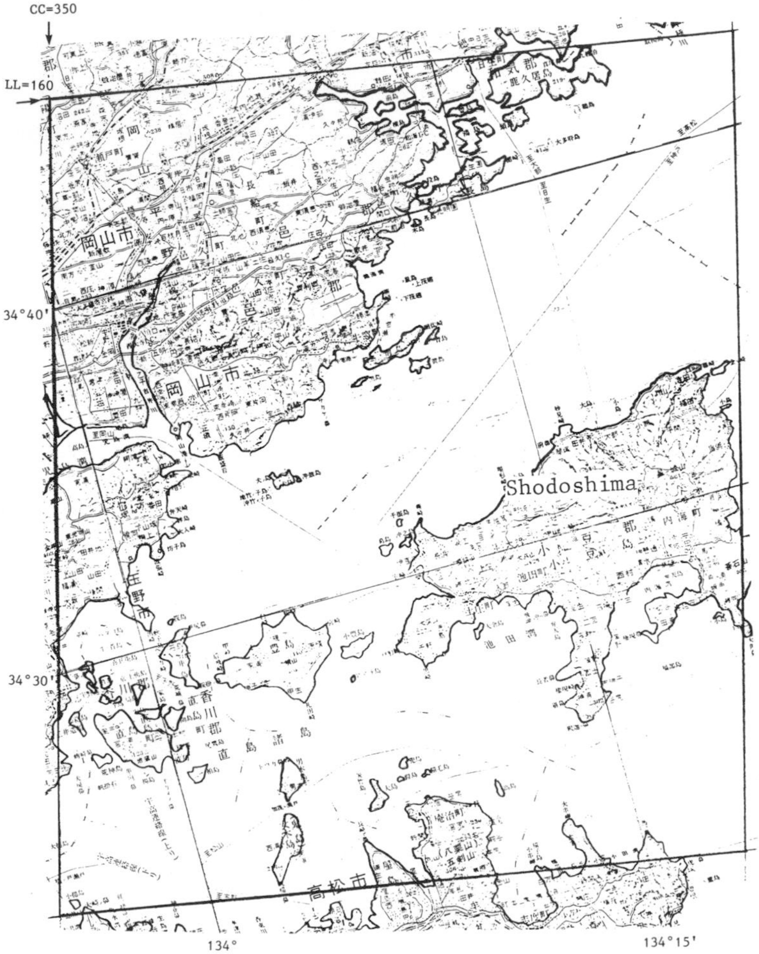

Fig. 9 Map of Shodoshima and Other Islands

5.2.3 MAPPING IMAGES

SOAR has a function to create as many sets as appropriate for various conditions. Therefore, not just simply for locating clouds and islands, SOAR can also create various sets corresponding to cities and forests. If sets are created, an output can be obtained by mapping such sets using MAP command. The following example is an analysis of Yoshino Plain. 'T' designates trees, '.' for urban,blank for sea and 'Q' for others. If several output, each of which is obtained using one character are copied on colored film, simple color image can be obtained by mapping all such output.

```
* TYPE COMMAND
$FILE IMAGE;
$FIND L4C4 LL=300 THRU 500 AND CC=400 THRU 660;
$FILE L4C4;
$FIND AAA B4=9 THRU 11;
$FIND BBB B7=12 THRU 28;
$COMPARE TREE=AAA*BBB;
$FIND UBAN A1=U;
$FIND SEA A1=W;
$COMPARE OTHR=L4C4-(UBAN+SEA+TREE);
$MAP UBAN='.' TREE=T OTHR=Q
     LINE=300 COLUMN=400 FA=2 WIDTH=130 DEPTH=200.
```

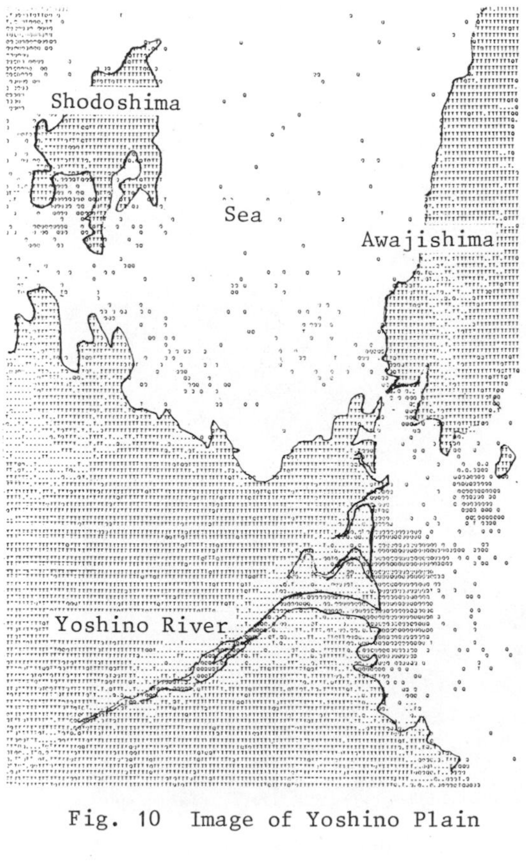

Fig. 10 Image of Yoshino Plain

Output is shown in Fig. 10.

Fig. 10 shows the Shodoshima Island which is also output in Fig. 8. The Awajishima Island is also distinctly shown in Fig. 10. Also, as shown in Fig. 10 the Yoshino River flows into the Inland Sea, contaminating the Sea. Comparing with the map, the coast line is drawn for easy reference. The dots in the Sea may have appeared due to sea contamination.

In order to survey how far the Yoshino River is contaminating the Sea, we had the river portion output in white (Fig. 11). This can be obtained through a simple set operation.

As a reference, real image output is attached in Fig. 12. Comparing the location of clouds (Fig. 7), Sea and Shodoshima Island (Fig. 8) and Yoshino Plain (fig. 10) with real image, the map obtained from the experiment is confirmed to be very accurate.

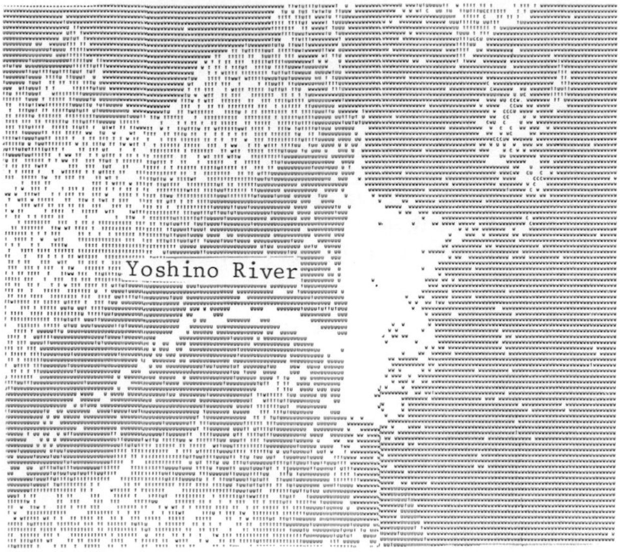

Fig. 11 Image of Yoshino River

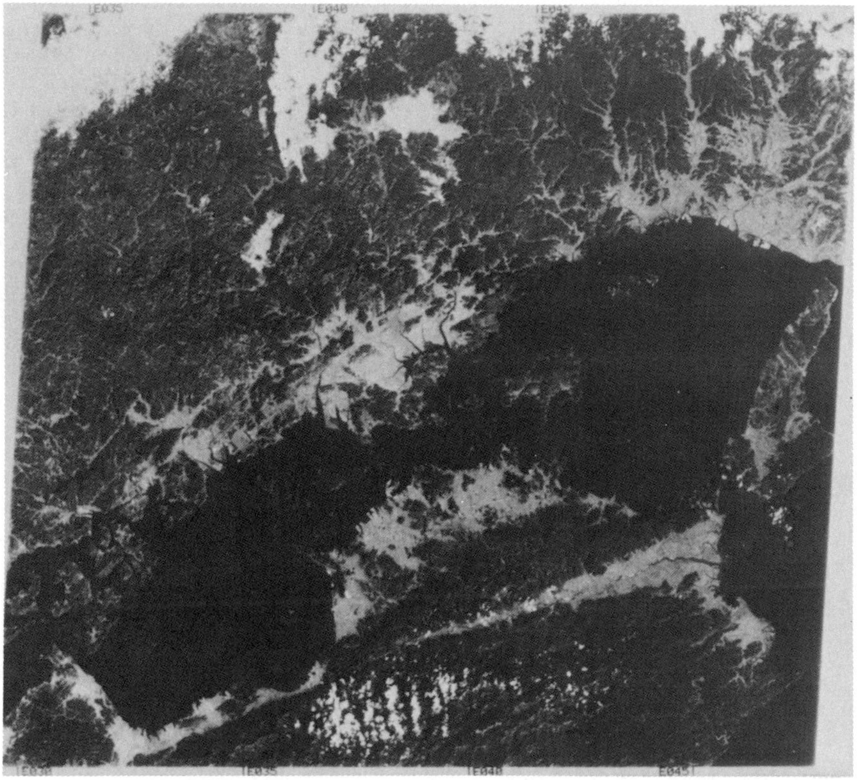

Fig. 12 Real LANDSAT Image of the Scene at PATH 119, ROW 36

6. CONCLUSION

We experimented an approach to store the LANDSAT image data and output part of the image to a terminal printer. The image data is made up of a set of Pixels, and the data is stored in an ADABAS database. SOAR, the interactive set-oriented language is utilized for operations on Pixels as well as for output of image. We also experimented an approach to map several images.

We believe the approaches used in the experiment will become one of the key approaches for interactive processing of image data from a regular terminal, utilizing image data stored in a database.

ACKNOWLEDGEMENT

We would like to express our deep appreciation to Mr. Aida of Software AG of Far East, Inc. for offering various assistance in database creation, terminal retrieval, etc. for the experiment. We would also like to thank Ms. Kojima and Ms. Kitagawa for assisting us in translating and typing of this paper.

REFERENCES

[1] E. F. Codd (1970); "A Relational Model of Data for Large Shared Data Banks", Commun. ACM, Vol. 13, No. 6, Jan. 1970, pp. 377-387.

[2] T. L. Kunii, Y. Ishii and H. Kitagawa; "A Description of the Logical ADABAS Architecture" (draft version).

[3] Y. Ishii and M. Nishibayashi (1978); "SOIR Language" (in Japanese) Proc. of 20th Programming Symposium, IPSJ, Dec. 1978.

[4] Y. Ishii and K. Yokota (1981); "Interactive IR Language SOAR" (in Japanese) Proc. of 25th DBMS Research Meeting, IPSJ, July 1981.

[5] T. Hoshi and K. Nakayama (1982); "Retrieval of LANDSAT Image Data in the Data Cartridge" (in Japanese) Proc. of 8th Annual Conference on Remote Sensing, Society of Instrument and Control Engineerings, 1982.

3 DIMENSIONAL IMAGE PROCESSING OF ULTRASONOTOMOGRAMS

Shohei Nakamura

Department of Urology, Faculty of Medicine
The University of Tokyo
Tokyo 113, JAPAN

ABSTRACT

Ultrasonography is a very powerful technique to obtain cross-section image of the body and some other objects in the water. Thirty images are produced in a second , which can be recorded by video-disk at once. Hundreds of these sequential cross-section images with very narrow intervals make a complete three-dimentional information of the object. A computer program was developed to make a molded three-dimentional images, which were displayed by contour lines like a map and by simulation technique of light reflection like a photo. For the three-dimentional imaging of the hollow organ like a bladder, projection method of world map was applied. The inner structure of the bladder was projected into two circule images. Another computer program was developed which displayed tomograms of the object sectioned in any direction. Not only the tomograms sectioned by plane surface but also by curved surface were obtained. These programming was written in assembler language of 6502 micro-processor of Apple II computer.

I. INTRODUCTION

Ultrasonography is a method to display the tomograms of the body using ultrasound. Recently, this technique have made rapid progress and widely used in many hospitals for the detection of the diseases. Fig. 1 shows ultrasonic apparatus.

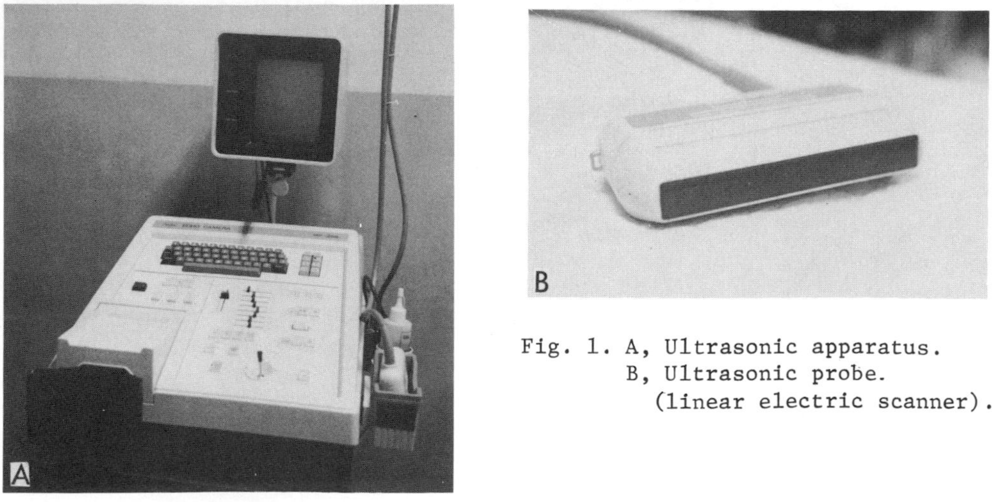

Fig. 1. A, Ultrasonic apparatus.
B, Ultrasonic probe.
(linear electric scanner).

Brief electrical impulses produced by a pulse generator are converted to pulsed ultrasound in the transducer and directed into the object to be examined in the form of a narrow beam. For medical diagnostic purpose, frequencies of 2 10 MHz are employed. When the beam strikes a boundary surface between tissues of different densities and sound velocity (acoustic impedance = densities of medium x velocity of sound), a portion of the ultrasound beam is reflected as echoes. When detected by transducer, now functioning as a receiver, the amplitude of the echoes are converted to electrical voltage. These signals are transmitted to the CRT via an amplifier as a corresponding series of dots. The arrangement and the intensity of the dots are displayed the same as that of the echoes generated in the body. The distance from the boundary surface to the transducer can easily be determined from the known velocity of sound in tissue. The derection of the beam is detected by potentiometer or by some other devices.

During the examination of the body, the transducer is oriented and moved in desired sectional planes so that sectional ultrasonic images (ultrasonotomograms) are obtained. Conventionally, the transducer is moved manually, taking one or two seconds for one image. Recent high-speed mechanical scanner can display about 30 images per second, which allows the image to be viewed in "real time" so that the movement of organs can be seen as a movie picture. Another method for real time imaging of ultrasound is a phased array system. It is consisted of many minute transducers and they are electrically switched one by one making an effect as if a single transducer is moved. Recent ultrasonograms are displayed on a ordinary TV monitor, which is advantageous for the image processing by computor, because no special interface is needed between the ultrasonic equipment and the digital TV frame memory to be accessed by a computer.

If the ultrasonograms are sequentially recorded at narrow slice intervals such as 0.5 mm, then complete three-dimentional information of the body can be obtained. In this paper these data were processed three-dimentionally by electric computer. Image processing by computer in X-ray CT (computed Tomography) has already been reported.1)2)3) But X-ray CT takes several seconds to display one tomograms. Irradiation hazard is another disadvantage to obtain many sequential images.

We used video-disc system for storage of ultrasonograms. It can record TV frame images at once and play again any time at the requent of the computer. As the ultrasonic apparatus produces 30 images/sec, high-speed image recording system is needed. Recording system by digital data seems inappropriate for this purpose. Video-tape recorder has also disadvantage, since it is difficult to play back the images at the requent of the computer.

II. THREE-DIMENTIONAL PORTRAYAL

An experimental system is consisted of ultrasonic apparatus, video-disc system, digital TV frame memory and microcomputer (Apple II). Block diagram of the system is shown on Fig. 2. The frame memory provides 8 bits for each X and Y axis, namely 256 x 256 = 65536 picture elements, and also 8 bits for the gradient of monochromatic tones.

A glass head (Fig. 3) was used for the object of the ultrasonic scanning in this study. It was immersed in water since ultrasound does not propagate well in the air. The scanning area of the ultrasonogram is 9 cm (width) x 12 cm (depth). The scanning planes are pararell and the distances of each planes were 0.5 mm. As 240 frames of the sonograms were recorded in video-disc system, three-dimentional information of 12 cm length were obtained.

To portray the object, surface boundaries of the object must be detected automatically. One of the many tomograms of the glass head is shown on Fig. 4. No echoes were detected in the water, making the water area white. As any material shows comparatively high echoic level than water, the surface boundary was easily detected by judging the level of picture elements higher or not than the threshold level, which was set in advance a little higher than that in water.

CRT---Ultrasonic Apparatus
|
CRT---Video-disc System
|
A-D Converter
|
CRT---Digital TV Frame Memory
|
Microcomputer
|
Key Board

Fig. 2. (left), Block diagram of the system used for the 3D image processing of ultrasonograms. Fig. 3. (right), Glass head used for 3D portrayal.

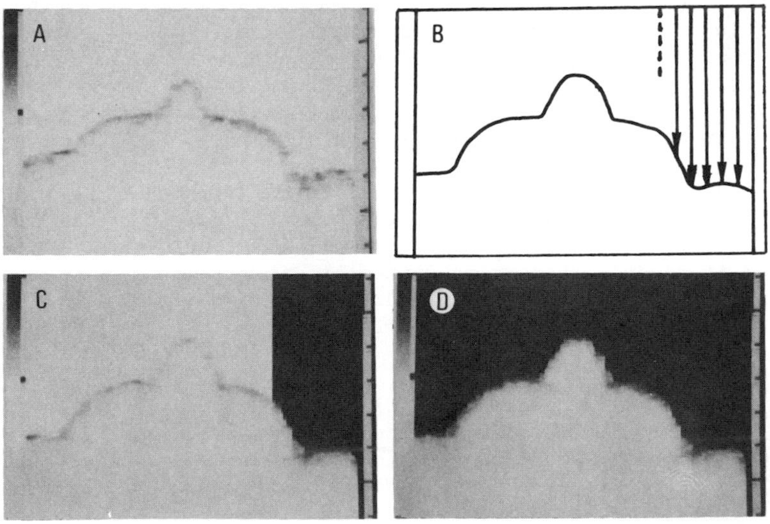

Fig. 4. A, One of the sequential ultrasonograms of the glass head. B, Schema of distance measurement. C, Image during distance measurement. The length of the black lines are stored in computer memory. D, Image after distance measurement.

A horizontal standard line was determined for measuring the distance to the object. The measuring starts from the right and upper margine as indicated by arrows on Fig. 4. B. If the level of the picture element is higher than the threshold level, the element was turned to black. These black dots indicates whether the measurement is correctly performed or not. If the level is not higher, then the co-ordinate of the elements is registered in the memory of the computer and the measurements in the next left line starts. It takes about two seconds to examine one image. Fig. 4. C and D show images during and after distance measuring. For each image, 256 bitesdata are stored in computer memory. After processing 240 images, 256 x 240 bites data are accumulated. The image of the object comes to appear on the TV monitor, if these data are transferred to the frame memory just in the order as the data have been recorded. Protruding and hollow portion are displayed in darker and brighter tones respectively (Fig. 5. A). Fig. 5. B shows an image after smoothing process, which makes the level of elements averaged of 8 neighboring elements in X and Y direction. On Fig. 5. C gradient gray tones were limited to 32 tones. In this picture, an information like a contour lines in the map is added. By counting the number of contour lines, the hight and depth of the surface structure is easily determined.

For the portrayal like a photo, a source of light is supposed. The surface element facing the light ray becomes the brightest, while one facing in a direction perpendicular to the light ray is the darkest. In our computer program, the light ray which is to illuminate the object was supposed just parallel to the direction of distance measuring, namely just vertical to the photo plane of Fig. 5.

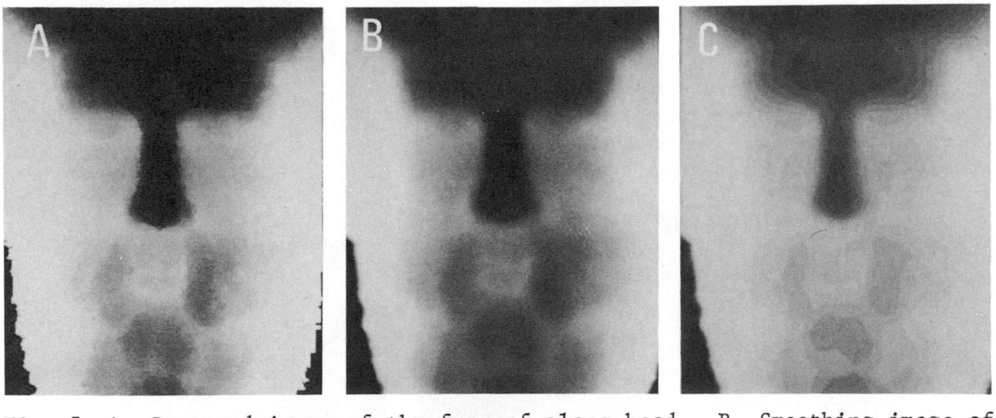

Fig. 5. A, Composed image of the face of glass head. B, Smoothing image of A. C, Gray tones were limited to 32 in the image of B, representing contour lines.

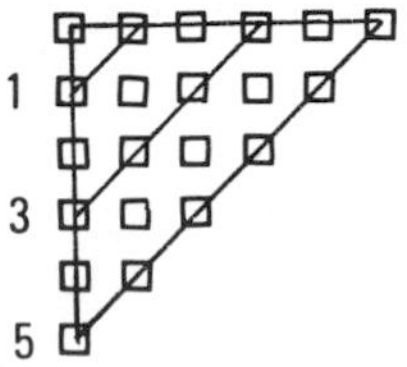

Fig. 6. Minute triangle size to calculate the angle of surface elements. (size 1, size 3 and size 5).

To calculate the angle of surface element against illuminating light ray, vareous sizes of little triangle are tried. Fig. 6 shows 3 kinds of triangle size (size 1, size 3 and size 5). Fig. 7. A is obtained, processing non-smoothed gray tone image (Fig. 5. A) by size 1 triangle. Fig. 7. A seems to have much noise on the image, because slight measuring errors are exaggerated. Size 3 triangle make the image more stable (Fig. 7. B). Fig. 7. C is obtained, processing smoothed gray tone image (Fig. 5. B) by size 3 triangle.

If size 1 triangle is applied to Fig. 5. C, only contour lines are extracted and Fig. 8. A is obtained. Making the contour lines much more dense, some minute surface structure comes to appear only by contour lines (Fig. 8. B).

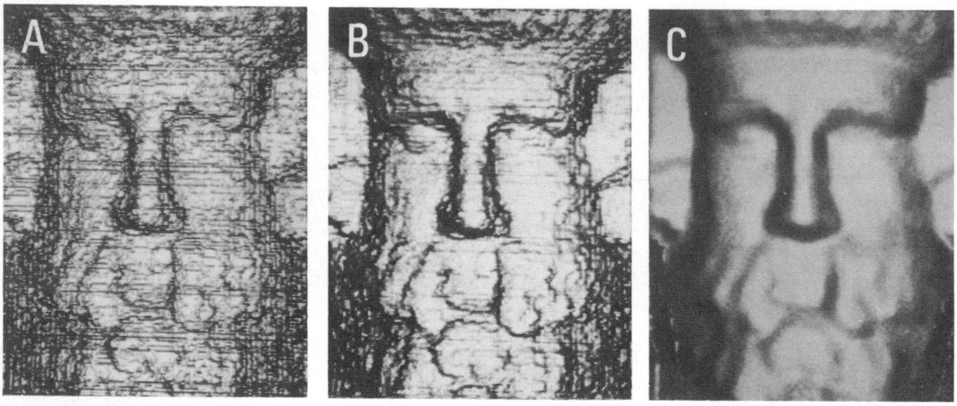

Fig. 7. A, Molded picture presentation of Fig. 5. A, using size 1 triangular elements. B, Molded picture presentation of Fig. 5. A, using size 3 triangular elements. C, Molded picture presentation of Fig. 5. B, using size 3 triangular elements.

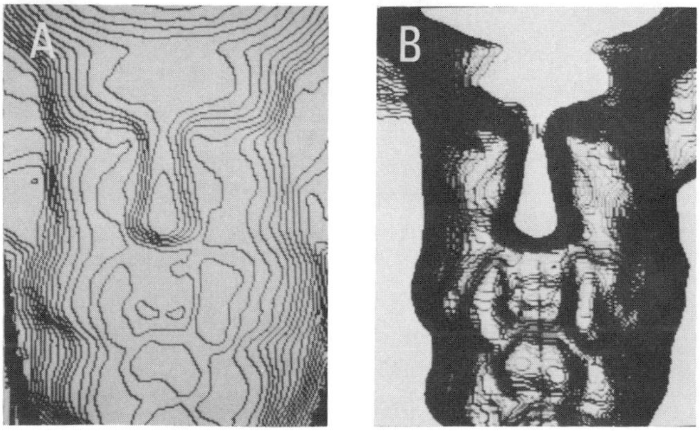

Fig. 8. A, Contour line presentation of the face, obtained by processing Fig. 5. C by size 1 triangular elements. B, Presentation of the face by dense contour lines.

III. PORTRAYAL OF CYSTOSCOPIC FINDINGS

Cystoscopic observation is limited to a specific angle and the other side of the tumor cannot be observed. Some large tumors are difficult to recognize even by the experienced. The illustration of the findings are usually influenced by subjective impression. Based on the application of transurethral ultrasonography and a simple data processing system, we developed a new method capable of determining the location, size and morphology of the

The tumor morphology, or contour, can be mapped by a computer by, first of all, establishing the reference point from which distances are to be measured accurately. To make a map of the bottom of a lake, the best way is to run a boat across it as it emits an ultrasonic beam (Fig. 9). In this case, the water surface is our reference point. This sweeping method is the most reliable way. However, the bladder, with its extreme curvature at the bottom, requires techniques different from those for drawing a map of bottom of the lake. The ultrasonic transducer, placed at the center of the bladder, must rotate, like radar, while emitting pulses. The most desirable way, of realising this, is to make cross-section images by inserting a rotating ultrasonic probe transurethrally into the bladder.[4)5)6)] Fig. 10 shows the transurethral scanner.

Clinically, a probe was removed from the dome of the bladder towards the neck as approximately 120 ultrasonic tomograms were taken at 0.5 to 1 mm intervals, with the assistance of a scanner stand. These images were stor ed in video-disc system.

In order to obtain tumor image illustrations similar to cystoscopic findings from ultrasonotomograms made by transurethral intravesical scanning, it is, generally speaking, necessary to consider the following three factors: First, an accurate measurement of the distance is required. Secondly, we need a display method for making a graphical representation of the inner surface of the bladder from these measured distances. And finally, a method of projection which corresponds to the conventional cystoscopic findings. We were able to solve these three problems by applying a simple data processing system. To measure the distance, a specific point must be designated in a bladder. Measurement is started from the scanning probe. As a result, the surface of the tumor can be viewed as in the case of cystoscopy.

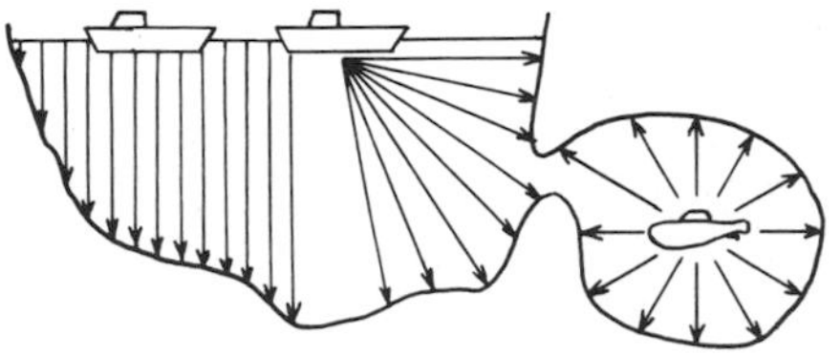

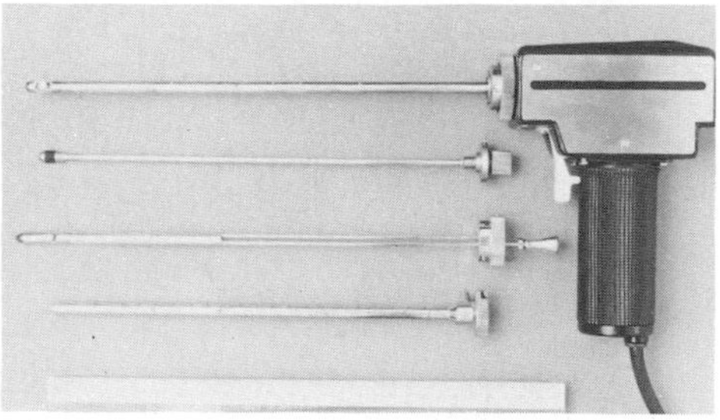

Fig. 9. (left), Schema of measuring distance for drawing a map of lake bottom. Fig. 10. (right), Transurethral ultrasonic scanner.

First, the cross-section image of the bladder is stored into the frame memory (Fig. 11. A). A microcomputer measures the distance from the probe. If the threshold of the image density is set in advance in the micro-computer, measurements will be made automatically, and the measurement data will be stored in the computer's memory. Measurements can be made freely, either by horizontal scanning, which is like moving a boat on a lake (Fig. 11. B), or by radial scanning, which is like radar (Fig. 11. C). Also, measurement data can be transferred to the frame memory and viewed on a CRT.

For the next problem, the conversion of measurements into three-dimensional representations, we tried the following three approaches: One is to make a presentation with countour lines, as in a map. The next possible solution is to make depths correspond to grades of image density. In other words, the depth is represented by coloring deeper places with darker grey tones and shallower places with lighter grey tones. Another possibility is to shine a light from a certain place and to draw the distribution of its re-flections.

In the horizontal (linear) scan of measurement, the ultrasonotomogram of the bladder is divided at the central line into two sections (Fig. 11. B), posterior and anterior wall. Then, distances are measured horizontally, and an image of the tumor is displayed. Fig. 12. A is a display of posteri-

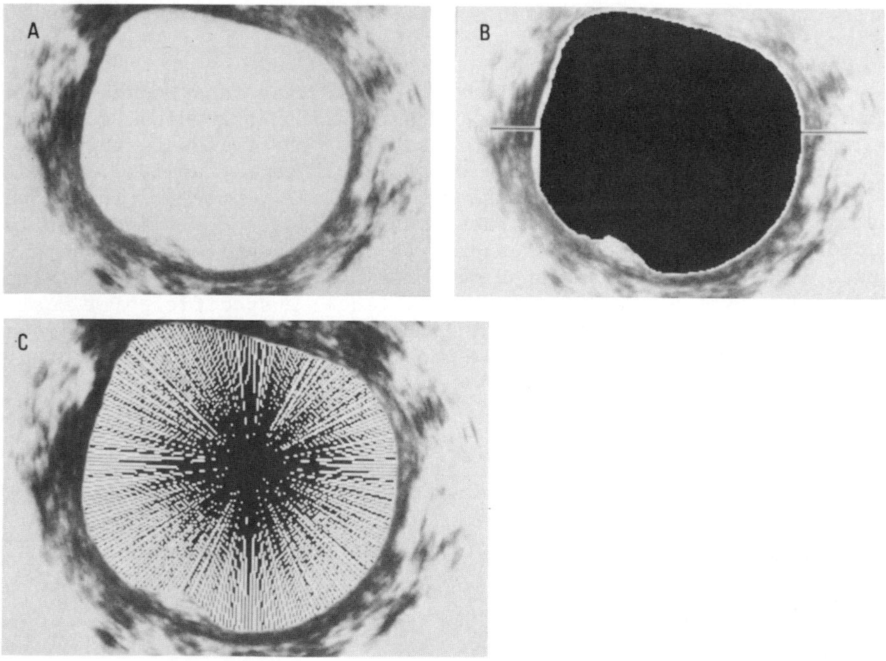

Fig. 11. A, Tomogram of bladder tumor. B, Horizontal (linear) measuring of the distances from the central line to the bladder surface. Locuses of the measurements are indicated by black lines. C, Radial measuring of the distances from the probe to the bladder surface. Locuses of the measurements are indicated by black lines.

or wall using 32 gray tones, which correspond to various distances. In other words, it is a display method which combines grey tones and contour line methods. The tumor is visualized as a white image. Fig. 12. B is an image employed by the distribution of reflected light. This image is like a vesical hemisphere as viewed from the top. Therefore, it is not completely analogous to a cystoscopy view. Tumors which are located at the bottom can be clearly recognized. But it is difficult to display a tumor accurately when it is located on the lateral side of the wall.

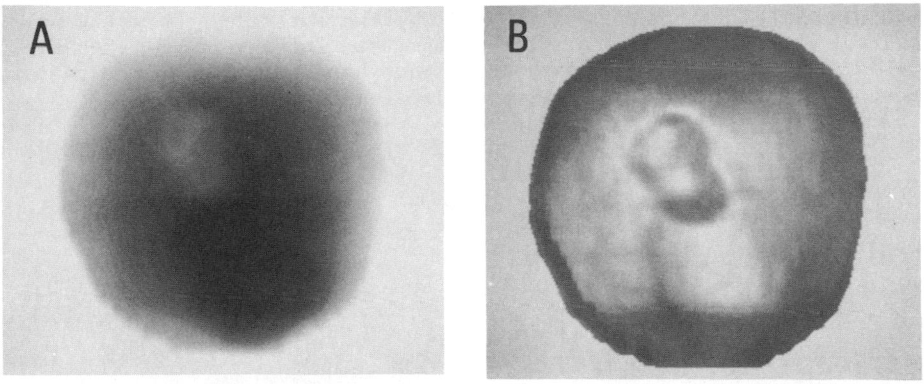

Fig. 12. A, Composed image of posterior wall by horizontal (linear) measuring. Displaying is a combination of gray tones and contour lines. B, Composed image of posterior wall by horizontal (linear) measuring. For displaying, similation technique of drawing the distribution of reflected light is used.

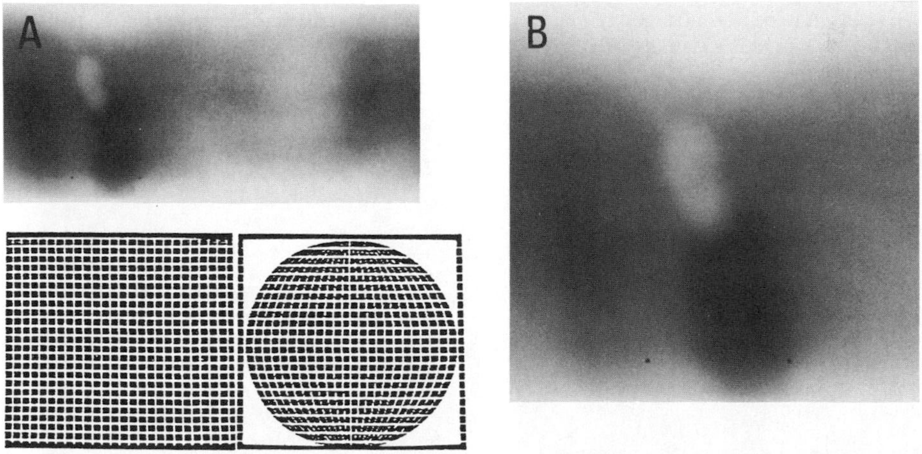

Fig. 13. A, Image of radially measured distances. Left and right half of the image show the posterior and anterior wall of the bladder respectively. The projection method is similar to the world map of eastern and western hemisphere. B, Left half of Fig. 13. A (posterior wall), is enlarged by twice. Fig. 14. (left bottom), Schema of the image deformation from square to circle.

In order to obtain comparable cystoscopic findings in which views are obtained through a fish-eye lens in the bladder, it is necessary to measure the distance radially from the central point of the bladder (Fig. 11. C). When these measurements are transferred to their corresponding grey tones on the CRT, a rectangular figure is obtained (Fig. 13. A). The ratio of two sides is designed 2 : 1. Dark and light tones correspond to the long and short distances in this image. The interior views of the anterior and posterior walls of the bladder are developed and observed side by side, similar to one type of a world map. The left half of Fig. 13. A shows the posterior wall, which was magnified on Fig. 13. B. The black points are marks indicating the openings of urethers. They provide good reference points for determining the location of tumors. In Fig. 13. B, the shining image of the tumor, which appears white, can be recognized on the posterior wall of the bladder, in a central position closer to the top.

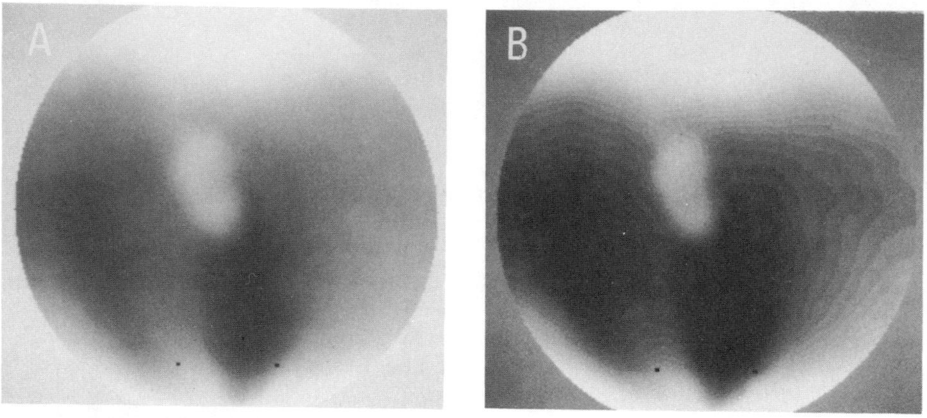

Fig. 15. A, Deformed image of Fig. 13. B (from square into circle image). B, Image of radial measurement deformed into circle, displayed by 32 varying gray tones.

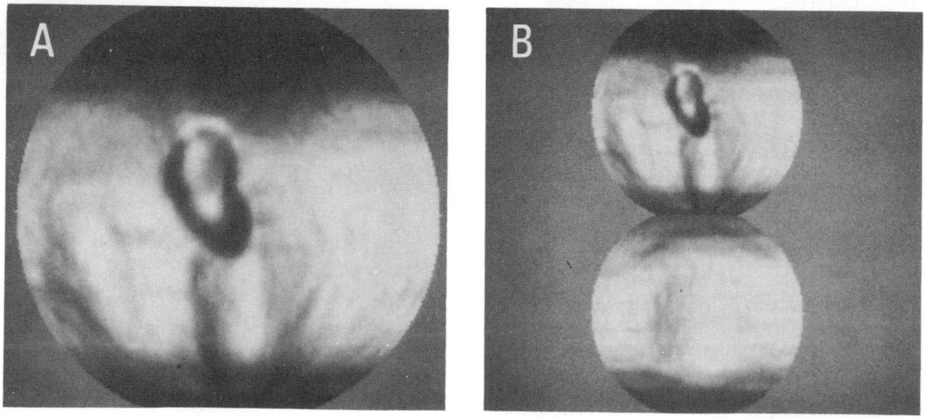

Fig. 16. A, Image of radial measurement deformed in circle, displayed through distribution of reflected light. B, Final image of the shape of the bladder surface. Posterior and anterior images displayed like cystoscopic findings.

When this square image is transformed into a round shape (Fig. 15. A), a comparison with a cystoscopic finding naturally becomes possible. Transformation of square image into circle is schematically shown on Fig. 14. Fig. 15. is an interior view of the posterior wall hemisphere of the bladder after transformation. Fig. 15. B is displayed by 32 grey tones. Fig. 16. A is an image displayed through distribution of reflected light. The swelling of the tumor may be seen with greater clarity. Fig. 16. B shows posterior and anterior wall like cystoscopic findings, which contains no subjective element at all. This would be considered an ideal description of a cystoscopic finding.

IV. COMPOSITION OF NEW CROSS-SECTION IMAGE IN DESIRED DIRECTION

Ultrasonogram is a cross-section image of the body or any other objects in water scanned by ultrasound. It had been desired to obtaine a new sectional image not only in the scanning direction but also any direction

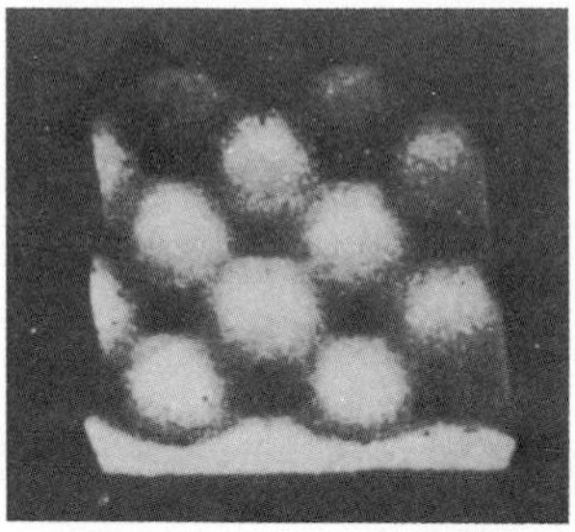

Fig. 17. An wave-shaped sponge

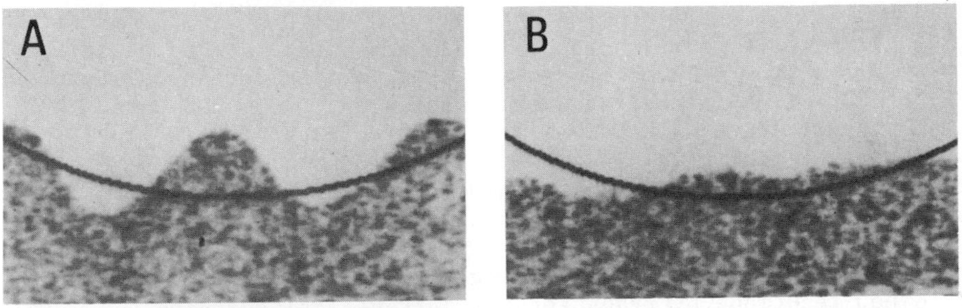

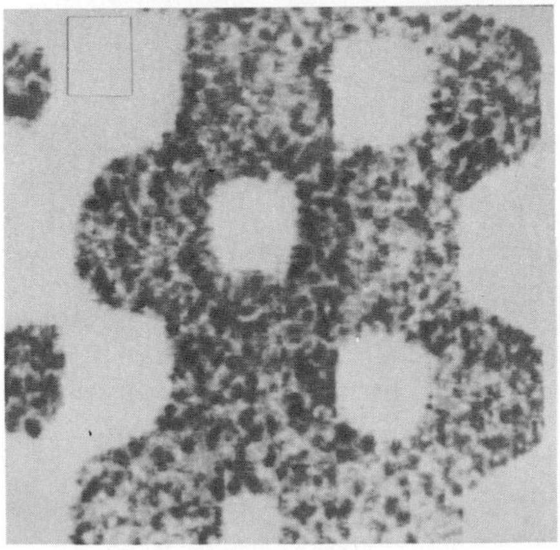

Fig. 18. (Top), Two tomograms out of 240 sequential ultrasonograms of sponge. Black line indicates the curved surface to make a new cross-section. Fig. 19. (bottom), New cross-section image.

just as to cut an apple in vareous directions by a knife. Several methods were reported to realize this purpose.[7] Their methods were to obtain a new image during the scan of the whole area of interest. As the result, they must scan again and review all the tomograms to make an image. We propose a new method which enables one scanning of the whole area, complete image store by a video-disc system and afterwards image processing by computer.

A wave shaped sponge (Fig. 17) in water was scanned at 0.5 mm slice intervals and 240 ultrasonograms were recorded in video-disc system. Two of them were shown on Fig. 18. The shape and the direction of the new cross-section is determined as is indicated by black line in Fig. 18. The cross-section is possible either by plane or curved surface.

The level of gray tones on the black line are stored in computer memory. These line data of 240 sequential ultrasonogram makes another cross-sectional image (Fig. 19), if arranged densely. Resolution of the image was not reduced by such a processing. As ultrasound does not propagate well through bone or air in intestine, the scanning site of the body surface (skin) is restricted. It is clinically significant to obtaine a new cross-section image in less scanning time. This technique have been already applied to the image of prostate by us.[8]

REFERENCES

1) Huang, H.K. and Ledley, R.S.: Coronal and sagittal planes display from in-vivo consecutive transverse axial sections. Proc. of the RSNA, 30 Nov.-5 Dec., 1975, Chicago, Ill.

2) Ledley, R.S., Park, C.M., Molded picture representation of whole body organs generated from CT scan sequences, Proc. of the 1st Annual Symp. of Computer Applications in Medical Care, Washington, D.C., 3-5 Oct., 1977, pp.363-367. Institute of Electrical and Electronics Engineers, Inc.

3) Ledley, R.S., Park, C.M. and Ray, R.D.: Application of the ACTA-scanner to visualization of the spine. Computerized Tomography, 3: 57, 1979.

4) Nakamura, S. and Niijima, T.: Staging of bladder cancer by ultrasonography: a new technique by transurethral intravesical scanning. J. Urol., 124: 341, 1980.

5) Nakamura, S. and Niijima, T.: Transurethral real-time scanner. J. Urol., 125: 781, 1981.

6) Niijima, T., Nakamura, S. and Shiraishi, T.: Transurethral scanning and scanning via abdominal wall. in Watanabe, H., Holmes, J.H., Holm, H.H. and Goldberg, B.B., editor: Diagnostic ultrasound in Urology and Nephrology, 1981, Igaku-shoin Ltd., Tokyo, pp.96-104.

7) Yokoi, H., Ito, K., Shibuya, N., Tamura, K., Yuta, S., Hirafuku, S.: Clinical Application of the high-speed C-and F-mode ultrasonography using the electric scanning transducer (mammary and thyroid gland tumors). Abstract of 2nd Meeting of WFUMB, 442, 1979.

8) Nakamura, S., Niizuma, M., Kimura, A., Hoshino, T. and Niijima, T.: Composition of C & F mode image by processing many tomograms stored in video-disc system — clinical application to prostate. Proc. of 41th Meeting of JSUM, 41: 113, 1982.

Author Index

The page numbers refer to the list of references provided by each contributor.